AF856311

CONSTITUTIONS
of
NATIONS

VOLUME III-EUROPE

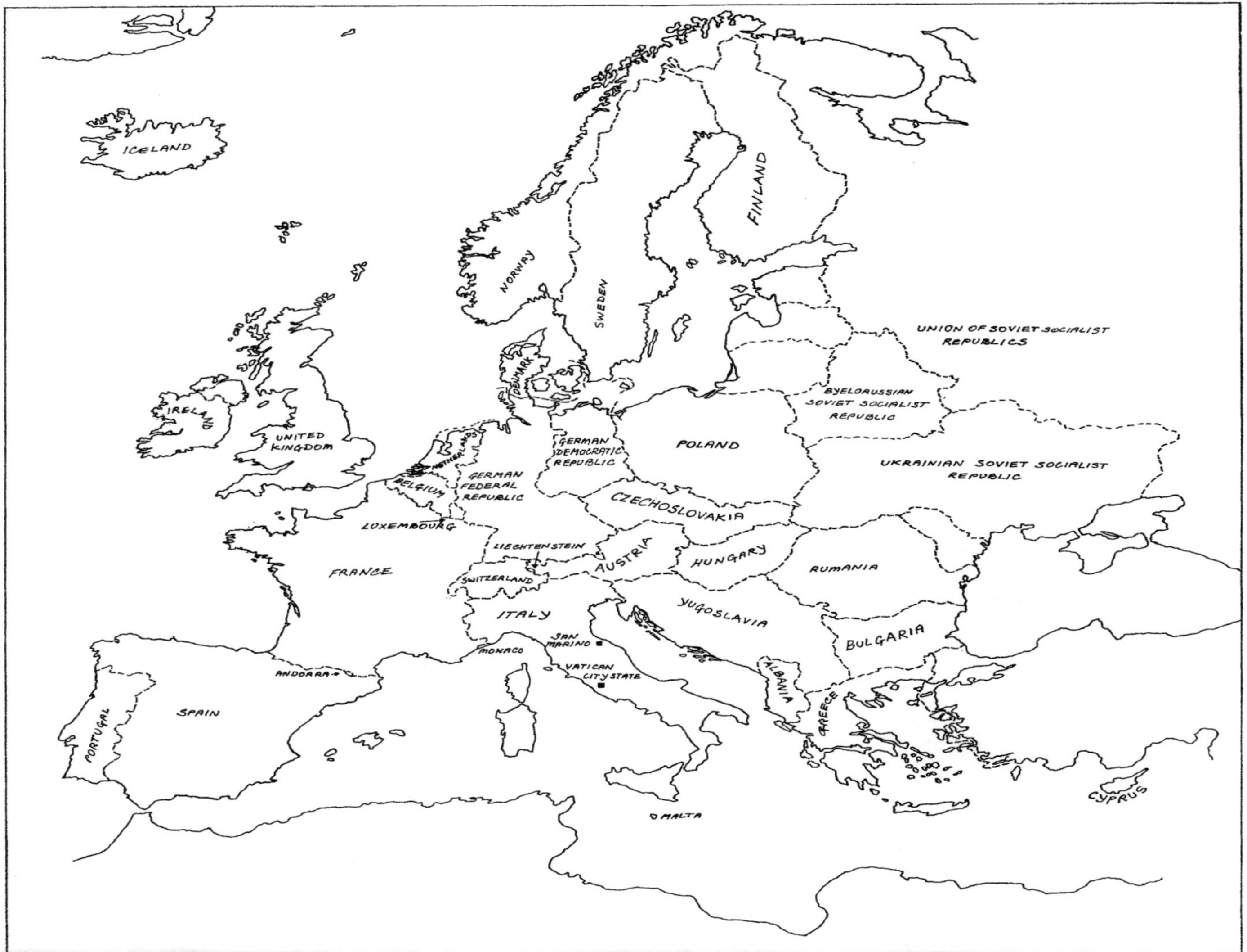
ICELAND
IRELAND
UNITED KINGDOM
NORWAY
SWEDEN
FINLAND
DENMARK
NETHERLANDS
BELGIUM
LUXEMBOURG
GERMAN FEDERAL REPUBLIC
GERMAN DEMOCRATIC REPUBLIC
POLAND
UNION OF SOVIET SOCIALIST REPUBLICS
BYELORUSSIAN SOVIET SOCIALIST REPUBLIC
UKRAINIAN SOVIET SOCIALIST REPUBLIC
CZECHOSLOVAKIA
FRANCE
LIECHTENSTEIN
SWITZERLAND
AUSTRIA
HUNGARY
RUMANIA
ITALY
SAN MARINO
MONACO
VATICAN CITY STATE
YUGOSLAVIA
BULGARIA
ALBANIA
GREECE
ANDORRA
SPAIN
PORTUGAL
MALTA
CYPRUS

CONSTITUTIONS

of

NATIONS

VOLUME III - EUROPE

by

AMOS J. PEASLEE

Formerly Ambassador of the United States of America to Australia, Secretary-General of the International Bar Association, Member of the American Council of Learned Societies, President of the American Branch of the International Law Association, Representative of the American Society of International Law at the San Francisco Conference of 1945, Associate of the American Commission to Negotiate Peace at Versailles in 1919

Author of INTERNATIONAL GOVERNMENTAL ORGANIZATIONS-THEIR CONSTITUTIONAL DOCUMENTS (*Martinus Nijhoff, The Hague; and Justice House, New York, 2nd Ed., 1961*), A PERMANENT UNITED NATIONS (*Putnams, 1942*), UNITED NATIONS GOVERNMENT (*Putnams, 1945*), *and co-author of* THREE WARS WITH GERMANY (*Putnams, 1944*)

★

REVISED THIRD EDITION

In four Volumes

Prepared by Dorothy Peaslee Xydis

Formerly officer in the Secretariat of the General Agreement on Tariffs and Trade

Unchanged reprint 1974

ISBN 978-94-017-1151-7 ISBN 978-94-017-1149-4 (eBook)
DOI 10.1007/978-94-017-1149-4

© *1974 Springer Science+Business Media Dordrecht*
All rights reserved, including the right to translate or to reproduce this book or parts thereof in any form

Originally published by Martinus Nijhoff, The Hague, Netherlands in 1974.

Softcover reprint of the hardcover 1st edition 1974

FOREWORD TO VOLUME III

Volume III of the new edition covers thirty five countries. Two, Cyprus and Malta, are new entries and a third, Albania, which had a section but no text in the second edition now has its constitution reproduced. Six countries [1] have new constitutions and the constitutions of twenty have been amended. A number of additional constitutional texts have been included in the section for the United Kingdom. Only in the case of four countries [2] has there been no change since the second edition and for these countries the revised edition contains the latest edition of the Constitution as supplied by the government in question or a more recent translation.

The texts of the constitutions reproduced in this volume are all as supplied by the Governments concerned to the editor up to November 15, 1966. The editor is indebted to the Foreign Ministries which supplied most of the texts, almost all of them in English, and a certain amount of background material and bibliographies. As is the case with all the volumes, the editor has used for background material particularly the *Série Outremer* of the *Documentation française*, the *Statesman's Yearbook*, the *Encyclopaedia Americana* and *Le Monde*. The figures for area are taken from the Statesman's Yearbook, for population from the United Nations Yearbook for United Nations members and from the Statesman's Yearbook for non-members.

The selected bibliographies have been entirely revised and the books listed in the bibliography, now consolidated at the end of the volume, are, in many cases, those indicated as appropriate by the governments in question.

Dorothy Peaslee Xydis
Athens, November 15, 1966

[1] Czechoslovakia, France, Monaco, Rumania, San Marino, Yugoslavia.
[2] Belgium, Denmark, Greece, Ireland.

TABLE OF CONTENTS

VOLUME III - EUROPE

ALBANIA

SUMMARY

INTERNATIONAL STATUS

Albania is a member of the United Nations (December 14, 1955). It is a member of other international organizations. It was a member of the League of Nations.

Albania became independent on November 28, 1912, after centuries of Ottoman domination. Its existence was recognized internationally after the First Balkan War on July 28, 1913, and an international control commission drew up a constitution in 1914, providing for a monarchy with a National Assembly most of whose members were elected by the people.

Although a neutral state, Albania became involved in the First World War, after which, in January 1920, the Albanian chiefs drew up a new constitution providing for a monarchy. In 1925, Albania was proclaimed a republic and a new constitution, based on the United States constitution, was promulgated. In 1928, the President became King and a new constitution followed. On April 7, 1939, Italy occupied Albania and imposed a constitution providing that Albania was a monarchy under the House of Savoy. On April 6, 1941, martial law was proclaimed throughout the country. After the Italian capitulation in 1943, Albania was occupied by Germany.

The Albanian Communist Party was founded in November 1941, and the bases of the communist regime were laid at the second national conference in July 1943 of the Movement for National Liberation, created by the Party to unite and control all the forces opposing foreign occupation. This conference created Councils of National Liberation. On October 22, 1944, the Executive Committee of the General Council of National Liberation, which had taken over all the nationalist groups following a civil war between communist and non-communist ones during 1943–1944, and was acting as a provisional government, became the Albanian Democratic Government. On December 2, 1945, elections were organized for a Constituent Assembly in which the Democratic Front obtained 96% of the votes. The sovietization of the entire country began immediately after the elections and on January 10, 1946, the Constituent Assembly proclaimed the Popular Republic of Albania.

FORM OF NATIONAL GOVERNMENT

The Constitution of March 14, 1946, revised on July 4, 1950, and amended in 1953, 1954 and 1958, states that Albania is a people's republic, a state of workers and laboring peasants, the political basis of which are the people's Councils.[1] Power belongs to the working people.[2] A chapter relates to the social and economic order.[3]

RIGHTS OF THE PEOPLE

The Constitution provides equality before the law, universal suffrage, equal rights for women, freedom of conscience and faith, separation of church and state, protection of marriage and the family, freedom of speech, press, association, assembly, petition, inviolability of person and due process of law, inviolability of domicile, secrecy of correspondence, right to work and rest, freedom of science and art, protection of minorities, right of asylum.[4] Citizens are required to safeguard state and co-operative property, defend the country and pay taxes.[5]

[1] Constitution, Art. 2, 3.
[2] Id., Art. 4.
[3] Id., Art. 7–13.
[4] Id., Art. 14–34, 39, 40.
[5] Id., Art. 35–37.

LEGISLATIVE DEPARTMENT

Legislative power is exercised by the People's Assembly which is the highest organ of state power.[1] It is composed of one representative for every 8000 inhabitants elected by universal suffrage in electoral districts for a term of four years, subject to dissolution by itself.[2] It meets in two regular sessions a year.[3] Immunities of representatives are provided.[4]

EXECUTIVE DEPARTMENT

Executive power is exercised by the Presidium of the People's Assembly, elected by it and composed of a President, two Vice-Presidents, a secretary and ten members.[5] It promulgates laws, has the right of pardon, grants honors, has the power of appointment.[6] It is responsible to the People's Assembly.[7] The highest administrative and executive organ is the Government, appointed by and responsible to the People's Assembly, composed of the Chairman and ministers and the Chairmen of the State Committee of Control and of the Planning Committee.[8] A chapter relates to local administration.[9]

JUDICIAL DEPARTMENT

Justice is administered by the High Court, by district courts, people's courts and courts-martial; courts are independent and in all degrees are separated from the administration.[10] The question of the conformity of laws to the Constitution is decided by the Presidium of the People's Assembly.[11]

AREA, POPULATION, ETC.

The area of Albania is 28,738 square kilometres, its population (1964) is 1,814,000. The Constitution specifies that Albanian shall be used in all courts of justice.[12] The capital is Tirana.[13]

[1] Id., Art. 41, 43. [2] Id., Art. 44, 45, 54. [3] Id., Art. 47. [4] Id., Art. 53.
[5] Id., Art. 57. [6] Id., Art. 58. [7] Id., Art. 59. [8] Id., Art. 61–70.
[9] Id., Art. 71–78. [10] Id., Art. 79, 80. [11] Id., Art. 58 (3). [12] Id., Art. 84.
[13] Id., Art. 97.

CONSTITUTION
of
ALBANIA[1]

March 14, 1946, revised July 4, 1950, and amended in 1953, 1954 and 1958

FIRST PART—BASIC PRINCIPLES

CHAPTER I

THE PEOPLE'S REPUBLIC OF ALBANIA

Art. 1. Albania is a people's republic.

Art. 2. The People's Republic of Albania is a state of workers and laboring peasants.

Art. 3. The political basis of the People's Republic of Albania are the people's councils which sprang up during the war of national liberation against fascism and reaction and were consolidated after the historic victory of this war and during the construction of the bases of socialism.

Art. 4. All power in the People's Republic of Albania belongs to the working people of town and countryside represented by the people's councils.

Art. 5. All the representative organs of state power are elected by the citizens in free elections and by general, equal, direct and secret ballots.

The representatives of the people in all the organs of state power are responsible to their electors.

The electors have a right to revoke their representatives at any time. The norms to exercise this power will be set by special law.

Art. 6. All the organs of state power exercise their functions on the basis of the Constitution, of the laws and general provisions issued by the high organs of state power.

[1] Published in English by the Albanian Committee for Cultural Relations and Friendship with Foreign Countries, Tirana 1964. Supplied by the Ministry of Foreign Affairs in January 1966. Ed.

CHAPTER II

THE SOCIAL AND ECONOMIC ORDER

Art. 7. The means of production in the People's Republic of Albania is made up of the common property of the people in the hands of the State, of the property of the people's co-operative organizations and of the property of the private persons, natural or legal.

All mines and other resources of the subsoil, waters, natural springs, forests and pasture-grounds, the means of air, rail and maritime communication, posts, telegraph, telephone, broadcasting stations and banks make up the joint property of the people.

Foreign trade is under the state control. The State also governs and controls the entire interior trade of the country.

Art. 8. In order to safeguard the vital interests of the people and to raise the level of their well-being as well as to make full use of all the economic possibilities and powers, the State directs the economic life and development on the basis of a general economic plan. Relying on the state economic and co-operative sectors it exercises a general control on the private sector of economy.

In fulfilling the general economic plan the State lays its trust on the trade unions of the workers and employees, on the co-operatives of the peasants as well as on the other organizations of the laboring masses.

Art. 9. The management of state property is governed by law. State property enjoys special support by the State.

Art. 10. The State shows special concern about the co-operative movement, sponsors and favors it.

Art. 11. Private property and private enterprise in economy are guaranteed. The right of succession to private property is guaranteed. No one can use the right of private property to the prejudice of the community.

Private property may be limited and expropriated by law when the common good demands it.

In what cases and how much the proprietor will be remunerated will be specified by law.

Certain branches of economy or enterprises may be nationalized by the State under the same conditions if public interests demand it.

Monopolies, trusts, combines and so forth set up for the purpose of dictating prices and of monopolizing markets to the prejudice of national economy are prohibited.

Art. 12. The land belongs to those who till it. When an institution or person who does not till the land may remain in possession of this land or of part of it, is specified by law.

Large estates can by no means be in the hands of private owners.

The maximum area of land that can be under private ownership is determined by law.

The State sponsors the socialist development of agriculture by setting up state agricultural enterprises, machine and tractor stations and by aiding agricultural co-operatives and other forms of union of laboring peasants created on the basis of free choice.

The State gives special protection and aid to the poor and medium peasants by its economic policy, its credits and its system of taxation.

Art. 13. Work is the basis of the social order of the People's Republic of Albania.

Work is both a duty and an honor for all able-bodied citizens according to the principle of "who works not, eats not".

The socialist principle of "from each according to his capacity and to each according to his work" is carried out in the People's Republic of Albania.

CHAPTER III

THE RIGHTS AND DUTIES OF CITIZENS

Art. 14. All citizens are equal before the law. It is their duty to comply with the Constitution and the laws.

No privileges are recognized for reasons of origin, position, wealth or cultural standard.

Art. 15. All citizens are equal with no differences of nationality, race or religion. Any act which brings about privileges in favor of citizens or limits their rights on account of differences of nationality, race or religion is contrary to the Constitution and incurs punishment foreseen by law. Any attempt to sow hatred and cause dissension among nationalities, races and religions is contrary to the Constitution and liable to punishment according to law.

Art. 16. All citizens, without distinction of sex, nationality, belief, cultural standard or residence, and who have reached the age of 18 years, have the right to vote and stand for election to all the organs of state power.

These rights are enjoyed also by citizens serving in the army.

The right of the ballot is universal, equal, direct and secret.

The right of the ballot is refused to persons who are excluded by law.

Art. 17. Women enjoy equal rights with men in all spheres of private, political and social life.

Women enjoy the rights of equal pay with men for the same work. They enjoy the same right in social insurances.

The State gives special protection to the interests of mother and child by securing the right for a paid leave before and after childbirth and by setting up homes for expectant mothers and homes for bringing up and sheltering children.

Art. 18. All the citizens are guaranteed the freedom of conscience and of faith.

The church is separated from the State.

The religious communities are free in matters of their belief as well as in their outer exercise and practice.

It is prohibited to use the church and religion for political purposes.

Political organizations on a religious basis are likewise prohibited.

The State may give material aid to religious communities.

Art. 19. Marriage and the family are under the protection of the State. The State determines by law the legal conditions of marriage and the family.

Lawful marriage can be contracted only before the competent organs of the State. After the celebration of lawful marriage the citizens may also celebrate religious marriage according to the rules of their religion.

Only the state courts have jurisdiction on all the matters connected with marriage.

Parents have the same obligations and duties towards the children born outside their marriage as they have towards children born within their marriage. Children born outside marriage enjoy the same rights as children born within marriage.

Art. 20. All the citizens are guaranteed the freedom of speech, of the press, of organization, of meetings, of assembly and of public manifestations.

Art. 21. In order to develop the initiative of the working masses in the field of organization and their political activity, the State guarantees to the citizens the right to join in social organizations: the Democratic Front, the Trade Unions, the co-operatives, the organizations of Youth and of Women, the organizations of Sport and of Defence, cultural, scientific and technical societies; the more active and conscientious citizens of the working class and of the other working masses join the ranks of the Albanian Party of Labor, the vanguard organization of the working class and of all the working masses in their endeavors to build the bases of socialism and the leading nucleus of all the organizations of the working masses, both social as well as of the State.

Art. 22. All the citizens are guaranteed the inviolability of the person. No one can be detained under arrest more than three days without a decision of the court or without the approval of the public attorney.

Nobody can be condemned for a crime without a sentence of the court having jurisdiction according to the law which fixes the jurisdiction and specifies the crime.

No sentences can be passed except on the basis of law.

Nobody can be convicted without being heard and without being called to defend himself according to the provisions of law, except when his absence is legally verified.

The organs of the state administration may, within bounds specified by law, pass sentences to imprisonment for slight violations of common law.

No citizen can be banished abroad or within the State except in cases considered by law.

The People's Republic of Albania protects the Albanian citizens residing abroad.

Art. 23. Dwelling houses cannot be violated.

Nobody can enter one's domicile and make searches without the consent of the owner of the house, except when he is in possession of a search warrant.

Searches cannot be made except in the presence of two witnesses. The owner of the house also has the right to be present.

Art. 24. The secrecy of correspondence and other means of communication cannot be violated, except in cases of inquiries on crimes, of mobilization and of a state of war.

Art. 25. The State guarantees to the citizens the right of work for a remuneration according to the amount and quality of the work they yield.

The State guarantees to the citizens the right to rest through a shortening of the hours of work, through granting an annual paid vacation, and through setting up sanatoria, rest homes, clubs, etc.

Through social insurance the State guarantees to the citizens likewise, the material means of subsistence in old age and in case of illness and disability.

Art. 26. Under conditions specified by law, all the citizens have equal rights to be admitted to state posts.

The citizens charged with public functions or appointed to public service are bound to carry out their missions conscientiously.

Art. 27. The State is duty-bound to provide better living conditions to the invalids of the war and make them capable of work at its own expense. The State shows special concern for the children of the fighters fallen in the battle-field and of the other victims of the war.

Art. 28. The State takes care of the health of the people by setting up and supervising health service, hospitals and sanatoria.

Art. 29. The State takes care of the physical culture of the people, particularly of the youth, so that the health and the vigor of the people for work and the defence of the State may be improved.

Art. 30. The freedom of scientific and art work is guaranteed. The State supports science and arts so that the culture and welfare of the people may develop.

Copyright is protected by law.

Art. 31. In order to raise the general cultural standard of the people the State provides opportunities to attend schools and other cultural institutions for all ranks of the people.

The State shows special concern for the education of youth.

Children of tender age are under the protection of the law.

The schools are under the dependence of the State. No private schools can be opened except by law. Their activity is under the supervision of the State.

Primary education is compulsory and is given free of charge.

The school is separated from the church.

Art. 32. Citizens have a right to lodge petitions and complaints to the state organs.

Citizens have a right to complain against all decisions contrary to law or irregular, taken by the organs of state administration as well as when functionaries act unlawfully.

Art. 33. Every citizen has the right to claim for damages before the competent courts against the state employees for unlawful deeds they incur in the exercise of their functions.

Art. 34. Under conditions specified by law, citizens are entitled to indemnities from the State or its employees for damages incurred due to carrying out of services contrary to law or in an irregular way.

Art. 35. Every citizen is duty-bound to safeguard and consolidate social property (state and co-operative property), the sacred and inviolable basis of the people's democracy, the source of power of the Fatherland, of the welfare and culture of all the working people.

Those who lay hands on social property are enemies of the people.

Art. 36. Protection of the Fatherland is the supreme duty and the highest honor of every citizen.

Betrayal of the people is the greatest felony.

Military service is compulsory for all citizens.

Art. 37. All citizens are obliged to pay taxes in proportion to their economic possibilities.

State taxes and exemptions from payment of taxes are stated by law.

Art. 38. Citizens are not entitled to use the rights granted to them by this Constitution, in order to change the constitutional order of the People's Republic of Albania for anti-democratic purposes.

Every act in this direction is considered contrary to law and incurs punishments foreseen by law.

Art. 39. National minorities in the People's Republic of Albania enjoy all the rights, the protection of their cultural development and the free use of their language.

Art. 40. The People's Republic of Albania grants the right to asylum in its territory to foreign citizens persecuted on account of their activity in favor of democracy, of the struggle for national liberation, of the rights of working people or in favor of the freedom in scientific and cultural work.

SECOND PART—ORGANIZATION OF THE STATE

CHAPTER I

THE HIGH ORGANS OF STATE POWER

(a) The People's Assembly

Art. 41. The People's Assembly is the highest organ of state power in the People's Republic of Albania.

Art. 42. The sovereignty of the nation and of the State is invested in the People's Assembly which exercises its sovereign rights on the basis of the Constitution with the exception of those rights which the Constitution itself has left to the competence of the Presidium of the People's Assembly or of the Government.

Art. 43. Legislative power is exercised only by the People's Assembly.

The Presidium of the People's Assembly, the Government and the representatives have the exclusive right of proposal of new laws.

Art. 44. The People's Assembly is elected by universal suffrage in electoral districts in the ratio of one representative for every 8,000 inhabitants.

Art. 45. The People's Assembly is elected for a term of four years.

Art. 46. The People's Assembly elects one chairman, two vice-chairmen and a secretary. The chairman presides at the meetings in conformity with the rules.

Art. 47. The People's Assembly is convened by decree of its Presidium in two regular sessions a year.

It may be convened in extraordinary sessions by decision of the Presidium of the People's Assembly or at the request of one third of the representatives.

Art. 48. The People's Assembly draw up their own rules and regulations.

Art. 49. No draft law can have legal power if it is not voted upon by the relative majority of the representatives at a meeting of the People's Assembly attended by the majority of its members.

Art. 50. Laws become effective fifteen days after they have been published in the Official Gazette, except when the law provides otherwise.

Art. 51. The People's Assembly appoints special committees for specific missions.

At its first meeting the People's Assembly appoints a committee to verify the mandates of the representatives.

On the proposal of this Committee the People's Assembly confirms or annuls the mandates of the representatives.

Art. 52. The People's Assembly may hold inquests on matters of general importance through a committee of investigation.

All organs of the State are obliged to respond to the queries of the Committee with regard to establishing facts and gathering evidence.

Art. 53. The representatives to the People's Assembly enjoy parliamentary immunity.

They cannot be arrested or prosecuted without the approval of the People's Assembly or its Presidium, except when caught in the act.

Art. 54. In case of war in or similar cases of emergency the People's Assembly may prolong their legislature beyond the normal term as long as the state of emergency lasts.

The People's Assembly may take a decision to dissolve itself before the end of the term for which it is elected.

Art. 55. Elections for a new People's Assembly must be held not later than three months after the day of the dissolution of the People's Assembly.

Art. 56. Amendments or additions to the Constitution can be made only by decision of the People's Assembly.

Bills on amendments or additions to the Constitution may be submitted by the Presidium of the People's Assembly, by the Government or by two thirds of the number of representatives.

Bills on amendments or additions to the Constitution are adopted by a two-thirds majority of all the representatives of the People's Assembly.

(b) The Presidium of the People's Assembly

Art. 57. The People's Assembly elects its Presidium which is made up of a President, two Vice-Presidents, a secretary and ten members.

Art. 58. The Presidium of the People's Assembly exercises the following functions:

(1) Convenes the sessions of the People's Assembly;

(2) Decrees the elections to the People's Assembly;

(3) Decides on the conformity of laws to the Constitution provided that this decision is later approved by the People's Assembly;

(4) Interprets laws;

(5) Promulgates laws that have been enacted;

(6) Issues decrees. When decrees contain juridical rules they must be submitted for approval to the People's Assembly at its next session;

(7) Exercises the right of pardon in conformity with the provisions of the law;

(8) Grants decorations and titles of honor;

(9) Ratifies and denounces international treaties except in cases when it deems it advisable to have these ratifications or denunciations passed on by the People's Assembly;

(10) Appoints or recalls Envoys Extraordinary and Ministers Plenipotentiary on the proposal of the Government;

(11) Receives credential letters and letters of recall of the diplomatic representatives of foreign states;

(12) Appoints and discharges the Supreme Command of the Armed Forces of the People's Republic of Albania;

(13) During the interval between two sessions of the People's Republic of Albania decrees general mobilization and a state of war in case of an armed aggression against the People's Republic of Albania or when this is necessary to fulfil the obligations that arise from international treaties of mutual defence against an aggression;

(14) Appoints and discharges ministers between two sessions of the People's Assembly on the proposal of the Head of the Government;

(15) On the proposal of the Head of the Government it sets up committees within the Government and appoints their chairmen;

(16) On the proposal of the Government it designates which enterprises of general importance to the State should come under the direct supervision of a ministry or of a government committee;

(17) Decrees people's referendums on various questions, on the basis of the decision of the People's Assembly or on the proposal of the Government.

The decrees of the Presidium of the People's Assembly are signed by the President and the Secretary.

Art. 59. The Presidium of the People's Assembly is responsible to the People's Assembly for its doings. The latter may revoke its Presidium and elect another, may revoke its members and may substitute them also before the end of the term for which they are elected.

Art. 60. In case of the dissolution of the People's Assembly the Presidium remains in power until the new Presidium of the People's Assembly is elected.

The Presidium convenes the newly-elected People's Assembly not later than three months after its election.

CHAPTER II

ORGANS OF THE STATE ADMINISTRATION

Art. 61. The Government is the highest executive organ and authority of the People's Republic of Albania.

The Government is appointed and discharged by the People's Assembly.

The Government is responsible to the People's Assembly and should render account to it for its activity. During the interval between two sessions of the People's Assembly it is responsible to the Presidium of the Assembly to which it should render account for its activity.

Art. 62. The Government acts on the basis of the Constitution and in conformity with the laws.

The Government issues decisions and orders on the basis of and for the implementation of the laws in force and checks on their implementation.

The decisions and orders of the Government are signed by the Head of the Government and are published in the Official Gazette.

Art. 63. The Government directs and co-ordinates the work of the Ministries, of the committees and of the services of other institutions which are under its direct supervision.

The Government draws up the general economic plan of the State and the general budget of the State which it submits to the People's Assembly for approval and supervises their implementation; directs the system of credits and the monetary system; takes all the necessary measures to assure and protect the constitutional order and the rights of citizens; directs the general organization of the army; maintains relations with foreign states; sees to it that international treaties and obligations are carried out; submits to the People's Assembly the drafts of laws drawn up by it or by the different ministers; determines the internal organization of the ministries and of the institutions dependent on it; sets up committees and institutions to carry out economic, cultural and national defence measures.

Art. 64. The Government is made up of the chairman, the deputy chairmen, the ministers, the Chairman of the State Committee of Control and the Chairman of the Planning Committee.

The members of the Government take oath before the People's Assembly.

Art. 65. The Head of the Government represents the Government, presides at its meetings and directs the affairs of the Government.

Art. 66. The members of the Government head the various departments of the state administration.

The Government may also have ministers without portfolio.

Art. 67. The members of the Government are penally responsible for the violation of the Constitution and the laws in force in connection with the exercise of their functions.

They are responsible also for damages they may cause to the State through their activities contrary to the law.

The norms on the responsibility of the members of the Government will be specified in detail by a special law.

Art. 68. Within the bounds of the competence of their departments, the Ministers issue orders and directions based on the laws and aiming at carrying out the laws in force, the decisions and orders of the Government and supervise their execution.

The orders and instructions of the Ministers are published in the Official Gazette.

Art. 69. The Ministries of the People's Republic of Albania are:

(1) The Ministry of Foreign Affairs;
(2) The Ministry of Internal Affairs;
(3) The Ministry of People's Defence;

(4) The Ministry of Justice;
(5) The Ministry of Finances;
(6) The Ministry of Education and Culture;
(7) The Ministry of Industry;
(8) The Ministry of Commerce;
(9) The Ministry of Agriculture;
(10) The Ministry of Health and Sanitation;
(11) The Ministry of Construction;
(12) The Ministry of Communications;
(13) The Ministry of Mines and Geology.

The Committee of State Control and the State Planning Committee are of ministerial rank.

Other ministries may be set up or those already in existence may be suppressed only by law.

Art. 70. The Government may decide to charge a more restricted ministerial council to take up certain matters concerning economy and national defence.

The decision to set up a restricted ministerial council will determine its make-up and its competence.

CHAPTER III

ORGANS OF STATE POWER OF THE LOCAL ADMINISTRATIVE UNITS

Art. 71. The people's councils are the organs of state power in villages, counties, cities, townships and districts.

The people's councils of villages, counties, cities, townships and districts are elected by the citizens for a term of three years.

The above administrative units may be suppressed or new administrative units may be set up, too, by law.

Art. 72. The people's councils direct the affairs of the administrative organs dependent on them, they are charged with economic and cultural matters within the bounds of their competence, keep public order, supervise the implementation of laws, protect the rights of citizens and draw up the local budgets.

Art. 73. Within the bounds of their competence the people's councils issue decrees and orders in conformity with the Constitution, the laws and general provisions of the higher organs of state power.

Art. 74. In the exercise of their general and local functions the people's councils must collaborate with the people and the organizations of the laboring masses and be inspired by their initiatives.

Art. 75. The executive committees of the people's councils are the executive organs of authority of the people's councils.

The composition and functions of the executive committees of the people's councils are specified by law.

The executive organs of authority in minor administrative units may be made up of the chairman and the secretary of the people's councils.

Art. 76. The local people's councils call meetings of their electorate at the times set by law before which they render account of their activity.

Art. 77. The executive committees of the people's councils are dependent on both the people's councils which have elected them as well as the executive organs of authority of the higher organs of state power.

Art. 78. In order to direct the various departments of administration the people's councils may set up offices or sections. The activities of these offices or sections are directed by the executive committees and supervised by the people's councils and at the same time by the corresponding offices and sections of the higher people's councils and the competent ministry.

CHAPTER IV

COURTS OF JUSTICE AND PUBLIC ATTORNEYS

(a) Courts of Justice

Art. 79. Justice in the People's Republic of Albania is administered by the High Court of the People's Republic of Albania, by district courts, by people's courts and by courts-martial.

Special courts may also be set up by law for a given category of questions.

Art. 80. Courts of justice are independent in the exercise of their functions. Courts of justice in all degrees are separated from the Administration. Their judgements and sentences cannot be changed except by the higher courts having jurisdiction.

Within the bounds of law the higher courts of justice have the right to control the lower courts.

The Minister of Justice directs and supervises the activity of the judiciary administration and sees to it that the courts of justice are organized and function as they should.

Art. 81. The courts of justice try cases on the basis of the law and pass sentences and judgements in the name of the people.

Art. 82. The courts as a rule try their cases in public sittings.

The accused is assured the right of defence.

Art. 83. The courts of justice try cases with the participation of the jury (assistant-judges) except cases specifically envisaged by law.

Art. 84. The Albanian language is used in all courts of justice. The citizens that do not speak Albanian may use their own language and make use of an interpreter.

Art. 85. The High Court is elected by the People's Assembly for a four-year term.

Courts-martial are elected by the People's Assembly and, between its two sessions, by the Presidium of the People's Assembly, for a three-year term.

District courts are elected by the people's councils of the district for a three-year term.

The people's courts are elected by citizens by universal, equal, direct and secret ballot for a three-year term.

Art. 86. The High Court of Justice is the highest organ of justice in the People's Republic of Albania.

It is determined by law when the High Court of Justice will hold trials of the first or of the second grade.

Art. 87. The High Court of Justice will decide whether the final judgements of all the courts of the Republic are lawful or not.

(b) Public Attorneys

Art. 88. Public attorneys are organs of the People's Assembly whose mission it is to check on the exact implementation of the law by the Ministers and other administrative organs as well as by the public service men and by all the citizens.

Art. 89. The Attorney-General of the People's Republic of Albania and his assistants are appointed by the People's Assembly.

Public attorneys are appointed by the Attorney-General.

Art. 90. All public attorneys are independent towards all local organs and are dependent on the Attorney-General from whom they receive orders and instructions.

CHAPTER V

RELATIONS BETWEEN THE ORGANS OF STATE POWER AND STATE ADMINISTRATION

Art. 91. The Presidium of the People's Assembly may declare the decisions and the ordinances of the Government null and void when they are contrary to the Constitution and to the laws.

The Government may annul the orders and instructions of the Ministers when they are contrary to the Constitution and to the laws as well as to the decisions and orders of the Government.

Art. 92. The Presidium of the People's Assembly and the higher people's councils may annul every unlawful or irregular act of the lower people's councils. The Government may annul all unlawful and irregular acts of the executive committees of the people's councils. The executive committees of the higher people's councils have the same right towards the lower executive committees.

The people's councils may quash every unlawful or irregular act of their executive committees.

The Government and the executive committees of the higher people's councils may suspend the execution of all unlawful and irregular acts of the lower people's councils and propose to their people's councils or to the Presidium of the People's Assembly to declare these acts null and void.

Art. 93. The Presidium of the People's Assembly and the higher people's councils may dissolve the lower people's councils and order the election of new people's councils. They may likewise dismiss the executive committees of the lower people's councils and order the election of new executive committees.

CHAPTER VI

THE PEOPLE'S ARMY

Art. 94. The People's Army is the armed force of the People's Republic of Albania. Its function is to secure and protect the independence of the State and the freedom of the people.

Its stands guard over the state boundaries so that they should not be violated and serves the cause of peace and security.

THIRD PART—NATIONAL EMBLEM, NATIONAL FLAG, CAPITAL

Art. 95. The national emblem of the People's Republic of Albania represents a field wrapped by two sheaves of ears of wheat. The sheaf of wheat is bound at the lower end with a ribbon which bears the inscription of the date May 24, 1944. A five-pointed red star stands among the tops of the tufts of the ears of wheat. A black double-headed eagle stands in the center of the field.

Art. 96. The national flag of the People's Republic of Albania represents a red field with a double-headed eagle in the center. Above the eagle there is a five-pointed red star, gold-embroidered all around. The ratio between the width and the length of the flag is one to one and forty-hundredths.

Art. 97. The Capital of the People's Republic of Albania is Tirana.

AUSTRIA

SUMMARY

INTERNATIONAL STATUS

Austria is a member of the United Nations (December 14, 1955). It is a member of other international organizations. It was a member of the League of Nations.

The Hapsburg Emperor renounced the title of Holy Roman Emperor on August 6, 1806, and retained only the title of Emperor of Austria which he had assumed in 1804. The 1814 and 1815 treaties restored to Austria certain of the lands lost to Napoleon. Growing national sentiment led to the Galician revolt in 1846 and the 1848 revolutions in Hungary, Vienna and Lombardy. By the end of 1849, they had been put down and a unitary centralized empire established. A period of absolutism followed which was discredited by the defeats by Napoleon III and in the war with Prussia, which resulted in the loss of the Italian provinces — Lombardy in 1859 and Venetia in 1866—and of Austria's position of primacy in Germany. In 1867, the Compromise with Hungary was reached granting the latter full internal autonomy, the empire to continue as a single state for war and foreign affairs. In December 1867, Constitutional laws were passed regarding individual rights and an impartial judiciary some of which are still in force. The remainder of the Empire, which had become Austria-Hungary, was only formally consulted over the arrangement with Hungary and there was growing dissatisfaction in Czechoslovakia and the Balkans. Following the First World War the Empire was dissolved, the Emperor renounced on November 11 and 13, 1918 his powers as ruler of Austria and Hungary, the Austrian German Republic was proclaimed on November 12, 1918. The Treaty of St. Germain laid down the borders of the new Austria and forbade union with Germany. The Constitution of 1920 created a federal state with a bicameral legislature. In 1933, political and economic crises led to the dissolution of Parliament and the imposition of authoritarian rule, the Constitution of May 1, 1934, established a fascist corporate state. On March 12, 1938, Austria was annexed by Germany and even its name abolished. It was liberated in the spring of 1945 and on April 27, 1945, the provisional government restored the Republic of Austria in the spirit of the Constitution of 1920–29. A Four-Power Allied Control Council remained in Austria with certain powers until the conclusion of the Austrian State Treaty of July 27, 1955, between the United Kingdom, the United States, the U.S.S.R., France and Austria, restored the latter's sovereignty and independence. The Treaty included a prohibition of *anschluss* and a declaration of neutrality.

FORM OF NATIONAL GOVERNMENT

The Austrian Constitution of October 26, 1955, as amended to 1964, states that Austria is a democratic republic, a federal state composed of autonomous *Länder* which are named.[1] Law emanates from the people.[2] The generally recognized rules of international law are considered component parts of Federal Law.[3] Article 149 lists other laws which are to be regarded as constitutional laws, including laws of 1862, 1867, regarding rights, laws of 1919 banishing the dynasty of Hapsburg-Lorraine, abolishing the nobility, concerning the coat of arms and seal, and articles of the Treaty of St. Germain concerning the protection of minorities.

[1] Const., Art. 1, 2. [2] Id., Art. 1. [3] Id., Art. 9.

RIGHTS OF THE PEOPLE

The Constitution provides equality before the law.[1] Noone may be withheld from his legal judge, military jurisdictions are abolished in time of war, capital punishment is abolished.[2] The laws of 1862 concerning the protection of personal liberty and the inviolability of the home and the State Fundamental Act of 1867 providing for equality of citizens, freedom of persons and property, freedom of travel and residence, inviolability of property, of the domicile, secrecy and inviolability of correspondence, freedom of petition, assembly, association, expression, the press, religion, teaching, profession, and the equality of peoples and their right to language and nationality, are regarded as constitutional laws.[3]

LEGISLATIVE DEPARTMENT

The federal legislative power is exercised by the bicameral legislature composed of the *Nationalrat* (National Council) and the *Bundesrat* (Federal Council).[4] The legislative jurisdiction and powers of the Federation and the *Länder* are described.[5] The *Nationalrat* is elected by equal, direct, universal suffrage and proportional representation for a term of four years subject to dissolution.[6] It meets in two regular annual sessions.[7] The *Bundesrat* is composed of representatives of the *Länder* according to their population elected by the *Land* Diets for the same term as the latter.[8] The two bodies meet together as the Federal Assembly for specified purposes.[9] There are provisions regarding finances.[10] Immunities of deputies are provided.[11] There are provisions concerning the legislative powers of the *Länder*; the *Land* Diets may be dissolved by the Federal President.[12] There are provisions concerning Vienna [13] and the municipalities.[14]

EXECUTIVE DEPARTMENT

Supreme executive functionaries are the Federal President, the Federal Ministers, the Secretaries of State and the members of *Land* governments.[15] The Federal President is elected by direct, secret and compulsory suffrage for a term of six years and may be immediately re-elected once only.[16] The Federal President represents the Republic in international relations, has the power of appointment, grants titles, has the power of clemency, the right to legitimize illegitimate children and is Commander in Chief of the Federal Army.[17] He is responsible to the Federal Assembly for the exe-

[1] Id., Art. 7. [2] Id., Art. 83, 84, 85. [3] Id., Art. 149.
[4] Id., Art. 24. [5] Id., Art. 10–15. [6] Id., Art. 26, 27, 29.
[7] Id., Art. 28. [8] Id., Art. 34, 35. [9] Id., Art. 38–40.
[10] Id., Art. 51, 121–128. [11] Id., Art. 57, 58. [12] Id., Art. 95–100.
[13] Id., Art. 108–111. [14] Id., Art. 115–120. [15] Id., Art. 19. [16] Id., Art. 60.
[17] Id., Art. 65, 80.

cution of his office.[1] The highest administrative functions of the Federation are entrusted to the Federal Chancellor, Vice-Chancellor and other Federal Ministers forming the Government.[2] The Federal Chancellor is appointed by the Federal President and the Federal Government must have the confidence of the *Nationalrat.*[3] Ministers have access to all the legislative bodies and are responsible to the *Nationalrat.*[4] There are provisions regarding the Army.[5] The Constitution provides for the executive powers of the *Länder.*[6] Educational matters fall under the direction of the Federation.[7]

JUDICIAL DEPARTMENT

The judicial power emanates from the Federation, judges are appointed by the Federal President on the nomination of the Federal Government.[8] Judges are independent in the exercise of their judicial functions.[9] Courts may not examine the validity of duly promulgated laws.[10] The Supreme Court is the court of final appeal in civil and criminal cases.[11] The Administrative Court of Vienna safeguards the legality of acts of the public administration.[12] There is provision for a Constitutional Court to rule upon, among other things, the constitutionality of laws, violations of international law, conflicts of jurisdiction and contested elections.[13]

AREA, POPULATION, ETC.

The area of Austria is 83,849 square kilometres, its population (1964) 7,237,000. Vienna is the federal capital.[14] German is the official language without prejudice to the rights conceded by Federal law to linguistic minorities.[15]

[1] Id., Art. 68.
[2] Id., Art. 69.
[3] Id., Art. 70, 74.
[4] Id., Art. 75, 76.
[5] Id., Art. 79–81.
[6] Id., Art. 101–107.
[7] Id., Art. 102a.
[8] Id., Art. 82, 86.
[9] Id., Art. 87.
[10] Id., Art. 89
[11] Id., Art. 92..
[12] Id., Art. 129–136.
[13] Id., Art. 137–148.
[14] Id., Art. 5
[15] Id., Art. 8.

CONSTITUTION
of
AUSTRIA

Federal Constitutional Law[1]

October 26, 1955, as amended to 1964

CHAPTER I

GENERAL PROVISIONS

Art. 1. Austria is a democratic republic. Its law emanates from the people.

Art. 2. (1) Austria is a Federal State.

(2) The Federal State is composed of the autonomous *Länder* (States) of Burgenland, Carinthia, Lower Austria, Upper Austria, Salzburg, Styria, Tyrol, Vorarlberg and Vienna.

Art. 3. (1) The territory of the Federal State comprises the territories of the Austrian *Länder.*

(2) An alteration of Federal boundaries, affecting also the boundaries of a *Land,* as well as an alteration of *Land* boundaries within the Federal territory can take place—except as provided by peace treaties—only by concurrent constitutional laws of the *Bund* (Federation) and the *Land,* the boundaries of which are affected thereby.

Art. 4. (1) The Federal territory forms a uniform currency, economic and customs area.

(2) Inter-*Land* custom barriers or other restrictions of traffic shall not be established within the Federal territory.

Art. 5. (1) Vienna is the Federal capital and the seat of the supreme Federal authorities.

(2) For the duration of a state of emergency, the Federal President may, at the request of the Federal Government, transfer the seat of the supreme Federal authorities to another place in the Federal territory.

[1] *BundesVerfassungsgesetz.* Provisional English translation prepared by Austrian Ministry of Foreign Affairs, supplied by them in May 1967. Amendments of 1964 translated by Editor. Ed.

Art. 6. There shall exist a *Land* citizenship for each *Land.* The qualification requisite for *Land* citizenship shall be the *Heimatrecht* (right of domicile) in a *Gemeinde* (municipality) of the *Land.* The conditions for the acquisition and loss of *Land* citizenship shall be the same in each *Land.*

(2) An acquisition of *Land* citizenship shall carry with it the acquisition of Federal citizenship.

(3) In each *Land* every Federal citizen shall have the same rights and duties as the citizens of the *Land* itself.

(4) An alien shall, by assuming a professorship at an Austrian university or at another school of the same rank, acquire the *Land* citizenship of the *Land,* in which the school is situated and at the same time the *Heimatrecht* in the *Gemeinde* of his place of office.

Art. 7. (1) All Federal citizens shall be equal before the law. Privileges based upon birth, sex, social position, class, or creed shall be excluded.

(2) All public employees, including the members of the Federal army, shall be guaranteed the unrestricted exercise of their political rights.

Art. 8. Without prejudice to the rights conceded by Federal law to linguistic minorities, the German language shall be the official language of the Republic.

Art. 9. The generally recognized rules of international law shall be considered as component parts of the Federal law.

Art. 10. (1) The *Bund* (Federation) shall have powers of legislation and execution with respect to the following matters:

1. The Federal Constitution, in particular election to the *Nationalrat* (National Council); plebiscites as provided by the Federal Constitution; Constitutional jurisdiction.
2. Foreign relations, including political and commercial representation in relation with foreign countries, in particular, the conclusion of all treaties, marking of boundaries, trade in goods and livestock with foreign countries, and customs.
3. Regulation and control of entry into and exit from the Federal territory; immigration and emigration; passports; deportation, interdiction of sojourn, expulsion and extradition from or through the Federal territory.
4. Federal finances, in particular, taxes to be collected exclusively or in part for the *Bund*; monopolies.
5. Money; matters pertaining to commodities and stock exchanges; banking; weights and measures; standards and hallmarking.
6. Civil law, including the law of economic associations; criminal law with the exception of administrative penal law and administrative penal procedure in matters falling within the autonomous sphere of competence of the *Länder,* administration of justice; institutions for the protection of society from criminals, neglected or other dangerous persons, such as workhouses and similar establishments; administrative

jurisdiction; copyright; press-affairs; expropriations for slum clearance; other expropriations unless they concern matters falling within the autonomous sphere of competence of the *Länder*; matters pertaining to public notaries, lawyers, and related professions.

7. Maintenance of public peace, order and safety, exclusive of the local safety police; laws of association and assembly; matters concerning the personal status of individuals, including registration of births, marriages, and deaths, and change of name; alien police and matters pertaining to registration of residence; matters pertaining to arms, ammunition and explosives; use of firearms.

8. Matters concerning trade and industry; professional acting as agent before public authorities and brokerage; measures against unfair competition; patent matters as well as the protection of designs, trademarks and other designations of commodities; matters relating to patent attorneys; matters pertaining to civil and consulting engineers; chambers for commerce, trade and industry; establishment of professional representations in so far as they extend over the whole Federal territory, except those in the field of agriculture and forestry.

9. Traffic by rail, water and air; motor transport; matters concerning roads declared by Federal law as Federal highways on account of their importance in intercommunication; river and navigation police; post, telegraph, and telephone affairs.

10. Mining; forestry including floating of timber, water rights; conservancy of water-courses for the purpose of flood control or for the purpose of navigation and rafting; regulation of torrents; construction and maintenance of water-ways; standardization and systematization of electrical establishments and plants, safety measures in this field; right of way for electric power transmission in so far as the transmission extends across the boundary of two or more *Länder*; matters concerning steam boilers and power engines; surveying.

11. Labor law and protection of workers and employees in so far as they are not engaged in agriculture or forestry; social insurance and contractual insurance; chambers for workers and employees.

12. Public health, exclusive of the disposal or burial of the dead, as well as of municipal sanitation and first aid services; however with respect to hospitals and sanatoria, health resorts, and medicinal springs only their sanitary supervision; veterinary affairs; foodstuffs, including food inspection.

13. Scientific and technical archives and libraries; art collections and institutions, scientific collections and institutions, all matters pertaining to the Federal theatres, however not including the determination of the alignment and the level nor the supervision by building authorities of constructions affecting the exterior of the theatres buildings; protection of monuments; matters pertaining to religion; census as well as other

statistics, unless they serve only the interests of one *Land;* endowments and foundations not intended to serve the interests of one *Land* only and not hitherto autonomously administered by the *Länder*.

14. Organization and operation of the Federal police and the Federal gendarmerie; establishment and organization of other guards, including their armament and right to make use of their weapons.

15. Military affairs; war damages and welfare measures concerning veterans and their surviving dependents; care of war graves; measures to be taken because of or in wake of a war in order to safeguard the uniform administration of economic affairs, in particular, the supply of necessary commodities to the population.

16. Establishment of Federal authorities and other Federal agencies; Federal employment regulations.

(2) In the Federal laws issued according to paragraph 1, clause 10, the *Land* legislature may be authorized to enact enabling laws with regard to certain specifically designated provisions of the Federal law. The provisions of Article 15, paragraph 6, shall be applied with any necessary modifications to these *Land* laws. The execution of these enabling laws shall fall within the sphere of competence of the *Bund*. Enabling ordinances which are based on the enabling provisions of the *Land* law shall, however, require a previous agreement with the *Land* Government concerned.

Art. 11. (1) The *Bund* (Federation) shall have the power of legislation, but the *Land* shall have the power of execution in respect to the following matters:

1. Citizenship and *Heimatrecht*.
2. Professional representations not included in Article 10 but exclusive of those pertaining to agriculture and forestry.
3. Public housing.

(2) Administrative procedure, the general rules of administrative penal law, administrative penal procedure and administrative execution shall be regulated by Federal laws. Provided there exists a need for the enactment of uniform rules, this shall also apply to matters which otherwise are within the legislative power of the *Länder*, especially matters pertaining to taxation.

(3) Enabling ordinances to the laws enacted under paragraphs 1 and 2 shall be issued by the Federal Government save as otherwise provided in these laws.

(4) The administration of the laws and enabling ordinances issued under paragraph 2 shall fall within the sphere of competence of the *Bund* or the *Länder* according to whether the executive powers for the matters forming the subject of the procedure fall within the sphere of competence of the *Bund* or of the Länder.

(5) Final decision in proceedings before administrative authorities for administrative offenses shall be exercised by special administrative penal

boards to be established at the competent authorities. The members of these boards shall be independent in the exercise of their office, and shall not be bound by any order. The board is presided over by the head of the administrative authority concerned or by a deputy appointed by him who shall have legal training. The *Bund* shall appoint two members also in those cases in which the boards are not established at Federal authorities. The right of pardon provided for by the law shall be exercised, on recommendation of the administrative penal boards, in penal administrative cases falling within the indirect Federal administration by the *Landeshauptmänner* (Governors), in cases falling within the autonomous sphere of competence of the *Land* by the *Landesregierungen* (*Land* Governments).

Details concerning the organization and operation of the administrative penal boards shall be ruled by Federal law.

Art. 12. (1) The *Bund* (Federation) shall have legislative power as to basic principles, but the *Länder* shall have the power of enabling legislation and execution with respect to the following matters:

1. Organization of the administration in the *Länder*.
2. Poor relief; population policy; national welfare establishments; maternity, infant, and adolescent welfare; hospitals and nursing homes; matters pertaining to health-resorts and medicinal springs;
3. Public institutions for the extra-judicial adjustment of controversies.
4. Labor law and protection of workers and employees in agriculture and forestry.
5. Land reform, including, in particular, agrarian re-adjustment operations and resettlement.
6. Protection of plants against disease and pests.
7. Matters concerning electric power, insofar as they are not included in Article 10.
8. Highway police with the exception of the highway police on Federal highways which comes under Article 10, clause 9.
9. Employment regulations for *Land* employees performing official duties.

(2) In matters pertaining to land reform (paragraph 1, clause 5), the decision on the supreme level and on the *Land* level shall rest with boards composed of a chairman and of judges, civil servants and experts; the board which acts on the supreme level shall be established at the competent Federal Ministry. The organization, the functions and the procedure of the boards, as well as the principles concerning the organization of the other authorities engaged in land reform, shall be ruled by Federal law.

(3) If and in so far as decisions of *Land* authorities in matters pertaining to electric power differ from one another, or if the *Land* Government was the only competent *Land* authority the right of decision shall pass to the appropriate Federal Ministry, if a party concerned submits a request to this effect within a time limit which shall be fixed by Federal law. Upon

the decision of the Federal Ministry, the previous decisions of the *Land* authorities shall be invalidated.

Art. 13. The competences of the *Bund* and of the *Länder* in the field of taxation shall be ruled by a special Federal Constitutional Law (Constitutional Finance Law).

Art. 14. A special Federal Constitutional Law shall rule the competences of the *Bund* and of the *Länder* in matters pertaining to schools, education, and adult education.

Art. 15. (1) Unless a subject matter has been specifically entrusted by the Federal Constitution to the *Bund* as to legislation or execution, it shall remain within the autonomous sphere of competence of the *Länder.*

(2) In matters of local safety police (*Sicherheitspolizei*), i.e. that part of the police which affects in the first place the interest of the *Gemeinde* (municipality) and which the *Gemeinde* can exercise within its boundaries by its own resources, the *Bund* shall have authority to supervise the administration of these affairs by the *Gemeinde* and redress any deficiencies perceived by orders given to the *Landeshauptmann* (Article 103). For this purpose, Federal inspectors may be sent to the *Gemeinden*; the *Landeshauptmann* shall be informed thereof in each case.

(3) The laws of the *Länder* in matters concerning theaters, cinemas as well as public shows, displays and entertainment shall, within the jurisdictional district of Federal police authorities, transfer to these Federal police authorities at least the supervision of such performances in so far as it does not concern technical equipment, building and fire protection matters and also permit these authorities to concur on the lowest level, in issuing such licenses as may be required by such laws.

(4) Corresponding laws of the *Bund* and of the *Land* concerned shall rule to what extent executive power shall be conferred upon Federal police authorities within their jurisdictional districts in matters concerning highway police on highways other than Federal highways.

(5) In so far as executive acts in building matters affect Federally-owned buildings which serve public purposes, such as giving accomodation to Federal authorities and Federal offices or to public institutions—including schools and hospitals—or which serve for accomodating in barracks members of the Armed Forces or other Federal employees, such acts shall fall within the indirect Federal administration. The final decision on appeals shall rest with the competent Federal Minister. The determination of the alignment and level, however, shall even in this case fall within the executive power of the *Länder.*

(6) In so far as only the legislative power concerning the basic principles has been reserved to the *Bund* the *Länder* shall have the power of enabling legislation within the scope determined by Federal Law. The Federal law may fix a time-limit for the enactment of enabling legislation which period, without the consent of the *Bundesrat*, shall not be less than six

months and not more than one year. If a *Land* does not observe this time limit the power of enabling legislation for such *Land* shall pass to the *Bund*. Upon the enactment by the *Land* of the enabling law, the Federal enabling law shall cease to be effective.

(7) If an act of execution on the part of a *Land* in the matters covered by Articles 11 and 12 shall be effective in several *Länder*, the interested *Länder* shall first of all proceed in mutual agreement. If an agreement cannot be reached within six months from the day the legal affair arose, the power to perform such an act shall pass, at the request of one of the *Länder* concerned or of one of the interested parties, to the appropriate Federal Ministry. The details may be ruled by the Federal laws enacted under Articles 11 and 12.

(8) The *Bund* shall have the right to enforce the observance of the regulations issued by it with respect to such subjects as are reserved to Federal legislation under Articles 11 and 12.

(9) The *Länder* are empowered to issue all rules necessary for the regulation of matters which are within the scope of their legislative competence, even in the field of criminal and civil law.

Art. 16. (1) The *Länder* are bound, within the limits of their autonomous sphere of competence, to take such measures as are necessary for the execution of international treaties. Should a *Land* fail to comply in due time with this obligation, its competence for such measures, in particular, for the enactment of the necessary legislation, shall pass to the *Bund*.

(2) Likewise, the *Bund*, when carrying out treaties with foreign states, shall have the right of supervision even with respect to such matters as come within the autonomous sphere of competence of the *Länder*. In this case the *Bund* shall have the same rights towards the *Länder* as in matters of indirect Federal administration (Article 102).

Art. 17. (1) The provisions of Articles 10 to 15 with respect to the powers of legislation and execution shall in no way affect the status of the *Bund* as holder of private rights.

(2) The *Bund* may never, in all these legal relations, be placed by the legislation of any *Land* in a less favorable position than the *Land* concerned.

Art. 18. (1) The entire public administration shall be carried on only on the basis of the laws.

(2) Every administrative authority may issue ordinances within its sphere of competence on the basis of the laws.

(3) If, for the prevention of an obvious and irreparable damage to the common welfare, the immediate enactment of measures which according to the Constitution require a decision of the *Nationalrat* becomes necessary at a time when the latter is not convened, or is not able to meet in due time, or is obstructed in its activity by *force majeure* the Federal President, on the proposal of the Federal Government and on his and the Federal

Government's responsibility, may take these measures by way of provisional law-amending ordinances. The proposal of the Federal Government shall be made in agreement with the permanent subcommittee (Article 55, paragraph 2) to be appointed by the Main Committee of the *Nationalrat*. Such an ordinance shall be countersigned by the Federal Government.

(4) Every ordinance issued under paragraph 3 shall be submitted without delay by the Federal Government to the *Nationalrat* which shall be convened by the Federal President, if it is not in session at that time, however, if it is in session, by the President of the Nationalrat, for one of the eight days following the day of submission. Within four weeks after the submission the *Nationalrat* shall either enact an appropriate Federal law in lieu of the ordinance or demand, by a resolution, that the ordinance be immediately repealed by the Federal Government. In the latter case, the Federal Government shall at once comply with this demand. In order that the resolution of the *Nationalrat* may be adopted in due time, the President of the *Nationalrat* has to submit the motion to the vote not later than on the last but one day of the four weeks time-limit; detailed provisions shall be prescribed by the rules of procedure of the *Nationalrat*. If the ordinance is repealed by the Federal Government according to the preceding provisions, the legal provisions which were repealed by the ordinance shall re-enter into force from the day of the entry into force of the repeal.

(5) The ordinances referred to in paragraph 3 shall not contain provisions which would involve an amendment of provisions of Federal constitutional law, nor a permanent financial burden on the *Bund*, nor a financial burden on the *Länder*, *Bezirke* (districts) or *Gemeinden*, nor the imposition of financial obligations on Federal citizens, nor the alienation of public property, nor measures concerning matters referred to in Article 10, clause 11, nor, finally, measures concerning the right of free association, or the protection of tenants.

Art. 19. (1) The supreme executive functionaries are the Federal President, the Federal Ministers and Secretaries of State, and the members of the *Land* Governments.

(2) The activity in private business of functionaries mentioned in paragraph 1 and other public functionaries may be restricted by Federal law.

Art. 20. (1) Under the direction of the supreme functionaries of the *Bund* and of the *Länder*, the administration shall be carried on in accordance with the provisions of the laws, by officers elected for a certain period or by appointed professional officers. Unless otherwise provided by Constitutional law they shall be bound by the instructions of their superiors and shall be responsible to them for the exercise of their office. The subordinate officer may refuse to obey an instruction if this instruction is either given by an unauthorized officer or if the obedience to the instruction would violate regulations under criminal law.

(2) Unless otherwise provided by law, all officers entrusted with duties within the Federal, *Land* or *Gemeinde* administration shall be bound to treat as confidential all facts of which they obtain knowledge exclusively through their official duties if it is in the interest of the *Bund, Länder or Gemeinden* or a party to treat these facts as confidential (official obligation to secrecy). Functionaries appointed by a general representative body shall not be bound by this obligation to secrecy in relation to this representative body if the latter expressly asks for information on such facts.

Art. 21. (1) The employment regulations including the salary system and the disciplinary regulations concerning those employees of the *Bund* and of the *Länder* who have to carry out administrative duties, shall be made by Federal law according to uniform principles (Article 10, clause 16 and Article 12, clause 9). This law shall, in particular, also contain provisions determining the extent to which representatives of employees may participate in the regulation of the rights and duties of such employees without prejudice to the supreme authority of the *Bund* and the *Länder* in matters pertaining to public service.

(2) Supreme authority in matters pertaining to public service over the employees of the *Bund* shall be exercised by the supreme functionaries of the *Bund*; over employees of the *Länder* by the supreme functionaries of the *Länder*. The president of the Court of Accounts shall exercise the supreme authority of the *Bund* in service matters concerning the employees of this court.

(3) The appointment of employees of district and local *Gemeinden* who perform administrative duties and the service regulations concerning such employees, shall be ruled in connection with the organization of the administration.

(4) The possibility of an interchange of service between the *Bund*, the *Länder* and the *Gemeinden* shall always be open to public employees. Such transfer shall take place with the consent of the authorities exercising the supreme authority in matters pertaining to public service. Special arrangements to facilitate interchange of service may be made by Federal law.

(5) Official titles for the functionaries of the *Bund*, the *Länder* or the *Gemeinden* may be created in a uniform manner by Federal law. Such titles shall be protected by law.

Art. 22. All agencies of the *Bund*, the *Länder* or the *Gemeinden* shall render mutual assistance within the framework of their legal sphere of competence.

Art. 23. (1) The *Bund*, the *Länder*, the districts, the *Gemeinden*, and the other corporations and establishments under public law shall be liable for the tort which the persons acting as their officers have inflicted through their fault to whomever by an illegal conduct while engaged in the execution of the laws.

(2) Persons acting as officers of an holder of legal authority mentioned in paragraph 1 shall, as far as they are guilty of malice or gross negligence, be liable to the holder for the damage for which the holder of legal authority has indemnified the victimized person.

(3) Persons acting as officers of an holder of legal authority mentioned in paragraph 1 shall be liable for the damage which they directly inflicted to the holder of legal authority by an illegal conduct while engaged in the execution of the laws.

(4) Detailed provisions to paragraphs 1 to 3 shall be made by Federal Law.

(5) A Federal law may also determine how far, in the field of post-telegraph, and telephone matters, special provisions differing from the principles established in paragraphs 1 to 3 shall apply.

CHAPTER II

FEDERAL LEGISLATION

A. The Nationalrat (National Council)

Art. 24. The Federal legislation shall be exercised by the *Nationalrat* (National Council), together with the *Bundesrat* (Federal Council).

Art. 25. (1) The seat of the *Nationalrat* shall be Vienna, the Federal capital.

(2) For the duration of a state of emergency the Federal President may at the request of the Federal Government convene the *Nationalrat* at any other place within the Federal territory.

Art. 26. (1) The *Nationalrat* shall be elected by the people of the *Bund* according to the principles of proportional representation upon equal, direct, secret and personal suffrage of the men and women who have completed their twenty first year [1] of age. The Federal electoral law shall determine whether and on which conditions persons who do not possess the Federal citizenship may hold the right to vote on the basis of reciprocity guaranteed by treaty. Voting shall be compulsory in the *Länder* in which such compulsory voting has been enacted by *Land* law. Detailed regulations concerning electoral procedure and compulsory voting, if any, shall be stipulated by Federal law. This Federal law shall also determine the reasons which excuse abstention from voting in spite of the existence of compulsory voting.

[1] Under the Federal Election Law of 1949, reduced to 20 years.

(2) The Federal territory shall be divided into contiguous electoral districs, whose boundaries shall not overlap the boundaries of the *Länder*. The number of representatives allotted to the qualified voters of an electoral district (electoral body) shall be in proportion to the number of citizens who, in accordance with the results of the last census, had their domicile in the electoral district. A division of the electorate into other electoral bodies shall not be admissible.

(3) The polling day shall be a Sunday or other public holiday.

(4) Every qualified voter who is more than twenty-nine years[1] of age before the 1st of January of the year in which the election is held, shall be eligible for election.

(5) Exclusion from the right to vote and from eligibility can only be the consequence of a sentence or an order of the courts.

(6) Election boards shall be appointed which shall have to carry out and conduct the elections for the *Nationalrat,* the election of the Federal President and referendums under Article 46, as well as to co-operate in the scrutiny of popular initiatives. These election boards shall include representatives of the electioneering parties as assessors entitled to vote; the main election board shall, moreover, include assessors who are or have been members of the Judiciary. The number of these assessors to be fixed in the election regulations—setting aside the assessors coming from the Judiciary—shall be divided up among the electioneering parties according to their strength resulting from the last election for the *Nationalrat.*

(7) The electoral registers shall be drawn up by the *Gemeinden* (however, in *Gemeinden* which are the seat of a Federal police authority they shall be drawn up by this authority in co-operation with the *Gemeinde*).[2]

Art. 27. (1) The legislative period of the *Nationalrat* shall last four years, beginning with the day of its first meeting, and in any case, up to the day on which the new *Nationalrat* meets.

(2) The newly elected *Nationalrat* shall be convened by the Federal President not later than on the thirtieth day after the election. The election shall be fixed by the Federal Government in such a manner as to enable the newly elected *Nationalrat* to meet on the day after the expiration of the fourth year of the legislative period.

Art. 28. (1) The Federal President shall convene the *Nationalrat* in each year for two regular sessions, i.e. a spring session and an autumn session. The spring session shall last at least two months but should not last longer than June 15th; the autumn session shall last at least four months but should not begin prior to October 15th.

(2) The Federal President may convene the *Nationalrat* also for extra-

[1] Under the Federal Election Law of 1949, reduced to 26 years.
[2] Superseded by § 29(5) of the Federal Election Law of 1949.

ordinary sessions. If the Federal Government or at least one third of the members of the *Nationalrat* or if the *Bundesrat* so demand, the Federal President shall convene the *Nationalrat* for an extraordinary session within two weeks.

(3) Upon resolution of the *Nationalrat* the Federal President shall declare the sessions of *the Nationalrat* closed.

(4) When within the same legislative period a new session of the *Nationalrat* is opened, the *Nationalrat* shall resume its work at that stage in which it was left at the end of the preceeding session. At the end of a session, individual committees may be instructed by the *Nationalrat* to continue their work.

(5) Within the same session, the meetings of the *Nationalrat* shall be convened and closed by its President. Within the same session, the latter shall convene a meeting at the latest within five days if at least one fourth of the members of the *Nationalrat* or if the Federal Government should so demand.

Art. 29. (1) The Federal President may dissolve the *Nationalrat,* however, he shall be authorized to do so only once for the same reason. In this case the election of the new *Nationalrat* shall be fixed by the Federal Government in such a way that the newly elected *Nationalrat* may meet at the latest on the hundredth day after the dissolution.

(2) Before the expiration of the legislative period the *Nationalrat* may dissolve itself by ordinary law.

(3) After a dissolution under paragraph 2 as well as after expiration of the period for which the *Nationalrat* has been elected, the legislative period shall last till the day on which the newly elected *Nationalrat* meets.

Art. 30. (1) The *Nationalrat* shall elect from among its members the President, the Second and Third Presidents.

(2) The business of the *Nationalrat* shall be conducted in accordance with a special law and an autonomous set of rules of procedure to be adopted by the *Nationalrat* within the framework of this law. The law concerning the rules of procedure can be passed only if one half of the members are present, and by a majority of two thirds of the votes cast.

(3) The appointment of the employees of the Chancellery of the President of the *Nationalrat* shall rest with the President of the *Nationalrat.*

Art. 31. A resolution of the *Nationalrat* shall require the presence of at least one third of the members and the absolute majority of the votes cast unless this law otherwise provides.

Art. 32. (1) The meetings of the *Nationalrat* shall be public.

(2) Upon demand made by the chairman or by one fifth of the members present, the public shall be excluded if the *Nationalrat* so resolves after the withdrawal of the audience.

Art. 33. No one shall be held responsible for publishing truthful reports of the proceedings at the public meetings of the *Nationalrat* or its committees.

B. The Bundesrat (Federal Council)

Art. 34. (1) The Länder shall be represented in the *Bundesrat* in proportion to the number of citizens in each *Land* in accordance with the following provisions.

(2) The *Land* having the largest number of citizens shall delegate twelve members and each other *Land* as many members as corresponds to the proportion of the number of its citizens to the first-mentioned number of citizens; any remainders exceeding one half of the proportional number shall count as full. Each *Land* shall, however, be entitled to a minimum representation of three members. For each member a substitute shall be appointed.

(3) The number of members to be thus delegated by each *Land* shall be fixed by the Federal President after each general census.

Art. 35. (1) The members of the *Bundesrat* and their substitutes shall be elected by the *Landtage* (*Land* Diets) for the duration of their own legislative period according to the principle of proportional representation, however, at least one seat shall fall to the party having the second highest number of seats in the *Landtag* or, if several parties have an equal number of seats, the second highest number of votes at the last election for the *Landtag*. When the claims of several parties are equal, the issue shall be decided by lot.

(2) The members of the *Bundesrat* must not necessarily be members of the *Landtag* which delegated them; they shall, however, be eligible for election to that *Landtag*.

(3) After the expiration of the legislative period of a *Landtag* or after its dissolution, the members of the *Bundesrat* delegated by it shall continue in office until the new *Landtag* has held the election for the *Bundesrat*.

(4) The provisions of Article 34 and 35 can be amended only if, in the *Bundesrat*—apart from the majority of votes normally required for the passing of a measure in that body—the majority of representatives of at least four *Länder* have approved the amendment.

Art. 36. (1) The Chairmanship of the *Bundesrat* shall pass in turn every six months to each of the different *Länder* in alphabetical order.

(2) The office of Chairman shall be assumed by the member heading the list of the *Land* entitled to the Chairmanship; the appointment of the deputies shall be regulated by the rules of procedure of the *Bundesrat*.

(3) The *Bundesrat* shall be convened by its Chairman at the seat of the *Nationalrat*. The Chairman shall be bound to convene the *Bundesrat* immediately at the request of at least one fourth of its members or of the Federal Government.

Art. 37. (1) A resolution of the *Bundesrat* shall require the presence of at least one third of the members and the absolute majority of the votes cast unless this law otherwise provides.

(2) The *Bundesrat* shall give itself its rules of procedure by resolution. This resolution can be adopted only if one half of the members are present, and by a majority of two third of the votes cast.

(3) The meetings of the *Bundesrat* shall be public. Under the provisions of the rules of procedure the public can however be excluded by resolution. The provisions of Article 33 shall also apply to the public meetings of the *Bundesrat* and its Committees.

C. The Bundesversammlung (Federal Assembly)

Art. 38. The *Nationalrat* and the *Bundesrat* shall meet as the *Bundesversammlung* in a joint public meeting at the seat of the *Nationalrat* for accepting the solemn promise of the Federal President to fulfil the duties of his office as well as for a resolution on a declaration of war.

Art. 39. (1) Apart from the cases provided for by Article 60, paragraph 6, Article 63, paragraph 2, Article 64, paragraph 2, and Article 68, paragraph 2, the *Bundesversammlung* shall be convened by the Federal President. The chairmanship shall be assumed alternately by the President of the *Nationalrat* and the chairman of the *Bundesrat*, beginning with the former.

(2) In the *Bundesversammlung* the rules of procedure of the *Nationalrat* shall be applied with any necessary modifications.

(3) The provisions of Article 33 shall apply also to the meetings of the *Bundesversammlung*.

Art. 40. (1) The resolutions of the *Bundesversammlung* shall be authenticated by its chairman and countersigned by the Federal Chancellor.

(2) The resolutions of the *Bundesversammlung* on a declaration of war shall be officially promulgated by the Federal Chancellor.

D. Federal Legislative Procedure

Art. 41. (1) Draft laws shall be introduced in the *Nationalrat* either as motions of its members or as bills of the Federal Government. The *Bundesrat* may introduce bills in the *Nationalrat* through the channel of the Federal Government.

(2) Every proposal signed by 200,000 voters or by one half of the voters of each of three *Länder* (popular initiative) shall be submitted by the Federal Government to the *Nationalrat* for action in accordance with its rules of procedure. The popular initiative shall be couched in the form of a draft law.

Art. 42. (1) Every enactment of the *Nationalrat* shall be communicated without delay by its President to the Federal Chancellor, who shall immediately communicate it to the *Bundesrat.*

(2) Save as otherwise provided under constitutional law, an enactment may be authenticated and promulgated only if the *Bundesrat* has not raised a motivated objection to this enactment.

(3) Such an objection shall be communicated in writing to the *Nationalrat* through the agency of the Federal Chancellor within eight weeks after the enactment has reached the *Bundesrat.*

(4) If the *Nationalrat* in the presence of at least one half of its members reiterates its original enactment, the enactment shall be authenticated and promulgated. Should the *Bundesrat* resolve not to raise any objection or if no motivated objection has been raised within the time limit prescribed by paragraph 3, the enactment shall be authenticated and promulgated.

(5) The *Bundesrat* cannot object to resolutions of the *Nationalrat* which concern a law under Article 64, paragraph 1, relating to the substitution of the Federal President, or a law concerning the rules of procedure of the *Nationalrat,* the dissolution of the *Nationalrat,* the appropriation of the federal budget estimates, the approval of the final budget accounts, the raising or conversion of Federal loans, or the disposal of Federal property. These enactments of the *Nationalrat* shall be authenticated and promulgated without further procedure.

Art. 43. If the *Nationalrat* so resolves, or if a majority of the members of the *Nationalrat* so demands, any enactment of the *Nationalrat* shall upon conclusion of the procedure under Article 42, but before its authentication by the Federal President, be submitted to a referendum.

Art. 44. (1) Constitutional laws or constitutional provisions contained in ordinary laws may be enacted by the *Nationalrat* only in the presence of at least one half of its members and by a majority of two thirds of the votes cast. They shall be explicitly designated as such ("constitutional law," "constitutional provision");

(2) Any total revision of the Federal Constitution shall upon conclusion of the procedure under Article 42, before, however, authentication by the Federal President, be submitted to a referendum of the entire people of the Federal State; but a Constitutional amendment need be so submitted only on demand of one third of the members of the *Nationalrat* or of the *Bundesrat.*

Art. 45. (1) An absolute majority of the valid votes cast in the referendum shall decide.

(2) The result of the referendum shall be officially promulgated.

Art. 46. (1) Regulations concerning the procedure for the popular initiative and for the referendum shall be prescribed by Federal law.

(2) Every citizen of the Federal State qualified to vote at the elections for the *Nationalrat* shall be qualified to vote at the popular initiative and referendum.

(3) The Federal President shall order the referendum.

Art. 47. (1) The signature of the Federal President shall authenticate that the Federal laws have been enacted in accordance with the Constitution.

(2) The submission of Federal laws for authentication shall be effected by the Federal Chancellor.

(3) The authentication shall be countersigned by the Federal Chancellor and the appropriate Federal Ministers.

Art. 48. Federal laws and the treaties referred to in Article 50 shall be promulgated with reference to the enactment of the *Nationalrat*; Federal laws based on a referendum shall be promulgated with reference to the result of the referendum.

Art. 49. (1) The Federal laws and the treaties referred to in Article 50 shall be promulgated by the Federal Chancellor in the Federal Law Gazette (*Bundesgesetzblatt*). Unless explicitly otherwise provided, they shall become effective after the expiration of the day on which the issue of the Federal Law Gazette containing the promulgation is issued and distributed; and, unless explicitly otherwise provided, they shall apply to the entire Federal territory; this shall not hold, however, for treaties which are to be implemented by the promulgation of laws (Article 50, paragraph 2).

(2) There shall be enacted a special Federal law concerning the Federal Law Gazette.

E. Co-operation of the Nationalrat and the Bundesrat in the Executive of the Bund

Art. 50. (1) Political treaties and other treaties only in so far as they contain provisions modifying or completing existing laws, shall require for their validity the approval of the *Nationalrat.*

(2) At the time of its approval of a treaty falling under paragraph (1), the *Nationalrat* may decide that such a treaty should be implemented by the promulgation of laws.

(3) The provisions of Article 42, paragraphs (1) to (4), and, if a constitutional law be modified or completed by a treaty, those of Article 44, paragraph (1), shall be applicable with any necessary modifications, to resolutions of the *Nationalrat,* under paragraph (1) and (2) above, concerning the approval of treaties; any such treaties or any such provisions contained in a treaty approved in accordance with paragraph (1), must be expressly described as modifying the constitutional laws.

Art. 51. (1) The Federal Government shall submit to the *Nationalrat,* not later than ten weeks before the expiration of the current fiscal year an estimate of the revenue and expenditure of the *Bund* for the ensuing fiscal year.

(2) Federal expenses which are not provided for by the Federal Finance

Law or by a special law, shall require, before their execution the constitutional approval of the *Nationalrat* which shall be obtained by the Federal Minister of Finance. If there is danger in delay, such Federal expenditure, if not exceeding 666,666 schillings, may be made with the consent of the Main Committee of the *Nationalrat*; the approval of the *Nationalrat* shall be requested subsequently.

(3) If the draft of the Federal budget estimate submitted in due time (paragraph 1) to the *Nationalrat* by the Federal Government is not constitutionally approved by the *Nationalrat* before the close of the fiscal year and if no provisional arrangement is made by Federal law until that date, then during the first two months of the ensuing fiscal year the taxes, rates and dues shall be collected according to the existing provisions, and the Federal expenditure shall be defrayed on account of the appropriations to be legally determined, except expenditure of a kind not especially provided for in the last Federal Finance Law. The ceiling of the admissible Federal expenditure shall be formed by the appropriations contained in the draft of the budget submitted to the *Nationalrat.* One twelfth of these appropriations shall be the basis of the Federal expenditure of one month. Expenditure for meeting legal liabilities shall be defrayed according to their due date. Appointments of officials likewise, are to be made on the basis of the draft of the Federal Finance Law submitted to the *Nationalrat.* In all other respects the provisions of the last Federal Finance Law, in so far as they do not concern budget figures, shall be applied, with any necessary modifications, also during the two abovementioned months.

Art. 52. The *Nationalrat* and the *Bundesrat* are entitled to examine the conduct of public business by the Federal Government, to interrogate the members of the Federal Government on all matters relating to the execution of the laws, and to demand all pertinent information as well as to express by declaration their wishes in respect of the exercise of the executive power.

Art. 53. (1) By resolution the *Nationalrat* may set up committees of investigation.

(2) The courts and all other public authorities shall be obliged to comply with requests of these committees for the taking of evidence; upon their demands, all public authorities shall produce their files to them.

(3) The procedure of the committees of investigation shall be regulated by the law concerning the rules of procedure of the *Nationalrat.*

Art. 54. The *Nationalrat* shall co-operate in fixing railroad, postal, telegraph and telephone rates and prices of articles subject to monopoly, as well as salaries of persons permanently employed in enterprises of the *Bund.* This co-operation shall be ruled by Federal constitutional law.

Art. 55. (1) The *Nationalrat* shall elect from among its own members, according to the principles of proportional representation, the Main Committee; by a Federal law it may provide that certain ordinances of the Federal Government or of a Federal Minister require the agreement of the Main Committee. If it is necessary, the Main Committee shall also be convened between sessions of the *Nationalrat* (Article 28).

(2) The Main Committee shall elect from among its own members a permanent sub-committee whose powers are determined by this law. The election shall take place according to the principle of proportional representation. This principle shall be so applied that at least one member of each party represented in the Main Committee shall be a member of the sub-committee. The members and the substitute-members of the permanent sub-committee shall have their residence at the seat of the *Nationalrat*. The rules of procedure shall provide that the permanent sub-committee may be convened and may meet at any time. If the *Nationalrat* is dissolved by the Federal President according to Article 29, paragraph 1, it shall be the duty of the permanent subcommittee to co-operate in the executive power, which co-operation is normally according to this law vested in the *Nationalrat* (Main Committee).

F. Status of the Members of the Nationalrat and of the Bundesrat

Art. 56. The members of the *Nationalrat* and the members of the *Bundesrat* shall not be bound by any instructions in the exercise of their office.

Art. 57. (1) The members of the *Nationalrat* shall never be held responsible for any votes cast in the exercise of their office, and they shall be held responsible only by the *Nationalrat* for any oral utterances made in this capacity.

(2) No member of the *Nationalrat* may, without the consent of this body, be arrested or otherwise officially prosecuted for a punishable act except if caught in the very act of committing a crime. In case the authority competent for prosecution asks the *Nationalrat* to consent to the arrest or to any other official prosecution of any of its members, that body shall decide on the question within six weeks. Unless the *Nationalrat* demands within this time limit that the prosecution be postponed for the duration of the legislative period, the arrest or other official prosecution may take place. The time during which the *Nationalrat* is not in session shall not be included either in this time limit or in the term of limitation.

(3) In case a member of the *Nationalrat* has been caught in the very act of committing a crime, the authority concerned shall immediately notify the President of the *Nationalrat* of the arrest. The arrest shall be cancelled or the entire prosecution deferred for the duration of the legislative period, if the *Nationalrat*, or—at the time during which the *Nationalrat* is not in

session—the permanent committee entrusted with this function so demands.

(4) In order to give the *Nationalrat* the opportunity of taking its decision in due time. the President shall put the request for extradition to the vote at the latest on the day before the last day of the six weeks period; the rules of procedure shall contain more detailed regulations.

(5) The immunity of the members of the *Nationalrat* (paragraphs 1 to 3) shall cease on the day on which the newly elected *Nationalrat* meets, in the case of functionaries of the *Nationalrat* whose functions extend beyond this date, with the expiration of their functions.

Art. 58. During the entire term of their function the members of the *Bundesrat* shall enjoy the immunity of members of the *Landtag* which delegated them.

Art. 59. (1) No one can be a member of the *Nationalrat* and of the *Bundesrat* at the same time.

(2) Public employees including the members of the Federal Army, shall need no leave of absence for the exercise of their functions as members of the *Nationalrat* or of the *Bundesrat.* Should they seek election to the *Nationalrat* they shall be granted the time off necessary for this purpose. Detailed regulations shall be provided by the public service regulations.

CHAPTER III

THE EXECUTIVE POWER OF THE BUND

A. Administration

1. THE FEDERAL PRESIDENT

Art. 60. (1) The Federal President shall be elected by the people of the Federal State by direct and secret suffrage. Every voter qualified to vote in elections for the *Nationalrat* shall be entitled to vote. For the election of the Federal President voting shall be compulsory. A Federal Law shall provide for detailed regulations for the electoral procedure and for the compulsory voting. That law shall especially determine the reasons which excuse abstention from the election.

(2) The candidate who polls more than half of all valid votes shall be elected. If no such majority results, a second ballot shall take place. In this second ballot valid votes may be given only to one of the two candidates who have polled the largest numbers of votes in the first ballot; however, in the second ballot each of the two groups of voters which have put up these two candidates may nominate another person instead of the candidate orginally put up by this group.

(3) Only a person who is qualified to vote in the elections for the *Na-*

tionalrat and who has passed the thirty fifth year of age before the first of January of the year of the election may be elected Federal President. Members of reigning houses or of families that have formerly reigned shall be excluded from eligibility.

(4) The result of the election for the Federal President shall be officially promulgated by the Federal Chancellor.

(5) The Federal President shall hold his office six years. Re-election for the immediately following term of office shall be admissible only once.

(6) Before the expiration of his term of office, the Federal President may be deposed by referendum. The referendum shall be held upon demand of the *Bundesversammlung*. The *Bundesversammlung* shall be convened by the Federal Chancellor for this purpose if the *Nationalrat* has adopted a resolution to this effect. The resolution of the *Nationalrat* shall require the presence of at least half of the members and a majority of two thirds of the votes cast. By such a resolution the Federal President shall be prevented from the further exercise of his office. The rejection of the deposition by referendum shall be considered as a new election of the Federal President and shall entail the dissolution of the *Nationalrat* (Article 29, Paragraph 1). Also in this case the total term of office of the Federal President shall not exceed twelve years.

Art. 61. (1) During his term of office the Federal President shall not be a member of any general representative body nor exercise any other profession.

(2) The title "Federal President" shall not be used by anyone else—not even with an addition or in connection with another designation. This title is protected by law.

Art. 62. (1) When entering on his duties the Federal President before the *Bundesversammlung* shall make the following solemn promise to fulfil the duties of his office. "I vow that I will faithfully observe the Constitution and all laws of the Republic and will fulfil my duty to the best of my knowledge and conscience."

(2) A religious affirmation may be added.

Art. 63. (1) An official prosecution of the Federal President shall be admissible only with the consent of the *Bundesversammlung*.

(2) The motion for the prosecution of the Federal President shall be presented by the competent authority to the *Nationalrat* which decides whether the motion shall be submitted to the *Bundesversammlung*. If the *Nationalrat* declares for it, the Federal Chancellor shall convene the *Bundesversammlung* immediately.

Art. 64. (1) If the Federal President is prevented or in case of a permanent vacancy of his office, the functions of the Federal President shall devolve for the time being on the Federal Chancellor. If the prevention will presumably last more than twenty days the substitution shall be regulated by Federal law.

(2) In case of a permanent vacancy of the post of Federal President the Federal Government shall immediately arrange for the election of a new Federal President and after the new Federal President has been elected, the Federal Chancellor shall immediately convene the *Bundesversammlung* for accepting the solemn promise of the Federal President to fulfil the duties of his office.

Art. 65. (1) The Federal President shall represent the Republic in international relations, shall receive and accredit the diplomatic envoys, approve the appointment of foreign consuls, appoint the consular representatives of the Republic abroad and conclude treaties. Upon the conclusion of a treaty not falling under Article 50, he may rule that such treaty shall be implemented by decrees.

(2) Moreover, in addition to the powers conferred upon him by other provisions of this Constitution, he shall be vested with:

a) the appointment of the Federal employees including army officers and the other Federal functionaries, and the bestowal of official titles on them;

b) the creation and bestowal of professional titles;

c) in individual cases: powers of clemency with respect to persons convicted by final judgments of the courts, powers to mitigate or commute sentences pronounced by the courts, to remit the legal consequences of a conviction and to strike convictions from the criminal record, further to quash criminal proceedings in case of penal offenses to be prosecuted *ex officio*;

d) the legitimization of illegimate children at the request of the parents.

(3) Special laws shall provide to what extent the Federal President shall further be vested with rights to confer honorary rights and to grant extraordinary gratifications, allowances and pensions, to appoint or to confirm, and with other powers in personnel matters.

Art. 66. (1) The Federal President may delegate to the appropriate members of the Federal Government his right to appoint certain categories of Federal employees.

(2) The Federal President may empower the Federal Government or the appropriate members thereof to conclude certain categories of treaties not covered by the provisions of Article 50; such authorization may also include the power to issue decrees in accordance with the second part of Article 65 paragraph (1).

Art. 67. (1) Save as otherwise provided by the Constitution, all official acts of the Federal President shall take place upon the proposal of the Federal Government or of the Federal Minister empowered by it. The law shall provide to what extent the Federal Government or the appropriate Federal Minister themselves shall in this respect be bound by proposals emanating from other agencies.

(2) Save as otherwise provided under Constitutional law all official

acts of the Federal President shall require for their validity the countersignature of the Federal Chancellor or of the appropriate Federal Ministers.

Art. 68. (1) In accordance with Article 142, the Federal President shall be responsible to the *Bundesversammlung* for the exercise of his office.

(2) For the purpose of asserting this responsibility the *Bundesversammlung* shall be convened by the Federal Chancellor upon resolution of the *Nationalrat* or of the *Bundesrat.*

(3) A resolution of impeachment within the meaning of Article 142 shall require the presence of more than one half of the members of each of the two representative bodies and a majority of two thirds of the votes cast.

II. THE FEDERAL GOVERNMENT

Art. 69. (1) The highest administrative functions of the *Bund,* insofar as they are not conferred upon the Federal President, shall be entrusted to the Federal Chancellor, the Vice-Chancellor, and the other Federal Ministers. Taken collectively they form the Federal Government under the chairmanship of the Federal Chancellor.

(2) The Vice-Chancellor shall be called to act as deputy of the Federal Chancellor in respect to all his functions. If both the Federal Chancellor and the Vice-Chancellor are prevented from exercising the duties of their offices at the same time, the Federal President shall appoint a member of the Federal Government to act as deputy for the Federal Chancellor.

Art. 70. (1) The Federal Chancellor and, upon his proposal, the other members of the Federal Government shall be appointed by the Federal President. No proposal shall be required for the dismissal of the Federal Chancellor or of the entire Federal Government; the dismissal of individual members of the Federal Government shall take place upon proposal of the Federal Chancellor. The appointment of the Federal Chancellor and of the entire Federal Government shall be countersigned by the newly appointed Federal Chancellor; no countersignature shall be required for the dismissal.

(2) Only persons eligible to the *Nationalrat* may be appointed Federal Chancellor, Vice-Chancellor or Federal Ministers; the members of the Federal Government shall not necessarily be members of the *Nationalrat.*

(3) If a new Federal Government is appointed by the Federal President at a time when the *Nationalrat* is not in session, the Federal President shall convene the *Nationalrat* for an extraordinary session (Article 28, paragraph 2) within one week to enable the new Federal Government to present itself before the *Nationalrat.*

Art. 71. If the Federal Government has gone out of office, the Federal President shall, until a new Federal Government has been formed, entrust members of the outgoing Government or high officials of the Federal departments with the carrying on of the administration and one of them with the chairmanship of the provisional Federal Government. This provision shall be applied with any necessary modifications if individual members of the Federal Government have gone out of office.

Art. 72. (1) Before entering on their duties the members of the Government shall make a solemn promise to the Federal President to fulfil the duties of their office. A religious affirmation may be added.

(2) The official commissions of the Federal Chancellor, of the Vice-Chancellor and of the other Federal Ministers shall be issued by the Federal President on the day of their solemn promise to fulfil the duties of their office and shall be countersigned by the newly appointed Federal Chancellor.

(3) These provisions shall also apply with any necessary modifications to the cases mentioned in Article 71.

Art. 73. In case a Federal Minister is temporarily prevented from discharging his duties the Federal President shall authorize a Federal Minister or a high official of a Federal department to act as deputy of this Minister. This deputy shall bear the same responsibility as a Federal Minister (Article 76).

Art. 74. (1) If the *Nationalrat* by explicit resolution refuses confidence to the Federal Government, or to individual members thereof the Federal Government or the Federal Minister concerned shall be removed from office.

(2) The presence of one half of the members of the *Nationalrat* shall be required for a resolution of the *Nationalrat* by which confidence is refused. Upon demand, however, of one fifth of the members present, the vote shall be postponed to the next working day but one. A new adjournment of the vote can take place only by resolution of the *Nationalrat.*

(3) Without prejudice to the power otherwise vested in the Federal President under Art. 70, paragraph 1, the Federal Government or its individual members shall be removed from office by the Federal President in the cases provided by law or at their request.

Art. 75. The members of the Federal Government, as well as the deputies delegated by them, shall be authorized to participate in all deliberations of the *Nationalrat,* of the *Bundesrat* and of the *Bundesversammlung,* as well as of the committees of these representative bodies; they may, however, participate only on special invitation in such deliberations of the Main Committee of the *Nationalrat* as according to the provisions of the Federal law concerning the rules of procedure of the *Nationalrat,* are in principle non-public. At their request they shall always be heard. The *Nationalrat,* the *Bundesrat* and the *Bundesversammlung,* as well as their committees, may demand the presence of the members of the Federal Government.

Art. 76. (1) The members of the Federal Government (Articles 69 and 71) shall be responsible to the *Nationalrat* in accordance with Artilce 142.

(2) A resolution of impeachment in accordance with Article 142 shall require the presence of more than one-half of the members.

Art. 77. (1) The Federal Ministries and the offices subordinated to them shall conduct the affairs of the Federal administration.

(2) The number of the Federal Ministries, their competence and their organization shall be determined by Federal law.

(3) The Federal Chancellor shall be entrusted with the direction of the Federal Chancellery and a Federal Minister shall be entrusted with the direction of each of the other Federal Ministries. The Federal President may entrust the actual direction of specified matters which fall within the competence of the Federal Chancellery to special Federal Ministers notwithstanding that these matters continue to belong to the sphere of competence of the Federal Chancellery. In respect of these matters such Federal Ministers shall have the status of a competent Federal Minister.

(4) The Federal Chancellor and any other Federal Minister may in exceptional cases be entrusted with the direction of a second Federal Ministry.

Art. 78. (1) In special cases Federal Ministers may be appointed without being entrusted at the same time with the direction of a Federal Ministry.

(2) Secretaries of State who are appointed and removed from office in the same way as the Federal Ministers may be assigned to the Federal Ministers to assist them in the conduct of the affairs of the Ministry and to represent them in Parliament.

(3) The Secretary of State shall be subordinated to the Federal Minister and shall be bound by his instructions.

3. THE FEDERAL ARMY

Art. 79. (1) The protection of the frontiers of the Republic shall be the duty of the Federal Army.

(2) Insofar as the lawful civil power requires its co-operation, the Federal Army shall protect the constitutional institutions, as well as maintain order and safety within the country in general and shall give assistance in case of disasters due to natural forces and in case of accidents of unusual extent.

(3) Which authorities and functionaries are authorized to request directly the assistance of the Federal Army for the purposes mentioned in paragraph 2 shall be determined by the law on national defense.

(4) An independent military action for purposes mentioned in paragraph 2 may be taken only if the competent authorities are prevented by *force majeure* from bringing about the military action and if further delay would

cause irreparable damage to the public welfare, or if such action is taken in order to repel an assault or to overcome active resistance directed against a component of te Federal Army.

Art. 80. (1) The Federal President shall be the Commander-in-Chief of the Federal Army.

(2) Insofar as the law on national defense does not reserve the employment of the Army to the Federal President, the appropriate Federal Minister shall be entitled to employ the Army within the limits of the authorization conferred upon him by the Federal Government.

(3) The ordinary power of command over the Federal Army is exercised by the appropriate Federal Minister (Article 76, paragraph 1).

Art. 81. Federal Law shall determine to what extent the *Länder* shall participate in recruiting, provisioning, and quartering the Army and in providing its other requirements.

B. Judicial Power

Art. 82. (1) All judicial power shall emanate from the *Bund.*

(2) The sentences and judgments shall be pronounced and issued in the name of the Republic.

Art. 83. (1) The organization and jurisdiction of the courts shall be determined by Federal law.

(2) No one may be withheld from the jurisdiction of the judge assigned to him by law.

(3) Extraordinary courts shall be admissible only in the cases provided by the laws on the procedure in criminal matters.

Art. 84. Military jurisdiction is abolished except in time of war.

Art. 85. Capital punishment in ordinary procedure is abolished.

Art. 86. (1) Save as otherwise provided by this law, the judges shall be appointed upon nomination of the Federal Government by the Federal President, or upon his authorization by the appropriate Federal Minister; for this purpose the Federal Government or the Federal Minister shall obtain proposals of appointment from the boards provided for by the law on the organization of the courts.

(2) The proposal of appointment, to be submitted to the competent Federal Minister and to be forwarded by him to the Federal Government, shall comprise, if there is a sufficient number of applicants, at least three names, and, if more than one post is to be filled, at least twice as many names as there are judges to be appointed.

Art. 87. (1) Judges shall be independent in the exercise of their judicial functions.

(2) A judge shall be deemed to exercise his judicial functions when performing any judicial business entrusted to him by law and by the apportionment of business, with the exception of such matters of judicial

administration as shall not be discharged, in accordance with the provisions of the law, by boards or commissions.

(3) Business shall be apportioned in advance among the judges of a court for a term designated by the law on the organization of the courts. Any matter thus assigned to a judge may be taken off his jurisdiction by administrative decree only in case he should be unable to discharge his functions.

Art. 88. (1) A limit of age shall be fixed by the law on the organization of the courts upon the attainment of which judges shall be permanently retired.

(2) In all other cases, judges may be removed from office, or be transferred against their will to another post or be retired only by a formal judicial decision and only in the cases and according to the forms prescribed by law. These provisions, however, shall not apply to transfers or retirements which become necessary through changes in the law on the organization of the courts. In such cases the law shall prescribe within what period of time judges may be transferred and or retired without the formalities otherwise prescribed.

(3) Temporary removal of judges from office may take place only by decree of the president of the court or of the superior judicial authority. Simultaneously the matter shall be referred to the competent court.

Art. 89. (1) The courts shall not be entitled to examine the validity of duly promulgated laws.

(2) If a court has doubts to apply an ordinance on the ground of its being in conflict with a law, the court shall suspend the proceedings and file an application to the Constitutional Court for the rescinding of this ordinance.

(3) If the ordinance to be applied by the court has already ceased to be in force, the application of the court shall ask for the decision that the ordinance had been in conflict with a law.

(4) If the ordinance to be applied by the court has been rescinded on account of its illegality by a decision of the Constitutional Court, the court shall be bound in this matter by the legal opinion of the Constitutional Court, without filing the application mentioned in paragraph 3.

(5) Paragraphs (2) to (4) shall be applied, with any necessary modifications, in accordance with the provisions of Article 140a to treaties which have been concluded without the approval of the *Nationalrat* as stipulated in Article 50.

Art. 90. (1) Hearings in civil and criminal cases before the trial court shall be oral and public. Exceptions may be prescribed by law.

(2) Criminal proceedings shall be by indictment.

Art. 91. (1) The people shall participate in the administration of justice.

(2) In case of crimes punishable by severe penalties—which crimes shall

be specified by law—and in case of all political crimes and offenses, a jury shall render the verdict as to the guilt of the accused person.

(3) In criminal procedure for other penal acts, lay assessors (*Schöffen*) shall participate in the administration of justice, if the penalty to be imposed exceeds a limit to be determined by law.

Art. 92. (1) The Supreme Court shall be the court of final appeal in civil and criminal cases.

(2) Members of the Federal Government, of a *Land* Government or of a general representative body cannot be members of the Supreme Court. For members of a general representative body who were elected for a fixed legislation or function period the incompatibility shall continue, even if they prematurely resign their seat until the term has expired for which they had been elected. A person who has exercised one of the functions just mentioned during the last four years cannot be appointed President or Vice-President of the Supreme Court.

Art. 93. Amnesties for judicially punishable acts shall be granted by Federal law.

Art. 94. Judicial and administrative powers shall be separated in all stages of judicial and administrative proceedings.

CHAPTER IV

THE LEGISLATIVE POWER

AND THE EXECUTIVE POWER OF THE *LÄNDER*

A. General Provisions

Art. 95. (1) The legislative power of the *Länder* shall be exercised by the *Landtage* (Diets). Their members shall be elected in accordance with the principle of proportional representation by equal, direct, secret and personal suffrage of all Federal citizens of both sexes, who are qualified to vote under the *Landtag* election laws and who have their domicile in the *Land* concerned. The provision of Article 26, paragraph 1, last sentence, shall be applied with any necessary modifications; there shall, however, not be more reasons which excuse abstention from the election than in the election regulations for the *Nationalrat.*

(2) The *Landtag* election regulations shall not stipulate stricter conditions for the right to vote and to be elected than the *Nationalrat* election regulations.

(3) The voters shall exercise their right to vote in electoral districts, which shall each encompass a contiguous territory. The number of representatives shall be apportioned among the electoral districts in proportion

to the number of their citizens. A breaking down of the electorate into other electoral bodies shall not be admissible.

(4) The number of members of the *Landtage* shall be determined by *Land* legislation according to the number of citizens in a way as not to exceed:

In *Länder* with a number of citizens up to 250,000: twenty six,
in *Länder* with a number of citizens up to 500,000: thirty six,
in *Länder* with a number of citizens up to 1,000,000: forty eight,
in *Länder* with a number of citizens up to 1,500,000: fifty six.

(5) If public employees, including the members of the Federal Army, seek election to a *Landtag*, or have been elected member of a *Landtag*, they shall be granted the time off necessary for seeking election or for exercising the function of a member of the Landtag. Detailed regulations shall be provided by the public service regulations.

Art. 96. (1) The members of the *Landtage* shall enjoy the same immunity as the members of the *Nationalrat*. The provisions of Article 57 shall be applied with any necessary modifications.

(2) The provisions of Articles 32 and 33 shall apply also to the meetings of the *Landtage* and of their committees.

Art. 97. (1) A *Land* law shall require for its validity a resolution of the *Landtag*, the authentication and countersignature in accordance with the provisions of the *Land* Constitution and the promulgation by the *Landeshauptmann* (*Land* Governor) in the *Land* Law Gazette (*Landesgesetzblatt*).

(2) In so far as a *Land* law provides for its implementation the co-operation of functionaries of the *Bund*, the consent of the Federal Government shall be obtained for this co-operation. It may be assumed that the Federal Government has given its consent if within eight weeks of the day of receipt of the enacted law by the appropriate Federal Ministry the Federal Government has not informed the *Landeshauptmann*, that the co-operation of Federal functionaries is denied. Before the expiration of this time limit, the enacted law may be promulgated only if the Federal Government has explicitly consented thereto.

Art. 98. (1) All enactments of the *Landtage* shall be communicated to the appropriate Federal Ministry by the *Landeshauptmann* immediately after their enactment by the *Landtag* before their promulgation.

(2) Within eight weeks from the day on which the appropriate Federal Ministry has received the enactment of a *Landtag* the Federal Government may raise a motivated objection thereto, on the ground, that the enactment endangers Federal interests. In such a case the enactment shall be promulgated only if the *Landtag*, in the presence of at least one half of its members, re-enacts the law.

(3) Before expiration of the time allowed for raising an objection the

promulgation shall be admissible only if the Federal Government explicitly consents thereto.

(4) Resolutions of the *Landtage* concerning matters of taxation shall be subject to the provisions of the Constitutional Finance Law.

Art. 99. (1) The *Land* Constitution to be enacted by a *Land* Constitutional Law may be amended by a *Land* Constitutional Law in so far as the Federal Constitution is not affected thereby.

(2) A *Land* Constitutional Law may be enacted only in the presence of one half of the members of the *Landtag* and by a majority of two thirds of the votes cast.

Art. 100. (1) Every *Landtag* may be dissolved by the Federal President on the proposal of the Federal Government and with the consent of the *Bundesrat.* The consenting vote of the *Bundesrat* requires the presence of one half of the members and a majority of two thirds of the votes cast. The representatives of the *Land* whose *Landtag* is to be dissolved shall not participate in the vote.

(2) In case of dissolution writs for new elections shall be issued according to the provisions of the *Land* Constitution, within three weeks. The newly-elected *Landtag* shall be convened within four weeks after the election.

Art. 101. (1) The executive power of each *Land* shall be exercised by a *Land* Government (*Landesregierung*) to be elected by the *Landtag.*

(2) The members of the *Land* Government shall not necessarily be members of the *Landtag.* However, only persons eligible to the *Landtag* may be elected members of the *Land* Government.

(3) The *Land* Government shall consist of the *Landeshauptmann,* the requisite number of deputies and other members.

(4) Before accession to office the *Landeshauptmann* shall make before the Federal President, the other members of the *Land* Government before the *Landeshauptmann,* the solemn promise to observe strictly the Federal Constitution. A religious affirmation may be added.

Art. 102. (1) Within the *Länder* the executive power of the *Bund* shall be exercised—in so far as no Federal authorities exist (direct Federal administration)—by the *Landeshauptmann* and the *Land* authorities subordinated to him (indirect Federal administration). In so far as Federal authorities, and especially Federal police authorities, are entrusted with the execution of matters which are carried out in indirect Federal administration, these Federal authorities in the matters concerned are subordinated to the *Landeshauptmann* and are bound by his instructions (Article 20, paragraph 1); the Federal laws to be enacted in accordance with Article 10 shall determine whether and to what extent such Federal authorities shall be entrusted with acts of execution. In those cases in which Federal police authorities are to perform executive acts in matters of the autonomous sphere of competence of the *Land* the *Landeshauptmann* shall be entitled to issue instructions to them.

(2) The following matters may be administered directly by Federal authorities within the framework of their constitutional sphere of competence:

Marking out of boundaries, trade in goods and livestock with foreign countries, customs, regulation and supervision of entry into and exit from the Federal territory, Federal finances, monopolies, weights and measures, standards and hall-marking, technical experiments, administration of justice, passports, registration of residence, matters pertaining to weapons, ammunition and explosives, use of firearms, patent matters, protection of designs, trademarks and other designations of commodities, engineers and consulting engineers, traffic, Federal highways, river and navigation police, post, telegraph, and telephone, mining, regulation and conservancy of the Danube, regulation of torrents, construction and conservancy of waterways, surveying, labor law, protection of workers and other employees, social insurance, protection of monuments, organization and operation of the Federal Police and the Federal Gendarmerie; finally, under extraordinary circumstances, in such places where on the day when this constitutional law comes into force, the jurisdictional district of a Federal police authority does not coincide with the territory of a *Land*: Maintenance of public peace, order and safety exclusive of the local safety police, press-affairs, association and assembly matters, alien police, military affairs, welfare measures for veterans and their surviving dependents.

(3) The *Bund* may authorize the *Landeshauptmann* to exercise the executive power of the *Bund*, also in the matters enumerated in paragraph 2

(4) The establishment of special Federal authorities as organs of the direct Federal administration in matters other than those enumerated in paragraph 2, is admissible only with the consent of the *Länder* affected thereby.

(5) Within the jurisdictional district of a Federal police authority to which a Federal police force is attached, no other regional authority shall set up and entertain guards of its own. The dissolution of guards whose setting up or retention is contrary to this provision shall fall within the executive competence of the *Bund*.

(6) The setting up of Federal police authorities, the fixing of their jurisdictional districts and, in administrative fields in which the Federal laws to be enacted in accordance with Article 10 provide for execution by Federal police authorities, the fixing of their material competence, as well as the issue of the special service regulations for their functionaries, shall take place by ordinance of the Federal Government. Insofar as such a authority is to be entrusted with the performance of duties in matters which fall into the autonomous sphere of competence of the *Gemeinden* or

otherwise into the autonomous sphere of executive competence of the *Land*, such ordinance may be issued only if the performance of the duties has been transferred to the Federal police authorities by a law of the *Land* concerned.

(7) If, on account of danger to public peace and order, an emergency arises in individual *Gemeinden* which requires special measures, the appropriate Federal Minister may, for the period of such danger, entrust special federal functionaries with the execution of these measures.

Art. 102a. (1) Supreme direction and supervision of the administration in all matters of education and instruction shall be vested in the *Bund*. The *Landesschulräte* (Land school boards), (the *Stadtschulrat* (City school board) of Vienna) and the school authorities subordinate to these authorities shall be subordinated to the appropriate Federal Minister.

(2) The chairmen of the *Landesschulräte* (of the *Stadtschulrat* of Vienna) and of the *Bezirksschulräte* (district school boards) and their deputies shall obey the instructions (Article 20, paragraph 1) of the superior school authorities. Such instructions may be issued only insofar as they do not interfere with the decision on a matter which by law is reserved to the collegiate decision of the subordinate school authorities, unless the instruction concerns the exercise of the powers conferred by law to the chairman with regard to the decisions of the board.

(3) Impeachment proceedings may be brought before the Constitutional Court by a resolution of the Federal Government against the Chairmen of the *Land* school authorities (*Stadtschulrat* of Vienna) and their deputies in matters which by law are to be disposed of under their responsibility. The provisions of Article 142, paragraph 2, clause d, shall be applied with any necessary modifications, to these impeachment proceedings.

(4) If the execution of a collegiate decision of a school authority is suspended by the chairman in pursuance of an instruction of the superior school authority, then the decision of the superior school authority containing the instruction can be contested, on the strength of a collegiate decision of the school authority which has passed the decision, through the successive stages of appeal, and finally by complaint before the Administrative Court.

(5) The appropriate Federal Minister may occasionally satisfy himself personally, or through officials of the Federal Ministry directed by him as to the condition and accomplishments of those secondary and elementary schools that are not under the direct administration of the Federal Ministry; the competent *Land* school authority (*Stadtschulrat of Vienna*) shall participate in this official act through one of its officials. The observations made by the official of the Federal Ministry shall be communicated to the competent *Land* school authorities (to the *Stadtschulrat* of Vienna).

Art. 103. (1) In the matters of the indirect Federal administration, the

Landshauptmann shall be bound by the instructions of the Federal Government as well as of the several Federal Ministers (Article 20). He shall be obliged to use towards the carrying out of these instructions also such powers as are available to him in his capacity as functionary of the autonomous sphere of competence of the *Land*.

(2) In establishing its rules of procedure the *Land* Government may decree that certain categories of matters of the indirect Federal administration on account of their close relationship with matters of the autonomous sphere of competence of the *Land* shall be conducted in the name of the *Landeshauptmann* by members of the *Land* Government. In these matters these members of the *Land* Government shall be bound by the instructions of the *Landeshauptmann* in the same way (Article 20) as the latter is bound by the instructions of the Federal Government or of individual Federal Ministers.

(3) Instructions issued by the Federal Government or by individual Federal Ministers according to paragraph 1 shall be addressed to the *Landeshauptmann* also in cases of paragraph 2. The latter, if he does not himself conduct the indirect Federal administration in this matter, shall be obliged under his responsibility (Article 142, paragraph 2, clause d) to refer immediately such instructions unchanged and in writing to the appropriate member of the *Land* Government and to supervise their execution. If the instruction is not complied with, though the *Landeshauptmann* has taken the necessary steps, the member concerned of the *Land* Government shall also be responsible to the Federal Government according to Article 142.

(4) In matters of the indirect Federal administration, the successive stages of appeal shall go up to the appropriate Federal Ministers unless otherwise explicitly provided for by Federal law.

Art. 104. (1) The provisions of Article 102 shall not apply to agencies set up for the performance of affairs of the *Bund* designated in Article 17.

(2) The Federal Ministers entrusted with the administration of Federal property may, however, delegate the performance of such affairs to the *Landeshauptmann* and to the authorities in the *Land* subordinated to him. Such delegation may be revoked wholly or partly at any time. A Federal law shall determine to what extent in special exceptional cases the Bund shall reimburse the costs incurred by the performance of such affairs.

Art. 105. (1) The *Land* shall be represented by the *Landeshauptmann*. In matters of indirect Federal administration, he shall be responsible to the Federal Government according to Article 142. The *Land* Government shall appoint one of its members as deputy for the *Landeshauptmann* (Deputy *Landeshauptmann*). This appointment shall be communicated to the Federal Chancellor. If this member of the *Land* Government has to deputize for the *Landeshauptmann* he shall be likewise responsible to the Federal Government in matters of the indirect Federal administration according to Article 142. This responsibility of the *Landeshauptmann* or of the member of the *Land* Government deputizing for him may be enforced notwithstanding any immunity. Likewise the immunity shall not prevent the enforcement of the responsibility of a member of the *Land* Government in the case of Article 103, paragraph 3.

(2) The members of the *Land* Government shall be responsible to the *Landtag* in accordance with Article 142.

(3) A resolution of impeachment in accordance with Article 142 shall require the presence of one half of the members.

Art. 106. An administrative official with legal training shall be appointed as *Landesamtsdirektor* (*Land* Administrative Director) to direct the internal service of the Office of the *Land* Government. He shall also be the assistant of the *Landeshauptmann* in matters of indirect Federal administration.

Art. 107. The *Länder* shall enter into compacts with each other only in respect of matters within their autonomous sphere of competence and shall bring such compacts, to the knowledge of the Federal Government without delay.

B. The Federal Capital, Vienna

Art. 108. (1) As regards the Federal capital, Vienna, in its capacity of *Land*, the *Gemeinderat* (City Council) shall also have the function of the *Landtag*; the *Stadtsenat* (City Government) also the function of the *Land* Government, the *Bürgermeister* also the function of the *Landeshauptmann*; the *Magistrat* (City Office) also the function of the Office of the *Land* Government; the *Magistratsdirektor* (City Administrative Director) also the function of the *Landesamtsdirektor*.

(2) The number of the members of the *Gemeinderat* shall not exceed one hundred.

Art. 109. In the field of the indirect Federal administration in the *Land* Vienna, the affairs on the district level and on the *Land* level shall be conducted on one level by the *Bürgermeister* as *Landeshauptmann* and by the *Magistrat* subordinated to him. Appeal may be made from any decision of the *Bürgermeister* as *Landeshauptmann* to the appropriate Federal Minister, except in cases in which an appeal against the decision of the district authority is excluded. Abridgements of the stages of appeal, otherwise generally provided by Federal law (Article 103, paragraph 4) shall not apply. These provisions shall not apply to matters of the indirect Federal administration in so far as Federal authorities are entrusted with their execution (Article 102, paragraph 1, second and third sentence.)

Art. 110. The administrative penal board, which according to Article 11, paragraph 5, is to be established at the *Magistrat* of the Federal capital Vienna as office of the *Land* Government, in order to pass final decisions in administrative penal matters arising in the autonomous sphere of competence of the *Land* shall at the same time pass final decisions in administrative penal matters which arise in the field of the indirect Federal administration; in these cases the right of pardon provided by law shall be exercised by the *Bürgermeister* as *Landeshauptmann* upon proposals of the administrative penal board.

Art. 111. The final decision in building and tax matters shall rest with special boards. The composition and appointment of these boards shall be ruled by *Land* law.

Art. 112–114. Repealed.

C. The Gemeinden (Municipalities)

Art. 115. General public administration in the *Länder* shall, in accordance with the following provisions be organized according to the principle of self-government.

Art. 116. (1) Administrative districts and units of self-government into which the *Länder* are divided shall be the *Ortsgemeinden* (local municipalities) and the *Gebietsgemeinden* (district municipalities).

(2) The *Ortsgemeinden* shall be subordinated to the *Gebietsgemeinden* and these to the *Länder*.

Art. 117. (1) *Ortsgemeinden* of more than 20.000 inhabitants shall at their request be declared *Gebietsgemeinden.* In such *Ortsgemeinden* district administration shall coincide with municipal administration.

(2) Towns heretofore governed under their own charters shall become *Gebietsgemeinden.*

Art. 118. The *Ortsgemeinde* and *Gebietsgemeinde* shall also be independent economic unites. They shall have the right to own and to acquire property of all kinds and to dispose thereof within the limits of Federal and *Land* laws, to engage in economic enterprises, to manage their own finances and to levy taxes.

Art. 119. (1) The agencies of the *Ortsgemeinden* shall be the local municipal council and the local municipal administration office (*Ortsgemeindeamt*) the agencies of the *Gebietsgemeinde* shall be the district municipal council and the district municipal administration office (*Gebietsgemeindeamt*).

(2) Elections to all municipal councils shall take place in accordance with the principle of proportional representation and upon equal, direct, secret and personal suffrage of all Federal citizens who have their domicile within the territorial jurisdiction of the municipal council to be elected. The election regulations shall be issued by *Land* legislation. The right to vote or to be elected shall not be restricted by these election regulations to a greater extent than by the *Landtag* election regulations. *Land* laws may, however, provide that persons who have lived in the *Gemeinde* less than

one year shall have no right to vote or to be elected to the local municipal council if their residence in the *Gemeinde* is obviously only transient. The provisions concerning compulsory voting in the elections for the *Landtag* (Article 95, paragraph 1, last sentence) shall apply with any necessary modifications to the elections for all municipal councils. The election regulations may provide that the voters shall exercise their votes in electoral districts which shall each encompass a contiguous territory. A breaking down of the electorate into other electoral bodies shall not be admissible. For elections for the district municipal council the judicial district shall be the electoral district. The number of representatives shall be apportioned among the electoral districts on the basis of the number of their citizens.

(3) Only persons who have their domicile in the *Gebietsgemeinde* and who are eligible for the *Landtag* shall be eligible for the district municipal councils.

(4) The municipal councils may elect, in accordance with the principle of proportional representation from among their members, for the different branches of the administration, special administrative committees, which insofar as definite professional or interest groups are concerned, may still be enlarged by the admission of representatives of such professional or interest groups.

(5) The heads of the district municipal administration offices shall be administrative officials with legal training.

Art. 120. (1) The laying down of further principles for the organization of the general public administration in the *Länder* in accordance with Article 115–119 shall fall within the competence of the Federal constitutional legislation; the implementation shall be entrusted to the *Land* legislatures.

(2) Federal and *Land* laws, respectively, shall within their sphere of competence as defined by the Constitution, determine what matters of administration, as to subject matter and administrative organization, shall be administered by representative assemblies, administrative committees, and administrative offices, respectively.

(3) In this respect, however, the *Ortsgemeinden* shall be guaranteed a scope of first action in the following matters:

1. Care for the safety of persons and property (local safety police);
2. First aid;
3. Maintenance of streets, roads, public squares, and bridges of the *Gemeinde*;
4. Local highway police;
5. Protection and policing of the fields;
6. Market and food police;
7. Sanitary police;
8. Building and fire police.

CHAPTER V

CONTROL OF PUBLIC ACCOUNTS AND FINANCIAL ADMINISTRATION

Art. 121. (1) The audit of the financial administration of the *Bund*, of the *Länder*, of groupings of *Gemeinden*, and of other holders of legal authority determined by law shall be the responsibility of the Court of Accounts (*Rechnungshof*).

(2) The Court of Accounts shall draw up the final Federal budget accounts and submit them to the *Nationalrat.*

(3) All documents concerning financial debts of the *Bund*, in so far as they authenticate a liability of the *Bund*, shall be countersigned by the President of the Court of Accounts and in case he should be prevented, by his deputy. The countersignature guarantees only the lawfulness of the contraction of the debt and its lawful entry in the ledger of the State Debt.

Art. 122. (1) The Court of Accounts shall be directly subordinated to the *Nationalrat.* The Court shall act in matters of the Federal Financial Administration as agency of the *Nationalrat*, in matters of the financial administration of the *Länder*, groupings of *Gemeinden*, and *Gemeinden* as agency of the *Landtag* concerned.

(2) The Court of Accounts shall be independent of the Federal Government and of the Governments of the *Länder* and shall be subject only to the provisions of the law.

(3) The Court of Accounts shall consist of a President, a Vice-President and the otherwise requisite officials and ancillary personnel.

(4) The President of the Court of Accounts shall be elected by the *Nationalrat* upon nomination by the Main Committee. Before entering on his duties he shall give a solemn promise to fulfil the duties of his office to the Federal President.

(5) The President of the Court of Accounts shall not belong to any general representative body shall and, during the last four years, not have been a member of the Federal Government or of a *Land* Government.

Art. 123. (1) The President of the Court of Accounts shall have the same responsibility as the members of the Federal Government or as the members of the *Land* Government concerned, according as to whether the Court acts as agency of the *Nationalrat* or of a *Landtag.*

(2) He may be recalled by resolution of the *Nationalrat.*

Art. 124. (1) In case the President of the Court of Accounts should be prevented the Vice-President shall deputize for him, and if the latter is also prevented the highest-ranking official of the Court of Accounts shall deputize for him. This shall also apply if the office of the President is vacant.

(2) In case a deputy acts for the President the provisions of Article 123, Paragraph 1 shall apply to the deputy.

Art. 125. (1) The Vice-President and the other officials of the Court of Accounts shall be appointed by the Federal President upon nomination and with the countersignature of the President of the Court of Accounts; the same applies to the bestowal of titles designating their office. The Federal President may, however, authorize the President of the Court of Accounts to appoint officials of specified categories.

(2) The ancillary personnel shall be appointed by the President of the Court of Accounts.

Art. 126. No member of the Court of Accounts shall take part in the management and administration of enterprises, which are subject to control by the Court of Accounts. Neither shall a member of the Court of Accounts participate in the management and administration of other profit seeking enterprises.

Art. 126a. If divergences of opinion concerning the interpretation of the legal provisions on the competence of the Court of Accounts arise between the Court of Accounts and the Federal Government or a Federal Minister or a *Land* Government, the Constitutional Court shall decide in non-public proceedings upon appeal by the Federal (*Land*) Government or by the Court of Accounts. The procedure shall be ruled by Ordinance.

Art. 126b. (1) The Court of Accounts shall audit the entire public administration of the *Bund,* further the financial administration of endowments, funds, and institutions which are administered by agencies of the *Bund* or by persons (groups of persons) who are appointed thereto by agencies of the *Bund.*

(2) The financial administration of enterprises which are carried on by the *Bund* without any partners or in which the *Bund* has a financial interest shall also be subject to the control of the Court of Accounts. If the Court of Accounts audits the financial administration of such enterprises, it may also audit the administration of enterprises in which this enterprise has a financial interest. The administration of Federal property under trusteeship, the assuming of a guaranty of profit or against loss in favor of an enterprise, the grant of a loan from Federal funds for carrying on an enterprise or the grant of a subsidy from Federal funds for the same purpose shall be deemed equivalent to a financial interest of the *Bund.*

(3) The Court of Accounts shall be entitled to audit the financial administration of Federal funds by corporations under public law.

(4) Upon substantiated request of the Federal Government or of a Federal Minister, the Court of Accounts shall carry out special auditing measures coming under its competence and shall report the result to the requesting authority.

(5) The audit by the Court of Accounts shall cover the correctness of

the figures of the accounts, their compliance with the existing regulations and, furthermore, the observance of economy, thriftiness and expediency.

Art. 126c. The Court of Accounts shall be entitled to audit the financial administration of the bearers of social insurance.

Art. 126d. (1) The Court of Accounts shall submit to the *Nationalrat* every year a report on its activity at the latest before the first meeting of the autumn session. Moreover the Court of Accounts may at any time report to the *Nationalrat* its observations about individual facts and, if necessary, submit proposals. The Court of Accounts shall inform the Federal Chancellor of each report at the same time as it submits this report to the *Nationalrat.* The Annual Report on the activity of the Court of Accounts shall be published after having been submitted to the *Nationalrat.*

(2) The *Nationalrat* shall set up a permanent Committee for the discussion of the reports of the Court of Accounts. This committee shall be set up according to the principle of proportional representation. The committee shall complete the discussion of each report within six weeks whereupon it shall report to the *Nationalrat.*

Art. 127. (1) The Court of Accounts shall audit the financial administration coming under the autonomous sphere of competence of the *Länder* as well as the financial administration of endowments, funds, and institutions which are administered by agencies of a *Land* Government or by persons (groups of persons) who are appointed thereto by agencies of a *Land* Government. The audit shall cover the correctness of the figures of the accounts, their compliance with the existing regulations and, furthermore, the observance of economy, thriftiness and expediency of the financial administration; it shall, however, not include the control of the resolutions conclusive on the financial administration adopted by the representative bodies competent under the Constitution.

(2) The *Land* Governments shall transmit every year the budget estimates and the final budget accounts to the Court of Accounts.

(3) Enterprises carried on by a *Land* without any partners or which are under the exclusive financial control of one *Land* shall be subject to the audit like the rest of the financial administration of the *Land.* This shall also apply to those enterprises, wherein apart from a *Land* only territorial corporations under public law have a financial interest. Other enterprises in which the *Land* has a financial interest shall be audited by the Court of Accounts only upon substantiated request of the *Land* Government. As regards the *notion* of such financial interest Article 126b paragraph 2 shall apply with any necessary modifications.

(4) The Court of Accounts shall be entitled to audit the financial administration of *Land* funds by corporations under public law.

(5) The Court of Accounts shall inform the *Land* Government of the result of its audit for submission to the *Landtag* and for possible comments.

Such comments shall be made within three weeks. The *Land* Government shall inform the Court of Accounts within three months of the measures taken as the result of the audit.

(6) The Court of Accounts shall also inform the Federal Government of the report made to the *Landtag* together with the comments of the *Land* Government, if any.

(7) Upon substantiated request of a *Land* Government the Court of Accounts shall carry out special auditing measures coming under the competence of the Court of Accounts and shall report the result to the requesting authority.

(8) The provisions of this Article shall apply also to the audit of the financial administration of the City of Vienna, the *Gemeinderat* taking the place of the *Landtag* and the *Stadtsenat* taking the place of the *Land* Government.

Art. 127a. (1) The financial administration of *Gemeinden* with at least 20,000 inhabitants as well as the financial administration of endowments, funds, and institutions which are administered by agencies of a *Gemeinde* or by persons (groups of persons) appointed thereto by agencies of a *Gemeinde* shall be subject to the control of the Court of Accounts. The audit shall cover the correctness of the figures of the account, their compliance with the existing regulations, and, furthermore, the observance of economy, thriftiness and expediency of the financial administration.

(2) The *Bürgermeister* shall transmit every year the budget estimates and the final budget accounts to the Court of Accounts and at the same time to the *Land* Government.

(3) Enterprises carried on by a *Gemeinde* without any partners or which are under the exclusive financial control of such a *Gemeinde* shall be subject to the audit of the Court of Audits like the rest of the financial administration of the *Gemeinde*. This shall also apply to those enterprises wherein, apart from a *Gemeinde* with at least 20,000 inhabitants, only territorial corporations under public law have a financial interest insofar as such enterprises are not already subject to the audit by the Court of Accounts in virtue of Article 127 paragraph 3 second sentence. Other enterprises in which the *Gemeinde* has a financial interest shall be audited by the Court of Accounts only upon substantiated request of the *Land* Government. As regards the notion of such financial interest, Article 126b, paragraph 2, shall apply with any necessary modifications.

(4) The Court of Accounts shall be entitled to audit the financial administration by corporations under public law of funds of a *Gemeinde* with at least 20,000 inhabitants.

(5) The Court of Accounts shall inform the *Bürgermeister* of the result of its audit for submission to the *Gemeinderat* and for possible comments. Such comments shall be made within three weeks. Upon expiration of this term the Court of Accounts shall transmit the result of the audit together

with the comments, if any, to the *Land* Government which shall inform the *Landtag* accordingly. The *Bürgermeister* shall inform the Court of Accounts within three months of the measures taken as the result of the audit.

(6) The Court of Accounts shall also inform the Federal Government of the result of its audit.

(7) Upon substantiated request of the competent *Land* Government the Court of Accounts shall also audit in individual cases the financial administration of *Gemeinden* with less than 20,000 inhabitants and inform the *Land* Government of the result of this audit. The paragraphs 1 and 3 of this article shall apply.

(8) The provisions concerning the audit of the financial administration of the *Gemeinden* with at least 20,000 inhabitants shall apply with any necessary modifications to the audit of the financial administration of the groupings of *Gemeinden.*

Art. 128. Detailed provisions concerning the organization and activity of the Court of Accounts shall be laid down by Federal law.

CHAPTER VI

GUARANTIES OF THE CONSTITUTION AND ADMINISTRATION

Art. 129. The Administrative Court in Vienna shall safeguard the legality of all acts of the entire public administration.

Art. 130. (1) The Administrative Court shall pronounce judgment upon complaints, by which it is asserted that decisions of administrative authorities are illegal or that administrative authorities have failed in their duty to issue a decision.

(2) An act cannot be illegal in so far as legislation refrains from laying down binding rules for the policy to be adopted by the administrative authority, and leaves it to the discretion of the authority itself to establish such policy and insofar as the authority has used this discretion in conformity with the law.

Art. 131. (1) After the complainant has exhausted all administrative remedies, a complaint asserting illegality of a decision of an administrative authority may be filed:

(a) by the person asserting that his rights have been violated by the decision;

(b) in matters under Articles 11 and 12, also by the competent Federal Minister.

(2) The conditions under which complaints asserting the illegality of decisions of administrative authorities may be brought also in other cases

than in those mentioned in paragraph 1, shall be regulated by Federal or *Land* laws governing the several fields of administration.

Art. 132. Complaints asserting that an authority failed in its duty to issue a decision, may be brought by the party, who in the administrative proceedings was entitled to claim such a decision.

Art. 133. The following matters shall be excluded from the jurisdiction of the Administrative Court:

1. matters which belong to the jurisdiction of the Constitutional Court,
2. disciplinary matters concerning the employees of the *Bund,* of the *Länder,* of the districts and *Gemeinden,*
3. patent matters,
4. matters the final decision of which rests with a collegiate authority if, according to the Federal or *Land* law which determines the organization of this authority, at least one of its members is a judge and if in the execution of their office the other members are not bound by instructions, if, further, the decisions of the authority cannot be rescinded or modified by an administrative authority and if, notwithstanding the fact that these conditions have been met, an appeal to the Administrative Court has not explicitly been declared admissible.

Art. 134. (1) The Administrative Court shall consist of a President, a Vice President and the requisite number of other members (Presidents of Chambers of the Court and Councillors).

(2) The President, the Vice-President and the other members of the Administrative Court shall be appointed by the Federal President upon nomination by the Federal Government. The Federal Government shall make its nomination with the exception of the nominations concerning the post of the President or the Vice-President, on the basis of proposals containing the names of three candidates made by the plenary meeting of the Administrative Court.

(3) All members of the Administrative Court shall be law school graduates and shall already have served for at least ten years in a position for which a law degree is required. At least one third of the members shall have the qualification for a judge; at least one fourth shall be taken from positions in the several *Länder,* if possible from the administrative service of the *Länder.*

(4) Members of the Federal Government, of a *Land* Governments or of a general representative body shall not be members of the Administrative Court; for members of the general representative bodies who were elected for a certain term the incompatibility continues, even in case of premature resignation, until the term has expired for which they have been elected.

(5) A person who has exercised one of the functions mentioned in paragraph 4 during the last four years may not be appointed President or Vice-President of the Administrative Court.

(6) By their appointment all members of the Administrative Court

become professional judges. The provisions of Article 87, paragraphs 1 and 2, and Article 88, paragraph 2 shall apply to them. On December 31st of the year in which they complete their 65th year of age the members of the Administrative Court shall be permanently retired in virtue of the law.

Art. 135. (1) The Administrative Court shall pronounce judgment in chambers which shall be formed from the plenary meeting of members of the Court.

(2) Business shall be assigned to the chambers by the plenary meeting within the time limit fixed by federal law.

(3) A matter assigned to a member in such a distribution may be withdrawn from the member only in case of his inability to act.

Art. 136. Detailed regulations concerning the organization, jurisdiction and procedure of the Administrative Court shall be stipulated in a special Federal law and in rules based thereon to be decided by the plenary of the Court.

B. The Constitutional Court

Art. 137. The Constitutional Court shall pronounce judgment upon pecuniary claims against the *Bund,* the *Länder,* districts, *Gemeinden* and groupings of *Gemeinden,* which can neither be brought to a decision by ordinary court action nor be disposed of by decision of an administrative authority.

Art. 138. (1) Furthermore the Constitutional Court shall pronounce judgment upon disputes about competence:

(a) between courts and administrative authorities;

(b) between the Administrative Court and all other courts, especially also between the Administrative Court and the Constitutional Court itself, as well as between the ordinary courts and other courts;

(c) between the *Länder* amongst themselves as well as between a *Land* and the *Bund.*

(2) On application of the Federal Government or of a *Land* Government, the Constitutional Court shall declare whether an act of legislation or execution falls, according to Articles 10–15, within the sphere of competence of the *Bund* or of the *Länder.*

Art. 139. (1) The Constitutional Court shall pronounce judgment: at the request of a court upon the illegality of ordinances made by a Federal or *Land* authority; if, however, such an ordinance is to form the basis of a judgment of the Constitutional Court the judgment shall be pronounced *ex officio;*

upon the illegality of ordinances of a *Land* authority also at the request of the Federal Government;

upon the illegality of ordinances of a Federal authority also at the request of a *Land* Government.

(2) The judgment of the Constitutional Court by which an ordinance is rescinded as being illegal, shall oblige the competent authority to promulgate the rescission immediately. The rescission shall become effective on the day of promulgation unless the Constitutional Court fixes a time limit for the rescission which shall not exceed six months.

(3) If the ordinance to be applied by the court has already ceased to be in force and if consequently the application has been made according to Article 89, paragraph 3, the judgment of the Constitutional Court shall be limited to the decision of the question as to whether the ordinance was illegal.

Art. 140. (1) The Constitutional Court shall pronounce judgment: upon the unconstitutionality of a Federal or *Land* law at the request of the Supreme Court or of the Administrative Court if such a law shall constitute the basis of a judgment of the applying court; further *ex officio* if such a law constitutes the basis of a judgment of the Constitutional Court itself;

upon the unconstitutionality of *Land* laws also at the request of the Federal Government;

upon the unconstitutionality of Federal laws also at the request of a *Land* Government.

(2) The request mentioned in paragraph 1 may be made at any time; the authority that makes the request shall communicate it immediately to the *Land* Government concerned or to the Federal Government.

(3) The judgment of the Constitutional Court by which a law or a certain part thereof is annulled as being unconstitutional, shall oblige the Federal Chancellor or the *Landeshauptmann* concerned to promulgate the annulment immediately. The annulment shall become effective on the date of the promulgation, unless the Constitutional Court fixes a time limit for the annulment. This time limit shall not exceed one year.

(4) If by a decision of the Constitutional Court, a law or a part thereof is annulled as being unconstitutional, the legal provisions which were repealed by the law which the Constitutional Court has found unconstitutional shall re-enter into force on the day of the entry into force of the annulment unless the judgment provides otherwise. In the promulgation concerning the annulment of the law it shall also be announced whether and which legal provisions shall re-enter into force.

(5) The Constitutional Finance Law determines to what extent resolutions of a *Landtag* concerning *Land* surtaxes to Federal taxes may be contested before the Constitutional Court and which legal effects are connected with any judgment of the Constitutional Court which pronounces the annulment of such a resolution of the *Landtag* or of a *Land* law concerning *Land* or *Gemeinde* taxes.

(6) The provision of Article 89, paragraph 1, shall not apply to the review by the Constitutional Court of the constitutionality of laws.

Art. 140a. (1) The Constitutional Court shall pronounce judgment upon the illegality of treaties. The provisions of Article 140 shall be applied to treaties concluded with the approval of the *Nationalrat* as stipulated in Article 50, and the provisions of Article 139 shall be applied to all other treaties, with the necessary modifications; treaties whose illegality or unconstitutionality has been adjudged by the Constitutional Court shall cease to be applied by the competent authorities from the day the decision is notified, except if the Constitutional Court fixes a time limit during which the treaty may continue to be applied. Such a time limit may not exceed two years in the case of treaties described in Article 50, and one year in the case of all other treaties.

(2) If the Constitutional Court adjudges the illegality or unconstitutionality of a treaty which is implemented by laws or decrees, any decision reached in accordance with Article 50, paragraph (2) or decree promulgated in accordance with Article 65, paragraph (1), second sentence, shall cease to be valid.

Art. 141. (1) The Constitutional Court shall pronounce judgment if the results of elections of the Federal President, for the *Nationalrat,* for the *Bundesrat* and for the *Landtage* are contested as well as, upon request of one of these legislative bodies, upon the unseating of one of its members. It shall also pronounce judgment if the result of elections for all other general representative bodies are contested further, upon application of one of these bodies, upon the unseating of one of its members, finally, upon the rescission of decisions of administrative authorities by which the loss of membership in these bodies was pronounced, after the exhaustion of the administrative stages of appeal. The body concerned shall be a party to the proceedings before the administrative authorities.

(2) A Federal Law shall rule under which conditions the Constitutional Court shall decide if the results of a popular initiative or referendum are contested. By Federal law it may also be provided how long the promulgation of a Federal law on which a referendum took place shall be delayed in view of the possibility of contesting the results.

Art. 142. (1) The Constitutional Court shall pronounce judgment in impeachment proceedings by which the constitutional responsibility of the highest Federal and *Land* officers for wilful violations of law during their tenure of office is being asserted.

(2) Impeachment proceedings may be brought:

(a) against the Federal President for violation of the Federal Constitution: by resolution of the *Bundesversammlung*;

(b) against the members of the Federal Government and the officers of equal standing regarding their responsibility, for infringement of the law: by resolution of the *Nationalrat*;

(c) against the members of a *Land* Government and the officers of equal standing according to this law or to the *Land* constitution, as regards their responsibility, for infringement of the law: by resolution of the *Landtag* concerned;

(d) against a *Landeshauptmann,* his deputy (Article 105, paragraph 1) or a member of the *Land* Government (Article 103, paragraphs 2 and 3) for infringement of the law as well as for non-compliance with the ordinances or other orders (instructions) of the *Bund* in matters of indirect Federal administration, if a member of the *Land* Government is concerned, also for non-compliance with directions of the *Landeshauptmann* in these matters: by resolution of the Federal Government.

(3) If the impeachment proceedings are brought by the Federal Government according to paragraph 2, clause d, only against the *Landeshauptmann* or his deputy, and if it becomes evident that another member of the *Land* Government entrusted with matters of indirect Federal administration according to Article 103, paragraph 2, is guilty of an offense within the meaning of paragraph 2, clause d, the Federal Government may at any time, pending the passing the judgment of the Constitutional Court extend the impeachment also to this member of the *Land* Government.

(4) The condemning judgment of the Constitutional Court shall declare the loss of office and under particularly aggravating circumstances also the temporary loss of political rights. In the event of minor infringements in the cases mentioned in paragraph 2, clause d, the Constitutional Court may limit its finding to the declaration that the law has been infringed.

(5) In the cases of the clauses a, b and c of the 2nd paragraph of this Article the Federal President may avail himself of the right conferred upon him by Article 65, paragraph 2, clause c, only upon application of the representative body which has adopted the resolution of impeachment; in case of clause d only on proposal of the Federal Government; in all cases, however, only with the consent of the accused.

Art. 143. The impeachment against the persons mentioned in Article 142 may also be brought for acts falling under criminal prosecution if these acts are connected with the official activities of the person to be impeached. In this case, the Constitutional Court shall have exclusive jurisdiction; any criminal investigations which may be pending before an ordinary criminal court shall then devolve upon the Constitutional Court. The latter may apply in such cases, beside Article 142, paragraph 4, also the criminal law provisions.

Art. 144. (1) The Constitutional Court shall pronounce judgment upon complaints against decisions (or orders) of the administrative authorities insofar as the complainant asserts that one of his rights guaranteed by the Constitution has been violated by the decision. The complaint can be filed only after all administrative remedies have been exhausted, unless a Federal law provides otherwise.

(2) If the Constitutional Court finds that a right guaranteed by the Constitution has not been violated by the contested decision of the ad-

ministrative authority and if it is not a case which according to Article 133 is excluded from the jurisdiction of the Administrative Court the Constitutional Court shall reject the complaint and at the same time, at the request of the complainant, assign the complaint to the Administrative Court for decision whether any other right of the complainant has been violated by the decision.

Art. 145. The Constitutional Court shall pronounce judgment upon violations of international law in accordance with the provisions of a special Federal law.

Art. 146. (1) The judgments of the Constitutional Court upon claims according to Article 137 shall be enforced by the ordinary courts.

(2) The enforcement of the other judgments of the Constitutional Court shall rest with the Federal President. It shall be carried out according to his instructions by such Federal or *Land* agencies as he may choose to select, including the Federal Army. The Constitutional Court shall apply to the Federal President for the enforcement of such judgments. The above mentioned instructions by the Federal President shall, if they concern the enforcement of judgments against the *Bund* or against Federal officers, require no countersignature according to Article 67.

Art. 147. The Constitutional Court shall consist of a President, a Vice-President, twelve other members and six substitute members.

(2) The President, the Vice-President, six other members and three substitute members shall be appointed by the Federal President upon nomination by the Federal Government; these members shall be selected from among judges, administrative civil servants and professors of the law and political sciences faculties of the universities. The other six members and three substitute members shall be appointed by the Federal President upon proposals made, as regards three members and two substitute members, by the *Nationalrat* and, as regards three members and one substitute member, by the *Bundesrat.* Each proposal shall contain the names of three candidates for each post. Three members and two substitute members shall have their permanent residence outside the Federal capital of Vienna. Administrative civil servants who are appointed members of the Constitutional Court shall be put on the retired list in so far and as long as they are not retired.

(3) The President, the Vice-President, as well as the other members and the substitute members shall be law school graduates and shall have already served for at least ten years in a position for which a law degree is required.

(4) The following persons cannot be members of the Constitutional Court: members of the Federal Government or of a *Land* Government, members of the *Nationalrat,* of the *Bundesrat* or of any general representative body. For members of these representative bodies who were elected for a certain term of legislation or office period the incompatibility shall

continue even in case of a premature resignation until that term has expired. Finally, employees or other functionaries of a political party cannot be members of the Constitutional Court.

(5) A person who has exercised one of the functions mentioned in paragraph 4 during the last four years may not be appointed President or Vice-President of the Constitutional Court.

(6) Article 87, paragraphs 1 and 2, and Article 88, paragraph 2, shall apply to the members of the Constitutional Court; detailed provisions will be made in the Federal law to be issued according to Article 148. The office of a member of the Constitutional Court shall end on December 31st of the year in which the judge completes his 70th year of age.

(7) If a member or a substitute member without satisfactory excuse, does not attend three consecutive meetings of the Constitutional Court to which he was invited, the court shall issue a formal declaration concerning this fact after hearing the member or substitute member concerned. This declaration entails the loss of membership or substitute membership.

Art. 148. Detailed regulations concerning the organization and procedure of the Constitutional Court shall be stipulated in a special Federal law and in rules based thereon to be decided by the plenary of the Court.

CHAPTER VII

FINAL PROVISIONS

Art. 149. (1) In addition to this law the following laws shall, within the meaning of Article 44, paragraph 1, be regarded as constitutional laws with due consideration for the modifications necessitated by this law:

State Fundamental Act of December 21st, 1867, R.G.Bl. No. 142, concerning the general rights of citizens, for the kingdoms and territories represented in the *Reichsrat* (Imperial Diet).

Law of October 27th, 1862, R.G.Bl. No. 87, for the protection of personal liberty.

Law of October 27th, 1862, R.G.Bl. No. 88, for the protection of the inviolability of the home.

Resolution of the Provisional National Assembly of October 30th, 1918, St.G. Bl. No. 3.

Law of April 3rd, 1919, St.G.Bl. No. 209, concerning the banishment and the confiscation of the property of the dynasty of Hapsburg-Lorraine.

Law of April 3rd, 1919, St.G.Bl. No. 211, concerning the abolition of the nobility, of the secular orders of knights and ladies, and of certain titles and honors.

Law of May 8th, 1919, St.G.Bl. No. 257, concerning the Coat of Arms and the Seal of State of the German-Austrian Republic with the modifications resulting from Articles 2, 5 and 6 of the Law of October 21st, 1919, St.G.Bl. No. 484.

Section V of part III of the Treaty of St. Germain, of September 10th, 1919, St.G.Bl. 1920, No. 303.

Constitutional Law of November 30th, 1945, B.G.Bl. 1946, No. 6 concerning the application of the Law of October 27th, 1862, R.G.Bl. No. 87 in the proceedings before the People's Court.

(2) Article 20 of the State Fundamental Act of December 21st, 1867, R.G.Bl. No. 142, as well as the Law of May 5th, 1869, R.G.Bl. No. 66, enacted on the basis of the aforementioned Article shall cease to be in force.

Art. 150. The transition to the Federal Constitution introduced by this law shall be regulated by a special constitutional law, which shall become effective at the same time as this law.

Art. 151. (*Abrogated*).

Art. 152. The execution of this law is entrusted to the Government.

BELGIUM

SUMMARY

INTERNATIONAL STATUS

Belgium is a member of the United Nations (December 27, 1945).[1] It is a member of the European Economic Community, of Benelux and of other international organizations. It was a member of the League of Nations.

The Protocol of London of June 21, 1814, ratified by the Congress of Vienna, united Belgium and Holland to form, together with Luxembourg,

[1] It accepts the compulsory jurisdiction of the International Court under Article 36 of the Statute.

the Kingdom of the Netherlands. On August 25, 1830, the Belgians revolted against Dutch rule on and September 25, the provisional government declared the independence of Belgium. On October 14, 1831, a conference in London declared the dissolution of the United Kingdom of the Netherlands. The Constitution was voted in 1831 and on June 4, 1831, Prince Leopold of Saxe Coburg-Saalfeld was elected King and took the oath to defend the Constitution. The international status of Belgium was fully recognized by the Treaty of London of April 19, 1839, which guaranteed Belgian neutrality. In 1885 the Congo Free State was established under the sovereignty of the King of Belgium. Germany violated Belgian neutrality in 1914 and invaded and occupied the country. Belgium was occupied by Germany from 1940 to 1944. The Belgian Congo joined the Allied powers.

An Economic Union was formed with Luxembourg on July 25, 1921, and reestablished in 1945. The Benelux Economic Union was established by Protocol of February 3, 1958 between Belgium, Luxembourg and the Netherlands following upon the customs union initiated by the Protocol of September 5, 1944, which entered into force on January 1, 1948. The Congo became independent in 1960.

FORM OF NATIONAL GOVERNMENT

The Belgian Constitution was promulgated on February 7, 1931, and amended in 1893, 1920 and 1921. It provides for a constitutional monarchy and a system of separation of powers. It lists the provinces of Belgium.[1] All powers stem from the nation.[2] In January 1964, a Commission for Institutional Reform was set up composed of delegates from the three national parties to examine proposals for the reform of the Constitution made by a political working party set up on April 6, 1962. After a favorable vote on the Commissions' report by two of the parties in February 1965, the Government tabled in the Lower House a draft statement of intent to revise the Constitution, and Parliament ratified the government's proposals, published in the Moniteur on April 17, 1965.

RIGHTS OF THE PEOPLE

The Constitution guarantees equality before the law, individual liberty, due process of law and the right to the judge assigned by law, inviolability of domicile, the right to property, freedom of worship, education, press, the right of assembly, association and petition, secrecy of correspondence.[3]

[1] Const., Art. 1. [2] Id., Art. 25. [3] Id., Art. 4–22.

LEGISLATIVE DEPARTMENT

Legislative authority is exercised collectively by the King and a bicameral Parliament composed of the House of Representatives and the Senate.[1] Only the Legislature may interpret the laws.[2] Members represent the nation.[3] Immunities of deputies are provided.[4] Parliament meets in one regular session a year.[5]

Members of the House of Representatives are elected by universal direct suffrage for a term of four years subject to dissolution.[6] The Senate is composed of (1) members elected by universal suffrage from specified groups of persons on the basis of the population of each province, (2) members elected by the provincial councils, (3) members elected by the Senate itself; the total of its members amounts to half the members of the House of Representatives; its term is four years subject to dissolution.[7] There are provisions concerning finances.[8]

EXECUTIVE DEPARTMENT

Executive authority is vested in a hereditary King.[9] The King is inviolable and his ministers are responsible.[10] He has the power of appointment, commands the Armed Forces, promulgates the laws, has the right of pardon, confers honors.[11] There is a cabinet with a Prime Minister collectively answerable to Parliament. Members of the royal family may not be ministers.[12] An Inner Cabinet on General Policy was created by Decree in 1961 and also a Ministerial Committee on Economic and Social Co-ordination. The former became in 1966 the Restricted Cabinet.

The Constitution contains provisions relating to provincial and municipal institutions.[13]

JUDICIAL DEPARTMENT

Judicial authority is exercised by the courts and tribunals.[14] Judges are appointed for life.[15] The Constitution provides for a Court of Cassation.[16] Decrees and regulations must not be applied save as they are in accordance with the law.[17]

[1] Id., Art. 26. [2] Id., Art. 28. [3] Id., Art. 32. [4] Id., Art. 45.
[5] Id., Art. 70. [6] Id., Art. 47, 51, 71.
[7] Id., Art. 53–56B, 56D, 71. [8] Id., Art. 110–117.
[9] Id., Art. 29, 60. [10] Id., Art. 63. [11] Id., Art. 65–69, 73–76.
[12] Id., Art. 87. [13] Id., Art. 108, 109. [14] Id., Art. 31. [15] Id., Art. 100.
[16] Id., Art. 95. [17] Id., Art. 107.

AREA, POPULATION, ETC.

The area of Belgium is 30,513 square kilometres, its population (1963) 9,328,000. The capital is Brussels.[1] The Constitution provides that the use of the languages spoken in Belgium is optional.[2] Since 1898, laws and decrees are passed, approved and promulgated in both French and Flemish. In 1963, Parliament passed three laws regulating the use of languages in the administrative, educational and legal sectors. In 1962, a law fixed the linguistic boundary and divided Belgium into four linguistic regions, Dutch speaking, French speaking, German speaking and the bilingual region of Brussels and its environs.

[1] Id., Art. 126. [2] Id., art. 23.

CONSTITUTION of BELGIUM [1]

February 7, 1831, as amended September 7, 1893, November 15, 1920, February 7, August 24 and October 15, 1921

HEADING I

CONCERNING THE TERRITORY AND ITS DIVISIONS

Art. 1. Belgium is divided into provinces.

Its provinces are: Antwerp, Brabant, East Flanders, West Flanders, Hainaut, Liège, Limburg, Luxemburg, Namur.

It is up to the law, if necessary, to divide the territory into a larger number of provinces.

The colonies, overseas possessions or protectorates which Belgium may acquire are governed by special laws. Belgian troops destined for their defence may only be recruited through voluntary engagement.

Art. 2. The subdivisions of the provinces can only be established by law.

Art. 3. The boundaries of the State, the provinces and the boroughs can only be modified or rectified by means of a law.

HEADING II

CONCERNING THE BELGIANS AND THEIR RIGHTS

Art. 4. Belgian nationality is acquired, retained and withdrawn in accordance with the rules laid down by civil law.

The present Constitution and the other laws governing political rights determine what conditions, apart from nationality, are necessary for the exercise of those rights.

Art. 5. Naturalization is granted by the legislative power.

[1] In *The Political and Economic Structure of Belgium*, Robert Senelle. No. 73–74–75, February, March, April 1966, of *Memo from Belgium* issued by the Ministry of Foreign Affairs and External Trade, Brussels. Supplied by them in July 1966. Ed.

Only full naturalization places the foreigner on an equal footing with the Belgian citizen where the exercise of political rights is concerned.

Art. 6. There is no distinction between orders in the State.

All Belgians are equal in the eyes of the law; they alone are acceptable for civil and military posts, with some exceptions which may be established by law in special cases.

Art. 7. Individual liberty is guaranteed.

No person may be prosecuted except in cases laid down by the law and in the form it prescribes.

Apart from the case of *flagrante delicto*, no person may be arrested save on a motivated order by a judge, which must be signified at the time of the arrest or within twenty-four hours at latest.

Art. 8. No person may be withdrawn from the judge assigned to him by the law, save with his consent.

Art. 9. No penalty may be decreed nor applied save in accordance with the law.

Art. 10. The home is inviolable; no entrance into a private house may be made save in those cases laid down by the law and in the manner it prescribes.

Art. 11. No person may be deprived of his property save in the public interest, in cases laid down by the law and in the manner it prescribes, and on condition that just compensation is made previously.

Art. 12. The penalty consisting of confiscation of property may not be decreed.

Art. 13. The civilian death penalty is abolished and may not be reinstated.

Art. 14. Freedom of worship and its public exercise, together with freedom to manifest personal opinions in every way, are guaranteed save for the punishment of offences perpetrated in exercising those liberties.

Art. 15. No person may be constrained to assist in any way in the acts and ceremonies of any form of worship, nor to observe its days of rest.

Art. 16. The State has no right to intervene either in the appointment or the induction of ministers of any form of worship, nor to forbid them to correspond with their superiors and to publish their acts save, in the latter case, for the ordinary responsibility bound up with the press and publishing.

The civil wedding must always precede the nuptial benediction, save in exceptional cases to be established, where necessary, by law.

Art. 17. Education is free; any preventive measure is forbidden; the punishment of misdemeanours is regulated only by law.

Public education provided at the expense of the State is also regulated by law.

Art. 18. The press is free; no form of censorship may ever be instituted: no cautionary deposit may be demanded from writers, publishers or printers.

When the author is known and is resident in Belgium, the publisher, printer or distributor may not be prosecuted.

Art. 19. Belgians have the right to hold peaceful, unarmed meetings; they must comply with the laws which may regulate the exercise of this right without, however, subjecting it to prior authorization.

This clause does not apply to open-air meetings which remain entirely subject to the police laws.

Art. 20. Belgians have the right to associate; this right may not be subjected to any preventive measure.

Art. 21. Every person has the right to address petitions signed by one or several people to the public authorities.

The constituted authorities alone have the right to send in collective petitions.

Art. 22. The secrecy of letters is inviolable. The law shall determine what agents are responsible for the violation of secrecy in the case of letters sent by post.

Art. 23. The use of the languages spoken in Belgium is optional; it may only be regulated by law and only in the case of acts by the public authorities and of legal matters.

Art. 24. No prior authorization is necessary to bring an action against civil servants with regard to their administrative acts, except as elsewhere specified for Ministers.

HEADING III

CONCERNING THE AUTHORITIES

Art. 25. All powers stem from the nation.

They are exercised in the manner laid down by the Constitution.

Art. 26. Legislative authority is exercised collectively by the King, the House of Representatives and the Senate.

Art. 27. The right of initiation is vested in each of the three branches of the Legislative authority.

Art. 28. The authoritative interpretation of laws is solely the prerogative of the Legislative authority.

Art. 29. The Executive authority is vested in the King as laid down by the Constitution.

Art. 30. The Judiciary authority is exercised by the courts and tribunals.

Their decisions and judgments are delivered in the name of the King.

Art. 31. Interests which are exclusively municipal or provincial are regulated by the municipal or provincial councils in accordance with the principles laid down by the Constitution.

CHAPTER I. CONCERNING THE HOUSES OF PARLIAMENT

Art. 32. The members of both Houses represent the nation, and not merely the province or subdivision of a province which elected them.

Art. 33. The sessions of both Houses are public.

Nevertheless, each House may go into secret committee at the request of its president or of ten members.

It then decides, on the basis of an absolute majority, whether the sitting is to be resumed in public on the same subject.

Art. 34. Each House verifies the powers of its members and pronounces judgment on any contestations that may arise in this regard.

Art. 35. No person may be a member of both Houses simultaneously.

Art. 36. The member of either House who is appointed by the government to any salaried post other than that of Minister, and who accepts, ceases to sit immediately and does not resume his functions save as the result of a new election.

Art. 37. At each session, each House nominates its president, its vice-presidents and makes up its steering committee.

Art. 38. Every resolution is passed on the basis of an absolute majority of votes cast, except as shall be prescribed by the House and Senate rules with respect to elections and candidatures.

Should there be an equal number of votes on both sides, the proposal under discussion is thrown out.

Neither of the two Houses may adopt any resolution without the majority of its members being present.

Art. 39. Voting is done either by word of mouth or by sitting and standing; all laws generally are voted on by the calling of names and word of mouth. The election and presentation of candidates are voted on by secret ballot.

Art. 40. Each House has the right of investigation.

Art. 41. No bill may be passed by either House except after being voted on article by article.

Art. 42. The Houses have the right to amend and to divide up the articles and amendments proposed.

Art. 43. It is prohibited to present petitions to the Houses personally.

Each House has the right to refer the petitions addressed to it back to the Ministers. The latter are bound to provide explanations regarding their contents whenever the House shall request it.

Art. 44. No member of either of the two Houses may be prosecuted or sought out as a result of the opinions and votes he has expressed in the exercise of his functions.

Art. 45. No member of either of the two Houses may, during the session, be prosecuted or arrested as a punishment save with the permission of the House to which he belongs, except in the case of *flagrante delicto*.

No bodily constraint may be used towards a member of either of the two Houses during the session, save with the same permission as above.

The detention or prosecution of a member of either of the two Houses is suspended during the session and throughout its duration if the House shall so require.

Art. 46. Each House, through its own rules, shall determine the way in which it shall exercise its powers.

Section I. Concerning the House of Representatives

Art. 47. Members of the House of Representatives are directly elected by all citizens aged 21 years and over, resident for at least six months in the same borough, and who do not come under any of the causes of disenfranchisement laid down by the law.

Each elector is entitled to only one vote.

A law may, under the same conditions, attribute voting rights to women. This last must secure at least two thirds of the votes cast.

Art. 48. The constitution of the electoral bodies is regulated by law in each province.

Elections are held on the basis of the proportional representation system as specified by the law.

Voting is compulsory and secret. It takes place in the borough, save in exceptional cases to be specified by law.

Art. 49. The electoral law fixes the number of members of Parliament according to the population: this number may not exceed the proportion of one member to every 40.000 inhabitants. It also specifies the conditions required to become an elector and the conduct of electoral operations.

Art. 50. To be eligible, it is necessary:

(1) to be a Belgian by birth or to have been granted full naturalization;
(2) to enjoy civil and political rights:
(3) to be aged twenty-five years or over;
(4) to be legally resident in Belgium.

No other condition of eligibility may be required.

Art. 51. The members of the House of Representatives are elected for a term of four years. The House is renewed every four years.

Art. 52. Every member of the House of Representatives is entitled to an annual indemnity of 12,000 francs.

He is furthermore entitled to travel free on all lines of communication that are operated or contracted out by the State.

The law specifies those methods of transportation which members may use free of charge apart from those mentioned above. An annual indemnity, chargeable to the endowment destined to cover the expenses of the House of Representatives, may be attributed to the president of that assembly.

The House determines the amounts that may be levied on the indemnity under the heading of contributions to the retirement or pension funds it has deemed useful to set up.

Section II. Concerning the Senate

Art. 53. The Senate is composed:

(1) of members elected on the basis of the population in each province, in accordance with article 47. The provisions of article 48 are applicable to the election of those senators;

(2) of members elected by the provincial councils in the proportion of one senator to every 200,000 inhabitants.

Every surplus of at least 125,000 inhabitants confers the right to elect an additional senator. However, every provincial council shall nominate at least three senators;

(3) of members elected by the Senate on the basis of half the number of senators elected by the provincial councils. If the number is an odd one, it is increased by one digit. These members are designated by the senators who were elected according to the provisions of (1) and (2) of the present article.

The election of senators who are elected according to the provisions of (2) and (3) of the present article, is carried out according to the proportional representation system as laid down by the law.

Art. 54. The number of Senators directly elected by the electorate is equal to half the number of members of the House of Representatives.

Art. 55. The senators are elected for a term of four years. The Senate is entirely renewed every four years.

Art. 56. To be elected senator, it is necessary:

(1) to be Belgian by birth or to have been granted full naturalization;

(2) to enjoy civil and political rights;

(3) to be legally resident in Belgium;

(4) to be at least forty years of age.

Art. 56(B). To be elected senator under paragraph (1) of article 53, it is also necessary to belong to one of the following categories:

(1) Ministers, former Ministers, and Ministers of State;

(2) Members and former members of the House of Representatives and the Senate;

(3) Holders of a diploma of secondary education awarded by one of the higher educational establishments, a list of which is laid down by law;

(4) Former senior officers in the Army and Navy;

(5) Regular members and former members of the commercial courts who have served for at least two terms;

(6) Those who have, for at least ten years, performed the office of minister of one of the forms of worship whose members are entitled to a salary chargeable to the State;

(7) Regular members and former regular members of one of the royal academies, and professors and former professors of one of the higher educational establishments, a list of which is laid down by law;
(8) Former provincial governors; members and former members of the Permanent Deputations; former district commissioners;
(9) Members and former members of the provincial councils who have served for at least two terms;
(10) Mayors and former mayors, town councillors and former town councillors of those boroughs which are the chief towns of districts and those with over 4,000 inhabitants;
(11) Former Governors-General and Vice-Governors-General of the Belgian Congo; members and former members of the Colonial Council;
(12) Former directors-general, former directors and former inspectors-general of the various ministerial departments;
(13) The owners and usufructuaries of real estate and landed property located in Belgium, the rateable value of which amounts to at least 12,000 francs; those taxpayers who pay at least 3,000 francs in direct taxes annually to the State Treasury;
(14) Those who, with the rank of managing director, director or similar rank, have been placed for five years in charge of the day-to-day management of a Belgian commercial joint-stock company, the capital of which is paid up in the amount of at least one million francs;
(15) The heads of industrial enterprises permanently employing at least 100 workers, and agricultural enterprises with an area of at least 50 hectares (123.5 acres);
(16) Those who, with the rank of director-manager or some similar rank, have been placed for three years in charge of the day-to-day management of a Belgian co-operative society having at least 500 members over the past five years;
(17) Those who, as effective members, have for five years held the post of president or secretary of a mutual benefit society or federation with at least 1,000 members over the past five years;
(18) Those who, as effective members, have for five years held the post of president or secretary of a professional, industrial or agricultural association with at least 500 members over the past five years;
(19) Those who, for five years, have acted as president of a chamber of commerce or industry with at least 300 members over the last five years;
(20) Members of industrial and labour councils and of provincial agricultural commissions and conciliation boards who have served in that capacity for at least two terms;
(21) Elected members of one of the advisory councils set up alongside ministerial departments.

A law may create new categories of eligibility; it must be passed by a two-thirds majority vote at least.

Art. 56(c). Senators elected by the provincial councils may not belong to the assembly which elected them nor have been a member of it during the year of election or during the two previous years.

Art. 56(D). In the event of a dissolution of the Senate, the King may dissolve the provincial councils.

The act of dissolution contains a summons to the provincial electors within forty days and to the provincial councils within two months.

Art. 57. Senators receive no salary.

They are, however, entitled to the reimbursement of their expenses. This indemnity is fixed at four thousand francs a year.

They are furthermore entitled to travel free of charge on all lines of communication operated or contracted out by the State.

The law lays down those means of transportation which they may use free of charge apart from the lines mentioned above.

Art. 58. The sons of the King or, failing these, Belgian princes of that branch of the royal family which is in the line of succession, are senators by right at the age of eighteen years. They are only entitled to speak and vote at the age of twenty-five years.

Art. 59. Any assembly of the Senate which is held outside the time of the session of the House of Representatives shall automatically be null and void.

CHAPTER II. CONCERNING THE KING AND HIS MINISTERS

Section I. Concerning the King

Art. 60. The constitutional powers of the King are hereditary in the direct line of natural, legitimate heirs of H.M. Léopold Georges Chrétien Frédéric of Saxe-Coburg, from male heir to male heir, in order of primogeniture, to the perpetual exclusion of women and their descendants.

Shall be deprived of his right of succession any prince who marries without the consent of the King or of those people who, failing him, exercise his powers in the cases laid down by the Constitution.

However, he may be relieved from this disqualification by the King or by those who, failing him, exercise his powers in the cases laid down by the Constitution, on condition that both Houses agree thereto.

Art. 61. Should there be no male descendants of H.M. Léopold Georges Chrétien Frédéric of Saxe-Cobourg, the King may nominate his heir with the consent of both Houses, which is expressed in the manner prescribed by the following article.

If no nomination has been made according to the method outlined above, the throne shall be vacant.

Art. 62. The King may not simultaneously be the Head of another State save with the consent of both Houses.

Neither of the Houses may debate on this subject unless at least two thirds of its total number of members are present, and the resolution is only passed if it secures at least two thirds of the total number of votes cast.

Art. 63. The King's person is inviolable; his Ministers are responsible.

Art. 64. No act of the King's is effective unless it is countersigned by a Minister who, in doing so, renders himself responsible therefor.

Art. 65. The King appoints and dismisses his Ministers.

Art. 66. He confers rank in the Armed Forces.

He appoints persons to posts in the general administrative departments and those connected with external relations, except in such cases are laid down by law.

He does not make appointments to other offices except under the express ruling of a law.

Art. 67. He issues the regulations and decrees necessary for the implementation of laws, without ever being able to suspend the laws themselves nor exempt people from implementing them.

Art. 68. The King commands the Armed Forces on land and sea, declares war, makes treaties of peace, alliance and commerce. He advises the House of the contents thereof as soon as the interest and security of the State shall permit, enclosing all relevant documents. Commercial treaties and those which might affect the State or individually become binding on certain Belgians, only become effective after they have received the consent of both Houses.

No cession, exchange or addition of territory may take place save under a law. In no cases may the secret clauses of a treaty render the public clauses null and void.

Art. 69. The King sanctions and promulgates the laws.

Art. 70. The Houses automatically assemble every year on the second Tuesday of November, unless they have been convened previously by the King.

The Houses must sit during at least forty days of every year.

The King pronounces the closure of the session.

The King has the right to convene the Houses in an extraordinary session.

Art. 71. The King has the right to dissolve the Houses, either together or separately. The act of dissolution contains a summons to the electorate within forty days, and to the Houses within two months.

Art. 72. The King may prorogue the Houses. However, this adjournment may not exceed one month in duration, nor be repeated during the same session, without the consent of the Houses.

Art. 73. He has the right to reprieve or reduce the sentences delivered by judges, except in regard to what has been laid down for the Ministers.

Art. 74. He has the right to coin currency in implementation of the law.

Art. 75. He has the right to confer titles of nobility, without ever being able to grant privileges on that account.

Art. 76. He awards military decorations in obedience to the prescriptions of the law in this respect.

Art. 77. The law fixes the amount of the civil list for the duration of each reign.

Art. 78. The King has no other powers save those formally vested in him by the Constitution and the special laws passed in accordance with the Constitution itself.

Art. 79. On the death of the King, the Houses shall meet automatically by the tenth day at latest following the date of decease. If the Houses have been dissolved previously and a summons has been included in the act of dissolution for a time which is later than the tenth day, the outgoing Houses will resume their functions up to the assembly of those which are to replace them.

If only one House has been dissolved, the same rule shall be followed in respect of that House.

Dating from the death of the King and until the oath of office is taken either by his successor to the throne or by the regent, the constitutional powers of the King are exercised, in the name of the Belgian people, by the Ministers meeting in Council and on their own responsibility.

Art. 80. The King comes of age on his eighteenth birthday. He does not mount the throne until he has formally taken the following oath before both Houses meeting together:

"I swear to observe the Constitution and the laws of the Belgian people, to maintain national independence and the integrity of the territory."

Art. 81. If, on the death of the King, his successor is a minor, the two Houses shall meet in a single assembly in order to arrange for the regency and the guardianship of the new King.

Art. 82. If the King is unavoidably prevented from reigning, the Ministers, after establishing that impossibility, shall immediately convene both Houses.

Arrangements are made for the regency and guardianship of the King by both Houses meeting together.

Art. 83. The regency can only be conferred on one person. The regent does not take office until he has taken the oath laid down in article 80.

Art. 84. No alteration to the Constitution may be made during a regency.

Art. 85. When the throne is vacant, the House shall meet in a joint session to make temporary arrangements for the regency until the Houses meet again after they have been entirely renewed; this meeting shall take place at latest within two months. The new Houses, meeting together, shall make definite arrangements in regard to the vacancy.

Section II. Concerning the Ministers

Art. 86. No person may become a Minister if he is not Belgian by birth or has been granted full naturalization.

Art. 87. No member of the royal family may become a minister.

Art. 88. Ministers are only entitled to speak and vote in one or other of the Houses when they are a member of it.

They are authorized to enter either House and must be heard whenever they so request.

The Houses may request the presence of the ministers.

Art. 89. In no case may any verbal or written order from the King exempt a minister from his responsibility.

Art. 90. The House of Representatives has the right to impeach Ministers and to bring them before the Court of Cassation, which alone has the right to judge them in the presence of both Houses, except as it shall be laid down by the law with regard to the exercise of civil proceedings by the injured party and to the crimes and misdemeanors that the ministers may have committed outside the exercise of their official functions.

A law shall specify the cases of responsibility, the penalties to be imposed on ministers, and the procedure to be adopted in their regard, either on the basis of an accusation accepted by the House of Representatives or on the legal action brought by the injured parties.

Art. 91. The King may not reprieve a minister sentenced by the Court of Cassation save at the request of one of the two Houses.

CHAPTER III. CONCERNING THE JUDICIARY POWER

Art. 92. Contestations arising out of civil rights come under the exclusive jurisdiction of the law courts.

Art. 93. Contestations arising out of political rights come under the jurisdiction of the law courts except in such cases as are laid down by the law.

Art. 94. No tribunal nor court of arbitration may be set up save under a law. No extraordinary commissions or courts may be set up under any denomination whatsoever.

Art. 95. There is one Court of Cassation for the whole of Belgium. This court does not deal with the content of the affairs submitted to it, save in regard to the judgment of ministers.

Art. 96. Hearings in the courts and tribunals are public unless such publicity is prejudicial to good order or morals; in this case, the court shall so declare in an official ruling.

In matters connected with political or press misdemeanors, a session *in camera* can only be ordered on a unanimous basis.

Art. 97. Every judgment shall be motivated. It is pronounced in open court.

Art. 98. A jury is empanelled for all criminal affairs and for political and press misdemeanors.

Art. 99. Justices of the peace and judges of the various courts are directly appointed by the King.

Counsellors of the Courts of Appeal, the presidents and vice-presidents of the Courts of First Instance within their jurisdiction, are appointed by the King on the basis of two double lists, one submitted by the courts concerned and the other by the provincial councils.

Counsellors of the Court of Cassation are appointed by the King on the basis of two double lists, one submitted by the Senate and the other by the Court of Cassation.

In both cases, candidates named on one list may also be named on the other list.

The names of all candidates are made public at least fifteen days before the appointment is made. The courts shall choose their own presidents and vice-presidents from among themselves.

Art. 100. Judges are appointed for life.

No judge may be deprived of his office or suspended except by a specific judgment.

The transfer of a judge can only be made on the basis of a new appointment and with his consent.

Art. 101. The King appoints and dismisses the officials of the Public Prosecutor's department in the courts and tribunals.

Art. 102. The salaries of members of the Judiciary are fixed by law.

Art. 103. No judge may accept a salaried post from the government unless he exercises it without charge, and except for the cases of incompatibility laid down by the law.

Art. 104. There are three Courts of Appeal in Belgium.

The law defines their respective jurisdictions and the places in which they are located.

Art. 105. Special laws regulate the organization of military tribunals, their powers, the rights and obligations of the members of such tribunals, and the duration of their term of office. There shall be commercial courts set up in places to be specified by the law which also regulates their organization, their powers, the method of appointing their members and the duration of the latters' term of office.

Art. 106. The Court of Cassation delivers its verdict on conflicts of authority in the manner laid down by the law.

Art. 107. The courts and tribunals shall not apply any general, provincial or local decrees and regulations save insofar as they are in accordance with the law.

CHAPTER IV. CONCERNING PROVINCIAL AND MUNICIPAL INSTITUTIONS

Art. 108. Provincial and municipal institutions are regulated by laws. These laws consecrate the application of the following principles:
(1) Direct election, save in the case of such exceptions as the law may establish in regard to the heads of municipal administrations and government commissioners on the provincial councils;
(2) The attribution to the provincial and municipal councils of all matters of provincial or municipal interest, without prejudice to the approval of their acts in cases and in the manner laid down by the law. Several provinces or several boroughs may reach an agreement or enter into an association under conditions and in the manner to be laid down by the law, in order to regulate and manage on a joint basis those matters which are of provincial or municipal interest. However, it is not permissible for several provincial councils or several municipal councils to debate in joint meetings.
(3) The public nature of sessions of the provincial and municipal councils within the limits established by the law;
(4) The publication of budgets and accounts;
(5) The intervention of the King or the Legislative Authority to prevent the provincial and municipal councils from going beyond their attributions and injuring the general interest.

Art. 109. The establishing of certificates of birth, marriage and death, and the keeping of the registers, are attributions exclusively vested in the municipal authorities.

HEADING IV

CONCERNING FINANCES

Art. 110. No tax for the benefit of the State may be levied save under a law.

No provincial levy or imposition may be established save with the consent of the provincial council.

No municipal levy or imposition may be established save with the consent of the municipal council.

The law determines the exceptions, the necessity of which is revealed by experience, in respect of provincial and municipal taxes.

Art. 111. Taxes for the benefit of the State are voted annually. The laws establishing them are effective during one year only unless the are renewed.

Art. 112. No privilege may be established where taxes are concerned.

No exemption nor moderation of taxes may be established save through a law.

Art. 113. Apart from cases formally excepted by law, no remuneration can be required of citizens except under the heading of taxes for the benefit of the State, the province or the borough. No innovation is made to the existing system in force where reclaimed land and drainage are concerned, as this remains subject to ordinary legislation.

Art. 114. No pension and no gratuity chargeable to the public treasury may be granted save in accordance with a law.

Art. 115. Each year the Houses pass the law on State accounting and vote on the budgets.

All the receipts and expenditures of the State must be included in the budgets and in the accounting.

Art. 116. The members of the Audit Office are appointed by the House of Representatives and for a term of office laid down by the law.

This office is in charge of the examination and winding up of the accounts of the general administration and of all vouchers on the public treasury. It ensures that no article of expenditure in the budget is exceeded, and that no transfer takes place. It winds up the accounts of the various State administrative offices and is in charge of collecting, for this purpose, any information and accountable receipts that may be necessary. The general accounts of the State are submitted to the Houses along with the comments of the Audit Office.

This office is organized by a law.

Art. 117. The salaries and pensions of ministers of religion are chargeable to the State; the sums necessary for this purpose are included in the annual budget.

HEADING V

CONCERNING THE ARMED FORCES

Art. 118. The method of recruiting for the Armed Forces is laid down by law. It also regulates the promotion, rights and obligations of the military.

Art. 119. The armed forces contingent is voted annually. The law which establishes it is only effective for one year unless it is renewed.

Art. 120. The organization and attributions of the gendarmerie are the subject of a law.

Art. 121. No foreign troops may be admitted to the service of the State, nor may they occupy or pass through the territory, save under the terms of a law.

Art. 122. The organization of a civic guard, if necessary, is regulated by law.

Art. 123. Abrogated.

Art. 124. The military may not be deprived of their rank, honors and decorations, or pensions save in the manner laid down by the law.

HEADING VI

GENERAL CLAUSES

Art. 125. The Belgian nation has adopted the colours red, yellow and black, and for its coat of arms, the Lion of Belgium with the device: "Unity is strength."

Art. 126. The city of Brussels is the capital of Belgium and the seat of the government.

Art. 127. No oath may be imposed save in accordance with the law, which lays down the wording thereof.

Art. 128. Any foreigner who is on Belgian territory enjoys the same protection afforded to persons and property, save in exceptional cases to be established by law.

Art. 129. No law, decree or administrative regulation of a general, provincial or municipal character is compulsory until it has been published in the manner laid down by the law.

Art. 130. The Constitution may not be suspended, either in whole or in part.

HEADING VII

CONCERNING THE REVISION OF THE CONSTITUTION

Art. 131. The legislative Power has the right to state that it is necessary to revise this or that constitutional clause as it shall designate.

Following this statement, both Houses are automatically dissolved. Two new Houses will be convened in accordance with Article 71. These Houses, in agreement with the King, shall pronounce judgment on the points submitted for revision.

In this case, the Houses may not debate unless at least two thirds of the members of each of them are present; and no alteration shall be adopted unless it secures at least two thirds of the total votes cast.

HEADING VIII

TRANSITIONAL ARRANGEMENTS

Art. 132. For the first choice of the Head of the State, a derogation of the first clause of Article 80 is permissible.

Art. 133. Foreigners who were established in Belgium prior to January 1, 1814 and who have continued to reside there, are regarded as Belgians by birth on condition that they declare their intention of enjoying the privileges provided for under the present clause.

This declaration must be made within six months dating from the day on which the present Constitution becomes compulsory, if the persons concerned have reached their majority, or in the year following their majority if the persons concerned are minors.

This declaration shall be made in the presence of the provincial authority whose jurisdiction includes their place of residence.

It shall be made in person or by proxy, the latter to be in possession of special and authentic powers of attorney.

Art. 134. Until a law has been passed in this regard, the House of Representatives shall exercise discretionary powers in impeaching a minister, and the Court of Cassation shall exercise similar powers in judging him, the misdemeanor being specified and the penalty being determined.

Nevertheless, the penalty may not exceed that of penal internment, without prejudice to cases expressly provided for under the penal laws.

Art. 135. The personnel of courts and tribunals is maintained in its existing form until a law has been passed in this regard.

This law shall be enacted during the first legislative session.

Art. 136. A law enacted during the same session shall determine the method governing the first appointment of the members of the Court of Cassation.

Art. 137. The fundamental law of August 24, 1815 is abolished, as also the provincial and local statutes. However, the provincial and local authorities shall retain their powers until such time as other arrangements have been made by law.

Art. 138. Dating from the day on which the Constitution comes into force, all laws, decrees, ordinances, regulations and other acts which are contrary to it shall be abolished.

COMPLEMENTARY CLAUSES

Art. 139. The National Congress declares that it is necessary to establish laws governing the following subjects within the shortest possible time:

(1) the press;
(2) the empanelling of juries;
(3) finances;
(4) provincial and municipal organization;
(5) the responsibility of ministers and other government officials;
(6) the organisation of the judiciary;
(7) the revision of the list of pensions;

(8) measures designed to prevent abuses arising out of plurality of office;
(9) the revision of legislation pertaining to bankruptcies and suspensions;
(10) the organization of the Armed Forces, rights to promotion and retirement; and the Military Penal Code;
(11) the revision of the Codes, and instructs the Executive Power to proceed with the implementation of the present decree.

BULGARIA

SUMMARY

INTERNATIONAL STATUS

Bulgaria is a member of the United Nations (December 14, 1955). It is a member of the Council for Mutual Economic Aid, and other international organizations. It was a member of the League of Nations.

Bulgaria declared its independence on October 5, 1908. It had been an autonomous principality under Ottoman suzerainty since the Congress of Berlin in 1878, which reduced the frontiers granted to it previously by Russia in the Treaty of San Stefano. An autocephalous and independent Bulgarian church had been granted by Turkey in 1870 and the Bulgarian church remained in schism with the Patriarch in Constantinople until 1945. A constitution was adopted on April 28, 1879. Bulgarian ambition to achieve the boundaries granted by the San Stefano Treaty led to the Second Balkan War. By the Treaty of Neuilly in 1919, certain territories were ceded. Bulgaria joined the Axis powers in the Second World War but did not declare war on the Soviet Union. In July 1942, the Communist party and other groups of the left formed the Fatherland Front and organized guerrilla activity. On September 5, 1944, the U.S.S.R. declared war on Bulgaria and occupied strategic parts of the country. By a revolution on September 9, the Fatherland Front came to power as the provisional government. By elections on November 18, 1945, in which the opposition did not participate, the Fatherland Front gained 86% of the votes. On September 8, 1946, a plebiscite abolished the monarchy and established a People's Republic. The Constitutional Assembly was elected on October 27, 1946 and the Peace Treaty signed on February 10, 1947.

FORM OF NATIONAL GOVERNMENT

The Constitution of December 4, 1947, as amended in 1961, and 1965, states that Bulgaria is a People's Republic with a representative government.[1] All power derives from and belongs to the people.[2] A chapter relates to the social and economic structure.[3]

RIGHTS OF THE PEOPLE

The Constitution provides equality before the law, equal rights of women, the right to work, rest, pensions and social insurance, protection of the family, freedom of conscience and religion, the right to education, freedom and inviolability of the individual, the right of asylum, inviolability of the domicile, secrecy of correspondence, freedom of association, press, speech, assembly, the right to petition.[4] Citizens are bound to defend the country, observe the Constitution and laws and pay taxes.[5]

LEGISLATIVE DEPARTMENT

The legislative body is the National Assembly which is the supreme organ of government.[6] Deputies are elected by universal suffrage, one for every 20,000 inhabitants, for a term of four years subject to dissolution.[7] Immunities of deputies are provided.[8]

[1] Const., Art. 1.
[2] Id., Art. 2.
[3] Id., Art. 6–24.
[4] Id., Art. 71–89.
[5] Id., Art. 90–94.
[6] Id., Art. 15, 16.
[7] Id., Art. 18, 30.
[8] Id., Art. 29.

EXECUTIVE DEPARTMENT

The Presidium of the National Assembly is elected by that body and responsible to it.[1] It acts as Head of State, summons the legislature, publishes the laws, has the right of pardon, confers decorations, has the power of appointment.[2] The supreme executive and administrative organ is the Government composed of the Council of Ministers.[3] It is responsible to the National Assembly.[4] A section relates to local government.[5]

JUDICIAL DEPARTMENT

Judges are independent and subject only to law.[6] Supreme judicial control is exercised by the Supreme Court of the People's Republic whose members are elected by the National Assembly for a five year term.[7] The constitutionality of laws is decided by the National Assembly.[8]

AREA, POPULATION, ETC.

The area of Bulgaria is 110,927,7 square kilometres, its population (1964) is 8,178,000. The capital is Sofia.[9] Natonal minorities have the right to education in their mother-tongue, the study of Bulgarian is compulsory.[10]

[1] Id., Art. 33, 34. [2] Id., Art. 35. [3] Id., Art. 38, 39. [4] Id., Art. 40.
[5] Id., Art. 47–55. [6] Id., Art. 56. [7] Id., Art. 61. [8] Id., Art. 25.
[9] Id., Art. 98. [10] Id., Art. 79.

CONSTITUTION of BULGARIA[1]

December 4, 1947, amended 1961 and 1965

CHAPTER I

THE PEOPLE'S REPUBLIC OF BULGARIA

Art. 1. Bulgaria is a People's Republic with a representative government, firmly established as a result of the heroic struggles of the Bulgarian peoples against the monarcho-fascist dictatorship and of the victorious people's uprising of September, 9, 1944.

Art. 2. All power in the People's Republic of Bulgaria derives from the people and belongs to the people.

This power is exercised through freely elected representative organs and through referenda.

All representative organs of the state authority are elected by the citizens on the basis of universal, equal and direct suffrage by secret ballot.

Art. 3. All citizens of the People's Republic, who have completed their eighteenth year of age, irrespective of sex, nationality, race, creed, education, occupation, social or property status have the right to vote and to be elected, with the exception of those placed under tutelage or deprived of civil and political rights.

Art. 4. The representatives of the people in all representative bodies are responsible to the electors. They may be recalled before the end of the term for which they are elected.

The manner of holding elections as well as the order of recalling the people's elected candidates are established by law.

Art. 5. The People's Republic of Bulgaria is governed in exact accordance with the Constitution and the laws of the country.

[1] Published in English (translation by Zdravko Stankov) by the Foreign Language Press, Sofia, 1964. Supplied, together with 1965 amendments, by the Ministry of Foreign Affairs in January 1966. Ed.

CHAPTER II

SOCIAL AND ECONOMIC STRUCTURE

Art. 6. The means of production in the People's Republic of Bulgaria belong to the state (national property), to the co-operatives, or to private individuals or juridical persons.

Art. 7. All mineral and other underground natural resources, forests, waters, including mineral and curative springs, sources of natural power, railways and communications, posts, telegraphs, telephones and radio broadcasting are state-owned, i.e. national property.

A special law shall regulate the exploitation of forests by the population.

Art. 8. National property is the mainstay of the country's economic development and enjoys special protection.

The state can itself manage or concede to another the management of the means of production at its disposal.

Art. 9. The state aids and fosters co-operative associations.

Art. 10. Private property and its inheritance, as well as private initiative in economy, are recognized and protected by law.

Private property acquired by labor and thrift and the right to inherit it enjoy special protection.

No one can exercise his right of ownership to the detriment of the public interest.

Private monopoly agreements and associations, such as cartels, trusts and concerns, are prohibited. Private property may be subject to compulsory restrictions or expropriations solely for the state and public use and against fair indemnity.

The state can nationalize, fully or in part, certain branches or individual enterprises of industry, trade, transport and credit. The indemnity is determined by the Law on Nationalization.

Art. 11. The land belongs to those who till it. The law determines how much land private persons may own, as well as the cases in which non-farmers may own arable land. Private ownership of large landed estates is not permitted. Co-operative farms are fostered and aided by the state and enjoy special protection.

The state may organize state farms.

Art. 12. All state, co-operative and private economic activity is directed by the state by means of a state economic plan, with a view to the most expedient development of the nation's economy and the promotion of the public welfare. In drawing up and implementing the state economic plan, the state avails itself of the active collaboration of professional, economic and social organizations and institutions.

Art. 13. Foreign and domestic trade are directed and controlled by the state.

The state may reserve to itself the exclusive right to produce or trade in any goods which are of prime importance to the national economy and the needs of the people.

Art. 14. Labor is recognized as a basic social and economic factor and is the object of the state's care in every respect.

The state directly aids the working people—workers, farmers, craftsmen and intellectuals—by means of its general economic and social policy, cheap credit, tax system and co-operative association.

For the all-round improvement of the life of the working people, the state encourages their associations, creative self-initiative and amateur art activities.

CHAPTER III

SUPREME ORGANS OF GOVERNMENT

Art. 15. The National Assembly is the supreme organ of government. Within the framework of the Constitution, it is the repository of government in its entirety, insofar as certain particular functions do not fall within the competence of other and subordinate organs of the government and of the state administration by virtue of the Constitution.

Art. 16. The National Assembly is the sole legislative body of the People's Republic of Bulgaria.

Art. 17. The National Assembly:

(1) Elects the Presidium of the National Assembly.

(2) Appoints the Government of the People's Republic.

(3) Amends the Constitution.

(4) Resolves the establishment of new Ministries and the abolition, fusion or renaming of existing Ministries.

(5) Resolves the question of the cession, exchange or increase of the territory of the People's Republic.

(6) Votes the State Economic Plan.

(7) Votes the State budget and the laws for the application of the budget program, determines taxes and tax-collection procedure.

(8) Resolves the nationalization of economic enterprises and the introduction of state monopolies.

(9) Resolves questions of war and peace.

(10) Resolves the holding of referenda.

(11) Grants amnesties.

Art. 18. The National Assembly is elected for a term of four years. It consists of deputies elected by the people, one for every 20,000 inhabitants.

Art. 19. The National Assembly is convened at sessions by the Presidium of the National Assembly at least twice a year.

It may be convened also on the request of at least one fifth of the number of the deputies.

The newly elected National Assembly is convened at session not later than two months after the date of the elections.

Art. 20. Immediately after its opening, the National Assembly, under the chairmanship of the oldest national representative, elects from its number a bureau consisting of a President and three Vice-Presidents.

The President, or in his absence the Vice-Presidents, conducts the proceedings in the National Assembly in accordance with the Rules of Procedure worked out by the National Assembly.

The National Assembly also elects the necessary number of secretaries and tellers in accordance with the Rules of Procedure.

Art. 21. The National representatives take the following oath:

"I swear in the name of the people and of the People's Republic of Bulgaria that I will serve them devotedly and selflessly, that I will observe and hold sacred and inviolable the Constitution, that in my activity as national representative I will keep in view only the national and state interests and will spare no effort in defence of the freedom and independence of my country. I have sworn."

Art. 22. Immediately after it has been constituted, the National Assembly elects an auditing committee which, within a three-month period, reports the confirmation or annulment of the election of each national representative individually.

Art. 23. Legislative initiative is vested in the Government and in the national representatives. National representatives can introduce bills if they bear the signature of at least one fifth of their total number.

Art. 24. Laws passed by the National Assembly are signed by the President and Secretary of the Presidium of the National Assembly and published in the State Gazette.

A law enters into force three days after its publication unless a different term is set by the law itself.

Art. 25. The National Assembly has the sole right to decide whether all the requirements of the Constitution have been observed for the issuance of a law and whether it is constitutional or not.

Art. 26. The National Assembly can hold a session if more than half of the total number of representatives are present. Decisions are then taken by a simple majority of the national representatives except in cases for which the Constitution has made special provision.

Art. 27. The Sessions of the National Assembly are public unless it decides that important state interests call for the sitting to be secret.

Art. 28. The National Assembly can make investigations and inquiries into any question through special committees.

All state organs and private persons are obliged to give the information and submit the documents requested by the inquiry committees.

Art. 29. National representatives cannot be detained or prosecuted except for grave offenses and then with the consent of the National Assembly, or if it is not in session, with the consent of the Presidium. Such permission is not necessary if a deputy has been apprehended in the commission of a grave criminal offence, in which case it suffices to notify the Presidium of the National Assembly forthwith.

National representatives are immune from penal proceedings for their opinions expressed in the National Assembly or for their vote.

Art. 30. The National Assembly is dissolved on the expiry of its mandate, or earlier if it so decides.

In case of war or other exceptional circumstances, the National Assembly can prolong its mandate for their duration.

The dissolved National Assembly can be recalled by its Presidium and its mandate prolonged in case of war or other exceptional circumstances.

Art. 31. A new National Assembly is elected within three months after the dissolution of the previous Assembly.

Art. 32. National representatives receive remuneration as determined by the National Assembly.

Art. 33. The National Assembly, by a majority of more than half of the total number of national representatives, elects the Presidium of the National Assembly consisting of a President, two Vice-Presidents, a Secretary and 15 Members.

Art. 34. The Presidium of the National Assembly is responsible to the National Assembly for its entire activity.

The National Assembly may at any time change the Presidium or its individual members.

Art. 35. The Presidium of the National Assembly has the following functions:

(1) Summons the National Assembly.

(2) Fixes the date of elections for the National Assembly.

(3) Publishes the laws passed by the National Assembly.

(4) Interprets the laws in a way binding to all.

(5) Issues decrees.

(6) Exercises the right of pardon.

(7) Institutes medals and decorations and awards them.

(8) Represents the People's Republic in its international relations; appoints and recalls diplomatic and consular representatives abroad on the recommendation of the Government and receives foreign representatives accredited to it.

(9) Ratifies and denounces international treaties concluded by the Government.

(10) When the National Assembly is not in session, the Presidium can, on the proposal of the Government, declare a state of war in the event of an armed aggression against the People's Republic, or in the event of

an urgent necessity of fulfilling international obligations relating to common defence against aggression; in such a case the Presidium immediately summons the National Assembly to pronounce on the measure taken.

(11) Proclaims, on the proposal of the Government, general or partial mobilization and martial law.

(12) When the National Assembly is not in session, the Presidium may, on the proposal of the Prime Minister, relieve of duty and appoint individual members of the Government; the Presidium is obliged to submit this measure to the National Assembly for ratification at its nearest session.

(13) Repeals the decisions and directives of the Government which do not conform to the Constitution or the laws.

(14) Fixes the date of a referendum on the decision of the National Assembly.

(15) Appoints and discharges, on the proposal of the Government, the Staff of the High Command of the Armed Forces of the People's Republic.

(16) Appoints and discharges, on the proposal of the Government, the Commander-in-Chief of the Armed Forces.

(17) Remits uncollectable debts.

(18) Decides upon matters which the National Assembly has entrusted to it.

(19) Discharges all functions which have been assigned to it by law.

Art. 36. Edicts issued by the Presidium of the National Assembly are signed by its President and Secretary.

Art. 37. After the expiry of the mandate of the National Assembly, or if it is dissolved before the expiry of its term, the Presidium which it has elected continues to exercise its functions until the newly elected National Assembly elects a new Presidium.

CHAPTER IV

ORGANS OF THE STATE EXECUTIVE

Art. 38. The Government (Council of Ministers) is the supreme executive and administrative organ of the state in the People's Republic of Bulgaria.

Art. 39. The Government consists of the:

President of the Council of Ministers,
Vice-Presidents of the Council of Ministers,
President of the State Planning Commission,
President of the Commission for State Control,
Ministers and
President of the Committee for Science, Art and Culture.

The President and Vice-Presidents of the Council of Ministers can head a ministry, as well as the State Planning Commission, the Commission for State Control, or the Committee for Science, Arts and Culture, or they can be Ministers without Portfolio.

The Ministries are:

(1) Ministry of Foreign Affairs
(2) Ministry of the Interior
(3) Ministry of Education
(4) Ministry of Finance
(5) Ministry of Justice
(6) Ministry of National Defence
(7) Ministry of Commerce and Supplies
(8) Ministry of Agriculture and Forests
(9) Ministry of Construction and Roads
(10) Ministry of Communal Economy and Public Works
(11) Ministry of Railway, Road and Water Communications
(12) Ministry of Posts, Telegraphs and Telephones
(13) Ministry of Industry and Handicrafts
(14) Ministry of Electrification and Land Reclamation
(15) Ministry of Mines and Mineral Wealth
(16) Ministry of Public Health
(17) Ministry of Labor and Social Welfare.

The National Assembly may, by a vote of more than half of the total number of national representatives, set up new Ministries, or abolish, fuse or rename the existing Ministries.

The Presidium of the National Assembly can, on the recommendation of the Government, appoint Assistant Ministers to the various Ministries.

Art. 40. The National Assembly elects and relieves of their functions the Government or individual members of the Government.

The Government is responsible to the National Assembly and gives account of its activity to it. When the National Assembly is not in session, the Government is responsible and gives account to the Presidium of the National Assembly.

Art. 41. The members of the Government take the following oath before the National Assembly:

"I swear in the name of the people and the People's Republic of Bulgaria that I will serve them devotedly and selflessly, that in my activity as a member of the Government I will keep in view only the interests of the nation and the state, that I will strictly observe the Constitution and the laws of the People's Republic and will spare no effort in defence of the freedom and independence of the People's Republic of Bulgaria. I have sworn."

Art. 42. Members of the Government may also be persons who are not national representatives.

Art. 43. The Government directs the state administration by unifying and co-ordinating the work of the various Ministries, of the State Planning Commission, the Commission for State Control and the Committee for Science, Arts and Culture; takes measures for the implementation of the State Economic Plan and of the State budget, as well as for maintaining public order, defending the state interests and protecting the rights of the citizens; it exercises general guidance of the foreign policy of the People's Republic of Bulgaria and of national defence, and also supervises the execution of the laws and of various acts of the government.

The various members of the Government direct their respective Ministries within the framework and on the basis of the general policy and directives of the Council of Ministers.

The Council of Ministers may take under its direct control certain branches of the administration by setting up for the purpose commissions, committees, councils, head departments, departments, administrations and services directly subordinate to it.

Art. 44. Every national representative has the right to question and interpellate the Government or its members.

The latter are obliged to answer the questions within the term set down by the Rules of Procedure, and interpellations when put on the agenda.

Art. 45. The members of the Government are penally responsible for any violation of the Constitution and the laws, and for any criminal offence committed in the discharge of their functions.

They bear civil responsibility for damage caused by them to the state or to private citizens by their unlawful acts.

The responsibilities of the members of the Government and the procedure for their prosecution are regulated in greater detail by a special law.

Art. 46. Officials take an oath of loyalty to the People's Republic.

They bear disciplinary penal and civil responsibility for offences committed in the discharge of their functions.

CHAPTER V

LOCAL ORGANS OF GOVERNMENT

Art. 47. The territory of the People's Republic of Bulgaria is divided into municipalities and districts.

Other administrative units may be established by law.

Art. 48. Organs of Government in the municipalities are the municipal and district councils, which are elected by the local population for a three-year term.

Art. 49. The municipal and district councils direct the implementation of all economic, social and cultural undertakings of local significance in accordance with the laws of the country. They draft the economic plan and budget of the municipality and the district within the frame of the State Economic Plan and the State budget and direct their implementation. They supervise the proper administration of state property and the economic enterprises in their area; they supervise the maintenance of public order for the observance of the laws and the defence of the citizens' rights; they direct the activity of the subordinate executive and administrative organs.

Art. 50. Within the limits of their competence, the local people's councils take decisions and issue orders in conformity with the laws and general directives of the superior organs of government.

Art. 51. Executive and administrative organs of the municipal and district councils are the municipal and district executives consisting of a president, vice-president, a secretary and members.

Art. 52. In the execution of their functions, the municipal and district councils rely on the initiative and broad participation of the people and their political, professional and other mass organizations.

At least once a year, in the manner and order regulated by law, municipal and district councils give an account of their past activity to the electors.

Art. 53. The sessions of the municipal and district councils are regular or extraordinary. Municipal councils meet for a regular session every month, and district councils every two months. The municipal and district executives may summon the councils to extraordinary session on their own initiative, on the demand of one third of the councillors or on order of the respective superior state organ.

Art. 54. Municipal and district executives are subordinate both to the people's councils which have elected them and to the superior state organs.

Art. 55. Departments for the various administrative branches may be established at the municipal and district councils; they are then directed by the executives of the council. In their work these departments are subordinate both to the executive of the people's council to which they are attached and to the corresponding department at the superior people's councils and the corresponding Ministry or Government service of the People's Republic.

CHAPTER VI

PEOPLE'S COURTS AND PROSECUTION

Art. 56. The courts apply the laws exactly and equally to all citizens. Judges are independent: in issuing their warrants, they act only according to the dictates of the law. They pronounce their decisions and sentences in the name of the people.

Art. 57. Assessors also take part in the dispensation of justice. The cases and procedure for their participation are determined by law.

Art. 58. Judges of all ranks and assessors are elected except in the cases explicitly laid down by law.

The law determines which judges and assessors are directly elected by the citizens in accordance with the rules and regulations on the general, equal, direct and secret ballot, and which—by the local people's councils, or by the National Assembly, as well as the term for which they shall be elected.

Art. 59. Special courts for the judgment of specific law-suits and crimes may be established only by law.

Art. 60. The constitution of courts, legal proceedings, the conditions of eligibility of court officials and the procedure for electing and recalling judges and assessors, as well as the grading of courts are determined by law.

Art. 61. Supreme judicial control over every kind and grade of courts is exercised by the Supreme Court of the People's Republic, the members of which are elected by the National Assembly for a five-year term.

Art. 62. Supreme supervision of the strict application of the laws by different government organs and officials and by the citizens is exercised by the Chief Prosecutor of the People's Republic.

The Chief Prosecutor of the People's Republic has the particular duty to attend to the prosecution and punishment of crimes against the state, national and economic interests of the People's Republic, as well as the crimes and acts detrimental to the independence and sovereignty of the nation.

Art. 63. The Chief Prosecutor of the People's Republic is elected by the National Assembly for a five-year term and is subordinate to it alone.

Art. 64. All other prosecutors at courts of every grade are appointed and discharged by the Chief Prosecutor of the People's Republic, and in the exercise of their duty are subordinate only to prosecutors who are their immediate superiors, while all prosecutors are subordinate to the Chief Prosecutor.

CHAPTER VII

RELATIONS BETWEEN GOVERNMENTAL AND ADMINISTRATIVE ORGANS

Art. 65. The Presidium of the National Assembly may repeal all decisions and orders of the Council of Ministers which do not conform to the Constitution and the laws of the country. The Council of Ministers may repeal all decisions and orders of any one of its members which do not conform to the Constitution, the laws, or the decisions and orders of the Government.

Art. 66. The Presidium of the National Assembly and the superior people's councils have the right to repeal unlawful and irregular acts of the inferior people's councils.

Art. 67. The Government or its individual members may, within the limits of their competence, repeal the unlawful and irregular acts of the municipal and district executives.

The executives of superior people's councils have the same right with regard to the executives at the inferior councils.

Art. 68. Each municipal and district council may repeal the unlawful and irregular acts of its own executive.

Art. 69. The Government or its individual members, within the limits of their competence, as well as the executive of a superior people's council may suspend the execution of the unlawful and irregular acts of an inferior local people's council and refer the question of repeal to the Presidium of the National Assembly, or to the people's council of the same rank.

Art. 70. A superior local people's council, as well as the Presidium of the National Assembly, may dissolve an inferior people's council in its area and hold elections for a new people's council.

Superior people's councils as well as the Presidium of the National Assembly may discharge the executive of an inferior people's council in its area and hold elections for a new executive.

CHAPTER VIII

FUNDAMENTAL RIGHTS AND DUTIES OF CITIZENS

Art. 71. All citizens of the People's Republic of Bulgaria are equal before the law.

No privileges based on nationality, origin, faith or property status shall be recognized.

Propagation of racial, national or religious hatred is punishable by law.

Art. 72. Women enjoy equal rights with men in all spheres of state, private, economic, public, cultural and political life.

This equality is realized by guaranteeing to women, on an equality with men, the right to labor, equal pay for equal work, the right to rest, to social insurance, a pension and education.

Mothers enjoy special protection in respect to work. The state takes special care of mothers and their children by establishing maternity homes, nurseries, kindergartens, and out-patient clinics, guarantees paid leave to mothers before and after childbirth and free obstetrical and medical aid.

Art. 73. Citizens have the right to work.

The state guarantees this right to all citizens by planning the national economy, by systematically and continually developing the forces of production and by creating public works.

Labor is paid according to the quantity and quality of the work done.

Work is a duty and a matter of honor for every able-bodied citizen. It is the duty of every citizen to engage in socially useful labor and work according to his powers and ability.

Citizens' labor service obligations are determined by a special law.

Art. 74. Citizens have the right to rest.

This right is guaranteed by the limitation of the working day, by paid annual leave, and by the establishment of a wide network of rest homes, clubs, etc.

Art. 75. Citizens have the right to pensions, aid and indemnities in case of illness, accident, disablement, unemployment and old age.

The state puts this right into practical effect through social insurance and medical aid.

Art. 76. Marriage and the family are under state protection.

Only civil marriage performed by the competent organs is legally valid.

Children born out of wedlock enjoy equal rights with the issue of lawful marriage.

Art. 77. The state takes special care of the social, cultural, labor, physical and health education of the youth.

Art. 78. Citizens are guaranteed freedom of conscience and religion, and of performing religious rites.

The church is separated from the state.

A special law regulates the legal status, the questions of material support and the right of self-government of the various religious communities. Misusing the church and religion for political purposes, or forming political organizations on a religious basis is prohibited,

Art. 79. Citizens have the right to education. Education is secular, democratic and progressive in spirit. National minorities have the right to be educated in their mother tongue and to develop their national culture, while the study of Bulgarian is compulsory.

Elementary education is compulsory and free.

The schools are state-owned. The establishment of private schools may be permitted only by law in which case they are under state supervision. The right to education is guaranteed by schools, educational institutions, universities, as well as by scholarships, student hostels, material aid and special encouragement for gifted students.

Art. 80. The state promotes the development of science and arts by establishing research institutes, publishing houses, libraries, theatres, museums, reading clubs, art galleries, film studios, cinemas, etc. and by aiding persons who have shown ability in this field.

Art. 81. The state promotes public health by organizing and directing health services and institutions, propagating health education among the people and paying special attention to the physical education of the people.

Art. 82. The freedom and inviolability of the individual are guaranteed.

No one may be detained for more than 48 hours without a warrant of the judicial authorities or the prosecutor.

Punishment may be inflicted only in virtue of the existing laws.

Punishment is personal and corresponds to the crime committed.

Punishment for crimes may only be inflicted by the established courts.

The defendant has the right to defence.

Art. 83. All Bulgarian citizens abroad enjoy the protection of the People's Republic of Bulgaria.

Art. 84. Foreigners residing in the People's Republic of Bulgaria enjoy the right of sanctuary when they are persecuted for upholding democratic principles, for struggling for their national liberation, for the people's right or for scientific and cultural freedom.

Art. 85. Homes are inviolable. Without the consent of the householder no one may enter his home or premises and conduct a search there, unless all conditions required by law are observed.

Art. 86. The secrecy of correspondence is inviolable, except in the event of mobilization, martial law, or special permission given by the judicial authorities or the prosecutor.

Art. 87. Bulgarian citizens have the right to form societies, associations and organizations, provided they are not contrary to the state and public order established by the present Constitution.

The law forbids and punishes the formation of and participation in organizations aiming at depriving the Bulgarian people of their rights and liberties gained by the people's uprising of September 9, 1944, and guaranteed by the present Constitution or to encroach on these rights and liberties, or to imperil the nation's independence or sovereignty, or of organizations which openly or secretly propagate a fascist and anti-democratic ideology or facilitate imperialist aggression.

Art. 88. The citizens of the People's Republic are guaranteed freedom of the press, of speech and of assembly, including meetings and demonstrations.

Art. 89. Citizens have the right to make requests, complaints and petitions.

Every citizen has the right to demand court proceedings against officials for offences committed in the discharge of their duties.

Citizens have a right to indemnity from officials for injury caused them by the latter, owing to unlawful or irregular execution of their duties.

Art. 90. The defence of the country is a supreme duty and a matter of honor for every citizen.

Treason to the country is the gravest crime against the people and is punished with the full severity of the law.

Art. 91. Military service is compulsory for all citizens in accordance with the special laws.

Art. 92. Citizens are bound to observe the Constitution and the laws of the country strictly and conscientiously.

Art. 93. Citizens are bound to protect national property and by all their actions to help promote the nation's economic, cultural and defensive power and the welfare of the people.

Art. 94. The citizens' tax obligations are repartitioned in accordance with their paying ability. The obligations and exemptions from them are established only by law.

CHAPTER IX

COAT-OF-ARMS, SEAL, FLAG, CAPITAL

Art. 95. The coat-of-arms of the People's Republic of Bulgaria is round; in the center, a lion rampant beset on both sides by ears of corn, above the lion a five-pointed red star, and below, in gold figures, 9.IX.1944.

Art. 96. The state seal bears the state coat-of-arms.

Art. 97. The flag of the People's Republic of Bulgaria is tricolored—white, green and red, placed horizontally. The upper left-hand corner of the white stripe bears the coat-of-arms of the People's Republic.

Art. 98. The capital of the People's Republic of Bulgaria is the city of Sofia.

CHAPTER X

AMENDMENT TO THE CONSTITUTION

Art. 99. The Constitution may be amended on the proposal of the Government or of at least one quarter of the national representatives.

The Constitutional amendment bill is put on the agenda one week after its introduction in the Assembly at the earliest.

It may be passed by a majority of two thirds of the total number of national representatives.

The Constitutional amendment law enters into force on the day of its publication in the State Gazette.

CHAPTER XI

TEMPORARY PROVISIONS

Art. 100. After the present Constitution enters into force, the Grand National Assembly elected on October 27, 1946, elects a Presidium of the Grand National Assembly in accordance with Article 33; the Presidium immediately assumes the functions provided for by the Constitution. This terminates the functions of the Presidency of the Grand National Assembly elected in accordance with Article 2 of the Rules of Procedure of the Grand National Assembly. The Grand National Assembly elects, in accordance with Article 20 of the present Constitution, a President and Vice-Presidents for conducting the proceedings.

Art. 101. The Presidium of the Grand National Assembly appoints temporary municipal and district administrations with the prerogatives of people's councils, until the municipal and district councils provided by the present Constitution are elected.

BYELORUSSIAN SOVIET SOCIALIST REPUBLIC

SUMMARY

INTERNATIONAL STATUS

The Byelorussian Soviet Socialist Republic is a member of the United Nations (October 24, 1945). It is a member of other international organizations.

On December 30, 1918, the Sixth Conference of the Bolshevik Party of the Northwest opened at Smolensk, declared itself the First Congress of the Communist Party of Byelorussia and adopted a decision to form the Byelorussian S.S.R. on January 1, 1919. The Provisional Workers' and Peasants' Government of Byelorussia issued a manifesto on the form of the Byelorussian S.S.R. and on February 4, 1919, the First All-Byelorussian Congress of Soviets issued a declaration concerning federative ties with the Russian Socialist Federative Soviet Republic and approved a Byelorussian constitution. Poland invaded western Byelorussia and seized several towns in the eastern part. On July 11, 1920, Minsk was liberated by the Red Army and on August 1, 1920, the Byelorussian S.S.R. restored (Poland retaining the western parts until the second World War). On January 16, 1921, a treaty of union relations signifying the establishment of federative ties between the Byelorussian S.S.R. and the R.S.F.S.R. was drawn up and on December 29, 1922 the formation of the U.S.S.R. was sanctioned by a Conference of delegates of the R.S.F.S.R., the Ukrainian S.S.R., Byelorussian S.S.R. and Trans-Caucasia. Byelorussia was invaded and devastated by Germany during the war. At the San Francisco Conference in 1945, at the request of the U.S.S.R., it was accorded separate representation and separate membership in the United Nations.

FORM OF NATIONAL GOVERNMENT

The Constitution of February 19, 1937, as amended to 1960, states that the Byelorussian Soviet Socialist Republic is a socialist state of workers and peasants.[1] Its political foundation is the Soviets of Working People's Deputies and all power is vested in the working people of town and country as represented therein.[2] The socialist system of economy and socialist ownership of the instruments and means of production is described.[3] The Constitution states that the B.S.S.R. has voluntarily united with other equal Soviet Socialist Republics, which are named, and has delegated to the U.S.S.R. the rights set forth in Article 14 of the latter's Constitution; beyond those provisions, the B.S.S.R., preserves fully its sovereign rights, including the right to secede.[4] The provinces are listed.[5]

RIGHTS OF THE PEOPLE

The Constitution guarantees the right to work, rest and leisure, social security, education, equal rights of women and equality of all citizens, freedom of conscience, freedom of speech, press, assembly, demonstration, association.[6] Inviolability of the person, domicile, the right of asylum are guaranteed.[7] Citizens must abide by the Constitution and the laws, maintain labor discipline, safeguard socialist property, perform military service and defend the country.[8] The right to own and inherit specified personal

[1] Const., Art. 1. [2] Id., Art. 2, 3. [3] Id., Art. 4–11. [4] Id., Art. 13, 15.
[5] Id., Art. 14. [6] Id., Art. 93–101. [7] Id., Art. 102–104. [8] Id., Art. 105–108.

property is protected by[1] law. Work is a duty and honor for all able-bodied citizens, and the socialist principle "from each according to his ability, to each according to his work" applies.[2]

LEGISLATIVE DEPARTMENT

The highest organ of state power and sole legislative organ is the Supreme Soviet of the B.S.S.R. whose members are elected in electoral districts for a term of four years by universal, equal and direct suffrage by secret ballot.[3] It meets in two regular sessions a year.[4] Immunities of members are provided.[5] The local organs of state power are described.[6] There are provisions for the state budget.[7]

EXECUTIVE DEPARTMENT

The Supreme Soviet of the B.S.S.R. elects the Presidium of the Supreme Soviet composed of a President, two Vice-Presidents, a Secretary and fifteen members which exercises the functions of Head of State; it convenes sessions of the Supreme Soviet, issues decrees and interprets the laws, awards honors, grants pardons, appoints representatives to foreign states.[8]

The highest executive and administrative organ is the Council of Ministers appointed by the Supreme Soviet of the B.S.S.R. and accountable to it.[9] The Ministers are listed and the Constitution states that they issue orders and instructions on the basis and in pursuance of laws, decisions and orders of the U.S.S.R. and B.S.S.R.[10] Union-Republican Ministries are subordinate to the Council of Ministers of the B.S.S.R. and to the corresponding Union-Republican Ministry of the U.S.S.R.[11] There are also Republic Ministries subordinate to the Council of Ministers of the B.S.S.R.[12] A Soviet of National Economy is provided.[13]

JUDICIAL DEPARTMENT

Justice is administered by the Supreme Court of the B.S.S.R., the Provincial and People's Courts and the special courts of the U.S.S.R.[14] The Supreme Court is elected by the Supreme Soviet of the B.S.S.R. for a term of five years.[15] Judges are independent and subject only to the law.[16] There is provision for people's assessors to participate in all court cases,[17] and for a Procurator's Office.[18]

[1] Id., Art. 9, 10. [2] Id., Art. 12. [3] Id., Art. 20–23, 110.
[4] Id., Art. 28. [5] Id., Art. 34. [6] Id., Art. 52–75. [7] Id., Art. 76–79.
[8] Id., Art. 29–31. [9] Id., Art. 39, 40. [10] Id., Art. 47, 48 [11] Id., Art. 49.
[12] Id., Art. 50. [13] Id., Art. 50A. [14] Id., Art. 80. [15] Id., Art. 83.
[16] Id., Art. 88. [17] Id., Art. 81. [18] Id., Art. 89–92.

AREA, POPULATION, ETC.

The area of the B.S.S.R. is 207,600 square kilometres, its population (1964) 8,533,000. Laws are published in Byelorussian and Russian.[1] The capital is Minsk.[2]

[1] Id., Art. 121 Id., Art. 25.

CONSTITUTION of the BYELORUSSIAN SOVIET SOCIALIST REPUBLIC[1]

February 19, 1937, as amended to 1960

CHAPTER I

THE SOCIAL STRUCTURE

Art. 1. The Byelorussian Soviet Socialist Republic is a socialist state of workers and peasants.

Art. 2. The political foundation of the B.S.S.R. is the Soviets of the Working People's Deputies, which grew and became strong as a result of the overthrow of the power of the landlords and capitalists, the attainment of the dictatorship of the proletariat, the freeing of the Byelorussian people from the national yoke of czarism and the Russian imperialist bourgeoisie, and the destruction of Byelorussian nationalist counter-revolution.

Art. 3. All power in the B.S.S.R. is vested in the working people of town and country as represented by the Soviets of Working People's Deputies.

Art. 4. The economic foundation of the B.S.S.R. is the socialist system of economy and the socialist ownership of the instruments and means of production, firmly established as a result of the abolition of the capitalist system of economy, private ownership of the instruments and means of production, and the annihilation of the exploitation of man by man.

Art. 5. Socialist property in the B.S.S.R. exists either in the form of state property (belonging to the whole people) or in the form of co-operative and collective-farm property (the property of collective farms or co-operative societies).

Art. 6. The land, its mineral wealth, waters, forests, the factories and

[1] Constitution (Basic Law) of the Byelorussian Soviet Socialist Republic, published in Russian in Minsk 1960. Translation contained in second edition revised by L. Kipouridis and the Editor. Ed.

mines, rail, water and air transport facilities, the banks, means of communication, large state-organized agricultural enterprises (state farms, machine and tractor stations, etc.) as well as municipal enterprises and the bulk of the dwelling-houses in the cities and industrial localities, are state property, that is, belong to the whole people.

Art. 7. The enterprises of the collective farms and co-operative organizations, with their livestock, buildings, implements, and output, as well as their buildings for common use are the common, socialist property of the collective farms and co-operative organizations.

Every collective-farm household, in addition to its basic income from the collective farms, has for its own use a small plot of land attached to the house and, as its own property, a dwelling-house, livestock, poultry and minor agricultural implements—in conformity with the rules of the Agricultural Artel.

Art. 8. The land occupied by the collective farms is made over to them for their free use for an unlimited time, that is, in perpetuity.

Art. 9. In addition to the socialist system of economy, which is the predominant form of economy in the B.S.S.R., the law permits the small private undertakings of individual peasants and handicraftsmen based on their own labor and precluding the exploitation of the labor of others.

Art. 10. The right of citizens to own, as their personal property, income and savings derived from work, to own a dwelling house and a supplementary husbandry, articles of household and articles of personal use and convenience, is protected by law, as is also the right of citizens to inherit personal property.

Art. 11. The economic life of the B.S.S.R. is determined and guided by the state economic plan for the purpose of increasing the wealth of society as a whole, steadily raising the material and cultural standards of the working people and strengthening the independence of the B.S.S.R. and its capacity for defense, and the independence of the U.S.S.R.

Art. 12. Work in the B.S.S.R. is a duty and a matter of honor for every able-bodied citizen, in accordance with the principle: "He who does not work, neither shall he eat."

The principle applied in the B.S.S.R. is that of socialism: "From each according to his ability, to each according to his work."

CHAPTER II

THE STATE STRUCTURE

Art. 13. For the purpose of reciprocal assistance in economic and political matters, as well as in questions of defense, the B.S.S.R. has voluntarily united with the other equal, Soviet Socialist Republics, namely:

The Russian Soviet Federative Socialist Republic,

The Ukrainian Soviet Socialist Republic,
The Uzbek Soviet Socialist Republic,
The Kazakh Soviet Socialist Republic,
The Georgian Soviet Socialist Republic,
The Azerbaijan Soviet Socialist Republic,
The Lithuanian Soviet Socialist Republic,
The Moldavian Soviet Socialist Republic,
The Latvian Soviet Socialist Republic,
The Kirghiz Soviet Socialist Republic,
The Tajik Soviet Socialist Republic,
The Armenian Soviet Socialist Republic,
The Turkmen Soviet Socialist Republic,
The Estonian Soviet Socialist Republic,
into a united state, the Union of Soviet Socialist Republics.

In accordance with the above, the B.S.S.R. delegates to the U.S.S.R. in the person of its higher organs of government authority and administration, the rights set forth in Article 14 of the Constitution of the U.S.S.R.

Outside the provisions of Article 14 of the Constitution of the U.S.S.R., the B.S.S.R. exercises state authority independently, preserving fully its sovereign rights.

Art. 14. The Byelorussian Soviet Socialist Republic consists of the following provinces: Brest, Vitebsk, Gomel, Grodno, Minsk and Mogilev.

Art. 15. The B.S.S.R. reserves the right freely to secede from the U.S.S.R.

Art. 16. The territory of the B.S.S.R. may not be altered without its own consent.

Art. 16A. The B.S.S.R. has the right to enter into direct relations with foreign states and to conclude agreements and exchange diplomatic and consular representatives with them.

Art. 16B. The B.S.S.R. has its own Republican military formations.

Art. 17. The laws of the U.S.S.R. are binding within the territory of the B.S.S.R.

Art. 18. Every citizen of the B.S.S.R. is a citizen of the U.S.S.R.

Citizens of the other Union Republics have equal rights with the citizens of the B.S.S.R. in the territory of the B.S.S.R.

Art. 19. The highest executive and administrative organs of the B.S.S.R. have the following functions:

a) To adopt the Constitution of the B.S.S.R. and supervise its execution;

b) To create the provinces within the B.S.S.R., to define the boundaries and regional divisions of the provinces of the B.S.S.R. and also the disions into economical administrative units;

c) To legislate for the B.S.S.R.;

d) To preserve order in the state and the rights of citizens;

e) To approve the economic plan of the B.S.S.R.;

f) To draw up and supervise the execution of the budget of the B.S.S.R. and to direct the operations of accounting;

g) To establish, in accordance with the laws of the U.S.S.R. state and local taxes, their collection, and non-tax income, and to supervise the local provincial budgets;

h) To supervise insurance and savings;

i)To supervise banking, industrial, farming, trade enterprises, and the regulatory organizations of the Republic, to direct industry and construction subordinate to the Union, and generally to supervise local industry;

j) To control and supervise the conditions and management of all-Republic enterprises;

k) To establish management methods for land, mines, forests and waters;

l) To supervise housing and communal enterprises, building and the general welfare of cities and other inhabited places;

m) To supervise road construction, Republic and local transportation and communication;

n) To draw up labor legislation;

o) To supervise social security;

p) To supervise primary, secondary and higher education;

q) To supervise cultural, educational and scientific organizations and foundations in the B.S.S.R. and to administer those of an all-Republic character;

r) To supervise public health and administer public health foundations of an all-Republic character;

s) To supervise and create organizations for sport and physical culture;

t) To legislate concerning the organization and functioning of the courts and judicial bodies and to approve the civil and criminal codes of the B.S.S.R.;

u) To confer B.S.S.R. citizenship;

v) To exercise the right of amnesty and pardon of citizens sentenced by the judicial organs of the B.S.S.R.;

w) To decide questions of representation of the B.S.S.R. in its international relations;

x) To determine the manner of organizing the B.S.S.R.'s military formations;

y) To legislate concerning marriage and the family.

CHAPTER III

THE HIGHER ORGANS OF STATE POWER IN THE B.S.S.R.

Art. 20. The highest organ of state power in the B.S.S.R. is the Supreme Soviet of the B.S.S.R.

Art. 21. The members of the Supreme Soviet of the B.S.S.R. are elected by the citizens of the B.S.S.R. in electoral districts for a term of four years on the basis of one deputy for each twenty thousand of the population.

Art. 22. The Supreme Soviet of the B.S.S.R. exercises all the rights vested in the Republic according to Articles 13 and 19 of its Constitution, insofar as they do not fall within the constitutionally defined jurisdiction of bodies of the Republic which are subordinate to the Supreme Soviet of the Republic, namely, the Presidium of the Supreme Soviet of the B.S.S.R. the Council of Ministers and the Ministries of the B.S.S.R.

Art. 23. The Supreme Soviet of the B.S.S.R. is the sole legislative organ of the Republic.

Art. 24. A law is considered adopted if passed by a simple majority vote of the Supreme Soviet.

Art. 25. Laws passed by the Supreme Soviet of the B.S.S.R. are published over the signatures of the President and Secretary of the Presidium of the Supreme Soviet of the B.S.S.R. in the Byelorussian and Russian languages.

Art. 26. The Supreme Soviet of the B.S.S.R. elects a Chairman of the Soviet and four Vice-Chairmen.

Art. 27. The Chairman of the Supreme Soviet of the B.S.S.R. presides at the sittings of the Supreme Soviet and has charge of the conduct of its business and proceedings and internal order.

Art. 28. Sessions of the Supreme Soviet of the B.S.S.R. are convened twice a year by its Presidium. Extraordinary sessions are convened by the Presidium of the Supreme Soviet of the B.S.S.R. at its discretion, or the demand of at least one third of the deputies of the Supreme Soviet.

Art. 29. The Supreme Soviet of the B.S.S.R. elects the Presidium of the Supreme Soviet consisting of a President of the Presidium, two Vice-Presidents, a Secretary of the Presidium and fifteen members of the Presidium of the Supreme Soviet.

Art. 30. The Presidium of the Supreme Soviet of the B.S.S.R. is accountable to the Supreme Soviet of the B.S.S.R. for all its activities.

Art. 31. The Presidium of the Supreme Soviet of the B.S.S.R.:

a) Convenes the sessions of the Supreme Soviet of the B.S.S.R.;

b) Issues decrees and interprets the laws of the B.S.S.R. in operation;

c) Conducts national referendums;

d) Annuls decisions and orders of the Council of Ministers and of the Provincial Soviets of Working People's Deputies if they do not conform to law;

e) In the intervals between sessions of the Supreme Soviet of the B.S.S.R., releases and appoints Ministers of the B.S.S.R. on the recommendation of the Chairman of the Council of Ministers of the B.S.S.R., subject to subsequent confirmation by the Supreme Soviet of the B.S.S.R.;

f) Issues certificates of commendation on behalf of the Supreme Soviet of the B.S.S.R. and awards honorary titles of the B.S.S.R.;

g) exercises the right of pardon of citizens sentenced by the judicial organs of the B.S.S.R.;

i) Appoints and recalls plenipotentiary representatives of the B.S.S.R. to foreign states;

j) Receives letters of credence and recall of diplomatic representatives accredited to it by foreign states.

Art. 32. The Supreme Soviet of the B.S.S.R. elects a Credentials Committee to verify the credentials of the deputies.

On the report of the Credentials Committee, the Supreme Soviet decides whether to recognize the credentials of deputies or to annul their election.

Art. 33. The Supreme Soviet of the B.S.S.R., when it deems necessary, appoints commissions of investigation and audit on any matter. It is the duty of all institutions and officials to comply with the demands of such commissions and to submit to them all necessary materials and documents.

Art. 34. A member of the Supreme Soviet of the B.S.S.R. may not be prosecuted or arrested without the consent of the Supreme Soviet of the B.S.S.R. or, when the Supreme Soviet is not in session, without the consent of the Presidium of the Supreme Soviet.

Art. 35. On the expiration of the term of office of the Supreme Soviet of the B.S.S.R. the Presidium of the Supreme Soviet orders new elections to be held within a period not exceeding two months from the date of expiration of the term of office.

Art. 36. On the expiration of the term of office of the Supreme Soviet of the B.S.S.R., the Presidium of the Supreme Soviet retains its powers until the newly-elected Supreme Soviet of the B.S.S.R. shall have formed a new Presidium.

Art. 37. The newly elected Supreme Soviet of the B.S.S.R is convened by the out-going Presidium of the Supreme Soviet not later than three months after the elections.

Art. 38. The Supreme Soviet of the B.S.S.R. appoints the Government of the B.S.S.R., namely the Council of Ministers of the B.S.S.R.

CHAPTER IV

THE ORGANS OF STATE ADMINISTRATION OF THE B.S.S.R.

Art. 39. The highest executive and administrative organ of the state power of the B.S.S.R. is the Council of Ministers of the B.S.S.R.

Art. 40. The Council of Ministers is responsible and accountable to the Supreme Soviet of the B.S.S.R. or, in the intervals between sessions of the Supreme Soviet, to the Presidium of the Supreme Soviet of the B.S.S.R.

Art. 41. The Council of Ministers of the B.S.S.R. issues decisions and orders on the basis and in pursuance of the laws in operation of the U.S.S.R. and of the B.S.S.R., and of the decisions and orders of the Council of Ministers of the U.S.S.R., and verifies their execution.

Art. 42. Decisions and orders of the Council of Ministers of the B.S.S.R. are binding throughout the territory of the B.S.S.R.

Art. 43. The Council of Ministers of the B.S.S.R.:

a) Co-ordinates and directs the work of the Union-Republican and Republican Ministries of the B.S.S.R. and of other institutions under its jurisdiction;

b) Draws up the program of the national economy of the B.S.S.R., submits it for approval to the Supreme Soviet of the B.S.S.R., and takes steps towards its execution;

c) Draws up the state budget of the B.S.S.R. and a summary of local budgets of the B.S.S.R.; submits the state budget for approval to the Supreme Soviet of the B.S.S.R.; and takes steps toward execution of the state and local budgets;

d) Adopts measures for the maintenance of law and order, for the protection of the interests of the state, and for the safeguarding of the rights of citizens;

e) Directs and supervises the work of the provincial Executive Committee of the Soviets of Working People's Deputies;

f) Sets up, whenever necessary, special Committees and Central Boards under the Council of Ministers of the B.S.S.R. for economic and cultural affairs;

g) Directs the relations of the B.S.S.R. with foreign states in accordance with the general procedure established by the U.S.S.R. concerning the relations of the Union Republics with foreign states;

h) Directs the general organization of the Armed Forces of the B.S.S.R.

Art. 44. The Council of Ministers of the B.S.S.R. has the right to suspend decisions and orders of the provincial Executive Committees of the provincial Soviets of Working People's Deputies as well as of the local Soviets of Working People's Deputies.

The Council of Ministers of the B.S.S.R. has the right to approve decrees and orders of the Ministers of the B.S.S.R. and decisions and orders of the Soviets of Working People's Deputies of the B.S.S.R.

Art. 45. The Council of Ministers of the B.S.S.R. is appointed by the Supreme Soviet of the B.S.S.R. and consists of:

The Chairman of the Council of Ministers of the B.S.S.R.;

The First Vice-Chairman of the Council of Ministers;

The Vice-Chairmen of the Council of Ministers;

The Chairman of the State Planning Committee of the B.S.S.R.;

The Chairman of the State Committee for construction and architecture of the Council of Ministers of the B.S.S.R.;

The Chairman of the Committee of the Council of Ministers of the B.S.S.R. of Control;

The Chairman of the State Committee of the Council of Ministers of the B.S.S.R. for Science and Technology;

The Chairman of the State Security Committee of the Council of Ministers of the B.S.S.R.

The Chief of the Central Statistical Board under the Council of Ministers.

Art. 46. The Ministers of the B.S.S.R. direct the branches of the State administration which come within the jurisdiction of the B.S.S.R.

Art. 47. The Ministers of the B.S.S.R., within the limits of the jurisdiction of their respective Ministries, issue orders and instructions on the basis and in pursuance of the laws in operation in the U.S.S.R. and the B.S.S.R., and also of decisions and orders of the Council of Ministers of the U.S.S.R. and the B.S.S.R. and of the Union-Republican Ministries of the U.S.S.R. and verify their execution,

Art. 48. The Ministries of the B.S.S.R. are either Union-Republican or Republican Ministries.

The following Ministries of the B.S.S.R. are Union-Republican Ministries:

Higher and Secondary Special Education;

Health

Foreign Affairs

Culture

Defense

Co-ordination

Agricultural economy

Finance

The following Ministries are Republican Ministries:

Interior

Enlightenment

Social insurance

Public works

Commerce

Cereal products

Art. 49. Each Union-Republican Ministry of the B.S.S.R. directs the branch of state administration entrusted to it and is subordinate both to the Council of Ministers of the B.S.S.R. and to the corresponding Union-Republic Ministry of the U.S.S.R.

Art. 50. Each Republican Ministry directs the branch of state administration entrusted to it, and is directly subordinate to the Council of Ministers of the B.S.S.R.

Art. 50A. The Soviet of National Economy of the B.S.S.R. supervises the activities of the branches of the national economy subordinate to it, and is itself immediately accountable to the Council of Ministers of the B.S.S.R.

The Soviet of National Economy of the B.S.S.R., within the limits of its jurisdiction, issues orders and instructions on the basis and in pursuance of the laws in operation in the U.S.S.R. and also of decisions and orders of the Council of Ministers of the U.S.S.R. and the B.S.S.R.

Art. 51. The Government of the B.S.S.R. or a Minister of the B.S.S.R. to whom a question of a member of the Supreme Soviet of the B.S.S.R. is addressed must give a verbal or written reply in the Supreme Soviet within a period not exceeding three days.

CHAPTER V

THE LOCAL ORGANS OF STATE POWER

Art. 52. The organs of state power in provinces, regions, districts, cities, towns, villages and hamlets are the Soviets of Working People's Deputies.

Art. 53. The Soviets of Working People's Deputies of provinces, regions, districts, cities and rural localities are elected by the working people of the respective provinces, regions, districts, cities and rural localities for a term of two years.

Art. 54. The Soviet of Working People's Deputies (of a province, region, district, city or rural locality) directs local economic and cultural affairs, determines the local budget, directs the work of subordinate organs of administration, ensures the maintenance of law and order, co-operates in the defense and improvement of the land, and protects the rights of citizens.

Art. 55. The Soviets of Working People's Deputies adopt decisions and issue orders within the limits of the powers vested in them by the laws of the U.S.S.R. and the B.S.S.R.

Art. 56. The executive and administrative organ of the Soviet of Working People's Deputies of a province, district, city or rural locality is the Executive Committee elected by it, consisting of a Chairman, Vice-Chairmen, a Secretary and members.

Art. 57. The executive and administrative organ of the Soviet of Working People's Deputies in a small locality, is the Chairman, the Vice-Chairman and the Secretary elected by the Soviet of Working People's Deputies.

Art. 58. The executive organs of the Soviets of Working People's Deputies direct local economic and cultural affairs on the basis of decisions of their respective Soviets of Working People's Deputies and of higher organs of state power.

Art. 59. Sessions of the provincial Soviets of Working People's Deputies are convened by their Executive Committees at least four times a year.

Sessions of the regional Soviets of Working People's Deputies are convened by their Executive Committees at least six times a year.

Art. 60. Sessions of the city, city district and rural Soviets of Working People's Deputies are convened by their executive organs at least six times a year; in the case of Soviets of Working People's Deputies of cities comprising districts, at least four times a year.

Art. 61. The Soviets of Working People's Deputies of provinces, regions, districts and cities elect a Chairman and Vice-Chairman to conduct their sittings.

Art. 62. Repealed.

Art. 63. The executive organs of the Soviets of Working People's Deputies of the provinces, regions, districts, cities and towns, are directly accountable both to the Soviets of Working People's Deputies which elected them and to the executive organ of the superior Soviet of Working People's Deputies.

Art. 64. The Executive Committees of the superior Soviets of Working People's Deputies have the right to annul decisions and orders of the lower executive organs and to suspend decisions and orders of the lower Soviets of Working People's Deputies.

Art. 65. The superior Soviets of Working People's Deputies have the right to annul decisions and orders of the lower Soviets of Working People's Deputies and of their executive committees.

Art. 66. The Provincial Soviets of Working People's Deputies create the following sections and departments subordinate to their Executive Committees:

Motor transport and roads
Interior
Health
Communal economy
Culture
Land improvement
Industry
Popular education
General affairs

Organization and guidance
Building and architecture
Building in communal property
Agricultural economy
Social insurance
Commerce
Finance
Planning commission
Departmental staff of the Chairman of the Executive Committee.

In addition, the provincial Soviets of Working People's Deputies may, with the approval of the Council of Ministers of the B.S.S.R., recommend other sections and departments of their Executive Committees in connection with the special needs of the economy of the region.

Art. 67. In conformity with the conditions in a province and with the laws of the U.S.S.R. and the B.S.S.R., the Republican Ministries and the State Security Committee of the Council of Ministers of the B.S.S.R. may establish their administrative organs in the provincial Soviets of Working People's Deputies.

Art. 68. The departments and administrative organs of a provincial Soviet of Working People's Deputies are directly accountable for their activities both the to provincial Soviet of Working People's Deputies and its Executive Committee and to the corresponding Ministry of the B.S.S.R.

Art. 69. The district Soviets of Working People's Deputies create the following departments subordinate to their Executive Committees:

Culture
Militia
Popular education
General affairs
Social insurance
Finance
Planning commission

and in addition, in accordance with the special needs of the economy of the district, the district Soviets of Working People's Deputies may recommend the following departments:

Communal affairs
Local industry and fuel

Art. 70. Repealed.

Art. 71. The departments of a district Soviet of Working People's Deputies are directly accountable for their activities both to the district Soviet of Working People's Deputies and its Executive Committee and to the corresponding department of the provincial Soviet of Working People's Deputies.

Art. 72. The city Soviets of Working People's Deputies create the following departments subordinate to their Executive Committees:

Health
Culture
Communal economy
Militia
Popular education
General affairs
Social insurance
Commerce
Finance
Planning commission
Departmental staff of the Chairman of the Executive Committee,

And, in accordance with the special needs of the economy of the city and of its suburbs, may create the following departments:

Local industry and fuel
Agricultural economy

Art. 73. The departments of a city Soviet of Working People's Deputies are directly accountable for their activities both to the city Soviet of Working People's Deputies and its Executive Committee and to the corresponding department of the provincial Soviet of Working People's Deputies.

Art. 74. The departments of the city Soviets of Working People's Deputies of the cities of Baranovich, Bobruisk, Borisov, Bresht, Vileiki, Vitebsk, Gomel, Grodno, Lidda, Mogilev, Mozir, Molodetsno, Orsi, Pinsk, Polotsk, Retsitsa and Sloutsk, are subordinate in their activity to the respective Soviets of Working People's Deputies of those cities, to their respective Executive Committees, as well as to the corresponding department of the district Soviet of Working People's Deputies.

Art. 74A. The departments of the city Soviets of Working People's Deputies of Minsk are subordinate in their activity to the Soviet of Working People's Deputies of the City of Minsk and to its Executive Committee, as well as directly to the related Ministry of the B.S.S.R.

Art. 75. On the expiration of the term of office of the provincial, district, city or rural Soviet of Working People's Deputies, their executive and administrative organs retain their power until the newly-elected Soviets of Working People's Deputies shall have formed new executive and administrative organs.

CHAPTER VI

BUDGET OF THE BYELORUSSIAN S.S.R.

Art. 76. The state budget of the B.S.S.R. is drawn up by the Council of Ministers of the B.S.S.R. and is submitted by it to the Supreme Soviet of the B.S.S.R. for approval. The state budget as approved by the Supreme

Soviet of the B.S.S.R. is published for general information.

Art. 77. The Supreme Soviet of the B.S.S.R. elects the budgetary commission which reports to the Supreme Soviet its conclusions in regard to the state budget.

Art. 78. On completion of its study, the state budget of the B.S.S.R. is approved by the Supreme Soviet of the B.S.S.R. and is then published for general information.

Art. 79. The budgets of the provincial, district, city and village Soviets must show the income from the local economy separately from the state income received in their territory, and must also show the income from local taxes and levies in amounts established by the laws of the U.S.S.R. and of the B.S.S.R.

CHAPTER VII

THE COURTS AND THE PROCURATOR'S OFFICE

Art. 80. In the B.S.S.R. justice is administered by the Supreme Court of the B.S.S.R., the Provincial Courts, the People's Courts and the Special Courts of the U.S.S.R. established by decision of the Supreme Soviet of the U.S.S.R.

Art. 81. In all courts cases are tried with the participation of people's assessors, except in cases specially provided for by law.

Art. 82. The Supreme Court of the B.S.S.R. is the highest judicial organ of the B.S.S.R. The Supreme Court of the B.S.S.R. is charged with the supervision of the judicial activities of all the judicial organs of the B.S.S.R.

Art. 83. The Supreme Court of the B.S.S.R. is elected by the Supreme Soviet of the B.S.S.R. for a term of five years.

Art. 84. The Provincial Courts are elected by the provincial Soviets of Working People's Deputies for a term of five years.

Art. 85. People's judges of District (City) People's Courts are elected by the citizens of the districts (cities) on the basis of universal, direct and equal suffrage by secret ballot for a term of five years.

People's Assessors of District (City) People's Courts are elected at general meetings of industrial, office and professional workers, and peasants in the place of work or residence, and of servicemen in military units, for a term of two years.

Art. 86. Judicial proceedings in the B.S.S.R. are conducted in the White Russian and Russian languages, persons not knowing these languages being guaranteed the opportunity of fully acquainting themselves with the material of the case through an interpreter and likewise the right to use their own language in court.

Art. 87. In all courts of the B.S.S.R. cases are heard in public, unless otherwise provided for by law, and the accused is guaranteed the right to defense.

Art. 88. Judges are independent and subject only to the law.

Art. 89. Supreme supervisory power to ensure the strict observance of the law by all Ministries and institutions subordinated to them, as well as by people in office and citizens of the B.S.S.R. generally, is vested in the Procurator-General of the U.S.S.R. and in the Procurator of the B.S.S.R.

Art. 90. The Procurator of the B.S.S.R. and the provincial Procurators are appointed by the Procurator-General of the U.S.S.R. for a term of five years.

Art. 91. The procurators of the regions, and cities are appointed by the Procurator of the B.S.S.R., subject to the approval of the Procurator-General of the U.S.S.R., for a term of five years.

Art. 92. The organs of the Procurator's Office perform their functions independently of any local organs whatsoever, being subordinate solely to the Procurator-General of the U.S.S.R.

CHAPTER VIII

FUNDAMENTAL RIGHTS AND DUTIES OF CITIZENS

Art. 93. Citizens of the B.S.S.R. have the right to work, that is the right to guaranteed employment and payment for their work in accordance with its quantity and quality.

The right to work is ensured by the socialist organization of the national economy, the steady growth of the productive forces of Soviet society, the elimination of the possibility of economic crises, and the abolition of unemployment.

Art. 94. Citizens of the B.S.S.R. have the right to rest and leisure.

The right to rest and leisure is ensured by the establishment of a seven-hour day for industrial, office and professional workers, the reduction of the working day to six hours for arduous trades and to four hours in shops where conditions of work are particularly arduous; by the institution of annual vacations with full pay for industrial, office and professional workers, and by the provision of a wide network of sanatoriums, holiday homes and clubs for the accomodation of the working people.

Art. 95. Citizens of the B.S.S.R. have the right to maintenance in old age and in case of sickness or disability.

This right is ensured by the extensive development of social insurance of industrial, office and professional workers at state expense, free medical service for the working people, and the provision of a wide network of health resorts for the use of the working people.

Art. 96. Citizens of the B.S.S.R. have the right to education.

This right is ensured by universal compulsory eight-year education; by extensive development of secondary polytechnical education, vocational-technical education, and secondary special and higher education based on close ties between the school, real life and production activities; by the utmost development of evening and extramural education; by free education in all schools; by a system of state grants; by instruction in schools in the native language, and by the organization of free vocational, technical and agronomic training for the working people in the factories, state farms, and collective farms.

Art. 97. Women in the B.S.S.R. are accorded all rights on an equal footing with men in all spheres of economic, government, cultural, political and other social activity.

The possibility of exercising these rights is ensured by women being accorded the same rights as men to work, payment for work, rest and leisure, social insurance and education, and also by state protection of the interests of mother and child, state aid to mothers of large families and to unmarried mothers, maternity leave with full pay, and the provision of a wide network of maternity homes, nurseries and kindergartens.

Art. 98. Equality of rights of citizens of the B.S.S.R., irrespective of their nationality or race, in all spheres of economic, government, cultural, political and other social activity, is an indefeasible law.

Any direct or indirect restriction of the rights of, or, conversely, the establishment of any direct or indirect privileges for, citizens on account of their race or nationality, as well as any advocacy of racial or national exclusiveness or hatred and contempt, are punishable by law.

Art. 99. In order to ensure to citizens freedom of conscience, the church in the B.S.S.R. is separated from the state, and the school from the church. Freedom of religious worship and freedom of anti-religious propaganda is recognized for all citizens.

Art. 100. In conformity with the interests of the working people, and in order to strengthen the socialist system, the citizens of the B.S.S.R. are guaranteed by law:

a) freedom of speech;
b) freedom of the press;
c) freedom of assembly, including the holding of mass meetings;
d) freedom of street processions and demonstrations.

These civil rights are ensured by placing at the disposal of the working people and their organizations printing presses, stocks of paper, public buildings, the streets, communications facilities and other material requisites for the exercise of these rights.

Art. 101. In conformity with the interests of the working people, and in order to develop the organizational initiative and political activity of the masses of the people, citizens of the B.S.S.R. are guaranteed the right to unite in public organizations: trade unions, co-operative societies, youth organizations, sport and defense organizations, cultural, technical and scientific societies; and the most active and politically-conscious citizens in the ranks of the working class, working peasants and working intelligentsia voluntarily unite in the Communist Party of the Soviet Union, which is the vanguard of the working people in their struggle to build communist society and is the leading core of all organizations of the working people, both public and state.

Art. 102. Citizens of the B.S.S.R. are guaranteed inviolability of the person. No person may be placed under arrest except by decision of a court or with the sanction of a procurator.

Art. 103. The inviolability of the homes of citizens and privacy of correspondence are protected by law.

Art. 104. The B.S.S.R. affords the right of asylum to foreign citizens persecuted for defending the interests of the working people, or for scientific activities, or for struggling for national liberation.

Art. 105. It is the duty of every citizen of the B.S.S.R. to abide by the Constitution of the B.S.S.R., to observe the laws, to maintain labor discipline, honestly to perform public duties, and to respect the rules of socialist society.

Art. 106. It is the duty of every citizen of the B.S.S.R. to safeguard and fortify public, socialist property as the sacred and inviolable foundation of the Soviet system, as the source of the wealth and might of the country, as the source of the prosperity and culture of all the working people.

Persons committing offences against public, socialist property are enemies of the people.

Art. 107. Universal military service is law.

Military service in the Armed Forces of the U.S.S.R. is the honorable duty of citizens of the B.S.S.R.

Art. 108. To defend the country is the sacred duty of every citizen of the B.S.S.R. Treason to the Motherland—violation of the oath of allegiance, desertion to the enemy, impairing the military power of the state, espionage—is punishable with all the severity of the law as the most heinous of crimes.

CHAPTER IX

THE ELECTORAL SYSTEM

Art. 109. Members of all Soviets of Working People's Deputies—of the Supreme Soviet of the B.S.S.R., the Soviets of Working Peopl'es Deputies of the regions, districts, cities and rural areas—are chosen by electors on the basis of universal, equal, and direct suffrage by secret ballot.

Art. 110. Elections of deputies are universal: all citizens of the B.S.S.R. who have reached the age of eighteen, irrespective of race or nationality, sex, religion, education, domicile, social origin, property status or past activities, have the right to vote in the election of deputies, with the exception of persons who have been legally certified insane.

Every citizen of the B.S.S.R. who has reached the age of twenty one is eligible for election to the Supreme Soviet of the B.S.S.R., irrespective of race or nationality, sex, religion, education, domicile, social origin, property status or past activities.

Art. 111. Elections of deputies are equal: each citizen has one vote; all citizens participate in elections on an equal footing.

Art. 112. Women have the right to elect and be elected on equal terms with men.

Art. 113. Citizens serving in the Armed Forces of the U.S.S.R. have the right to elect and be elected on equal terms with all other citizens.

Art. 114. Elections of deputies are direct: all Soviets of Working People's Deputies, from rural and city Soviets of Working People's Deputies to the Supreme Soviet of the B.S.S.R., are elected by the citizens by direct vote.

Art. 115. The voting for election of the deputies is secret.

Art. 116. Candidates are nominated for each constituency.

The right to nominate candidates is secured to public organizations and societies of the working people: Communist Party organizations, trade unions, co-operatives, youth organizations and cultural societies.

Art. 117. It is the duty of every deputy to report to his electors on his work and on the work of his Soviet of Working People's Deputies, and he may be recalled at any time upon decision of a majority of the electors in the manner established by law.

Art. 118. Elections to the Soviets of Working People's Deputies of the B.S.S.R. are conducted in constituencies. The electoral norms for each region, district, city and rural area Soviet of Working People's Deputies are established by the Electoral Law for provincial, district, city and rural area Soviets of Working People's Deputies of the B.S.S.R.

CHAPTER X

ARMS, FLAG, CAPITAL

Art. 119. The state emblem of the Byelorussian Soviet Socialist Republic consists of the rays of the rising sun over a sickle and hammer, encircled by a wreath; the left side of this wreath consists of ears of wheat intertwined with clover, and on the right, of ears of wheat intertwined with flax; underneath, between both halves of the wreath is shown a portion of the earth's globe. Both halves of the wreath are intertwined with a red ribbon bearing in the Byelorussian and Russian languages the inscription "Workers of the World, Unite!", and below them, the initials of the B.S.S.R. At the top of the emblem is shown a five-pointed star.

Art. 120. The state flag of the Byelorussian Soviet Socialist Republic consists of a fabric in two colored horizontal stripes, the upper one which forms two thirds of the whole is red, and the lower one forming one third of the whole is green. In the upper left hand corner of the red stripe there is a golden hammer and sickle and above them a red five-pointed star with a golden border. Near and parallel to the staff is the Byelorussian national ornament, white on a red background, composing one ninth of the length of the flag. The ratio of width to length is 1:2.

Art. 121. The capital of the Byelorussian Soviet Socialist Republic is Minsk.

CHAPTER XI

PROCEDURE FOR AMENDING THE CONSTITUTION

Art. 122. The Constitution of the B.S.S.R. may be amended only by decision of the Supreme Soviet of the B.S.S.R. adopted by a majority of not less than two thirds of the votes of the members of the Supreme Soviet.

CYPRUS

SUMMARY

INTERNATIONAL STATUS

Cyprus is a member of the United Nations (September 20, 1960). It is a member of the Commonwealth of Nations and of other international organizations.

Cyprus became independent on August 16, 1960, in accordance with the Agreement drawn up at the Tripartite Conference of London between Greece, Great Britain and Turkey on February 19, 1959.

Cyprus passed from Turkish to British control in 1878 while remaining under Ottoman suzerainty until 1914. The movement for union (*enosis*) with Greece, coupled with efforts to secure greater rights of self-government, continued throughout the nineteenth century. From 1922, when the annexation in 1914 by Great Britain of Cyprus as a colony was recognized by the Treaties of Sèvres and Lausanne, Cyprus claimed, in addition to *enosis*, an autonomous and representative government. This was refused and after a general revolt throughout the island in October 1931 such liberties and participation in government as existed were abolished and the Archbishop, as Ethnarch, was deported together with other leaders. After the second World War, expectations of union with Greece were again deceived. In 1954, the question of Cyprus was placed for the first time on the agenda of the United Nations by Greece. In 1955, the EOKA was organized and for four years fought a guerrilla war against the British. In February 1959, a meeting took place in Zurich between the premiers of Greece and Turkey, immediately followed by the London Conference which provided for Cypriot independence without union with Greece and subject to guarantees giving the three guaranteeing powers the right of joint or unilateral intervention, empowering Greece and Turkey to maintain contingents of their own forces in Cyprus and Great Britain to keep sovereign bases in the island. The Constitution drawn up to take account of the London agreements soon showed itself to be unworkable. On November 30, 1963, the President proposed to the Turkish-Cypriot leaders discussions on amendments to eliminate some of the difficulties, among them the abolition of separate majorities for certain laws, unified municipalities, unification of justice, the abolition of the Greek Communal Chamber, etc. The proposals were rejected by the Government of Turkey before the expression of any views by the Turkish-Cypriots, and on December 22, 23, 1963, a Turkish-Cypriot insurrection broke out. Turkey announced its intention to intervene and Cyprus requested the immediate intervention of the Security Council. A United Nations Peace-keeping Force was sent to the island in March 1964. The United Nations Mediator's report in 1965 was not accepted by Turkey.

FORM OF NATIONAL GOVERNMENT

The Constitution was drawn up by a Constitutional Committee during the transitional period following the London Conference. Everything agreed upon at the Zurich conference was required to be incorporated as basic articles. It entered into force on April 16, 1960 and was operative until the outbreak of the anomalous situation in December 1963. Since then certain parts of the Constitution are being treated as inoperative. Laws have been passed to meet the new situation in certain respects, such as, for instance, the Courts of Justice Law of 1964.

The Constitution states that Cyprus is an independent and sovereign Republic with a presidential regime, the President being Greek Cypriot and the Vice-President being Turkish Cypriot.[1] It states that the territory of the Republic is indivisible and union with any other State or separatist independence is excluded.[2] It describes the Greek and Turkish communities and provides for other citizens to opt for one or the other.[3] The Zurich and London agreements are to be considered in all interpretations of the Constitution and the Treaty between Cyprus, Greece, Turkey and the United Kingdom granting independence, territorial integrity and a constitution has constitutional force as has the treaty of military alliance with Greece and Turkey.[4] Certain articles are listed as unamendable.[5]

RIGHTS OF THE PEOPLE

The Constitution provides that there shall be no discrimination between the Communities except as the Constitution provides.[6] It guarantees the right to life, a decent existence and social security, forbids inhuman or degrading punishment, slavery and forced labor, guarantees the right to liberty and security of the person, due process of law, no retroactive punishment, freedom of movement and travel, no banishment, respect for private and family life, inviolability of the dwelling, secrecy of correspondence, freedom of thought, conscience and religion, speech and expression, education and free and compulsory primary education, peaceful assembly and association, freedom of marriage, property, occupation, to strike, equality before the law, the right to petition, the right to vote.[7] All citizens must pay taxes.[8]

LEGISLATIVE DEPARTMENT

Legislative power is exercised by the House of Representatives in all matters not reserved to the Communal Chambers.[9] Fifty representatives are elected by universal suffrage on separate electoral lists of the Greek and Turkish communities, 70% elected by the Greek community and 30% elected by the Turkish community separately from amongst their members for a term of five years subject to dissolution.[10] The President of the House of Representatives is Greek Cypriot, the Vice-President Turkish Cypriot.[11] It meets in one ordinary session a year.[12] Immunities of deputies are provided.[13]

The Communal Chambers have, in respect of their communities, legislative powers in matters of religion, education, personal status and courts relating thereto, communal associations and taxes for community purposes, certain municipal regulations, co-operatives.[14]

[1] Const., Art. 1. [2] Id., Art. 185. [3] Id., Art. 2. [4] Id., Art. 180, 181.
[5] Id., Art. 182, Annex III. [6] Id., Art. 6. [7] Id., Art. 7–31.
[8] Id., Art. 24. [9] Id., Art. 61. [10] Id., Art. 62, 63, 65, 67.
[11] Id., Art. 72. [12] Id., Art. 74. [13] Id., Art. 83. [14] Id., Art. 87.

There are financial provisions.[1] It is provided that separate municipalities be created in the five largest towns by the Turkish inhabitants thereof.[2] All laws relating to municipalities, duties and taxes must be passed by separate majorities vote of the representatives elected by the Greek and Turkish communities respectively.[3]

Since December 1963, the legislative organs provided by the Constitution are functioning without the participation of the Turkish members.

EXECUTIVE DEPARTMENT

Executive power is exercised by the Greek President, and the Turkish Vice President as Head and Vice-Head of State, elected respectively and separately by the Greek and Turkish communities by direct universal, secret suffrage for a term of five years.[4] The Council of Ministers is composed of 7 Greek and 3 Turkish ministers.[5] The Constitution describes the joint and separate executive powers of the President and Vice President.[6] Other executive powers are exercised by the Council of Ministers [7] or by the Communal Chambers.[8] There are provisions concerning the independent officers of the Republic, namely the Attorney General, the Auditor General, the Governor of the Bank of Cyprus and their deputies, stipulating that in each case the officer and deputy must be of different communities.[9] There are provisions concerning the public service which must be composed of 70% Greeks and 30% Turks;[10] the forces of the Republic, of which the Army must comprise 60% Greeks and 40% Turks and the police and gendarmerie 70% Greeks and 30% Turks.[11] Since December 1963, the executive organs provided by the Constitution are functioning without the participation of the Turkish members.

JUDICIAL DEPARTMENT

The Constitution provides a Supreme Constitutional Court composed of a Greek, Turk and a neutral judge which functions as a constitutional and as an administrative court.[12] There are a High Court and subordinate courts [13], and provisions concerning the judges in cases where plaintiff and defendant are of the same or of different communities.[14] In case of ambiguity of the Constitution, interpretation shall be made by the Supreme Constitutional Court with due regard to the letter and spirit of the Zurich and London agreements.[15]

[1] Id., Art. 165–168. [2] Id., Art. 173–178. [3] Id., Art. 78.
[4] Id., Art. 36, 1, 2, 39, 43, 46. "Greek-Cypriot" and "Turkish-Cypriot" are understood in all references to "Greek" and "Turk". [5] Id., Art. 46. [6] Id., Art. 47–54.
[7] Id., Art. 54. [8] Id., Art. 54, 89, 90. [9] Id., Art. 112–121.
[10] Id., Art. 122–128. [11] Id., Art. 129–132.
[12] Id., Art. 133, 136–146, 149. [13] Id., Art. 152. [14] Id., Art. 159.
[15] Id., Art. 180.

The provisions contained in the Constitution are not being applied for the present and the Administration of Justice Law of July 9, 1964, was enacted in order that justice should continue to be administered unhampered by the situation created by recent events.[1] The latter law provides for a Supreme Court to exercise the jurisdiction hitherto exercised by the Supreme Constitutional Court and the High Court, composed of from five to seven judges and deemed to be duly constituted during and notwithstanding any vacancy in the office of any members thereof.[2] Its jurisdiction is described.[3] A Supreme Council of the Judicature is provided.[4] Inferior courts shall be composed of such judge or judges as the Supreme Court may direct irrespective of the community to which parties to a proceeding belong.[5]

AREA, POPULATION, ETC.

The area of Cyprus is 9,251 square kilometres, its population (1964) 588,000. The official languages are Greek and Turkish.[6] The capital is Nicosia.

[1] Ad. of Justice, Preamble. [2] Id., Art. 3–8, 16. [6][3] Id., Art. 9.
[4] Id., Art. 10. [5] Id., Art. 12. Const. Art. 73.

CONSTITUTION
of
CYPRUS[1]

April 6, 1960

PART I

GENERAL PROVISIONS

Art. 1. The State of Cyprus is an independent and sovereign Republic with a presidential régime, the President being Greek and the Vice President being Turk elected by the Greek and the Turkish Communities of Cyprus respectively as hereinafter in this Constitution provided.

Art. 2. For the purposes of this Constitution:

(1) the Greek Community comprises all citizens of the Republic who are of Greek origin and whose mother tongue is Greek or who share the Greek cultural traditions or who are members of the Greek-Orthodox Church;

(2) the Turkish Community comprises all citizens of the Republic who are of Turkish origin and whose mother tongue is Turkish or who share the Turkish cultural traditions or who are Moslems;

(3) citizens of the Republic who do not come within the provisions of paragraph (1) or (2) of this Article shall, within three months of the date of the coming into operation of this Constitution, opt to belong to either the Greek or the Turkish Community as individuals, but, if they belong to a religious group, shall so opt as a religious group and upon such option they shall be deemed to be members of such Community:

Provided that any citizen of the Republic who belongs to such a religious group may choose not to abide by the option of such group and by a written and signed declaration submitted within one month of the date of such option to the appropriate officer of the Republic and to the Presidents of the Greek and the Turkish Communal Chambers opt to belong to the Community other than that to which such group shall be deemed to belong:

Provided further that if an option of such religious group is not accepted on the ground that its members are below the requisite number any mem-

[1] *Cyprus.* Cmd. 1093. HMSO, London, July 1960. Supplied by the Offices of the Supreme Court, Nicosia, in May 1966. Ed.

ber of such group may within one month of the date of the refusal of acceptance of such option opt in the aforesaid manner as an individual to which Community he would like to belong.

For the purposes of this paragraph a "religious group" means a group of persons ordinarily resident in Cyprus professing the same religion and either belonging to the same rite or being subject to the same jurisdiction thereof the number of whom, on the date of the coming into operation of this Constitution, exceeds one thousand out of which at least five hundred become on such date citizens of the Republic;

(4) a person who becomes a citizen of the Republic at any time after three months of the date of the coming into operation of this Constitution shall exercise the option provided in paragraph (3) of this Article within three months of the date of his so becoming a citizen;

(5) a Greek or a Turkish citizen of the Republic who comes within the provisions of paragraph (1) or (2) of this Article may cease to belong to the Community of which he is a member and belong to the other Community upon:

(a) a written and signed declaration by such citizen to the effect that he desires such change, submitted to the appropriate officer of the Republic and to the Presidents of the Greek and the Turkish Communal Chambers;

(b) the approval of the Communal Chamber of such other Community;

(6) any individual or any religious group deemed to belong to either the Greek or the Turkish Community under the provisions of paragraph (3) of this Article may cease to belong to such Community and be deemed to belong to the other Community upon:

(a) a written and signed declaration by such individual or religious group to the effect that such change is desired, submitted to the appropriate officer of the Republic and to the Presidents of the Greek and the Turkish Communal Chambers;

(b) the approval of the Communal Chamber of such other Community;

(7) (a) a married woman shall belong to the Community to which her husband belongs;

(b) a male or female child under the age of twenty-one who is not married shall belong to the Community to which his or her father belongs, or, if the father is unknown and he or she has not been adopted, to the Community to which his or her mother belongs.

Art. 3. 1. The official languages of the Republic are Greek and Turkish.

2. Legislative, executive and administrative acts and documents shall be drawn up in both official languages and shall, where under the express provisions of this Constitution promulgation is required, be promulgated by publication in the official Gazette of the Republic in both official languages.

3. Administrative or other official documents addressed to a Greek or

a Turk shall be drawn up in the Greek or the Turkish language respectively.

4. Judicial proceedings shall be conducted or made and judgments shall be drawn up in the Greek language if the parties are Greek, in the Turkish language if the parties are Turkish, and in both the Greek and the Turkish languages if the parties are Greek and Turkish. The official language or languages to be used for such purposes in all other cases shall be specified by the Rules of Court made by the High Court under Article 163.

5. Any text in the official Gazette of the Republic shall be published in both official languages in the same issue.

6. (1) Any difference between the Greek and the Turkish texts of any legislative, executive or administrative act or document published in the official Gazette of the Republic, shall be resolved by a competent court.

(2) The prevailing text of any law or decision of a Communal Chamber published in the official Gazette of the Republic shall be that of the language of the Communal Chamber concerned.

(3) Where any difference arises between the Greek and the Turkish texts of an executive or administrative act or document which, though not published in the official Gazette of the Republic, has otherwise been published, a statement by the Minister or any other authority concerned as to which text should prevail or which should be the correct text shall be final and conclusive.

(4) A competent court may grant such remedies as it may deem just in any case of a difference in the texts as aforesaid.

7. The two official languages shall be used on coins, currency notes and stamps.

8. Every person shall have the right to address himself to the authorities of the Republic in either of the official languages.

Art. 4. 1. The Republic shall have its own flag of neutral design and colour, chosen jointly by the President and the Vice-President of the Republic.

2. The authorities of the Republic and any public corporation or public utility body created by or under the laws of the Republic shall fly the flag of the Republic and they shall have the right to fly on holidays together with the flag of the Republic both the Greek and the Turkish flags at the same time.

3. The Communal authorities and institutions shall have the right to fly on holidays together with the flag of the Republic either the Greek or the Turkish flag at the same time.

4. Any citizen of the Republic or any body, corporate or unincorporate other than public, whose members are citizens of the Republic, shall have the right to fly on their premises the flag of the Republic or the Greek or the Turkish flag without any restriction.

Art. 5. The Greek and the Turkish Communities shall have the right to celebrate respectively the Greek and the Turkish national holidays.

PART II

FUNDAMENTAL RIGHTS AND LIBERTIES

Art. 6. Subject to the express provisions of this Constitution no law or decision of the House of Representatives or of any of the Communal Chambers, and no act or decision of any organ, authority or person in the Republic exercising executive power or administrative functions, shall discriminate against any of the two Communities or any person as a person or by virtue of being a member of a Community.

Art. 7. 1. Every person has the right to life and corporal integrity.

2. No persons shall be deprived of his life except in the execution of a sentence of a competent court following his conviction of an offence for which this penalty is provided by law. A law may provide for such penalty only in cases of premeditated murder, high treason, piracy *jure gentium* and capital offences under military law.

3. Deprivation of life shall not be regarded as inflicted in contravention of this Article when it results from the use of force which is no more than absolutely necessary:

(a) in defence of person or property against the infliction of a proportionate and otherwise unavoidable and irreparable evil;

(b) in order to effect an arrest or to prevent the escape of a person lawfully detained;

(c) in action taken for the purpose of quelling a riot or insurrection, when and as provided by law.

Art. 8. No person shall be subjected to torture or to inhuman or degrading punishment or treatment.

Art. 9. Every person has the right to a decent existence and to social security. A law shall provide for the protection of the workers, assistance to the poor and for a system of social insurance.

Art. 10. 1. No person shall be held in slavery or servitude.

2. No person shall be required to perform forced or compulsory labour.

3. For the purposes of this Article the term "forced or compulsory labour" shall not include:

(a) any work required to be done in the ordinary course of detention imposed according to the provisions of Article 11 or during conditional release from such detention;

(b) any service of a military character if imposed or, in case of conscientious objectors, subject to their recognition by a law, service exacted instead of compulsory military service;

(c) any service exacted in case of an emergency or calamity threatening the life or well-being of the inhabitants.

Art. 11. 1. Every person has the right to liberty and security of person.

2. No person shall be deprived of his liberty save in the following cases when and as provided by law:

(a) the detention of a person after conviction by a competent court;

(b) the arrest or detention of a person for non-compliance with the lawful order of a court;

(c) the arrest or detention of a person effected for the purpose of bringing him before the competent legal authority on reasonable suspicion of having committed an offence or when it is reasonably considered necessary to prevent his committing an offence or fleeing after having done so:

(d) the detention of a minor by a lawful order for the purpose of educational supervision or his lawful detention for the purpose of bringing him before the competent legal authority;

(e) the detention of persons for the prevention of spreading of infectious diseases, of persons of unsound mind, alcoholics or drug addicts or vagrants;

(f) the arrest or detention of a person to prevent him effecting an unauthorised entry into the territory of the Republic or of an alien against whom action is being taken with a view to deportation or extradition.

3. Save when and as provided by law in case of a flagrant offence punishable with death or imprisonment, no person shall be arrested save under the authority of a reasoned judicial warrant issued according to the formalities prescribed by the law.

4. Every person arrested shall be informed at the time of his arrest in a language which he understands of the reasons for his arrest and shall be allowed to have the services of a lawyer of his own choosing.

5. The person arrested shall, as soon as is practicable after his arrest, and in any event not later than twenty-four hours after the arrest, be brought before a judge, if not earlier released.

6. The judge before whom the person arrested is brought shall promptly proceed to inquiry into the grounds of the arrest in a language understandable by the person arrested and shall, as soon as possible and in any event not later than three days from such appearance, either release the person arrested on such term as he may deem fit or where the investigation into the commission of the offence for which he has been arrested has not been completed remand him in custody and may remand him in custody from time to time for a period not exceeding eight days at any one time:

Provided that the total period of such remand in custody shall not exceed three months of the date of the arrest on the expiration of which every person or authority having the custody of the person arrested shall forthwith set him free.

Any decision of the judge under this paragraph shall be subject to appeal.

7. Every person who is deprived of his liberty by arrest or detention shall be entitled to take proceedings by which the lawfulness of his detention shall be decided speedily by a court and his release ordered if the detention is not lawful.

8. Every person who has been the victim of arrest or detention in contravention of the provisions of this Article shall have an enforceable right to compensation.

Art. 12. 1. No person shall be held guilty of any offence on account of any act or omission which did not constitute an offence under the law at the time when it was committed; and no person shall have a heavier punishment imposed on him for an offence than that expressly provided for it by law at the time when it was committed.

2. A person who has been acquitted or convicted of an offence shall not be tried again for the same offence. No person shall be punished twice for the same act or omission except where death ensues from such act or omission.

3. No law shall provide for a punishment which is disproportionate to the gravity of the offence.

4. Every person charged with an offence shall be presumed innocent until proved guilty according to law.

5. Every person charged with an offence has the following minimum rights:

(a) to be informed promptly and in a language which he understands and in detail of the nature and grounds of the charge preferred against him;

(b) to have adequate time and facilities for the preparation of his defence;

(c) to defend himself in person or through a lawyer of his own choosing or, if he has no sufficient means to pay for legal assistance, to be given free legal assistance when the interests of justice so require;

(d) to examine or have examined witnesses against him and to obtain the attendance and examination of witnesses on his behalf under the same conditions as witnesses against him;

(e) to have the free assistance of an interpreter if he cannot understand or speak the language used in court.

6. A punishment of general confiscation of property is prohibited.

Art. 13. 1. Every person has the right to move freely throughout the territory of the Republic and to reside in any part thereof subject to any restrictions imposed by law and which are necessary only for the purposes of defence or public health or provided as punishment to be passed by a competent court.

2. Every person has the right to leave permanently or temporarily the territory of the Republic subject to reasonable restrictions imposed by law.

Art. 14. No citizen shall be banished or excluded from the Republic under any circumstances.

Art. 15. 1. Every person has the right to respect for his private and family life.

2. There shall be no interference with the exercise of this right except such as is in accordance with the law and is necessary only in the interests of the security of the Republic or the constitutional order or the public safety or the public order or the public health or the public morals or for the protection of the rights and liberties guaranteed by this Constitution to any person.

Art. 16. 1. Every person's dwelling house is inviolable.

2. There shall be no entry in any dwelling house or any search therein except when and as provided by law and on a judicial warrant duly reasoned or when the entry is made with the express consent of its occupant or for the purpose of rescuing the victims of any offence of violence or of any disaster.

Art. 17. 1. Every person has the right to respect for, and to the secrecy of, his correspondence and other communication if such other communication is made through means not prohibited by law.

2. There shall be no interference with the exercise of this right except in accordance with the law and only in cases of convicted and unconvicted prisoners and business correspondence and communication of bankrupts during the bankruptcy administration.

Art. 18. 1. Every person has the right to freedom of thought, conscience and religion.

2. All religions whose doctrines or rites are not secret are free.

3. All religions are equal before the law. Without prejudice to the competence of the Communal Chambers under this Constitution, no legislative, executive or administrative act of the Republic shall discriminate against any religious institution or religion.

4. Every person is free and has the right to profess his faith and to manifest his religion or belief, in worship, teaching, practice or observance, either individually or collectively, in private or in public, and to change his religion or belief.

5. The use of physical or moral compulsion for the purpose of making a person change or preventing him from changing his religion is prohibited.

6. Freedom to manifest one's religion or belief shall be subject only to such limitations as are prescribed by law and are necessary in the interests of the security of the Republic or the constitutional order or the public safety or the public order or the public health or the public morals or for the protection of the rights and liberties guaranteed by this Constitution to any person.

7. Until a person attains the age of sixteen the decision as to the religion

to be professed by him shall be taken by the person having the lawful guardianship of such person.

8. No person shall be compelled to pay any tax or duty the proceeds of which are specially allocated in whole or in part for the purposes of a religion other than his own.

Art. 19. 1. Every person has the right to freedom of speech and expression in any form.

2. This right includes freedom to hold opinions and receive and impart information and ideas without interference by any public authority and regardless of frontiers.

3. The exercise of the rights provided in paragraphs 1 and 2 of this Article may be subject to such formalities, conditions, restrictions or penalties as are prescribed by law and are necessary only in the interests of the security of the Republic or the constitutional order or the public safety or the public order or the public health or the public morals or for the protection of the reputation or rights of others or for preventing the disclosure of information received in confidence or for maintaining the authority and impartiality of the judiciary.

4. Seizure of newspapers or other printed matter is not allowed without the written permission of the Attorney-General of the Republic, which must be confirmed by the decision of a competent court within a period not exceeding seventy-two hours, failing which the seizure shall be lifted.

5. Nothing in this Article contained shall prevent the Republic from requiring the licensing of sound and vision broadcasting or cinema enterprises.

Art. 20. 1. Every person has the right to receive, and every person or institution has the right to give, instruction or education subject to such formalities, conditions or restrictions as are in accordance with the relevant communal law and are necessary only in the interests of the security of the Republic or the constitutional order or the public safety or the public order or the public health or the public morals or the standard and quality of education or for the protection of the rights and liberties of others including the right of the parents to secure for their children such education as is in conformity with their religious convictions.

2. Free primary education shall be made available by the Greek and the Turkish Communal Chambers in the respective communal primary schools.

3. Primary education shall be compulsory for all citizens of such school age as may be determined by a relevant communal law.

4. Education, other than primary education, shall be made available by the Greek and the Turkish Communal Chambers, in deserving and appropriate cases, on such terms and conditions as may be determined by a relevant communal law.

Art. 21. 1. Every person has the right to freedom of peaceful assembly.

2. Every person has the right to freedom of association with others,

including the right to form and to join trade unions for the protection of his interests. Notwithstanding any restriction under paragraph 3 of this Article, no person shall be compelled to join any association or to continue to be a member thereof.

3. No restrictions shall be placed on the exercise of these rights other than such as are prescribed by law and are absolutely necessary only in the interests of the security of the Republic or the constitutional order or the public safety or the public order or the public health or the public morals or for the protection of the rights and liberties guaranteed by this Constitution to any person, whether or not such person participates in such assembly or is a member of such association.

4. Any association the object or activities of which are contrary to the constitutional order is prohibited.

5. A law may provide for the imposition of restrictions on the exercise of these rights by members of the Armed Forces, the police or gendarmerie.

6. Subject to the provisions of any law regulating the establishment or incorporation, membership (including rights and obligations of members), management and administration, and winding up and dissolution, the provisions of this Article shall also apply to the formation of companies, societies and other associations functioning for profit.

Art. 22. 1. Any person reaching nubile age is free to marry and to found a family according to the law relating to marriage, applicable to such person under the provisions of this Constitution.

2. The provisions of paragraph 1 of this Article shall, in the following cases, be applied as follows:

(a) if the law relating to marriage applicable to the parties as provided under Article 111 is not the same, the parties may elect to have their marriage governed by the law applicable to either of them under such Article;

(b) if the provisions of Article 111 are not applicable to any of the parties to the marriage and neither of such parties is a member of the Turkish Community, the marriage shall be governed by a law of the Republic which the House of Representatives shall make and which shall not contain any restrictions other than those relating to age, health, proximity of relationship and prohibition of polygamy;

(c) if the provisions of Article 111 are applicable only to one of the parties to the marriage and the other party is not a member of the Turkish Community, the marriage shall be governed by the law of the Republic as in sub-paragraph (b) of this paragraph provided:

Provided that the parties may elect to have their marriage governed by the law applicable, under Article 111, to one of such parties in so far as such law allows such marriage.

3. Nothing in this Article contained shall, in any way, affect the rights, other than those on marriage, of the Greek-Orthodox Church or of any

religious group to which the provisions of paragraph 3 of Article 2 shall apply with regard to their respective members as provided in this Constitution.

Art. 23. 1. Every person, alone or jointly with others, has the right to acquire, own, possess, enjoy or dispose of any movable or immovable property and has the right to respect for such right.

The right of the Republic to underground water, minerals and antiquities is reserved.

2. No deprivation or restriction or limitation of any such right shall be made except as provided in this Article.

3. Restrictions or limitations which are absolutely necessary in the interest of the public safety or the public health or the public morals or the town and country planning or the development and utilization of any property to the promotion of the public benefit or for the protection of the rights of others may be imposed by law on the exercise of such right.

Just compensation shall be promptly paid for any such restrictions or limitations which materially decrease the economic value of such property; such compensation to be determined in case of disagreement by a civil court.

4. Any movable or immovable property or any right over or interest in any such property may be compulsorily acquired by the Republic or by a municipal corporation or by a Communal Chamber for the educational, religious, charitable or sporting institutions, bodies or establishments within its competence and only from the persons belonging to its respective Community or by a public corporation or a public utility body on which such right has been conferred by law, and only:

(a) for a purpose which is to the public benefit and shall be specially provided by a general law for compulsory acquisition which shall be enacted within a year from the date of the coming into operation of this Constitution; and

(b) when such purpose is established by a decision of the acquiring authority and made under the provisions of such law stating clearly the reasons for such acquisition; and

(c) upon the payment in cash and in advance of a just and equitable compensation to be determined in case of disagreement by a civil court.

5. Any immovable property or any right over or interest in any such property compulsorily acquired shall only be used for the purpose for which it has been acquired. If within three years of the acquisition such purpose has not been attained, the acquiring authority shall, immediately after the expiration of the said period of three years, offer the property at the price it has been acquired to the person from whom it has been acquired. Such person shall be entitled within three months of the receipt of such offer to signify his acceptance or non-acceptance of the offer, and if he signifies acceptance, such property shall be returned to him immediately

after his returning such price within a further period of three months from such acceptance.

6. In the event of agricultural reform, lands shall be distributed only to persons belonging to the same Community as the owner from whom such land has been compulsorily acquired.

7. Nothing in paragraphs 3 and 4 of this Article contained shall affect the provisions of any law made for the purpose of levying execution in respect of any tax or penalty, executing any judgment, enforcing any contractual obligation or for the prevention of danger to life or property.

8. Any movable or immovable property may be requisitioned by the Republic or by a Communal Chamber for the purposes of the educational, religious, charitable or sporting institutions, bodies or establishments within its competence and only where the owner and the person entitled to possession of such property belong to the respective Community, and only:

(a) for a purpose which is to the public benefit and shall be specially provided by a general law for requisitioning which shall be enacted within a year from the date of the coming into operation of this Constitution; and

(b) when such purpose is established by a decision of the requisitioning authority and made under the provisions of such law stating clearly the reasons for such requisitioning; and

(c) for a period not exceeding three years; and

(d) upon the prompt payment in cash of a just and equitable compensation to be determined in case of disagreement by a civil court.

9. Notwithstanding anything contained in this Article no deprivation, restriction or limitation of the right provided in paragraph 1 of this Article in respect of any movable or immovable property belonging to any See, monastery, church or any other ecclesiastical corporation or any right over it or interest therein shall be made except with the written consent of the appropriate ecclesiastical authority being in control of such property and the provisions of paragraphs 3, 4, 7 and 8 of this Article shall be subject to the provisions of this paragrpah:

Provided that restrictions or limitations for the purposes of town and country planning under the provisions of paragraph 3 of this Article are exempted from the provisions of this paragraph.

10. Notwithstanding anything contained in this Article, no deprivation, restriction or limitation of any right provided in paragraph 1 of this Article in respect of any *vakf* movable or immovable property, including the objects and subjects of the *vakfs* and the properties belonging to the Mosques or to any other Moslem religious institutions, or any right thereon or interest therein shall be made except with the approval of the Turkish Communal Chamber and subject to the Laws and Principles of *Vakfs* and the provisions of paragraphs 3, 4, 7 and 8 of this Article shall be subject to the provisions of this paragraph:

Provided that restrictions or limitations for the purposes of town and country planning under the provisions of paragraph 3 of this Article are exempted from the provisions of this paragraph.

11. Any interested person shall have the right of recourse to the court in respect of or under any of the provisions of this Article, and such recourse shall act as a stay of proceedings for the compulsory acquisition; and in case of any restriction or limitation imposed under paragraph 3 of this Article, the court shall have power to order stay of any proceedings in respect thereof.

Any decision of the court under this paragraph shall be subject to appeal.

Art. 24. 1. Every person is bound to contribute according to his means towards the public burdens.

2. No such contribution by way of tax, duty or rate of any kind whatsoever shall be imposed save by or under the authority of a law.

3. No tax, duty or rate of any kind whatsoever shall be imposed with retrospective effect:

Provided that any import duty may be imposed as from the date of the introduction of the relevant Bill.

4. No tax, duty or rate of any kind whatsoever other than customs duties shall be of a destructive or prohibitive nature.

Art. 25. 1. Every person has the right to practise any profession or to carry on any occupation, trade or business.

2. The exercise of this right may be subject to such formalities, conditions or restrictions as are prescribed by law and relate exclusively to the qualifications usually required for the exercise of any profession or are necessary only in the interests of the security of the Republic or the constitutional order or the public safety or the public order or the public health or the public morals or for the protection of the rights and liberties guaranteed by this Constitution to any person or in the public interest:

Provided that no such formalities, conditions or restrictions purporting to be in the public interest shall be prescribed by a law if such formality, condition or restriction is contrary to the interests of either Community.

3. As an exception to the aforesaid provisions of this Article a law may provide, if it is in the public interest, that certain enterprises of the nature of an essential public service or relating to the exploitation of sources of energy or other natural resources shall be carried out exclusively by the Republic or a municipal corporation or by a public corporate body created for the purpose by such law and administered under the control of the Republic, and having a capital which may be derived from public and private funds or from either such source only:

Provided that, where such enterprise has been carried out by any person, other than a municipal corporation or a public corporate body, the installations used for such enterprise shall, at the request of such person, be acquired, on payment of a just price, by the Republic or such municipal corporation or such public corporate body, as the case may be.

Art. 26. 1. Every person has the right to enter freely into any contract subject to such conditions, limitations or restrictions as are laid down by the general principles of the law of contract. A law shall provide for the prevention of exploitation by persons who are commanding economic power.

2. A law may provide for collective labour contracts of obligatory fulfilment by employers and workers with adequate protection of the rights of any person, whether or not represented at the conclusion of such contract.

Art. 27. 1. The right to strike is recognised and its exercise may be regulated by law for the purposes only of safeguarding the security of the Republic or the constitutional order or the public order or the public safety or the maintenance of supplies and services essential to the life of the inhabitants or the protection of the rights and liberties guaranteed by this Constitution to any person.

2. The members of the Armed Forces, of the police and of the gendarmerie shall not have the right to strike. A law may extend such prohibition to the members of the public service.

Art. 28. 1. All persons are equal before the law, the administration and justice and are entitled to equal protection thereof and treatment thereby.

2. Every person shall enjoy all the rights and liberties provided for in this Constitution without any direct or indirect discrimination against any person on the ground of his community, race, religion, language, sex, political or other convictions, national or social descent, birth, colour, wealth, social class, or on any ground whatsoever, unless there is express provision to the contrary in this Constitution.

3. No citizen shall be entitled to use or enjoy any privilege of any title of nobility or of social distinction within the territorial limits of the Republic.

4. No title or nobility or other social distinction shall be conferred by or recognised in the Republic.

Art. 29. 1. Every person has the right individually or jointly with others to address written requests or complaints to any competent public authority and to have them attended to and decided expeditiously; an immediate notice of any such decision taken duly reasoned shall be given to the person making the request or complaint and in any event within a period not exceeding thirty days.

2. Where any interested person is aggrieved by any such decision or where no such decision is notified to such person within the period specified in paragraph 1 of this Article, such person may have recourse to a competent court in the matter of such request or complaint.

Art. 30. 1. No person shall be denied access to the court assigned to him by or under this Constitution. The establishment of judicial committees or exceptional courts under any name whatsoever is prohibited.

2. In the determination of his civil rights and obligations or of any criminal charge against him, every person is entitled to a fair and public hearing within a reasonable time by an independent, impartial and competent court established by law. Judgment shall be reasoned and pronounced in public session, but the press and the public may be excluded from all or any part of the trial upon a decision of the court where it is in the interest of the security of the Republic or the constitutional order or the public order or the public safety or the public morals or where the interests of juveniles or the protection of the private life of the parties so require or, in special circumstances where, in the opinion of the court, publicity would prejudice the interests of justice.

3. Every person has the right:

(a) to be informed of the reasons why he is required to appear before the court;

(b) to present his case before the court and to have sufficient time necessary for its preparation;

(c) to adduce or cause to be adduced his evidence and to examine witnesses according to law;

(d) to have a lawyer of his own choice and to have free legal assistance where the interests of justice so require and as provided by law;

(e) to have free assistance of an interpreter if he cannot understand or speak the language used in court.

Art. 31. Every citizen has, subject to the provisions of this Constitution and any electoral law of the Republic or of the relevant Communal Chamber made thereunder, the right to vote in any election held under this Constitution or any such law.

Art. 32. Nothing in this Part contained shall preclude the Republic from regulating by law any matter relating to aliens in accordance with International Law.

Art. 33. 1. Subject to the provisions of this Constitution relating to a state of emergency, the fundamental rights and liberties guaranteed by this Part shall not be subjected to any other limitations or restrictions than those in this Part provided.

2. The provisions of this Part relating to such limitations or restrictions shall be interpreted strictly and shall not be applied for any purpose other than those for which they have been prescribed.

Art. 34. Nothing in this Part may be interpreted as implying for any Community, group or person any right to engage in any activity or perform any act aimed at the undermining or destruction of the constitutional order established by this Constitution or at the destruction of any of the rights and liberties set forth in this Part or at their limitation to a greater extent than is provided for therein.

Art. 35. The legislative, executive and judicial authorities of the Republic shall be bound to secure, within the limits of their respective competence, the efficient application of the provisions of this Part

PART III

THE PRESIDENT OF THE REPUBLIC, THE VICE-PRESIDENT OF THE REPUBLIC AND THE COUNCIL OF MINISTERS

Art. 36. 1. The President of the Republic is the Head of the State and takes precedence over all persons in the Republic.

The Vice-President of the Republic is the Vice-Head of the State and takes precedence over all persons in the Republic next after the President of the Republic.

Deputizing for or replacing the President of the Republic in case of his temporary absence of temporary incapacity to perform his duties is made as provided in paragraph 2 of this Article.

2. In the event of a temporary absence or a temporary incapacity to perform the duties of the President or of the Vice-President of the Republic, the President or the Vice-President of the House of Representative and, in case of his absence or pending the filling of a vacancy in any such office, the Representative acting for him under Article 72 shall act for the President or the Vice-President of the Republic respectively during such temporary absence or temporary incapacity.

Art. 37. The President of the Republic as Head of the State:

(a) represents the Republic in all its official functions;

(b) signs the credentials of diplomatic envoys appointed under Article 54 and receives the credentials of foreign diplomatic envoys who shall be accredited to him;

(c) signs:

(i) the credentials of delegates appointed under Article 54 for the negotiation of international treaties, conventions or other agreements, or for signing any such treaties, conventions or agreements already negotiated, in accordance with, and subject to, the provisions of this Constitution;

(ii) the letter relating to the transmission of the instruments of ratification of any international treaties, conventions or agreements approved as provided in this Constitution;

(d) confers the honours of the Republic.

Art. 38. 1. The Vice-President of the Republic as Vice-Head of the State has the right to:

(a) be present in all official functions;

(b) be present at the presentation of the credentials of the foreign diplomatic envoys;

(c) recommend to the President of the Republic the conferment of honours of the Republic on members of the Turkish Community which recommendation the President shall accept unless there are grave reasons to the contrary. The honours so conferred will be presented to the recipient by the Vice-President if he so desires.

2. For the purposes of sub-paragraphs (a) and (b) of paragraph 1 of this Article, the necessary information shall be given to the Vice-President of the Republic in writing in sufficient time before any such event.

Art. 39. 1. The election of the President and the Vice-President of the Republic shall be direct, by universal suffrage and secret ballot, and shall, except in the case of a by-election, take place on the same day but separately:

Provided that in either case if there is only one candidate for election that candidate shall be declared as elected.

2. The candidate who receives more than fifty per centum of the votes validly cast shall be elected. If none of the candidates attains the required majority the election shall be repeated on the corresponding day of the week next following between the two candidates who received the greater number of the votes validly cast and the candidate who receives at such repeated election the greatest number of the votes validly cast shall be deemed to be elected.

3. If the election cannot take place on the date fixed under this Constitution owing to extraordinary and unforeseen circumstances such as earthquake, floods, general epidemic and the like, then such election shall take place on the corresponding day of the week next following.

Art. 40. A person shall be qualified to be a candidate for election as President or Vice-President of the Republic if at the time of election such person:

(a) is a citizen of the Republic;

(b) has attained the age of thirty-five years;

(c) has not been, on or after the date of the coming into operation of this Constitution, convicted of an offence involving dishonesty or moral turpitude or is not under any disqualification imposed by a competent court for any electoral offence;

(d) is not suffering from a mental disease incapacitating such person from acting as President or Vice-President of the Republic.

Art. 41. 1. The office of the President and of the Vice-President of the Republic shall be incompatible with that of a Minister or of a Representative or of a member of a Communal Chamber or of a member of any municipal council including a Mayor or of a member of the armed or security forces of the Republic or with a public or municipal office.

For the purposes of this Article "public office" means any office of profit in the public service of the Republic or of a Communal Chamber, the emoluments of which are under the control either of the Republic or of a Communal Chamber, and includes any office in any public corporation or public utility body.

2. The President and the Vice-President of the Republic shall not, during their term of office, engage either directly or indirectly, either for their own account or for the account of any other person, in the exercise of any profit or non-profit making business or profession.

Art. 42. 1. The President and the Vice-President of the Republic are invested by the House of Representatives before which they make the following affirmation:

"I do solemnly affirm faith to, and respect for, the Constitution and the laws made thereunder, the preservation of the independence and the territorial integrity, of the Republic of Cyprus."

2. For this purpose the House of Representatives shall meet on the date the five years' period of office of the outgoing President and the outgoing Vice-President of the Republic expires, and in the case of a by-election under paragraph 4 of Article 44 on the third day from the date of such by-election.

Art. 43. 1. The President and the Vice-President of the Republic shall hold office for a period of five years commencing on the date of their investiture and shall continue to hold such office until the next elected President and Vice-President of the Republic are invested.

2. The President or the Vice-President of the Republic elected at a by-election under paragraph 4 of Article 44 shall hold office for the unexpired period of office of the President or the Vice-President of the Republic, as the case may be, whose vacancy he has been elected to fill.

3. The election of a new President and Vice-President of the Republic shall take place before the expiration of the five years' period of office of the outgoing President and the outgoing Vice-President of the Republic so as to enable the newly-elected President and Vice-President of the Republic to be invested on the date such period expires.

Art. 44. 1. The office of the President or the Vice-President of the Republic shall become vacant:

(a) upon his death;

(b) upon his written resignation addressed to the House of Representatives through, and received by, its President or Vice-President respectively;

(c) upon his conviction of high treason or any other offence involving dishonesty or moral turpitude;

(d) upon such permanent physical or mental incapacity or such absence, other than temporary, as would prevent him to perform effectively his duties.

2. In the event of a vacancy in the office of the President or the Vice-President of the Republic, the President or the Vice-President of the House of Representatives respectively shall act, during such vacancy, as President or Vice-President of the Republic, respectively.

3. The Supreme Constitutional Court shall decide on any question arising out of sub-paragraph (d) of paragraph 1 of this Article on a motion by the Attorney-General and the Deputy Attorney-General of the Republic upon a resolution of the Representatives belonging to the same Community as the President or the Vice-President of the Republic respectively, carried by a simple majority:

Provided that no such resolution shall be taken and no item shall be entered on the agenda or debated in the House of Representatives in connexion therewith unless the proposal for such resolution is signed by at least one fifth of the total number of such Representatives.

4. In the event of a vacancy in the office of either the President or the Vice-President of the Republic, the vacancy shall be filled by a by-election which shall take place within a period not exceeding forty-five days of the occurrence of such vacancy.

Art. 45. 1. The President or the Vice-President of the Republic shall not be liable to any criminal prosecution during his term of office except under the provisions of this Article.

2. The President or the Vice-President of the Republic may be prosecuted for high treason on a charge preferred by the Attorney-General and the Deputy Attorney-General of the Republic before the High Court upon a resolution of the House of Representatives carried by a secret ballot and a majority of three fourths of the total number of Representatives:

Provided that no such resolution shall be taken and no item shall be entered on the agenda or debated in the House of Representatives in connexion therewith unless the proposal for such resolution is signed by at least one fifth of the total number of Representatives.

3. The President or the Vice-President of the Republic may be prosecuted for an offence involving dishonesty or moral turpitude upon a charge preferred by the Attorney-General and the Deputy Attorney-General of the Republic before the High Court with the leave of the President of the High Court.

4. (1) The President or the Vice-President of the Republic upon being prosecuted under paragraph 2 or 3 of this Article shall be suspended from the performance of any of the functions of his office and thereupon the provisions of paragraph 2 of Article 36 shall apply.

(2) The President or the Vice-President of the Republic on any such prosecution shall be tried by the High Court; on his conviction his office shall become vacant and on his acquittal he shall resume the performance of the functions of his office.

5. Subject to paragraphs 2 and 3 of this Article the President or the

Vice-President of the Republic shall not be liable to prosecution for any offence committed by him in the execution of his functions but he may be prosecuted for any other offence committed during his term of office after he ceases to hold office.

6. No action shall be brought against the President or the Vice-President of the Republic in respect of any act or omission committed by him in the exercise of any of the functions of his office:

Provided that nothing in this paragraph contained shall be construed as in any way depriving any person of the right to sue the Republic as provided by law.

Art. 46. The executive power is ensured by the President and the Vice-President of the Republic.

The President and the Vice-President of the Republic in order to ensure the executive power shall have a Council of Ministers composed of seven Greek Ministers and three Turkish Ministers. The Ministers shall be designated respectively by the President and the Vice-President of the Republic who shall appoint them by an instrument signed by them both. The Ministers may be chosen from outside the House of Representatives.

One of the following Ministries that is to say the Ministry of Foreign Affairs, the Ministry of Defence or the Ministry of Finance, shall be entrusted to a Turkish Minister. If the President and the Vice-President of the Republic agree they may replace this system by a system of rotation.

The Council of Ministers shall exercise executive power as in Article 54 provided.

The decisions of the Council of Ministers shall be taken by an absolute majority and shall, unless the right of final veto or return is exercised by the President or the Vice-President of the Republic or both in accordance with Article 57, be promulgated immediately by them by publication in the official Gazette of the Republic in accordance with the provisions of Article 57.

Art. 47. The executive power exercised by the President and the Vice-President of the Republic conjointly consists of the following matters that is to say:

(a) determining the design and colour of the flag of the Republic as in Article 4 provided;

(b) creation or establishment of the honours of the Republic;

(c) appointment by an instrument signed by them both of the members of the Council of Ministers as in Article 46 provided;

(d) promulgation by publication in the official Gazette of the Republic of the decisions of the Council of Ministers as in Article 57 provided;

(e) promulgation by publication in the official Gazette of the Republic of any law or decision passed by the House of Representatives as in Article 52 provided;

(f) appointments in Articles 112, 115, 118, 124, 126, 131, 133, 153 and

184 provided; termination of appointments as in Article 118 provided and of appointments made under Article 131;

(g) institution of compulsory military service as in Article 129 provided;

(h) reduction or increase of the security forces as in Article 130 provided:

(i) exercise of the prerogative of mercy in capital cases where the injured party and the convicted person are members of different Communities as in Article 53 provided; remission, suspension and commutation of sentences as in Article 53 provided;

(j) right of reference to the Supreme Constitutional Court as in Article 140 provided;

(k) publication in the official Gazette of the Republic of decisions of the Supreme Constitutional Court as in Articles 137, 138, 139 and 143 provided;

(l) replacement by a system of rotation of the system of appointment of a Turkish Minister to one of the three Ministries of Foreign Affairs or of Defence or of Finance as in Article 46 provided;

(m) exercise of any of the powers specified in paragraphs (d), (e), (f) and (g) of Articles 48 and 49 and in Articles 50 and 51 which the President or the Vice-President of the Republic respectively can exercise separately;

(n) address of messages to the House of Representatives as in Article 79 provided.

Art. 48. The executive power exercised by the President of the Republic consists of the following matters, that is to say:

(a) designation and termination of appointment of Greek Ministers;

(b) convening the meetings of the Council of Ministers as in Article 55 provided, presiding at such meetings and taking part in the discussions thereat without any right to vote;

(c) preparing the agenda of such meetings as in Article 56 provided;

(d) right of final veto on decisions of the Council of Ministers concerning foreign affairs, defence or security as in Article 57 provided;

(e) right of return of decisions of the Council of Ministers as in Article 57 provided;

(f) right of final veto on laws or decisions of the House of Representatives concerning foreign affairs, defence or security as in Article 50 provided;

(g) right of return of laws or decisions of the House of Representatives or of the Budget as in Article 51 provided;

(h) right of recourse to the Supreme Constitutional Court as in Articles 137, 138 and 143 provided;

(i) right of reference to the Supreme Constitutional Court as in Article 141 provided;

(j) publication of the communal laws and decisions of the Greek Communal Chamber as in Article 104 provided;

(k) right of reference to the Supreme Constitutional Court of any law or decision of the Greek Communal Chamber as in Article 142 provided;

(l) right of recourse to the Supreme Constitutional Court in connection with any matter relating to any conflict or contest of power or competence arising between the House of Representatives and the Communal Chambers or any of them and between any organs of, or authorities in, the Republic as in Article 139 provided;

(m) the prerogative of mercy in capital cases as in Article 53 provided;

(n) the exercise of any of the powers specified in Article 47 conjointly with the Vice-President of the Republic;

(o) addressing messages to the House of Representatives as in Article 79 provided.

Art. 49. The executive power exercised by the Vice-President of the Republic consists of the following matters, that is to say:

(a) designation and termination of appointment of Turkish Ministers;

(b) asking the President of the Republic for the convening of the Council of Ministers as in Article 55 provided and being present and taking part in the discussions at all meetings of the Council of Ministers without any right to vote;

(c) proposing to the President of the Republic subjects for inclusion in the agenda as in Article 56 provided;

(d) right of final veto on decisions of the Council of Ministers concerning foreign affairs, defence or security as in Article 57 provided;

(e) right of return of decisions of the Council of Ministers as in Article 57 provided;

(e) right of return of decisions of the Council of Ministers as in Article 57 provided;

(f) right of final veto on laws or decisions of the House of Representatives concerning foreign affairs, defence or security as in Article 50 provided;

(g) right of return of laws or decisions of the House of Representatives or of the Budget as in Article 51 provided;

(h) right of recourse to the Supreme Constitutional Court as in Articles 137, 138 and 143 provided;

(i) right of reference to the Supreme Constitutional Court as in Article 141 provided;

(j) publication of the communal laws and decisions of the Turkish Communal Chamber as in Article 104 provided;

(k) right of reference to the Supreme Constitutional Court of any law or decision of the Turkish Communal Chamber as in Article 142 provided;

(l) right of recourse to the Supreme Constitutional Court in connection with any matter relating to any conflict or contest of power or compe tence arising between the House of Representatives and the Communal

Chambers or any of them and between any organs of, or authorities in, the Republic as in Article 139 provided;

(m) the prerogative of mercy in capital cases as in Article 53 provided;

(n) the exercise of any of the powers specified in Article 47 conjointly with the President of the Republic;

(o) addressing messages to the House of Representatives as in Article 79 provided.

Art. 50. 1. The President and the Vice-President of the Republic, separately or conjointly, shall have the right of final veto on any law or decision of the House of Representatives or any part thereof concerning:

(a) foreign affairs, except the participation of the Republic in international organisations and pacts of alliance in which the Kingdom of Greece and the Republic of Turkey both participate.

For the purposes of this sub-paragraph "foreign affairs" includes:

(i) the recognition of States, the establishment of diplomatic and consular relations with other countries and the interruption of such relations. The grant of acceptance to diplomatic representatives and of *exequatur* to consular representatives. The assignment of diplomatic representatives and of consular representatives, already in the diplomatic service, to posts abroad and the entrusting of functions abroad to special envoys already in the diplomatic service. The appointment and the assignment of persons, who are not already in the diplomatic service, to any posts abroad as diplomatic or consular representatives and the entrusting of functions abroad to persons, who are not already in the diplomatic service, as special envoys;

(ii) the conclusion of international treaties, conventions and agreements;

(iii) the declaration of war and the conclusion of peace;

(iv) the protection abroad of the citizens of the Republic and of their interests;

(v) the establishment, the status and the interests of aliens in the Republic;

(vi) the acquisition of foreign nationality by citizens of the Republic and their acceptance of employment by, or their entering the service of, a foreign Government;

(b) the following questions of defence:

(i) composition and size of the armed forces and credits for them;

(ii) (*nominations des cadres—διορισμοί στελεχῶν—kadrolara tayinler*) and their promotions (*καί ἡ προαγωγή αὐτῶν—ve bunlardaki terfiler*);

(iii) importation of war materials and also explosives of all kinds;

(iv) cession of bases and other facilities to allied countries;

(c) the following questions of security:

(i) (*nominations des cadres—διορισμοί στελεχῶν—kadrolara tayinler*) and their promotions (*καί ἡ προαγωγή αὐτῶν—ve bunlardaki terfiler*);

(ii) distribution and stationing of forces;
(iii) emergency measures and martial law;
(iv) police laws.

It is specified that the right of veto under sub-paragraph (c) above shall cover all emergency measures or decisions, but not those which concern the normal functioning of the police and the gendarmerie.

2. The above right of veto may be exercised either against the whole of a law or decision or against any part thereof, and in the latter case such law or decision shall be returned to the House of Representatives for a decision whether the remaining part thereof will be submitted, under the relevant provisions of this Constitution, for promulgation.

3. The right of veto under this Article shall be exercised within the period for the promulgation of laws or decisions of the House of Representatives as in Article 52 provided.

Art. 51. 1. The President and the Vice-President of the Republic shall have the right, either separately or conjointly, to return any law or decision or any part thereof of the House of Representatives to the House for reconsideration.

2. On the adoption of the Budget by the House of Representatives the President and the Vice-President of the Republic, either separately or conjointly, may exercise his or their right to return it to the House of Representatives on the ground that in his or their judgment there is a discrimination.

3. In case a law or decision or any part thereof is returned to the House of Representatives as in paragraph 1 of this Article provided, the House of Representatives shall pronounce on the matter so returned within fifteen days of such return and in the case of return of the Budget as in paragraph 2 of this Article provided the House of Representatives shall pronounce on the matter so returned within thirty days of such return.

4. If the House of Representatives persists in its decision the President and the Vice-President of the Republic shall, subject to the provisions of this Constitition, promulgate the law or decision or the Budget, as the case may be, within the time limit fixed for the promulgation of laws and decisions of the House of Representatives by publication of such law or decision or Budget in the official Gazette of the Republic.

5. Whenever the President or the Vice-President of the Republic exercises his right to return as provided in this Article he shall immediately notify the other of such return.

6. The right of return under this Article shall be exercised within the period for the promulgation of laws or decisons of the House of Representatives as in Article 52 provided.

Art. 52. The President and the Vice-President of the Republic shall, within fifteen days of the transmission to their respective offices of any law or decision of the House of Representatives, promulgate by publication in the official Gazette of the Republic such law or decision unless in the meantime they exercise, separately or conjointly, as the case may be, their right of veto as in Article 50 provided or their right of return as in Article 51 provided or their right of reference to the Supreme Constitutional Court as in Articles 140 and 141 provided or in the case of the Budget their right of recourse to the Supreme Constitutional Court as in Article 138 provided.

Art. 53. 1. The President or the Vice-President of the Republic shall have the right to exercise the prerogative of mercy with regard to persons belonging to their respective Community who are condemned to death.

2. Where the person injured (*βλαβέν πρόσωπον—zarar gōren kimse—mağdur*) and the offender are members of different Communities such prerogative of mercy shall be exercised by agreement between the President and the Vice-President of the Republic; in the event of disagreement between the two the vote for clemency shall prevail.

3. In case the prerogative of mercy is exercised under paragraph 1 or 2 of this Article the death sentence shall be commuted to life imprisonment.

4. The President and the Vice-President of the Republic shall, on the unanimous recommendation of the Attorney-General and the Deputy Attorney-General of the Republic, remit, suspend, or commute any sentence passed by a court in the Republic in all other cases.

Art. 54. Subject to the executive power expressly reserved, under Articles 47, 48 and 49, to the President and the Vice-President of the Republic, acting either separately or conjointly, the Council of Ministers shall exercise executive power in all other matters other than those which, under the express provisions of this Constitution, are within the competence of a Communal Chamber, including the following:

(a) the general direction and control of the government of the Republic and the direction of general policy;

(b) foreign affairs as in Article 50 set out;

(c) defence and security, including questions thereof as in Article 50 set out;

(d) the co-ordination and supervision of all public services;

(e) the supervision and disposition of property belonging to the Republic in accordance with the provisions of this Constitution and the law;

(f) consideration of Bills to be introduced to the House of Representatives by a Minister;

(g) making of any order or regulation for the carrying into effect of any law as provided by such law;

(h) consideration of the Budget of the Republic to be introduced to the House of Representatives.

Art. 55. The President of the Republic convenes the meetings of the Council of Ministers. Such convening is made by the President of the Republic on his own motion or on being asked by the Vice-President of the Republic in due time for a specific subject.

Art. 56. The agenda of any meeting of the Council of Ministers is prepared by the President of the Republic at his discretion and is communicated to all concerned prior to such meeting. The Vice-President of the Republic may propose to the President any subject for inclusion in the agenda of any meeting. The President of the Republic shall include such subject in the agenda if it can conveniently be dealt with at such meeting, otherwise such subject shall be included in the agenda of the meeting next following.

Art. 57. 1. On a decision being taken by the Council of Ministers such decision shall be transmitted forthwith to the office of the President and of the Vice-President of the Republic respectively.

2. The President or the Vice-President of the Republic or both shall have the right of return, within four days of the date when the decision has been transmitted to their respective offices, of such decision to the Council of Ministers for reconsideration, whereupon the Council of Ministers shall reconsider the matter and if they persist in such decision the President and the Vice-President of the Republic shall, subject to paragraph 4 of this Article, promulgate by publication such decision:

Provided that the exercise of the right of return shall not, in cases where the right of veto exists, prevent either the President or the Vice-President of the Republic or both from exercising the right of veto, within four days of the transmission to their respective offices, of the decision persisted upon.

3. If a decision relates to foreign affairs, defence or security as in Article 50 set out, the President or the Vice-President of the Republic or both shall have a right of veto which they shall exercise within four days of the date when the decision has been transmitted to their respective offices.

4. If the decision is enforceable and no right of veto or return has been exercised as in paragraph 2 or 3 of this Article provided, such decision shall be forthwith promulgated by the President and the Vice-President of the Republic by publication in the official Gazette of the Republic unless the Council of Ministers otherwise states in that decision.

Art. 58. 1. A Minister is the Head of his Ministry.

2. Subject to the executive power expressly reserved, under this Constitution, to the President and the Vice-President of the Republic, acting either separately or conjointly, and to the Council of Ministers, the executive power exercised by each Minister includes the following matters:

(a) the execution of laws relating to, and the administration of all matters and affairs usually falling within, the domain of his Ministry;

(b) preparation of orders or regulations concerning his Ministry for submission to the Council of Ministers;

(c) the issuing of directions and general instructions for the carrying out of the provisions of any law relating to his Ministry and of any order or regulation under such law;

(d) the preparation for submission to the Council of Ministers of the part of the Budget of the Republic relating to his Ministry.

Art. 59. 1. No person shall be appointed as a Minister unless he is a citizen of the Republic and has the qualifications required for a candidate for election as a member of the House of Representatives.

2. The office of a Minister shall be incompatible with that of a Representative or of a member of a Communal Chamber or of a member of any municipal council including a Mayor or of a member of the armed or security forces of the Republic or with a public or municipal office or in the case of a Turkish Minister with that of a religious functionary (*din adami*).

For the purposes of this paragraph "public office" has the same meaning as in Article 41.

3. The Ministers shall hold office in the case of the Greek Ministers until their appointment is terminated by the President of the Republic and in the case of the Turkish Ministers until their appointment is terminated by the Vice-President of the Republic.

4. Any person appointed as a Minister shall, before entering upon his office, make before the President and the Vice-President of the Republic the following affirmation:

"I do solemnly affirm faith to, and respect for, the Constitution and the laws made thereunder, the preservation of the independence and the territorial integrity, of the Republic of Cyprus."

Art. 60. 1. There shall be a Joint Secretariat of the Council of Ministers headed by two Secretaries, one belonging to the Greek Community and the other belonging to the Turkish Community, who shall be public officers.

2. The two Secretaries of the Joint Secretariat of the Council of Ministers shall have charge of the Council of Ministers' Office and shall, in accordance with any instructions as may be given to them by the Council of Ministers, attend its meetings and keep the minutes thereof and convey the decision of the Council of Ministers to the appropriate organ or authority or person.

PART IV

THE HOUSE OF REPRESENTATIVES

Art. 61. The legislative power of the Republic shall be exercised by the House of Representatives in all matters except those expressly reserved to the Communal Chambers under this Constitution.

Art. 62. 1. The number of Representatives shall be fifty:

Provided that such number may be altered by a resolution of the House of Representatives carried by a majority comprising two thirds of the Representatives elected by the Greek Community and two thirds of the Representatives elected by the Turkish Community.

2. Out of the number of Representatives provided in paragraph 1 of this

Article seventy per centum shall be elected by the Greek Community and thirty per centum by the Turkish Community separately from amongst their members respectively, and in the case of a contested election, by universal suffrage and by direct and secret ballot held on the same day.

The proportion of Representatives stated in this paragraph shall be independent of any statistical data.

Art. 63. 1. Subject to paragraph 2 of this Article every citizen of the Republic who has attained the age of twenty-one years and has such residential qualifications as may be prescribed by the Electoral Law shall have the right to be registered as an elector in either the Greek or the Turkish electoral list:

Provided that the members of the Greek Community shall only be registered in the Greek electoral list and the members of the Turkish Community shall only be registered in the Turkish electoral list.

2. No person shall be qualified to be registered as an elector who is disqualified for such registration by virtue of the Electoral Law.

Art. 64. A person shall be qualified to be a candidate for election as a Representative if at the time of the election that person:

(a) is a citizen of the Republic;

(b) has attained the age of twenty-five years;

(c) has not been, on or after the date of the coming into operation of this Constitution, convicted of an offence involving dishonesty or moral turpitude or is not under any disqualification imposed by a competent court for any electoral offence;

(d) is not suffering from a mental disease incapacitating such person from acting as a Representative.

Art. 65. 1. The term of office of the House of Representatives shall be for a period of five years.

The term of office of the first House of Representatives shall commence on the date of the coming into operation of this Constitution.

2. The outgoing House shall continue in office until the newly-elected House assumes office under paragraph 1 of this Article.

Art. 66. 1. A general election for the House of Representatives shall be held on the second Sunday of the month immediately preceding the month in which the term of office of the outgoing House expires.

2. When a vacancy occurs in the seat of a Representative such vacancy shall be filled by a by-election to be held within a period not exceeding forty-five days of the occurrence of such vacancy on a date to be fixed by the House of Representatives.

3. If an election under paragraph 1 or 2 of this Article cannot take place on the date fixed by or under this Constitution owing to extraordinary and unforeseen circumstances such as earthquake, floods, general epidemic and the like, then such election shall take place on the corresponding day of the week next following.

Art. 67. 1. The House of Representatives may dissolve itself only by its own decision carried by an absolute majority including at least one third of the Representatives elected by the Turkish Community.

2. Any such decision shall, notwithstanding anything contained in paragraph 1 of Article 65 and paragraph 1 of Article 66, provide for the date of the holding of the general election, which shall not be less than thirty days and not more than forty days from the date of such decision, and also for the date of the first meeting of the newly elected House which shall not be later than fifteen days after such general election and until such date the outgoing House shall continue to be in office.

3. Notwithstanding anything in paragraph 1 of Article 65 contained, the term of office of the House of Representatives to be elected after dissolution shall be for the unexpired period of the term of office of the dissolved House. In case of dissolution within the last year of the five years' term of office, a general election for the House of Representatives shall take place both for the unexpired part of the term of office of the dissolved House, during which any session of the newly elected House shall be considered to be an extraordinary session, and for the subsequent five years' term of office.

Art. 68. Whenever a House of Representatives continues to be in office until the assumption of office by a newly elected House under either paragraph 2 of Article 65 or paragraph 2 of Article 67, such House shall not have power to make any laws or to take any decisions on any matter except only in case of urgent and exceptional unforeseen circumstances to be specifically stated in the relevant law or decision.

Art. 69. A Representative before assuming duties as such in the House of Representatives and at a public meeting thereof shall make the following affirmation:

"I do solemnly affirm faith to, and respect for, the Constitution and the laws made thereunder, the preservation of the independence and the territorial integrity, of the Republic of Cyprus."

Art. 70. The office of a Representative shall be incompatible with that of a Minister or of a member of a Communal Chamber or of a member of any municipal council including a Mayor or of a member of the armed or security forces of the Republic or with a public or municipal office or, in the case of a Representative elected by the Turkish Community, of a religious functionary (*din adami*).

For the purposes of this Article "public office" means any office of profit in the service of the Republic or of a Communal Chamber the emoluments of which are under the control either of the Republic or of a Communal Chamber, and includes any office in any public corporation or public utility body.

Art. 71. The seat of a Representative shall become vacant:

(a) upon his death;

(b) upon his written resignation;

(c) upon the occurrence of any of the circumstances referred to in paragraph (c) or (d) of Article 64 or if he ceases to be a citizen of the Republic;

(d) upon his becoming the holder of an office mentioned in Article 70.

Art. 72. 1. The President of the House of Representatives shall be a Greek, and shall be elected by the Representatives elected by the Greek Community, and the Vice-President shall be a Turk and shall be elected by the Representatives elected by the Turkish Community. Each shall be elected separately as above at the same meeting at the beginning and for the whole period of the term of office of the House of Representatives.

2. In case of any vacancy in either of the offices provided in paragraph 1 of this Article, an election as provided in such paragraph shall take place with all due speed and at an extraordinary session if necessary in order to fill such vacancy.

3. In case of temporary absence or pending the filling of a vacancy as provided in paragraph 2 of this Article in either of the offices of the President or the Vice-President of the House, their functions shall be performed by the eldest Representative of the respective Community unless the Representatives of such Community should otherwise decide.

4. In addition to the President and the Vice-President of the House there shall be appointed from amongst the Representatives and by the President and the Vice-President of the House respectively two Greek and one Turkish Clerks of the House and two Greek and one Turkish Administrative Clerks of the House who shall be attached respectively to the office of the President and the Vice-President of the House.

Art. 73. 1. Subject to the ensuing provisions of this Article, the House of Representatives by its Standing Orders regulates any matter of parliamentary procedure and of functions of its offices.

2. There shall be a Committee to be known as the Committee of Selection consisting of the President of the House as Chairman, the Vice-President of the House as Vice-Chairman and eight other members elected by the House of Representatives at its meeting after the election of the President and the Vice-President of the House, six from amongst the Representatives elected by the Greek Community and two from amongst the Representatives elected by the Turkish Community.

3. The Committee of Selection shall set up the Standing Committees and any other temporary, *ad hoc* or special Committee of the House of Representatives and shall appoint Representatives to be members thereof and in so doing due regard should be had to the proposals made by the Greek and the Turkish Communal groups or political party groups in the House for such setting up and appointments. The appointments to such Committees shall be subject to the provisions of the paragraph next following.

4. The Greek and the Turkish Communal groups and political party

groups in the House of Representatives shall be adequately represented on each of the Standing, and of any other temporary, *ad hoc* or special, Committee of the House:

Provided that the total number of the seats on such Committees distributed respectively to the Representatives elected by the Greek and the Turkish Communities shall be in the same proportion as that in which the seats in the House are distributed to the Representatives elected by the Greek and the Turkish Communities respectively.

5. Every Bill on being introduced in the House of Representatives shall be referred for debate in the first instance before the appropriate Committee.

With the exception of those which are considered to be of an urgent nature, no Bill shall be debated by a Committee before the lapse of forty-eight hours after its being distributed to the Representatives constituting such a Committee.

With the exception of those which are considered to be of an urgent nature, no Bill which has passed the Committee stage shall be debated in the House of Representatives before the lapse of forty-eight hours after it has been distributed to the Representatives together with the report of the Committee.

6. The agenda of the meetings of the House of Representatives, which shall include any additional subject proposed by the Vice-President of the House, shall be drawn up and presented to the House of Representatives by the President of the House.

After the presentation of the agenda to the House of Representatives, any Representative may move any addition or amendment to such agenda, and such motion shall be decided upon by the House of Representatives.

7. No Representative can speak at any meeting of the House of Representatives unless he registers his name in the proper Register or unless he obtains the permission of the person presiding at such meeting.

Every Representative who has complied with such formality is entitled to be given reasonably sufficient time, having regard to the particular subject, to speak and to be heard at the relevant meeting.

The speeches shall be made in order of the registration or of oral request, as the case may be, of those who desire to speak:

Provided that where there are opposite views held, a speaker shall, as far as practicable, follow another one who supports the opposite view. But Representatives speaking on behalf of the Committees or of the political party groups of the House of Representatives shall not be subject to such order of precedence.

Representatives desiring to speak in connexion with motions with regard to any matter relating to the agenda, the application of the Standing Orders or the closure of the debate shall be given precedence in time over the Representatives desiring to speak in connexion with the subject of the debate, and in such a case two Representatives, one in favour and one against the motion, shall be allowed fifteen minutes each for their respective speeches.

8. All speeches in the House of Representatives shall be made from the rostrum of the House and addressed to the House of Representatives. All speeches and other proceedings in the House and at all the Committee meetings shall, simultaneously as they are being made or taking place, be translated from the official language in which they are being made or taking place into the other official language.

9. Save as otherwise provided in the Standing Orders, interruptions of the speech of a Representative or personal attacks against any Representative unconnected with the subject under debate, both in the House and at the Committee meetings, are prohibited.

10. The votes in the House of Representatives shall be jointly counted and recorded by one Greek and the Turkish Clerk of the House.

11. The minutes of the debates in the House of Representatives shall comprise all proceedings fully.

The minutes of the proceedings of the Committees shall be kept in a summary form. Upon objection to the minutes of a meeting of the House of Representatives through the oral submission of a Representative at the first following meeting or by a written objection sent to the President of the relevant meeting, the House of Representatives may decide to correct such minutes accordingly.

12. Any political party which is represented at least by twelve per centum of the total number of the Representatives in the House of Representatives can form and shall be entitled to be recognised as a political party group.

Art. 74. 1. The House of Representatives shall meet on the fifteenth day next following a general election and thereafter in each year on the corresponding day in such year without summons for its ordinary session.

2. The ordinary session of the House of Representatives shall last for a period of three to six months in each year, as the House of Representatives may determine.

3. The House of Representatives shall be summoned to an extraordinary session by the President or the Vice-President of the House on the request of ten Representatives addressed to both the President and the Vice-President of the House.

Art. 75. 1. The meetings of the House of Representatives shall be open to the public and the minutes of its debates shall be published.

2. The House of Representatives may, if it thinks necessary, hold secret sessions on a resolution carried by a three-quarters majority vote of the total number of Representatives.

Art. 76. 1. The President of the House shall declare the commencement and the end of every meeting.

2. The President of the House in declaring the end of a meeting shall at the same time announce the date and time fixed, with the consent of the House of Representatives, of the meeting next following and shall present to the House of Representatives the agenda of such meeting and thereupon the provisions of paragraph 6 of Article 73 shall apply.

3. Any agenda shall be printed and distributed to the Representatives at least twenty-four hours prior to the meeting, but if such agenda relates to the topic already under debate such distribution may be made at any time prior to the meeting.

Art. 77. 1. The quorum of the House of Representatives shall consist of at least one third of the total number of its members.

2. The debate relating to any particular topic shall be adjourned once for twenty-four hours at the request of the majority of the Representatives of either Community who are present at a meeting.

Art. 78. 1. The laws and the decisions of the House of Representatives shall be passed by a simple majority vote of the Representatives present and voting.

2. Any modification of the Electoral Law and the adoption of any law relating to the municipalities and of any law imposing duties or taxes shall require a separate simple majority of the Representatives elected by the Greek and the Turkish Communities respectively taking part in the vote.

Art. 79. 1. The President or the Vice-President of the Republic may address the House of Representatives by message, or transmit to the House of Representatives their views through the Ministers.

2. The Ministers may follow the proceedings of the House of Representatives or any Committee thereof, and make a statement to, or inform, the House of Representatives or any Committee thereof, on any subject within their competence.

Art. 80. 1. The right to introduce Bills belongs to the Representatives and to the Ministers.

2. No Bill relating to an increase in budgetary expenditure can be introduced by any Representative.

Art. 81. 1. The Budget is introduced to the House of Representatives at least three months before the day fixed by law for the commencement of the financial year and is voted by it not later than the day so fixed.

2. Within three months from the end of the financial year the final accounts shall be submitted to the House of Representatives for approval.

Art. 82. A law or decision of the House of Representatives shall come into operation on its publication in the official Gazette of the Republic unless another date is provided by such law or decision.

Art. 83. 1. Representatives shall not be liable to civil or criminal proceedings in respect of any statement made or vote given by them in the House of Representatives.

2. A Representative cannot, without the leave of the High Court, be

prosecuted, arrested or imprisoned so long as he continues to be a Representative. Such leave is not required in the case of an offence punishable with death or imprisonment for five years or more in case the offender is taken in the act. In such a case the High Court being notified forthwith by the competent authority decides whether it should grant or refuse leave for the continuation of the prosecution or detention so long as he continues to be a Representative.

3. If the High Court refuses to grant leave for the prosecution of a Representative, the period during which the Representative cannot thus be prosecuted shall not be reckoned for the purposes of any period of prescription for the offence in question.

4. If the High Court refuses to grant leave for the enforcement of a sentence of imprisonment imposed on a Representative by a competent court, the enforcement of such sentence shall be postponed until he ceases to be a Representative.

Art. 84. 1. Representatives receive from the Public Revenue remuneration defined by law.

2. Any increase of such remuneration shall not become operative during the term of office of the House of Representatives in which such increase has been made.

Art. 85. Any question with regard to the qualifications of candidates for election and election petitions shall be finally adjudicated by the Supreme Constitutional Court.

PART V

THE COMMUNAL CHAMBERS

Art. 86. The Greek and the Turkish Communities respectively shall elect from amongst their own members a Communal Chamber which shall have the competence expressly reserved for it under the provisions of this Constitution.

Art. 87. 1. The Communal Chambers shall, in relation to their respective Community, have competence to exercise within the limits of this Constitution and subject to paragraph 3 of this Article, legislative power solely with regard to the following matters:

(a) all religious matters;

(b) all educational, cultural and teaching matters;

(c) personal status;

(d) the composition and instances (*βαθμούς δικαιοδοσίας—dereceleri*) of courts dealing with civil disputes relating to personal status and to religious matters;

(e) in matters where the interests and institutions are of purely communal nature such as charitable and sporting foundations, bodies and associations created for the purpose of promoting the well-being of their respective Community;

(f) imposition of personal taxes and fees on members of their respective Community in order to provide for their respective needs and for the needs of bodies and institutions under their control as in Article 88 provided;

(g) in matters where subsidiary legislation in the form of regulations or bye-laws within the framework of the laws relating to municipalities will be necessary to enable a Communal Chamber to promote the aims pursued by municipalities composed solely of members of its respective Community;

(h) in matters relating to the exercise of the authority of control of producers' and consumers' co-operatives and credit establishments and of supervision in their functions of municipalities consisting solely of their respective Community, vested in them by this Constitution:

Provided that:

(i) any communal law, regulation, bye-law or decision made or taken by a Communal Chamber under this sub-paragraph (h) shall not directly or indirectly be contrary to or inconsistent with any law by which producers' and consumers' co-operatives and credit establishments are governed or to which the municipalities are subject;

(ii) nothing in paragraph (i) of this proviso contained shall be construed as enabling the House of Representatives to legislate on any matter relating to the exercise of the authority vested in a Communal Chamber under this sub-paragraph (h);

(i) in such other matters as are expressly provided by this Constitution.

2. Nothing in sub-paragraph (f) of paragraph 1 of this Article contained shall be construed as in any way curtailing the power of the House of Representatives to impose, in accordance with the provisions of this Constitution, any personal taxes.

3. Any law or decision of a Communal Chamber made or taken in exercise of the power vested in it under paragraph 1 of this Article shall not in any way contain anything contrary to the interests of the security of the Republic or the constitutional order or the public safety or the public order or the public health or the public morals or which is against the fundamental rights and liberties guaranteed by this Constitution to any person.

Art. 88. 1. The power of imposing taxes under sub-paragraph (f) of paragraph 1 of Article 87 of a Communal Chamber shall be exercised for the purposes of meeting the part of its expenditure provided in its budget in each financial year which is not met by the payment made to such Communal Chamber in respect of such financial year by the Republic out of its Budget as provided in paragraph 2 of this Article or by any other revenue which such Chamber may have in that financial year.

2. The House of Representatives shall, in respect of each financial year, provide in the Budget and make available for payment to both Communal Chambers in respect of their respective financial year for the purposes of their respective needs relating to matters within their respective competence an amount not less than two million pounds to be allocated to the Greek and the Turkish Communal Chambers as follows:

(a) to the Greek Communal Chamber an amount not less than the sum of one million and six hundred thousand pounds; and

(b) to the Turkish Communal Chamber an amount not less than the sum of four hundred thousand pounds:

Provided that in the case of the increase of the minimum total amount payable to both Communal Chambers the allocation to each of the Communal Chambers of such increased amount shall be made in such manner as the House of Representatives may decide.

3. If a Communal Chamber so requests the taxes imposed by it shall be collected on its behalf and paid to such a Communal Chamber by the authorities of the Republic.

4. For the purposes of this Article and of sub-paragraph (f) of paragraph 1 of Article 87 "member" includes corporate and unincorporate bodies to the extent of the interest held in such bodies by such members.

Art. 89. 1. The Communal Chambers shall, in relation to their respective Community, also have competence:

(a) (i) to direct policy ("*determiner les principes directeurs*") within their communal laws;

(ii) to exercise administrative powers in the manner and through such persons as may be provided by a communal law,

with respect to any matter on which they are competent to exercise legislative power under the provisions of Article 87 other than those provided in sub-paragraphs (g) and (h) of paragraph 1 of such Article for which specific provisions is made in the ensuing sub-paragraphs;

(b) to exercise control on producers' and consumers' co-operatives and credit establishments created for the purpose of promoting the well-being of their respective Community and which will be governed by the laws;

(c) to promote the aims pursued by municipalities composed solely of members of their respective Community and to supervise in their functions such municipalities to which the laws shall apply.

2. Nothing in sub-paragraph (e) of paragraph 1 of Article 87 and in sub-paragraph (b) of paragraph 1 of this Article contained shall be construed as precluding the creation of mixed and common institutions of the nature therein provided if the inhabitants so desire.

3. In the case where the central administration shall, on its part, proceed to control the institutions, establishments or municipalities mentioned in sub-paragraphs (b) and (c) of paragraph 1 of this Article by virtue of

legislation in force, such control shall be carried out through public officers belonging to the same Community as that to which the institution, establishment or municipality in question belongs.

Art. 90. 1. Subject to the ensuing provisions of this Article each Communal Chamber shall have power by or in its own communal laws to provide for the application (*ἐφαρμογή—tatbik*) of its laws and decisions.

2. A Communal Chamber shall have no power to provide in any of its laws or decisions for imprisonment or detention for any violation thereof or failure to comply with any directions given by a Communal Chamber in exercise of any power vested in it under this Constitution.

3. The Communal Chambers shall have no competence to use measures of constraint (*ἀναγκαστικά μέτρα—cebir*) to secure compliance with their respective communal laws or decisions and of the judgments of the Courts dealing with civil disputes relating to personal status and to religious matters within their respective competence.

4. Where it becomes necessary to use measures of constraint in compelling compliance with any law or decision of a Communal Chamber or with any matter connected with the exercise of the authority of control or supervision by a Communal Chamber such measures of constraint shall, on the application by or on behalf of the Communal Chamber, be applied by the public authorities of the Republic which shall have exclusive competence to apply such measures of constraint.

5. The execution of any judgment or order of a court in connexion with any matter within the exclusive competence of a Communal Chamber shall be carried out through the public authorities of the Republic.

Art. 91. 1. Each Communal Chamber shall once yearly prepare and adopt a budget of its revenue and expenditure for the ensuing financial year.

(2) Such budget shall be voted by the Communal Chamber not later than the day fixed by a communal law for the commencement of the communal financial year.

Art. 92. The number of the members of each Communal Chamber shall be determined by a communal law carried by a two-thirds majority of the total number of the members of the Communal Chamber concerned.

Art. 93. The elections for both the Communal Chambers shall be by universal suffrage and by direct and secret ballot.

Art. 94. 1. Subject to paragraph 2 of this Article every citizen of the Republic who has attained the age of twenty-one years and has such residential qualifications as may be prescribed by the respective communal electoral law shall have the right to be registered as an elector in the respective communal electoral list:

Provided that the members of the Greek Community shall only be registered in the Greek communal electoral list and the members of the Turkish Community shall only be registered in the Turkish communal electoral list.

2. No person shall be qualified to be registered as an elector who is disqualified for such registration by virtue of the respective communal electoral law.

Art. 95. A person shall be qualified to be a candidate for election as a member of a Communal Chamber if at the time of the election that person:

(a) is a citizen of the Republic and is registered in the respective communal electoral list;

(b) has attained the age of twenty-five years;

(c) has not been, on or after the date of the coming into operation of this Constitution, convicted of an offence involving dishonesty or moral turpitude or is not under any disqualification imposed by a competent court for an electoral offence;

(d) is not suffering from a mental disease incapacitating such person from acting as a member of a Communal Chamber.

Art. 96. 1. The term of office of the Communal Chambers shall be for a period of five years commencing on such date as a communal law respectively shall appoint.

2. The outgoing Communal Chambers shall continue in office until the newly elected Communal Chambers assume office under paragraph 1 of this Article.

Art. 97. 1. A communal general election for a Communal Chamber shall be held at least thirty days before the expiration of the term of office of the outgoing Chamber.

2. When a vacancy occurs in the seat of a member of a Communal Chamber such vacancy shall be filled by a by-election to be held within a period not exceeding forty-five days of the occurrence of such vacancy.

3. If an election under paragraph 1 or 2 of this Article cannot take place on the date fixed by or under this Constitution owing to extraordinary and unforeseen circumstances such as earthquake, floods, general epidemic and the like, then such election shall take place on the corresponding day of the week next following.

Art. 98. 1. Either Communal Chamber may dissolve itself only by its own decision carried by an absolute majority.

2. Any such decision shall, notwithstanding anything contained in paragraph 1 of Article 96 and paragraph 1 of Article 97, provide for the date of the holding of the communal general election with respect to the Communal Chamber in question which shall not be less than thirty days and not more than forty days from the date of such decision and also for the date of the first meeting of the newly-elected Communal Chamber which shall not be later than fifteen days after such communal general election and until such date the outgoing Communal Chamber shall continue to be in office.

3. Notwithstanding anything contained in paragraph 1 of Article 96, the term of office of the Communal Chamber to be elected after dissolution

shall be for the unexpired period of the term of office of the dissolved Communal Chamber. In case of dissolution within the last year of the five years' term of office of the Communal Chamber concerned a communal general election for such Chamber shall take place for the unexpired part of the term of office of the dissolved Communal Chamber and for the subsequent five years' period of office of such Communal Chamber.

Art. 99. Whenever a Communal Chamber continues to be in office until the assumption of office by a newly-elected Communal Chamber, either under paragraph 2 of Article 96 or paragraph 2 of Article 98, it shall not have power to make any laws or take any decisions on any matter except only in case of urgent and exceptional unforeseen circumstances to be specifically stated in the relevant law or decision.

Art. 100. A member of a Communal Chamber before assuming duties as such in the Communal Chamber and at a public meeting thereof shall make the following affirmation:

"I do solemnly affirm faith to, and respect for, the Constitution and the laws made thereunder, the preservation of the independence and the territorial integrity, of the Republic of Cyprus."

Art. 101. 1. The office of a member of a Communal Chamber shall be incompatible with that of a Minister or of a Representative or of a member of any municipal council including a Mayor or of a member of the armed or security forces of the Republic or with a public or municipal office and, in the case of that of a member of the Turkish Communal Chamber, with that of a religious functionary (*din adami*).

2. For the purposes of this Article "public office" means any office of profit in the public service of the Republic or of a Communal Chamber the emoluments of which are under the control either of the Republic or of a Communal Chamber and includes any office in any public corporation or public utility body.

Art. 102. The Communal Chambers shall, by Standing Orders, make rules relating to all matters of procedure including the holding of ordinary and extraordinary meetings, the dates and duration of such meetings, the manner of voting and the transaction of business.

Art. 103. 1. The meetings of the Communal Chambers shall be open to the public and the minutes of its debates shall be published.

2. Any Communal Chamber may, if it thinks necessary, hold secret sessions on a resolution carried by a two-thirds majority vote of the total number of its members.

Art. 104. 1. The laws or decisions passed by the Greek or the Turkish Communal Chamber shall be published in the official Gazette of the Republic immediately after being signed by the President or the Vice-President of the Republic respectively within fifteen days of the receipt by him of such laws or decisions.

2. A communal law shall come into operation on its publication in the

official Gazette of the Republic unless another date is provided by such law.

Art. 105. 1. The President of the Republic with regard to the Greek Communal Chamber and the Vice-President of the Republic with regard to the Turkish Communal Chamber may, within fifteen days of the receipt by him of any law or decision passed by the respective Communal Chamber, return such law or decision to such Chamber for reconsideration.

2. If the Communal Chamber concerned maintains that the law or decision so returned to it shall stand, the President or the Vice-President of the Republic, as the case may be, shall sign and publish such law or decision in accordance with the provisions of the immediately preceding Article.

Art. 106. 1. A member of a Communal Chamber shall not be liable to civil or criminal proceedings in respect of any statement made or vote given by him in the Chamber.

2. A member of a Communal Chamber cannot without the leave of the High Court, be prosecuted, arrested or imprisoned, so long as he continues to be a member. Such leave is not required in the case of an offence punishable with death or imprisonment for five years or more in case the offender is taken in the act. In such a case the High Court, being notified forthwith by the competent authority, decides whether it should grant or refuse leave for the continuation of the prosecution or detention, as the case may be, so long as he continues to be a member.

3. If the High Court refuses to grant leave for the prosecution of a member of a Communal Chamber, the period during which such member cannot thus be prosecuted shall not be reckoned for the purposes of any period of prescription for the offence in question.

4. If the High Court refuses to grant leave for the enforcement of a sentence of imprisonment imposed on a member of a Communal Chamber by a competent court, the enforcement of such sentence shall be postponed until he ceases to be such member.

Art. 107. The seat of a member of a Communal Chamber shall become vacant:

(a) upon his death; or

(b) upon his written resignation; or

(c) upon the occurrence of any of the circumstances referred to in paragraph (c) or (d) of Article 95, or if he ceases to be a citizen of the Republic or if he ceases to be qualified to be registered as an elector in the respective Communal electoral list; or

(d) upon his becoming the holder of an office mentioned in Article 101.

Art. 108. 1. The Greek and the Turkish Communities shall have the right to receive subsidies from the Greek or the Turkish Government respectively for institutions of education, culture, athletics and charity belonging to the Greek or the Turkish Community respectively.

2. Also where either the Greek or the Turkish Community considers that it has not the necessary number of schoolmasters, professors or clergymen (*κληρικοὶ—din adami*) for the functioning of its institutions, such Community shall have the right to obtain and employ such personnel to the extent strictly necessary to meet its needs as the Greek or the Turkish Government respectively may provide.

Art. 109. Each religious group which under the provisions of paragraph 3 of Article 2 has opted to belong to one of the Communities shall have the right to be represented, by elected member or members of such group, in the Communal Chamber of the Community to which such group has opted to belong as shall be provided by a relevant communal law.

Art. 110. 1. The Autocephalous Greek-Orthodox Church of Cyprus shall continue to have the exclusive right of regulating and administering its own internal affairs and property in accordance with the Holy Canons and its Charter in force for the time being and the Greek Communal Chamber shall not act inconsistently with such right.

2. The institution of *Vakf* and the Principles and Laws of, and relating to, *Vakfs* are recognised by this Constitution.

All matters relating to or in any way affecting the institution or foundation of *Vakf* or the *vakfs* or any *vakf* properties, including properties belonging to Mosques and any other Moslem religious institution, shall be governed solely by and under the Laws and Principles of *Vakfs* (*ahkâmül evkaf*) and the laws and regulations enacted or made by the Turkish Communal Chamber, and no legislative, executive or other act whatsoever shall contravene or override or interfere with such Laws or Principles of *Vakfs* and with such laws and regulations of the Turkish Communal Chamber.

3. Any right with regard to religious matters possessed in accordance with the law of the Colony of Cyprus in force immediately before the date of the coming into operation of this Constitution by the Church of a religious group to which the provisions of paragraph 3 of Article 2 shall apply shall continue to be so possessed by such Church on and after the date of the coming into operation of this Constitution.

Art. 111. 1. Subject to the provisions of this Constitution any matter relating to betrothal, marriage, divorce, nullity of marriage, judicial separation or restitution of conjugal rights or to family relations other than legitimation by order of the court or adoption of members of the Greek-Orthodox Church or of a religious group to which the provisions of paragraph 3 of Article 2 shall apply shall, on and after the date of the coming into operation of this Constitution, be governed by the law of the Greek-Orthodox Church or of the Church of such religious group, as the case may be, and shall be cognizable by a tribunal of such Church and no Communal Chamber shall act inconsistently with the provisions of such law.

2. Nothing in paragraph 1 of this Article contained shall preclude the

application of the provisions of paragraph 5 of Article 90 to the execution of any judgment or order of any such tribunal.

PART VI

THE INDEPENDENT OFFICERS OF THE REPUBLIC

Chapter I. The Attorney-General of the Republic and the Deputy Attorney-General of the Republic

Art. 112. 1. The President and the Vice-President of the Republic shall appoint jointly two persons who are qualified for appointment as a judge of the High Court one to be the Attorney-General of the Republic and the other to be the Deputy Attorney-General of the Republic:

Provided that the Attorney-General and the Deputy Attorney-General of the Republic shall not belong to the same Community.

2. The Attorney-General of the Republic shall be the Head and the Deputy Attorney-General of the Republic shall be the Deputy Head of the Law Office of the Republic which shall be an independent office and shall not be under any Ministry.

3. The Attorney-General and the Deputy Attorney-General of the Republic shall have the right of audience in, and shall take precedence over any other persons appearing before, any court:

Provided that the Attorney-General of the Republic shall always take precedence over the Deputy Attorney-General of the Republic.

4. The Attorney-General and the Deputy Attorney-General of the Republic shall be members of the permanent legal service of the Republic and shall hold office under the same terms and conditions as a judge of the High Court other than its President and shall not be removed from office except on the like grounds and in the like manner as such judge of the High Court.

5. In all matters affecting persons belonging to the Community of the Attorney-General of the Republic or of the Deputy Attorney-General of the Republic, as the case may be, the one belonging to such Community shall be consulted by the other before any decision is taken by the Attorney-General of the Republic:

Provided that for the prosecutions in the courts exercising criminal jurisdiction composed of judges of one Community, the Attorney-General of the Republic or the Deputy Attorney-General of the Republic, as the case may be, belonging to that Community, shall have the effective charge and responsibility.

Art. 113. 1. The Attorney-General of the Republic assisted by the Deputy Attorney-General of the Republic shall be the legal adviser of the Republic and of the President and of the Vice-President of the Republic and of the Council of Ministers and of the Ministers and shall exercise all such other powers and shall perform all such other functions and duties as are conferred or imposed on him by this Constitution or by law.

2. The Attorney-General of the Republic shall have power, exercisable at his discretion in the public interest, to institute, conduct, take over and continue or discontinue any proceedings for an offence against any person in the Republic. Such power may be exercised by him in person or by officers subordinate to him acting under and in accordance with his instructions.

Art. 114. 1. The Deputy Attorney-General of the Republic shall have such powers and shall perform such duties as normally appertain to his office and also shall, subject to the directions of the Attorney-General of the Republic, exercise all the powers and perform all the functions and the duties vested in the Attorney-General of the Republic under the provisions of this Constitution or by law.

2. The Deputy Attorney-General of the Republic shall act for the Attorney-General of the Republic in case of his absence or his temporary incapacity to perform his duties.

Chapter II. The Auditor-General and the Deputy Auditor-General

Art. 115. 1. The President and the Vice-President of the Republic shall appoint jointly two fit and proper persons one to be the Auditor-General and the other to be the Deputy Auditor-General:

Provided that the Auditor-General and the Deputy Auditor-General shall not belong to the same Community.

2. The Auditor-General shall be the Head and the Deputy Auditor-General shall be the Deputy Head of the Audit Office of the Republic which shall be an independent office and shall not be under any Ministry.

3. The Auditor-General and the Deputy Auditor-General shall be members of the permanent public service of the Republic and shall not be retired or removed from office except on the like grounds and in like manner as a judge of the High Court.

Art. 116. 1. The Auditor-General assisted by the Deputy Auditor-General shall, on behalf of the Republic, control all disbursements and receipts and audit and inspect all accounts of moneys and other assets administered, and of liabilities incurred, by or under the authority of the Republic and for this purpose he shall have the right of access to all books, records and returns relating to such accounts and to places where such assets are kept.

2. The Auditor-General assisted by the Deputy Auditor-General shall exercise all such other powers and shall perform all such other functions and duties as are conferred or imposed on him by law.

3. The powers, functions and duties of the Auditor-General provided in this Chapter may be exercised by him in person or by such subordinate officers acting under and in accordance with his instructions.

4. The Auditor-General shall submit annually a report on the exercise of his functions and duties under this Chapter to the President and the Vice-President of the Republic who shall cause it to be laid before the House of Representatives.

Art. 117. 1. The Deputy Auditor-General shall have such powers and shall perform such functions and duties as normally appertain to his office and also shall, subject to the directions of the Auditor-General, exercise all the powers and perform all the functions and duties vested in the Auditor-General under the provisions of this Constitution or by law.

2. The Deputy Auditor-General shall act for the Auditor-General in case of his absence or his temporary incapacity to perform his duties.

Chapter III. The Governor and the Deputy Governor of the Issuing Bank of the Republic

Art. 118. 1. The President and the Vice-President of the Republic shall appoint jointly two fit and proper persons one to be the Governor and the other to be the Deputy-Governor of the Issuing Bank of the Republic:

Provided that the Governor and the Deputy-Governor of the Issuing Bank of the Republic shall not belong to the same Community.

2. The Governor of the Issuing Bank of the Republic shall be the Head and the Deputy-Governor of the Issuing Bank shall be the Deputy Head of the Issuing Bank of the Republic which shall not be under any Ministry.

3. The Governor and the Deputy-Governor of the Issuing Bank of the Republic shall be either members of the permanent public service or shall be persons appointed under such terms and conditions as laid down in the instruments of their appointment.

4. The President and the Vice-President of the Republic acting jointly may, at any time, terminate the appointment of either the Governor or the Deputy-Governor of the Issuing Bank of the Republic or both as such Governor or Deputy-Governor, as the case may be.

5. In the case of such termination the Governor or the Deputy-Governor of the Issuing Bank of the Republic or both, as the case may be, shall, subject to paragraph 6 of this Article, and to the provisions of this Constitution relating to the public service of the Republic, be given other suitable post in the permanent public service of the Republic if such Governor or Deputy-Governor was, immediately before such termination, a member of such service.

6. Any disciplinary matter in connexion with the exercise of the functions of the Governor and the Deputy-Governor of the Issuing Bank of the

Republic shall be within the competence of the Council established under paragraph 8 of Article 153.

Art. 119. 1. The Governor of the Issuing Bank of the Republic assisted by the Deputy-Governor of the Issuing Bank of the Republic shall administer the currency laws of the Republic and shall be in charge of the management of the Issuing Bank of the Republic and shall exercise all other powers and perform all other functions and duties within the domain of the Issuing Bank of the Republic.

2. The Governor of the Issuing Bank of the Republic assisted by the Deputy-Governor of the Issuing Bank of the Republic shall exercise all such powers and shall perform all such other functions as are conferred or imposed on him by law.

3. The powers, functions and duties of the Governor of the Issuing Bank of the Republic provided in this Chapter may be exercised by him in person or by such subordinate officers acting under and in accordance with his instructions.

4. The Governor assisted by the Deputy-Governor of the Issuing Bank of the Republic shall, with regard to the financial policy relating to his office, carry out the decisions of the Council of Ministers in this respect and the provisions of any law and, with regard to the manner of the carrying out of such policy, he shall consult and be guided by the advice of the Minister of Finance.

5. The Governor of the Issuing Bank of the Republic shall submit half yearly reports on the state of currency, funds and securities of the Republic to the President and the Vice-President of the Republic who shall cause such reports to be laid before the House of Representatives.

Art. 120. 1. The Deputy-Governor of the Issuing Bank of the Republic shall have such powers and shall perform such functions and duties as normally appertain to his office and also shall, subject to the directions of the Governor of the Issuing Bank of the Republic, exercise all the powers and perform all the functions and duties vested in the Governor of the Issuing Bank of the Republic under the provisions of this Constitution or by law.

2. The Deputy-Governor of the Issuing Bank of the Republic shall act for the Governor of the Issuing Bank of the Republic in case of his absence or his temporary incapacity to perform his duties.

Art. 121. Nothing in this Chapter contained shall be construed as precluding the Issuing Bank of the Republic from becoming a Central Bank:

Provided that in such a case, subject to the provisions of this Chapter, the Governor and the Deputy-Governor of the Issuing Bank of the Republic shall be respectively the Governor and the Deputy-Governor of the Central Bank of the Republic.

PART VII

THE PUBLIC SERVICE

Chapter I. General

Art. 122. For the purposes of this Chapter, unless the context otherwise requires:

"public office" means an office in the public service;

"public officer" means the holder, whether substantive or temporary or acting, of a public office;

"public service" means any service under the Republic other than service in the army or the security forces of the Republic and includes service under the Cyprus Broadcasting Corporation, the Cyprus Inland Telecommunications Authority and the Electricity Authority of Cyprus and any other public corporate or unincorporate body created in the public interest by a law and either the funds of which are provided or guaranteed by the Republic or, if the enterprise is carried out exclusively by such body, its administration is carried out under the control of the Republic, but does not include service in an office the appointment to or the filling of which is, under this Constitution, made jointly by the President and the Vice-President of the Republic or service by workmen except those who are regularly employed in connexion with permanent works of the Republic or any such body as aforesaid.

Art. 123. 1. The public service shall be composed as to seventy per centum of Greeks and as to thirty per centum of Turks.

2. This quantitative distribution shall be applied, so far as this will be practically possible, in all grades of the hierarchy in the public service.

3. In regions or localities where one of the two Communities is in a majority approaching one hundred per centum the public officers posted for, or entrusted with, duty in such regions or localities shall belong to that Community.

Art. 124. 1. There shall be a Public Service Commission consisting of a Chairman and nine other members appointed jointly by the President and the Vice-President of the Republic.

2. Seven members of the Commission shall be Greeks and three members shall be Turks.

3. Each member of the Commission shall be appointed for a period of six years, but he may at any time resign his office by writing under his hand addressed to the President and the Vice-President of the Republic.

4. The remuneration and other conditions of service of a member of the Commission shall be provided by a law and shall not be altered to his disadvantage after his appointment.

5. A member of the Commission shall not be removed from office except

on the like grounds and in the like manner as a judge of the High Court.

6. (1) No person shall be appointed as a member of the Commission unless he is a citizen of the Republic, of high moral character and has the qualifications for election as a member of the House of Representatives.

(2) No person shall be appointed as, or be, a member of the Commission who is, or within the preceding twelve months in the case of the Chairman or six months in the case of any other member, has been:

(a) a Minister;

(b) a member of the House of Representatives or of any Communal Chamber;

(c) a public officer or a member of any of the armed forces;

(d) an officer or employee of any local authority or of a body corporate or authority established by law for public purposes;

(e) a member of a trade union or of a body or association affiliated to a trade union.

7. Where, during any period, a member of the Commission has been granted leave of absence or is unable, owing to absence from the Republic, or to any other cause, to discharge his functions as a member, the President and the Vice-President of the Republic may jointly appoint at his place any person who would be qualified to be appointed to exercise such functions, during that period.

Art. 125. 1. Save where other express provision is made in this Constitution with respect to any matter set out in this paragraph and subject to the provisions of any law, it shall be the duty of the Public Service Commission to make the allocation of public office between the two Communities and to appoint, confirm, emplace on the permanent or pensionable establishment, promote, transfer, retire and exercise disciplinary control over, including dismissal or removal from office of, public officers.

2. The Chairman shall convene the meetings of the Commission and shall preside thereat:

Provided that:

(a) no meeting shall be held unless prior notice thereof has been given to all the members;

(b) on an equality of votes the Chairman shall not have a second or casting vote.

3. (1) Subject to the ensuing provisions of this paragraph any decision of the Commission shall be taken by an absolute majority vote of its members.

(2) If the question relates to an appointment or promotion to fill a vacant or newly created post, the decision whether such post shall be filled, under the provisions of this Constitution, by a Greek or a Turk, shall be taken by such absolute majority vote including at least the votes of two Turkish members of the Commission:

Provided that if such a decision cannot be taken on such majority, the question shall be referred by the Commission to the Supreme Constitutional Court for a decision; the decision of such Court shall be final and binding on the Commission.

(3) Where the question relates solely to a Turk any decision of the Commission shall be taken by such an absolute majority vote including the votes of at least two Turkish members. Where the question relates solely to a Greek, any decision of the Commission shall be taken by such an absolute majority vote including the votes of at least four Greek members.

(4) Where the question relates to the selection of the Greek or the Turk to be appointed or promoted, the decision shall, subject to sub-paragraph (3) of this paragraph, be taken by an absolute majority vote:

Provided that the unanimous recommendation, of five Greek members in the case of the selection of a Greek, or of the three Turkish members in the case of the selection of a Turk, shall be acted upon by the Commission.

Chapter II. The Accountant-General and the Deputy Accountant-General

Art. 126. 1. The President and the Vice-President of the Republic shall appoint jointly two fit and proper persons one to be the Accountant-General and the other to be the Deputy Accountant-General:

Provided that the Accountant-General and the Deputy Accountant-General shall not belong to the same Community.

2. The Accountant-General shall be the Head and the Deputy Accountant-General shall be the Deputy Head of the Treasury.

3. The Accountant-General and the Deputy Accountant-General shall be members of the permanent public service of the Republic.

4. The retirement and any disciplinary control, including dismissal or removal from office, of the Accountant-General and the Deputy Accountant-General shall be within the competence of the Public Service Commission.

Art. 127. 1. The Accountant-General assisted by the Deputy Accountant-General shall manage and supervise all accounting operations in respect of all moneys and other assets administered, and of liabilities incurred, by or under the authority of the Republic and, subject to the provisions of this Constitution or of any law, shall receive and make all the disbursements of moneys of the Republic.

2. The Accountant-General assisted by the Deputy Accountant-General shall exercise all such other powers and shall perform all such other functions and duties as are conferred or imposed on him by law.

3. The powers, functions and duties of the Accountant-General provided in this Chapter may be exercised by him in person or by such subordinate officers acting under and in accordance with his instructions.

Art. 128. 1. The Deputy Accountant-General shall have such powers and shall perform such functions and duties as normally appertain to his office and also shall, subject to the directions of the Accountant-General, exercise all the powers and perform all the functions and duties vested in the Accountant-General under the provisions of this Constitution or by law.

2. The Deputy Accountant-General shall act for the Accountant-General in case of his absence or his temporary incapacity to perform his duties.

PART VIII

THE FORCES OF THE REPUBLIC

Art. 129. 1. The Republic shall have an army of two thousand men of whom sixty per centum shall be Greeks and forty per centum shall be Turks.

2. Compulsory military service shall not be instituted except by common agreement of the President and the Vice-President of the Republic.

Art. 130. 1. The security forces of the Republic shall consist of the police and gendarmerie and shall have a contingent of two thousand men which may be reduced or increased by common agreement of the President and the Vice-President of the Republic.

2. The security forces of the Republic shall be composed as to seventy per centum of Greeks and as to thirty per centum of Turks:

Provided that for an initial period and in order not to discharge those Turks serving in the police on the 11th February, 1959, except those serving in the auxiliary police, the percentage of Turks may be kept up to a maximum of forty per centum and consequently that of the Greeks may be reduced to sixty per centum.

Art. 131. 1. The Heads and Deputy Heads of the army, the police and the gendarmerie of the Republic shall be appointed jointly by the President and the Vice-President of the Republic.

2. One of the Heads of the army, the police and the gendarmerie shall be a Turk and where the Head of the army, the police and the gendarmerie belongs to one Community the Deputy Head shall belong to the other Community.

Art. 132. Forces which are stationed in parts of the territory of the Republic inhabited in a proportion approaching one hundred per centum only by members of one Community shall belong to that Community.

PART IX

THE SUPREME CONSTITUTIONAL COURT

Art. 133. 1. (1) There shall be a Supreme Constitutional Court of the Republic composed of a Greek, a Turk and a neutral judge. The neutral judge shall be the President of the Court.

(2) The President and the other judges of the Supreme Constitutional Court shall be appointed jointly by the President and the Vice-President of the Republic:

Provided that in the case of a vacancy solely in the post of either the Greek or the Turkish judge the proposal of the President or the Vice-President of the Republic to whose Community the judge to be appointed shall belong shall prevail if the President and the Vice-President of the Republic do not agree on the appointment within a week of such proposal.

2. The seat of the Supreme Constitutional Court shall be in the capital of the Republic.

3. The neutral judge shall not be a subject or a citizen of the Republic or of the Kingdom of Greece or of the Republic of Turkey or of the United Kingdom and the Colonies.

4. The Greek and the Turkish judge of the Supreme Constitutional Court shall be a citizen of the Republic.

5. The President and the other judges of the Supreme Constitutional Court shall be appointed from amongst lawyers of high professional and moral standard.

6. (1) The President of the Court shall be appointed for a period of six years.

(2) The remuneration and other conditions of service of the President of the Court shall be laid down in the instrument of his appointment.

(3) The conditions of service of the President of the Court to be laid down in the instrument of his appointment as provided in sub-paragraph (2) of this paragraph shall include:

(a) provision for this retirement on the same grounds as those on which the Greek or the Turkish judge may be retired under sub-paragraph (3) of paragraph 7 of this Article; and

(b) provision for his dismissal on the same grounds as those on which such Greek or Turkish judge may be dismissed under sub-paragraph (4) of paragraph 7 of this Article.

7. (1) The Greek and the Turkish judge of the Court shall be permanent members of the judicial service of the Republic and shall hold office until they attain the age of sixty-eight.

(2) Without prejudice to any retirement pension, gratuity or any other like benefit he may have acquired under the provisions of any law, the reek or the Turkish judge of the Court may at any time resign his office

by writing under his hand addressed to the President and the Vice-President of the Republic.

(3) The Greek or the Turkish judge of the Court shall be retired on account of such mental or physical incapacity or infirmity as would render him incapable of discharging the duties of his office either permanently or for such period of time as would render it impracticable for him to continue in office. A judge so retired shall be entitled to all benefits and emoluments provided by any law in force the time being.

(4) The Greek or the Turkish judge of the Court may be dismissed on the ground of misconduct.

8. (1) There shall be established a Council consisting of the President of the High Court as Chairman and the senior in appointment Greek judge and the Turkish judge of the High Court as members.

(2) This Council shall have exclusive competence to determine all matters relating to:

(a) the retirement, dismissal or otherwise the termination of the appointment of the President of the Court in accordance with the conditions of service laid down in the instrument of his appointment;

(b) the retirement or dismissal of the Greek or the Turkish judge of the Court on any of the grounds provided in sub-paragraphs (3) and (4) of paragraph 7 of this Article.

(3) The proceedings of the Council under sub-paragraph (2) of this paragraph shall be of a judicial nature and the judge concerned shall be entitled to be heard and present his case before the Council.

(4) The decision of the Council taken by a majority shall be binding upon the President and the Vice-President of the Republic who shall jointly act accordingly.

9. In the case of temporary absence or incapacity of the President or of the Greek judge or of the Turkish judge of the Court, the President of the High Court or the senior in appointment of the two Greek judges or the Turkish judge thereof respectively shall act in his place during such temporary absence or incapacity.

10. No action shall be brought against the President or any other judge of the Court for any act done or words spoken in his judicial capacity.

11. The remuneration and other conditions of service of the Greek and the Turkish judge of the Court shall be fixed by a law.

12. The remuneration and other conditions of service of any judge of the Court shall not be altered to his disadvantage after his appointment.

Art. 134. 1. The sittings of the Supreme Constitutional Court for the hearing of all proceedings shall be public but the Court may hear any proceedings in the presence only of the parties, if any, and the officers of the Court if it considers that such a course will be in the interest of the orderly conduct of the proceedings or if the security of the Republic or public morals so require.

2. When a recourse appears to be *prima facie* frivolous the Court may, after hearing arguments by or on behalf of the parties concerned, unanimously dismiss such recourse without a public hearing if satisfied that such recourse is in fact frivolous.

Art. 135. The Supreme Constitutional Court shall make Rules of Court for regulating the practice and procedure of the Court in the exercise of jurisdiction conferred upon it by this Constitution, for prescribing forms and fees in respect of proceedings in the Court and for prescribing and regulating the composition of its registry and the powers and the duties of the officers thereof.

Art. 136. The Supreme Constitutional Court shall have exclusive jurisdiction to adjucate finally on all matters as provided in the ensuing Articles.

Art. 137. 1. The President and the Vice-President of the Republic, either separately or conjointly, shall have a right of recourse to the Supreme Constitutional Court under the provisions of this Article on the ground that any law or decision of the House of Representatives or any provision thereof discriminates against either of the two Communities.

2. A recourse under paragraph 1 of this Article shall be made within seventy-five days of the promulgation of any such law or decision.

3. Notice of the filing of such a recourse shall be published in the official Gazette of the Republic by the President and the Vice-President of the Republic within a period of twenty-four hours from such filing. Upon the publication of such notification in the official Gazette of the Republic the operation of such law or decision shall be suspended from the day following such publication until the Supreme Constitutional Court determines such recourse.

4. Upon such recourse the Court may confirm or annul such law or decision or any provision thereof or return it to the House of Representatives for reconsideration, in whole or in part:

Provided that in the case of annulment of a law or decision or any provision thereof such annulment shall operate from the date of the publication of the decision of the Supreme Constitutional Court under paragraph 5 of this Article without prejudice to anything done or left undone under such law or decision or provision thereof.

5. The decision of the Court shall be notified forthwith to the President and the Vice-President of the Republic and to the President and the Vice-President of the House of Representatives and shall be published forthwith by the President and the Vice-President of the Republic in the official Gazette of the Republic.

Art. 138. 1. Where on the adoption of the Budget by the House of Representatives the President and the Vice-President of the Republic, either separately or conjointly, has or have exercised his or their right to return it to the House of Representatives on the ground that in his or their judgment there is a discrimination and the House has persisted in its decision, the President and the Vice-President of the Republic, either separately or conjointly, as the case may be, shall have a right of recourse to the Supreme Constitutional Court on such ground.

2. Such recourse shall be made within the period fixed by this Constitution for the promulgation of the laws or decisions of the House of Representatives.

3. Upon such a recourse the Court may annul or confirm the Budget or return it to the House of Representatives, in whole or in part.

4. The decision of the Court shall be notified forthwith to the President and the Vice-President of the Republic and to the President and the Vice-President of the House of Representatives and shall be published forthwith by the President and the Vice-President of the Republic in the official Gazette of the Republic.

Art. 139. 1. The Supreme Constitutional Court shall have jurisdiction to adjudicate finally on a recourse made in connexion with any matter relating to any conflict or contest of power or competence arising between the House of Representatives and the Communal Chambers or any one of them and between any organs of, or authorities in, the Republic:

Provided that nothing in this paragraph contained shall apply to any conflict or contest between any courts or judicial authorities in the Republic, which conflict or contest shall be decided by the High Court.

For the purposes of this paragraph the expression "courts or judicial authorities in the Republic" does not include the Supreme Constitutional Court.

2. Where any question arises as to the competence of the Supreme Constitutional Court regarding any matter, such question shall be determined by the Supreme Constitutional Court.

3. Recourse to the Court under paragraph 1 of this Article may be made by:

(a) the President or the Vice-President of the Republic; or

(b) the House of Representatives; or

(c) one of, or both the Communal Chambers; or

(d) any other organ of, or authority in, the Republic,

if involved in such conflict or contest.

4. Such recourse shall be made within thirty days of the date when such power or competence is contested.

5. Upon such a recourse the Court may declare that the law or the decision or the act, the subject or the recourse, is void, either from the time when the conflict or contest arose or *ab initio*, and without any legal effect whatsoever, either in whole or in part, on the ground that such law or decision or act was made or taken or done without power or competence, and in either case the Court may give directions as to the effect of anything done or left undone under such law or decision or act.

6. Any decision of the Court upon such recourse shall be forthwith noti-

fied to the parties concerned and to the President and the Vice-President of the Republic who shall forthwith publish it in the official Gazette of the Republic.

7. Upon a recourse under this Article the Court may order that the operation of the law or decision or act, as the case may be, which is the subject matter of such recourse, shall be suspended until the determination of the recourse; such order shall be published forthwith in the official Gazette of the Republic.

Art. 140. 1. The President and the Vice-President of the Republic acting jointly may, at any time prior to the promulgation of any law or decision of the House of Representatives, refer to the Supreme Constitutional Court for its opinion the question as to whether such law or decision or any specified provision thereof is repugnant to or inconsistent with any provision of this Constitution, otherwise than on the ground that such law or decision or any provision thereof discriminates against either of the two Communities.

2. The Supreme Constitutional Court shall consider every question referred to it under paragraph 1 of this Article and having heard arguments on behalf of the President and the Vice-President of the Republic and on behalf of the House of Representatives shall give its opinion on such question and notify the President and the Vice-President of the Republic and the House of Representatives accordingly.

3. In case the Supreme Constitutional Court is of the opinion that such law or decision or any provision thereof is repugnant to or inconsistent with any provision of this Constitution such law or decision or such provision thereof shall not be promulgated by the President and the Vice-President of the Republic.

Art. 141. 1. The President or the Vice-President of the Republic may, at any time prior to the promulgation of any law imposing any formalities, conditions or restrictions on the right guaranteed by Article 25, refer to the Supreme Constitutional Court for its opinion the question as to whether such formality, condition or restriction is not in the public interest or is contrary to the interests of his Community.

2. The Supreme Constitutional Court shall consider such question and having heard arguments on behalf of the President or the Vice-President of the Republic, as the case may be, and on behalf of the House of Representatives shall give its opinion and notify the President and the Vice-President of the Republic and the House of Representatives accordingly.

3. In case the Supreme Constitutional Court is of opinion that such formality, condition or restriction is not in the public interest or is contrary to the interests of such Community such law or any provision thereof prescribing such formality, condition or restriction shall not be promulgated by the President and the Vice-President of the Republic.

Art. 142. 1. The President of the Republic with regard to any law or decision of the Greek Communal Chamber and the Vice-President of the Republic with regard to any law or decision of the Turkish Communal Chamber, may, at any time prior to the publication of such law or decision, refer to the Supreme Constitutional Court for its opinion the question as to whether such law or decision or any specified provision thereof is repugnant to or inconsistent with any provision of this Constitution.

2. The Supreme Constitutional Court shall consider every question referred to it under paragraph 1 of this Article and having heard arguments on behalf of the President or the Vice-President of the Republic, as the case may be, and on behalf of the Communal Chamber concerned, shall give its opinion on such question and notify accordingly the President or the Vice-President of the Republic, as the case may be, and the Communal Chamber concerned.

3. In case the Supreme Constitutional Court is of the opinion that such law or decision or any provision thereof is repugnant to or inconsistent with any provision of this Constitution such law or decision or such provision thereof shall not be published by the President or the Vice-President of the Republic, as the case may be.

Art. 143. 1. The President or the Vice-President of the Republic or Representatives consisting of at least one fifth of the total number of a newly-elected House of Representatives shall have a right of recourse to the Supreme Constitutional Court on the question whether there exist such urgent and exceptional unforeseen circumstances as to justify a House of Representatives which continues to be in office until the assumption of office of a newly-elected House to make any laws or take any decisions as in Article 68 provided.

2. Such recourse, if made by the President or the Vice-President of the Republic shall be made within the period provided by this Constitution for the promulgation of the laws and decisions of the House of Representatives, and if made by such Representatives shall be made within fifteen days of the date when the new House first meets.

3. The decision of the Court shall be notified forthwith to the President and the Vice-President of the Republic and to the President and the Vice-President of the House of Representatives and shall be published forthwith by the President and the Vice-President of the Republic in the official Gazette of the Republic.

Art. 144. 1. A party to any judicial proceedings, including proceedings on appeal, may, at any stage thereof, raise the question of the unconstitutionality of any law or decision or any provision thereof material for the determination of any matter at issue in such proceedings and thereupon the Court before which such question is raised shall reserve the question for the decision of the Supreme Constitutional Court and stay further proceedings until such question is determined by the Supreme Constitutional Court.

2. The Supreme Constitutional Court, on a question so reserved, shall, after hearing the parties, consider and determine the question so reserved and transmit its decision to the Court by which such question has been reserved.

3. Any decision of the Supreme Constitutional Court under paragraph 2 of this Article shall be binding on the court by which the question has been reserved and on the parties to the proceedings and shall, in case such decision is to the effect that the law or decision or any provision thereof is unconstitutional, operate as to make such law or decision inapplicable to such proceedings only.

Art. 145. The Supreme Constitutional Court shall have exclusive jurisdiction to adjudicate finally on any election petition, made under the provisions of the Electoral Law, with regard to the elections of the President or the Vice-President of the Republic or of members of the House of Representatives or of any Communal Chamber.

Art. 146. 1. The Supreme Constitutional Court shall have exclusive jurisdiction to adjudicate finally on a recourse made to it on a complaint that a decision, an act or omission of any organ, authority or person, exercising any executive or administrative authority is contrary to any of the provisions of this Constitution or of any law or is made in excess or in abuse of powers vested in such organ or authority or person.

2. Such a recourse may be made by a person whose any existing legitimate interest, which he has either as a person or by virtue of being a member of a Community, is adversely and directly affected by such decision or act or omission.

3. Such a recourse shall be made within seventy-five days of the date when the decision or act was published or, if not published and in the case of an omission, when it came to the knowledge of the person making the recourse.

4. Upon such a recourse the Court may, by its decision:

(a) confirm, either in whole or in part, such decision or act or omission; or

(b) declare, either in whole or in part, such decision or act to be null and void and of no effect whatsoever; or

(c) declare that such omission, either in whole or in part, ought not to have been made and that whatever has been omitted should have been performed.

5. Any decision given under paragraph 4 of this Article shall be binding on all courts and all organs or authorities in the Republic and shall be given effect to and acted upon by the organ or authority or person concerned.

6. Any person aggrieved by any decision or act declared to be void under paragraph 4 of this Article or by any omission declared thereunder that it ought not to have been made shall be entitled, if his claim is not

met to his satisfaction by the organ, authority or person concerned, to institute legal proceedings in a court for the recovery of damages or for being granted other remedy and to recover just and equitable damages to be assessed by the court or to be granted such other just and equitable remedy as such court is empowered to grant.

Art. 147. The Supreme Constitutional Court shall have exclusive jurisdiction to adjudicate finally on a motion made by the Attorney-General and the Deputy Attorney-General of the Republic, in accordance with the provisions of paragraph 3 of Article 44, with regard to the question of the existence of such permanent or temporary incapacity, or absence, otherwise than temporary, of the President or the Vice-President of the Republic, as would prevent him to perform effectively his duties as in sub-paragraph (d) of paragraph 1 of Article 44 provided.

Art. 148. Subject to the provisions of paragraph 3 of Article 144, any decision of the Supreme Constitutional Court on any matter within its jurisdiction or competence shall be binding on all courts, organs, authorities and persons in the Republic.

Art. 149. The Supreme Constitutional Court shall have exclusive jurisdiction:

(a) to determine any conflict between the two texts of this Constitution by reference to the text of the draft of this Constitution signed at Nicosia on the 6th April, 1960, in the Joint Constitutional Commission together with the schedule of amendments thereto signed on 6 July 1960, by representatives of the Kingdom of Greece, the Republic of Turkey and the Greek and Turkish Cypriot communities, due regard being had to the letter and spirit of the Zurich Agreement dated the 11th February, 1959, and of the London Agreement dated the 19th of February, 1959;

(b) to make, in case of ambiguity, any interpretation of this Constitution, due regard being had to the letter and spirit of the Zurich Agreement dated the 11th February, 1959, and of the London Agreement dated the 19th February, 1959.

Art. 150. The Supreme Constitutional Court shall have jurisdiction to punish for contempt of itself.

Art. 151. 1. Notwithstanding anything in the foregoing provisions of this Part, the Supreme Constitutional Court shall have exclusive competence to decide finally on a reference made to it by the Public Service Commission under sub-paragraph (2) of paragraph 3 of Article 125.

2. Nothing in this Article contained shall preclude any recourse to the Supreme Constitutional Court under Article 146 on a complaint concerning any decision, act or omission of the Public Service Commission.

PART X

THE HIGH COURT AND THE SUBORDINATE COURTS

Art. 152. 1. The judicial power, other than that exercised under Part IX by the Supreme Constitutional Court and under paragraph 2 of this Article by the courts provided by a communal law, shall be exercised by a High Court of Justice and such inferior courts as may, subject to the provisions of this Constitution, be provided by a law made thereunder.

2. The judicial power with respect to civil disputes relating to personal status and to religious matters which are reserved under Article 87 for the Communal Chambers shall be exercised by such courts as a communal law made under the provisions of this Constitution shall provide.

Art. 153. 1. (1) There shall be a High Court of Justice composed of two Greek judges, one Turkish judge and a neutral judge. The neutral judge shall be the President of the Court and shall have two votes.

(2) The President and the other judges of the High Court shall be appointed jointly by the President and the Vice-President of the Republic:

Provided that in the case of a vacancy solely in the post of either a Greek judge or the Turkish judge the proposal of the President or the Vice-President of the Republic to whose Community the judge to be appointed shall belong shall prevail if the President and the Vice-President of the Republic do not agree on the appointment within a week of such proposal.

2. The seat of the High Court shall be in the capital of the Republic.

3. The neutral judge shall not be a subject or a citizen of the Republic or of the Kingdom of Greece or of the Republic of Turkey or of the United Kingdom and the Colonies.

4. The Greek judges and the Turkish judge of the High Court shall be citizens of the Republic.

5. The President and the other judges of the High Court shall be appointed from amongst lawyers of high professional and moral standard.

6. (1) The President of the High Court shall be appointed for a period of six years.

(2) The remuneration and other conditions of service of the President of the High Court shall be laid down in the instrument of his appointment.

(3) The conditions of service of the President of the High Court to be laid down in the instrument of his appointment as provided in sub-paragraph (2) of this paragraph shall include:

(a) provision for his retirement on the same grounds as those on which a Greek or the Turkish judge may be retired under sub-paragraph (3) of aragraph 7 of this Article; and

(b) provision for his dismissal on the same grounds as those on which such Greek or Turkish judge may be dismissed under sub-paragraph (4) of paragraph 7 of this Article.

7. (1) The Greek judges and the Turkish judge of the High Court shall be permanent members of the judicial service of the Republic and shall hold office until they attain the age of sixty-eight.

(2) Without prejudice to any retirement pension, gratuity or any other like benefit he may have acquired under the provisions of any law, any Greek judge or the Turkish judge of the High Court may at any time resign his office by writing under his hand addressed to the President and the Vice-President of the Republic.

(3) Any Greek or the Turkish judge of the High Court shall be retired on account of such mental or physical incapacity or infirmity as would render him incapable of discharging the duties of his office either permanently or for such period of time as would render it impracticable for him to continue in office. A judge so retired shall be entitled to all benefits and emoluments provided by any law in force for the time being.

(4) A Greek or the Turkish judge of the High Court may be dismissed on the ground of misconduct.

8. (1) There shall be established a Council consisting of the President of the Supreme Constitutional Court as Chairman and the Greek and the Turkish judge of the Supreme Constitutional Court as members.

(2) This Council shall have exclusive competence to determine all matters relating to:

(a) the retirement, dismissal or otherwise the termination of the appointment of the President of the High Court in accordance with the conditions of service laid down in the instrument of his appointment;

(b) the retirement or dismissal of any Greek judge or the Turkish judge of the High Court on any of the grounds provided in sub-paragraphs (3) and (4) of paragraph 7 of this Article.

(3) The proceedings of the Council under sub-paragraph (2) of this paragraph shall be of a judicial nature and the judge concerned shall be entitled to be heard and present his case before the Council.

(4) The decision of the Council taken by a majority shall be binding upon the President and the Vice-President of the Republic who shall jointly act accordingly.

9. In the case of temporary absence or incapacity of the President of the High Court or of one of the Greek judges or of the Turkish judge thereof the President of the Supreme Constitutional Court or the Greek judge or the Turkish judge thereof respectively shall act in his place during such temporary absence or incapacity:

Provided that if it is impracticable or inconvenient for the Greek or the Turkish judge of the Supreme Constitutional Court to act, the senior in office Greek or Turkish judge in the judicial service of the Republic shall so act respectively.

10. No action shall be brought against the President or any other judge of the High Court for any act done or words spoken in his judicial capacity.

11. The remuneration and other conditions of service of the Greek judges and of the Turkish judge of the High Court shall be fixed by a law.

12. The remuneration and other conditions of service of any judge of the High Court shall not be altered to his disadvantage after his appointment.

Art. 154. The sittings of the High Court for the hearing of all proceedings shall be public but the court may hear any proceedings in the presence only of the parties, if any, and the officers of the court if it considers that such a course will be in the interest of the orderly conduct of the proceedings or if the security of the Republic or public morals so require.

Art. 155. 1. The High Court shall be the highest appellate court in the Republic and shall have jurisdiction to hear and determine, subject to the provisions of this Constitution and of any Rules of Court made thereunder, all appeals from any court other than the Supreme Constitutional Court.

2. Subject to paragraphs 3 and 4 of this Article the High Court shall have such original and revisional jurisdiction as is provided by this Constitution or as may be provided by a law:

Provided that where original jurisdiction is so conferred, such jurisdiction shall, subject to Article 159, be exercised by such judge or judges of the High Court as the High Court shall determine:

Provided further that there shall be a right of appeal to the High Court from their decision.

3. The High Court shall, to the exclusion of any other court, determine the composition of the court which is to try a civil case where the plaintiff and the defendant belong to different Communities and of the court which is to try a criminal case in which the accused and the injured party belong to different Communities. Such court shall be composed of judges belonging to both the Greek and the Turkish Communities.

4. The High Court shall have exclusive jurisdiction to issue orders in the nature of *habeas corpus*, *mandamus*, prohibition, *quo warranto* and *certiorari*.

Art. 156. The following offences in the first instance shall be tried by a court composed of such judges belonging to both Communities as the High Court shall determine presided over by the President of the High Court:

(a) treason and other offences against the security of the Republic;

(b) offences against the Constitution and the constitutional order:

Provided that in the appeal from any decision of such court the High Court shall be presided over by the President of the Supreme Constitutional Court in the place of the President of the High Court and in such a case the President of the Supreme Constitutional Court shall have all the powers vested in the President of the High Court.

Art. 157. 1. Save as otherwise provided in this Constitution with regard to the Supreme Constitutional Court, the High Court shall be the Supreme Council of Judicature, and its President shall have two votes.

2. The appointment, promotion, transfer, termination of appointment, dismissal and disciplinary matters of judicial officers are exclusively within the competence of the Supreme Council of Judicature.

3. No judicial officer shall be retired or dismissed except on the like grounds and in the same manner as a judge of the High Court.

Art. 158. 1. A law shall, subject to the provisions of this Constitution, provide for the establishment, jurisdiction and powers of courts of civil and criminal jurisdiction other than courts to be provided by a communal law under Article 160.

2. Any such law shall provide for the establishment of adequate courts in sufficient number for the proper and undelayed administration of justice and for securing within the limits of their respective competence the efficient application of the provisions of this Constitution guaranteeing the fundamental rights and liberties.

3. A law shall provide for the remuneration and other conditions of service of the judges of the courts to be established under paragraph 1 of this Article. The remuneration and other conditions of service of any such judge shall not be altered to this disadvantage after his appointment.

Art. 159. 1. A court exercising civil jurisdiction in a case where the plaintiff and the defendant belong to the same Community shall be composed solely of a judge or judges belonging to that Community.

2. A court exercising criminal jurisdiction in a case where the accused and the person injured belong to the same Community, or where there is no person injured, shall be composed of a judge or judges belonging to that Community.

3. Where in a civil case the plaintiff and the defendant belong to different Communities the court shall be composed of such judges belonging to both Communities as the High Court shall determine.

4. Where in a criminal case the accused and the person injured belong to different Communities the court shall be composed of such judges belonging to both Communities as the High Court shall determine.

5. A coroner's inquest where the deceased belonged to the Greek Community shall be conducted by a Greek coroner and where the deceased belonged to the Turkish Community shall be conducted by a Turkish coroner. In case there are more than one deceased belonging to different Communities the inquest shall be conducted by such coroner as the High Court may direct.

6. The execution of any judgment or order of a court exercising civil or criminal jurisdiction, if the court is composed of a Greek judge or Greek judges shall be carried out through Greek officers of the court, if the court is composed of a Turkish judge or Turkish judges shall be carried out through Turkish officers of the court, and in any other case such execution shall be carried out by such officers as the court of trial shall direct.

Art. 160. 1. A communal law made by the Communal Chamber concerned shall, subject to the provisions of this Constitution, provide for the establishment, composition and jurisdiction of courts to deal with civil disputes relating to personal status and to religious matters which are reserved for the competence of the Communal Chambers by the provisions of this Constitution.

2. By such law provision shall be made for appeals against the decisions of such courts and for the composition of the courts by which such appeals are to be heard and determined and for the jurisdiction and powers of such appellate courts. A communal law made under this paragraph may provide that such appellate court may be composed of a judge or judges or the High Court either sitting alone or with such other judge or judges in the judicial service of the Republic as such law may determine.

3. Any such court as aforesaid in the exercise of its jurisdiction, shall apply the laws made by the Communal Chamber concerned:

Provided that nothing in this paragraph contained shall preclude a court of the Republic from applying in a case, where an issue relating to personal status or to religious matters is raised incidentally, the relevant communal law.

Art. 161. Subject to paragraph 3 of Article 160 the courts of the Republic shall have power to apply also the relevant communal laws other than those relating to personal status and to religious matters.

Art. 162. The High Court shall have jurisdiction to punish for any contempt of itself, and any other court of the Republic, including a court established by a communal law under Article 160, shall have power to commit any person disobeying a judgment or order of such court to prison until such person complies with such judgment or order and in any event for a period not exceeding twelve months.

A law or a communal law, notwithstanding anything in Article 90 contained, as the case may be, may provide for punishment for contempt of court.

Art. 163. 1. The High Court shall make Rules of Court for regulating the practice and procedure of the High Court and of any other court established by or under this Part of this Constitution, other than a court established under Article 160.

2. Without prejudice to the generality of paragraph 1 of this Article the High Court may make Rules of Court for the following purposes:

(a) for regulating the sittings of the courts and the selection of judges for any purpose;

(b) for providing for the summary determination of any appeal or other proceedings which appear to the High Court or such other court before which such proceedings are pending to be frivolous or vexatious or to have been instituted for the purpose of delaying the course of justice;

(c) for prescribing forms and fees in respect of proceedings in the courts and regulating the costs of, and incidental to, any such proceedings;

(d) for prescribing and regulating the composition of the registries of the courts and the powers and duties of officers of the courts;

(e) for prescribing the time within which any requirement of the Rules of Court is to be complied with;

(f) for prescribing the practice and procedure to be followed by the Supreme Council of Judicature in the exercise of its competence with regard to disciplinary matters relating to judicial officers.

3. Rules of Court made under this Article may fix the number of judges of the High Court who are to hear any specified matter:

Provided that in the exercise of the jurisdiction conferred on the High Court by or under this Constitution no matter shall be determined unless the provisions of Article 159 are complied with and for the hearing of any appeal, including an appeal under Article 156, the High Court shall, subject to paragraph 2 of Article 160, be composed of all its members.

Art. 164. Any appellate court created under paragraph 2 of Article 160 shall make Rules of Court for regulating the practice and procedure of such court and the practice and procedure of any court from which any appeal shall lie to it.

2. Without prejudice to the generality of paragraph 1 of this Article such appellate court may make Rules of Court for itself and for the Courts from which an appeal shall lie to it for the following purposes:

(a) for regulating the sittings of such courts;

(b) for prescribing forms and fees in respect of proceedings in such courts and for regulating the costs of, and incidental to, any such proceedings;

(c) for prescribing and regulating the composition of registries of such courts and the powers and duties of officers of such courts;

(d) for prescribing the time within which any requirement of such Rules of Court is to be complied with.

PART XI

FINANCIAL PROVISIONS

Art. 165. 1. All revenues and moneys, howsoever raised or received by the Republic, shall, subject to the provisions of this Constitution and of the law, be paid into and form one fund to be known as the Consolidated Fund of the Republic.

2. All revenues and moneys, howsoever raised or received by a Communal Chamber, shall, subject to any communal law, be paid into and form one fund, to be known as the Consolidated Fund of that Communal Chamber.

3. Unless the context otherwise requires any reference in this Constitution to the Consolidated Fund shall be construed as a reference to the

Consolidated Fund of the Republic provided in paragraph 1 of this Article.

Art. 166. 1. There shall be charged on the Consolidated Fund, in addition to any grant, remuneration or other moneys charged by any other provision of this Constitution or law:

(a) all pensions and gratuities for which the Republic is liable;

(b) the emoluments of the President and the Vice-President of the Republic and the salaries of the judges of the Supreme Constitutional Court and of the High Court, of the Attorney-General and of the Deputy Attorney-General of the Republic, of the Auditor-General and of the Deputy Auditor-General, of the Governor and the Deputy Governor of the Issuing Bank of the Republic and of the members of the Public Service Commission;

(c) all debt charges for which the Republic is liable; and

(d) any moneys required to satisfy any judgment, decision or award against the Republic by any court.

2. For the purposes of this Article debt charges include interest, sinking fund charges, the repayment of amortisation of debt and all expenditure in connexion with the raising of loans on the security of the Consolidated Fund and the service and redemption of debt created thereby.

Art. 167. 1. The Minister of Finance shall, upon receipt of the estimates of each Ministry and of each Independent Office of the Republic, cause to be prepared in respect of every financial year a comprehensive Budget of the Republic for that year which, when approved by the Council of Ministers, shall be laid before the House of Representatives.

2. The estimates of expenditure in the Budget shall show separately:

(a) the total sums required to meet expenditure charged on the Consolidated Fund; and

(b) the sums respectively required to meet other expenditure.

3. The said Budget shall also show, so far as is practicable, the assets and liabilities of the Republic at the end of the last completed financial year, the manner in which those assets are invested or held and particulars in respect of outstanding liabilities.

4. The expenditure to be met from the Consolidated Fund but not charged thereon shall be submitted to the House of Representatives for adoption and if adopted shall be included in the Budget in respect of that financial year.

5. If in respect of any financial year it is found that the amount adopted by the House of Representatives for any purpose is insufficient or that a need has arisen for expenditure for a purpose for which no amount has been adopted a supplementary budget showing the sums required shall be laid before the House of Representatives for adoption and if adopted by the House of Representatives shall be included in the Budget in respect of that financial year.

6. The House of Representatives may approve or refuse its approval to

any expenditure contained in a supplementary Budget but may not vote an increased amount or an alteration in its destination.

Art. 168. 1. No expenditure shall be met from the Consolidated Fund or other Public Funds except upon the authority of a warrant under the hand of the Minister of Finance:

Provided that the Minister of Finance shall not refuse to sign any such warrant for an expenditure provided for in the Budget.

2. Subject to the provisions of paragraph 3 of this Article, no such warrant shall be issued unless such expenditure has been adopted in the Budget for the financial year to which the warrant relates in the Budget.

3. If the Budget has not been adopted by the House of Representatives by the first day of the financial year to which it relates, the House of Representatives may, subject to the provisions of this Constitution, by a resolution, authorise the meeting of any expenditure required, for a period not exceeding one month at any one time but in any event not exceeding two months in the aggregate, from the Consolidated Fund or other Public Funds as they may consider essential for the continuance of the public services shown in the Budget until the expiration of such period:

Provided that the expenditure so authorised for any service shall not exceed the proportion with respect to such period of the amount voted for that service in the Budget for the preceding financial year.

PART XII

MISCELLANEOUS PROVISIONS

Art. 169. Subject to the provisions of Article 50 and paragraph 3 of Article 57:

(1) every international agreement with a foreign State or any International Organisation relating to commercial matters, economic co-operation (including payments and credit) and *modus vivendi* shall be concluded under a decision of the Council of Ministers;

(2) any other treaty, convention or international agreement shall be negotiated and signed under a decision of the Council of Ministers and shall only be operative and binding on the Republic when approved by a law made by the House of Representatives whereupon it shall be concluded;

(3) treaties, conventions and agreements concluded in accordance with the foregoing provisions of this Article shall have, as from their publication in the official Gazette of the Republic, superior force to any municipal law on condition that such treaties, conventions and agreements are applied by the other party thereto.

Art. 170. 1. The Republic shall, by agreement on appropriate terms, accord most-favoured-nation treatment to the Kingdom of Greece, the

Republic of Turkey and the United Kingdom of Great Britain and Northern Ireland for all agreements whatever their nature might be.

2. The provisions of paragraph 1 of this Article shall not apply to the Treaty concerning the Establishment of the Republic of Cyprus between the Republic, the Kingdom of Greece, the Republic of Turkey and the United Kingdom of Great Britain and Northern Ireland concerning the bases and military facilities accorded to the United Kingdom.

Art. 171. 1. In sound and vision broadcasting there shall be programmes both for the Greek and the Turkish Communities.

2. The time allotted to programmes for the Turkish Community in sound broadcasting shall not be less than seventy-five hours in a seven-day week, spread to all days of such week in daily normal periods of transmission:

Provided that if the total period of transmissions has to be reduced so that the time allotted to programmes for the Greek Community should fall below seventy-five hours in a seven-day week, then the time allotted to programmes for the Turkish Community in any such week should be reduced by the same number of hours as that by which the time allotted to programmes for the Greek Community is reduced below such hours:

Provided further that if the time allotted to programmes for the Greek Community is increased above one hundred and forty hours in a seven-day week, then the time allotted to programmes for the Turkish Community shall be increased in the ratio of three hours for the Turkish Community to every seven hours for the Greek Community.

3. In vision broadcasting there shall be allotted three transmission days to the programmes for the Turkish Community of every ten consecutive transmission days and the total time allotted to the programmes for the Turkish Community in such ten transmission days shall be in the ratio of three hours to seven hours allotted to programmes for the Greek Community in such ten transmission days.

4. All official broadcasts in sound and vision shall be made both in Greek and Turkish and shall not be taken into account for the purposes of calculating the time under this Article.

Art. 172. The Republic shall be liable for any wrongful act or omission causing damage committed in the exercise or purported exercise of the duties of officers or authorities of the Republic.

A law shall regulate such liability.

Art. 173. 1. Separate municipalities shall be created in the five largest towns of the Republic, that is to say, Nicosia, Limassol, Famagusta, Larnaca and Paphos by the Turkish inhabitants thereof:

Provided that the President and the Vice-President of the Republic shall within four years of the date of the coming into operation of this Constitution examine the question whether or not this separation of municipalities in the aforesaid towns shall continue.

2. The council of the Greek municipality in any such town shall be elected by the Greek electors of the town and the council of the Turkish municipality in such town shall be elected by the Turkish electors of the town.

3. In each such town a co-ordinating body shall be set up composed of two members chosen by the council of the Greek municipality, two members chosen by the council of the Turkish municipality and a President chosen by agreement between the two councils of such municipalities in such town. Such co-ordinating body shall provide for work which needs to be carried out jointly, shall carry out joint services entrusted to it by agreement of the councils of the two municipalities within the town and shall concern itself with matters which require a degree of co-operation.

Art. 174. Within the limits of any such town no municipal tax, rate, fee or any other revenue shall be imposed or levied upon or collected from any person by any such municipality unless such person belongs to the same Community as the municipality concerned:

Provided that:

(a) fees payable in connexion with the use of municipal markets, slaughter houses and other municipal places which are in the region within which the council of one of such municipalities in any such town exercises its jurisdiction;

(b) entertainment fees payable in connexion with premises or places in the region within which the council of one of such municipalities in any such town exercises its jurisdiction;

(c) such fees as may be agreed upon between the two councils of such municipalities in any such town for any services additional to, or in excess of, those usually rendered by a municipality, to a person not belonging to the Community thereof,

shall be paid to the council of such municipality:

Provided further that in case any service in the way of control, inspection and the like is rendered by one of the municipalities to a person belonging to the Community of the other municipality in any such town any fees in respect thereof shall be payable to the municipality rendering such service.

Art. 175. No licence or permit shall be issued to any person by a municipality in any such town not belonging to the Community of such municipality:

Provided that licences or permits relating to premises, places or building operations in the region within which one of such municipalities in any such town exercises its jurisdiction shall be issued by the council of such municipality and any service, control or supervision in connexion with such licences or permits shall be performed by the council of such municipality and any such fee payable in respect thereof shall be collected by council.

Art. 176. Nothing in Articles 173 to 178, both inclusive, contained shall be construed as precluding a law to provide for town planning with respect to any such municipalities subject to the following conditions:

(a) the planning authority for any such town shall consist of ten members, out of whom seven shall be Greeks and three shall be Turks;

(b) all decisions of such authority shall be taken by an absolute majority: Provided that no decision affecting a Greek municipality shall be taken unless such majority includes the votes of at least four Greek members, and no decision affecting a Turkish municipality shall be taken unless such majority includes the votes of at least two Turkish members;

(c) all matters of a town planning nature affecting any such town and any regulation of any such matter shall be entrusted exclusively to such planning authority.

Art. 177. Subject to the provisions of Articles 173 to 178, both inclusive, each municipality in any such town shall exercise its jurisdiction and perform all its functions respectively within a region the limits of which shall be fixed for each municipality by agreement of the President and the Vice-President of the Republic.

Art. 178. With regard to other localities, a special provision shall be made for the constitution of the organs of the municipalities in accordance, as far as possible, with the rule of proportional representation of the two Communities.

PART XIII

FINAL PROVISIONS

Art. 179. 1. This Constitution shall be the supreme law of the Republic.

2. No law or decision of the House of Representatives or of any of the Communal Chambers and no act or decision of any organ, authority or person in the Republic exercising executive power or any administrative function shall in any way be repugnant to, or inconsistent with, any of the provisions of this Constitution.

Art. 180. 1. The Greek and the Turkish texts of this Constitution shall both be originals and shall have the same authenticity and the same legal force.

2. Any conflict between the two texts of this Constitution shall be determined by the Supreme Constitutional Court by reference to the text of the draft of this Constitution signed at Nicosia on the 6th April, 1960, in the Joint Constitutional Commission together with the Schedule of amendments thereto signed on 6 July 1960, by representatives of the Kingdom of Greece, the Republic of Turkey and the Greek and Turkish Cypriot communities, due regard being had to the letter and spirit of the

Zurich Agreement dated the 11th February, 1959, and of the London Agreement dated the 19th February, 1959.

3. In case of ambiguity any interpretation of the Constitution shall be made by the Supreme Constitutional Court due regard being had to the letter and spirit of the Zurich Agreement dated the 11th February, 1959, and of the London Agreement dated the 19th February, 1959.

Art. 181. The Treaty guaranteeing the independence, territorial integrity and Constitution of the Republic concluded between the Republic, the Kingdom of Greece, the Republic of Turkey and the United Kingdom of of Great Britain and Northern Ireland, and the Treaty of Military Alliance concluded between the Republic, the Kingdom of Greece and the Republic of Turkey, copies of which are annexed to this Constitution as Annexes I and II, shall have constitutional force.

Art. 182. 1. The Articles or parts of Articles of this Constitution set out in Annex III hereto which have been incorporated from the Zurich Agreement dated 11th February, 1959, are the basic Articles of this Constitution and cannot, in any way, be amended, whether by way of variation, addition or repeal.

2. Subject to paragraph 1 of this Article any provision of this Constitution may be amended, whether by way of variation, addition or repeal, as provided in paragraph 3 of this Article.

3. Such amendment shall be made by a law passed by a majority vote comprising at least two thirds of the total number of the Representatives belonging to the Greek Community and at least two thirds of the total number of the Representatives belonging to the Turkish Community.

Art. 183. 1. In case of war or other public danger threatening the life of the Republic or any part thereof, the Council of Ministers shall have power, by a decision taken in this respect, to issue a Proclamation of Emergency:

Provided that the President and the Vice-President of the Republic shall, separately or conjointly, have a right of veto against any such decision which they shall exercise within forty-eight hours of the date when the decision has been transmitted to their respective offices.

2. Any such Proclamation shall specify the Articles of the Constitution which shall be suspended for the duration of such Emergency:

Provided that only the following Articles of the Constitution may be suspended by any such Proclamation that is to say:

Article 7, only in so far as it relates to death inflicted by a permissible act of war; Article 10, paragraphs 2 and 3; Article 11; Article 13; Article 16; Article 17; Article 19; Article 21; Article 23, paragraph 8, sub-paragraph (d); Article 25 and Article 27.

3. The President and the Vice-President of the Republic shall, unless, separately or conjointly, they have exercised their right of veto as provided in paragraph 1 of this Article, promulgate forthwith such Proclamation by publication in the official Gazette of the Republic.

4. A Proclamation promulgated under the foregoing provisions of this Article shall be laid forthwith before the House of Representatives. If the House of Representatives is not sitting it must be convened as soon as possible for this purpose.

5. The House of Representatives shall have the right to reject or confirm such Proclamation of Emergency. In the case of rejection the Proclamation of Emergency shall have no legal effect. In the case of confirmation the President and the Vice-President of the Republic shall promulgate forthwith such decision of the House of Representatives by publication in the official Gazette of the Republic.

6. The Proclamation of Emergency shall cease to operate at the expiration of two months from the date of confirmation by the House of Representatives unless the House, at the request of the Council of Ministers, decides to prolong the duration of the state of emergency, whereupon the President and the Vice-President of the Republic, separately or conjointly, shall have a right of veto against such decision of prolongation to be exercised in accordance with Article 50.

7. (1) While a Proclamation is in operation, notwithstanding anything in this Constitution, the Council of Ministers if satisfied that immediate action is required may, subject to the right of veto of the President and the Vice-President of the Republic under Article 57 to be exercised, separately or conjointly, make any ordinance strictly connected with the state of emergency having the force of law.

(2) If no right of veto is exercised under sub-paragraph (1) of this paragraph the President and the Vice-President of the Republic shall forthwith promulgate by publication in the official Gazette of the Republic such ordinance.

(3) Such ordinance if not sooner revoked shall cease to be in force at the expiration of the emergency.

Art. 184. 1. Where any ordinance promulgated in pursuance of sub-paragraph (2) of paragraph 7 of Article 183 provides for preventive detention:

(a) the authority on whose order any person is detained under that ordinance shall, as soon as may be, inform him of the grounds for his detention and, subject to paragraph 3 of this Article, the allegations of fact on which the order is based, and shall give him the opportunity of making representations against the order as soon as may be;

(b) no citizen shall be detained under that ordinance for a period exceeding one month unless an advisory board constituted as mentioned in paragraph 2 of this Article has considered any representations made by him under sub-paragraph (a) of this paragraph and has reported, before the expiration of that period, that there is in its opinion sufficient cause for the detention.

2. An advisory board constituted for the purposes of this Article shall

consist of a Chairman, who shall be appointed jointly by the President and the Vice-President of the Republic from among persons who are or have been judges of the High Court or are qualified to be judges of such Court, and two other members, who shall be appointed jointly by the President and the Vice-President of the Republic after consultation with the President of the High Court.

3. This Article does not require any authority to disclose facts of which disclosure would in its opinion be against the national interest.

Art. 185. 1. The territory of the Republic is one and indivisible.

2. The integral or partial union of Cyprus with any other State or the separatist independence is excluded.

Art. 186. 1. In this Constitution, unless it is otherwise expressly provided or required by the context:

(1) "Community" means the Greek or the Turkish Community;

"court" includes any judge thereof;

"Greek" means a member of the Greek Community as defined in Article 2;

"law" when used in relation to the period after the coming into operation of this Constitution means a law of the Republic;

"person" includes any company, partnership, association, society, institution or body of persons, corporate or unincorporate;

"Republic" means the Republic of Cyprus;

"Turk" or "Turkish" means a member of the Turkish Community as defined in Article 2;

(2) words importing the masculine gender include females and words in the singular include the plural and vice-versa.

2. Where a power is conferred by this Constitution to make any order, rules, regulations or bye-laws or to give any directions the power shall be construed as including a power exercisable in like manner to amend or revoke any such order, rules, regulations, bye-laws or directions.

TRANSITIONAL PROVISIONS

Art. 187. 1. Any person elected:

(a) as first President or first Vice-President of the Republic;

(b) as a member of the House of Representatives or of any Communal Chamber,

under any law in force immediately before the date of the coming into operation of this Constitution shall be deemed to be the President of the Republic or the Vice-President of the Republic, a member of the House of Representatives or a member of the Communal Chamber concerned, elected respectively under the provisions of this Constitution.

2. All laws and regulations relating to elections expired on the date of the coming into operation of this Constitution and notwithstanding such

expiration shall continue to be in force until a new electoral law is made by the House of Representatives or by any Communal Chamber, as the case may be, and in any case not later than eighteen months of the date of the coming into operation of this Constitution with regard to any by-election to fill any vacancy occurring during such period in the office of the President of the Republic, the Vice-President of the Republic, any Representative or any member of a Communal Chamber.

Art. 188. 1. Subject to the provisions of this Constitution and to the following provisions of this Article, all laws in force on the date of the coming into operation of this Constitution shall, until amended, whether by way of variation, addition or repeal, by any law or communal law, as the case may be, made under this Constitution, continue in force on or after that date, and shall, as from that date be construed and applied with such modification as may be necessary to bring them into conformity with this Constitution.

2. Save where otherwise provided in the Transitional Provisions of this Constitution no provision in any such law which is contrary to, or inconsistent with, any provision of this Constitution and no law which under Article 78 requires a separate majority shall so continue to be in force:

Provided that the laws relating to the municipalities may continue to be in force for a period of six months after the date of the coming into operation of this Constitution and any law imposing duties or taxes may continue to be in force until the 31st day of December, 1960.

3. In any such law which continues in force under paragraph 1 of this Article, unless the context otherwise requires:

(a) any reference to the Colony of Cyprus or to the "Crown" shall, in relation to any period beginning on or after the date of the coming into operation of this Constitution, be construed as a reference to the Republic;

(b) any reference to the Governor or the Governor in Council shall, in relation to any such period, be construed as a reference to the President and the Vice-President of the Republic, separately or conjointly, according to the express provisions in this Constitution, to the House of Representatives in matters relating to exercise of legislative power other than those expressly reserved to the Communal Chambers, to the Communal Chamber concerned in all matters within its competence under this Constitution, and to the Council of Ministers in matters relating to exercise of executive power;

(c) any reference to the Administrative Secretary or the Financial Secretary, shall in relation to any such period, be construed as a reference to the Ministry or Independent Office of the Republic for the time being charged with responsibility for the subject in relation to which reference is made;

(d) any reference to the Attorney-General or the Solicitor-General, shall, in relation to any such period, be construed as a reference to the Attorney-General of the Republic or the Deputy Attorney-General of the Republic respectively;

(e) any reference to any other person holding a public office or to any authority or body, shall, in relation to any such period, be construed as a reference to the corresponding public officer or corresponding authority, body or office of the Republic.

4. Any court in the Republic applying the provisions of any such law which continues in force under paragraph 1 of this Article, shall apply it in relation to any such period, with such modification as may be necessary to bring it into accord with the provisions of this Constitution including the Transitional Provisions thereof.

5. In this Article:

"law" includes any public instrument made before the date of the coming into operation of this Constitution by virtue of such law;

"modification" includes amendment, adaptation and repeal.

Art. 189. Notwithstanding anything in Article 3 contained, for a period of five years after the date of the coming into operation of this Constitution:

(a) all laws which under Article 188 will continue to be in force may continue to be in the English language;

(b) the English language may be used in any proceedings before any court in the Republic.

Art. 190. 1. Subject to the ensuing provisions of this Article any court existing immediately before the date of the coming into operation of this Constitution shall, notwithstanding anything in this Constitution, as from that date and until a new law is made regarding the constitution of the courts of the Republic and in any event not later than four months from that date, continue to function as hitherto but constituted, as far as practicable, in accordance with the provisions of this Constitution:

Provided that any pending proceedings, civil or criminal, part heard on the date of the coming into operation of this Constitution shall continue and be disposed of, notwithstanding anything contained in this Constitution, by the court as constituted in such a case.

2. Notwithstanding anything in this Constitution and until the Supreme Constitutional Court established thereunder is constituted within a period not later than three months of the date of the coming into operation of this Constitution, the registry of the High Court shall be the registry of the Supreme Constitutional Court.

3. The registry of the High Court shall be deemed to be the registry of the Supreme Constitutional Court for all its purposes, including a recourse, until such Court is constituted; the constitution of such Court shall be effected not later than three months of the date of the coming into operation of this Constitution.

4. In computing any time with regard to a recourse to the Supreme Constitutional Court under the provisions of this Constitution, the period between the date of the coming into operation of this Constitution and the constitution of such Court as aforesaid shall not be counted.

5. The Supreme Court existing immediately before the date of the coming into operation of this Constitution shall be deemed to be the High Court as established under this Constitution until the constitution of such Court under the provisions thereof; the constitution of such Court shall be made not later than three months of the date of the coming into operation of this Constitution:

Provided that a reference to the Chief Justice shall be a reference to the senior member of such Court, and such Court shall be deemed to be validly constituted during such period notwithstanding that its membership shall be below four.

Art. 191. Any proceedings pending on the date of the coming into operation of this Constitution in which the Attorney-General on behalf of the Government of the Colony of Cyprus or any Department or officer thereof is a party shall continue, on and after such date, with the Republic or its corresponding office or officer being substituted as a party.

Art. 192. 1. Save where other provision is made in this Constitution any person who, immediately before the date of the coming into operation of this Constitution, holds an office in the public service shall, after that date, be entitled to the same terms and conditions of service as were applicable to him before that date and those terms and conditions shall not be altered to his disadvantage during his continuance in the public service of the Republic on or after that date.

2. Subject to paragraph 1 of this Article the judges of the Supreme Court other than the Chief Justice and the judges and magistrates of the subordinate courts holding office immediately before the date of the coming into operation of this Constitution shall, notwithstanding anything contained in Articles 153 and 157, as from that date continue to hold their respective offices as if they had been duly appointed thereto under the provisions of those Articles until an appointment is made under the provisions of those Articles and the provisions of this Constitution shall apply to them accordingly.

3. Where any holder of an office mentioned in paragraphs 1 and 2 of this Article is not appointed in the public service of the Republic he shall be entitled, subject to the terms and conditions of service applicable to him, to just compensation or pension on abolition of office terms out of the funds of the Republic whichever is more advantageous to him.

4. Subject to paragraph 5 of this Article any holder of an office mentioned in paragraphs 1 and 2 of this Article whose office comes, by the operation of this Constitution, within the competence of a Communal Chamber, may, if he so desires, waive his rights under paragraph 3 of this

Article and choose to serve under such Communal Chamber and in such a case such holder of such office shall be entitled to receive from the Republic any retirement pension, gratuity or other like benefit to which he would have been entitled under the law in force immediately before the date of the coming into operation of this Constitution in respect of the period of his service before such date if such period by itself or together with any period of service under such Communal Chamber would, under such law, have entitled him to any such benefit.

5. Any teacher who, immediately before the date of the coming into operation of this Constitution, was a serving teacher and was in receipt of remuneration out of the public funds of the Colony of Cyprus and whose office comes, by the operation of this Constitution, within the competence of a Communal Chamber shall be entitled to recieve from the Republic any retirement pension, gratuity or other like benefit to which he would have been entitled under the law in force before the date of the coming into operation of this Constitution in respect of the period of his service before such date if such period by itself or together with any period of service under such Communal Chamber would, under such law, have entitled him to any such benefit.

6. Any person who, immediately before the date of the coming into operation of this Constitution, being in the public service of the Colony of Cyprus is on leave prior to retirement therefrom or on transfer from that service to any service other than that of the Republic shall, irrespective of whether he is a citizen of the Republic or not, continue to be entitled to the same terms and conditions of service as were applicable to him under such circumstances before that date and such terms and conditions shall not be altered to his disadvantage.

7. For the purposes of this Article:

(a) "public service" in relation to service before the date of the coming into operation of this Constitution means service under the Government of the Colony of Cyprus and in relation to service after that date means service in a civil capacity under the Republic and includes service as a member of the security forces of the Republic;

(b) "terms and conditions of service" means, subject to the necessary adaptations under the provisions of this Constitution, remuneration, leave, removal from service, retirement pensions, gratuities or other like benefits.

8. Save as provided in paragraph 6 of this Article nothing in this Article shall apply to a person who is not a citizen of the Republic.

Art. 193. Any person who, immediately before the date of the coming into operation of this Constitution, was in receipt of any pension or other retirement benefit out of the public Funds, including the Widows' and Orphans' Pension Fund, of the Colony of Cyprus shall on and after the date of the coming into operation of this Constitution, continue to be paid such pension or other retirement benefit out of the public Funds of the Republic under the same terms and conditions as were applicable to such pensions or other retirement benefits immediately before the date of the coming into operation of this Constitution or under terms and conditions made thereafter not less favourable to that person and applicable to his case.

Art. 194. The eligibility of any person to receive a pension under the Widows' and Orphans' Pension Fund shall, on and after the date of the coming into operation of this Constitution, continue to be subject to the same terms and conditions as were in force immediately before the date of the coming into operation of this Constitution and shall not be altered to the disadvantage of any such person so long as such eligibility remains.

Art. 195. Notwithstanding anything in this Constitution contained, the person elected as first President of the Republic and the person elected as first Vice-President of the Republic, who under Article 187 are deemed to be the first President and the first Vice-President of the Republic, whether before or after their investiture as in Article 42 provided, conjointly shall have, and shall be deemed to have had, the exclusive right and power to sign and conclude on behalf of the Republic the Treaty concerning the Establishment of the Republic of Cyprus between the Republic, the Kingdom of Greece, the Republic of Turkey and the United Kingdom of Great Britain and Northern Ireland together with the Exchanges of Notes drawn up for signature with that Treaty, and the Treaty guaranteeing the independence, territorial integrity and Constitution of the Republic, between the Republic, the Kingdom of Greece, the Republic of Turkey and the United Kingdom of Great Britain and Northern Ireland, the Treaty of Military Alliance between the Republic, the Kingdom of Greece and the Republic of Turkey and the Agreement between the Republic, the Kingdom of Greece and the Republic of Turkey for the application of the Treaty of Alliance concluded between these countries, and such Treaties, Agreements and Notes exchanged shall be thus validly concluded on behalf of the Republic and shall be operative and binding as from the date on which they have been so signed.

Art. 196. The term of office of the first Communal Chambers shall commence on the date of the coming into operation of this Constitution.

Art. 197. 1. Any movable or immovable property, or any right or interest thereon, which, immediately before the date of the coming into operation of this Constitution, was vested in, held by, or registered in the name of, the Government of the Colony of Cyprus or any other person or body, for and on behalf of, or in trust for, any school, or other body or institution which come, by or under the provisions of this Constitution, within the competence of the Communal Chambers shall, as from that date, be vested in, and be held by such person, body or authority as provided by a law of the respective Communal Chamber subject to such terms and conditions as such communal law may provide:

Provided that no such law shall direct that any such property shall vest in, or be held by, the Communal Chamber itself.

2. Nothing in this Article contained shall apply to any bequest or other donation administered by trustees or to any *vakf* in connexion with any educational purposes.

Art. 198. 1. The following provisions shall have effect until a law of citizenship is made incorporating such provisions:

(a) any matter relating to citizenship shall be governed by the provisions of Annex D to the Treaty of Establishment;

(b) any person born in Cyprus, on or after the date of the coming into operation of this Constitution, shall become on the date of his birth a citizen of the Republic if on that date his father has become a citizen of the Republic or would but for his death have become such a citizen under the provisions of Annex D to the Treaty of Establishment.

2. For the purposes of this Article "Treaty of Establishment" means the Treaty concerning the Establishment of the Republic of Cyprus between the Republic, the Kingdom of Greece, the Republic of Turkey and the United Kingdom of Great Britain and Northern Ireland.

Art. 199. The Turkish Communal Chamber shall have the right to receive from the Government of the United Kingdom of Great Britain and Northern Ireland the sums specified in the Notes exchanged between the Governor of the Colony of Cyprus, on behalf of the Government of the United Kingdom and the representatives of the Turkish Community of Cyprus drawn up for signature on.

Annex I—Article 181

Treaty guaranteeing the independence, territorial integrity and Constitution of the Republic concluded between the Republic, the Kingdom of Greece, the Republic of Turkey and the United Kingdom of Great Britain and Northern Ireland.

Not reproduced

Annex II—Article 181

Treaty of Military Alliance concluded between the Republic, the Kingdom of Greece and the Republic of Turkey.

Not reproduced

Annex III—Article 182

LIST OF BASIC ARTICLES OF THE CONSTITUTION

Articles		
1		
3	paragraphs 1 and 2	
4	paragraph 1	
	paragraph 2	in so far as it relates to the Authorities of the Republic
	paragraph 3	in so far as it relates to Communal authorities
	paragraph 4	in so far as it relates to citizens of the Republic
5		
23	paragraph 4	in so far as it relates to the Republic or a municipal corporation and sub-paragraph (c) thereof
	paragraph 5	in so far as it relates to the use of compulsorily acquired property by the Republic or a municipal corporation and its restoration to the owner
	paragraph 6	
	paragraph 11	in so far as the compulsory acquisition is made by the Republic or a municipal corporation and in so far as this paragraph relates to the recourse to the courts and its suspending effect
36	paragraph 2	
39	paragraph 1	in so far as it relates to universal suffrage
42	paragraph 1	except the text of the affirmation other than its part relating to faith to, and respect for, the Constitution
	paragraph 2	
43	paragraph 1	in so far as it relates to the five years' period
44	paragraphs 2 and 4	
46		except its fourth paragraph
50	paragraph 1	except the part of its sub-paragraph (a) items (i) to (vi) both inclusive
51	paragraphs 1 and 2	
	paragraph 3	except for the time of thirty days provided for the Budget
	paragraphs 4 and 6	
52		except its part relating to the recourse to the Supreme Constitutional Court under Article 140
53	paragraphs 1, 2 and 3	
57	paragraph 2	except its part relating to time limits and its proviso
	paragraph 3	except its part relating to time limits

Articles		
	paragraph 4	in so far as it relates to promulgation
61		
62	paragraph 2	in so far as it relates to the percentages, to the separate and universal suffrage and to the proportion being independent of any statistical data
65	paragraph 1	in so far as it relates to the five years' period
78		
86		
87	paragraph 1	sub-paragraphs (a) to (e) both inclusive and sub-paragraph (f) except its final words referring to Article 88
89	paragraph 1	sub-paragraphs (b) and (c) and paragraphs 2 and 3
92		in so far as it relates only to the determination of the number of its members by the Communal Chambers
108		
112	paragraph 1	except its part relating to qualifications
115	paragraph 1	except its part relating to qualifications
118	paragraph 1	except its part relating to qualifications
123		
126	paragraph 1	except its part relating to qualifications
129		
130		
131		
132		
133	paragraph 1	except the proviso to its sub-paragraph (2)
137	paragraph 1	
	paragraph 3	only in so far as it relates to the suspension of the laws or decisions
	paragraph 4	except its proviso
138	paragraph 1	
139	paragraph 1	in so far as it relates to conflict of competence between the House of Representatives and the Communal Chambers
153	paragraph 1	except the proviso to its sub-paragraph (2)
157	paragraphs 1 and 2	
159	paragraphs 1, 2, 3, and 4	
160	paragraph 1	its part which provides the matter with which the courts are dealing
	paragraph 3	except its proviso
170		
173	paragraph 1	except the names of the towns
	paragraph 3	except its part relating to the carrying out of joint services entrusted to the co-ordinating body

178
181
182
185 paragraph 2

Administration of Justice (Miscellaneous Provisions) Law 1964[1]

July 9, 1964

Whereas recent events have rendered impossible the functioning of the Supreme Constitutional Court and of the High Court of Justice and the administration of justice in some other respects:

And whereas it is imperative that justice should continue to be administered unhampered by the situation created by such events and that the judicial power hitherto exercised by the Supreme Constitutional Court and by the High Court of Justice should continue to be exercised:

And whereas it has become necessary to make legislative provision in this respect until such time as the people of Cyprus may determine such matters:

Now, therefore, the House of Representatives enacts as follows:

PART I

PRELIMINARY

1. This Law may be cited as the Administration of Justice (Miscellaneous Provisions) Law, 1964.

2. (1) In this Law, unless the context otherwise requires:

"Court" means the Supreme Court established under section 3;

"High Court" means the High Court of Justice established under Article 153 of the Constitution;

"Judge" means the President or any other Judge of the Court;

"law" means the Constitution or any Law and includes a public instrument;

"proceedings" includes civil and criminal proceedings;

"Supreme Constitutional Court" means the Supreme Constitutional Court established under Article 133 of the Constitution.

[1] *A law to remove certain difficulties, arising out of recent events, impeding the administration of justice and to provide for other matters connected therewith.* No. 33 of 1964. Supplied by the Offices of the Supreme Court, Nicosia, in May 1966. Ed.

(2) Expressions not otherwise defined in this Law shall, unless the context otherwise requires, have the meaning assigned to such expressions by the Courts of Justice Law, 1960.

PART II

SUPREME COURT

3. (1) For the purpose of having the jurisdiction hitherto exercised by the Supreme Constitutional Court and the High Court continued to be exercised, there shall be established in the Republic a Supreme Court to exercise, subject to the provisions of this Law, such jurisdiction.

(2) The Court shall consist of five or more, but not exceeding seven, Judges one of whom shall be the President.

(3) Any member of the Supreme Constitutional Court and of the High Court holding office on the date of the coming into operation of this Law shall, as from that date, be a member of the Court and shall hold office under the same terms and conditions as were applicable to him before that date.

(4) The senior member of the Court shall be the first President of the Court and thereafter in case of vacancy or temporary incapacity or absence of the President of the Court the President of the Republic shall designate the President of the Court from amongst its members.

(5) All the Judges shall, save as in this Law otherwise expressly provided, have in all respects equal power, authority and jurisdiction and shall be addressed in the manner formerly customary in addressing the Judges of the Supreme Constitutional Court and of the High Court.

(6) The President of the Court shall take precedence over all the Judges of the Court and the Judges shall rank among themselves according to their seniority.

(7) For the purposes of this Law seniority shall be determined as follows:

(a) in the case of Judges who become members of the Court under subsection (3) their seniority shall be determined by the date of the publication of their appointment as Judges of the Supreme Constitutional Court or the High Court, as the case may be, in the official Gazette of the Republic:

Provided that if the publication of their appointment was made on the same date, their seniority shall be determined by reference to their respective length of service in the judicial service of Cyprus, and in the case of persons who had held no judicial office before their appointment their seniority shall be determined by the priority of the instrument of their appointment;

(b) in any other case, seniority shall be determined by the date of the publication of his appointment as a Judge in the official Gazette of the Republic.

4. (1) Whenever the office of a Judge is vacant a new Judge shall be appointed by the President of the Republic to fill the vacancy.

(2) The office of a Judge shall be vacant when no one is appointed to that office or on the death, retirement, resignation, removal from or refusal to act in the office of its holder.

(3) Any appointment under this section shall be made in consultation with the Court.

(4) Any appointment under this section shall be made on the same terms and conditions as are applicable to a Judge under sub-section (3) of section 3.

5. (1) No person shall be appointed as a Judge unless he is a qualified lawyer with at least twelve years' practice and of high moral standard.

(2) For the purposes of sub-section (1) "practice" shall include service in the permanent judicial or legal service of Cyprus.

6. A Judge shall be a permanent member of the judicial service of the Republic.

7. (1) The President of the Republic shall, if advised by the Court that it is expedient, owing to an existing vacancy and until the office is filled, or to the temporary incapacity or absence of a Judge, that a temporary appointment should be made, appoint a person having the appropriate qualifications provided by section 5 to be a Judge for such time as may be specified in the instrument of his appointment.

(2) Any person appointed under subsection (1) shall, whilst so acting, have all the powers and may perform all the duties of a Judge.

(3) A person appointed under this section may be allowed as remuneration an amount not exceeding the amount provided for the office to which he is so appointed and such remuneration shall be a charge on the Consolidated Fund of the Republic.

8. Any Judge, appointed under section 4 or 7 shall, before assuming the duties of his office, make and subscribe before the President of the Republic the affirmation of faith to the Republic and the judicial oath in the form prescribed by the Schedule to the Courts of Justice Law, 1960.

PART III

JURISDICTION AND POWERS

9. There shall be vested in the Court:

(a) the jurisdiction and powers, which have been hitherto vested in, or capable of being exercised by, the Supreme Constitutional Court and the High Court;

(b) the competence and the powers vested in, and exercised by, a

Council for determining all matters relating to the retirement, dismissal or otherwise of a Judge of the Supreme Constitutional Court or of the High Court on account of such mental or physical incapacity or infirmity as would render him incapable of discharging the duties of his office either permanently or for such period of time as would render it impracticable for him to continue in office or on the ground of misconduct.

10. (1) The Supreme Council of Judicature for the exercise of the competence and the powers in respect of appointments, promotions, transfers, termination of appointments, dismissals and disciplinary matters of judicial officers shall be composed of:

(a) the Attorney-General of the Republic;

(b) the President and the two senior Judges of the Court;

(c) the senior President of a District Court and the senior District Judge; and

(d) a practising advocate of at least twelve years' practice elected at a general meeting, convened for the purpose, of the Cyprus Bar Association for a period of six months and not being eligible for re-election for the next five years:

Provided that in case of absence or temporary incapacity of the President or a Judge of the Court or of a President of the District Court, or the senior District Judge, the Judge or President of a District Court, or District Judge, the Judge or President of a District Court, or District Judge, as the case may be, next in seniority shall act as a member of the Council:

Provided further that in case of absence or temporary incapacity of the practising advocate provided by paragraph (d) of this subsection the practising advocate elected as an alternate member of the Council at the same meeting of the Bar Association shall act.

(2) The Supreme Council of Judicature shall be deemed to be duly constituted during and notwithstanding any vacancy in the office of any member thereof.

(3) For the purposes of this section seniority of Judges shall be determined in accordance with the provisions of subsection (7) of section 3 and seniority of a President of a District Court or a District Judge shall be determined by seniority in that office.

(4) The Supreme Council of Judicature may make rules regulating its own procedure.

11. (1) Any jurisdiction, competence or powers vested in the Court under section 9 shall, subject to subsections (2) and (3) and to any Rules of Court, be exercised by the full Court.

(2) Any original jurisdiction vested in the Court under any aw in force and any revisional jurisdiction, including jurisdiction the nadjloudication of a recourse made against an act or omission of any organ, authority or

person exercising executive or administrative authority as being contrary to the law in force or in excess or abuse of power, may be exercised, subject to any Rules of Court, by such Judge or Judges as the Court shall determine:

Provided that, subject to any Rules of Court, there shall be an appeal to the Court from his or their decision.

(3) Any appellate jurisdiction vested in the Court shall, subject to any Rules of Court, be exercised by at least three Judges nominated by the Court.

Each such nomination shall be made in respect of a period of four months at the beginning of such period.

PART IV

MISCELLANEOUS

12. (1) Any Court, established by the Courts of Justice Law, 1960, or any other Law shall, in the exercise of its civil or criminal jurisdiction under such Law, be composed of such judge or judges, irrespective of the community to which the parties to the proceedings belong, as the Court may direct.

(2) Any judge of a District Court may hear and determine any case falling within his jurisdiction irrespective of the community to which the parties to the proceedings belong.

13. (1) The Court shall have and use, as occasion requires, a seal bearing the style of the Court and such device as may be approved by the Minister of Justice.

(2) The Court may have as many duplicates of the seal of the Court as may be required, not exceeding one duplicate for each member of the Court.

(3) The Court shall direct in whose custody every duplicate of the seal of the Court shall be kept.

14. The sittings of the Court shall be held at Nicosia in such building as the Minister of Justice shall from time to time assign as a Court House for that purpose.

15. For any reference in any law in force to the Supreme Constitutional Court or the High Court or any Judge thereof respectively a reference to the Court or a Judge, as the case may be, shall be substituted and where there is any conflict between the provisions of this Law and of any other Law, the provisions of this Law shall prevail.

16. The Court shall be deemed to be duly constituted during and notwithstanding any vacancy in the office of any member thereof.

17. The Court may make Rules (in this Law referred to as "Rules of Court") to be published in the official Gazette of the Republic for the better carrying out of this Law into effect:

Provided that any Rules of Court duly made and in force on the date of the coming into operation of this Law shall, until revoked or amended by any new Rules made under this Law, continue to be in force.

18. Any proceedings pending on the date of the coming into operation of this Law before the Supreme Constitutional Court or the High Court shall be transferred at the stage they have reached to be heard and determined, under the provisions of this Law, by the Court.

CZECHOSLOVAKIA

SUMMARY

INTERNATIONAL STATUS

Czechoslovakia is a member of the United Nations (October 24, 1945). It is a member of the Council of Mutual Economic Assistance and other international organizations. It was a member of the League of Nations.

The establishement of a free and united Republic of Czechoslovakia was proclaimed by the Czechoslovak National Council in Prague on October 28, 1918, the Slovak membership of which was reaffirmed by a Declaration of October 30. From 1620 to 1918, Bohemia, Moravia and Slovakia had been under Hapsburg rule. The Constitution was promulgated on

February 29, 1920. The position of Czechoslovakia became precarious after the advent of Hitler and the organization of a Sudeten German party. Following the German occupation of Austria came the Munich agreement and on September 29, 1938, the first partition of Czechoslovakia. On March 15, 1939, Germany occupied all of Czechoslovakia except for some lands which were annexed by Hungary. The Czechoslovak National Committee in London was recognized as the government-in-exile. The first government of the National Front of Czechs and Slovaks was formed in the town of Kosice on April 4, 1945. In the May 1946 elections, the Communists emerged as the strongest single party and the Communist leader became Prime Minister. In February 1948, a government crisis was followed by a coup d'etat in which the Communist party took complete control of the government.

On May 9, 1948, the National Constitutional Assembly accepted a new constitution proclaiming a People's Democratic Republic.

FORM OF NATIONAL GOVERNMENT

The Constitution of July 11, 1960, replacing the Constitution of May 9, 1948, states that Czechoslovakia is a socialist state founded on the alliance of workers, farmers and intelligentsia with the working class at its head.[1] It is a unitary state of two fraternal nations, the Czechs and the Slovaks, each possessing equal rights.[2] All power belongs to the working people.[3] The guiding force in the country is the Communist Party.[4] The socialist economic system is described.[5]

RIGHTS OF THE PEOPLE

The Constitution provides the right and duty to work, equal rights and duties and equality of men and women, the right to leisure, protection of health and old age, the right to education, protection for minorities, of motherhood and the family, freedom of speech and press "consistent with the interests of the working people," the right of petition, inviolability of the person and due process of law, inviolability of the home, privacy of communication, freedom of domicile, faith, the right of asylum.[6] Citizens must uphold the constitution and the laws, protect socialist ownership, defend the country.[7]

LEGISLATIVE DEPARTMENT

The National Assembly is the supreme organ of state power and is composed of 300 deputies, elected by universal, direct and secret suffrage

[1] Const., Art. 1. [2] Id., Art. 1. [3] Id., Art. 2. [4] Id., Art. 4.
[5] Id., Art. 7–18. [6] Id., Art. 19–33. [7] Id., Art. 34–38.

for a term of four years.[1] It meets in at least two sessions a year.[2] Immunities of deputies are provided.[3]

Provision is made for a Slovak National Council as the national organ of state power and administration in Slovakia, elected for a term of four years.[4] It enacts special legislation for Slovakia, may introduce bills to the National Assembly, ensures the overall economic and cultural development of Slovakia and favorable conditions for citizens of Hungarian and Ukrainian nationality.[5]

EXECUTIVE DEPARTMENT

The President of the Republic is elected by the National Assembly for a term of five years and is responsible to it.[6] He summons and prorogues the National Assembly, has the power of appointment, of pardon, is Commander-in-Chief of the Armed Forces.[7] The supreme executive organ of state power is the Government composed of the Premier, the Vice-Premiers and the ministers; it is responsible to the National Assembly.[8]

Provision is made for national committees as organs of state power and administration in local government.[9]

JUDICIAL DEPARTMENT

The execution of justice is vested in elected and independent people's courts, consisting of the Supreme Court, regional courts, military courts and local people's courts.[10] Judges of the Supreme Court are elected by the National Assembly for a term of four years; they are independent, bound only by the legal order of the Socialist State.[11] The right of defence is guaranteed.[12]

AREA, POPULATION, ETC.

The area of Czechoslovakia is 127,863 square kilometres, its population (1965) is 14,159,000. The capital is Prague.[13] The languages are Czech and Slovak; citizens of Hungarian, Ukrainian and Polish nationality are ensured the means for education in their mother tongue.[14]

[1] Id., Art. 3, 39. [2] Id., Art. 50. [3] Id., Art. 58. [4] Id., Art. 73–85.
[5] Id., Art. 74. [6] Id., Art. 43, 61, 63. [7] Id., Art. 62.
[8] Id., Art. 66, 67. [9] Id., Art. 86–96. [10] Id., Art. 98. [11] Id., Art. 99, 102.
[12] Id., Art. 103. [13] Id., Art. 109. [14] Id., Art. 25.

CONSTITUTION of CZECHOSLOVAKIA [1]

July 11, 1960

DECLARATION

I. We, the working people of Czechoslovakia, solemnly declare:

The social order for which whole generations of our workers and other working people fought, and which they have had before them as an example since the victory of the Great October Socialist Revolution, has become a reality in our country, too, under the leadership of the Communist Party of Czechoslovakia.

Socialism has triumphed in our country!

We have entered a new stage in our history, and we are determined to go forward to new and still higher goals. While completing the socialist construction of our country, we are proceeding towards the construction of an advanced socialist society and gathering strength for the transition to communism.

We shall continue along this road hand in hand with our great ally, the fraternal Union of Soviet Socialist Republics, and all the other friendly countries of the world socialist system, of which our Republic is a firm part.

We desire to live in peace and friendship with all nations of the world and contribute to peaceful co-existence and to good relations among countries with different social systems. Through a consistently peaceful policy and through the comprehensive development of our country we shall help to convince all nations of the advantages of socialism, which alone can bring well-being for all mankind.

II. Fifteen years ago, in 1945, our working people, following their liberation by the heroic Soviet Army from the yoke of fascist occupation, decided in the light of their experience with a bourgeois republic to build up their newly-liberated country as a people's democracy whose objective

[1] *Constitution of the Czechoslovak Socialist Republic*, third edition, published in English by Orbis, Prague, 1964. Supplied by the Ministry of Foreign Affairs in April 1966. Ed.

would be to ensure peaceful development towards socialism. The Communist Party of Czechoslovakia, the proved vanguard of the working class, steeled in struggle under the bourgeois Republic and during the occupation, took its stand at the head of the Republic. The last major attempt of international and domestic reaction to reverse this development was defeated by the determined action of the working people in February, 1948.

Thus our working people first freed themselves from the shackles of foreign rule and then from capitalist exploitation and became masters of their country. In the last fifteen years they have, by their work and purposeful efforts, achieved successes in all fields of human endeavor which would be inconceivable under capitalism. The advantages of the socialist system have been demonstrated clearly and convincingly in this country, too.

The face of our country has undergone a fundamental transformation. Our economy is expanding as never before. Production is increasing from year to year and the living standard of all working people is constantly rising. There are no longer any exploiting classes, exploitation of man by man has been eliminated forever. There are no longer economic crises or unemployment. Education and culture are becoming the common property of all the working people.

The two nations, Czechs and Slovaks, which created the Czechoslovak Republic, live in fraternal harmony. By building socialism together they have made it possible for Slovakia rapidly to overcome its former backwardness and achieve an advanced level of industry and agriculture.

The Czechoslovak State, into which the working people led by the working class organized itself, has become a people's organization in the truest sense of the word—a socialist State.

In our country all the main tasks of the transition from capitalist to socialist society have already been solved. Emancipated human labor has become the basic factor throughout our society. It is now not only a duty but a matter of honor for every citizen. We are already practising the the socialist principle:

> "From each according to his ability,
> to each according to his work."

People's democracy, as a way to socialism, has fully proved its worth; it has led us to the victory of socialism.

III. All our efforts are now directed at creating the material and moral conditions for the transition of our society to communism.

While developing socialist statehood we shall perfect our socialist democracy by increasing the direct participation of the working people in the administration of the State and in the management of the economy, consolidating the political and moral unity of our society, safeguarding the defence of our country, cherishing the revolutionary achievements of the people and providing conditions for the development of all their creative abilities.

At a later stage, in which work becomes the primary necessity of life, it is our intention to expand the forces of production and multiply the wealth of society to such a degree that it will be possible to provide for all the growing requirements of society and for the full development of each of its members. It will then be possible to proceed to the realization of the highest principle of distribution—the principle of communism:

> "From each according to his ability,
> to each according to his needs."

In order to consolidate the results achieved by the struggle and labor of our people, and at the same time to show our unbreakable will to advance to still higher objectives, we enact this day the following socialist Constitution of our Republic.

CHAPTER ONE

THE SOCIAL ORDER

Art. 1. (1) The Czechoslovak Socialist Republic is a socialist State founded on the firm alliance of the workers, farmers and intelligentsia, with the working class at its head.

(2) The Czechoslovak Socialist Republic is a unitary State of two fraternal nations possessing equal rights, the Czechs and the Slovaks.

(3) The Czechoslovak Socialist Republic is part of the world socialist system; it works for friendly relations with all nations and to ensure lasting peace throughout the world.

Art. 2. (1) All power in the Czechoslovak Socialist Republic shall belong to the working people.

(2) The working people shall exercise state power through representative bodies which are elected by them, controlled by them, and accountable to them.

(3) Representative bodies of the working people in the Czechoslovak Socialist Republic shall be: the National Assembly, the Slovak National Council, and national committees. The authority of other state organs shall be derived from them.

(4) Representative bodies and all other state organs shall rely in their activity on the initiative and direct participation of the working people and their organizations.

Art. 3. (1) The right to elect all representative bodies shall be universal, equal, direct and by secret ballot. Every citizen shall have the right to vote on reaching the age of 18. Every citizen shall be eligible for election on reaching the age of 21.

(2) Members of representative bodies, deputies, shall maintain constant contact with their constituents, shall heed their suggestions, shall be accountable to them for their activity, and shall report to them on the activity of the body of which they are members.

(3) A member of any representative body may be recalled by his constituents at any time.

Art. 4. The guiding force in society and in the State is the vanguard of the working class, the Communist Party of Czechoslovakia, a voluntary militant alliance of the most active and most politically conscious citizens from the ranks of the workers, farmers and intelligentsia.

Art. 5. For the development of joint activities, for full and active participation in the life of society and the State, and to ensure the exercise of their rights, the working people form voluntary associations, particularly the Revolutionary Trade Union Movement, co-operative, youth, cultural, physical training and other organizations; some of the duties of the state organs shall gradually be transferred to these organizations of the people.

Art. 6. The National Front of Czechs and Slovaks, in which the people's organizations are associated, is the political expression of the alliance of the working people of town and country, led by the Communist Party of Czechoslovakia.

Art. 7. (1) The economic foundation of the Czechoslovak Socialist Republic shall be the socialist economic system, which excludes every form of exploitation of man by man.

(2) The socialist economic system, in which the means of production are socially owned and the entire national economy directed by plan, ensures, with the active co-operation of all citizens, a tremendous development of production and a continuous rise in the living standard of the working people.

(3) Labor in a socialist society is always labor for the benefit of the community, and at the same time for the benefit of the worker himself.

Art. 8. (1) Socialist ownership has two basic forms: state ownership, which is ownership by the people as a whole (national property), and co-operative ownership (property of people's co-operatives).

(2) National property is particularly: the mineral wealth and basic sources of power; the main areas of forests, rivers, natural therapeutic sources; means of industrial production, public transport and communications; banks and insurance institutions; broadcasting, television and motion picture enterprises, and the most important social institutions, such as health facilities, schools and scientific institutes.

(3) Land joined for the purpose of joint co-operative cultivation shall be in the joint use of unified agricultural co-operatives.

Art. 9. Within the limits of the socialist economic system small private enterprises, based on the labor of the owner himself and excluding exploitation of another's labor power, shall be permitted.

Art. 10. (1) The citizen's personal ownership of consumer goods, particularly articles of personal and domestic use, family houses, as well as savings derived from labor, shall be inviolable.

(2) Inheritance of such personal property shall be guaranteed.

Art. 11. (1) The State shall establish economic organizations, particularly national enterprises, which shall, as independent legal persons, be entrusted with the administration of part of the national property.

(2) Unified agricultural co-operatives shall be voluntary associations of working farmers for joint socialist agricultural production. The State shall support their development in every way and shall effectively assist co-operative farmers to advance large-scale socialist agricultural production, making use of modern science and technology. The State shall support the development of other people's co-operatives in accordance with the interests of society.

(3) All economic activity of state and other socialist economic organizations is carried out in mutual harmony and directed according to the principle of democratic centralism. At the same time, the participation and enterprise of the working people and their organizations, particularly the Revolutionary Trade Union Movement, shall be exercised in full measure and systematically at all levels of management.

Art. 12. (1) The entire national economy shall be directed by the state plan for the development of the national economy, which shall be drawn up and implemented with the widest active participation of the working people.

(2) The plan for the development of the national economy and culture, usually worked out for a period of five years, shall be promulgated as law and shall be binding for that period as the basis of all planning activity by state organs and economic organizations.

(3) A state budget shall be drawn up each year in conformity with the state plan for the development of the national economy, and promulgated as law.

Art. 13. (1) Every organization and every citizen who is allotted any task connected with the fulfilment of the state plan for the development of the national economy shall exert every effort and show the utmost initiative to carry out this task with the maximum success.

(2) All economic organizations shall systematically create the material, technological and organizational conditions for their activity, in accordance with the long-term plans for the development of the national economy, in such a way that their planned tasks may be fulfilled.

Art. 14. (1) The State shall direct its entire policy, and particularly its economic policy, so that the all-round development of production on the basis of the continuous advance of science and technology and increasing labor productivity shall secure the full development of socialist society and create the conditions for the gradual transition to communism. Particular attention shall be paid to eliminating the substantial differences between physical and mental labor and between town and country.

(2) The realization of these aims is made possible by fraternal co-operation between the Czechoslovak Socialist Republic and the Union of Soviet Socialist Republics and the other countries of the world socialist system. The Czechoslovak Socialist Republic shall systematically develop and strengthen this co-operation, which is based on mutual assistance and the international socialist division of labor.

Art. 15. (1) The State shall carry out an economic, health, social and cultural policy enabling the physical and mental capabilities of all the people to develop continuously together with the growth of production, the rise in the living standard, and the gradual reduction of working hours.

(2) The State shall make provision for the conservation of nature and the preservation of the beauties of the country so as to create an increasingly rich source of benefit to the people and suitable surroundings for the working people with a view to their health and their right to recreation.

Art. 16. (1) The entire cultural policy of Czechoslovakia, the development of all forms of education, schooling and instruction shall be directed in the spirit of the scientific world outlook, Marxism, Leninism, and closely linked to the life and work of the people.

(2) The State, together with the people's organizations, shall give all possible support to creative activity in science and art, shall endeavor to achieve an increasingly high educational level of the working people and their active participation in scientific and artistic work, and shall see to it that the results of this work serve all the people.

(3) The State and the people's organizations shall systematically endeavor to free the minds of the people from surviving influences of a society based on exploitation.

Art. 17. (1) All citizens and all state and people's organizations shall direct all their activity according to the legal order of the socialist State, and shall see to the full enforcement of socialist legality in the life of society.

(2) People's organizations, in fulfilling their purpose, shall guide citizens to uphold the law, to maintain working discipline and the rules of socialist conduct, and shall endeavor to forestall and prevent their violation.

Art. 18. (1) The central direction of society and the State in accordance with the principle of democratic centralism shall be effectively combined with the broad authority and responsibility of lower organs, drawing on the initiative and active participation of the working people.

(2) In conformity with the scientific world outlook, the results of scientific research shall be fully applied in the direction of the society of the working people and in planning its further development.

CHAPTER TWO

RIGHTS AND DUTIES OF CITIZENS

Art. 19. (1) In a society of the working people in which exploitation of man by man has been abolished, the advancement and interests of each member are in accord with the advancement and interests of the whole community. The rights, freedoms and duties of citizens shall therefore serve both the free and complete expression of the personality of the individual and the strengthening and growth of socialist society; they shall be broadened and deepened with its development.

(2) In a society of the working people the individual can fully develop his capabilities and assert his true interests only by active participation in the development of society as a whole, and particularly by undertakiúg an appropriate share of social work. Therefore, work in the interests of the community shall be a primary duty and the right to work a primary right of every citizen.

Art. 20. (1) All citizens shall have equal rights and equal duties.

(2) The equality of all citizens without regard to nationality and race shall be guaranteed.

(3) Men and women shall have equal status in the family, at work and in public activity.

(4) The society of the working people shall ensure the equality of all citizens by creating equal possibilities and equal opportunities in all fields of public life.

Art. 21. (1) All citizens shall have the right to work and to remuneration for work done according to its quantity, quality and social importance.

(2) The right to work and to remuneration for work done is secured by the entire socialist economic system, which does not experience economic crises or unemployment and guarantees a continuous rise in the real value of remuneration.

(3) The State shall follow a policy which, as production and productivity increase, will permit the gradual reduction of working hours without reduction in wages.

Art. 22. (1) All working people shall have the right to leisure after work

(2) This right shall be secured by the legal regulation of working hours and paid holidays, as well as by the attention paid by the State and people's organizations to ensuring the most fruitful use of the free time of the working people for recreation and for cultural life.

Art. 23. (1) All working people shall have the right to the protection of their health and to medical care, and to material security in old age and when incapable of work.

(2) The State and people's organizations shall secure these rights by the prevention of disease, the whole health system, the provision of medical

and social facilities, by continuous expansion of free medical services and by the organization of safety measures at work, by health insurance and pension security.

Art. 24. (1) All citizens shall have the right to education.

(2) This right shall be secured by compulsory free basic school education for all children up to the age of 15 years, and by a system of free education which shall to an increasing extent provide complete secondary education, general or specialized, and university-level education. The organization of courses for employed persons, free specialized training in industrial enterprises and agricultural co-operatives and the cultural and educational activities undertaken by the State and the people's organizations shall serve further to advance the level of education.

(3) All education and schooling shall be based on the scientific world outlook and on close ties between school and the life and work of the people.

Art. 25. The State shall ensure citizens of Hungarian, Ukrainian and Polish nationality every opportunity and all means for education in their mother tongue and for their cultural development.

Art. 26. (1) Motherhood, marriage and the family shall be protected by the State.

(2) The State and society shall ensure that the family provides a sound foundation for the development of young people. Large families shall be granted special relief and assistance by the State.

(3) Society shall ensure to all children and youth every opportunity for full physical and mental development. This development shall be secured through the care provided by the family, the State and the people's organizations, and by the special adjustment of working conditions for young people.

Art. 27. The equal status of women in the family, at work and in public life shall be secured by special adjustment of working conditions and special health care during pregnancy and maternity, as well as by the development of facilities and services which will enable women fully to participate in the life of society.

Art. 28. (1) Freedom of expression in all fields of public life, in particular freedom of speech and of the press, consistent with the interests of the working people, shall be guaranteed to all citizens. These freedoms shall enable citizens to further the development of their personalities and their creative efforts, and to take an active part in the administration of the State and in the economic and cultural development of the country. For this purpose freedom of assembly, and freedom to hold public parades and demonstrations shall be guaranteed.

(2) These freedoms shall be secured by making publishing houses and printing presses, public buildings, halls, assembly grounds, as well as broadcasting, television and other facilities available to the working people and their organizations.

Art. 29. Citizens and organizations shall have the right to submit their proposals, suggestions and complaints to representative bodies and to other state organs; it shall be the duty of state organs to take responsible and prompt action.

Art. 30. (1) Inviolability of the person shall be guaranteed. No one shall be prosecuted except in cases authorized by law and by due process of law. No one shall be taken into custody except in cases prescribed by law and on the basis of a decision of the court or the Procurator.

(2) Offenders can be punished only by due process of law.

Art. 31. Inviolability of the home, the privacy of the mails and all other forms of communication, as well as freedom of domicile shall be guaranteed.

Art. 32. (1) Freedom of confession shall be guaranteed. Every one shall have the right to profess any religious faith or to be without religious conviction, and to practise his religious beliefs in so far as this does not contravene the law.

(2) Religious faith or conviction shall not constitute grounds for anyone to refuse to fulfil the civic duties laid upon him by law.

Art. 33. The Czechoslovak Socialist Republic shall grant the right of asylum to citizens of a foreign state persecuted for defending the interests of the working people, for participating in the national liberation movement, for scientific or artistic work, or for activity in defence of peace.

Art. 34. Citizens shall be in duty bound to uphold the Constitution and other laws, and in all their actions to pay heed to the interests of the socialist State and the society of the working people.

Art. 35. Citizens shall be in duty bound to protect and strengthen socialist ownership as the inviolable foundation of the socialist social order and the source of the welfare of the working people, the wealth and strength of the country.

Art. 36. Citizens shall be in duty bound to discharge the public functions entrusted to them by the working people conscientiously and honestly, and to consider their fulfilment in the interests of society as a matter of honour.

Art. 37. (1) The defence of the country and its socialist social order shall be the supreme duty and a matter of honor for every citizen.

(2) Citizens shall be in duty bound to serve in the Armed Forces as prescribed by law.

Art. 38. An essential part of the duty of every citizen shall be respect for rights of his fellow citizens and the careful observance of the rules of socialist conduct.

CHAPTER THREE

THE NATIONAL ASSEMBLY

Art. 39. (1) The National Assembly shall be the supreme organ of state power in the Czechoslovak Socialist Republic. It shall be the sole state-wide legislative body.

(2) The National Assembly shall consist of 300 deputies, who shall be elected by the people, shall be accountable to the people, and may be recalled by the people.

(3) The National Assembly shall be elected for a term of four years.

(4) Provisions regarding the exercise of the right to elect and be elected to the National Assembly and the manner in which the election and recall of deputies shall be conducted, shall be prescribed by law.

The Competence of the National Assembly

Art. 40. (1) The National Assembly shall discuss and decide on fundamental questions of the home and foreign policy of the State.

(2) All the activity of the National Assembly and the work of its organs and deputies shall be directed towards fulfilling the tasks of the socialist State.

Art. 41. (1) The National Assembly shall enact the Constitution and other laws, and shall supervise their implementation. It shall in particular approve the long-term plans for the development of the national economy and the state budget, investigate their fulfilment, and discuss the reports of the Government on the fulfilment of annual plans and the state financial account.

(2) The National Assembly shall see to it that the Constitution is upheld. It may annul a law of the Slovak National Council, an order or decision of the Government and a generally binding order of a regional national committee if they contravene the Constitution or another law.

Art. 42. The National Assembly shall approve international political treaties, economic treaties of a general nature and such treaties as require implementation by legislation.

Art. 43. (1) The National Assembly shall elect the President of the Republic. The President of the Republic shall be responsible to it for the discharge of his office.

(2) The President of the Republic shall have the right to speak in the National Assembly whenever he requests it.

Art. 44. (1) After being appointed by the President of the Republic, the Government shall present its program to the National Assembly and ask for its approval.

(2) The National Assembly shall supervise and control the activities of

the Government and its members. The Government, and its members as well, shall be accountable for their activities to the National Assembly, which shall debate their statements of policy and reports.

(3) The National Assembly may propose to the President of the Republic recall of the Government or of its individual members.

Art. 45. (1) The National Assembly shall be entitled to question the Premier and the other members of the Government regarding matters within their competence. The Premier and the other members of the Government shall be required to answer the questions of deputies.

(2) A member of the Government shall be required to appear in person at a meeting of the National Assembly, of the Presidium or of a committee at the request of the National Assembly, the Presidium, or any of its committies.

(3) The Premier and other members of the Government shall be entitled to take part in meetings of the National Assembly, its Presidium. or any of its committees, and shall have the right to speak if they so request.

Art. 46. (1) The National Assembly shall elect the Supreme Court and may recall its members.

(2) The Procurator General shall be responsible to the National Assembly for the exercise of his office. The National Assembly may propose to the President of the Republic that he recall the Procurator General.

(3) The National Assembly shall discuss reports of the Supreme Court and the Procurator General on the state of socialist legality.

Art. 47. The National Assembly shall enact laws establishing ministries and other central organs.

Art. 48. The National Assembly, as the supreme representative body in the Republic, shall consider the suggestions of the national committees, discuss their activities, draw general conclusions from their experience and pass measures to improve their structure and methods of work.

Art. 49. The National Assembly shall have the power te declare war in case of an attack on the Czechoslovak Socialist Republic or in fulfilment of international treaty obligations concerning joint defence against aggression.

Sessions of the National Assembly

Art. 50. (1) The President of the Republic shall convene the National Assembly at least twice a year. The National Assembly must be convened if at least one third of the deputies request it.

(2) The President of the Republic shall prorogue the session of the National Assembly.

Art. 51. (1) A majority of the deputies to the National Assembly shall constitute a quorum.

(2) Enactments of the National Assembly shall require a straight majority vote of deputies present.

(3) Adoption or amendment of the Constitution, a declaration of war, changes in the state boundaries and election of the President shall require a three-fifths majority of all the deputies.

(4) The meetings of the National Assembly shall as a rule be public.

(5) The principles of work of the National Assembly shall be laid down in the National Assembly Rules of Procedure and Work.

Laws

Art. 52. (1) Bills may be introduced by deputies of the National Assembly, its committees and its Presidium, the President of the Republic, the Government and the Slovak National Council.

(2) Laws shall be signed by the President of the Republic, the Chairman of the National Assembly and the Premier.

(3) A law shall take effect only when promulgated in the manner prescribed by law. Laws shall be promulgated by the Presidium of the National Assembly within 14 days after their adoption.

Committees of the National Assembly

Art. 53. (1) The National Assembly shall establish committees for the principal sectors of state and social activity as its working and initiatory organs.

(2) The National Assembly shall elect the chairman and the other members of its committees and shall have the power to recall them at any time.

(3) The committees of the National Assembly shall supervise and discuss the fulfilment of economic and cultural tasks and make recommendations for the activity of state organs.

Art. 54. (1) The committees of the National Assembly shall rely in their activities on the co-operation of the working people and their organizations.

(2) The committees shall have the right to invite members of the Government and representatives of other state organs to their meetings and request from them information and reports.

(3) The committees shall invite scientists, innovators, technicians and other leading workers in economic and cultural life to participate in their work.

Deputies of the National Assembly

Art. 55. The National Assembly shall verify the validity of the election of its deputies. It shall do so on the recommendation of the Mandates Committee, which it shall elect.

Art. 56. A deputy of the National Assembly shall take the following oath at the first meeting of the National Assembly which he attends:

"I swear on my honor and conscience to be loyal to the Czechoslovak Socialist Republic and to the cause of socialism. I will respect the will and the interests of the people, uphold the Constitution and the other laws of the Republic and work for their implementation."

Art. 57. (1) It shall be the duty of a deputy of the National Assembly to work in his constituency, maintain constant contact with his constituents, heed their suggestions and account to them regularly for his activity. A deputy shall co-operate with the national committees in his constituency and help them to fulfil their tasks.

(2) It shall be the duty of a deputy of the National Assembly to take an active part and show initiative in the work of the National Assembly. As a general rule it shall be the duty of every deputy to serve on one of the committees of the National Assembly.

Art. 58. No penal or disciplinary proceedings shall be instituted against a deputy, nor can he be taken into custody, without the assent of the National Assembly.

The Presidium of the National Assembly

Art. 59. (1) The National Assembly shall elect a Presidium of 30 from the deputies. The Presidium shall consist of the Chariman of the National Assembly, the Vice-Chairmen, the charimen of the committees, and other members.

(2) The Presidium shall be elected for the entire electoral term of the National Assembly. It shall remain in office after the expiration of the electoral term until a new National Assembly has elected its Presidium.

(3) The Presidium of the National Assembly and its members shall be accountable for their activity to the National Assembly. The National Assembly shall have the power to recall the Presidium and its members at any time.

(4) Decisions of the Presidium of the National Assembly shall require an absolute majority of all its members.

Art. 60. (1) The Presidium shall direct the work of the National Assembly.

(2) At a time when the National Assembly is not in session because it has been adjourned or because its electoral term has expired, the Presidium shall exercise the competence of the National Assembly. It shall not, how-

ever, be competent to elect the President of the Republic or to amend the the Constitution. It may make a decision regarding a declaration of war only if the convening of the National Assembly is prevented by exceptional circumstances; such a decision shall require the approval of three fifths of all members of the Presidium. Measures of the Presidium of the National Assembly resulting from the exercise of this competence must be approved at the next session of the National Assembly, otherwise they shall become null and void. Measures which require legislation shall take the form of legal measures of the Presidium and shall be signed by the President of the Republic, the Chairman of the National Assembly and the Premier; they shall be promulgated in the same manner als laws.

(3) At a time when the Government is discharging the office of President of the Republic, the Presidium of the National Assembly shall be competent to appoint and recall the Government and its members and invest in them the direction of ministries and other central organs.

(4) The Presidium of the National Assembly shall order elections to the National Assembly and general elections to representative bodies.

CHAPTER FOUR

THE PRESIDENT OF THE REPUBLIC

Art. 61. (1) At the head of the State shall be the President of the Republic, elected by the National Assembly as the representative of state power.

(2) The President shall be accountable to the National Assembly for the discharge of his office.

Art. 62. (1) The President of the Republic shall:

1. represent the State in foreign relations, negotiate and ratify international treaties. The negotiation of international treaties and agreements which do not require approval of the National Assembly may be delegated by the President to the Government or, with its approval, to its individual members;
2. receive and accredit envoys;
3. summon and prorogue sessions of the National Assembly;
4. sign laws of the National Assembly and legal measures of its Presidium;
5. have the right to submit to the National Assembly reports on the state of the Republic and on important political questions, recommend necessary measures, and be present at meetings of the National Assembly;
6. appoint and recall the Premier and the other members of the Government and entrust them with the direction of ministries and other central organs;
7. have the right to be present and to take the chair at meetings of the

Government, to request reports from the Government and its individual members, and to discuss with the Government or its members matters requiring action;

8. appoint high state officials in cases laid down by law; appoint and promote generals;

9. award decorations unless he authorizes another organ to do so;

10. have the right to proclaim an amnesty, to grant a pardon or mitigate a sentence imposed by a criminal court and order the cancellation or suspension of criminal proceedings;

11. be the Commander-in-Chief of the Armed Forces;

12. proclaim a state of war on the recommendation of the Government and declare war in pursuance of a decision of the National Assembly if Czechoslovakia is attacked or in fulfilment of international treaty obligations concerning joint defence against aggression.

(2) The President of the Republic shall also exercise authority which is not explicitly reserved to him in the Constitution if the law so provides.

Art. 63. (1) Any citizen of the State who is eligible for election to the National Assembly may be elected President of the Republic. A candidate shall be declared elected if he receives three fifths of the votes of all the deputies of the National Assembly.

(2) The President of the Republic shall be elected for a term of five years. He shall assume his function by taking the oath of office.

(3) The President of the Republic may not at the same time be a deputy of the National Assembly, the Slovak National Council, or of a national committee or a member of the Government.

(4) If a deputy or a member of the Government is elected President of the Republic he shall cease to exercise his previous office from the day of his election. His mandate or membership in the Government shall lapse on the day on which he takes the oath of office.

Art. 64. The President of the Republic shall take the following oath before the National Assembly: "I swear upon my honor and conscience to be loyal to the Czechoslovak Socialist Republic and the cause of socialism. I will discharge my duties in accordance with the will of the people and in the interests of the people. I will cherish the welfare of the Republic and abide by the Constitution and the other laws of the socialist State."

Art. 65. If the office of the President of the Republic has been vacated and a new President has not yet been elected and has not taken the oath of office, or if the President is unable to exercise his function for serious reasons, the exercise of his function shall fall to the Government. The Government shall have the authority in such an event to delegate some of the powers of the President to the Premier; the supreme command of the Armed Forces shall, during this time, pass to the Premier.

CHAPTER FIVE

THE GOVERNMENT

Art. 66. (1) The Government shall be the supreme executive organ of state power in the Czechoslovak Socialist Republic.

(2) The Government and its members are accountable for the exercise of their office to the National Assembly.

Art. 67. The Government shall consist of the Premier, the Vice-Premiers, and the ministers.

Art. 68. The Government shall organize and ensure fulfilment of the economic and cultural tasks of socialist construction, the raising of the standard of living of the working people, strengthening of the country's security, and pursuance of a peaceful foreign policy.

To this end it shall, specifically,

1. unify, direct and control the activities of the ministries and other central organs of state administration;
2. direct and control the work of the national committees;
3. prepare long-term plans for the development of the national economy and the state budget and ensure and control their fulfilment; it shall set forth annual plans necessary for the carrying out of the long-term plans for development of the national economy and submit reports to the National Assembly on their fulfilment;
4. ensure observance of the laws and the maintenance of state discipline, the protection of the rights of citizens and the interests of the State;
5. issue decisions and orders on the basis of laws and for their implementation, and supervise their execution;
6. have the right to introduce bills in the National Assembly and drafts of legal measures to the Presidium of the National Assembly;
7. appoint state officials and heads of economic organizations where provided by law and propose officials who are appointed by the President of the Republic.

Art. 69. Members of the Government shall take the following oath administered by the President: "I swear upon my honor and conscience to be loyal to the Czechoslovak Socialist Republic and to the cause of socialism. I will perform my duties in accordance with the will of the people and in the interests of the people. I will abide by the Constitution and other laws and work for their implementation."

Art. 70. (1) The National Assembly may propose that the President of the Republic recall the Government or any of its members. In such an event the President of the Republic shall recall the Government or the member concerned.

(2) The Government and its members shall fulfil their tasks in close co-operation with the National Assembly and its organs.

Art. 71. After being appointed by the President of the Republic, the Government shall present its program to the National Assembly and ask for its approval.

Art. 72. Ministries and other central organs of state administration may on the basis of laws and government orders and in pursuance of them issue generally binding legal regulations.

CHAPTER SIX

THE SLOVAK NATIONAL COUNCIL

Art. 73. (1) The Slovak National Council shall be the national organ of state power and administration in Slovakia.

(2) The Slovak National Council shall be composed of deputies of the Slovak National Council, who shall be elected by the people of Slovakia, shall be accountable to the people and may be recalled by the people.

(3) The Slovak National Council shall be elected for a term of four years.

(4) The number of deputies of the Slovak National Council, provisions regarding the exercise of the right to elect and be elected to the Slovak National Council and the manner in which the election and recall of deputies shall be conducted shall be prescribed by law of the Slovak National Council.

(5) The seat of the Slovak National Council shall be Bratislava.

Competence of the Slovak National Council

Art. 74. The Slovak National Council shall have the competence to:

(a) enact, in conformity with state-wide legislation, laws of the Slovak National Council concerning matters of a national or regional nature where special legislation is required to ensure the full economic and cultural development of Slovakia;

(b) enact laws of the Slovak National Council where empowered to do so by law of the National Assembly;

(c) participate in the drawing up of the state plan for the development of the national economy and discuss, within the limits of the state plan, the overall economic and cultural development of Slovakia;

(d) discuss and approve the budget of the Slovak National Council, of its organs and of institutions in Slovakia under its immediate jurisdiction;

(e) introduce bills in the National Assembly;

(f) exercise control within the limits of its own authority;

(g) ensure, in the spirit of equality, favorable conditions for the full development of the life of citizens of Hungarian and Ukrainian nationality;

(h) elect a Presidium and from its members commissioners of the Slovak National Council;

(i) discuss reports of the Presidium, of the commissions, and of commissioners of the Slovak National Council.

Sessions of the Slovak National Council

Art. 75. (1) The Presidium of the Slovak National Council shall convene the Slovak National Council at least twice a year. The Slovak National Council must be convened if at least one third of the deputies request it.

(2) The Presidium of the Slovak National Council shall prorogue the session of the Slovak National Council.

Art. 76. (1) A majority of the deputies of the Slovak National Council shall constitute a quorum. Enactments shall require a straight majority vote of deputies present.

(2) Meetings of the Slovak National Council shall, as a rule, be public.

(3) The fundamental rules of procedure of the Slovak National Council shall be set forth in the Slovak National Council Rules of Procedure and Work.

Laws of the Slovak National Council

Art. 77. (1) Bills of the Slovak National Council may be introduced by deputies, commissions, and the Presidium of the Slovak National Council.

(2) Laws shall be signed by the Chairman of the Slovak National Council.

(3) A law shall take effect only when promulgated in the manner prescribed by law of the Slovak National Council. Laws shall be promulgated by the Presidium of the Slovak National Council within 14 days after their adoption.

Commissions of the Slovak National Council

Art. 78. (1) The Slovak National Council shall establish commissions for the particular sectors of its activities as its initiatory, controlling and executive organs.

(2) Commissions of the Slovak National Council shall supervise the carrying out of tasks evolving from the economic and cultural development of Slovakia, discuss them and make decisions concerning them, help to execute them and submit their decisions and recommendations to the Slovak National Council and its Presidium.

(3) Commissions of the Slovak National Council shall rely in their activities on the co-operation of the working people and their organizations.

(4) Members of the commissions of the Slovak National Council shall be elected by the Slovak National Council from among its deputies and from the ranks of political, economic, cultural and other workers in Slovakia.

The Slovak National Council shall as a rule elect commissioners of the Slovak National Council to be chairmen of commissions.

Deputies of the Slovak National Council

Art. 79. The Slovak National Council shall verify the validity of the election of its deputies. It shall do so on the recommendation of the Mandates Commission which it shall elect.

Art. 80. A deputy of the Slovak National Council shall take the following oath at the first meeting of the Slovak National Council which he attends:

"I swear on my honor and conscience to be loyal to the Czechoslovak Socialist Republic, the cause of socialism and the heritage of the Slovak National Uprising. I will respect the will and interests of the people, uphold the Constitution and the other laws of the Republic, and work for their implementation."

Art. 81. (1) It shall be the duty of a deputy of the Slovak National Council to work in his constituency, maintain constant contact with his constituents, heed their suggestions and account to them regularly for his activity. He shall co-operate with the national committees in his constituency and help them to fulfil their tasks.

(2) It shall be the duty of a deputy of the Slovak National Council to take an active part in the work of the Slovak National Council and its organs. As a general rule it shall be the duty of every deputy to serve on one of the commissions of the Slovak National Council.

(3) A deputy of the Slovak National Council may also be a deputy of the National Assembly.

Art. 82. Penal or disciplinary proceedings shall not be instituted against a deputy of the Slovak National Council, nor can he be taken into custody, without the assent of the Slovak National Council.

The Presidium of the Slovak National Council

Art. 83. (1) The Presidium of the Slovak National Council shall have 16 members. It shall consist of the Chairman of the Slovak National Council, the Vice-Chairmen and other members.

(2) The Presidium of the Slovak National Council shall be elected by the Slovak National Council from among its members for the entire electoral term. The Presidium shall remain in office after the expiration of the electoral term until a new Slovak National Council has elected its Presidium.

(3) The Presidium of the Slovak National Council and its members shall be accountable for their activity to the Slovak National Council. The

Slovak National Council shall have the power to recall the Presidium and its members at any time.

(4) A member of the Presidium of the Slovak National Council may also be a member of the Government.

Art. 84 (1) The Presidium shall be the executive organ of the Slovak National Council within the limits of the latter's authority. It shall ensure the implementation of laws and shall particularly see to the balanced fulfilment of the tasks of the state economic plan in Slovakia in complete conformity with the plan.

(2) The Presidium of the Slovak National Council shall direct and co-ordinate the work of the commissions and the commissioners of the Slovak National Council, discuss their reports and prepare recommendations for the sessions of the Slovak National Council.

(3) The Presidium of the Slovak National Council shall issue decisions and orders on the basis of laws of the Slovak National Council and in pursuance of them.

(4) The Presidium of the Slovak National Council shall appoint and propose state officials for Slovakia within limits set by the Government.

Art. 85. (1) The Slovak National Council shall elect commissioners of the Slovak National Council from among the members of the Presidium of the Slovak National Council. The Council shall have the power to recall a commissioner of the Slovak National Council at any time.

(2) Commissioners of the Slovak National Council shall hold office in those branches of the state administration laid down by law.

(3) Commissioners shall discharge the tasks entrusted to them within the limits of the authority of the Slovak National Council. They shall discharge other tasks connected with the economic and cultural life of Slovakia within limits set by the Government.

CHAPTER SEVEN

THE NATIONAL COMMITTEES

Art. 86. (1) The national committees—the broadest organization of the working people—are the organs of state power and administration in the regions, districts and localities.

(2) The national committees shall be composed of deputies who shall be elected by the people, shall be accountable to the people and may be recalled by the people.

(3) The national committees shall be elected for a term of four years.

(4) Provisions regarding the exercise of the right to elect and be elected to the national committees and the manner in which the election and recall of deputies shall be conducted shall be prescribed by law.

Art. 87. (1) The national committees shall rely in all their work on the constant and active participation of the working people of their area. In this way they shall gain the fullest co-operation of the working people in the administration of the State, draw on their experience and learn from it.

(2) The national committees shall work closely with other organizations of the working people, rely on their co-operation and help them fulfil their tasks.

Art. 88. (1) The national committees and their deputies shall be accountable to their constituents for their activities.

(2) It shall be the duty of a deputy of a national committee to work in his constituency, maintain constant contact with his constituents, take their advice, heed their suggestions, account to them for his activity and report to them on the work of the national committee.

(3) It shall be the duty of a deputy of a national committee to take an active part in the work of the national committee and to work in one of its commissions.

(4) A deputy of a national committee shall take the following oath at the first meeting of the national committee which he attends:

> "I swear on my honor and conscience to be loyal to the Czechoslovak Socialist Republic and to the cause of socialism. I shall respect the will and the interests of the people, uphold the Constitution and the laws of the Republic and work for their implementation."

Art. 89. The national committees shall, with the broadest participation of the citizens,

– direct, organize and ensure in a planned manner the development of their area as regards economic affairs, culture, health and social services; their primary responsibilities shall include satisfaction of the material and cultural requirements of the working people to a continuously-increasing degree; to this end they shall establish economic institutions and cultural, health and social institutions and direct their work;

– ensure the protection of socialist ownership and all the achievements of the working people, the maintenance of socialist order in society, see that the rules of socialist conduct are upheld, and strengthen the defence potential of the Republic;

– ensure the implementation of laws and see to their observance, ensure the protection and realization of the rights and the assertion of the true interests of the working people and of socialist organizations.

Art. 90. (1) The national committees shall be guided in their work by the state plan for the development of the national economy. They shall take part in drafting and carrying it out. They shall draw up the plan of development for their areas in accordance with and on the basis of the state plan.

(2) They shall have at their disposal the necessary material and financial resources to carry out the planned tasks and shall employ them as responsible managers.

(3) The basis of the financial management of the national committees shall be their budgets, which they shall draft and which shall be part of the state budget.

Art. 91. National committees shall be regional, district, and municipal or local in localities. In Prague there shall be the National Committee of the City of Prague, for the districts of Prague and in certain other cities there shall be district national committees.

Art. 92. The authority and responsibility of the national committees at the various levels shall be laid down so that they may, most effectively and with the broadest possible participation of the working people, ensure the economic and cultural advancement and satisfy the requirements of the citizens of their areas.

Art. 93. (1) The national committees shall combine in their work the fulfilment of the state-wide tasks with satisfaction of the special needs of their areas and the interests of their citizens.

(2) The national committees shall be guided by the principle that the interests of all the people of the Czechoslovak Socialist Republic stand above sectional and local interests, and shall in all their activity educate citizens for the politically-conscious and voluntary fulfilment of their responsibilities towards society and the State.

Art. 94. In the exercise of their functions, the national committees may issue generally binding orders for their respective districts.

Art. 95. (1) National committees shall establish a council, commissions and other organs and direct their work.

(2) The council shall, under the direction of the national committee, direct and co-ordinate the work of the other organs of the national committee and its organizations and institutions. The council shall be elected by the national committee from among its members for the whole term of office. The council and its members shall be accountable to the national committee, which may recall the council or its individual members at any time.

(3) The commissions shall be the initiatory, controlling and executive organs of the national committee for individual fields or branches of its activity. They shall be furnished with the necessary authority to this end. The commissions, to which a national committee shall elect its members and other citizens, shall systematically intensify the participation of the working people in the activity of the national committee. The commissions shall be accountable to the national committee and its council.

Art. 96. (1) National committees of superior levels shall guide and direct the work of national committees of subordinate levels. In so doing they shall respect the authority and responsibility of the latter. They shall rely on their initiative and experience and carry out their tasks in constant co-operation with them.

(2) National committees shall be guided in their activity by the laws

and orders and the decisions of the Government, as well as the decisions and directives of higher state organs; decisions of national committees of a subordinate level which conflict with these may be annulled by a national committee of a superior level or by the Government.

CHAPTER EIGHT

THE COURTS AND THE OFFICE OF THE PROCURATOR

Art. 97. (1) The courts and the office of the Procurator shall protect the socialist State, its social order and the rights and true interests of its citizens and of the organizations of the working people.

(2) The courts and the Procurator's office shall in all their activity educate citizens to be loyal to their country and the cause of socialism, to abide by the laws and the rules of socialist conduct, and honorably to fulfil their duties towards the State and society.

The Courts

Art. 98. (1) The execution of justice in the Czechoslovak Socialist Republic shall be vested in elected and independent people's courts.

(2) The courts shall be the Supreme Court, regional courts, district courts, military courts and local people's courts.

Art. 99. (1) The Supreme Court shall be the highest court; it shall supervise the judicial activities of all other courts. Judges of the Supreme Court shall be elected by the National Assembly.

(2) Judges of the regional courts shall be elected by regional national committees.

(3) Judges of the district courts shall be elected by citizens by universal, direct, equal vote and by secret ballot.

(4) The Supreme Court, regional and district courts shall be elected for a term of four years.

(5) Military courts shall be elected under special regulations.

Art. 100. (1) The courts shall, as a rule, make decisions through benches.

(2) Benches of the Supreme Court, regional, district and military courts shall be composed both of judges who carry out their function as a profession and of judges who carry it out in addition to their regular employment. Both categories of judges are equal in making decisions.

Art. 101. (1) To ensure increased participation of the working people in the work of the judiciary, local people's courts shall be elected in the localities and at places of work.

(2) Local people's courts shall contribute to the consolidation of socialist legality, to the safeguarding of social order and the rules of socialist conduct.

(3) The extent of the jurisdiction of the local people's courts, the manner of their instalment, their electoral term and the principles of their organization and proceedings shall be prescribed by law.

Art. 102. Judges shall be independent in the discharge of their office and shall be bound solely by the legal order of the socialist State. They shall be in duty bound to act in accordance with the laws and other legal regulations and to interpret them in the spirit of socialist legality.

(2) Judges shall be in duty bound to submit reports on the activities of the courts of which they are members to their electors or to the representative body that has elected them. Judges may be recalled by their electors or by the representative body that has elected them; the conditions for and manner of recall of judges shall be prescribed by law.

Art. 103. (1) The courts shall proceed so that the true facts of the case shall be determined and shall base their judgements on these findings.

(2) All court proceedings shall in principle be oral and public. The public may be excluded only in cases prescribed by law.

(3) The accused shall be guaranteed the right of defence.

(4) Judgements shall be pronounced in the name of the Republic and shall always be pronounced in public.

The Office of the Procurator

Art. 104. The supervision of the precise fulfilment and observance of the laws and other legal regulations by ministries and other organs of state administration, national committees, courts, economic and other organizations and by individual citizens, shall rest with the office of the Procurator, headed by the Procurator General.

Art. 105. (1) The Procurator General shall be appointed and recalled by the President of the Republic.

(2) The Procurator General shall be accountable to the National Assembly.

Art. 106. The organs of the Procurator's office shall be subordinated to the Procurator General only and shall discharge their functions independently of local organs. In all their activities they shall rely on the initiative of the working people and their organizations.

CHAPTER NINE

GENERAL AND CONCLUDING PROVISIONS

Art. 107. (1) The territory of the Czechoslovak Socialist Republic shall constitute a single and indivisible whole.

(2) The state frontiers may be altered by constitutional law only.

(3) The territorial organization of Czechoslovakia shall be determined

with a view to the economic, political, social and cultural needs of the whole of society, so as to aid its further development in every way and ensure the widest possible participation of the working people in the administration of the State and the direction of economic and cultural construction.

Art. 108. Conditions for the acquisition and loss of state citizenship shall be prescribed by law.

Art. 109. The capital of the Czechoslovak Socialist Republic shall be Prague.

Art. 110. (1) The state emblem of the Czechoslovak Socialist Republic shall consist of a red escutcheon in the form of a Hussite shield with a five-pointed star in the upper part, with a white, two-tailed lion bearing a red shield on its chest showing a blue outline of Kriváň Mountain and a golden fire of freedom. The emblem is outlined in gold.

(2) The flag of the Czechoslovak Socialist Republic shall consist of a lower red field and an upper white field, with a blue wedge between them extending from the hoist to the centre of the flag.

(3) Details of the state emblem and state flag and their proper display shall be enacted by law.

Art. 111. (1) The Constitution may be amended by constitutional law only.

(2) Laws and other legal regulations may not contravene the Constitution. Interpretation and application of all legal regulations must be in conformity with the Constitution.

Art. 112. (1) The Constitution shall take effect from the day of enactment by the National Assembly.

(2) As from that day the previous Constitution and all previous constitutional laws which amended and supplemented it shall cease to have effect.

DENMARK

SUMMARY

INTERNATIONAL STATUS

Denmark is a member of the United Nations (October 24, 1945).[1] It is a member of the Nordic Council, the European Free Trade Association and other international organizations. It was a member of the League of Nations.

After the Napoleonic wars, Denmark, Europe's most ancient kingdom, ceded Norway to Sweden by the Treaty of Kiel in 1814. In 1848, the King

[1] Denmark has accepted the compulsory jurisdiction of the International Court under Article 36 of its Statute.

was forced to appoint a responsible ministry and the Constitution of 1849 abolished absolutism and established a bicameral parliament; by 1901, the principle of cabinet responsibility was accepted by the King. A German-Danish conflict over Schleswig Holstein had been endemic; in 1863 a Constitution for Denmark and Schleswig was adopted and followed by Prussian conquest of the duchies which were ceded to Prussia and Austria by the Peace of Vienna of 1864. In 1917, the Danish West Indies were sold to the United States. In 1918, Iceland became independent while remaining, until 1939, in personal union with Denmark under the King. In 1920 the northern part of Schleswig was transferred, following a plebiscite, to Denmark. Denmark was invaded and occupied by Germany in 1940.

FORM OF NATIONAL GOVERNMENT

The Constitution of June 5, 1953 and the Succession to the Throne Act of March 27, 1953 comprise the constitutional documents of Denmark. The Constitution states that the form of government shall be that of a constitutional monarchy.[1] The Evangelical Lutheran Church is the established church.[2] Powers vested in the authorities of the Realm may be delegated to international authorities for the promotion of international rules of law and co-operation.[3]

RIGHTS OF THE PEOPLE

The Constitution provides freedom of religion.[4] It guarantees personal liberty and due process of law, inviolability of the dwelling, the right of property, free and equal access to trade, the right to work and public assistance, the right to free elementary education, freedom of speech and press, association, assembly, the abolition of privileges and estates tail.[5] Able-bodied males must contribute with their person to the defense of the state.[6]

LEGISLATIVE DEPARTMENT

The legislature is unicameral, consisting of the Folketing composed of not more than 179 members, two of whom from the Faeroe Islands and two from Greenland.[7] Members are elected by universal suffrage and general and direct ballot for a term of four years subject to dissolution.[8] Immunities of deputies are provided.[9] There are provisions concerning finance.[10]

[1] Const., Art. 2. [2] Id., Art. 4. [3] Id., Art, 20 [4] Id., Art. 67–70.
[5] Id., Art. 71–80, 83, 84. [6] Id., Art. 81. [7] Id., Art. 28.
[8] Id., Art. 29, 31, 32. [9] Id., Art. 57.
[10] Id., Art. 43, 45–47.

EXECUTIVE DEPARTMENT

Executive power is vested in the King who may not reign in other countries except with the consent of the Folketing and must be a member of the Evangelical Lutheran Church.[1] The King exercises his supreme authority through his ministers who are responsible; he is not answerable for his actions and his person is sacrosanct.[2] He has the power of appointment, promulgates the law, has the right of pardon.[3] The Prime Minister and other ministers form the Council of State which also includes the Heir to the throne when of age; ministers must have the confidence of the Folketing.[4]

JUDICIAL DEPARTMENT

The High Court of the Realm is composed of fifteen senior members of the highest courts of justice and fifteen members elected for a term of six years by the Folketing.[5] The administration of justice is independent of the executive power and courts may decide any question bearing upon the scope of the executive power.[6]

AREA, POPULATION, ETC.

The area of Denmark is 43,033 square kilometres, its population (1964) is 4,720,000. The capital is Copenhagen.

[1] Id., Art. 3, 5, 6. [2] Id., Art. 12, 13. [3] Id., Art. 14, 22, 24.
[4] Id., Art. 15, 17. [5] Id., Art. 59. [6] Id., Art. 62, 63.

CONSTITUTION
of the
KINGDOM OF DENMARK ACT[1]
June 5, 1953
and the
SUCCESSION TO THE THRONE ACT[1]
March 27, 1953

The Constitution of the Kingdom of Denmark Act
June 5, 1953

PART I

1. This Constitution Act shall apply to all parts of the Kingdom of Denmark.

2. The form of government shall be that of a constitutional monarchy. The Royal Power shall be inherited by men and women in accordance with the provisions of the Succession to the Throne Act, 27th March, 1953.

3. The legislative power shall be vested in the King and the Folketing conjointly. The executive power shall be vested in the King. The judicial power shall be vested in the courts of justice.

4. The Evangelical Lutheran Church shall be the Established Church of Denmark, and, as such, it shall be supported by the State.

PART II

5. The King shall not reign in other countries except with the consent of the Folketing.

6. The King shall be a member of the Evangelical Lutheran Church.

7. The King shall be of age when he has completed his eighteenth year. The same provision shall apply to the Successor to the Throne.

[1] Printed in English by J. H. Schultz Ltd, Copenhagen. Supplied by the Ministry of Foreign Affairs in January 1966. Ed.

8. The King, prior to his accession to the Throne, shall make a solemn Declaration in writing before the Council of State that he will faithfully adhere to the Constitution Act. Two identical originals of the Declaration shall be executed, one of which shall be handed over to the Folketing to be preserved in its archives, and the other shall be filed in the Public Record Office. Where the King, owing to his absence or for other reasons, is unable to sign the aforesaid Declaration immediately on his accession to the Throne, the government shall, unless otherwise provided by Statute, be conducted by the Council of State until such Declaration has been signed. Where the King already as Successor to the Throne has signed the aforesaid Declaration, he shall accede to the Throne immediately on its vacancy.

9. Provisions relating to the exercising of sovereign power in the event of the minority, illness, or absence of the King shall be laid down by Statute. Where on the vacancy of the Throne there is no Successor to the Throne, the Folketing shall elect a King and establish the future order of succession to the Throne.

10. (1) The Civil List of the King shall be granted for the duration of his reign by Statute. Such Statute shall also provide for the castles, palaces, and other State property which shall be placed at the disposal of the King for his use.

(2) The Civil List shall not be chargeable with any debt.

11. Members of the Royal House may be granted annuities by Statute. Such annuities shall not be enjoyed outside the Realm except with the consent of the Folketing.

PART III

12. Subject to the limitations laid down in this Constitution Act the King shall have the supreme authority in all the affairs of the Realm, and he shall exercise such supreme authority through the Ministers.

13. The King shall not be answerable for his actions; his person shall be sacrosanct. The Ministers shall be responsible for the conduct of the government; their responsibility shall be determined by Statute.

14. The King shall appoint and dismiss the Prime Minister and the other Ministers. He shall decide upon the number of Ministers and upon the distribution of the duties of government among them. The signature of the King to resolutions relating to legislation and government shall make such resolutions valid, provided that the signature of the King is accompanied by the signature or signatures of one or more Ministers. A Minister who has signed a resolution shall be responsible for the resolution.

15. (1) A Minister shall not remain in office after the Folketing has passed a vote of no confidence in him.

(2) Where the Folketing passes a vote of no confidence in the Prime

Minister, he shall ask for the dismissal of the Ministry unless writs are to be issued for a general election. Where a vote of censure has been passed on a Ministry, or it has asked for its dismissal, it shall continue in office until a new Ministry has been appointed. Ministers who continue in office as aforesaid shall do only what is necessary for the purpose of the uninterrupted conduct of official business.

16. Ministers may be impeached by the King or the Folketing with maladministration of office. The High Court of the Realm shall try cases of impeachment brought against Ministers for maladministration of office.

17. (1) The body of Ministers shall form the Council of State, in which the Successor to the Throne shall have a seat when he is of age. The Council of State shall be presided over by the King except in the instance mentioned in section 8, and in the instances where the Legislature in pursuance of section 9 may have delegated the conduct of the government to the Council of State.

(2) All Bills and important government measures shall be discussed in the Council of State.

18. If the King should be prevented from holding a Council of State he may entrust the discussion of a matter to a Council of Ministers. Such Council of Ministers shall consist of all the Ministers, and it shall be presided over by the Prime Minister. The vote of each Minister shall be entered in a minute book, and any question shall be decided by a majority of votes. The Prime Minister shall submit the Minutes, signed by the Minister present, to the King, who shall decide whether he will immediately consent to the recommendations of the Council of Ministers, or have the matter brought before him in a Council of State.

19. (1) The King shall act on behalf of the Realm in international affairs. Provided that without the consent of the Folketing the King shall not undertake any act whereby the territory of the Realm will be increased or decreased, nor shall he enter into any obligation which for fulfilment requires the concurrence of the Folketing, or which otherwise is of major importance; nor shall the King, except with the consent of the Folketing, terminate any international treaty entered into with the consent of the Folketing.

(2) Except for purposes of defence against an armed attack upon the Realm or Danish forces the King shall not use military force against any foreign state without the consent of the Folketing. Any measure which the King may take in pursuance of this provision shall immediately be submitted to the Folketing. If the Folketing is not in session it shall be convoked immediately.

(3) The Folketing shall appoint from among its Members a Foreign Affairs Committee, which the Government shall consult prior to the making of any decision of major importance to foreign policy. Rules applying to the Foreign Affairs Committee shall be laid down by Statute.

20. (1) Powers vested in the authorities of the Realm under this Constitution Act may, to such extent as shall be provided by Statute, be delegated to international authorities set up by mutual agreement with other states for the promotion of international rules of law and co-operation.

(2) For the passing of a Bill dealing with the above a majority of five sixths of the Members of the Folketing shall be required. If this majority is not obtained, whereas the majority required for the passing of ordinary Bills is obtained, and if the Government maintains it, the Bill shall be submitted to the Electorate for approval or rejection in accordance with the rules for Referenda laid down in section 42.

21. The King may cause Bills and other measures to be introduced in the Folketing.

22. A Bill passed by the Folketing shall become law if it receives the Royal Assent not later than thirty days after it was finally passed. The King shall order the promulgation of Statutes and shall see to it that they are carried into effect.

23. In an emergency the King may when the Folketing cannot assemble, issue provisional laws, provided that they shall not be at variance with the Constitution Act, and that they shall always immediately on the assembling of the Folketing be submitted to it for approval or rejection.

24. The King shall have the prerogative of mercy and of granting amnesty. The King may grant Ministers a pardon for sentences passed upon them by the High Court of the Realm only with the consent of the Folketing.

25. The King may either directly or through the relevant Government authorities make such grants and grant such exemptions from the Statutes as are either warranted under the rules existing before the 5th June, 1849, or have been warranted by a Statute passed since that date.

26. The King may cause money to be coined as provided by Statute.

27. (1) Rules governing the appointment of civil servants shall be laid down by Statute. No person shall be appointed a civil servant unless he is a Danish subject. Civil servants who are appointed by the King shall make a solemn declaration to the effect that they will adhere to the Constitution Act.

(2) Rules governing the dismissal, transfer, and pensioning of civil servants shall be laid down by Statute, confer section 64.

(3) Civil servants appointed by the King shall only be transferred without their consent if they do not suffer any loss in the income accruing from their posts or offices, and if they have been offered the choice of such transfer or retirement on pension under the general rules and regulations.

PART IV

28. The Folketing shall consist of one assembly of not more than one hundred and seventy-nine Members, of whom two Members shall be elected in the Faeroe Islands, and two Members in Greenland.

29. (1) Any Danish subject whose permanent residence is in the Realm, and who has the age qualification for suffrage provided for in subsection (2) of this section shall have the right to vote at Folketing elections, provided that he has not been declared incapable of conducting his own affairs. It shall be laid down by Statute to what extent conviction and public assistance amounting to poor relief within the meaning of the law shall entail disfranchisement.

(2) The age qualification for suffrage shall be such as has resulted from the Referendum held under the Act dated the 25th March, 1953. Such age qualification for suffrage may be altered at any time by Statute. A Bill passed by the Folketing for the purpose of such enactment shall receive the Royal Assent only when the provision on the alteration in the age qualification for suffrage has been put to a Referendum in accordance with subsection (5) of section 42, which has not resulted in the rejection of the provision.

30. (1) Any person who has a right to vote at Folketing elections shall be eligible for membership of the Folketing, unless he has been convicted of an act which in the eyes of the public makes him unworthy of being a Member of the Folketing.

(2) Civil servants who are elected Members of the Folketing shall not require permission from the Government to accept their election.

31. (1) The Members of the Folketing shall be elected by general and direct ballot.

(2) Rules for the exercise of the suffrage shall be laid down by the Elections Act, which, to secure equal representation of the various opinions of the Electorate, shall prescribe the manner of election and decide whether proportional representation shall be adopted with or without elections in single-member constituencies.

(3) In determining the number of seats to be allotted to each area regard shall be paid to the number of inhabitants, the number of electors, and the density of population.

(4) The Elections Act shall provide rules governing the election of substitutes and their admission to the Folketing, and also rules for the procedure to be adopted where a new election is required.

(5) Special rules for the representation of Greenland in the Folketing may be laid down by Statute.

32. (1) The members of the Folketing shall be elected for a period of four years.

(2) The King may at any time issue writs for a new election with the

effect that the existing seats shall be vacated upon a new election. Provided that writs for an election shall not be issued after the appointment of a new Ministry until the Prime Minister has presented himself to the Folketing.

(3) The Prime Minister shall cause a general election to be held before the expiration of the period for which the Folketing has been elected.

(4) No seats shall be vacated until a new election has been held.

(5) Special rules may be provided by Statute for the commencement and determination of Faeroe Islands and Greenland representation in the Folketing.

(6) If a Member of the Folketing becomes ineligible his seat in the Folketing shall become vacant.

(7) On approval of his election each new Member shall make a solemn declaration that he will adhere to the Constitution Act.

33. The Folketing itself shall determine the validity of the election of any Member and decide whether a Member has lost his eligibility or not.

34. The Folketing shall be inviolable. Any person who attacks its security or freedom, or any person who issues or obeys any command aiming thereat shall be deemed guilty of high treason.

PART V

35. (1) A newly elected Folketing shall assemble at twelve o'clock noon on the twelfth week-day after the day of election, unless the King has previously convoked a meeting of its Members.

(2) Immediately after the proving of the mandates the Folketing shall constitute itself by the election of a President and Vice-Presidents.

36. (1) The sessional year of the Folketing shall commence on the first Tuesday of October, and shall continue until the first Tuesday of October of the following year.

(2) On the first day of the sessional year at twelve o'clock noon the Members shall assemble for a new session of the Folketing.

37. The Folketing shall meet in the place where the Government has its seat. Provided that in extraordinary circumstances the Folketing may assemble elsewhere in the Realm.

38. (1) At the first meeting in the sessional year the Prime Minister shall render an account of the general state of the country and of the measures proposed by the Government.

(2) Such account shall be made the subject of a general debate.

39. The President of the Folketing shall convene the meetings of the Folketing, stating the Order of the Day. The President shall convene a meeting of the Folketing upon a requisition being made in writing by at least two fifths of the Members of the Folketing or the Prime Minister, stating the Order of the Day.

40. The Ministers shall *ex officio* be entitled to attend the sittings of the Folketing and to address the Folketing during the debates as often as they may desire, provided that they abide by the Rules of Procedure of the Folketing. They shall be entitled to vote only when they are Members of the Folketing.

41. (1) Any Member of the Folketing shall be entitled to introduce Bills and other measures.

(2) No Bill shall be finally passed until it has been read three times in the Folketing.

(3) Two fifths of the Members of the Folketing may request of the President that the third reading of a Bill shall not take place until twelve week-days after its passing the second reading. The request shall be made in writing and signed by the Members making it. Provided that there shall be no such postponement in connection with Finance Bills, Supplementary Appropriation Bills, Provisional Appropriation Bills, Government Loan Bills, Naturalization Bills, Expropriation Bills, Indirect Taxation Bills, and, in emergencies, Bills the enactment of which cannot be postponed owing to the intent of the Act.

(4) In the case of a new election and at the end of the sessional year all Bills and other measures which have not been finally passed, shall be dropped.

42. (1) Where a Bill has been passed by the Folketing, one third of the Members of the Folketing may within three week-days from the final passing of the Bill request of the President that the Bill be subjected to a Referendum. Such request shall be made in writing and signed by the Members making the request.

(2) Except in the instance mentioned in subsection 7, no Bill which may be subjected to a Referendum, confer subsection (6), shall receive the Royal Assent before the expiration of the time limit mentioned in subsection (1), or before a Referendum requested as aforesaid has taken place.

(3) Where a Referendum on a Bill has been requested the Folketing may within a period of five week-days from the final passing of the Bill resolve that the Bill shall be withdrawn.

(4) Where the Folketing has made no resolution in accordance with subsection (3), notice to the effect that the Bill will be put to a Referendum shall without delay be given to the Prime Minister, who shall then cause the Bill to be published together with a statement that a Referendum will be held. The Referendum shall be held in accordance with the decision of the Prime Minister not less than twelve and not more than eighteen week-days after the publication of the Bill.

(5) At the Referendum votes shall be cast for or against the Bill. For the Bill to be rejected a majority of the electors taking part in the voting, however, not less than thirty per centum of all persons entitled to vote, shall have voted against the Bill.

(6) Finance Bills, Supplementary Appropriation Bills, Provisional Appropriation Bills, Government Loan Bills, Civil Servants (Amendment) Bills, Salaries and Pensions Bills, Naturalization Bills, Expropriation Bills, Taxation (Direct and Indirect) Bills, as well as Bills introduced for the purpose of discharging existing treaty obligations shall not be subject to a decision by Referendum. This provision shall also apply to the Bills referred to in sections 8, 9, 10, and 11, and to such resolutions as are provided for in section 19, if existing in the form of a law, unless it has been provided by a special Act that such resolutions shall be put to a Referendum. Amendments of the Constitution Act shall be governed by the rules laid down in section 88.

(7) In an emergency a Bill that may be subjected to a Referendum may receive the Royal Assent immediately after it has been passed, provided that the Bill contains a provision to that effect. Where under the rules of subsection (1) one third of the Members of the Folketing request a Referendum on the Bill or on the Act to which the Royal Assent has been given, such Referendum shall be held in accordance with the above rules. Where the Act is rejected by the Referendum, an announcement to that effect shall be made by the Prime Minister without undue delay and not later than fourteen days after the Referendum was held. From the date of such announcement the Act shall become ineffective.

(8) Rules for Referenda, including the extent to which Referenda shall be held in the Faeroe Islands and in Greenland, shall be laid down by Statute.

43. No taxes shall be imposed, altered, or repealed except by Statute; nor shall any man be conscripted or any public loan be raised except by Statute.

44. (1) No alien shall be naturalized except by Statute.

(2) The extent of the right of aliens to become owners of real property shall be laid down by Statute.

45. (1) A Finance Bill for the next financial year shall be laid before the Folketing not later than four months before the beginning of such financial year.

(2) Where it is expected that the reading of the Finance Bill for the next financial year will not be completed before the commencement of that financial year, a Provisional Appropriation Bill shall be laid before the Folketing.

46. (1) Taxes shall not be levied before the Finance Act or a Provisional Appropriation Act has been passed by the Folketing.

(2) No expenditure shall be defrayed unless provided for by the Finance Act passed by the Folketing, or by a Supplementary Appropriation Act, or by a Provisional Appropriation Act passed by the Folketing.

47. (1) The Public Accounts shall be submitted to the Folketing not later than six months after the expiration of the financial year.

(2) The Folketing shall elect a number of Auditors. Such Auditors shall examine the annual Public Accounts and see that all the revenues of the State have been duly entered therein, and that no expenditure has been defrayed unless provided for by the Finance Act or some other Appropriation Act. The Auditors shall be entitled to demand all necessary information, and shall have a right of access to all necessary documents. Rules providing for the number of Auditors and their duties shall be laid down by Statute.

(3) The Public Accounts together with the Auditor's Report shall be submitted to the Folketing for its decision.

48. The Folketing shall lay down its own Rules of Procedure, including rules governing its conduct of business and the maintenance of order.

49. The sittings of the Folketing shall be public. Provided that the President, or such number of Members as may be provided for by the Rules of Procedure, or a Minister shall be entitled to demand the removal of all unauthorised persons, whereupon it shall be decided without a debate whether the matter shall be debated at a public or a secret sitting.

50. In order to make a decision more than one half of the Members of the Folketing shall be present and take part in the voting.

51. The Folketing may appoint committees from among its Members to investigate matters of general importance. Such committees shall be entitled to demand written or oral information both from private citizens and from public authorities.

52. The election by the Folketing of Members to sit on committees and of Members to perform special duties shall be according to proportional representation.

53. With the consent of the Folketing any Member thereof may submit for discussion any matter of public interest and request a statement thereon from the Ministers.

55. By Statute shall be provided for the appointment by the Folketing of one or two persons, who shall not be Members of the Folketing, to control the civil and military administration of the State.

56. The Members of the Folketing shall be bound solely by their own consciences and not by any directions given by their electors.

57. No Member of the Folketing shall be prosecuted or imprisoned in any manner whatsoever without the consent of the Folketing, unless he is caught in *flagrante delicto.* Outside the Folketing no Member shall be held liable for his utterances in the Folketing save by the consent of the Folketing.

58. The Members of the Folketing shall be paid such remuneration as may be provided for in the Elections Act.

PART VI

59. (1) The High Court of the Realm shall consist of up to fifteen of the eldest—according to seniority of office—ordinary members of the highest court of justice of the Realm, and an equal number of members elected for six years by the Folketing according to proportional representation. One or more substitutes shall be elected for each elected member. No Member of the Folketing shall be elected a member of the High Court of the Realm, nor shall a Member of the Folketing act as a member of the High Court of the Realm. Where in a particular instance some of the members of the highest court of justice of the Realm are prevented from taking part in the trial of a case, an equal number of the members of the High Court of the Realm last elected by the Folketing shall retire from their seats.

(2) The High Court of the Realm shall elect a president from among its members.

(3) Where a case has been brought before the High Court of the Realm, the members elected by the Folketing shall retain their seats in the High Court of the Realm for the duration of such case, even if the period for which they were elected has expired.

(4) Rules for the High Court of the Realm shall be provided by Statute.

60. (1) The High Court of the Realm shall try such actions as may be brought by the King or the Folketing against Ministers.

(2) With the consent of the Folketing the King may cause to be tried before the High Court of the Realm also other persons for crimes which he may deem to be particularly dangerous to the State.

61. The exercise of the judiciary power shall be governed only by Statute. Extraordinary courts of justice with judicial power shall not be established.

62. The administration of justice shall always remain independent of the executive power. Rules to this effect shall be laid down by Statute.

63. (1) The courts of justice shall be entitled to decide any question bearing upon the scope of the authority of the executive power. However, a person who wants to query such authority shall not, by bringing the case before the courts of justice, avoid temporary compliance with orders given by the executive power.

(2) Questions bearing upon the scope of the authority of the executive power may be referred by Statute for decision to one or more administrative courts. Provided that an appeal from the decision of the administrative courts shall lie to the highest court of the Realm. Rules governing this procedure shall be laid down by Statute.

64. In the performance of their duties the judges shall be directed solely by the law. Judges shall not be dismissed except by judgment, nor shall they be transferred against their will, except in the instances where a rearrangement of the courts of justice is made. However, a judge who has completed his sixty-fifth year may be retired, but without loss of income up to the time when he is due for retirement on account of age.

65. (1) In the administration of justice all proceedings shall be public and oral to the widest possible extent.

(2) Laymen shall take part in criminal procedure. The cases and the form in which such participation shall take place, including what cases are to be tried by jury, shall be provided for by Statute.

PART VII

66. The constitution of the Established Church shall be laid down by Statute.

67. The citizens shall be entitled to form congregations for the worship of God in a manner consistent with their convictions, provided that nothing at variance with good morals or public order shall be taught or done.

68. No one shall be liable to make personal contributions to any denomination other than the one to which he adheres.

69. Rules for religious bodies dissenting from the Established Church shall be laid down by Statute.

70. No person shall for reasons of his creed or descent be deprived of access to complete enjoyment of his civic and political rights, nor shall he for such reasons evade compliance with any common civic duty.

PART VIII

71. (1) Personal liberty shall be inviolable. No Danish subject shall in any manner whatever be deprived of his liberty because of his political or religious convictions or because of his descent.

(2) A person shall be deprived of his liberty only where this is warranted by law.

(3) Any person who is taken into custody shall be brought before a judge within twenty-four hours. Where the person taken into custody cannot be released immediately, the judge shall decide, stating the grounds in an order to be given as soon as possible and at the latest within three days, whether the person taken into custody shall be committed to prison, and in cases where he can be released on bail, the judge shall determine the nature and amount of such bail. This provision may be departed from by Statute as far as Greenland is concerned, if for local considerations such departure may be deemed necessary.

(4) The finding given by the judge may at once be separately appealed against by the person concerned to a higher court of justice.

(5) No person shall be remanded for an offence that can involve only punishment consisting of a fine or mitigated imprisonment (*haefte*).

(6) Outside criminal procedure the legality of deprivation of liberty which is not by order of a judicial authority, and which is not warranted by the legislation dealing with aliens, shall at the request of the person who has been deprived of his liberty, or at the request of any person acting on his behalf, be brought before the ordinary courts of justice or other judicial authority for decision. Rules governing this procedure shall be provided by Statute.

(7) The persons mentioned in subsection (6) shall be under supervision by a board set up by the Folketing, to which board the persons concerned shall be permitted to apply.

72. The dwelling shall be inviolable. House searching, seizure, and examination of letters and other papers as well as any breach of the secrecy to be observed in postal, telegraph, and telephone matters shall take place only under a judicial order unless particular exception is warranted by Statute.

73. (1) The right of property shall be inviolable. No person shall be ordered to cede his property except where required by the public weal. It can be done only as provided by Statute and against full compensation.

(2) Where a Bill relating to the expropriation of property has been passed, one third of the Members of the Folketing may within three week-days from the final passing of such Bill, demand that it shall not be presented for the Royal Assent until new elections to the Folketing have been held and the Bill has again been passed by the Folketing assembling thereupon.

(3) Any question of the legality of an act of expropriation and the amount of compensation may be brought before the courts of justice. The hearing of issues relating to the amount of the compensation may by Statute be referred to courts of justice established for such purpose.

74. Any restraint of the free and equal access to trade which is not based on the public weal, shall be abolished by Statute.

75. (1) In order to advance the public weal efforts should be made to afford work to every able-bodied citizen on terms that will secure his existence.

(2) Any person unable to support himself or his dependants shall, where no other person is responsible for his or their maintenance, be entitled to receive public assistance, provided that he shall comply with the obligations imposed by Statute in such respect.

76. All children of school age shall be entitled to free instruction in the elementary schools. Parents or guardians who themselves arrange for their children or wards receiving instruction equal to the general elementary school standard, shall not be obliged to have their children or wards taught n an elementary school.

77. Any person shall be entitled to publish his thoughts in printing, in writing, and in speech, provided that he may be held answerable in a court of justice. Censorship and other preventive measures shall never again be introduced.

78. (1) The citizens shall be entitled without previous permission to form associations for any lawful purpose.

(2) Associations employing violence, or aiming at attaining their object by violence, by instigation to violence, or by similar punishable influence on people of other views, shall be dissolved by judgment.

(3) No association shall be dissolved by any government measure. However, an association may be temporarily prohibited, provided that proceedings be immediately taken against it for its dissolution.

(4) Cases relating to the dissolution of political associations may without special permission be brought before the highest court of justice of the Realm.

(5) The legal effects of the dissolution shall be determined by Statute.

79. The citizens shall without previous permission be entitled to assemble unarmed. The police shall be entitled to be present at public meetings. Open-air meetings may be prohibited when it is feared that they may constitute a danger to the public peace.

80. In case of riots the armed forces, unless attacked, may take action only after the crowd in the name of the King and the Law has three times been called upon to disperse, and such warning has been unheeded.

81. Every male person able to carry arms shall be liable with his person to contribute to the defence of his country under such rules as are laid down by Statute.

82. The right of the municipalities to manage their own affairs independently under the supervision of the State shall be laid down by Statute.

83. All privileges by legislation attached to nobility, title, and rank shall be abolished.

84. In future no fiefs, estates tail in land or estates tail in personal property shall be created.

85. The provisions of sections 71, 78, and 79 shall only be applicable to the defence forces subject to such limitations as are consequential to the provisions of military laws.

PART IX

86. The age qualification for local government electors and congregational council electors shall be that applying at any time to Folketing electors. With reference to the Faeroe Islands and Greenland the age qualification for local government electors and congregational council electors shall be such as may be provided for by Statute or fixed in accordance with Statute.

87. Citizens of Iceland who enjoy equal rights with citizens of Denmark under the Danish-Icelandic Union (Abolition), etc. Act, shall continue to enjoy the rights attached to Danish citizenship under the provisions of the Constitution Act.

PART X

88. When the Folketing passes a Bill for the purposes of a new constitutional provision, and the Government wishes to proceed with the matter, writs shall be issued for the election of Members of a new Folketing. If the Bill is passed unamended by the Folketing assembling after the election, the Bill shall within six months after its final passing be submitted to the Electors for approval or rejection by direct voting. Rules for this voting shall be laid down by Statute. If a majority of the persons taking part in the voting, and at least 40 per centum of the Electorate has voted in favour of the Bill as passed by the Folketing, and if the Bill receives the Royal Assent it shall form an integral part of the Constitution Act.

PART XI

89. This Constitution Act shall come into operation at once. Provided that the Rigsdag last elected under the Constitution of the Kingdom of Denmark Act, 5th June, 1915, as amended on the 10th September, 1920, shall continue to exist until a general election has been held in accordance with the rules laid down in Part IV. Until a general election has been held the provisions laid down for the Rigsdag in the Constitution of the Kingdom of Denmark Act, 5th June, 1915, as amended on the 10th September, 1920, shall remain in force.

The Succession to the Throne Act March 27, 1953

1. The Throne shall be inherited by the descendants of King Christian X and Queen Alexandrine.

2. On the demise of a King the Throne shall pass to his son or daughter so that a son shall take precedence of a daughter, and where there are several children of the same sex the eldest child shall take precedence of a younger child.

Where one of the King's children has died the issue of the deceased shall take his place in accordance with the lineal descent and the rules laid down in subsection 1.

3. On the demise of a King who has left no issue entitled to succeed to the Throne, the Throne shall pass to his brother or sister with preference for the brother. Where the King has one or more brothers or one or more sisters, or where any of his brothers or sisters have died, the rules of section 2 shall apply correspondingly.

4. Where there is no person entitled to succeed to the Throne under the rules of sections 2 and 3, the Throne shall pass to the then nearest collateral line of the descendants of King Christian X and Queen Alexandrine in accordance with the lineal descent, and with preference correspondingly for men over women, and for the elder over the younger as laid down in sections 2 and 3.

5. Only children born of lawful marriage shall be entitled to succeed to the Throne.

The King shall not enter into marriage without the consent of the Rigsdag.

Where a person entitled to succeed to the Throne enters into marriage without the consent of the King given in the Council of State, the person in question shall forfeit his right of succession to the Throne for himself and the children born of the marriage and for their issue.

6. The provisions of sections 2–5 shall apply correspondingly in the case of the abdication of a King.

7. This Act shall come into operation at the same time as the Constitution of the Kingdom of Denmark Act, 5th June, 1953.

FINLAND

SUMMARY

INTERNATIONAL STATUS

Finland is a member of the United Nations (December 14, 1955).[1] It is a member of the Nordic Council and other international organizations. It was a member of the League of Nations.

Finland was a Grand Duchy of the Kingdom of Sweden until 1809 when, on the conclusion of peace between Sweden and Russia, Finland was joined to Russia as a Grand Duchy with autonomous national status.

[1] It accepts the compulsory jurisdiction of the International Court of Justice under Article 36 of its Statute.

Finland declared its independence on December 6, 1917. Finland's constitution continued, even after it had been joined to Russia, to be the Swedish Form of Government of 1772, supplemented by the Act of Union and Security of 1789. In the 1860's, growing demands for constitutional government were heard and on September 18, 1863, the Diet was convened and an era of peaceful reform began, including among other acts the Diet Act of 1869. From 1908, the growing reaction against the Russian empire was countered, on the Russian side, by attempts to narrow Finnish autonomy. After the February 1917 Russian Revolution, an extensive reform of Finland's institutions was prepared. The October Revolution was followed by independence and this was followed by civil war from January to May 1918 between the Whites and the Reds, the former aided by Germany and the latter by Soviet Russia. At the end of the war, Finland established relations with the Allies and set up a republican constitution—the Form of Government of 1919— under the Commander-in-Chief of the White Army, General Mannerheim, as Chief of State. In November 1939, the USSR invaded Finland and by the peace terms of March 1940 one tenth of Finland's territory was surrendered to Russia. In June 1941, Finland was again drawn into war with the USSR owing to the presence of German troops in the country. By an armistice in September 1944, the territorial losses of 1940 were increased and confirmed and an indemnity was imposed.

FORM OF NATIONAL GOVERNMENT

The Constitution Act of July 17, 1919, as amended in 1947, 1956 and 1957, together with theParliament Act of January 13, 1928, as amended in 1937, 1944, 1948 and 1955, constitute the Constitution of Finland. The Constitution Act states that Finland is a sovereign republic.[1] Sovereign power rests with the people.[2]

RIGHTS OF THE PEOPLE

The Constitution Act provides that Finnish citizens are equal before the law and protected by law as to life, honor, liberty and property, the labor of citizens being under the special protection of the State.[3] It guarantees the right of residence and travel, freedom of religion, speech, press, assembly, association, inviolability of the domicile, secrecy of communications, the right to one's natural judge.[4] Titles of nobility or hereditary honors are forbidden.[5] All citizens must take part in national defense.[6] There are provisions regarding education and it is provided that the University of Helsinki shall retain its right of self-government.[7]

[1] Const. Act, Art. 1. [2] Id., Art. 2. [3] Id., Art. 5, 6.
[4] Id., Art. 7–13. [5] Id., Art. 15. [6] Id., Art. 75, 76. [7] Id., Art. 77–82.

LEGISLATIVE DEPARTMENT

Parliament is unicameral, composed of 200 members elected by direct, universal and proportional suffrage for a term of four years subject to dissolution.[1] Immunities of Members of Parliament are provided.[2] Parliament meets in one ordinary session a year.[3] The Committees of Parliament are named and their duties described; they may not include members of the Government.[4] There are provisions relating to the Bank of Finland, the National Pensions Institute and the Parliament Library.[5] There are provisions relating to finance.[6]

EXECUTIVE DEPARTMENT

Executive power is vested in the President and Council of State for general government.[7] The President is elected by an electoral college for a term of six years.[8] He summons Parliament, has the right of pardon, is Commander-in-Chief of the Armed Forces, conducts foreign policy.[9] Members of the Council of State are appointed by the President and must have the confidence of Parliament.[10] It is responsible to Parliament.[11] There are provisions concerning public offices.[12]

JUDICIAL DEPARTMENT

Judicial power is exercised by independent tribunals and in final instance by the Supreme Court and the Supreme Administrative Court.[13] The Supreme Court is the highest court of appeal and also supervises judges and the executive authorities in their administration of justice.[14]

AREA, POPULATION, ETC.

The area of Finland is 305,396 square kilometres, its population (1964) is 4,579,000. The national languages are Finnish and Swedish.[15] The capital is Helsinki.

[1] Parl. Act., Art. 1–6.
[2] Id., Art. 13, 14, 15.
[3] Id., Art. 19.
[4] Id., Art. 40–53.
[5] Id., Art. 83–83b.
[6] Const. Act, Art. 61–74.
[7] Id., Art. 2.
[8] Id., Art. 23.
[9] Id., Art. 27–33, Parl Act, Art. 21, 22.
[10] Const. Act, Art. 36.
[11] Id., Art. 43.
[12] Id., Art. 84–93.
[13] Id., Art. 2.
[14] Id., Art. 53.
[15] Id., Art. 14.

CONSTITUTION
of
FINLAND[1]

July 17, 1919 and January 13, 1928

1. CONSTITUTION ACT OF FINLAND

July 17, 1919, as amended in 1947, 1956, 1957

Whereas Finland has become an independent and sovereign State, it has been deemed necessary to develop and consolidate its Constitution by new statutes having the character of Constitutional Laws, which, while securing the necessary stability of the State, enlarge the powers of the National Assembly, and guarantee the legal rights and liberties of the citizens. Therefore, in conformity with the decision of Parliament, taken in accordance with the procedure prescribed in Article 60 of the Parliament Act of July 20, 1906, the following Form of Government for Finland is hereby sanctioned.

CHAPTER I

GENERAL PROVISIONS

Art. 1. Finland is a sovereign Republic, its Constitution being established by this Constitution Act and by other Constitutional Laws.

Art. 2. The sovereign power in Finland rests with the people, represented by their delegates assembled in Parliament.

Legislative power shall be exercised by Parliament in conjunction with the President of the Republic.

The supreme executive power is vested in the President of the Republic. In addition to the President there shall be for the general government of the State a Council of State consisting of a Prime Minister and the necessary number of ministers.

[1] *Constitution Act and Parliament Act of Finland.* Published by the Ministry of Foreign Affairs, Helsinki, 1959. Confirmed as to date by the Ministry of Foreign Affairs in July 1966. Ed.

The judicial power shall be exercised by independent tribunals and, in the final instance, by the Supreme Court and the Supreme Administrative Court.

Art. 3. The territory of the Finnish Republic is indivisible. Its boundaries cannot be modified, except with the consent of Parliament.

Art. 4. The rights of Finnish citizenship belong to every person born of Finnish parents and to every woman of foreign nationality who has married a Finnish citizen.

A citizen of another country may be admitted to Finnish citizenship in accordance with the conditions and procedure laid down by law.

CHAPTER II

GENERAL RIGHTS AND LEGAL PROTECTION OF FINNISH CITIZENS

Art. 5. All Finnish citizens shall be equal before the law.

Art. 6. Every Finnish citizen shall be protected by law as to life, honor, personal liberty and property.

The labor of the citizens shall be under the special protection of the State.

Expropriation of property for the general need with full compensation shall be regulated by law.

Art. 7. Every Finnish citizen shall have the right of sojourn in his country, of freely choosing his place of residence and of travelling from one place to another, unless otherwise provided by law.

The right of Finnish citizens to leave the country is regulated by special provisions.

Art. 8. Every Finnish citizen shall have the right to worship in public and in private upon condition that he does not violate the law or good morals; he shall be at liberty also, in conformity with such special regulations as may govern the matter, to leave the religious community to which he belongs and to join another such community.

Art. 9. The fact of belonging to any special religious community or of not belonging to any such community shall in no way detract from the rights and duties of Finnish citizens. In respect to public posts and offices restrictions defined by law shall, however, remain in force until otherwise enacted.

Art. 10. Finnish citizens shall enjoy freedom of speech and the right to print and publish written or pictorial representations without interference. They shall also be free to meet, without any previous authorization, for the discussion of public affairs and for any other legitimate purpose. They shall also enjoy the right to form associations for purposes not contrary to law or good morals.

The rules concerning the exercise of these rights shall be prescribed by law.

Art. 11. The domicile of Finnish citizens shall be inviolable.

The conditions under which domiciliary searches may be ordered and carried out shall be determined by law.

Art. 12. The secrecy of postal, telegraphic and telephonic communications shall be inviolable, unless exceptions are provided by law.

Art. 13. A Finnish citizen shall be tried by no other court than that which has jurisdiction over him by law.

Art. 14. Finnish and Swedish shall be the national languages of the Republic.

The right of Finnish citizens to use their mother tongue, whether Finnish or Swedish, before the courts and the administrative authorities, and to obtain from them documents in these languages, shall be guaranteed by law; care shall be taken that the rights of the Finnish speaking population and the rights of the Swedish speaking population of the country shall be promoted by the State upon an identical basis.

The State shall provide for the intellectual and economic needs of the Finnish speaking and the Swedish speaking populations upon a similar basis.

Art. 15. No title of nobility nor other hereditary dignity shall be conferred in the Republic.

Art. 16. These provisions concerning the general rights of Finnish citizens shall constitute no obstacle to the establishment by law of restrictions which are necessary in time of war or insurrection and at any time whatsoever as far as persons on military service are concerned.

CHAPTER III

LEGISLATION

Art. 17. The organization and the functions of Parliament are regulated by the Parliament Act.

Art. 18. The right of proposing the enactment of a new law or the amendment, interpretation, or repeal of a law in force shall belong to the President as well as to Parliament.

The President of the Republic shall exercise his right to initiate legislation by introducing bills to Parliament. Bills shall be drafted by the Council of State. According to the nature of the matter the opinion of the Supreme Court or of the Supreme Administrative Court or of both these Courts may be requested upon such bills.

The exercise of the right of Parliament to initiate legislation is determined by the Parliament Act.

Art. 19. Bills adopted by Parliament shall be submitted to the President of the Republic for his sanction. The President may, on such bills, request the opinion of the Supreme Court or the Supreme Administrative Court or of both these Courts, according to the nature of the question involved.

The bill must be sanctioned in the wording adopted by Parliament. In case a bill is not sanctioned by the President, it shall nevertheless come into force without his sanction if, after a new election, Parliament readopts it without amendment by a majority vote. Otherwise the bill shall be regarded as having lapsed.

If the President has not sanctioned a bill within three months after is has been submitted for his sanction, this shall be regarded as a refusal of sanction.

Art. 20 The preamble of every law shall include a statement that it has been enacted in conformity with the decision of Parliament, and, if the law has been enacted in accordance with the procedure required for the enactment of Constitutional Laws, this too shall be stated.

Every law, whether it be sanctioned or whether it come into force without the sanction of the President, shall be signed by the President and countersigned by the competent Minister, after which it shall be published by the Council of State in the Statute Book of Finland.

Art. 21. The right of the President to issue decrees is determined by Article 28.

Art. 22. Laws and decrees as well as bills submitted by the Government to Parliament and the replies, recommendations, and other documents addressed by Parliament to the Government shall be drawn up in the Finnish and the Swedish languages.

CHAPTER IV

GOVERNMENT AND ADMINISTRATION

Art. 23. The President of the Republic shall be elected by the people of Finland from among the natural born citizens of Finland. His term of office shall be six years.

The election of the President shall be performed by three hundred Presidential Electors. In choosing these electors, the regulations in force for elections to Parliament shall be observed in respect to suffrage and eligibility and, in so far as applicable, also to the mode of election, the procedure of voting and the designation of deputy electors.

The choosing of the electors shall take place on the fifteenth and sixteenth of January; and on the fifteenth of the February following, the electors shall assemble under the chairmanship of the Prime Minister to elect the President. The vote shall be by secret ballot. If a candidate obtains more than half of the votes cast, he shall be declared elected; otherwise a new ballot shall be taken immediately, and if no candidate obtains an absolute majority this time, another ballot shall be taken between the two candidates who obtained the highest number of votes on the second count. In the case of a tie the decision shall be by lot.

If a Member of Parliament is elected President, his mandate as a Member shall cease. A State official who is elected President shall be regarded as having resigned his office.

If a day fixed in Paragraph 3 of this Article or elsewere in this Constiturion Act falls upon a Sunday or a public holiday, the nearest workday following shall be substituted for it.

Art. 24. The President shall assume the duties of his office on the first of March following his election, and on this date shall, in the presence of Parliament, make the following solemn vow:

"I, (full name), elected President of the Republic of Finland by the people of Finland, do hereby vow that in the execution of my office of President I will truly and faithfully obey and uphold the Constitution and the laws of the Republic, and that I will promote the welfare of the people of Finland to the utmost of my ability."

Art. 25. If the President is prevented from discharging the duties of his office, these shall be exercised by the Prime Minister; if the latter is also prevented, they shall be undertaken by the Minister who, in accordance with the provisions of Article 39, exercises the functions of deputy to the Prime Minister. If the disability is a lasting one, a new President shall be elected as soon as possible, and he shall assume the duties of his office immediately after the election.

During the period in which the Prime Minister or another Minister exercises the duties of President of the Republic, it will not be possible for him to exercise the duties of a Member of Parliament, if he is one.

Art. 26. For the exercise of his functions the President shall receive an annual emolument, the amount of which shall be fixed by law, and which shall be neither increased nor diminished during his term of office.

Art. 27. The President shall have the power to summon Parliament to an extraordinary session, to issue orders for elections to Parliament, to open and close the sessions of Parliament, to order new elections, and to dissolve Parliament.

Art. 28. In cases not otherwise provided for in this present Constitution Act and where such a right has not been vested in the Council of State, the President shall have the right to issue decrees upon matters which have heretofore been regulated by administrative provisions, as well as decrees regulating the execution of laws, the administration of State property, and the organization and operation of administrative services and public institutions. Decrees shall contain no provision implying a modification of a law.

The procedure for the issue and publication of decrees shall be the same as provided in Article 20, Paragraph 2, in respect to laws.

Art. 29. In particular cases, after hearing the opinion of the Supreme Court, the President may, by granting pardon, remit or reduce a sentence. In respect, however, to the pardoning of a member of the Council of State or the Chancellor of Justice, the existing special stipulations must be observed. A general amnesty may be granted only by special law.

The President may also grant dispensation from the provisions of the law in cases in which the law allows of such dispensations.

Art. 30. The President shall be Commander-in-Chief of the Armed Forces of Finland; he shall have the power in time of war to transfer his command to another.

Art. 31. The President may grant Finnish citizenship to a citizen of another country and may release a Finnish citizen from his citizenship.

Art. 32. The President shall supervise the administration of the State, and for this purpose he may require information from the heads or the governing bodies of public departments and institutions, and he may order inspections to be made.

Art. 33. The President shall determine the relations of Finland with foreign powers, yet treaties concluded with foreign powers must be approved by Parliament in so far as they contain stipulations falling within the domain of legislation or otherwise requiring, according to the Constitution, the consent of Parliament. Decisions of war and peace shall be taken by the President with the consent of Parliament.

All communications to foreign powers or the diplomatic representatives of Finland abroad must be made through the Minister to whose competency the management of foreign affairs belongs.

Art. 34. The decision of the President shall be made in the Council of State upon the report of the Minister to whose competency the question involved belongs.

To become valid, presidential decisions must be signed by the President and countersigned by the Minister who has reported upon the matter. This rule, however, shall not apply to the matters referred to in Articles 32 and 47.

If the decision of the President concerns the entire Council of State, it shall be countersigned by the appropriate *rapporteur* [1] of the Council.

Special rules are issued on the reporting of matters concerning the military command or military appointments, and also regarding the countersigning of presidential decisions on such matters.

The countersigner of a decision made by the President shall be responsible for the correctness of the document in which it is laid down.

Art. 35. If a Minister finds a decision made by the President to be contrary to law, he shall refer his opinion to the Council of State, which shall thereupon proceed as is set forth in Article 45. If the decision is con-

[1] The civil servant who reports on the matter concerned to the Council of State.

trary to a Constitutional Law the Minister must refuse his countersignature.

Art. 36. The members of the Council of State, who must enjoy the confidence of Parliament, shall be appointed by the President from among natural born citizens of Finland known for their honesty and ability. The Minister responsible for the administration of justice and at least one other Minister must have legal training.

Art. 37. The Council of State shall have a Chancellor of Justice, who must possess a mastery of the Law. The Chancellor of Justice shall have by his side a deputy Chancellor of Justice, who shall take his place in case of need.

Art. 38. The Council of State shall consist of as many Ministries as are necessary for the different branches of administration. Each Ministry shall be headed by a Minister.

The number of Ministries and the general determination of their spheres of competence shall be prescribed by law, but the detailed rules concerning the distribution of work among the Ministries and the organization of the Council of State in other respects shall be enacted by decree.

Art. 39. The Prime Minister shall be chairman of the Council of State. In the event of his being unable to attend, his place shall be taken by whoever is designated by the President of the Republic as his deputy, and, if the latter is also prevented from attending, by the highest-ranking Minister present. When the President of the Republic attends he shall preside over the Council.

During the period in which, by virtue of Article 25, the Prime Minister or another Minister exercises the duties of President of the Republic, it will not be possible for him to exercise the duties incumbent upon him as a Minister.

Art. 40. Matters devolving upon the Council of State shall be handled in plenary session, excepting when matters of a specific nature have been committed by decree to a Minister for decision in his capacity as head of the relevant Ministry.

A quorum of the Council shall consist of five members.

Art. 41. The Council of State shall execute the decisions of the President and decide upon matters which, according to the law, fall within its competence, as well as on other questions of government and administration which have not in the present Constitution Act or in any other law or decree been reserved for the President or committed either to a Minister in his capacity as head of a Ministry or to an inferior authority.

The extent to which matters relating to the administration of justice, the University of Helsinki and the Armed Forces are withdrawn from the competence of the Council of State is defined by special regulations.

Art. 42. If the Council of State is in doubt as to its competence to decide any matter, the President of the Republic shall settle this question of competence.

Art. 43. The members of the Council of State are responsible to Parliament for their administrative measures.

Every member of the Council of State who has taken part in the settlement of any matter by the Council of State shall be responsible for the decision reached, unless he has his dissension placed on record in the minutes.

Art. 44. All questions considered by the Council of State must have been prepared by the competent Ministry.

Each Ministry shall supervise the administration within its own sphere of activity and shall take measures to enforce laws, decrees and the decisions of the Council of State.

Art. 45. If it should happen that a decision taken by the President and to be executed by the Council of State is found to be contrary to law, the Council, after hearing the opinion of the Chancellor of Justice, shall request the President to withdraw or modify his decision, and, if the President nevertheless adheres to his decision, the Council must declare that the decision cannot be enforced.

Art. 46. The Chancellor of Justice must see that authorities and officials comply with the law and perform their duties so that no person shall suffer injury to his rights.

It shall be the duty of the Chancellor of Justice to act as public prosecutor in the Supreme Court and in the Supreme Administrative Court, and generally to guard the interests of the State as well as to institute prosecutions in other tribunals or cause them to be instituted when he shall deem it necessary. In his capacity as Supreme Public Prosecutor, the Chancellor of Justice must also exercise supervision over all public prosecutors and the latter must comply with his decisions.

The Chancellor of Justice shall have the right to assist at the sessions of the Council of State and those of all tribunals and public departments, and he shall have access to the minutes of the Council of State and its Ministries, of the tribunals and other public authorities.

Art. 47. If in the exercise of their functions the Council of State or any of its members act in a manner contrary to law, it is incumbent upon the Chancellor of Justice to make representation upon the subject and at the same time to indicate in what respect the act is illegal. If no heed is taken of such representation, the Chancellor of Justice shall have his opinion recorded in the minutes of the Council of State, and he shall also have the right to advise the President of the matter. If the illegality is of such a nature as to involve a prosecution against a member of the Council of State before the High Court mentioned in Article 59, and if the President orders such a prosecution to take place, it shall be carried out by the Chancellor of Justice. If the President finds that there is no ground for an indictment, the Chancellor of Justice shall be free to report on the case to Parliament. If the President decides upon an indictment of the Chancellor of Justice, the prosecution of the case shall be conducted by the person designated by the President for that purpose.

If in discharging the duties of his office the President should commit illegal acts, the Chancellor or Justice must make representation upon the subject as provided above. If the Chancellor of Justice or the Council of State finds that the President is guilty of high treason or treason, the Chancellor or the Council shall report on the matter to Parliament. And should Parliament, by a three-fourths majority vote, decide to arraign the President, the Chancellor shall prosecute him before the Supreme Court, and in the meantime the President shall abstain from the exercise of his functions. Except in such cases as are provided for above, the President shall not be arraigned for his administrative acts.

Art. 48. The Chancellor of Justice shall submit each year to the President and to Parliament a report upon the measures that he has taken and his comments on the observance of the laws.

The Chancellor of Justice shall upon request give the President and the Council of State information and advice.

Art. 49. At each regular session Parliament shall elect for a period of four years at a time, in accordance with the procedure provided for the election of its own Speaker, a person distinguished in law who shall be the Judicial Delegate to Parliament. The Judicial Delegate, in conformity with the instructions given him by Parliament, shall supervise the observance of the laws in the proceedings of courts and other authorities. There shall also be elected, for the same period and in accordance with the same procedure, a Deputy Judicial Delegate, who shall act for the Judicial Delegate in case of the latter's disability.

The Judicial Delegate to Parliament shall have the same right as the Chancellor of Justice to assist at the sessions of the Council of State and of tribunals and public departments, to have access to the minutes of the Council of State and its Ministries, of the tribunals and other authorities, and, under the responsibility imposed by law upon prosecutors, to prosecute or cause to be prosecuted complaints for malfeasance or nonfeasance in office.

The Judicial Delegate shall present to Parliament an annual report on the administration of his office, on the state of the administration of the law, and on the defects which he has noticed in legislation.

Art. 50. For the purpose of general administration Finland shall remain divided into provinces, circuits and communes.

Changes in the number of provinces shall be made by law; the Council of State shall decide all other changes concerning administrative divisions, unless otherwise provided by law.

In redrawing the boundaries of the administrative districts, it is to be observed that these shall, as far as circumstances permit, be so constituted as to contain populations speaking only one language, Finnish or Swedish, or to make their linguistic minorities as small as possible.

Art. 51. The administration of each province shall be headed by a Governor.

The administration of the communes shall rest on the principle of local self-government as prescribed by special laws. The manner and extent of application of local autonomy to larger districts than communes shall also be regulated by law; the regulations contained in Article 50, Paragraph 3, shall be followed in fixing the boundaries of these districts.

Art. 52. Public departments now existing or hereafter created for different branches of the administration of the State are governed by special regulations.

CHAPTER V

THE JUDICIARY

Art. 53. The Supreme Court is the highest court of appeal in suits at law; moreover it shall supervise judges and executive authorities in their administration of justice.

Art. 54. The Supreme Court shall be composed of a President and of the necessary number of Counsellors of Justice.

Matters pertaining to the judicial administration which, by reason of special regulations, fall within the jurisdiction of the Supreme Court shall be prepared by the Ministry to which questions concerning the administration of justice are assigned. The Head of this Ministry shall take part in the deliberations of the Supreme Court upon these matters.

In the Supreme Court decisions may be given by five members, unless for the settlement of certain questions participation of a larger or smaller number of members is specially required by law.

Art. 55. Provisions referring to general tribunals of first instance and of appeal are laid down in law.

Art. 56. The Supreme Administrative Court shall, with specially prescribed exceptions, be the court of last resort in cases of appeal involving administrative law. This Court shall also supervise the administration of justice by subordinate authorities in the field of administrative law.

Art. 57. The Supreme Administrative Court shall be composed of a President and of the necessary number of Counsellors of Administration. The provisions of Article 54, Paragraph 3, in regard to a quorum in the Supreme Court, shall apply also to this Court.

Art. 58. The Supreme Court and the Supreme Administrative Court, when they deem an amendment or interpretation of a law or decree necessary, shall address to the President a request for such a measure of legislation.

Art. 59. In the case of arraignment of the Chancellor of Justice, a member of the Council of State, of the Supreme Court or the Supreme Administrative Court, for an illegal act committed in the exercise of their functions, the case shall be tried by a special court called the High Court of Impeachment, governed by special constitutional provisions.

If an arraignment be decided upon by Parliament, the Judicial Delegate to Parliament shall act as prosecutor.

Art. 60. Special tribunals other than that mentioned in Article 59 shall be provided for by law.

No irregular tribunal may be established.

CHAPTER VI

PUBLIC FINANCE

Art. 61. Taxes, including customs dues, shall be fixed by law for an indeterminate or a limited period. The same applies to the abolition or modification of a previously imposed tax or compulsory levy.

A tax established for a limited period shall not be collected beyond such a period except in the case provided for in Article 69, Paragraph 1.

Art. 62. The general principles with regard to fees to be paid for the public services of Government officials and for documents issued by them, as well as for the use of postal services, railways, canals, hospitals, schools and other public institutions belonging to the State, shall be fixed by law.

Art. 63. Revenue-yielding properties and enterprises belonging to the State shall be managed and exploited according to general principles established by law.

Art. 64. The consent of Parliament shall be necessary for the raising of a public loan.

Art. 65. The principles governing new budgets for public departments and institutions, as well as the modification and abrogation of principles previously established, shall be regulated by law, as shall also the matter of pension rights. New public offices and departments shall be created only within the limits of the annual Budget.

New extraordinary pensions or subventions shall be granted only from appropriations voted for this purpose by Parliament.

Art. 66. The annual Budget, in which must be included the revenue and expenditure for the financial year, shall be adopted by Parliament and promulgated in the same manner as is prescribed for the promulgation of laws.

Special regulations determine whether a fund not designed to meet the annual needs of the State shall be excluded from the Budget.

Art. 67. No tax or other revenue which must be collected in accordance with the laws or decrees in force for the year may be excluded from the Budget of that year.

Art. 68. Interests and annuities on public debts and other grants designated to meet some State liability, as well as other expenditure which must be defrayed in accordance with regulations in effect during the fiscal year, must be included without deductions in the Budget. The Budget must also include an estimated grant for covering expenses based upon laws or decrees but not entered in the Budget as special items, as well as a sufficent grant to be placed at the disposal of the Government for unforeseen needs.

Other items of expenditure contained in the Budget shall be subjected to examination and decision by Parliament for each fiscal year.

Appropriations voted by Parliament on its own initiative shall be included in the Budget as facultative.

The Budget must show resources sufficient to meet the expenditure.

Art. 69. If the Budget is not adopted by Parliament before the beginning of the year, although the Budget Bill has been submitted by the Government at the least two months before the expiration of the Parliamentary session, the expenditure mentioned in Article 68, Paragraph 1, shall be defrayed, and the revenue necessary for this purpose shall be collected provisionally as before.

If alterations to the approved Budget appear to be absolutely necessary, a supplementary Budget Bill shall be submitted to Parliament.

Art. 70. The appropriations contained in the Budget shall not be exceeded, nor shall they be carried forward from one fiscal year to another, unless provisions for this are made in the Budget, nor shall an appropriation be transferred from a part separately voted on by Parliament to another part of the Budget.

Independently of the Budget, everyone shall have the right to demand from the State what is legally due to him.

Art. 71. For the examination of Treasury accounts and balance sheets there shall be an Auditing Office, which must satisfy itself that the figures in the accounts are correct, that the receipts and expenditure are legal, and that the Budget has been complied with.

At every regular session of Parliament there shall be appointed five State Auditors, who shall, on behalf of Parliament, supervise the observance of the Budget and examine the condition and administration of the Treasury. These Auditors shall follow instructions prescribed by Parliament, and they shall be entitled to obtain from the competent authorities any necessary information and documents. They shall be elected by proportional vote, by the Electors [1] of Parliament. In the same manner

[1] The Members of Parliament entrusted with electing the members of Parliamentary Committees.

there shall also be elected the necessary number of Deputy Auditors.

Art. 72. The rules concerning the monetary currency of Finland shall be enacted by law.

Art. 73. The Bank of Finland shall be placed under the guarantee and supervision of Parliament and under the supervision of Trustees appointed by Parliament.

The Bank of Finland shall be administrated by regulations adopted in accordance with the procedure prescribed for the enactment of laws.

Parliament shall determine how the profits of the Bank shall be used for the needs of the State.

Art. 74. Landed property, taxes, or revenue-yielding rights of the State shall not be alienated or mortgaged except as authorized by law.

The tenant of State-owned land shall nevertheless have the right to purchase such land in fee simple in accordance with special rulings.

CHAPTER VII

NATIONAL DEFENCE

Art. 75. Every Finnish citizen must take part in, or make his contribution to, the defence of the Country as prescribed by law.

Every conscript, unless he otherwise desires, shall if possible be enrolled in a military unit of which the rank and file speak his own mother tongue (Finnish or Swedish) and shall receive his training in that language. Finnish or Swedish) and shall receive his training in that language. Finnish shall be the language of command of the Armed Forces.

Art. 76. If the Armed Forces are to be mobilized the President shall issue an order in the Council of State to this effect. When this order has been given, the Council shall take measures to meet the expenditure which ensues, and Parliament shall be convoked if it is not in session.

CHAPTER VIII

EDUCATION

Art. 77. The University of Helsinki shall retain its right of self-government.

New regulations concerning the principles of the organization of the University shall be issued by law; but details concerning the University shall be regulated by decree. In both cases the Senate of the University must be previously consulted.

Art. 78. The State shall promote the study of and higher instruction in the technical, agricultural, and commercial sciences and other applied sciences, as well as the practice of and higher instruction in the fine arts, by maintaining and establishing for all these branches special schools of higher learning, in so far as they are not represented at the University, or by giving grants in aid to private institutions created for this purpose.

Art. 79. The State shall maintain at its own expense or, if necessary, subsidize schools for secondary education as well as for higher primary education. The principles of the organization of State-owned schools shall be established by law.

Art. 80. The principles governing the organization of primary education, the obligations of the State and the Communes to support schools as well as the establishment of compulsory education shall be determined by law.

Education in primary schools shall be free for everybody.

Art. 81. The State shall maintain, or if necessary, subsidize institutions for instruction in the technical professions, in agriculture and its subsidiary branches, in commerce and navigation, and in the fine arts.

Art. 82. The right to establish private schools or other private institutions of education and to organize instruction therein shall be regulated by law.

Instruction given at home shall be subject to no supervision by the authorities.

CHAPTER IX

RELIGIOUS COMMUNITIES

Art. 83. The organization and administration of the Evangelical Lutheran Church is regulated by Ecclesiastical Law.

Other existing religious communities shall be governed by rules which are or shall be prescribed on their behalf.

New religious communities may be founded subject to the provisions of the law.

CHAPTER X

PUBLIC OFFICES

Art. 84. Except where otherwise provided in this Article, only Finnish citizens shall be appointed to public office.

Employments of a technical nature, teaching posts in the University or comparable institutions, posts of teachers of foreign languages in schools, and of translators in public departments, as well as honorary consular posts and the posts of clerical assistants and other temporary staff positions in Legations and Consulates, may be held by other than Finnish citizens.

Art. 85. Examinations for appointment to public office shall be regulated by decree except where such matters are regulated by law. Exemption from the qualifications prescribed by decree may for special reasons be granted by the Council of State; this however, shall not apply to judicial appointments.

Art. 86. The general principles upon which appointment to public offices of the State may be made shall be ability, competence and proven civic virtue.

Art. 87. The President of the Republic shall appoint:

(1) The Chancellor of Justice and his Deputy;

(2) The Archbishop and Bishops and the Chancellor of the University;

(3) The Presidents of the Supreme Court and the Supreme Administrative Court, and, upon the recommendation of the Supreme Court, the members of that Court and the Presidents of the Courts of Appeal, as well as, upon the recommendation of the Supreme Administrative Court, the members of that Court;

(4) The members of the Courts of Appeal and the Professors of the University and of the Institute of Technology;

(5) The Heads of the Central Administrative Offices and the Provincial Governors, upon the recommendation of the Council of State, and the Members of the Central Administrative Offices;

(6) The Officials of the President's Secretarial Office and, upon the recommendation of the proper authority, the Reporters to the Council of State, to the Supreme Court, and to the Supreme Administrative Court; and

(7) Ministers Plenipotentiary and Consuls (*missi*), upon the recommendation of the Council of State.

Art. 88. Judges of Circuit Courts, Burgomasters, and Chairmen of Land-Partition Courts shall be appointed by the Supreme Court.

In compliance with special regulations, appointment to certain posts shall be made as follows:

(1) to tribunals, by the Supreme Court or by the superior Court within whose jurisdiction the employment falls, and to the Supreme Administrative Court, by that Court; and

(2) in the administration of schools, by the Council of State, the Minister, the Provincial Government, or the governing body of the Office to which the employment belongs.

Appointment to other public offices shall be made by the Council of State, unless the right of appointment has been reserved to the President or committed to some other authority.

Art. 89. Nominations of members of a Central Administrative Office and to posts mentioned in Article 87, Paragraph 4, and in Article 88, shall ensue subject to the reservations contained in Article 99. The post having been announced open for application, the authority to which the application is addressed shall put on a nomination list those three of the applicants who, in accordance with prescribed principles, have the greatest merits. The Supreme Court shall give its opinion on the nomination list for a post as member of a Court of Appeal.

If the appointment is made by the same authority to which the applications are addressed, no nomination list shall be drawn up. In accordance with special regulations, certain other administrative posts may also be filled by a procedure different from that prescribed in Paragraph 1 of this Article.

Art. 90. For appointments to posts in the University, in the Institute of Technology, in the Evangelical Lutheran Church and the Greek Orthodox Church, to the offices of Burgomaster and Alderman in towns, and to offices and employments in the Bank of Finland, special regulations are in force.

Officers of the Army and of the Navy shall be appointed by the President. Special regulations shall be issued concerning other matters of military promotion and instruction.

Art. 91. No judge shall be deprived of his office except by a lawful trial and judgement. Nor shall he, without his own consent, be transferred to another post, except in the case of a reorganization of the judiciary.

The right of other officials to retain their offices shall be regulated by a special law.

The law may impose, even for irremovable officials, an obligation to retire at a fixed age or because of infirmity involving incapacity.

Special regulations shall define the rights and duties of officials whose offices are abolished.

Art. 92. In the exercise of public functions the law must be strictly followed under penalty of the law.

If a provision in a decree is contrary to a constitutional or other law, it shall not be applied by a judge or other official.

Art. 93. Every official is responsible for the measures he has taken or to which he has contributed in his capacity as a member of a collegiate public office. A reporter is likewise responsible for a decision taken upon his report unless he has recorded his dissenting opinion in the minutes.

Whoever suffers a violation of his right or injury as a result of an illegal measure or negligence by an official has the right to demand that the official in question be punished and pay damages, or he can lay information against the official demanding his indictment in accordance with the formalities prescribed by law.

The responsibility, if any, of the State for damages caused by an official shall be governed by special regulations.

CHAPTER XI

FINAL PROVISIONS

Art. 94. The election of the first President of the Republic shall be made by Parliament, and shall take place immediately after the present Constitution Act comes into force. The election shall be by secret ballot. If a candidate obtains more than half of the votes cast he shall be proclaimed elected. Otherwise a new ballot shall immediately be held, and if no candidate obtains an absolute majority this time, another ballot shall be held between the two candidates who obtained the largest number of votes on the second count. In the case of a tie the decision shall be by lot.

Art. 95. The present Constitution Act shall be in all its parts an irrevocable Constitutional Law. It cannot be amended, interpreted or repealed, nor can it be departed from except in accordance with the procedure prescribed for Constitutional Laws in general.

The following laws are repealed by the present law: The Constitution Act of August 21, 1772, and the Act of Union and Security of February 21 and April 3, 1789, as well as provisions contained in other laws and decrees which are in conflict with the present Constitution Act.

The provisions necessary for bringing the present Constitution Act into effect shall be issued by law.

To be observed by whomsoever it may concern.

2. PARLIAMENT ACT

January 13, 1928, as amended in 1937, 1944, 1948 and 1955

Whereas, by reason of the adoption of the Constitution Act of July 17, 1919, and on the basis of the experience acquired, it has been judged necessary to bring certain modifications to the Parliament Act of July 20, 1906, there is hereby sanctioned, by the resolution of Parliament, taken in conformity with the dispositions of Article 60 of the said Act, the Parliament Act for the Republic of Finland, of which the following is the text:

CHAPTER I

GENERAL PRINCIPLES

Art. 1. Parliament represents the people of Finland.

Art. 2. Parliament is unicameral and is composed of two hundred Members of Parliament.

Art. 3. Elections to Parliament shall take place every four years and simultaneously throughout the country. The participation of Finnish citizens abroad in the parliamentary elections is determined by law.

The President of the Republic has, if he judges it necessary, the right to order new elections before the expiration of the period of four years provided for in Paragraph 1. In this case the following elections shall take place, if there is no new dissolution of Parliament, in the fourth year after the latest elections.

The mandate of a Member of Parliament shall take effect as soon as he has been declared elected and shall continue until the new elections have been held.

Art. 4. Members of Parliament are elected by direct and proportional suffrage; for these elections the country shall be divided into electoral districts numbering a minimum of twelve and a maximum of eighteen.

When local circumstances necessitate an exception to the proportional procedure, one or several districts, besides the number indicated above, can be established for the purpose of electing a single Member of Parliament.

At elections every elector shall have the same right to vote.

The right to vote cannot be exercised by proxy.

Detailed provisions relative to districts, to dates, and to the procedure of elections shall be given by special law.

Art. 5. Whosoever shall seek to disturb the freedom of voting by persuasion or bribery shall be liable to a maximum of three months' imprisonment. If he has employed force or threats, he shall be liable to a prison term of from one month to a year; if he is an official, he shall in addition be removed from his office.

An official who takes advantage of his public authority to influence the election of Members of Parliament shall be discharged.

An employer who does not grant an elector in his employment the opportunity to use his right to vote shall be liable to a fine.

Art. 6. Every Finnish citizen, man or woman, who has attained the age of 21 before the year in which the election takes place shall be an elector.

The following shall be deprived of the right to vote: whoever

(1) is under guardianship;

(2) has not during the last three years been entered on the civil register as a Finnish citizen;

(3) has been committed to a workhouse or forced labor for vagrancy, the right only being returned after the expiration of the third year counting from the year in which he has been set free;

(4) has been deprived by judicial decree of his right to vote or of his civil rights or has been declared unworthy of serving the country or of acting on behalf of another person, whether or not the decree be final;

(5) is convicted of having, at the time of the election of Members of Parliament, bought or sold votes or of having attempted to do so or has

voted in more than one place or has by force or threats disturbed the freedom of the vote, the right only being returned after the expiration of the sixth year counting from the year in which final judgement was rendered.

Art. 7. Every elector shall be eligible te become a Member of Parliament without regard to residence.

Eligibility shall not, however, extend to those who are on active military service.

Art. 8. Every person elected a Member of Parliament who forfeits his eligibility shall lose his mandate.

Art. 9. The Chancellor of Justice, members of the Supreme Court and of the Supreme Administrative Court as well as the Judicial Delegate to Parliament cannot be Members of Parliament. If a Member of Parliament is named or elected to any of these functions, he shall cease to be a Member of Parliament.

Art. 10. Whoever is, by virtue of the electoral law, declared elected a Member of Parliament, cannot resign except for a legal obstacle or other cause approved by Parliament.

Art. 11. Every Member of Parliament is obliged to act according to justice and truth in the exercise of his mandate. He should observe the Constitutional Laws and is not bound by any other instructions.

Art. 12. Access to the sessions and the exercise of his mandate cannot be refused a Member of Parliament.

Art. 13. No Member of Parliament should be prosecuted or deprived of his liberty because of opinions expressed by him in Parliament or because of his attitude during the proceedings, unless Parliament has authorized it by a vote of at least five sixths of the votes cast.

Art. 14. In the course of a session of Parliament no Member of Parliament should be arrested, without the consent of Parliament, for a criminal offence, unless a tribunal has ordered his arrest or he has been taken in the act of committing a criminal offence punishable by at least six months' imprisonment.

A Member of Parliament who, while proceeding to a session, is arrested for a cause other than that provided for in Paragraph 1 should be freed if Parliament decides upon it.

The Speaker should be informed immediately of the arrest of a Member of Parliament.

Art. 15. If anyone, knowing that a Member of Parliament is concerned, abuses by act or word a Member of Parliament while the latter is proceeding to a session of Parliament or returning from it or in the course of a session, or if anyone, once the session is ended, commits assault upon a Member of Parliament because of the way in which he has exercised his mandate, the fact that the infraction has been committed against a

Member of Parliament shall be considered a seriously aggravating circumstance.

What is stated here about Members of Parliament shall also apply to secretaries and to other officials and employees of Parliament.

Art. 16. Every Member of Parliament shall enjoy a parliamentary emolument paid by State funds and, in addition, his travelling expenses to and from a parliamentary session shall be reimbursed.

The parliamentary emolument and the reimbursement of travelling expenses shall be fixed by law; such a bill shall be dealt with as stipulated in Article 70.

In the said law shall also be determined the emolument to which, during a recess or after the close of a session, the following are entitled: members of the Finance Committee and the Foreign Affairs Committee as well as Members of Parliament appointed for the verification of communications and resolutions of Parliament.

The right of a Member of Parliament to a pension is prescribed by law.

Art. 17. On every Member of Parliament who does not present himself in due time at the session or who is, without authorization by Parliament and without recognized hindrance, absent from a sitting, Parliament can impose the loss of the parliamentary emolument or a part of it. Any Member of Parliament who does not amend his conduct as a consequence can be declared by Parliament to have forfeited his mandate.

Any Member of Parliament who undergoes a punishment depriving him of liberty shall forfeit his emolument during this time.

CHAPTER II

OPENING AND CLOSING OF SESSIONS OF PARLIAMENT AND DISSOLUTION OF PARLIAMENT

Art. 18. Parliament convenes in the capital of the State except when enemy action or any other serious cause makes it impossible or compromises the security of Parliament; in this case, another place of assembly shall be assigned by the President of the Republic.

Art. 19. The ordinary session of Parliament shall begin yearly, without special convocation, on February 1, unless the preceding session has appointed another date, and shall terminate after having continued for one hundred and twenty days, with or without interruption. Parliament shall nevertheless have the right to decide whether it will recess earlier or later.

Art. 20. If the President of the Republic, in the course of an ordinary session, orders new elections, Parliament shall be dissolved on the day which the President of the Republic has caused to be proclaimed. In this case, Parliament shall re-assemble in ordinary session, after the new elections, either on the first day of the first month which begins after a period of ninety days reckoning from the dissolution, or on an earlier day fixed by the President of the Republic.

If new elections are ordered after the closing of an ordinary session so that the elections cannot be concluded before the following February 1, the re-assembly of Parliament in ordinary session shall be postponed till the first day of the month which follows the publication of the results of the elections.

Art. 21. The President of the Republic shall have the right to convene Parliament in extraordinary session and to determine the date when this session shall end.

An extraordinary session of Parliament should not be convened for a date prior to the fifteenth day reckoning from the publication of the convocation and should not continue beyond the last working day preceding the beginning of the ordinary session.

An extraordinary session should not deal with matters other than those which caused the convocation or which otherwise are submitted to it by the Government or which are germane to the foregoing.

Art. 22. The decisions of the President of the Republic prescribed in Articles 18, 20, and 21 should be promulgated in the fashion established for the promulgation of laws and decrees.

The decision relative to new elections shall be made known to the provincial governors and to the authorities and commissions charged with the organization of elections.

Art. 23. On the day preceding the day when Parliament should assemble for the first time after the elections, all Members of Parliament shall be obliged, beginning at twelve o'clock noon and in the order named in the public notice, to present their credentials to the person or persons commissioned by the President of the Republic for this purpose. It should be proved at the time of the verification of credentials that these have been delivered by the competent authority and are in good and correct form.

An alphabetical list of duly accredited Members of Parliament should be put at the disposal of Parliament before twelve noon the following day.

Credentials presented later should be immediately verified in conformity with Paragraph 1 and shown to the Speaker as soon as they have been approved. Mention thereof and of any other change arising in the composition of Parliament should be made in the list provided by Paragraph 2.

Art. 24. If the credentials of a Member of Parliament have not been approved, Parliament shall have the right to consider whether this Member of Parliament can nevertheless take a seat in Parliament.

If, by virtue of the present law, the qualification of a Member of Parliament is contested, Parliament should likewise pronounce on this question, unless the same objection has been, by way of appeal made against the election, already submitted or is still liable to be submitted to the decision of the competent authority.

Any other question relative to the validity of the elections cannot be submitted to the examination of Parliament, except when it is claimed that an act manifestly criminal has been committed at the time of the elections or of any proceeding relating to the elections, or that an indubitable error has occurred at the verification of the results of the elections. In these cases, when it also appears that the criminal proceeding or error has affected the issue of the elections and that rectification can no longer be demanded by way of appeal, Parliament has the power to rectify the result in conformity with the electoral law.

A person whose qualification as a Member of Parliament is contested shall nevertheless hold his mandate until it has been invalidated.

Art. 25. On the first day of the session, Parliament assembles at noon in a plenary sitting, which shall begin with a roll-call following the list provided for in Article 23. At this sitting Parliament shall elect from among its Members the Speaker and two Deputy Speakers.

Then the Speaker and Deputy Speakers shall deliver one after the other before the assembled House this solemn declaration:

"I, . . ., affirm that in the exercise of my functions I shall maintain with all my power the rights of the people of Finland, of Parliament and of the Government in conformance with the Constitution."

Until this declaration has been made, the senior Member shall preside over Parliament.

In case of the death or resignation of the Speaker or of a Deputy Speaker in the course of the session, a new Speaker or Deputy Speaker should be immediately elected.

Art. 26. The President of the Republic causes the date and hour of the opening of the session to be proclaimed; the opening should not take place later than the third working day counted from the assembly of Parliament. On the day and hour indicated, Members of Parliament should assemble, after Divine Service, at the House, where the President of the Republic shall greet the Members of Parliament and declare open the session of Parliament. The Speaker, in the name of Parliament, shall reply to the speech of welcome.

Art. 27. At the time of the closing of the session the Members of Parliament shall assemble, after Divine Service, on the day and hour fixed by the President of the Republic, at the House, where the Speaker shall tender to the President of the Republic the greetings of Parliament and shall deliver the account of its decisions, after which the President of the Republic shall declare the closure of the session of Parliament.

CHAPTER III

INTRODUCTION OF BUSINESS IN PARLIAMENT

Art. 28. At the time of the opening of the session, the President of the Republic shall make known the Government Proposals which are submitted to Parliament.

Proposals which could not then be sent to Parliament can be submitted for consideration subsequently.

A Government Proposal can, if there is reason to do so, be withdrawn.

Art. 29. At every ordinary session of Parliament, at the time of its opening or within one month of the opening, a report should be delivered to Parliament concerning the measures taken by the Government as a result of the resolutions of Parliament and about any other important issue relating to public administration and to the country's relations with foreign powers.

Art. 30. At the time of every ordinary session a Budget Bill for the coming financial year shall be delivered.

At every ordinary session of Parliament there should likewise be presented a statement concerning the administration and state of the public finances.

The State Auditors appointed by Parliament are bound to report to it in conformity with the provisions in force on this subject.

Art. 31. Parliament shall have the right to admit for consideration any motion duly proposed by a Member of Parliament. Such a motion can be:

(1) a legislative motion, containing a bill, drawn up in legal form, aiming at the adoption of a new law or at the amendment, interpretation or abrogation of a law in force, or a bill on a matter regulated previously by administrative provisions;

(2) a financial motion, containing the proposal to include an appropriation in the Budget for the coming financial year;

(3) a petitionary motion, containing a proposal that Parliament request the Government to carry out certain measures in a matter which is within the competence of the Government.

Relative to the enactment of Ecclesiastical Laws, special provisions are in force.

Art. 32. Every motion should be presented in writing before noon on the fourteenth day counted from the opening of the first ordinary session after the elections, but on the tenth day at other ordinary sessions. A Member of Parliament shall not have the right to propose a motion after this date unless it be directly justified by a resolution of Parliament or a Government Proposal presented to Parliament or the resumption of a proposal or another issue arising in the course of the session. In any case, no motion can be presented later than noon on the seventh day counting from the day when the author of the motion may be considered as having been acquainted with the issue in question.

Every motion should be properly justified.

Questions of different characters should not be included in the same document.

Art. 33. Relative to the right of motion of the Representative Assembly (*Landsting*) of Aaland, special provisions are in force.

Art. 34. In a matter which is within the competence of the Government and which does not require the concurrence of Parliament, the Government can, through a proposal to this effect, request the opinion of Parliament.

Art. 35. If the consideration of a matter has not been terminated at an ordinary session, it shall be continued, with the exception of cases provided for in Articles 36 and 37, at the following ordinary session, unless elections intervene.

Art. 36. If the Government desires to make, beyond the orders of the day, a communication or account concerning the administration of public affairs or relations with foreign powers, this shall be read in the House and laid on the table for a subsequent sitting. The debate on the matter having been declared ended, the Speaker shall propose to Parliament to pass to the orders of the day by the adoption of a declaration formulated thus: "After having received the communication, Parliament passes to the orders of the day."

Parliament can either adopt this simple passage to the orders of the day or an amended passage proposed in the course of the debate or decide to refer the matter to a competent committee. If the matter is referred to a committee, the latter should propose an amended passage to the orders of the day; the final substance of this passage shall be determined by Parliament.

The consideration of a point in question here cannot be continued at a subsequent session.

Art. 37. If a Member of Parliament desires to address a question to a member of the Government on a matter which is within this Minister's competence, he shall present it in writing in precise terms to the Speaker, whose duty it is to forward it to the Minister concerned. The Minister shall answer orally or in writing within thirty days of being notified, on the day and hour agreed upon by the Speaker, unless he considers that he should refrain from answering; in this case, the motives for the refusal should be brought to the attention of Parliament within the same period. In a matter of this sort there can be neither debate nor resolution in Parliament.

If a Member of Parliament wishes to interpellate a member of the Government on a question which is within the competence of the latter, so that the matter may be considered by Parliament, he should present the interpellation to the Speaker in the form and substance provided by Paragraph 1.

When the interpellation has been read to Parliament and laid on the table until a subsequent sitting and if at least twenty Members of Parliament, including the authors, have approved it in writing, it shall without preliminary discussion in Parliament, through the good offices of the Speaker, be communicated to the Minister concerned. The Minister is bound to reply within fifteen days' notification, on the day and hour agreed upon by him and by the Speaker, unless the Government, within the same period, has made known that the character of the matter does not permit any reply; the motives for the refusal should be brought to the attention of Parliament. After a reply, or the communication that there is no reply, has been delivered and the debate is declared closed, the Speaker shall move to pass to the orders of the day in this form: "After having heard the explanation given, Parliament passes to the orders of the day."

Parliament can either adopt this simple passage to the orders of the day, or an amended passage proposed in the debates, or decide to refer the matter to the Constitutional Committee or, if the character of the matter demands it, to another committee. If the matter is referred to a committee, the latter should propose an amended passage to the orders of the day, of which the final substance shall be determined by Parliament.

The consideration of a point in question here cannot be continued at a subsequent session.

Art. 38. Special law shall prescribe the competence of Parliament to judge the legality of measures taken in the execution of their office by members of the Government and the Chancellor of Justice and the procedure to be followed in the examination of matters of this nature.

CHAPTER IV

PREPARATION OF BUSINESS FOR DISCUSSION IN PARLIAMENT

Art. 39. Within three days reckoning from the opening of the first session after the elections, Parliament shall appoint the Electors, at least forty-five in number, with the necessary number of substitutes, in view of the election of members to the Parliamentary committees.

The Electors and their substitutes shall be elected by proportional ballot, and their mandate shall continue during all sessions until new elections, unless Parliament decides, at the proposal of the Speaker's Conference, upon proceedings for a new election of Electors.

Art. 40. At the time of an ordinary session, there shall be constituted, within five days of the opening of the session, a Constitutional Committee, a Legislative Committee, a Foreign Affairs Committee, a Finance Committee and a Bank Committee. The Constitutional Committee, the Legislative Committee and the Foreign Affairs Committee should each be composed of at least seventeen members, the Finance Committee of at least twenty-one, and the Bank Committee of at least eleven members. At the same time substitutes numbering at least one quarter of the regular members of each committee shall be selected.

In addition to these standing committees, Parliament can also, in case of need, establish extraordinary committees; to such a committee, if it is composed of at least eleven members, there can also be referred matters which, considering their character, should otherwise be prepared by a standing committee.

If a committee deems it necessary that the number of its members or substitutes be increased, it should make a proposal to Parliament to this effect.

Every committee shall have the right to divide, when matters demand it, into sub-committees, of which each shall make reports in the name of the committee. Regarding the sub-committees, which should each consist of at least eleven members, the stipulations in the present law for committees shall be enforced.

In extraordinary sessions Parliament shall establish committees which are necessary for the preparation of matters submitted to that session.

Art. 41. If the Electors cannot agree on the designation of members of the committees, a proportional vote shall be applied.

Art. 42. Within five days of the opening of the session Parliament should establish, for the preparation of certain matters provided by Article 66, the Grand Committee, consisting of at least forty-five members; these, together with the necessary substitutes, shall be elected in the manner stipulated for the election of Electors.

Art. 43. The Finance Committee will, if Parliament so decides, continue its work even when Parliament is in recess or after the closing of a session.

The Foreign Affairs Committee likewise will, on the summons of the Government, meet during a recess of Parliament or after the closing of a session.

Art. 44. A member of the Government cannot be a member of a committee.

A member whose official activity is being examined by a committee or who is personally on trial should not participate in the handling of such a a matter within a committee.

Art. 45. The committees and Electors of Parliament as well as the examiners provided for in Article 85 shall elect from among themselves a chairman and a vice-chairman at each session.

The senior member of each committee shall convene the first meeting and preside over it until the chairman is chosen.

Every committee shall have the right to designate, for a certain matter, one or more reporters charged with communicating all necessary information to the plenary sitting of Parliament or to the Grand Committee.

Art. 46. The Constitutional Committee shall be charged with preparing matters which have been referred to it relative to the enactment, amendment, interpretation or abrogation of Constitutional Laws, or to all legislation intimately connected with Constitutional Laws.

It is the duty of this Committee also to examine bills which have been referred to it relative to the establishment, amendment, or abrogation of the rules of procedure of Parliament, or of dispositions concerning the elections within Parliament according to the proportional system, as well as of instructions for the Judicial Delegate to Parliament.

It is likewise the duty of this Committee to examine the report made by the Government and mentioned in Article 29 and to make proposals justified by this report.

Matters proceeding from the right of Parliament to examine the legality of official measures taken by members of the Government and the Chancellor of Justice shall likewise be prepared by this Committee.

It is the duty of the Constitutional Committee to arbitrate between Parliament and the Speaker, when the latter has refused to submit for consideration a question raised or to put a matter to the vote.

Art. 47. The Legislative Committee shall be charged with enactment, amendment, interpretation, or abrogation of laws.

Art. 48. The Foreign Affairs Committee shall be charged with preparing questions relating to the treaties or the provisions contained in treaties which, according to the Constitution, should be approved by Parliament; it shall also prepare other questions relating to foreign affairs, when the decision requires the consent of Parliament, as well as all matters of foreign policy which may be referred to it.

The Committee should receive, as often as circumstances require, a report by the Government concerning the relations of the country with foreign powers; the Committee can, if it judges it necessary, express its opinion on this report.

The Committee shall also examine the report referred to in Article 29, in as far as it concerns relations with foreign powers, and make such proposals as the matter may require.

The members of the Committee should observe the discretion that the Government may impose upon them in the case in point.

Art. 49. The Finance Committee should have access to all the accounts and acts of the Treasury. In the report which the Committee gives on the state of the public finances and on the report of the State Auditors, it will be its duty to pronounce on the manner in which the Budget has been observed and the public economy administered and to make proposals which may be justified by these facts.

The Budget Bill shall also be referred to the Finance Committee, as well as other financial propositions of the Government and motions of finance made by Parliament. In its report on the Budget Bill the Committee should treat all appropriations together. In this same report, the Committee should make proposals as to the manner of procuring the resources for the expenditure.

Every proposal for additions to the Budget should be treated by the Committee in the same manner as the Budget Bill.

It is also the duty of the Committee to examine proposals which may be referred to it relative to the establishment, amendment, or abrogation of instructions for the State Auditors.

Art. 50. The Bank Committee shall be charged with studying the administration and situation of the Bank of Finland, the action of the Bank Trustees and the Board of the Bank, and the state and management of funds under the guarantee of Parliament, and with making reports to Parliament thereon.

The Committee is bound to make any necessary proposals relating to the establishment, amendment, or abrogation of regulations for the Bank of Finland and of instructions for the Bank Trustees and regarding other provisions concerning the Bank of Finland, and to prepare Government Proposals and other proposals relating thereto. No decision should be taken on the disposal of the profit of the Bank of Finland before the Bank Committee has been heard.

It shall likewise be the duty of the Committee to prepare matters referred to it concerning the banks and the monetary system of the country.

Art. 51. Every committee should assemble two days after its formation at the latest and send to the plenary sitting of Parliament, in due order when ready, the report on each matter which that matter requires.

If a member is prevented from taking part in the consideration of a matter, a substitute shall be summoned in his place. A quorum is not constituted unless two thirds of the members are present.

If a member of a committee is absent from a meeting without excuse or special authorization, Parliament can condemn him to the forfeit in whole or in part of his parliamentary emolument, as stated in Article 17, and, if this conduct is repeated, can declare him deprived of his mandate as a member of the committee.

Every member who has not accepted the resolution of the committee shall have the right to express in writing his dissenting opinion and have it presented with the main report, but without retarding the report in that way.

Art. 52. Members of the Government shall have the right to attend meetings and take part in debates of the committees, unless the committee decides otherwise in the case in point.

The Speakers and Deputy Speakers shall have the right to attend the meetings of the committees.

All Members of Parliament as well as the Secretary and any other Parliamentary official assigned by the Speaker for this purpose shall have the right to attend meetings of the Grand Committee.

Art. 53. If a committee deems that it needs to have access to documents relating to a matter treated by a public authority or administration which is not under the jurisdiction of Parliament or to obtain oral or written information from these, the Prime Minister or Minister concerned shall, on the demand of the committee, take measures for these documents or this information to be communicated to it without delay. If they cannot be communicated, the refusal should be justified.

Art. 54. The Speaker and Deputy Speakers and the chairmen of the committees shall constitute the Speaker's Conference.

It shall be the duty of the Speaker's Conference to make any necessary proposals to Parliament regarding the general organization of the work of Parliament as well as regarding the establishment, amendment, or abrogation of the law concerning the basis of the budget for the Secretariat of Parliament, of the rules of procedure of Parliament and provisions relating to the elections within Parliament according to the proportional system, as well as of instructions for the officials of Parliament.

CHAPTER V

PROCEDURE FOR BUSINESS IN PLENARY SITTING AND IN THE GRAND COMMITTEE

Art. 55. It shall be the duty of the Speaker to issue the summons to plenary sittings; to present matters and conduct debates; to move resolutions; to maintain order at the sittings and to see that nothing contrary to Constitutional Law be discussed; and to close the plenary sitting.

The Speaker should not take part either in the debates or in the votes, nor make suggestions other than those which are necessary for enforcing Constitutional Laws, resolutions, or the rules of procedure of Parliament.

If the Speaker is unable to perform his duties, he shall be replaced by the first Deputy Speaker; if the latter is similarly prevented, he shall be replaced by the second Deputy Speaker.

Art. 56. The debates of the plenary sitting shall be public, unless Parliament has decided otherwise in the case in point.

Art. 57. Except for the contrary provisions below, each Member of Parliament shall have the right to take the floor in the order in which he demands it and to speak freely for inclusion in the record and express his opinion on all matters submitted for debate and on the legality of all that occurs in Parliament. No person should speak before the floor has been granted to him or off the record.

Art. 58. Every Member of Parliament should preserve a serious and dignified bearing. No one should be permitted to express himself about the Government or particular persons in a manner injurious, derogatory, or otherwise unseemly. Anyone who violates these provisions will be called to order by the Speaker and, if he persists, will be deprived of the floor. In other respects it shall be the duty of Parliament to judge whether a Member of Parliament who has disturbed order should receive the admonitions and remonstrance of the Speaker, be excluded for a specified period not exceeding two weeks from the sittings of Parliament or be brought to justice, or whether the matter should be dropped.

Art. 59. The members of the Government and the Chancellor of Justice, in the same manner as the Judicial Delegate to Parliament, shall have the right to attend plenary sittings and to take part in the debates, but not in resolutions, unless they are Members of Parliament. If one of the above persons requests the floor, he shall be given priority.

Art. 60. When a committee has elected, in conformity with Article 45, a reporter for a certain matter, he shall receive the benefit of priority of speech when he takes the floor concerning the same matter.

Art. 61. A person who is not of the Evangelical Lutheran Faith cannot take part in the consideration of proposals relating to the Ecclesiastical Law of the Evangelical Lutheran Church or to the ecclesiastical conditions of Evangelical Lutheran parishes in general.

Art. 62. A Member of Parliament may take part in a discussion concerning a matter in which he is personally interested, but not in the decision taken on this subject.

Art. 63. The proposals of the Government, in the same manner as legislative motions, should not be submitted to a final decision before the competent committee has given its opinion thereon.

Reports which must be submitted to Parliament according to Constitutional Law are also subject to preparatory examination by a committee.

Financial motions and petitionary motions which have not been rejected either without being laid on the table or after having been on the table should likewise be submitted for examination by a committee.

Art. 64. If a matter provided for in Paragraphs 1 and 2 of Article 63 is not immediately and unanimously referred to a committee upon its first presentation, it should be kept pending until one of the following sittings and should then be referred to a committee.

Art. 65. The report of a committee should on its first presentation be kept pending. At the following presentation, it should, whether or not there has been a debate, be kept pending again if two or more members demand it but at the third it can no longer be delayed.

The stipulations of the preceding paragraph shall not concern the report of the Grand Committee, which should, however, on its first presentation be kept pending if two or more Members of Parliament demand it.

Art. 66. If the opinion of a committee concerns the adoption or rejection of a bill, the matter should pass three distinct readings in plenary sitting.

At the first reading, the report of the committee shall be read, and the right of pronouncing upon it be given to Members of Parliament. After the debate has been declared closed, the matter shall be referred, without decision on points of substance, to the Grand Committee, which is obliged to give its opinion and make justified proposals.

At the second reading, the report of the Grand Committee shall be read, after which Parliament shall proceed to an examination of the bill and shall decide on each point of it. If the proposal of the Grand Committee is approved *in toto*, the second reading shall be declared closed. If the proposal of the Grand Committee is not approved without amendments, the bill shall be recommitted, in the wording it has received by the resolution of Parliament, to the Grand Committee, which is obliged to recommend the bill with or without amendments or to propose its rejection. If the Grand Committee has proposed amendments, Parliament shall decide on the adoption or rejection of these, after which the second reading is declared closed.

If the report of the Grand Committee contains a bill, the rejection of the bill in its entirety should not be proposed on the occasion of the second reading.

In the course of the second reading Parliament shall have the right to demand a further opinion from the special committee which first prepared the matter or from another special committee. The Grand Committee has the same right.

At the third reading, which shall take place not earlier than the third day after the completion of the second reading, the matter is presented for final decision; Parliament can either adopt the bill in the wording approved at the second reading or reject it.

A bill which has obtained a majority at the third reading can nevertheless be left pending. A proposal to this effect should be made before the proposal for the adoption or rejection of the bill is made; in this case, unless the bill has been rejected by vote, the matter should be delivered at the following plenary sitting; if the proposal to leave the matter pending is then urged by at least a third of all the Members of Parliament, the bill should, in the text approved at the third reading, remain pending until the first ordinary session after the elections.

Art. 67. In order to become a resolution of Parliament, every bill concerning the enactment, amendment, interpretation, or abrogation of a Constitutional Law should, after having been treated as provided in Article 66, at the third reading be approved by a majority of votes to be left pending until the first ordinary session after the elections and should be adopted without change at this session by a resolution assembling at least two thirds of the votes cast.

Nevertheless if a bill referring to a Constitutional Law has been declared urgent in plenary sitting by a resolution assembling at least five sixths of the votes cast, the matter should be resolved without being stood over, and the resolution on the adoption of the bill should be taken as stated in Paragraph 1.

The above stipulations relating to Constitutional Laws shall be applied to the privileges of the Estates.

Art. 68. The stipulations of Article 66 should likewise be observed when an impost is to be collected during a time either indeterminate or limited, or when the contracting of a State loan is concerned. Yet a bill referring to a new or increased impost, or to the indeterminate prolongation at the same rate of an impost fixed for a limited time, or to the contracting of a State loan, may not be left pending, and a bill referring to a new or increased impost destined to be collected for a time exceeding one year shall be considered lapsed if it has not received two thirds of the votes cast at the third reading.

In the case where a bill referring to a new or increased impost destined to be collected during a time exceeding one year becomes lapsed at the third reading, the matter shall be recommitted to the Finance Committee, which is obliged to give its advice on the question whether the impost should be fixed for one year and to propose the text of a bill relating to the collection of the impost.

In the case where a bill referring to an increased impost destined to be collected during a time of one year becomes lapsed at the third reading, the matter shall be recommitted to the Finance Committee, which is obliged to give its advice on the question whether the impost is to be prolonged at the same rate and to propose the text of a bill relating to the collection of the impost.

Parliament shall decide at the third adjourned reading on the adoption or rejection of the bill drafted by the Finance Committee as provided in Paragraphs 2 and 3; an opinion relating to it shall not be left pending, unless Parliament decides otherwise.

The stipulations herein provided for imposts shall be in force with relation to public encumbrances.

Art. 69. Proposals for the adoption of provisions contained in a treaty concluded between Finland and a foreign power which are within the legislative sphere shall be considered, whether the provisions be included in a peace treaty or other treaty, according to Article 66 and, if a Constitutional Law is concerned, according to Paragraph 1 of Article 67. However, in these cases, a bill should not be left pending.

A proposal for the adoption by Parliament of a provision contained in a treaty, by which the State is bound to maintain legal provisions in force during a certain time, as well as a proposal aiming at the adoption of a treaty, or of a provision contained in a treaty, which, without touching the legislative domain, requires by the terms of the Constitution the consent of Parliament or for which the Government desires the consent of Parliament, shall be considered without regard to the order stipulated in Article

66, and the matter shall be decided by the majority of votes. A proposal for a change in the frontiers of the State which constitutes a reduction of territory must nevertheless be carried by at least two thirds of the votes cast to be considered approved by Parliament.

Art. 70. On the examination of a bill relating to parliamentary emoluments, the provisions of Article 66 should likewise be observed, but with the reservation that a matter of this nature cannot be left pending and that the bill is considered lapsed if it is not approved at the third reading by at least two thirds of the votes cast.

Art. 71. Parliament also has the right to refer to the Grand Committee matters other than those provided for in Articles 66, 67, 68 and 70. In this case, the provisions of Article 66 shall be applied in such a way that the matter is submitted to only two readings and is decided at the second.

In a matter which has not been referred to the Grand Committee, Parliament can decide that the matter should be submitted to two readings and that the final decision should be taken at the second, which in this case shall take place not earlier than the third day after the first reading.

In matters of this nature a proposal to leave the matter pending should not be made.

Art. 72. A matter introduced by a Government Proposal at an extraordinary session and which does not concern a Constitutional Law cannot be left pending but should be decided at the same session.

Art. 73. A bill which has been left pending, or which has not been sanctioned by the President of the Republic, should be introduced at the first ordinary session after the election and should, after a report by the competent committee, be either adopted without amendment or rejected.

The decision relative to the adoption or rejection shall be taken by majority vote with the exception of the case provided for in Paragraph 1 of Article 67.

Art. 74. The fact that a bill has been left pending or that a bill adopted by Parliament has not been sanctioned shall not constitute an obstacle to a new proposal or motion on the same subject. If Parliament has, after such a proposal or motion, adopted a new bill, the bill left pending or not sanctioned shall be considered lapsed.

Art. 75. A proposal aiming at the assessment of a new impost or at the alteration of a previous impost or at the prolongation of an impost fixed for a limited time or at the contracting of a State loan should, even if the amount in question is included in the Budget Bill, be considered in Parliament as a separate matter.

A proposal made by a Member of Parliament and aiming to bring to the Budget a new appropriation not observed in the estimates of the Budget Bill can be taken up for final consideration only if it has been duly made by a financial motion which has been submitted to the examination of the Finance Committee and also, in case of need, preparatively to that of the special committee which the proposed appropriation particularly concerns.

Art. 76. If Parliament, in examining the proposal of the Finance Committee relating to the Budget, has not adopted it without change, the bill, in the amended form approved by resolution of Parliament, shall be recommitted to the Finance Committee, which is obliged to give its opinion on the amendments introduced by Parliament. If the Finance Committee proposes amendments to the resolution of Parliament, the latter will decide on the adoption or rejection of the Committee's proposal.

Art. 77. There should be no resolution on a matter debated until Parliament, on the proposal of the Speaker, has declared the debate closed.

Art. 78. When a question is to be decided, the Speaker shall put the matter to a vote, on the basis of the discussion, in such a way that "Yes" or "No" shall express the resolution of Parliament.

If several proposals for resolution exist, they shall be put to the vote one after the other until all have been voted upon. The text and order of the proposals should be approved by Parliament before they are put to the vote. Remarks on the text and order of the proposals can be made, but no renewed discussion on a point of substance is admissible.

There can be no vote on the question whether there should be a vote or not.

Art. 79. A member who has not supported a resolution shall have the right to have his dissension placed on record in the minutes; but such a communication should not be debated.

Art. 80. The Speaker should not refuse to introduce for consideration a question raised or to submit a proposal to the vote, unless he deems it contrary to a Constitutional Law or to another law or to a decision already taken by Parliament; the Speaker must give reasons for his refusal.

If Parliament does not approve the decision of the Speaker, the matter shall be referred to the Constitutional Committee, which should give its considered opinion without delay on the question whether a debate on the matter or the introduction of the proposal is contrary to a Constitutional Law, to another law or to a decision already taken by Parliament; the opinion expressed by the committee shall be decisive.

Art. 81. A resolution cannot be changed at the time of the verification of the record.

At the time of the verification of the record, the statement of any Member of Parliament and the debate following can be removed with his consent and with that of Parliament, unless the resolution is obviously based upon this same statement.

Art. 82. A Member of Parliament absent at the time of the resolution taken on a matter has the right to have the fact that he has not taken part in the resolution entered later in the record, but he cannot make any observation upon the resolution.

CHAPTER VI

MEASURES RELATING TO THE BANK OF FINLAND AND THE NATIONAL PENSIONS INSTITUTE AS WELL AS TO THE PARLIAMENT LIBRARY

Art. 83. In order to exercise control over the administration and activities of the Bank of Finland and over the administration of the funds under the guarantee of Parliament, the latter shall appoint nine Bank Trustees and determine their instructions.

Among the Trustees, three, who form the Reduced Committee of Trustees, should handle all questions which by the terms of the instructions do not devolve upon the Greater Committee, consisting of nine members. A quorum of the Greater Committee shall consist of six members.

If a member of the Reduced Committee is excused or resigns he shall be replaced by a member of the Greater Committee.

Trustees shall be elected at the first ordinary session of Parliament after the elections, and their mandate shall begin as soon as they have been elected and shall continue until the new election of Trustees. They are elected by the Electors of Parliament. There shall be designated at the time of the selection the three members of the Reduced Committee and two substitutes from the other six Trustees for each of the members of the Reduced Committee, as well as the order of this replacement. If no agreement is reached on the selection, a proportional vote shall be applied.

In the same manner as stipulated in the preceding paragraph for the selection of Trustees, the Electors of Parliament shall select annually, at the ordinary session, five Auditors who are to present an auditors' report for the current year. This report on the management of the Bank and the said funds should be submitted after the year has expired. A substitute for each Auditor shall similarly be selected.

Art. 83a. In order to exercise control over the administration and activities of the National Pensions Institute Parliament shall appoint twelve Trustees and determine their instructions.

The Trustees shall be selected at the first ordinary session of Parliament after the elections. Their mandate shall begin as soon as the selection has taken place and shall continue until Parliament has performed the new selection. There shall be appointed two substitutes for each Trustee.

The selection shall be performed by the Electors of Parliament. If no agreement is reached on the selection, a proportional vote shall be applied.

Art. 83b. The Parliament Library, a public institution administered and controlled by Parliament, which determines its regulations, is the subject of separate legislation.

CHAPTER VII

THE COMMUNICATION OF THE DECISIONS AND RESOLUTIONS OF PARLIAMENT

Art. 84. A bill adopted by Parliament shall be delivered, with a letter of advice, to the President of the Republic with a view to the sanction and promulgation of the law. If the bill is not sanctioned by the President, this fact should be brought to the attention of Parliament within four months counting from the submission of the bill for sanction. If Parliament is not assembled, notification of this fact should take place when Parliament has assembled.

Other resolutions of Parliament on proposals of the Government, as well as petitions addressed to the Government which Parliament has otherwise resolved to make, should also be brought to the attention of the President in a document issued by Parliament.

Art. 85. The communications and resolutions of Parliament shall be drawn up and forwarded by the Secretariat of Parliament under the supervision of five examiners elected by Parliament from its midst. Examiners shall be elected for one session.

The examiners and the necessary number of substitutes shall be elected, if Parliament cannot reach an agreement, by proportional vote.

No despatch should leave Parliament before being approved by Parliament or the five examiners provided for in the first paragraph.

Art. 86. The resolutions of Parliament shall be signed by all Members of Parliament, the other communications by the Speaker and Deputy Speakers alone.

CHAPTER VIII

SPECIFIC PROVISIONS

Art. 87. Government Proposals should be given priority of treatment both in plenary sittings and in the committees.

Art. 88. In the transaction of business in Parliament, the Finnish or Swedish language shall be used.

The opinions and reports of committees as well as the written proposals of the Speaker's Conference and of the Committee for the Secretariat should be drawn up in these two languages.

Written communications addressed by the Government to Parliament should likewise be drawn up in Finnish and Swedish.

Art. 89. The Secretariat of Parliament shall function under the supervision of the Committee for the Secretariat, composed of the Speaker, the

Deputy Speakers, and four Members of Parliament who, if Parliament cannot agree on their selection, are elected by proportional vote.

The basis for the budget of the Secretariat shall be prescribed by law.

Art. 90. The rule of procedure of Parliament, provisions relating to elections within Parliament according to the proportional system, as well as rulings for the officials of Parliament shall be determined by Parliament.

Art. 91. Government Proposals, committee reports, communications addressed by Parliament to the President of the Republic, the record and the resolutions of Parliament should be published in print.

Art. 92. All expenses occasioned by Parliament shall be paid from the public funds.

Art. 93. If a day fixed by the present law for a special case falls upon a Sunday or a public holiday, the following working day is understood.

If a period of time fixed by the present law for a measure to be taken at a session of Parliament begins while Parliament is assembled but expires during a recess, the remaining days of the fixed period shall be counted from the day when Parliament reassembles. The fixed period shall be counted in its totality from this day if it began during a recess.

FINAL PROVISION

Art. 94. The present Parliament Act, by which are repealed the Parliament Act of July 20, 1906, and the laws of December 31, 1917, May 29, 1918, October 22, 1918, and April 17, 1919, which amended the said Parliament Act, carries in all its parts the force of a Constitutional Law; it cannot be amended, interpreted, or repealed, nor can deviations be made from it except in the order stipulated in general for a Constitutional Law.

Provisions which in virtue of the laws are in force with relation to the Estates of Finland should be applied to Parliament in the composition that it has in virtue of the present Constitutional Law, unless otherwise stipulated by this Parliament Act.

FRANCE

SUMMARY

INTERNATIONAL STATUS

France is a member of the United Nations (October 24, 1945).[1] It is a member of the European Economic Community and other international organizations. It was a member of the League of Nations.

The first Constitution of France of 1791, established a constitutional monarchy. The French Republic was proclaimed on September 21, 1792. On August 22, 1795, a new constitution established a Republic with five

[1] France has accepted the compulsory jurisdiction of the International Court of Justice under Article 36 of its Statute.

Directors which was overthrown on 18 Brumaire, November 9, 1799, by Napoleon who established the Consulate. This became a hereditary empire on May 18, 1804. After the First Peace of Paris on May 30, 1814, France was reduced to approximately its 1792 boundaries. On June 4, 1814, Louis XVIII granted a Constitutional Charter. The Hundred Days saw a new constitution and the Second Peace of Paris on November 20, 1815, restored the monarchy with a bicameral legislature, a declaration of rights and the Napoleonic administrative system.

After the Paris insurrection of 1830, Louis Philippe accepted a revision of the Constitutional Charter and was proclaimed King on August 7, the principle of the divine right of kings being replaced by that of national sovereignty. The revolution of 1848, brought the proclamation of the Second Republic whose new constitution was debated and voted between June and November of that year. The Second Empire was instituted by the Constitution of January 14, 1852 following dissolution of the Assembly the month before. A series of partial reforms after 1859 attenuated the completely authoritarian character of the government in the direction of a parliamentary monarchy.

On September 4, 1870, after the defeat at Sedan and the collapse of the French armies, the Republican deputies led by Favre and Gambetta formed a provisional government to carry on the defense of France. The terms of the armistice of January 28, 1871, following the Siege of Paris, which included the loss of Alsace and Lorraine, led to the rising of the Commune. In 1875, the National Assembly adopted a series of fundamental laws which came to be the Constitution of the Third Republic. The end of the century saw a period of colonial expansion in Africa and Asia. Alsace and Lorraine were returned to France after the end of the first World War.

Following the German invasion, an armistice was granted on June 22, 1940, and on July 10 at Vichy, the National Assembly voted the end of the Third Republic and its replacement by an authoritarian regime. On November 22, 1942, the Germans occupied hitherto unoccupied France. On June 18, 1940, the Free French Movement was announced and on June 3, 1943, the French Committee of National Liberation was established in Algiers and recognized *de facto* as a provisional government, *de jure* on October 23, 1944, by the other Allied powers. On October 21, 1945, elections were held for a Constituent Assembly which rejected a return to the Third Republic. A second referendum (the first having been negative) on October 13, 1946, approved by a small majority the constitution of the Fourth Republic. Years followed of political and economic difficulties and colonial problems. On June 1, 1958, the National Assembly recalled General de Gaulle with virtually unlimited powers for a period of six months. By September 28, a Constitutional Committee had prepared the text of the Constitution of the Fifth Republic which was then presented to referendum. Between 1954 and 1962 almost all France's former colonies became independent nations.

FORM OF NATIONAL GOVERNMENT

The Constitution of October 4, 1958, as amended June 4, 1960, November 6, 1962, and December 30, 1963, adopted by referendum of September 28, 1958, replaces the Constitution of the Fourth Republic of September 28, 1946. It states that France is a Republic, indivisible, secular, democratic and social.[1] The Constitution institutes a Community composed of the Republic and the peoples of the Overseas territories who adopt it, and a chapter describes the Community, its jurisdiction and institutions.[2] Sovereignty belongs to the people.[3]

RIGHTS OF THE PEOPLE

The Preamble to the Constitution proclaims the attachment of the French people to the Rights of Man as defined by the Declaration of 1789 and complemented by the Preamble to the Constitution of 1946. The Constitution provides universal, equal and secret suffrage, free formation of political parties and groups, forbids arbitrary detention, and guarantees equality before the law.[4]

LEGISLATIVE DEPARTMENT

Parliament is bicameral, composed of the National Assembly and the Senate. Deputies to the National Assembly are elected by direct suffrage, Senators by indirect suffrage, for a term fixed by an organic law.[5] Parliament meets in two ordinary sessions a year.[6] The National Assembly may be dissolved by the President.[7] Immunities of deputies are provided.[8] Binding instructions on members of Parliament are forbidden.[9] Distinction is made between the domain of law and regulation and between laws and organic laws.[10] An Article relates to finance.[11]

EXECUTIVE DEPARTMENT

The President is elected for a term of seven years by direct universal suffrage and an absolute majority of the votes cast.[12] He has the power of appointment, promulgates laws, is Commander of the Armed Forces,

[1] Const., Art. 2. [2] Id., Art. 1, 77–87. [3] Id., Art. 3.
[4] Id., Art. 3, 4, 66, 77. [5] Id., Art. 24, 25. [6] Id., Art. 28.
[7] Id., Art. 12. [8] Id., Art. 26. [9] Id., Art. 27.
[10] Id., Art. 34, 37, 46. [11] Id., Art. 47. [12] Id., Art. 6, 7.

has the right of pardon, negotiates and ratifies treaties.[1] The Government determines and directs the policy of the nation and is responsible to Parliament.[2] The Premier is appointed by the President.[3] Members of the Government may not be members of Parliament but have access to the two Assemblies.[4] An Economic and Social Council is provided.[5] A chapter relates to local government.[6]

JUDICIAL DEPARTMENT

The President is guarantor of the independence of judicial authority assisted by the High Council of the Judiciary.[7] A High Court of Justice is provided to try the President for treason and members of the Government for crimes or misdemeanors.[8] A Constitutional Council is provided composed of nine members appointed equally by the President, the President of the National Assembly and the President of the Senate and of all former Presidents of the Republic.[9] It ensures the regularity of election and referendum procedures.[10] It rules on the constitutionality of laws and regulations.[11]

AREA, POPULATION, ETC.

The area of France is 551,601 square kilometres, its population (1965) is 49,030,000. The capital is Paris.

[1] Id., Art. 8, 10, 13, 15, 17, 52.
[2] Id., Art. 20, 49, 50
[3] Id., Art. 8.
[4] Id., Art. 23, 31.
[5] Id., Art. 69–71.
[6] Id., Art. 72–76.
[7] Id., Art. 64.
[8] Id., Art. 67, 68.
[9] Id., Art. 56.
[10] Id., Art. 58–60.
[11] Id., Art. 61, 62.

CONSTITUTION of FRANCE[1]

October 4, 1958, as amended June 4, 1960, November 6, 1962, December 30, 1963

PREAMBLE

The French people hereby solemnly proclaims its attachment to the Rights of Man and the principles of national sovereignty as defined by the Declaration of 1789, reaffirmed and complemented by the Preamble of the Constitution of 1946.

By virtue of these principles and that of the free determination of peoples, the Republic hereby offers to the Overseas Territories that express the desire to adhere to them, new institutions based on the common ideal of liberty, equality and fraternity and conceived with a view to their democratic evolution.

Art. 1. The Republic and the peoples of the Overseas Territories who, by an act of free determination, adopt the present Constitution thereby institute a Community.

The Community shall be based on the equality and the solidarity of the peoples composing it.

TITLE I

ON SOVEREIGNTY

Art. 2. France is a Republic, indivisible, secular, democratic and social. It shall ensure the equality of all citizens before the law, without distinction of origin, race or religion. It shall respect all beliefs.

The national emblem is the tricolor flag, blue, white and red.

The national anthem is the "Marseillaise."

The motto of the Republic is "Liberty, Equality, Fraternity."

[1] English Translation prepared and published by the French Embassy Press and Information Division, New York. Supplied by the Ministry of Foreign Affairs in April 1966. Ed.

Its principle is government of the people, by the people and for the people.

Art. 3. National sovereignty belongs to the people, which shall exercise this sovereignty through its representatives and by means of referendums.

No section of the people, nor any individual, may attribute to themselves or himself the exercise thereof.

Suffrage may be direct or indirect under the conditions stipulated by the Constitution. It shall always be universal, equal and secret.

All French citizens of both sexes who have reached their majority and who enjoy civil and political rights may vote under the conditions to be determined by law.

Art. 4. Political parties and groups shall be instrumental in the expression of the suffrage. They shall be formed freely and shall carry on their activities freely. They must respect the principles of national sovereignty and democracy.

TITLE II

THE PRESIDENT OF THE REPUBLIC

Art. 5. The President of the Republic shall see that the Constitution is respected. He shall ensure, by his arbitration, the regular functioning of the governmental authorities, as well as the continuance of the State.

He shall be the guarantor of national independence, of the integrity of the territory, and of respect for Community agreements and treaties.

Art. 6. The President of the Republic shall be elected for seven years by direct universal suffrage.

The procedures implementing the present article shall be determined by an organic law.

Art. 7. The President of the Republic shall be elected by an absolute majority of the votes cast. If this is not obtained on the first ballot, there shall be a second ballot on the second Sunday following. Only the two candidates who have received the greatest number of votes on the first ballot shall present themselves, taking into account the possible withdrawal of more favored candidates.

The voting shall begin at the summons of the Government.

The election of the new President shall take place twenty days at the least and thirty-five days at the most before the expiration of the powers of the President in office.

In the event that the Presidency of the Republic has been vacated, for any cause whatsoever, or impeded in its functioning as officially noted by the Constitutional Council, to which the matter has been referred by the Government, and which shall rule by an absolute majority of its members, the functions of the President of the Republic, with the exception of those provided for by the Articles 11 and 12 below, shall be temporarily exercised by the President of the Senate and, if the latter is in his turn impeded in the exercise of these functions, by the Government.

In the case of a vacancy, or when the impediment is declared definitive by the Constitutional Council, the voting for the election of a new President shall take place, except in case of *force majeure* officially noted by the Constitutional Council, twenty days at the least and thirty-five days at the most after the beginning of the vacancy or the declaration of the definitive character of the impediment.

There may be no application of either Articles 49 and 50 or of Article 89 of the Constitution during the vacancy of the Presidency of the Republic or during the period that elapses between the declaration of the definitive character of the impediment of the President of the Republic and the election of his successor.

Art. 8. The President of the Republic shall appoint the Premier. He shall terminate the functions of the Premier when the latter presents the resignation of the Government.

On the proposal of the Premier, he shall appoint the other members of the Government and shall terminate their functions.

Art. 9. The President of the Republic shall preside over the Council of Ministers.

Art. 10. The President of the Republic shall promulgate the laws within fifteen days following the transmission to the Government of the finally adopted law.

He may, before the expiration of this time limit, ask Parliament for a reconsideration of the law or of certain of its articles. This reconsideration may not be refused.

Art. 11. The President of the Republic, on the proposal of the Government during Parliamentary sessions, or on joint motion of the two assemblies, published in the *Journal Officiel,* may submit to a referendum any bill dealing with the organization of the governmental authorities, entailing approval of a Community agreement, or providing for authorization to ratify a treaty that, without being contrary to the Constitution, might affect the functioning of existing institutions.

When the referendum decides in favor of the bill, the President of the Republic shall promulgate it within the time limit stipulated in the preceding article.

Art. 12. The President of the Republic may, after consultation with the Premier and the Presidents of the Assemblies, declare the dissolution of the National Assembly.

General elections shall take place twenty days at the least and forty days at the most after the dissolution.

The National Assembly shall convene by right on the second Thursday following its election. If this meeting takes place between the periods provided for ordinary sessions, a session shall, by right, be held for a fifteen-day period.

There may be no further dissolution within a year following these elections.

Art. 13. The President of the Republic shall sign the ordinances and decrees decided upon in the Council of Ministers.

He shall make appointments to the civil and military posts of the State.

Councillors of State, the Grand Chancellor of the Legion of Honor, Ambassadors and Envoys Extraordinary, Master Councillors of the Audit Office, Prefects, representatives of the Government in the Overseas Territories, general officers, Rectors of Academies (regional divisions of the public educational system) and directors of central administrations shall be appointed in meetings of the Council of Ministers.

An organic law shall determine the other posts to be filled in meetings of the Council of Ministers, as well as the conditions under which the power of the President of the Republic to make appointments to office may be delegated by him and exercised in his name.

Art. 14. The President of the Republic shall accredit Ambassadors and Envoys Extraordinary to foreign powers; foreign Ambassadors and envoys Extraordinary shall be accredited to him.

Art. 15. The President of the Republic shall be Commander of the Armed Forces. He shall preside over the higher councils and committees of national defense.

Art. 16. When the institutions of the Republic, the independence of the nation, the integrity of its territory or the fulfilment of its international commitments are threatened in a grave and immediate manner and when the regular functioning of the constitutional governmental authorities is interrupted, the President of the Republic shall take the measures commanded by these circumstances, after official consultation with the Premier, the Presidents of the assemblies and the Constitutional Council.

He shall inform the nation of these measures in a message.

These measures must be prompted by the desire to ensure to the constitutional governmental authorities, in the shortest possible time, the means of fulfilling their assigned functions. The Constitutional Council shall be consulted with regard to such measures.

Parliament shall meet by right.

The National Assembly may not be dissolved during the exercise of emergency powers by the President.

Art. 17. The President of the Republic shall have the right of pardon.

Art. 18. The President of the Republic shall communicate with the two Assemblies of Parliament by means of messages, which he shall cause to be read, and which shall not be followed by any debate.

Between sessions, Parliament shall be convened especially for this purpose.

Art. 19. The acts of the President of the Republic, other than those provided for under Articles 8 (first paragraph), 11, 12, 16, 18, 54, 56 and 61, shall be countersigned by the Premier and, should circumstances so require, by the appropriate ministers.

TITLE III

THE GOVERNMENT

Art. 20. The Government shall determine and direct the policy of the Nation.

It shall have at its disposal the administration and the Armed Forces.

It shall be responsible to Parliament under the conditions and according to the procedures stipulated in Articles 49 and 50.

Art. 21. The Premier shall direct the operation of the Government. He shall be responsible for national defense. He shall ensure the execution of the laws. Subject to the provisions of Article 13, he shall have regulatory powers and shall make appointments to civil and military posts.

He may delegate certain of his powers to the ministers.

He shall replace, should the occasion arise, the President of the Republic as chairman of the councils and committees provided for under Article 15.

He may, in exceptional instances, replace him as chairman of a meeting of the Council of Ministers by virtue of an explicit delegation and for a specific agenda.

Art. 22. The acts of the Premier shall be countersigned, when circumstances so require, by the ministers responsible for their execution.

Art. 23. The office of member of the Government shall be incompatible with the exercise of any Parliamentary mandate, with the holding of any office at the national level in business, professional or labor organizations, and with any public employment or professional activity.

An organic law shall determine the conditions under which the holders of such mandates, functions or employments shall be replaced.

The replacement of members of Parliament shall take place in accordance with the provisions of Article 25.

TITLE IV

THE PARLIAMENT

Art. 24. The Parliament shall comprise the National Assembly and the Senate.

The deputies to the National Assembly shall be elected by direct suffrage.

The Senate shall be elected by indirect suffrage. It shall ensure the representation of the territorial units of the Republic. Frenchmen living outside France shall be represented in the Senate.

Art. 25. An organic law shall determine the term for which each Assembly is elected, the number of its members, their emoluments, the conditions of eligibility and ineligibility and the offices incompatible with membership in the assemblies.

It shall likewise determine the conditions under which, in the case of a vacancy in either Assembly, persons shall be elected to replace the deputy or senator whose seat has been vacated until the holding of new complete or partial elections to the Assembly concerned.

Art. 26. No member of Parliament may be prosecuted, sought, arrested, detained or tried as a result of the opinions or votes expressed by him in the exercise of his functions.

No member of Parliament may, during Parliamentary sessions, be prosecuted or arrested for criminal or minor offenses without the authorization of the Assembly of which he is a member except in the case of *flagrante delicto*.

When Parliament is not in session, no member of Parliament may be arrested without the authorization of the Secretariat of the Assembly of which he is a member, except in the case of *flagrante delicto*, of authorized prosecution or of final conviction.

The detention or prosecution of a member of Parliament shall be suspended if the Assembly of which he is a member so demands.

Art. 27. All binding instructions upon members of Parliament shall be null and void.

The right to vote of the members of Parliament shall be personal.

An organic law may, under exceptional circumstances, authorize the delegation of a vote. In this case, no member may be delegated more than one vote.

Art. 28. Parliament shall convene, by right, in two ordinary sessions a year.

The first session shall begin on October 2; it shall last eighty days.

The second session shall open on April 2; it may not last longer than ninety days.

If October 2 or April 2 is a holiday, the session shall begin on the first working day following.

Art. 29. Parliament shall convene in extraordinary session at the request of the Premier, or of the majority of the members comprising the National Assembly, to consider a specific agenda.

When an extraordinary session is held at the request of the members of the National Assembly, the closure decree shall take effect as soon as the Parliament has exhausted the agenda for which it was called, and at the latest twelve days from the date of its meeting.

Only the Premier may ask for a new session before the end of the month following the closure decree.

Art. 30. Apart from cases in which Parliament meets by right, extraordinary sessions shall be opened and closed by decree of the President of the Republic.

Art. 31. The members of the Government shall have access to the two assemblies. They shall be heard when they so request.

They may call for the assistance of Commissioners of the Government.

Art. 32. The President of the National Assembly shall be elected for the duration of the legislature. The President of the Senate shall be elected after each partial re-election of the Senate.

Art. 33. The meetings of the two Assemblies shall be public. An *in extenso* report of the debates shall be published in the *Journal Officiel.*

Each Assembly may sit in secret committee at the request of the Premier or of one tenth of its members.

TITLE V

ON RELATIONS BETWEEN PARLIAMENT AND THE GOVERNMENT

Art. 34. All laws shall be passed by Parliament.

Laws shall establish the regulations concerning:

– civil rights and the fundamental guarantees granted to the citizens for the exercise of their public liberties; the obligations imposed by the national defense upon the persons and property of citizens;

– nationality, status and legal capacity of persons, marriage contracts, inheritance and gifts;

– determination of crimes and misdemeanors as well as the penalties imposed therefor; criminal procedure; amnesty; the creation of new juridical systems and the status of magistrates;

– the basis, the rate and the methods of collecting taxes of all types; the issuance of currency.

Laws shall likewise determine the regulations concerning:

– the electoral system of the Parliamentary assemblies and the local assemblies;

– the establishment of categories of public institutions;

– the fundamental guarantees granted to civil and military personnel employed by the State;

– the nationalization of enterprises and the transfer of the property of enterprises from the public to the private sector.

Laws shall determine the fundamental principles of:

– the general organization of national defense;

– the free administration of local communities, the extent of their jurisdiction and their resources;
– education;
– property rights, civil and commercial obligations;
– legislation pertaining to employment, unions and social security.

The financial laws shall determine the financial resources and obligations of the State under the conditions and with the reservations to be provided for by an organic law.

Laws pertaining to national planning shall determine the objectives of the economic and social action of the State.

The provisions of the present article may be developed in detail and amplified by an organic law.

Art. 35. Parliament shall authorize the declaration of war.

Art. 36. Martial law shall be decreed in a meeting of the Council of Ministers.

Its prorogation beyond twelve days may be authorized only by Parliament.

Art. 37. Matters other than those that fall within the domain of law shall be of a regulatory character.

Legislative texts concerning these matters may be modified by decrees issued after consultation with the Council of State. Those legislative texts which may be passed after the present Constitution has become operative shall be modified by decree, only if the Constitutional Council has stated that they have a regulatory character as defined in the preceding paragraph.

Art. 38. The Government may, in order to carry out its program, ask Parliament to authorize it, for a limited period, to take through ordinances measures that are normally within the domain of law.

The ordinances shall be enacted in meetings of the Council of Ministers after consultation with the Council of State. They shall come into force upon their publication, but shall become null and void if the bill for their ratification is not submitted to Parliament before the date set by the enabling act.

At the expiration of the time limit referred to in the first paragraph of the present article, the ordinances may be modified only by law in those matters which are within the legislative domain.

Art. 39. The Premier and the members of Parliament alike shall have the right to initiate legislation.

Government bills shall be discussed in the Council of Ministers after consultation with the Council of State and shall be filed with the Secretariat of one of the two assemblies. Finance bills shall be submitted first to the National Assembly.

Art. 40. Bills and amendments introduced by members of Parliament shall not be considered when their adoption would have as a consequence either a diminution of public financial resources, or the creation or increase of public expenditures.

Art. 41. If it appears in the course of the legislative procedure that a Parliamentary bill or an amendment is not within the domain of law or is contrary to a delegation of authority granted by virtue of Article 38, the Government may declare its inadmissibility.

In case of disagreement between the Government and the President of the Assembly concerned, the Constitutional Council, upon the request of either party, shall rule within a time limit of eight days.

Art. 42. The discussion of Government bills shall pertain, in the first Assembly to which they have been referred, to the text presented by the Government.

An Assembly, given a text passed by the other assembly, shall deliberate on the text that is transmitted to it.

Art. 43. Government and Parliamentary bills shall, at the request of the Government or of the Assembly concerned, be sent for study to committees especially designated for this purpose.

Government and Parliamentary bills for which such a request has not been made shall be sent to one of the permanent committees, the number of which shall be limited to six in each Assembly.

Art. 44. Members of Parliament and of the Government shall have the right of amendment.

After the opening of the debate, the Government may oppose the examination of any amendment which has not previously been submitted to committee.

If the Government so requests, the Assembly concerned shall decide, by a single vote, on all or part of the text under discussion, retaining only the amendments proposed or accepted by the Government.

Art. 45. Every Government or Parliamentary bill shall be examined successively in the two Assemblies of Parliament with a view to the adoption of an identical text.

When, as a result of disagreement between the two Assemblies, it has become impossible to adopt a Government or Parliamentary bill after two readings by each Assembly, or, if the Government has declared the matter urgent, after a single reading by each of them, the Premier shall have the right to have a joint committee meet, composed of an equal number from both Assemblies and instructed to offer for consideration a text on the matters still under discussion.

The text prepared by the joint committee may be submitted by the Government for approval of the two Assemblies. No amendment shall be admissible except by agreement with the Government.

If the joint committee fails to approve a common text, or if this text is not adopted under the conditions set forth in the preceding paragraph, the Government may, after a new reading by the National Assembly and by the Senate, ask the National Assembly to rule definitively. In this case, the National Assembly may reconsider either the text prepared by the joint committee or the last text adopted by the National Assembly, modified, when circumstances so require, by one or several of the amendments adopted by the Senate.

Art. 46. The laws that the Constitution characterizes as organic shall be passed and amended under the following conditions:

A Government or Parliamentary bill shall be submitted to the deliberation and to the vote of the first Assembly to which it is submitted only at the expiration of a period of fifteen days following its introduction.

The procedure of Article 45 shall be applicable. Nevertheless, lacking an agreement between the two assemblies, the text may be adopted by the National Assembly on final reading only by an absolute majority of its members.

The organic laws relative to the Senate must be passed in the same manner by the two Assemblies.

Organic laws may be promulgated only after a declaration by the Constitutional Council on their constitutionality.

Art. 47. Parliament shall pass finance bills under the conditions to be stipulated by an organic law.

Should the National Assembly fail to reach a decision on first reading within a time limit of forty days after a bill has been filed, the Government shall refer it to the Senate, which must rule within a time limit of fifteen days. The procedure set forth in Article 15 shall then be followed.

Should Parliament fail to reach a decision within a time limit of seventy days, the provisions of the bill may be enforced by ordinance.

Should the finance bill establishing the resources and expenditures of a fiscal year not be filed in time for it to be promulgated before the beginning of that fiscal year, the Government shall immediately request Parliament for the authorization to collect the taxes and shall make available by decree the funds needed to meet the Government commitments already voted.

The time limits stipulated in the present article shall be suspended when Parliament is not in session.

The Audit Office shall assist Parliament and the Government in supervising the implementation of the finance laws.

Art. 48. The discussion of the bills filed or agreed upon by the Government shall have priority on the agenda of the Assemblies in the order set by the Government.

One meeting a week shall be reserved, by priority, for questions asked by members of Parliament and for answers by the Government.

Art. 49. The Premier, after deliberation by the Council of Ministers, may pledge the responsibility of the Government to the National Assembly with regard to the program of the Government, or with regard to a declaration of general policy, as the case may be.

The National Assembly may question the responsibility of the Government by the vote of a motion of censure. Such a motion shall be admissible only if it is signed by at least one tenth of the members of the National Assembly. The vote may only take place forty-eight hours after the motion has been filed; the only votes counted shall be those favorable to the motion of censure, which may be adopted only by a majority of the members comprising the Assembly. Should the motion of censure be rejected, its signatories may not introduce another motion in the course of the same session, except in the case provided for in the paragraph below.

The Premier may, after deliberation by the Council of Ministers, pledge the Government's responsibility to the National Assembly on the vote of a text. In this case, the text shall be considered as adopted, unless a motion of censure, filed in the succeeding twenty-four hours, is voted under the conditions laid down in the previous paragraph.

The Premier shall be entitled to ask the Senate for approval of a general policy declaration.

Art. 50. When the National Assembly adopts a motion of censure, or when it disapproves the program or a declaration of general policy of the Government, the Premier must submit the resignation of the Government to the President of the Republic.

Art. 51. The closure of ordinary or extraordinary sessions shall by right be delayed, should the occasion arise, in order to permit the application of the provisions of Article 49.

TITLE VI

ON TREATIES AND INTERNATIONAL AGREEMENTS

Art. 52. The President of the Republic shall negotiate and ratify treaties.

He shall be informed of all negotiations leading to the conclusion of an international agreement not subject to ratification.

Art. 53. Peace treaties, commercial treaties, treaties or agreements relative to international organization, those that imply a commitment for the finances of the State, those that modify provisions of a legislative nature, those relative to the status of persons, those that call for the cession, exchange or addition of territory may be ratified or approved only by a law.

They shall go into effect only after having been ratified or approved.

No cession, no exchange, no addition of territory shall be valid without the consent of the populations concerned.

Art. 54. If the Constitutional Council, the matter having been referred to it by the President of the Republic, by the Premier, or by the President of one or the other Assembly, shall declare that an international commitment contains a clause contrary to the Constitution, the authorization to ratify or approve this commitment may be given only after amendment of the Constitution.

Art. 55. Treaties or agreements duly ratified or approved shall, upon their publication, have an authority superior to that of laws, subject, for each agreement or treaty, to its application by the other party.

TITLE VII

THE CONSTITUTIONAL COUNCIL

Art. 56. The Constitutional Council shall consist of nine members, whose term of office shall last nine years and shall not be renewable. One third of the membership of the Constitutional Council shall be renewed every three years. Three of its members shall be appointed by the President of the Republic, three by the President of the National Assembly, three by the President of the Senate.

In addition to the nine members provided for above, former Presidents of the Republic shall be members *ex officio* for life of the Constitutional Council.

The President shall be appointed by the President of the Republic. He shall have the deciding vote in case of a tie.

Art. 57. The office of member of the Constitutional Council shall be incompatible with that of minister or member of Parliament. Other incompatibilities shall be determined by an organic law.

Art. 58. The Constitutional Council shall ensure the regularity of the election of the President of the Republic.

It shall examine complaints and shall announce the results of the vote.

Art. 59. The Constitutional Council shall rule, in the case of disagreement, on the regularity of the election of deputies and senators.

Art. 60. The Constitutional Council shall ensure the regularity of referendum procedures and shall announce the results thereof.

Art. 61. Organic laws, before their promulgation, and regulations of the Parliamentary Assemblies, before they come into application, must be submitted to the Constitutional Council, which shall rule on their constitutionality.

To the same end, laws may be submitted to the Constitutional Council, before their promulgation, by the President of the Republic, the Premier or the President of one or the other Assembly.

In the cases provided for by the two preceding paragraphs, the Constitutional Council must make its ruling within a time limit of one month.

Nevertheless, at the request of the Government, in case of emergency, this period shall be reduced to eight days.

In these same cases, referral to the Constitutional Council shall suspend the time limit for promulgation.

Art. 62. A provision declared unconstitutional may not be promulgated or implemented.

The decisions of the Constitutional Council may not be appealed to any jurisdiction whatsoever. They must be recognized by the governmental authorities and by all administrative and juridical authorities.

Art. 63. An organic law shall determine the rules of organization and functioning of the Constitutional Council, the procedure to be followed before it, and in particular the periods of time allowed for laying disputes before it.

TITLE VIII

ON JUDICIAL AUTHORITY

Art. 64. The President of the Republic shall be the guarantor of the independence of the judicial authority.

He shall be assisted by the High Council of the Judiciary.

An organic law shall determine the status of magistrates.

Magistrates may not be removed from office.

Art. 65. The High Council of the Judiciary shall be presided over by the President of the Republic. The Minister of Justice shall be its Vice President *ex officio*. He may preside in place of the President of the Republic.

The High Council shall, in addition, include nine members appointed by the President of the Republic in conformity with the conditions to be determined by an organic law.

The High Council of the Judiciary shall present nominations for judges of the Court of Cassation (Supreme Court of Appeal) and for First Presidents of Courts of Appeal. It shall give its opinion, under the conditions to be determined by an organic law, on proposals of the Minister of Justice relative to the nomination of the other judges. It shall be consulted on questions of pardon under conditions to be determined by an organic law.

The High Council of the Judiciary shall act as a disciplinary council for judges. In such cases, it shall be presided over by the First President of the Court of Cassation.

Art. 66. No one may be arbitrarily detained.

The judicial authority, guardian of individual liberty, shall ensure respect for this principle under the conditions stipulated by law.

TITLE IX

THE HIGH COURT OF JUSTICE

Art. 67. A High Court of Justice shall be instituted.

It shall be composed of members of Parliament elected, in equal number, by the National Assembly and the Senate after each general or partial election to these Assemblies. It shall elect its President from among its members.

An organic law shall determine the composition of the High Court, its rules, and also the procedure to be followed before it.

Art. 68. The President of the Republic shall not be held accountable for actions performed in the exercise of his office except in the case of high treason. He may be indicted only by the two Assemblies ruling by identical vote in open balloting and by an absolute majority of the members of said Assemblies. He shall be tried by the High Court of Justice.

The members of the Government shall be criminally liable for actions performed in the exercise of their office and deemed to be crimes or misdemeanors at the time they were committed. The procedure defined above shall be applied to them, as well as to their accomplices, in case of a conspiracy against the security of the State. In the cases provided for by the present paragraph, the High Court shall be bound by the definition of crimes and misdemeanors, as well as by the determination of penalties, as they are established by the criminal laws in force when the acts are committed.

TITLE X

THE ECONOMIC AND SOCIAL COUNCIL

Art. 69. The Economic and Social Council, whenever the Government calls upon it, shall give its opinion on the Government bills, ordinances and decrees, as well as on the Parliamentary bills submitted to it.

A member of the Economic and Social Council may be designated by the latter to present, before the Parliamentary Assemblies, the opinion of the Council on the Government or Parliamentary bills that have been submitted to it.

Art. 70. The Economic and Social Council may likewise be consulted by the Government on any problem of an economic or social character of interest to the Republic or to the Community. Any plan, or any bill dealing with a plan, of an economic or social character shall be submitted to it for its advice.

Art. 71. The composition of the Economic and Social Council and its rules of procedure shall be determined by an organic law.

TITLE XI

ON TERRITORIAL UNITS

Art. 72. The territorial units of the Republic are the communes, the Departments, the Overseas Territories. Other territorial units may be created by law.

These units shall be free to govern themselves through elected councils and under the conditions stipulated by law.

In the departments and the territories, the Delegate of the Government shall be responsible for the national interests, for administrative supervision, and for seeing that the laws are respected.

Art. 73. Measures of adjustment required by the particular situation of the Overseas Departments may be taken with regard to their legislative system and administrative organization.

Art. 74. The Overseas Territories of the Republic shall have a special organization, which takes into account their own interests within the general interests of the Republic. This organization shall be defined and modified by law after consultation with the Territorial Assembly concerned.

Art. 75. Citizens of the Republic who do not have ordinary civil status, the only status referred to in Article 34, may keep their personal status as long as they have not renounced it.

Art. 76. The Overseas Territories may retain their status within the Republic.

If they express the desire to do so by a decision of their Territorial Assemblies taken within the time limit set in the first paragraph of Article 91, they shall become Overseas Departments of the Republic or member States of the Community, either in groups or as single units.

TITLE XII

ON THE COMMUNITY

Art. 77. In the Community instituted by the present Constitution, the States shall enjoy autonomy; they shall administer themselves and manage their own affairs democratically and freely.

There shall be only one citizenship in the Community.

All citizens shall be equal before the law, whatever their origin, their race and their religion. They shall have the same duties.

Art. 78. The Community's jurisdiction shall extend over foreign policy, defense, currency, common economic and financial policy, as well as over policy on strategic raw materials.

It shall include, in addition, except in the case of specific agreements, the supervision of the tribunals, higher education, the general organization of external transportation and transportation within the Community, as well as of telecommunications.

Special agreements may create other common jurisdictions or regulate any transfer of jurisdiction from the Community to one of its members.

Art. 79. The member States shall benefit from the provisions of Article 77 as soon as they have exercised the choice provided for in Article 76.

Until the measures required for implementation of the present title go into force, matters within the common jurisdiction shall be regulated by the Republic.

Art. 80. The President of the Republic shall preside over and represent the Community.

The institutional organs of the Community shall be an Executive Council, a Senate and a Court of Arbitration.

Art. 81. The member States of the Community shall participate in the election of the President according to the conditions stipulated in Article 6.

The President of the Republic, in his capacity as President of the Community, shall be represented in each State of the Community.

Art. 82. The Executive Council of the Community shall be presided over by the President of the Community. It shall consist of the Premier of the Republic, the heads of Government of each of the member States of the Community, and the ministers responsible for the common affairs of the Community.

The Executive Council shall organize the co-operation of members of the Community at Government and administrative levels.

The organization and procedure of the Executive Council shall be determined by an organic law.

Art. 83. The Senate of the Community shall be composed of delegates whom the Parliament of the Republic and the legislative Assemblies of the other members of the Community shall choose from among their own membership. The number of delegates of each State shall be determined according to its population and the responsibilities it assumes in the Community.

The Senate of the Community shall hold two sessions a year, which shall be opened and closed by the President of the Community and may not last longer than one month each.

The Senate of the Community, when called upon by the President of the Community, shall deliberate on the common economic and financial policy before laws on these matters are voted upon by the Parliament of the Republic and, should circumstances so require, by the legislative Assemblies of the other members of the Community.

The Senate of the Community shall examine the acts and treaties or international agreements, which are specified in Articles 35 and 53, and which commit the Community.

The Senate of the Community shall make executory decisions in the domains in which it has received delegation of power from the legislative Assemblies of the members of the Community. These decisions shall be promulgated in the same form as the law in the territory of each of the States concerned.

An organic law shall determine the composition of the Senate and its rules of procedure.

Art. 84. A Court of Arbitration of the Community shall rule on litigation occurring among members of the Community.

Its composition and its jurisdiction shall be determined by an organic law.

Art. 85. By derogation from the procedure provided for in Article 89, the provisions of the present title that concern the functioning of the common institutions shall be amendable by identical laws passed by the Parliament of the Republic and by the Senate of the Community.

The provisions of the present title may also be amended by agreements concluded between al the States of the Community; the new provisions shall be put into force under the conditions required by the Constitution of each State.

Art. 86. A change of status of a member State of the Community may be requested, either by the Republic, or by a resolution of the legislative Assembly of the State concerned confirmed by a local referendum, the organization and supervision of which shall be ensured by the institutions of the Community. The procedures governing this change shall be determined by an agreement approved by the Parliament of the Republic and the legislative Assembly concerned.

Under the same conditions, a member State of the Community may become independent. It shall thereby cease to belong to the Community.

A member State of the Community may also, by means of agreements, become independent without thereby ceasing to belong to the Community.

An independent State not a member of the Community may, be means of agreements, join the Community without ceasing to be independent.

The position of these States within the Community shall by determined by agreements concluded to this end, in particular the agreements mentioned in the preceding paragraphs as well as, should the occasion arise, the agreements provided for in the second paragraph of Article 85.

Art. 87. The special agreements made for the implementation of the present title shall be approved by the Parliament of the Republic and the legislative assembly concerned.

TITLE XIII

ON AGREEMENTS OF ASSOCIATION

Art. 88. The Republic or the Community may make agreements with States that wish to associate themselves with the Community in order to develop their own civilizations.

TITLE XIV

ON AMENDMENT

Art. 89. The initiative for amending the Constitution shall belong both to the President of the Republic on the proposal of the Premier and to the members of Parliament.

The Government or Parliamentary bill for amendment must be passed by the two Assemblies in identical terms. The amendment shall become definitive after approval by a referendum.

Nevertheless, the proposed amendment shall not be submitted to a referendum when the President of the Republic decides to submit it to Parliament convened in Congress; in this case, the proposed amendment shall be approved only if it is accepted by a three-fifths majority of the votes cast. The Secretariat of the Congress shall be that of the National Assembly.

No amendment procedure may be undertaken or followed when the integrity of the territory is in jeopardy.

The republican form of government shall not be subject to amendment.

TITLE XV

TEMPORARY PROVISIONS

Art. 90. The ordinary session of Parliament is suspended. The mandate of the members of the present National Assembly shall expire on the day that the Assembly elected under the present Constitution convenes.

Until this meeting, the Government alone shall have the authority to convene Parliament.

The mandate of the members of the Assembly of the French Union shall expire at the same time as the mandate of the members of the present National Assembly.

Art. 91. The institutions of the Republic, provided for by the present Constitution, shall be established within four months after its promulgation.

This time limit shall be extended to six months for the institutions of the Community.

The powers of the President of the Republic now in office shall expire only when the results of the election provided for in Articles 6 and 7 of the present Constitution are proclaimed.

The member States of the Community shall participate in this first election under the conditions derived from their status at the date of the promulgation of the Constitution.

The established authorities shall continue to exercise their functions in these States according to the laws and regulations applicable when the Constitution becomes operative, until the authorities provided for by their new regimes are set up.

Until it is definitively constituted, the Senate shall consist of the present members of the Council of the Republic. The organic laws that determine the definitive composition of the Senate must be passed before July 31, 1959.

The powers conferred on the Constitutional Council by Articles 58 and 59 of the Constitution shall be exercised, until this Council is set up, by a committee composed of the Vice President of the Council of State, as chairman, the First President of the Court of Cassation, and the First President of the Audit Office.

The peoples of the member States of the Community shall continue to be represented in Parliament until the measures necessary to the implementation of Title XII have been put into effect.

Art. 92. The legislative measures necessary for the setting up of the institutions and, until they are set up, for the functioning of the governmental authorities, shall be taken in meetings of the Council of Ministers, after consultation with the Council of State, in the form of ordinances having the force of law.

During the time limit set in the first paragraph of Article 91, the Government shall be authorized to determine, by ordinances having the force of law and passed in the same way, the system of elections to the assemblies provided for by the Constitution.

During the same period and under the same conditions, the Government may also adopt measures, in all matters, which it may deem necessary to the life of the nation, the protection of citizens or the safeguarding of liberties.

GERMAN DEMOCRATIC REPUBLIC

SUMMARY

INTERNATIONAL STATUS[1]

The German Democratic Republic is not a member of the United Nations. It is a member of the Warsaw Treaty, the Council for Mutual Economic Assistance and other international organizations.

[1] See also German Federal Republic.

After the proclamation by the Allied Commanders on June 5, 1945, of the assumption of control over all Germany, the first three years of occupation saw the creation of a central administration for different aspects of government, the reorganization of the courts and the creation and unification of the Communist and Socialist parties. On April 20, 1946, the Constitutional Congress of the Unified Socialist Party (S.E.D.) was formed. From 1948 to 1952, the state organization was formed, Parliament constituted itself in the form of three Congresses of the German People held in 1947–1948 and 1949, economic powers were transferred from the occupying power to the Economic Commissions. The Berlin blockade began on March 31, 1948 and lasted until May 12, 1949. On June 23, 1948, a monetary reform was instituted. On July 1, 1948, the quadripartite Kommandatura for Berlin was ended and Berlin was henceforth divided into an eastern and western zone. On May 30, 1949, the Constitution of the German Democratic Republic was adopted by the Third Congress of the German People and entered into force on October 7 of that year. On July 6, 1950, the Goerlitz Agreement on the "peace frontier" was signed with Poland. On March 26, 1954, the German Democratic Republic became a sovereign state. On January 25, 1955, the USSR ended the state of war with Germany and on September 22, 1955 abolished the occupation regime. On January 27, 1956, the German Democratic Republic joined the Warsaw Pact. On August 13, 1961, began the building of the Berlin Wall.

FORM OF NATIONAL GOVERNMENT

The Constitution of October 7, 1949, as amended in 1955, 1958 and 1960, states that Germany is an indivisible democratic republic.[1] All power derives from the people.[2] The generally accepted rules of international law are binding on the state power and on citizens.[3] The economic structure is described.[4]

RIGHTS OF THE PEOPLE

The Constitution provides equality before the law, freedom of the person, inviolability of the domicile, privacy of correspondence, freedom of speech, press and assembly, freedom of development and use of their language by foreign language national groups, the right of association and trades unions, the right to work and protection of labor, the right to rest and social insurance, protection of labor conditions.[5] Activities against democratic institutions and organizations, militarist propaganda are penal crimes.[6] Citizens may not be extradited; all citizens have the right to emigrate subject to the laws.[7] The protection of the homeland is a national

[1] Const., Art. 1. [2] Id., Art. 3. [3] Id., Art. 5. [4] Id., Art. 19–29.
[5] Id., Art. 6–18. [6] Id., Art. 6. [7] Id., Art. 10.

duty of citizens.[1] The family and motherhood are protected.[2] The constitution provides for freedom of education and compulsory education up to the age of 18,[3] freedom of conscience and religious belief and exercise.[4]

LEGISLATIVE DEPARTMENT

The highest organ of the Republic is the People's Chamber composed of 400 deputies elected by proportional representation and universal, equal, direct and secret suffrage to represent the whole people for a term of four years subject to dissolution.[5] A constitutional committee of the People's Chamber verifies the constitutional character of laws and conflicts of jurisdiction between the Republic and the *laender*.[6] Immunities of deputies are provided.[7] There are provisions concerning the *laender* and their powers.[8]

EXECUTIVE DEPARTMENT

The government consists of the Prime Minister, nominated by the strongest parliamentary group in the People's Chamber, and the ministers who must be deputies.[9] The Constitution provides for a Council of State composed of a Chairman, six deputies and 16 members elected by the People's Chamber for a term of four years.[10] It promulgates laws, conducts international relations, exercises defence activities, makes appointments, awards honors, grants pardons.[11] It is accountable to the People's Chamber.[12] There are provisions concerning finances and the administration of the Republic.[13]

JUDICIAL DEPARTMENT

The execution of justice is vested in the Supreme Court of the Republic and courts of the *laender*; judges are independent subject only to the Constitution and the law.[14] Judges of the Supreme Court and the Attorney General are elected by the People's Chamber on the recommendation of the government.[15] Emergency courts are not permitted, citizens may not be withdrawn from their lawful judges, penalties may not be retroactive.[16] Judges may not examine the constitutional validity of laws.[17]

AREA, POPULATION, ETC.

The area of the German Democratic Republic is 108,298 square kilometres, its population (1963) 17,181,083. The capital is Berlin.

[1] Id., Art. 5. [2] Id., Art. 30–33. [3] Id., Art. 34–40. [4] Id., Art. 41–48.
[5] Id., Art. 50, 51, 52, 56. [6] Id., Art. 66. [7] Id., Art. 67.
[8] Id., Art. 109–116. [9] Id., Art. 91, 92. [10] Id., Art. 101, 102. [11] Id., Art. 104–106.
[12] Id., Art. 104. [13] Id., Art. 117–125. [14] Id., Art. 126, 127. [15] Id., Art. 131.
[16] Id., Art. 134, 135. [17] Id., Art. 89.

CONSTITUTION
of the
GERMAN DEMOCRATIC REPUBLIC[1]

October 7, 1949, as amended September 26, 1955, December 8, 1958 and September 12, 1960

Resolved to Ensure the Freedom and Rights of Man, to Create an Order of Society where Social and Economic Life is Governed by Social Justice, to Serve the Cause of Social Progress, to Promote Friendship with all Peoples and to Secure Peace, the German People have given themselves this Constitution.

A. FOUNDATIONS OF STATE POWER

Art. 1. Germany is an indivisible democratic Republic; its constituent parts are the German laender.

The Republic decides on all matters essential for the continued existence and development of the German people as a whole; all other matters fall within the competence of the laender.

The decisions arrived at by the Republic are binding on the laender.

There is only one German citizenship.

Art. 2. The colours of the German Democratic Republic are Black-Red-Gold.

The capital of the Republic is Berlin.

Art. 3. All power derives from the people.

Every citizen has the right and the duty to take an active part in the public affairs of his locality, his district, his land and of the German Democratic Republic.

The citizen's right to share in government finds expression in:

participation in plebiscites and referendums;

the right to vote and to stand for election;

the right to occupy public posts in administration and jurisdiction.

Every citizen has the right to petition the elected representative bodies.

[1] Published in English by *VEB Deutscher Zentralverlag,* Dresden 1962. Supplied by the Ministry of External Affairs in August 1966. Ed.

State power must be wielded in the interest of the people and serve the cause of freedom, peace and democratic progress.

All persons occupying public posts are servants of the people and not of any one party. They are subject to control by the elected representative bodies.

Art. 4. All measures taken by the state organs must be in conformity with the fundamental principles laid down in the Constitution as falling within the concept of state power. Parliament decides, in accordance with Article 66 of this Constitution, whether such measures are constitutional. Everyone has the right and the duty to resist measures in contradiction to the decisions of Parliament.

It is the duty of every citizen to act in the spirit of the Constitution and to defend it against its enemies.

Art. 5. The generally accepted rules of international law are binding upon the state power and upon every citizen.

The state organs have the duty of maintaining and preserving friendly relations with all peoples.

No citizen is permitted to take part in war-like activities aimed at the subjugation of another people.

Service for the protection of the Homeland and the achievements of the working people is an honorable national duty of the citizens of the German Democratic Republic.

B. CONTENT AND LIMITS OF STATE POWER

I. Rights of the Citizen

Art. 6. All citizens are equal before the law.

Incitement to boycott democratic institutions and organizations, incitement to murder democratic politicians, the profession of religious, racial or national hatred, militarist propaganda and incitement to war and all other acts directed against equal rights are crimes under the definition of the penal code. The exercise of democratic rights within the meaning of this Constitution is not to be regarded as incitement to boycott.

No person convicted of such crimes may be employed in public service, nor may he occupy a leading position in the economic or cultural field. He loses the right to vote and to stand for election.

Art. 7. Men and women have equal rights.

All laws and provisions infringing upon the equality of women are revoked.

Art. 8. The freedom of the person, the inviolability of the home, the privacy of correspondence and the right to choose one's place of residence are guaranteed. The state may only restrict or annul these rights on the basis of laws applying to all citizens.

Art. 9. All citizens have the right, within the limits of general law, to voice their opinion freely and publicly, and for this purpose to assemble peacefully and without arms. This right is not limited by position or employment; no person may suffer a disadvantage for making use of this right.

There shall be no censorship of the press.

Art. 10. No citizen may be extradited to a foreign power.

Foreign citizens who are persecuted abroad on account of their fight for the fundamental principles laid down in this Constitution may not be either extradited or expelled from the country.

Every citizen has the right to emigrate. This right can only be restricted by a law of the Republic.

Art. 11. The free development of the national characteristics of the foreign-language national groups in the Republic shall be encouraged by legislation and by the administration; in particular they may not be hindered in the use of their mother tongue in education, in the administration and in courts of law.

Art. 12. All citizens have the right to form associations or societies, provided their aims are not at variance with the provisions of the penal code.

Art. 13. Associations whose statutes stipulate as their aim the democratic development of public life on the basis of this Constitution and whose executive organs are appointed by their members are entitled to nominate candidates for the local councils, the district councils and the diets of the laender.

Candidates for the People's Chamber may only be nominated by associations aiming, according to the articles of their statutes, at the democratic development of the political and social life throughout the Republic and maintaining branches on the whole of its territory.

Art. 14. Every person is accorded the right to join associations striving for the improvement of wages and working conditions. All arrangements and measures designed to limit this freedom or to obstruct its exercise are contrary to law and prohibited.

The trade unions are guaranteed the right to strike.

Art. 15. Labor enjoys the protection of the state.

The right to work is guaranteed. By its guiding of the economy the state ensures work and the means of livelihood for every citizen. Where a suitable place of work cannot be made available the citizen will be provided with the necessary means of subsistence.

Art. 16. Every employed person has the right to rest and leisure, an annual paid vacation and maintenance in case of sickness and old age.

Sundays, public holidays and the 1st of May are days of rest and protected by law.

A uniform all-embracing social insurance system, organised as a self-governing body of the insured, provides for the preservation of the health and the capacity to work of the working population, protects the interests of mother and child and safeguards the insured against economic distress resulting from old age, disability, unemployment or other misfortunes.

Art. 17. All decisions on matters relating to production, wages and working conditions in factories are arrived at with full participation on the part of the workers and employees.

The workers and employees exercise these rights through their trade unions and shop councils.

Art. 18. With full participation by the working people the Republic evolves a uniform labor law, uniform labor jurisdiction and a uniform system of labor protection.

Labor conditions must be such as to meet the claims of health and to allow adequate time for cultural activities and family life.

Wages must be in accordance with the work done and ensure an adequate standard of living for the worker and his dependants.

Men and women, adults and youths are entitled to the same wage for doing the same work.

Women enjoy special protection in employment. A law of the Republic shall provide for the establishment of facilities enabling women to reconcile their tasks as citizens and workers with their duties as wives and mothers.

Young people are protected against exploitation and guarded from moral, physical and spiritual demoralization. Child labor is prohibited.

II. Economic Structure

Art. 19. The system of economy must be based on the principles of social justice and ensure an adequate standard of living for all.

The economy has to serve the interests of the people as a whole and to satisfy its wants; every person is to be ensured a share in the product of labor in conformity with his contribution.

The economic freedom of the individual is guaranteed within the framework of these tasks and aims.

Art. 20. The private initiative of peasants, tradesmen and artisans is to be encouraged. The system of co-operative mutual aid is to be further developed.

Art. 21. To ensure to citizens the material basis of existence and to raise their standard of living the state, through its legislative organs and with the direct participation of the citizens, draws up the public economic plan. It is the duty of the elected representative bodies to supervise its execution.

Art. 22. Property rights are protected by the Constitution. Their content and limits must be in harmony with the law and the social obligations towards the community.

The right of inheritance is guaranteed in accordance with the provisions of the civil code. The proportion of the inheritance which goes the state shall be fixed by law.

The work of the intellectual, the rights of the author, inventor and artist enjoy the protection, promotion and care of the Republic.

Art. 23. Restrictions on property rights, and dispossessions, are permissible only where they serve the common weal and are based on law. Adequate compensation will be given unless the law rules otherwise. Litigation in an ordinary court on the amount of compensation awarded is permissible unless the law rules otherwise.

Art. 24. Property rights entail responsibilities. Their exercise must not violate the interests of the community.

The misuse of property rights by building up a position of economic power to the detriment of the community will be met by dispossession without compensation and transfer of the property into the hands of the people.

The enterprises of war criminals and active nazis become the property of the people. The same procedure applies in the case of private undertakings aiding a warlike policy.

All private monopoly organizations, such as cartels, syndicates, combines, trusts and similar private organizations aiming at higher profits through the control of output, prices and markets are dissolved and prohibited.

Big private landed estates, in excess of one hundred hectares, are broken up into smaller parcels and distributed without compensation.

On completion of this land reform the peasants are guaranteed the private ownership of their land.

Art. 25. All mineral wealth and all economically exploitable natural resources, and the works of the mining, iron and steel, and power production industries needed for their utilization shall be transferred into the hands of the people.

Until such time, their operation shall be subject to the supervision by the laender, or the supervision by the Republic where all-German interests may be involved.

Art. 26. The distribution and use of the land are supervised and every abuse is prevented. Increase in the value of land, due to causes other than labor or capital investment, is to benefit the community as a whole.

Every citizen and every family is to be guaranteed a healthy dwelling commensurate with his requirements. Victims of fascism, severely disabled persons, persons who have suffered damage through war, and resettlers are to receive preferential treatment.

The maintenance and increase of agricultural yields is to be further secured by land preservation and amelioration schemes.

Art. 27. Private economic undertakings suitable for socialization can be transferred to common ownership by law in conformity with the provisions applying to expropriation.

On the authority of a law the Republic, the laender, the districts or localities can be ensured a decisive influence in enterprises or associations by participating in their administration or by some other suitable means.

Economic enterprises and associations may be merged by law on the basis of self-administration. This is to secure the participation of all sections of the working population, to allow workers and employers to share in the administration and to apply the communal principles to all questions concerning the production, manufacture, distribution, use, pricing as well as the import and export of commodities.

The consumers' co-operatives, purchasing co-operatives and co-operative industrial societies as well as the agricultural producers' co-operatives and their associations are to be integrated in the social economy with due regard paid to their statutes and individual character.

Art. 28. The disposal and mortgaging of nationally-owned land, or factories, or of shares therein requires the approval of the elected representative body responsible for the assignee. Such consent can only be given with the approval of a two-thirds majority of its members as required by law.

Art. 29. Property and income are taxed at a progressively advancing rate on social principles and with due regard given to family commitments.

Property and income earned by labor are to be given special consideration in respect of taxation.

III. Family and Motherhood

Art. 30. Marriage and family form the basic elements of communal life. They are protected by the state.

Laws and provisions infringing upon the equality of rights between husband and wife in the family are annulled.

Art. 31. The education of their children to mentally and physically fit persons in a democratic spirit is the natural right of parents and their first duty towards the society.

Art. 32. During maternity the mother has the right to special protection and care by the state.

The Republic enacts a law for the protection of mother and child. Institutions for the protection of mother and child are to be established.

Art. 33. Birth out of wedlock may not prejudice either the child or its parents.

Contrary laws and provisions are repealed.

IV. Education

Art. 34. The arts and sciences and their teaching are free.

The state shares in fostering them and protects them, especially against their misuse for purposes contrary to the provisions and the spirit of the Constitution.

Art. 35. Every citizen has equal rights to education and the free choice of his profession.

The education of youth and the intellectual and professional training of adults in all spheres of public and social life are ensured by public institutions.

Art. 36. The organisation of the public educational system and teaching in schools are matters falling within the competence of the laender. For this purpose the Republic issues unified legal directives. Public educational institutions can also be set up by the Republic itself.

For the training of teachers the Republic issues unified directives. Their training takes place at universities or colleges of a university standard.

Art. 37. It is the task of schools to educate the youth in the spirit of the Constitution. Their aim must be to turn out men and women capable of thinking independently and acting in a responsible manner, fitting them for a life within the community.

The school, as an institution serving to mediate culture, has the task of educating young people to real humanism in the spirit of peaceful and friendly co-existence of the nations, and the spirit of true democracy.

The parents assist, through parents' advisory committees, in the school education of their children.

Art. 38. Schooling is compulsory up to and including the age of eighteen years. After passing through elementary school, compulsory for all children, the pupil goes on to a trade or specialized school, senior school or some other public educational institution. Attendance at the trade school is compulsory up to and including the age of eighteen, where the pupil does not go to another grade of school. Private schools are impermissible as a substitute for state schools.

The trade and specialized schools give general and occupational advanced training.

The senior school prepares for entry to the university. Admission to university is not restricted, however, to persons who have passed through senior schools; it is also possible by means of study at other public educational institutions, which are to be extended or newly established for this purpose.

Pre-university institutions shall make it possible for all citizens to attend university.

Every person, regardless of social origin, is accorded the opportunity for educational advancement in evening schools without interruption of employment.

Art. 39. Every child must be given the opportunity of all-round development of physical, intellectual and moral faculties. The course of educational development of the youth must not be made dependent on the social and economic status of the parents. On the contrary, children handicapped by adverse social conditions shall receive special attention. Talented pupils from all social strata are to be enabled to attend specialised school, senior school or university.

No school fees are charged. At the compulsory schools books are free. In case of need pupils attending a specialised school, senior school or university may receive support in the form of maintenance grants or in some other way.

Art. 40. Religious instruction is a matter falling within the competence of religious communities. The exercise of this right is guaranteed.

V. Religion and Religious Communities

Art. 41. Every citizen enjoys full freedom of conscience and religious belief. The unhindered exercise of religion is protected by the Republic.

Institutions of religious communities, religious activities and religious instruction may not be misused for purposes contrary to the Constitution or for party-political ends. However, the right of religious communities to express their opinion on vital issues affecting the nation is undisputed.

Art. 42. Private or civil rights and duties are neither conditional upon religious worship nor can they be restricted on account of it.

The exercise of private or civil rights or the admission to public posts are independent of religious belief.

No person may be compelled to divulge his religious creed. The administrative organs have the right to inquire after membership in a religious community only to the extent to which certain rights or duties may devolve upon it or where such information is required for a statistical survey demanded by law.

Nobody may be forced to perform a church rite or celebration or to participate in religious exercises or to employ a religious form of oath.

Art. 43. There is no established church. The freedom to form religious associations is guaranteed.

Every religious congregation is a self-governing body and orders and conducts its own affairs within the legal framework applying to all citizens.

Religious congregations remain corporations under public law to the extent they have been so in the past. On application other religious congregations will be guaranteed the same rights provided their statutes and number of members give a fair guarantee of permanency. If several suc religious congregations under public law form a union, this union is also a corporation under public law.

Religious congregations under public law are entitled to collect taxes from their members on the basis of the official tax lists and in conformity with the general provisions.

Associations founded on the basis of a common philosophy of life and aiming at the propagation of such views are placed on the same footing as religious congregations.

Art. 44. The church is ensured the right to give religious instruction in rooms of the school. The teaching of religion is done by persons selected by the church. No person may be compelled to give or be prevented from giving religious instruction. The question of particiaption in religious instruction is decided by the parents or legal guardians.

Art. 45. Public contributions to religious congregations based upon law, contract, or special legal titles shall be compounded on the basis of law.

Religious communities and associations are guaranteed the right of ownership and other rights in institutions, foundations and other property intended for religious worship, instruction and charity.

Art. 46. Where there is a need of religious services and succour in hospitals, penitentiaties or other public institutions, religious associations are permitted to perform such religious functions. Nobody may be compelled to take part in such activities.

Art. 47. Anyone wishing to withdraw with civil effect from a religious congregation under public law must register his withdrawal with the court or file an officially attested written declaration.

Art. 48. Parents or legal guardians decide on the membership of a child up to the age of fourteen years in a religious association. From the age of fifteen the child itself decides its membership in a religious or philosophical association.

VI. Inviolability of Fundamental Rights

Art. 49. In so far as this Constitution admits the limitation by law of any of the above fundamental rights or reserves the right to legal delimitation, the fundamental right as such must remain untouched.

C. STRUCTURE OF STATE POWER

I. Parliamentary Representation of the Republic

Art. 50. The highest organ of the Republic is the People's Chamber.

Art. 51. The People's Chamber is composed of Deputies of the German people.

Deputies are elected in conformity with the principles of proportional representation on the basis of universal, equal and direct suffrage by secret ballot for a term of four years.

The Deputies are representatives of the whole people. They are bound only by their conscience and not bound by directions.

Art. 52. All citizens who have reached the age of eighteen years have the right to vote.

Every citizen who has reached the age of twenty-one years is eligible for election.

The People's Chamber consists of 400 Deputies. Details shall be laid down in an electoral law.

Art. 53. Nominations for election to the People's Chamber can be made only by associations fulfilling the provisions of Article 13, Paragraph 2.

Details shall be laid down in a law of the Republic.

Art. 54. The election takes place on a Sunday or legal holiday. Freedom to vote and electoral secrecy are guaranteed.

Art. 55. The People's Chamber meets at the latest on the thirtieth day following the election.

The President must summon the People's Chamber if this is demanded by the Government or by a minimum of one fifth of the Deputies of the People's Chamber.

Art. 56. A new election must be held at the latest on the sixtieth day after the expiration of the electoral period or on the forty-fifth day after the dissolution of the People's Chamber.

The People's Chamber can only be dissolved before the expiration of the electoral period on its own decision or as the result of a referendum, except in the case specified in Article 95, Paragraph 6.

The People's Chamber can only be dissolved on its own decision with the agreement of more than one half of the legal number of Deputies.

Art. 57. At its first sitting the People's Chamber elects the Presidium and agrees on the standing orders of the Chamber.

Every parliamentary group is represented in the Presidium provided it has a minimum of forty members.

The Presidium consists of the President, his deputies and the assessors.

The President conducts the business of the Presidium and presides over the People's Chamber. He exercises full authority in the People's Chamber.

Art. 58. Resolutions of the Presidium are adopted by majority vote.

A quorum is constituted by at least half the members of the Presidium.

The Acting President convokes the People's Chamber on the decision of the Presidium.

The Presidium continues in office until the new People's Chamber meets.

Art. 59. The People's Chamber verifies the credentials of the members and decides on the validity of the elections.

Art. 60. To conduct its business during the time the People's Chamber is not in session, and after the expiration of an electoral period or following dissolution, the People's Chamber appoints three standing committees:

a committee for general matters;

a committee for economic and financial matters;

a committee for foreign affairs.

These committees have the rights of committees of inquiry.

Art. 61. The People's Chamber adopts resolutions by majority vote, except in cases where the Constitution states otherwise.

A quorum is constituted by the presence of more than one half of the Deputies.

Art. 62. The business of the People's Chamber and its committees is conducted in public. The People's Chamber meets in closed session if this is demanded by two thirds of the members present; in committees a majority of the members is sufficient.

Nobody can be held to account for publishing true reports from open sittings of the People's Chamber or its committees.

Art. 63. The competence of the People's Chamber embraces:

the laying down of the fundamental principles of Government policy and its execution;

the confirmation of the Government, its supervision and recall;

the laying down of the fundamental principles of the administration and supervision of all state activity;

the right to legislate, except in cases where a referendum is held;

adoption of the state budget, of the economic plan, loans and state credits of the Republic and the approval of state treaties;

the promulgation of amnesties;

election of the Council of State of the Republic;

election of the members of the Supreme Court of the Republic and of the Attorney-General of the Republic as well as their recall.

Art. 64. The People's Chamber and any one of its committees may demand the presence of the Prime Minister, any Minister, their permanent deputies and the heads of administrations of the Republic for the purpose of eliciting information. Members of the Government and persons commissioned by them have at any time the right to be present at the sittings of the People's Chamber and its committees.

If they request it, the representatives of the Government must be heard at such sittings even outside the agenda.

They are subject to the rulings of the President.

Art. 65. The People's Chamber has the right to institute committees of inquiry to supervise the activities of state organs, and the duty to institute such committees on the request of one fifth of the legally established number of Deputies. These committees collect evidence considered essential by them or by the applicants.

For this purpose they can nominate commissioners. Courts and administrations are obliged to comply with the requests of these committees or their commissioners for the taking of evidence, and to place at their disposal official files and documents.

The relevant provisions of criminal court procedure are applicable to the taking of evidence by committees of inquiry.

Art. 66. For the duration of the electoral period the People's Chamber establishes a constitutional committee on which all parliamentary groups are represented proportionate to their size. In addition the committee includes three members of the Supreme Court of the Republic and three German experts on political law, but these may not be members of the People's Chamber.

The members of the constitutional committee are elected by the People's Chamber.

The constitutional committee verifies the constitutional character of laws of the Republic.

The constitutional character of laws of the Republic can only be questioned by at least one third of the members of the People's Chamber; by its Presidium; by the Council of State of the Republic or by the Government of the Republic.

Constitutional disputes between the Republic and the laender, and questions affecting the compatibility of laws of the Republic with laender laws are examined by the constitutional committee.

The report adopted by the constitutional committee is submitted to the People's Chamber for decision. Its decision is binding on everybody.

The People's Chamber decides also on the execution of its decision.

The establishement of the unconstitutional nature of measures instituted by the Government or the administration is the task of the People's Chamber and part of its function of supervising the administration.

Art. 67. No Deputy of the People's Chamber may be brought before a court of law or administratively prosecuted because of the way he voted or because of any utterance he made in the exercise of his duties as a Deputy, nor may he be held to account in any other way outside the assembly. This does not apply in cases of libel or slander within the meaning of the penal code if they have been established as such by a committee of inquiry of the People's Chamber.

Restrictions of the personal freedom, domiciliary searches, seizures or penal prosecution in respect of Deputies are conditional upon the consent of the People's Chamber.

Proceedings instituted against a Deputy of the People's Chamber, arrest and any other restraint placed on his personal freedom are suspended, on the demand of the Chamber to which the Deputy belongs, for the period the Chamber is in session.

Deputies of the People's Chamber have the right to refuse to testify on persons who have given them information in their capacity as Deputies, or to whom they have given information in the exercise of their function as Deputies; they also have the right to refuse testimony on this information itself. Regarding the seizure of documents they are on the same footing as those persons who are entitled under the law to refuse testimony.

Searches or seizures in the rooms of the People's Chamber are possible only with the consent of the Presidium.

Art. 68. Deputies of the People's Chamber need no leave from their place of employment for the execution of their duties.

Persons contesting a seat in the People's Chamber must be accorded sufficient leave to prepare for the election.

Salaries and wages must continue during the period.

Art. 69. Deputies of the People's Chamber receive a tax-free expenditure allowance.

The right to the expenditure allowance cannot be waived.

It is neither transferable nor attachable.

Art. 70. Deputies of the People's Chamber have the right to free travel on all public means of transport.

II. Laender Representation

Art. 71–80. Abrogated.

III. Legislation

Art. 81. Laws are passed either by the People's Chamber or directly by the people by means of a referendum.

Art. 82. Bills are introduced by the Government or by Deputies of the People's Chamber. Bills are given at least two readings.

Art. 83. The Constitution may be amended by legislation.

To become effective, resolutions of the People's Chamber involving a constitutional amendment require the presence of two thirds of the Deputies, of whom at least two thirds must support the Bill.

If a constitutional amendment is to be effected by means of a referendum the majority of the eligible voters must be in favour of it.

Art. 84. Abrogated.

Art. 85. The President of the People's Chamber has to engross the laws, passed in conformity with the Constitution, within a period of one month. They are promulgated without delay by the Chairman of the Council of State of the Republic in the Official Gazette of the Republic.

Engrossment and promulgation do not take place if, within the intervening period of one month, the unconstitutional character of the law in accordance with Article 66 has been established.

Unless stated otherwise laws come into force on the fourteenth day after promulgation.

Art. 86. Engrossment and promulgation of a law may be postponed for two months on request by one third of the Deputies of the People's Chamber.

On the expiration of this period the law must be engrossed and promulgated unless a successful demand has been made for the holding of a referendum against the promulgation.

Laws declared urgent by the majority of the Deputies of the People's Chamber must be engrossed and promulgated notwithstanding such demand.

Art. 87. A law, the promulgation of which has been suspended as a result of a motion backed by at least one third of the Deputies of the People's Chamber, must be put to a referendum on demand by one twentieth of all those entitled to vote.

A referendum is also to be held, if this is demanded by one tenth of all those entitled to vote or where an official demand for holding such a referendum is registered by recognized political parties or mass organizations who have a *bona fide* claim to represent one fifth of the electorate (demand for a referendum).

The demand for a referendum must be based on a Bill which the Government, with its comment, must introduce to the People's Chamber.

The referendum takes place only if the law aimed at is not passed by the People's Chamber in a form which meets with the approval of the applicants or their nominess.

The budget, the tax and dues laws and civil service payment regulations cannot be made the subject of a referendum.

The Bill on which the referendum is held is accepted if the majority of the voters are in favor.

The procedure to be adopted in both cases, demand for a referendum and the referendum itself, is set out in a special law.

Art. 88. The budget and the economic plan are adopted in the form of laws.

Amnesties require a law.

State treaties having matters of legislation as their content must be promulgated like laws.

Art. 89. Laws promulgated in the proper manner are not to be examined by judges regarding their constitutional validity.

On the initiation of an inquiry as to constitutional validity in conformity with Article 66 legal proceedings falling under this law must be suspended until the inquiry is closed.

Art. 90. Unless the law determines otherwise all general administrative provisions needed for the execution of the laws of the Republic are issued by the Government of the Republic.

IV. The Government of the Republic

Art. 91. The Government of the Republic consists of the Prime Minister and the Ministers.

Art. 92. The strongest parliamentary group in the People's Chamber nominates the Prime Minister; he forms the Government. Every group with at least forty members is represented by Ministers or State Secretaries proportional to its strength. State Secretaries participate in a consultative capacity in Government sessions.

In the event of any group excluding itself the Government is formed without it.

The Ministers shall be Deputies of the People's Chamber.

The People's Chamber confirms the Government and approves the program introduced by it.

Art. 93. On taking office the members of the Government are sworn in by the Chairman of the Council of State of the Republic to conduct their affairs impartially in the interests of the people and in strict conformity with the Constitution and the laws.

Art. 94. To carry out their governmental duties the Government and every Minister must have the confidence of the People's Chamber.

Art. 95. The period of office of the Government as a whole ends with the passing of a no-confidence motion by the People's Chamber.

The motion of no-confidence is put to the vote only if simultaneously with it the new Prime Minister and the principles of the political program to be followed by him are proposed. The decision on the no-confidence motion and the new policy proposals is taken by one and the same act of voting.

To become effective the decision on a no-confidence motion requires the support of at least half the legal number of Deputies.

The motion to take such a decision must bear the signatures of at least one quarter of the members of the People's Chamber. The motion can be put to the vote on the second day of the debate at the earliest. The motion must be brought to a close within one week from the day it was tabled.

If the new Government does not take office within twenty-one days after the passing of the no-confidence motion, the motion becomes ineffective.

In the event of a vote of no-confidence in the new Government the People's Chamber is considered dissolved.

Until a new Government takes office the affairs of state are conducted by the outgoing Government.

Art. 96. If the People's Chamber resolves to withdraw its confidence from a member of the Government, this member must resign. Unless the People's Chamber decides otherwise he must continue in office until relieved by his successor.

The provisions of Article 95, Paragraph 3, find corresponding application.

Every member of the Government can hand in his resignation at any time. Except where the People's Chamber decides otherwise his deputy is charged with carrying out his duties until his successor takes over.

Art. 97. The Prime Minister presides over the Government and conducts its affairs in conformity with standing orders to be decided on and made known by the Government to the People's Chamber.

Art. 98. The Prime Minister lays down the directives of Government policy in conformity with the fundamental principles adopted by the People's Chamber. He is accountable to the People's Chamber.

Guided by these directives every Minister conducts the affairs of his department independently and on his own responsibility but accountable to the People's Chamber.

Art. 99. The Ministers must submit to the Government for discussion and decision all Bills, and in addition all such matters as specified by the Constitution or by law, and disputes affecting the competence of more than one ministry.

Art. 100. The Government takes its decisions by majority vote. In the event of parity the casting vote of its chairman decides.

V. The Council of State of the Republic

Art. 101. The Council of State of the Republic is elected by the People's Chamber for a period of four years.

After expiration of the electoral period the Council of State continues in office until the new Council of State is elected by the People's Chamber.

Art. 102. The Council of State of the Republic consists of the Chairman, six deputies of the Chairman, sixteen members and the Secretary.

The Chairman directs the activity of the Council of State.

Art. 103. On taking office the Chairman, the deputies of the Chairman, the members and the Secretary of the Council of State take the following oath to the People's Chamber:

"I swear to devote my energies to the welfare of the German people, to safeguard the Constitution and the laws of the German Democratic Republic, faithfully to discharge my duties and do justice to all."

Art. 104. The Council of State of the Republic is accountable to the People's Chamber.

The Council of State of the Republic promulgates the laws of the Republic.

The Chairman of the Council of State signs them.

Art. 105. The Chairman of the Council of State of the Republic swears in the members of the Government when they take office.

Art. 106. The Council of State of the Republic:

issues the writ for elections to the People's Chamber and convenes the first meeting of the People's Chamber after such election;
may hold a general plebiscite;
ratifies and denounces international treaties entered into by the German Democratic Republic;
appoints and recalls the plenipotentiaries of the German Democratic Republic in foreign states;
accepts letters of credence and recall from diplomatic representatives of foreign states who are accredited to it;
issues generally binding interpretations of the laws;
promulgates decisions with legal force;
takes fundamental decisions on matters relating to the defence and security of the country;
endorses fundamental directions from the National Defence Council of the German Democratic Republic;
appoints the members of the National Defence Council of the German Democratic Republic;
specifies military ranks, diplomatic ranks and other special titles;
awards orders and other high distinctions and honorary titles;
exercises the right of reprieve.

Art. 107. The Council of State of the Republic is externally represented by its Chairman or his deputies.

The Chairman of the Council of State represents the Republic in international law.

Art. 108. The Chairman, the deputies of the Chairman, the members and the Secretary of the Council of State of the Republic may be recalled by a decision of the People's Chamber. Such decision requires a majority of two thirds of the legal number of Deputies.

VI. Republic and Laender

Art. 109. Every land must have a constitution in accord with the fundamental principles of the Constitution of the Republic. The land diet is the supreme and exclusive representation of the people of the land.

Members of the diet must be elected under a system of proportional representation in conformity with the fundamental principles of the electoral law of the Republic, that is, by all citizens entitled to vote and on the basis of universal, equal and direct suffrage by secret ballot.

Art. 110. Territorial changes of the laender and the formation of new laender within the borders of the Republic are effected by a law amending the Constitution of the Republic.

Given the consent of the laender directly affected an ordinary law is sufficient.

An ordinary law is sufficient also in the event of one of the affected laender dissenting but, where the territorial change or the new formation is demanded, as a result of a vote by the population living in that territory.

Art. 111. The Government may pass uniform laws for all spheres. But it shall confine itself in its legislation to the adoption of fundamental principles where this is considered adequate to meet the demand for uniformity.

To the extent that the right of legislation is not exercised by the Republic, the right may be exercised by the laender.

Art. 112. The Republic has the exclusive right of legislation in all matters concerning.

foreign relations;
customs and duties;
as well as the unity of the customs and trade territory and the free and unhindered exchange of goods;
citizenship, freedom of movement, immigration and emigration, extradition, the granting of passports and alien law;
personal status;
civil law, penal law, judicial organization and judicial proceedings;
labor law;
transport;
postal, telegraph and radio services;
film and press;
currency and coinage, weights, measures and standards;
social insurance;
war damage and occupation costs, and restitution.

Legislation relating to the military defence of the country and the protection of the civilian population falls within the jurisdiction of the Republic.

Art. 113. In the case of legislation relating to public finance and taxation the economic basis of existence of the laender, districts and local administrative units must be ensured.

Art. 114. All-German law prevails over laender law.

Art. 115. Unless stipulated otherwise in this Constitution or in the laws, the organs of the laender execute on principle the laws of the Republic. If considered desirable the Republic will, by law, set up its own administrations.

Art. 116. The Government of the Republic exercises a supervisory function in all matters falling within the legislative sphere of the Republic.

Insofar as the laws of the Republic are not executed by the administrative organs of the Republic, the Government of the Republic may issue general directives. It has the right to nominate persons authorized to supervise the putting into effect of these laws and decrees by the administrations charged with their execution. Regarding the rights of these authorized persons the provisions of Article 65 apply accordingly.

On request by the Republic the governments of the laender are under an obligation to remedy any short-comings that have arisen in the course of putting the laws of the Republic into effect.

Disputes in this respect are investigated and settled in accordance with the procedure described in Article 66, Paragraph 5.

VII. Administration of the Republic

Art. 117. The Republic is exclusively responsible for foreign relations.

In matters falling within the sphere of laender legislation the laender may conclude treaties with foreign states; the treaties must be approved by the People's Chamber.

Agreements with foreign states on changes in the frontier of the Republic are concluded by the Republic with the consent of the land affected. Frontier changes can only be made on the basis of a law of the Republic, except where they involve only boundary rectifications in uninhabited territory.

Art. 118. Germany constitutes a uniform customs and trade territory bounded by a common customs frontier.

Foreign states or parts thereof may be attached to the German customs territory as a result of state treaties or agreements. Areas may be excluded by law from the German customs territory.

All goods in free transit in the German customs territory may be freely imported and moved across the laender and district borders within the customs territory; the same applies in regard to attached foreign states or parts thereof referred to in Paragraph 2.

Art. 119. The customs dues and the taxes levied by virtue of a law of the Republic are administered by the Republic.

The authority to levy taxes is a prerogative of the Republic.

Taxes shall be levied by the Republic only to the extent necessary to meet its own requirements.

The Republic establishes its own tax administration. It is to include special institutions enabling the laender to safeguard specific laender interests in the fields of agriculture, commerce, trade and industry.

To the extent that this is necessary for the uniform execution of tax laws of the Republic, the Republic makes legal provisions regarding the institution of the tax administration of the laender, the institution and rights of administrative bodies charged with supervising the execution of the tax laws of the Republic, the settling of tax accounts with the laender and the payment of administrative expenses incurred in the course of executing the tax laws of the Republic.

Art. 120. Duties and taxes may be collected only on the basis of a law.

Property tax, income tax and purchase tax must be maintained in a proper balance to each other, and graduated progressively from a social point of view.

A steep graduation of death duties shall prevent the accumulation of large properties detrimental to the interests of the people.

Art. 121. For every fiscal year an estimate must be made of revenue and expenditure of the Republic and set down in the budget plan. Before the commencement of the fiscal year the budget plan is confirmed by a law.

Art. 122. For the Government the Minister of Finance is answerable to the People's Chamber about revenue and expenditure of the Republic. The audit takes place on the basis of a law of the Republic.

Art. 123. Funds may be raised by way of credit only in cases of urgent need. The procuring of such funds and the furnishing of securities in the form of charges against the Republic are permissible only on the basis of a law of the Republic.

Art. 124. Postal, telegraph and radio services as well as the railways are under the administration of the Republic.

The network of motor-traffic highways and roads of the former Reich, as well as all roads for overland motor services are under the administration of the Republic. Corresponding provisions obtain with regard to waterways.

Art. 125. The organization of merchant shipping, seaborne traffic and sea-marks falls under the administration of the Republic.

VIII. Administration of Justice

Art. 126. The ordinary exercise of jurisdiction is vested in the Supreme Court of the Republic and the courts of the laender.

Art. 127. In their jurisdiction the judges are independent and subject only to the Constitution and the law.

Art. 128. Only those persons may become judges who, by virtue of their personal character and activities, offer the guaranty that they will discharge their duties in accordance with the fundamental principles of the Constitution.

Art. 129. By extending the network of law schools the Republic creates the conditions enabling people from all sections of the population to acquire the qualification necessary to become judges, barristers and public prosecutors.

Art. 130. In jurisdiction lay judges are to participate to as large an extent as possible.

Lay judges are proposed by the democratic parties and organizations and elected by the respective elected representative bodies.

Art. 131. Judges of the Supreme Court and the Attorney General of the Republic are elected by the People's Chamber on the recommendation of the Government.

Judges of the supreme courts and the attorneys general of the laender are elected by the laender diets on the recommendation of the laender governments.

All other judges are nominated by the laender governments.

Art. 132. Judges of the Supreme Court and the Attorney General of the Republic can be recalled by the People's Chamber if they act counter to the Constitution and the laws or grossly violate their duties as judges or public prosecutors.

The recall takes place after an expert's opinion has been obtained from a juridical committee to be set up by the People's Chamber.

The juridical committee consists of the chairman of the law committee of the People's Chamber, three members of the People's Chamber, two members of the Supreme Court and one member of the Attorney-General's office. It is presided over by the chairman of the law committee. The other committee members are chosen by the People's Chamber for the duration of the electoral period. The members of the juridical committee belonging to the Supreme Court and the Attorney-General's office must not be members of the People's Chamber.

The judges chosen by the laender diets and appointed by the laender governments can be recalled by the respective laender diets. The recall takes place after an expert's opinion has been obtained from a juridical committee to be set up by the respective laender diet. The juridical committee consists of the chairman of the law committee of the laender diet, three members of the laender diet, two members of the supreme court and one member of the attorney general's office of the particular land. It is presided over by the chairman of the law committee. The other committee members are chosen by the respective laender diet for the duration of the electoral period. The members of the juridical committee representing the supreme court and the office of the attorney general must not be members of the laender diet.

The judges appointed by the laender governments may be recalled by the laender governments under the same conditions but only with the consent of the law committee of the respective laender diet.

Art. 133. Court cases are heard in public.

In the event of public security and order or public morality being endangered the public may be excluded by an order of the court.

Art. 134. No citizen may be withheld from his lawful judges. Emergency courts are not permitted. Courts of law for particular spheres may be established by the legislature only in cases where they are to deal with groups of persons or objects in dispute defined generally and in advance.

Art. 135. Penalties may be imposed only if they are specified by law at the time of the deed.

No penal law has a retroactive force.

Exceptions are measures and application of decrees aiming at the eradication of nazism, fascism and militarism or deemed necessary for the punishment of crimes against humanity.

Art. 136. In the case of provisional apprehensions, searches and attachments during preliminary proceedings the sanction of the judge is to be obtained without delay.

The judge alone has the decision on the admissibility and continuance of detention. Persons arrested must be brought before the judge not later than the day following the arrest. If detention on remand is ordered the judge must examine at regular intervals whether the continuance of the detention is justified.

The reason for the arrest must be made known to the person apprehended at the first hearing by the interrogating judge and, on his request, communicated to a person named by him, within a further period of twenty-four hours.

Art. 137. Punishment is to be in accordance with the idea of educating those capable of reform by means of communal productive labour.

Art. 138. Supervision by the elected representative bodies and administrative jurisdiction serves to protect citizens against unlawful acts committed by the administration.

The structure and competence of the administrative courts are defined by law.

Provisions corresponding to those regarding the election and recall of judges of ordinary courts apply also to the members of administrative courts.

IX. Local Government

Art. 139. Towns and villages have the right to self-government within the framework of the laws of the Republic and the laender.

Included in the sphere of self-government is the right to decide and put into effect all matters of public interest affecting the economic, social and cultural life of the town or village. The respective tasks are to be carried out by the lowest appropriate administrative unit.

Art. 140. The towns and villages have representative bodies formed on the basis of democratic principles.

To assist them, committees are set up in whose work representatives of the democratic parties and organizations take a responsible share.

Electoral franchise and electoral procedure accord with the provisions applying in the case of elections to the People's Chamber and the laender diets.

By virtue of a laender law the right to vote may, however, be made dependent on a term of residence in the town or village of up to six months.

Art. 141. To take office the elected executive organs of towns and villages must have the confidence of the representative bodies.

Art. 142. Control over the activities of local government bodies is limited to questions of legality of administration and observance of democratic principles of administration.

Art. 143. Towns and villages may be entrusted by the Republic and the laender with special tasks and the execution of laws.

X. Temporary and Final Provisions

Art. 144. All provisions of this Constitution constitute direct and valid law. Contrary provisions are annulled. The provisions replacing them and required for the execution of the Constitution are put into force simultaneously with the Constitution itself. Laws continuing to be in force are to be interpreted in accordance with the spirit of this Constitution.

The freedoms and rights of this Constitution cannot be claimed against decrees already adopted and those still to be issued with a view to eradicating nazism and militarism and making amends for the injustices committed by them.

The present Constitution of the German Democratic Republic, which was worked out and decided by the German People's Council with the participation of the whole German people on March 19th 1949, approved by the Third German People's Congress on May 30th 1949 and enacted by virtue of a law of the provisional People's Chamber dated October 7th 1949, is herewith promulgated.

GERMAN FEDERAL REPUBLIC

SUMMARY

INTERNATIONAL STATUS

The German Federal Republic is not a member of the United Nations. It is a member of the European Economic Community, NATO and other international organizations. It was a member of the League of Nations until 1932.

The first constitution of the German Reich was promulgated in Frankfurt in 1849. The North German Confederation was formed in 1867, following the war between Austria and Prussia in 1866. It excluded Austria and the southern German states the latter of which were however in a customs union with the Confederation. After the war with France in 1870, the south German states joined the Confederation and agreed to the King of Prussia as Kaiser. The Constitution of the German Reich was proclaimed at Versailles in 1871. After the First World War and the revolution in November 1918, the first German Republic was formed on June 18, 1919, and drew up the Weimar Constitution of August 11, 1919. In the 1932 elections the Nazi Party became the largest party in Parliament. In 1938 Austria was annexed, in 1939, Czechoslovakia.

After the Second World War, the four Allied Commanders met in Berlin on June 5, 1945, and proclaimed the assumption of control over all Germany with four zones of occupation within the frontiers of 1937. Following a Conference of Foreign Ministers of the four occupying powers, the United States Secretary of State, on September 6, 1946, recognized the impossibility of constituting a German economic unity, requested the fusion of the western zones and proposed formulas for neutralization. The English and American zones were fused on January 1, 1947 and all the western zones on August 1, 1948. On March 9, 1948, the Charter of Frankfurt created an embryo government. On March 31, the Berlin blockade crisis began. The monetary reform was instituted on June 18, 1948. On April 8, 1949, the Federal Republic of Germany was created by the Washington Agreement and on May 8, the Basic Law was adopted by the Parliamentary Council of Frankfurt. On May 12, 1949, the Berlin blockade ended. On November 22, 1949, the Petersburg Agreement replaced the military governments by High Commissioners and contained the "occupation statutes" forbidding remilitarization and foreign relations.

On July 9, 1951, the state of war between the western powers and Germany was ended. On May 26, 1952, the Bonn and Paris Agreements, in prevision of the creation of the European Defence Community, gave full sovereignty to Bonn with the exception of certain rights relating to the stationing of forces in Germany, Berlin, the question of unification, and a peace settlement. Following the rejection of the European Defense Community by the French Parliament, the London Agreements of October 3, 1954, provided for the incorporation of the Federal Republic into the Western European Union. On May 5, 1955, occupation status was terminated and on May 9 it became a member of NATO. On January 1, 1957, the Saar was reintegrated politically into Germany following the 1955 referendum.

FORM OF NATIONAL GOVERNMENT

The Basic Law of May 8, 1949, as amended to January 1, 1966, states that the Federal Republic is a democratic and social federal state; all state authority emanates from the people.[1] The laender to which the constitution applies are listed and it is stated that it shall be put in force in other parts of Germany on their accession.[2] Sovereign power may be transferred by legislation to inter-governmental institutions.[3] The general rules of international law are an integral part of federal law and have precedence there-over.[4] Federal law overrides land law.[5] Certain provisions of the Weimar Constitution relating to religion and forbidding a state church are listed as an integral part of the Basic law.[6]

RIGHTS OF THE PEOPLE

The Constitution guarantees the right to life, inviolability of the person and individual freedom, equality before the law, freedom of faith and religion, expression, art, science, research, teaching, protection of marriage and the family, freedom of assembly and association except those which conflict with the criminal laws, constitutional order or international understanding; secrecy of correspondence, freedom of movement, freedom of work, the inviolability of the home, the right of ownership and inheritance and the right of petition are assured.[7] Deprivation of citizenship and extradition of Germans is forbidden.[8] Capital punishment is abolished.[9]

LEGISLATIVE DEPARTMENT

The legislature is bicameral consisting of the Bundestag and the Bundesrat. The Bundestag is composed of deputies elected by general, direct, free, equal and secret elections for a term of four years subject to dissolution.[10] The Bundesrat is composed of members of the land governments which appoint and recall them, each land having three, four or five votes depending on population.[11] Immunities of deputies are provided.[12] There are provisions on finance.[13] The legislative powers of the Federation and the laender are described.[14]

EXECUTIVE DEPARTMENT

The President is elected for a term of five years by the Federal Convention consisting of members of the Bundestag and an equal number of

[1] Basic Law, Art. 20. [2] Id., Art. 23. [3] Id., Art. 24. [4] Id., Art. 25. [5] Id., Art. 31. [6] Id., Art. 140. [7] Id., Art. 1–15. [8] Id., Art. 16. [9] Id., Art. 102. [10] Id., Art. 38, 39. [11] Id., Art. 51. [12] Id., Art. 46. [13] Id., Art. 105–115. [14] Id., Art. 70–82.

members elected by representative assemblies of the laender by proportional representation.[1] He represents the Federation in international relations, has the power of appointment and pardon.[2] The Federal Government consists of the Federal Chancellor and ministers, the former elected by the Bundestag.[3] The command of the Armed Forces is vested in the Federal Ministry of Defense and devolves on the Federal Chancellor if a "case of defense" has been declared by the Bundestag.[4] The scope of federal administration is described.[5]

JUDICIAL DEPARTMENT

The judiciary is independent, subject only to and bound by the law.[6] The judicial authority is vested in the judges and exercised by the Federal Constitutional Court, the Supreme Federal Court, federal courts and courts of the laender.[7] The Federal Constitutional Court decides on disputes of jurisdiction or rights and duties of federal organs, between the Federation and the laender and between the laender, and on questions of unconstitutionality.[8] Half its members are elected by the Bundestag and half by the Bundesrat.[9] The Supreme Federal Court is established to preserve the uniformity of federal law; its judges are selected by the Federal Minister of Justice and a committee.[10] Extraordinary courts are inadmissible.[11]

AREA, POPULATION, ETC.

The area of the Federal Republic of Germany is 248,528 square kilometres, its population (1963) 57,864,500. The capital is Bonn.

[1] Id., Art. 54. [2] Id., Art. 59, 60. [3] Id., Art. 62, 63. [4] Id., Art. 59a, 65a.
[5] Id., Art. 87, 87a–d, 88–91. [6] Id., Art. 20, 97. [7] Id., Art. 92.
[8] Id., Art. 93, 99, 100. [9] Id., Art. 94. [10] Id., Art. 95.
[11] Id., Art. 101.

BASIC LAW
of the
FEDERAL REPUBLIC OF GERMANY[1]

May 8, 1949, as amended to January 1, 1966

PREAMBLE

The German People in the Laender Baden, Bavaria, Bremen, Hamburg, Hesse, Lower Saxony, Northrhine-Westphalia, Rhineland-Palatinate, Schleswig-Holstein, Wuerttemberg-Baden and Wuerttemberg-Hohenzollern, conscious of its responsibility before God and Men, animated by the resolve to preserve its national and political unity and to serve the peace of the World as an equal partner in a united Europe, desiring to give a new order to political life for a transitional period, has enacted, by virtue of its constituent power, this Basic Law of the Federal Republic of Germany.

It has also acted on behalf of those Germans to whom participation was denied.

The entire German people is called on to achieve in free self-determination the unity and freedom of Germany.

I. Basic Rights

Art. 1. (1) The dignity of man is inviolable. To respect and protect it shall be the duty of all state authority.

(2) The German people therefore acknowledges inviolable and inalienable human rights as the basis of every community, of peace and of justice in the world.

(3) The following basic rights shall bind the legislature, the executive and the judiciary as directly enforceable law.

Art. 2. (1) Everyone shall have the right to the free development of his personality insofar as he does not violate the rights of others or offend against the constitutional order or the moral code.

(2) Everyone shall have the right to life and to inviolability of his per-

[1] *The Bulletin*, special issue, published by the Press and Information Office of the German Federal Government, Bonn, 1966. Supplied by the Ministry of Foreign Affairs in September 1966. Ed.

son. The freedom of the individual shall be inviolable. These rights may only be encroached upon pursuant to a law.

Art. 3. (1) All persons shall be equal before the law.

(2) Men and women shall have equal rights.

(3) No one may be prejudiced or favored because of his sex, his parentage, his race, his language, his homeland and origin, his faith or his religious or political opinions.

Art. 4. (1) Freedom of faith and of conscience, and freedom of creed, religious or ideological (*weltanschaulich*), shall be inviolable.

(2) The undisturbed practice of religion is guaranteed.

(3) No one may be compelled against his conscience to render war service involving the use of arms. Details shall be regulated by a federal law.

Art. 5. (1) Everyone shall have the right freely to express and disseminate his opinion by speech, writing and pictures and freely to inform himself from generally accessible sources. Freedom of the press and freedom of reporting by radio and motion pictures are guaranteed. There shall be no censorship.

(2) These rights are limited by the provisions of the general laws, the provisions of law for the protection of youth, and by the right to inviolability of personal honor.

(3) Art and science, research and teaching shall be free. Freedom of teaching shall not absolve from loyalty to the constitution.

Art. 6. (1) Marriage and family enjoy the special protection of the state.

(2) The care and upbringing of children are the natural right of the parents and a duty primarily incumbent on them. The national community shall watch over the performance of this duty.

(3) Separation of children from the family against the will of the persons entitled to bring them up may take place only pursuant to a law, if those so entitled fail in their duty or if the children are otherwise threatened with neglect.

(4) Every mother shall be entitled to the protection and care of the community.

(5) Illegitimate children shall be provided by legislation with the same opportunities for their physical and spiritual development and their position in society as are enjoyed by legitimate children.

Art. 7. (1) The entire educational system shall be under the supervision of the state.

(2) The persons entitled to bring up a child shall have the right to decide whether it shall receive religious instruction.

(3) Religious instruction shall form part of the ordinary curriculum in state and municipal schools, except in secular (*bekenntnisfrei*) schools. Without prejudice to the state's right of supervision, religious instruction shall be given in accordance with the tenets of the religious communities. No teacher may be obliged against his will to give religious instruction.

(4) The right to establish private schools is guaranteed. Private schools, as a substitute for state or municipal schools, shall require the approval of the state and shall be subject to the laws of the Laender. This approval must be given if private schools are not inferior to the state or municipal schools in their educational aims, their facilities and the professional training of their teaching staff, and if a segregation of pupils according to the means of the parents is not promoted. This approval must be withheld if the economic and legal position of the teaching staff is not sufficiently assured.

(5) A private elementary school shall be admitted only if the educational authority finds that it serves a special pedagogic interest, or if, on the application of persons entitled to bring up children, it is to be established as an inter-denominational or denominational or ideological school and a state or municipal elementary school of this type does not exist in the commune (*Gemeinde*).

(6) Preparatory schools (*Vorschulen*) shall remain abolished.

Art. 8. (1) All Germans shall have the right to assemble peacefully and unarmed without prior notification or permission.

(2) With regard to open-air meetings this right may be restricted by or pursuant to a law.

Art. 9. (1) All Germans shall have the right to form associations and societies.

(2) Associations, the objects or activities of which conflict with the criminal laws or which are directed against the constitutional order or the concept of international understanding, are prohibited.

(3) The right to form associations to safeguard and improve working and economic conditions is guaranteed to everyone and to all trades and professions. Agreements which restrict or seek to hinder this right shall be null and void; measures directed to this end shall be illegal.

Art. 10. Secrecy of the mail and secrecy of posts and telecommunications shall be inviolable. Restrictions may be ordered only pursuant to a law.

Art. 11. (1) All Germans shall enjoy freedom of movement throughout the federal territory.

(2) This right may be restricted only by a law and only in cases in which an adequate basis of existence is lacking and special burdens would arise to the community as a result thereof or in which the restriction is necessary for the protection of youth against neglect, for combatting the danger of epidemics or for the prevention of crime.

Art. 12. (1) All Germans shall have the right freely to choose their trade or profession, their place of work and their place of training. The practice of trades and professions may be regulated by law.

(2) No one may be compelled to perform a particular work except within the framework of a traditional compulsory public service which applies

generally and equally to all. Anyone who refuses on conscientious grounds to render war service involving the use of arms, may be required to render an alternative service. The duration of this alternative service shall no exceed the duration of military service. Details shall be regulated by a law which shall not prejudice freedom of conscience and shall provide also for the possibility of an alternative service having no connection with any unit of the armed forces.

(3) Women shall not be required by law to render service in any unit of the armed forces. On no account shall they be employed in any service involving the use of arms.

(4) Forced labor may be imposed only in the event that a person is deprived of his freedom by the sentence of a court.

Art. 13. (1) The home shall be inviolable.

(2) Searches may be ordered only by a judge or, in the event of danger in delay, by other organs as provided by law and may be carried out only in the form prescribed by law.

(3) Otherwise, this inviolability may be encroached upon or restricted only to avert a common danger or a mortal danger to individuals, or, pursuant to a law, to prevent imminent danger to public security and order, especially to alleviate the housing shortage, to combat the danger of epidemics or to protect endangered juveniles.

Art. 14. (1) The rights of ownership and of inheritance are guaranteed. Their content and limits shall be determined by the laws.

(2) Property imposes duties. Its use should also serve the public weal.

(3) Expropriation shall be permitted only in the public weal. It may take place only by or pursuant to a law which provides for the nature and extent of the compensation. The compensation shall be determined upon just consideration of the public interest and of the interests of the persons affected. In case of dispute regarding the amount of compensation, recourse may be had to the ordinary courts.

Art. 15. Land, natural resources and means of production may for the purpose of socialization be transfered into public ownership or other forms of publicly controlled economy by a law which provides for the nature and extent of the compensation. In respect of such compensation Article 14, paragraph (3), sentences 3 and 4, shall apply *mutatis mutandis.*

Art. 16. (1) No one may be deprived of his German citizenship. Loss of citizenship may arise only pursuant to a law, and against the will of the person affected it may arise only if such person does not thereby become stateless.

(2) No German may be extradited to a foreign country. Persons persecuted for political reasons shall enjoy the right of asylum.

Art. 17. Everyone shall have the right individually or jointly with others to address written requests or complaints to the competent authorities and to the representative assemblies.

Art. 17a. (1) Laws concerning military service and alternative service may, by provisions applying to members of the Armed Forces and of alternative services during their period of military or alternative service, restrict the basic right freely to express and to disseminate opinions by speech, writing and pictures (Article 5, paragraph (1), first half-sentence), the basic right of assembly (Article 8), and the right of petition (Article 17) insofar as it permits to address requests or complaints jointly with others.

(2) Laws for defence purposes, including the protection of the civilian population, may provide for the restriction of the basic rights of freedom of movement (Article 11) and inviolability of the home (Article 13).

Art. 18. Whoever abuses freedom of expression of opinion, in particular freedom of the press (Article 5, paragraph (1)), freedom of teaching (Article 5, paragraph (3)), freedom of assembly (Article 8), freedom of association (Article 9), the secrecy of mail, posts and telecommunications (Article 10), ownership (Article 14), or the right of asylum (Article 16, paragraph (2)) in order to combat the free democratic basic order, shall forfeit these basic rights. The forfeiture and its extent shall be pronounced by the Federal Constitutional Court.

Art. 19. (1) Insofar as under this Basic Law a basic right may be restricted by or pursuant to a law, such law must apply generally and not solely to an individual case. Furthermore, the law must name the basic right, indicating the Article.

(2) In no case may a basic right be infringed upon in its essential content.

(3) The basic rights shall apply also to domestic juristic persons to the extent that the nature of such rights permits.

(4) Should any person's right be violated by public authority, recourse to the court shall be open to him. If no other court has jurisdiction, recourse shall be to the ordinary courts.

II. The Federation and the Leander

Art. 20. (1) The Federal Republic of Germany is a democratic and social federal state.

(2) All state authority emanates from the people. It shall be exercised by the people by means of elections and voting and by separate legislative, executive, and judicial organs.

(3) Legislation shall be subject to the constitutional order; the executive and the judiciary shall be bound by the law.

Art. 21. (1) The political parties shall participate in the forming of the political will of the people. They may be freely formed. Their internal organization must conform to democratic principles. They must publicly account for the sources of their funds.

(2) Parties which, by reason of their aims or the behavior of their

adherents, seek to impair or destroy the free democratic basic order or to endanger the existence of the Federal Republic of Germany are unconstitutional. The Federal Constitutional Court shall decide on the question of unconstitutionality.

(3) Details shall be regulated by federal legislation.

Art. 22. The federal flag shall be black-red-gold.

Art. 23. For the time being, this Basic Law shall apply in the territory of the Laender Baden, Bavaria, Bremen, Greater Berlin, Hamburg, Hesse, Lower Saxony, Northrhine-Westphalia, Rhineland-Palatinate, Schleswig-Holstein, Wuerttemberg-Baden, and Wuerttemberg-Hohenzollern. In other parts of Germany it shall be put into force on their accession.

Art. 24. (1) The Federation may, by legislation, transfer sovereign powers to inter-governmental institutions.

(2) For the maintenance of peace, the Federation may enter a system of mutual collective security; in doing so it will consent to such limitations upon its rights of sovereignty as will bring about and secure a peaceful and lasting order in Europe and among the nations of the world.

(3) For the settlement of disputes between states, the Federation will accede to agreements concerning a general, comprehensive and obligatory system of international arbitration.

Art. 25. The general rules of public international law are an integral part of federal law. They shall take precedence over the laws and shall directly create rights and duties for the inhabitants of the federal territory.

Art. 26. (1) Acts tending and undertaken with the intent to disturb the peaceful relation between nations, especially to prepare for aggressive war, are unconstitutional. They shall be made a punishable offence.

(2) Weapons designed for warfare may not be manufactured, transported or issued except with the permission of the Federal Government. Details shall be regulated by a federal law.

Art. 27. All German merchant vessels shall form one merchant fleet.

Art. 28. (1) The constitutional order in the Laender must conform to the principles of republican, democratic and social government based on the rule of law, within the meaning of this Basic Law. In each of the Laender, counties (*Kreise*) and communes (*Gemeinden*), the people must be represented by a body chosen in general, direct, free, equal, and secret elections. In the communes the Assembly of the commune may take the place of an elected body.

(2) The communes must be guaranteed the right to regulate on their own responsibility all the affairs of the local community within the limits set by law. The associations of communes (*Gemeindeverbände*) shall also have the right of self-government in accordance with the law and within the limits of the functions assigned to them by law.

(3) The Federation guarantees that the constitutional order of the

Laender shall conform to the basic rights and to the provisions of paragraphs (1) and (2).

Art. 29. (1) The federal territory shall be reorganized by a federal law with due regard to regional ties, historical and cultural connections, economic expediency and social structure. Such reorganization should create Laender which by their size and capacity are able effectively to fulfil the functions incumbent upon them.

(2) In areas which, upon the reorganization of the Laender after 8 May 1945, became, without plebiscite, part of another Land, a specific change in the decision then taken regarding the Land boundaries may be demanded by popular initiative within a year from the coming into force of this Basic Law. Such popular initiative shall require the assent of one tenth of the population entitled to vote in Landtag elections. If the popular initiative receives such assent, the Federal Government must include in the draft of the reorganization law a provision determining to which Land the area concerned shall belong.

(3) After the law has been passed, such part of the law as provides for the transfer of an area from one Land to another must be submitted to a referendum in that area. If a popular initiative received the assent required under paragraph (2), a referendum must in any event be held in the area concerned.

(4) Insofar as the law is rejected in at least one area, it must be reintroduced into the Bundestag. After it has been passed again, it shall require to that extent acceptance by a referendum in the entire federal territory.

(5) In a referendum the majority of the votes cast shall decide.

(6) The procedure shall be established by a federal law. The reorganization should be concluded before the expiration of three years after promulgation of the Basic Law and, should it become necessary as a result of the accession of another part of Germany, within two years after such accession.

(7) The procedure regarding any other change in Land boundaries shall be established by a federal law which shall require the consent of the Bundesrat and of the majority of the members of the Bundestag.

Art. 30. The exercise of governmental powers and the discharge of governmental functions shall be incumbent on the Laender insofar as this Basic Law does not otherwise prescribe or permit.

Art. 31. Federal law shall override Land law.

Art. 32. (1) The conduct of relations with foreign states shall be the concern of the Federation.

(2) Before the conclusion of a treaty affecting the special interests of a Land, this Land must be consulted in sufficient time.

(3) Insofar as the Laender have power to legislate, they may, with the consent of the Federal Government, conclude treaties with foreign states.

Art. 33. (1) Every German shall have in every Land the same civic (*staatsbürgerlich*) rights and duties.

(2) Every German shall be equally eligible to any public office according to his aptitude, qualifications, and professional achievements.

(3) Enjoyment of civil and civic rights, eligibility to public office, and rights acquired in the public service shall be independent of religious denomination. No one may suffer disadvantage by reason of his adherence or non-adherence to a denomination or ideology.

(4) The exercise of state authority as a permanent function shall as a rule be entrusted to members of the public service whose status, service and loyalty are governed by public law.

(5) The law of the public service shall be regulated with due regard to the traditional principles of the permanent civil service (*Berufsbeamtentum*)

Art. 34. If any person, in the exercise of a public office entrusted to him, violates his official obligations to a third party, liability shall rest in principle on the state or the public authority which employes him. In the case of wilful intent or gross carelessness the right of recourse is reserved. In respect of the claim for compensation or the right of recourse, the jurisdiction of the ordinary courts must not be excluded.

Art. 35. All Federal and Land authorities shall render each other legal and administrative assistance.

Art. 36. (1) Civil servants employed in the highest Federal authorities shall be drawn from all Laender in appropriate proportion. Persons employed in other Federal authorities should, as a rule, be drawn from the Land in which they serve.

(2) Military laws shall take into account the division of the Federation into Laender and the latter's particular ethnic conditions.

Art. 37. (1) If a Land fails to comply with its obligations of a federal character imposed by this Basic Law or another federal law, the Federal Government may, with the consent of the Bundesrat, take the necessary measures to enforce such compliance by the Land by way of federal compulsion.

(2) To carry out such federal compulsion the Federal Government or its commissioner shall have the right to give instructions to all Laender and their authorities.

III. The Bundestag

Art. 38. (1) The deputies to the German Bundestag shall be elected in general, direct, free, equal, and secret elections. They shall be representatives of the whole people, not bound by orders and instructions and shall be subject only to their conscience.

(2) Anyone who has attained the age of twenty-one shall be entitled to

vote; anyone who has attained the age of twenty-five shall be eligible for election.

(3) Details shall be regulated by a federal law.

Art. 39. (1) The Bundestag shall be elected for a four-year term. Its legislative term shall end four years after its first meeting or on its dissolution. The new election shall take place during the last three months of the term or within sixty days after dissolution.

(2) The Bundestag shall assemble within thirty days after the election, but not before the end of the term of the previous Bundestag.

(3) The Bundestag shall determine the termination and resumption of its meetings. The President of the Bundestag may convene it at an earlier date. He must do so if one third of the members, the Federal President, or the Federal Chancellor so demand.

Art. 40. (1) The Bundestag shall elect its President, Vice-Presidents, and secretaries. It shall draw up its rules of procedure.

(2) The President shall exercise the proprietary and police powers in the Bundestag building. No search or seizure may take place in the premises of the Bundestag without his permission.

Art. 41. (1) The scrutiny of elections shall be the responsibility of the Bundestag. It shall also decide whether a deputy has lost his seat in the Bundestag.

(2) Against the decision of the Bundestag an appeal shall lie to the Federal Constitutional Court.

(3) Details shall be regulated by a federal law.

Art. 42. (1) The meetings of the Bundestag shall be public. Upon a motion of one tenth of its members, or upon a motion of the Federal Government, the public may, by a two-thirds majority, be excluded. The decision on the motion shall be taken at a meeting not open to the public.

(2) Decisions of the Bundestag shall require a majority of the votes cast unless this Basic Law provides otherwise. For the elections to be made by the Bundestag the rules of procedure may provide exceptions.

(3) True and accurate reports of the public meetings of the Bundestag and of its committees shall not give rise to any liability

Art. 43. (1) The Bundestag and its committees may demand the presence of any member of the Federal Government.

(2) The members of the Bundesrat and of the Federal Government as well as persons commissioned by them shall have access to all meetings of the Bundestag and its committees. They must be heard at any time.

Art. 44. (1) The Bundestag shall have the right, and upon the motion of one fourth of its members the duty, to set up a committee of investigation which shall take the requisite evidence at public hearings. The public may be excluded.

(2) The rules of criminal procedure shall apply *mutatis mutandis* to the

taking of evidence. The secrecy of the mail, posts and telecommunications shall remain unaffected.

(3) Courts and administrative authorities shall be bound to render legal and administrative assistance.

(4) The decisions of the committees of investigation shall not be subject to judicial consideration. The courts shall be free to evaluate and judge the facts on which the investigation is based.

Art. 45. (1) The Bundestag shall appoint a Standing Committee which shall safeguard the rights of the Bundestag as against the Federal Government in the interval between two legislative terms. The Standing Committee shall also have the rights of a committee of investigation.

(2) Wider powers, such as the right to legislate, to elect the Federal Chancellor, and to impeach the Federal President, shall not be within the competence of the Standing Committee.

Art. 45a. (1) The Bundestag shall appoint a Committee on Foreign Affairs and a Committee on Defence. Both committees shall function also in the intervals between any two legislative terms.

(2) The Committee on Defence shall also have the rights of a committee of investigation. Upon the motion of one fourth of its members it shall have the duty to make a specific matter the subject of investigation.

(3) Article 44, paragraph (1), shall not be applied in matters of defence.

Art. 45b. A Defence Commissioner of the Bundestag shall be appointed to safeguard the basic rights and to assist the Bundestag in exercising parliamentary control. Details shall be regulated by a federal law.

Art. 46. (1) A deputy may not at any time be proceeded against in the courts or subjected to disciplinary action or otherwise called to account outside the Bundestag on account of a vote cast or an utterance made by him in the Bundestag or one of its committees. This shall not apply to defamatory insults.

(2) A deputy may be called to account or arrested for a punishable offence only by permission of the Bundestag, unless he is apprehended in the commission of the offence or during the course of the following day.

(3) The permission of the Bundestag shall also be necessary for any other restriction of the personal freedom of a deputy or for the initiation of proceedings against a deputy under Article 18.

(4) Any criminal proceedings and any proceedings under Article 18 against a deputy, any detention and any other restriction of his personal freedom shall be suspended upon the request of the Bundestag.

Art. 47. Deputies may refuse to give evidence concerning persons who have confided facts to them in their capacity as deputies or to whom they have confided facts in such capacity, as well as concerning these facts themselves. To the extent that this right to refuse to give evidence exists, no seizure of documents may take place.

Art. 48. (1) Any person standing for election to the Bundestag shall be entitled to the leave necessary for his election campaign.

(2) No one may be prevented from accepting and exercising the office of deputy. He may not be dismissed from employment, with or without notice, on this ground.

(3) Deputies shall be entitled to compensation adequate to ensure their independence. They shall be entitled to the free use of all state-owned means of transport. Details shall be regulated by a federal law.

Art. 49. In respect of the members of the Presidency, the Standing Committee, the Committee on Foreign Affairs, and the Committee on Defence, as well as their principal substitutes, Articles 46, 47, and paragraphs (2) and (3) of Article 48 shall apply also in the intervals between any two legislative terms.

IV. The Bundesrat

Art. 50. The Laender shall participate through the Bundesrat in the legislation and administration of the Federation.

Art. 51. (1) The Bundesrat shall consist of members of the Land Governments which appoint and recall them. Other members of such Governments may act as substitutes.

(2) Each Land shall have at least three votes; Laender with more than two million inhabitants shall have four, Laender with more than six million inhabitants five votes.

(3) Each Land may delegate as many members as it has votes. The votes of each Land may be cast only as a block vote and only by members present or their substitutes.

Art. 52. (1) The Bundesrat shall elect its President for one year.

(2) The President shall convene the Bundesrat. He must convene it if the members for at least two Laender or the Federal Government so demand.

(3) The Bundesrat shall take its decisions by at least a majority of its votes. It shall draw up its rules of procedure. Its meetings shall be public. The public may be excluded.

(4) Other members of, or persons commissioned by, Land Governments may serve on the committees of the Bundesrat.

Art. 53. The members of the Federal Government shall have the right, and on demand the duty, to take part in the debates of the Bundesrat and of its committees. They must be heard at any time. The Bundesrat must be currently kept informed by the Federal Government of the conduct of affairs.

V. The Federal President

Art. 54. (1) The Federal President shall be elected, without debate, by the Federal Convention (*Bundesversammlung*). Every German shall be eligible who is entitled to vote for the Bundestag and who has attained the age of forty.

(2) The term of office of the Federal President shall be five years. Reelection for a consecutive term shall be permitted only once.

(3) The Federal Convention shall consist of the members of the Bundestag and an equal number of members elected by the representative assemblies of the Laender according to the rules of proportional representation.

(4) The Federal Convention shall meet not later than thirty days before the expiration of the term of office of the Federal President or, in the case of premature termination, not later than thirty days after this date. It shall be convened by the President of the Bundestag.

(5) After expiration of the legislative term, the period specified in paragraph (4), first sentence, shall begin with the first meeting of the Bundestag.

(6) The person receiving the votes of the majority of the members of the Federal Convention shall be elected. If such majority is not obtained by any candidate in two ballots, the candidate who receives the largest number of votes in a further ballot shall be elected.

(7) Details shall be regulated by a federal law.

Art. 55. (1) The Federal President may not be a member of the Government or of a legislative body of the Federation or of a Land.

(2) The Federal President may not hold any other salaried office, nor engage in a trade, nor practise a profession, nor belong to the management or the board of directors of an enterprise carried on for profit.

Art. 56. On assuming his office the Federal President shall take the following oath before the assembled members of the Bundestag and the Bundesrat:

"I swear that I will dedicate my efforts to the well-being of the German people, enhance its benefits, ward harm from it, uphold and defend the Basic Law and the laws of the Federation, fulfil my duties conscientiously, and do justice to all. So help me God."

The oath may also be taken without religious affirmation.

Art. 57. If the Federal President is prevented from acting, or if his office falls prematurely vacant, his powers shall be exercised by the President of the Bundesrat.

Art. 58. (1) Orders and decrees of the Federal President shall require for their validity the countersignature of the Federal Chancellor or the appropriate Federal Minister. This does not apply to the appointment and dismissal of the federal Chancellor, the dissolution of the Bundestag under Article 63 and the request under Article 69, paragraph (3).

Art. 59. (1) The Federal President shall represent the Federation in its international relations. He shall conclude treaties with foreign states on behalf of the Federation. He shall accredit and receive envoys.

(2) Treaties which regulate the political relations of the Federation or relate to matters of federal legislation shall require the consent or participation, in the form of a federal law, of the bodies competent in any specific case for such federal legislation. For administrative agreements the provisions concerning the federal administration shall apply *mutatis mutandis.*

Art. 59a. (1) The Bundestag shall determine when a case of defence has occurred. Its decision shall be promulgated by the Federal President.

(2) If insurmountable difficulties prevent the Bundestag from assembling, the Federal President may, when there is danger in delay, make and promulgate this determination, subject to countersignature by the Federal Chancellor. The Federal President should previously consult the Presidents of the Bundestag and the Bundesrat.

(3) Statements concerning the existence of a case of defence which involve international relations shall not be issued by the Federal President until after such promulgation.

(4) Any decision on the conclusion of peace shall be taken by means of a federal law.

Art. 60. (1) The Federal President shall appoint and dismiss the federal judges, the federal civil servants, the officers and non-commissioned officers, unless otherwise provided for by law.

(2) He shall exercise the power of pardon on behalf of the Federation in individual cases.

(3) He may delegate these powers to other authorities.

(4) Paragraphs (2) to (4) of Article 46 shall apply *mutatis mutandis* to the Federal President.

Art. 61. (1) The Bundestag or the Bundesrat may impeach the Federal President before the Federal Constitutional Court for wilful violation of this Basic Law or any other federal law. The motion for impeachment must be brought forward by at least one fourth of the members of the Bundestag or one-fourth of the votes of the Bundesrat. The decision to impeach shall require a majority of two thirds of the members of the Bundestag or of two thirds of the votes of the Bundesrat. The prosecution shall be conducted by a person commissioned by the impeaching body.

(2) If the Federal Constitutional Court finds the Federal President guilty of a wilful violation of this Basic Law or of another federal law, it may declare him to have forfeited his office. After impeachment, it may issue an interim order preventing the Federal President from exercising his functions.

VI. The Federal Government

Art. 62. The Federal Government shall consist of the Federal Chancellor and the Federal Ministers.

Art. 63. (1) The Federal Chancellor shall be elected, without debate, by the Bundestag on the proposal of the Federal President.

(2) The person obtaining the votes of the majority of the members of the Bundestag is elected. The person elected must be appointed by the Federal President.

(3) If the person proposed is not elected, the Bundestag may elect within fourteen days of the ballot a Federal Chancellor by more than one half of its members.

(4) If no candidate has been elected within this period, a new ballot shall take place without delay, in which the person obtaining the largest number of votes is elected. If the person elected obtained the votes of the majority of the members of the Bundestag, the Federal President must appoint him within seven days of the election. If the person elected did not receive this majority, the Federal President must within seven days either appoint him or dissolve the Bundestag.

Art. 64. (1) The Federal Ministers shall be appointed and dismissed by the Federal President upon the proposal of the Federal Chancellor.

(2) The Federal Chancellor and the Federal Ministers, on assuming office, shall take before the Bundestag the oath provided in Article 56.

Art. 65. The Federal Chancellor shall determine, and be responsible for, general policy. Within the limits of this general policy, each Federal Minister shall conduct the business of his department autonomously and on his own responsibility. The Federal Government shall decide on differences of opinion between the Federal Ministers. The Federal Chancellor shall conduct the business of the Federal Government in accordance with rules of procedure adopted by it and approved by the Federal President.

Art. 65a. (1) Power of command in respect of the Armed Forces shall be vested in the Federal Minister of Defence.

(2) Upon promulgation of the determination concerning the case of defence, the power of command shall devolve on the Federal Chancellor.

Art. 66. The Federal Chancellor and the Federal Ministers may not hold any other salaried office, nor engage in a trade, nor practise a profession, nor belong to the management or, without the consent of the Bundestag, to the board of directors of an enterprise carried on for profit.

Art. 67. (1) The Bundestag can express its lack of confidence in the Federal Chancellor only by electing a successor with a majority of its members and by requesting the Federal President to dismiss the Federal Chancellor. The Federal President must comply with the request and appoint the person elected.

(2) Forty-eight hours must elapse between the motion and the election.

Art. 68. (1) If a motion of the Federal Chancellor for a vote of confidence is not assented to by the majority of the members of the Bundestag, the Federal President may, upon the proposal of the Federal Chancellor, dissolve the Bundestag within twenty-one days. The right to dissolve shall lapse as soon as the Bundestag by the majority of its members elects another Federal Chancellor.

(2) Forty-eight hours must elapse between the motion and the vote thereon.

Art. 69. (1) The Federal Chancellor shall appoint a Federal Minister as his deputy.

(2) The tenure of office of the Federal Chancellor or a Federal Minister shall end in any event on the first meeting of a new Bundestag; the tenure of office of a Federal Minister shall also end on any other termination of the tenure of office of the Federal Chancellor.

(3) At the request of the Federal President the Federal Chancellor, or at the request of the Federal Chancellor or of the Federal President a Federal Minister, shall be bound to continue to transact the business of his office until the appointment of a successor.

VII. Legislative Powers of the Federation

Art. 70. (1) The Laender shall have the power to legislate insofar as this Basic Law does not confer legislative powers on the Federation.

(2) The division of competence between the Federation and the Laender is determined by the provisions of this Basic Law concerning exclusive and concurrent legislative powers.

Art. 71. On matters within the exclusive legislative powers of the Federation the Laender shall have authority to legislate only if, and to the extent that, a federal law explicitly so authorizes them.

Art. 72. (1) On matters within the concurrent legislative powers the Laender shall have authority to legislate as long as, and to the extent that, the Federation does not use its legislative powers.

(2) The Federation shall have the right to legislate on these matters to the extent that a need for regulation by federal law exists because

1. a matter cannot be effectively regulated by the legislation of individual Laender, or
2. the regulation of a matter by a Land law might prejudice the interests of other Laender or of the entire community, or
3. the maintenance of legal or economic unity, especially the maintenance of uniformity of living conditions beyond the territory of a Land, necessitates such regulation.

Art. 73. The Federation shall have the exclusive power to legislate on:

1. foreign affairs as well as defence including both military service for

males from their completed age of 18 years and the protection of the civilian population;

2. citizenship in the Federation;

3. freedom of movement, passport matters, immigration and emigration, and extradition;

4. currency, money and coinage, weights and measures, as well as computation of time;

5. the unity of the customs and commercial territory, treaties on commerce and navigation, the freedom of movement of goods, and the exchanges of goods and payments with foreign countries, including customs and frontier protection;

6. federal railroads and air traffic;

7. postal and telecommunication services;

8. the legal status of persons employed by the Federation and by federal bodies-corporate under public law;

9. industrial property rights, copyrights and publication rights;

10. co-operation of the Federation and the Laender in matters of criminal police and of protection of the constitution, establishment of a federal office of the criminal police, as well as international control of crime;

11. statistics for federal purposes.

Art. 74. Concurrent legislative powers shall extend to the following matters:

1. civil law, criminal law and execution of sentences, the system of judicature, the procedure of the courts, the legal profession, notaries and legal advice (*Rechtsberatung*);

2. registration of births, deaths, and marriages;

3. the law of association and assembly;

4. the law relating to residence and establishment of aliens;

5. the protection of German cultural treasures against removal abroad;

6. refugee and expellee matters;

7. public welfare;

8. citizenship in the Laender;

9. war damage and reparation;

10. benefits to war-disabled persons and to dependents of those killed in the war, and assistance to former prisoners of war;

10a. war graves and graves of other victims of the war and of victims of despotism;

11. the law relating to economic matters (mining, industry, supply of power, crafts, trades, commerce, banking, stock exchanges, and private insurance);

11a. the production and utilization of nuclear energy for peaceful purposes, the construction and operation of installations serving these purposes, protection against dangers arising from the release of nuclear energy or from ionizing rays, and removal of radioactive material;

12. labor law, including the legal organization of enterprises, protection of workers, employment exchanges and agencies, as well as social insurance, including unemployment insurance;
13. the promotion of scientific research;
14. the law regarding expropriation, to the extent that matters enumerated in Articles 73 and 74 are concerned;
15. transfer of land, natural resources and means of production into public ownership or other forms of publicly controlled economy;
16. prevention of the abuse of economic power;
17. promotion of agricultural and forest production, safeguarding of the supply of food, the importation and exportation of agricultural and forest products, deep sea and coastal fishing, and preservation of the coasts;
18. real estate transactions, land law and matters concerning agricultural leases, housing, settlements and homesteads;
19. measures against epidemic and infectious diseases of humans and animals, admission to medical and other professions and practices in the field of healing, traffic in drugs, medicines, narcotics, and poisons;
20. protection with regard to traffic in food and stimulants as well as in necessities of life, in fodder, in agricultural and forest seeds and seedlings, and protection of trees and plants against diseases and pests;
21. ocean and coastal shipping as well as aids to navigation, inland shipping, meteorological services, sea waterways and inland waterways used for general traffic;
22. road traffic, motor transport, and construction and maintenance of long distance highways;
23. railroads other than federal railroads, except mountain railroads.

Art. 75. Subject to the conditions of Article 72 the Federation shall have the right to enact general rules concerning:

1. the legal status of persons in the public service of the Laender, communes, and other bodies-corporate under public law;
2. the general status of the press and motion pictures;
3. hunting, protection of nature, and care of the countryside;
4. land distribution, regional planning, and water management;
5. matters relating to registration (*Meldewesen*) and identity cards.

Art. 76. (1) Bills shall be introduced in the Bundestag by the Federal Government, by members of the Bundestag, or by the Bundesrat.

(2) Bills of the Federal Government shall be submitted first to the Bundesrat. The Bundesrat shall be entitled to state its position on these bills within three weeks.

(3) Bills of the Bundesrat shall be submitted to the Bundestag by the Federal Government. In doing so the Federal Government must state its own views.

Art. 77. (1) Federal laws are enacted by the Bundestag. Upon the adoption of a bill, it shall, without delay, be transmitted to the Bundesrat by the President of the Bundestag.

(2) The Bundesrat may, within two weeks of the receipt of the adopted bill, demand that a committee for joint consideration of bills, composed of members of the Bundestag and members of the Bundesrat, be convened. The composition and the procedure of this committee shall be regulated by rules of procedure to be adopted by the Bundestag and requiring the consent of the Bundesrat. The members of the Bundesrat on this committee shall not be bound by instructions. If the consent of the Bundesrat is required for a law, the demand for convening this committee may also be made by the Bundestag or the Federal Government. Should the committee propose any amendment to the adopted bill, the Bundestag must again vote on the bill.

(3) Insofar as the consent of the Bundesrat is not required for a law, the Bundesrat may, when the proceedings under paragraph (2) are completed, lodge an objection within one week against a bill adopted by the Bundestag. This period begins, in the case of paragraph (2), last sentence, on the receipt of the bill as readopted by the Bundestag, and in all other cases on the conclusion of the proceedings of the committee provided for in paragraph (2).

(4) If the objection is adopted by a majority of the votes of the Bundesrat, it can be rejected by a decision of the majority of the members of the Bundestag. If the Bundesrat adopted the objection by a majority of at least two thirds of its votes, its rejection by the Bundestag shall require a majority of two thirds, including at least the majority of the members of the Bundestag.

Art. 78. A law adopted by the Bundestag shall have been passed if the Bundesrat consents to it, or fails to make a demand pursuant to Article 77, paragraph (2), or fails to enter an objection within the period stipulated in Article 77, paragraph (3), or withdraws an objection so lodged, or if the objection is overridden by the Bundestag.

Art. 79. (1) This Basic Law can be amended only by a law which expressly amends or supplements the text thereof. In respect of international treaties the subject of which is a peace settlement, the preparation of a peace settlement, or the abolition of an occupation regime, or which are designed to serve the defence of the Federal Republic, it shall be sufficient, for the purpose of a clarifying interpretation to the effect that the provisions of the Basic Law are not contrary to the conclusion and entry into force of such treaties, to effect a supplementation of the text of the Basic Law confined to this clarifying interpretation.

(2) Such a law shall require the affirmative vote of two thirds of the members of the Bundestag and two thirds of the votes of the Bundesrat.

(3) An amendment of this Basic Law effecting the division of the Federation into Laender, the participation in principle of the Laender in legis-

lation, or the basic principles laid down in Articles 1 and 20, shall be inadmissible.

Art. 80. (1) The Federal Government, a Federal Minister or the Land Governments may be authorized by a law to issue ordinances having the force of law (*Rechtsverordnungen*). The content, purpose, and scope of the powers conferred must be set forth in the law. The legal basis must be stated in the ordinance. If a law provides that a power may be further delegated, an ordinance having the force of law shall be necessary in order to delegate the power.

(2) The consent of the Bundesrat shall be required, unless otherwise provided by federal legislation, for ordinances having the force of law issued by the Federal Government or a Federal Minister concerning basic rules for the use of facilities of the federal railroads and of postal and telecommunication services, or charges therefor, or concerning the construction and operation of railroads, as well as for ordinances having the force of law issued on the basis of federal laws that require the consent of the Bundesrat or that are executed by the Laender as agents of the Federation or as matters of their own concern.

Art. 81. (1) Should in the circumstances of Article 68 the Bundestag not be dissolved, the Federal President may, at the request of the Federal Government and with the consent of the Bundesrat, declare a state of legislative emergency with respect to a bill, if the Bundestag rejects the bill although the Federal Government has declared it to be urgent. The same shall apply if a bill has been rejected although the Federal Chancellor had combined with it the motion under Article 68.

(2) If, after a state of legislative emergency has been declared, the Bundestag again rejects the bill or adopts it in a version which has been stated by the Federal Government to be unacceptable to it, the law shall be deemed to have been passed insofar as the Bundesrat consents to it. The same shall apply if the bill is not adopted by the Bundestag within four weeks of its reintroduction.

(3) During the term of office of a Federal Chancellor, any other bill rejected by the Bundestag may be passed in accordance with paragraphs (1) and (2) within a period of six months after the first declaration of a state of legislative emergency. After expiration of this period, a further declaration of a state of legislative emergency shall be inadmissible during the term of office of the same Federal Chancellor.

(4) This Basic Law may not be amended, nor may it be repealed or suspended in whole or in part, by a law passed pursuant to paragraph (2).

Art. 82. (1) Laws passed in accordance with the provisions of this Basic Law shall, after countersignature, be signed by the Federal President and promulgated in the Federal Law Gazette. Ordinances having the force of law shall be signed by the agency which issues them, and, unless otherwise provided by law, shall be promulgated in the Federal Law Gazette.

(2) Every law and every ordinance having the force of law should specify its effective date. In the absence of such a provision, it shall become effective on the fourteenth day after the expiry of the day on which the Federal Law Gazette was published.

VIII. The Execution of Federal Laws of the Federal Administration

Art. 83. The Laender shall execute the Federal laws as matters of their own concern insofar as this Basic Law does not otherwise provide or permit.

Art. 84. (1) If the Laender execute the Federal laws as matters of their own concern, they shall provide for the establishment of authorities and the regulation of administrative procedures insofar as federal laws consented to by the Bundesrat do not otherwise provide.

(2) The Federal Government may, with the consent of the Bundesrat, issue general administrative rules.

(3) The Federal Government shall exercise supervision to ensure that the Laender execute the federal laws in accordance with applicable law. For this purpose the Federal Government may send commissioners to the highest Land authorities and, with their consent or, if this consent is refused, with the consent of the Bundesrat, also to subordinate authorities.

(4) Should any shortcomings which the Federal Government has found to exist in the execution of federal laws in the Laender not be corrected, the Bundesrat shall decide, on the application of the Federal Government or the Land, whether the Land has acted unlawfully. The decision of the Bundesrat may be challenged in the Federal Constitutional Court.

(5) For the execution of federal laws, the Federal Government may, by a federal law requiring the consent of the Bundesrat, be authorized to issue individual instructions for particular cases. They must be addressed to the highest Land authorities unless the Federal Government considers the matter urgent.

Art. 85. (1) Where the Laender execute federal laws as agents of the Federation, the establishment of the authorities shall remain the concern of the Laender except insofar as federal laws consented to by the Bundesrat otherwise provide.

(2) The Federal Government may, with the consent of the Bundesrat, issue general administrative rules. It may regulate the uniform training of civil servants and salaried government employees (*Angestellte*). The heads of authorities at intermediate level shall be appointed with its agreement.

(3) The Land authorities shall be subject to the instructions of the appropriate highest federal authorities. The instructions shall be addressed to the highest Land authorities unless the Federal Government considers

the matter urgent. Execution of the instructions shall be ensured by the highest Land authorities.

(4) Federal supervision shall extend to conformity with law and appropriateness of execution. The Federal Government may, for this purpose, require the submission of reports and documents and send commissioners to all authorities.

Art. 86. Where the Federation executes laws by means of direct federal administration or by federal bodies-corporate or institutions under public law, the Federal Government shall issue, insofar as the law contains no special provision, the general administrative rules. It shall provide for the establishment of authorities insofar as the law does not otherwise provide.

Art. 87. (1) The foreign service, the federal finance administration, the federal railroads, the federal postal service and, in accordance with the provisions of Article 89, the administration of federal waterways and of shipping shall be conducted as matters of direct federal administration with their own administrative substructure. Federal frontier protection authorities and central offices for police information and communications, for the compilation of data for the purpose of protecting the constitution and for the criminal police may be established by federal legislation.

(2) Social insurance institutions whose sphere of competence extends beyond the territory of one Land shall be conducted as federal bodies-corporate under public law.

(3) In addition, independent federal higher authorities as well as federal bodies-corporate and institutions under public law may be established by federal law for matters on which the Federation has the power to legislate. If new functions arise for the Federation in matters on which it has the power to legislate, federal authorities at intermediate and lower levels may be established, in case of urgent need, with the consent of the Bundesrat and of the majority of the members of the Bundestag.

Art. 87a. The numerical strength and general organizational structure of the Armed Forces raised for defence by the Federation shall be shown in the budget.

Art. 87b. (1) The Federal Armed Forces Administration shall be conducted as a direct federal administration with its own administrative substructure. Its function shall be to administer personnel matters and directly to meet the material requirements of the Armed Forces. Tasks connected with benefits to injured persons or with construction work shall not be assigned to the Federal Armed Forces Administration except by federal legislation which shall require the consent of the Bundesrat. Such consent shall also be required for any legislative provisions empowering the Federal Armed Forces Administration to interfere with rights of third parties; this shall, however, not apply in the case of laws concerning personnel.

(2) Moreover, federal laws concerning defence including recruitment for

military service and protection of the cilivian population may, with the consent of the Bundesrat, stipulate that they shall be carried out, wholly or in part, either by means of direct federal administration with its own administrative substructure or by the Laender acting as agents of the Federation. If such laws are executed by the Laender acting as agents of the Federation, they may, with the consent of the Bundesrat, stipulate that the powers vested by virtue of Article 85 in the Federal Government or appropriate highest federal authorities shall be transferred wholly or partly to higher federal authorities; in such an event it may be enacted that these authorities shall not require the consent of the Bundesrat in issuing general administrative rules as referred to in Article 85, paragraph (2), first sentence.

Art. 87c. Laws enacted under item 11a of Article 74 may, with the consent of the Bundesrat, stipulate that they shall be executed by the Laender acting as agents of the Federation.

Art. 87d. (1) The administration of air traffic shall be conducted as a matter of direct federal administratation.

(2) By federal law, which requires the consent of the Bundesrat, functions of the air traffic administration may be transferred to the Laender, which will carry out such functions as agents of the Federation.

Art. 88. The Federation shall establish a note-issuing and currency bank as the Federal Bank.

Art. 89. (1) The Federation shall be the owner of the former Reich waterways.

(2) The Federation shall administer the federal waterways through its own authorities. It shall exercise the governmental functions relating to inland shipping, which extend beyond the territory of one Land, and those relating to maritime shipping, which are conferred on it by law. Upon request, the Federation may transfer the administration of federal waterways, insofar as they lie within the territory of one Land, to this Land as its agent. If a waterway touches the territories of several Laender, the Federation may designate as its agent one Land if so requested by the Laender concerned.

(3) In the administration, development, and new construction of waterways the needs of soil cultivation and of water management shall be safeguarded in agreement with the Laender.

Art. 90. (1) The Federation shall be the owner of the former Reich motor roads (*Reichsautobahnen*) and Reich highways.

(2) The Laender, or such self-governing bodies-corporate as are competent under Land law, shall administer as agents of the Federation the federal motor roads and other federal highways used for long-distance traffic.

(3) At the request of a Land, the Federation may take under direct federal administration federal motor roads and other federal highways

used for long-distance traffic, insofar as they lie within the territory of that Land.

Art. 91. (1) In order to avert an imminent danger to the existence or to the free democratic basic order of the Federation or of a Land, a Land may request the services of the police forces of other Laender.

(2) If the Land in which the danger is imminent is not itself willing or able to combat the danger, the Federal Government may place the police in that Land and the police forces of other Laender under its own instructions. The order for this shall be rescinded after the danger is past, or else at any time on the demand of the Bundesrat.

IX. The Administration of Justice

Art. 92. The judicial authority shall be vested in the judges; it shall be exercised by the Federal Constitutional Court, by the Supreme Federal Court, by the federal courts provided for in this Basic Law and by the courts of the Laender.

Art. 93. (1) The Federal Constitutional Court shall decide:

1. on the interpretation of this Basic Law in the event of disputes concerning the extent of the rights and duties of a highest federal organ or of other parties concerned who have been endowed with rights of their own by this Basic Law or by rules of procedure of a highest federal organ;
2. in case of differences of opinion or doubts on the formal and material compatibility of federal law or Land law with this Basic Law, or on the compatibility of Land law with other federal law, at the request of the Federal Government, of a Land Government, or of one third of the Bundestag members;
3. in case of differences of opinion on the rights and duties of the Federation and the Laender, particularly in the execution of federal law by the Laender and in the exercise of federal supervision;
4. on other disputes involving public law, between the Federation and the Laender, between different Laender or within a Land, unless re course to another court exists;
5. in the other cases provided for in this Basic Law.

(2) The Federal Constitutional Court shall also act in such cases as are otherwise assigned to it by federal law.

Art. 94. (1) The Federal Constitutional Court shall consist of federal judges and other members. Half of the members of the Federal Constitutional Court shall be elected by the Bundestag and half by the Bundesrat. They may not belong to the Bundestag, the Bundesrat, the Federal Government, or the corresponding organs of a Land.

(2) Its constitution and procedure shall be regulated by a federal law, which shall specify in what cases its decisions shall have the force of law.

Art. 95. (1) To preserve the uniformity of federal law a Supreme Federal Court shall be established.

(2) The Supreme Federal Court shall decide cases in which the decision is of fundamental importance for the uniformity of the administration of justice by the higher federal courts.

(3) The judges of the Supreme Federal Court shall be selected jointly by the Federal Minister of Justice and a committee for the selection of judges consisting of the Land Ministers of Justice and an equal number of members elected by the Bundestag.

(4) In other respects, the constitution of the Supreme Federal Court and its procedure shall be regulated by federal legislation.

Art. 96. (1) Higher federal courts shall be established for the fields of ordinary, administrative, tax, labor, and social jurisdiction.

(2) Article 95, paragraph (3), shall apply to the judges of the higher federal courts, provided that the Ministers competent for the particular matter shall take the place of the Federal Minister of Justice and the Land Ministers of Justice. The terms of service of these judges shall be regulated by special federal legislation.

Art. 96a. (1) The Federation may establish a federal court for the field of industrial property rights.

(2) The Federation may establish military criminal courts for the Armed Forces as federal courts. They shall not exercise criminal jurisdiction except in the case of defence o rover members of the Armed Forces serving abroad or on board warships. Details shall be regulated by a federal law. These courts shall be within the sphere of business of the Federal Minister of Justice. Their full-time judges must be persons duly qualified to be judges.

(3) The Federal Court of Justice shall be the higher federal court for the courts referred to in paragraphs (1) and (2) above.

(4) The Federation may establish federal disciplinary courts for disciplinary proceedings against federal civil servants and federal judges (*Bundesdienststrafgerichte*) as well as federal service courts for disciplinary proceedings against soldiers and for proceedings in respect of complaints by soldiers (*Bundesdienstgerichte*).

Art. 97. (1) The judges shall be independent and subject only to the law.

(2) Judges appointed permanently on a full-time basis to an established post cannot, against their will, be dismissed, or permanently or temporarily suspended from office, or transferred to another post, or retired before the expiration of their term of office except by virtue of a judicial decision and only on the grounds and in the form provided for by law. Legislation may set age limits for the retirement of judges appointed for life. In the event of changes in the structure of the courts or their areas of jurisdiction, judges may be transferred to another court or removed from their office, provided they retain their full salary.

Art. 98. (1) The legal status of the federal judges shall be regulated by a special federal law.

(2) If a federal judge, in his official capacity or unofficially, infringes upon the principles of this Basic Law or the constitutional order of a Land, the Federal Constitutional Court may decide by a two-thirds majority, upon the request of the Bundestag, that the judge be transferred to another office or placed on the retired list. In a case of intentional infringement, his dismissal may be ordered.

(3) The legal status of the judges in the Laender shall be regulated by special Land laws. The Federation may enact general rules.

(4) The Laender may provide that the Land Minister of Justice together with a committee for the selection of judges shall decide on the appointment of judges in the Laender.

(5) The Laender may, in respect of Land judges, enact provisions consistent with paragraph (2). Existing Land constitutional law shall remain unaffected. The decision in a case of impeachment of a judge shall rest with the Federal Constitutional Court.

Art. 99. The decision on constitutional disputes within a Land may be assigned by Land legislation to the Federal Constitutional Court, and the decision of last instance, in matters involving the application of Land law, to the higher federal courts.

Art. 100. (1) If a court considers unconstitutional a law the validity of which is relevant to its decision, the proceedings shall be stayed, and a decision shall be obtained from the Land court competent for constitutional disputes if the matter concerns the violation of the Constitution of a Land, or from the Federal Constitutional Court if the matter concerns a violation of this Basic Law. This shall also apply if the matter concerns the violation of this Basic Law by Land law or the incompatibility of a Land law with a federal law.

(2) If, in the course of litigation, doubt exists whether a rule of public international law is an integral part of federal law and whether such rule directly creates rights and duties for the individual (Article 25), the court shall obtain the decision of the Federal Constitutional Court.

(3) If the constitutional court of a Land, in interpreting this Basic Law, intends to deviate from a decision of the Federal Constitutional Court or of the constitutional court of another Land, it must obtain the decision of the Federal Constitutional Court; if, in interpreting other federal law, it intends to deviate from the decision of the Supreme Federal Court or a higher federal court, it must obtain the decision of the Supreme Federal Court.

Art. 101. (1) Extraordinary Courts shall be inadmissible. No one may be removed from the jurisdiction of his lawful judge.

(2) Courts for special fields may be established only by a law.

Art. 102. Capital punishment shall be abolished.

Art. 103. (1) In the courts everyone shall be entitled to a hearing in accordance with the law.

(2) An act can be punished only if it was a punishable offence by law before the act was committed.

(3) No one may be punished for the same act more than once in pursuance of general penal legislation.

Art. 104. (1) The freedom of the individual may be restricted only on the basis of a formal law and only with due regard to the forms prescribed therein. Detained persons may be subjected neither to mental nor to physical ill-treatment.

(2) Only judges may decide on the admissibility or continuation of a deprivation of liberty. Where such deprivation is not based on the order of a judge, a judicial decision must be obtained without delay. The police may hold no one on their own authority in their own custody longer than the end of the day after the arrest. Details shall be regulated by legislation.

(3) Any person provisionally detained on suspicion of having committed a punishable offence must be brought before a judge at the latest on the day following the arrest; the judge shall inform him of the reasons for the detention, examine him, and give him an opportunity to raise objections. The judge must, without delay, either issue a warrant of arrest setting forth the reasons therefor or order the release from detention.

(4) A relative of the person detained or a person enjoying his confidence must be notified without delay of any judicial decision ordering or continuing a deprivation of liberty.

X. Finance

Art. 105. (1) The Federation shall have the exclusive power to legislate on customs matters and fiscal monopolies.

(2) The Federation shall have concurrent power to legislate on:

1. excise taxes and taxes on transport, motor-vehicles, and transactions (*Verkehrsteuern*), with the exception of taxes with localized application, in particular of real estate acquisition tax, increment value tax, and fire protection tax;
2. taxes on income, on property, on inheritances, and on donations;
3. taxes on real estate and business (*Realsteuern*), with the exception of the fixing of the tax rates,

if it claims the taxes in whole or in part to cover federal expenditure or if the conditions laid down in Article 72, paragraph (2), exist.

(3) Federal laws relating to taxes the receipts from which accrue in whole or in part to the Laender or the communes (associations of communes) shall require the consent of the Bundesrat.

Art. 106. (1) The yield of fiscal monopolies and receipts from the following taxes shall accrue to the Federation:

1. customs duties,
2. such excise taxes as do not accrue to the Laender in accordance with paragraph (2),
3. turnover tax,
4. transportation tax,
5. non-recurrent levies on property, and equalization taxes imposed for the purpose of implementing the Equalization of Burdens legislation,
6. Berlin emergency aid tax,
7. income and corporation surtaxes.

(2) Receipts from the following taxes shall accrue to the Laender:

1. property tax,
2. inheritance tax,
3. motor-vehicle tax,
4. such taxes on transactions (*Verkehrsteuern*) as do not accrue to the Federation in accordance with paragraph (1),
5. beer tax,
6. taxes on gambling establishments,
7. taxes with localized application.

(3) Receipts from income tax and corporation tax shall accrue:
until 31 March 1958, to the Federation and the Laender in a ratio of 33⅓ per cent to 66⅔ per cent, and
from 1 April 1958, to the Federation and the Laender in a ratio of 35 per cent to 65 per cent.

(4) The ratio of apportionment of the income and corporation taxes (paragraph (3)) should be modified by a federal law requiring the consent of the Bundesrat whenever the development of the relation of revenues to expenditures in the Federation differs from that in the Laender and the budgetary needs of the Federation or those of the Laender exceed the estimated revenues by a margin substantial enough to call for a corresponding adjustment of the ratio of apportionment in favor of either the Federation or the Laender. Any such adjustment shall be based on the following principles:

1. The Federation and the Laender shall each bear the expenditures resulting from the administration of their respective tasks; Article 120, paragraph (1), shall not be affected;
2. There shall be equality of rank between the claim of the Federation and the claim of the Laender to have their respective necessary expenditures covered from ordinary revenues;
3. The requirements of the Federation and of the Laender in respect of budget coverage shall be co-ordinated in such a way that a fair equalization is achieved, any overburdening of tax-payers precluded, and uniformity of living standards in the federal territory ensured.

The ratio of apportionment may be modified for the first time with effect from 1 April 1958, and subsequently at intervals of not less than two years after the entry into force of any law determining such ratio; provided that this stipulation shall not affect any modification of such ratio effected in accordance with paragraph (5).

(5) If a federal law imposes additional expenditure on, or withdraws revenue from, the Laender, the ratio of apportionment of the income and corporation taxes shall be modified in favor of the Laender, provided that conditions as envisaged in paragraph (4) have developed. If the additional burden placed upon the Laender is limited to a period of short duration, such burden may be compensated by grants from the Federation under a federal law requiring the consent of the Bundesrat and which shall lay down the principles for assessing the amounts of such grants and for distributing them among the Laender.

(6) Receipts from taxes on real estate and business shall accrue to the communes (*Gemeinden*). If no communes exist in a Land, such receipts shall accrue to the Land. Taxes on real estate and business may, in accordance with Land legislation, be taken as a basis for determining the amounts of assessments on or grants to communes. A percentage, to be determined by Land legislation, of the Land share in the income and corporation taxes shall accrue to the communes and associations of communes as a whole. Whether and to what extent receipts from Land taxes are to accrue to communes (associations of communes), shall be determined by Land legislation.

(7) If in individual Laender or communes (associations of communes) the Federation causes special facilities to be instituted which directly result in more expenditure or less revenue (special burdens) to these Laender or communes (associations of communes), the Federation shall grant the necessary compensation, if and insofar as the Laender or communes (associations of communes) cannot reasonably be expected to bear such special burden. In granting such compensation, due account shall be taken of indemnities by third parties or financial advantages accruing from such facilities to the Laender or communes (associations of communes) concerned.

(8) For the purposes of the present Article, revenues and expenditures of communes (associations of communes) shall be deemed to be Land revenues and expenditures.

Art. 107. (1) Receipts from Land taxes shall accrue to the individual Laender to the extent that such taxes are collected by revenue authorities within their respective territories (local receipts). Federal legislation requiring the consent of the Bundesrat may provide in detail for the determination and allotment of local receipts from specific taxes (tax shares).

(2) A federal law requiring the consent of the Bundesrat shall ensure a reasonable financial equalization between financially strong Laender and financially weak Laender, due account being taken of the financial capacity

and requirements of communes (associations of communes). Such law shall provide for equalization grants to be paid to financially weak Laender from equalization contributions made by financially strong Laender; it shall furthermore specify the conditions governing equalization claims and equalization liabilities as well as the criteria for determining the amounts of equalization payments. Such law may also provide for grants to be made by the Federation from federal funds to financially weak Laender in order to complement the coverage of their general financial requirements (complemental grants).

Art. 108. (1) Customs duties, fiscal monopolies, excise taxes subject to concurrent legislative powers, transportation tax, turnover tax, and non-recurrent levies on property shall be administered by federal revenue authorities. The organization of these authorities and the procedure to be applied by them shall be regulated by federal law. The heads of the authorities at intermediate level shall be appointed after consultation of the Land Governments. The Federation may transfer the administration of non-recurrent levies on property to the Land revenue authorities as its agents.

(2) To the extent that the Federation claims part of the income and corporation taxes for itself, it shall be entitled to administer them; it may, however, transfer the administration to the Land revenue authorities as its agents.

(3) The remaining taxes shall be administered by Land revenue authorities. The Federation may, by federal laws which require the consent of the Bundesrat, regulate the organization of these authorities, the procedure to be applied by them, and the uniform training of the civil servants. The heads of the authorities at intermediate level shall be appointed in agreement with the Federal Government. The administration of the taxes accruing to the communes (associations of communes) may be transferred by the Laender in whole or in part to the communes (associations of communes).

(4) To the extent that taxes accrue to the Federation, the Land revenue authorities shall act as agents of the Federation. The Laender shall be liable to the extent of their revenues for the proper administration of such taxes; the Federal Minister of Finance may supervise the proper administration, acting through authorized federal agents who shall be entitled to give instructions to the authorities at intermediate and lower levels.

(5) The jurisdiction of tax courts shall be uniformly regulated by federal law.

(6) The general administrative rules shall be issued by the Federal Government and, insofar as the administration is incumbent upon the Land revenue authorities, shall require the consent of the Bundesrat.

Art. 109. The Federation and the Laender shall be autonomous and independent of each other as regards their budgets.

Art. 110. (1) All revenues and expenditures of the Federation must be estimated for each fiscal year and included in the budget.

(2) The budget shall be established by a law before the beginning of the fiscal year. It must be balanced as regards revenue and expenditure. Expenditure shall as a rule be authorized for one year; in special cases, they may be authorized for a longer period. Otherwise no provisions may be inserted in the federal budget law which extend beyond the fiscal year or which do not relate to the revenues and expenditures of the Federation or its administration.

(3) Property and debts shall be set forth in an appendix to the budget.

(4) In the cases of commercially operated enterprises of the Federation the individual receipts and expenditures need not be included in the budget, but only the final balance.

Art. 111. (1) If, by the end of a fiscal year, the budget for the following year has not been established by a law, the Federal Government may, until such law comes into force, make all payments which are necessary:

(a) to maintain institutions existing by law and to carry out measures authorized by law;

(b) to meet legally established commitments of the Federation;

(c) to continue building projects, procurements, and other services, or to continue to grant subsidies for these purposes, provided amounts have already been authorized in the budget of a previous year.

(2) To the extent that revenues provided by special legislation and derived from taxes, duties, or any other charges or sources, or the working capital reserves, do not cover the expenditures referred to in paragraph (1), the Federal Government may borrow the funds necessary for the conduct of current operations to a maximum of one quarter of the total amount of the previous budget.

Art. 112. Expenditures in excess of budget authorizations and extra-budgetary expenditures shall require the consent of the Federal Minister of Finance. The consent may only be given if there exists an unforeseen and compelling necessity.

Art. 113. Decisions of the Bundestag and of the Bundesrat, which increase the budget expenditure proposed by the Federal Government or involve new expenditure or will cause new expenditure in the future, shall require the consent of the Federal Government.

Art. 114. (1) The Federal Minister of Finance must submit annually to the Bundestag and to the Bundesrat an account of all revenues and expenditures as well as of property and debts.

(2) This account shall be audited by an Audit Office (*Rechnungshof*) the members of which shall enjoy judicial independence. The general account and a summary of the property and debts shall be submitted to the Bundestag and the Bundesrat in the course of the following fiscal year together with the comments of the Audit Office in order to secure a discharge for

the Federal Government. The audit of accounts shall be regulated by a federal law.

Art. 115. Funds may be obtained by borrowing only in case of extraordinary need and as a rule only for expenditure for productive purposes and only pursuant to a federal law. The granting of credits and the provision of security by the Federation, the effect of which extends beyond the fiscal year, may take place only pursuant to a federal law. The amount of the credit, or the extent of the obligation for which the Federation assumes liability, must be fixed in the law.

XI. Transitional and Concluding Provisions

Art. 116. (1) Unless otherwise provided by law, a German within the meaning of this Basic Law is a person who possesses German citizenship or who has been admitted to the territory of the German Reich, as it existed on 31 December 1937, as a refugee or expellee of German stock (*Volkszugehorigkeit*) or as the spouse or descendant of such person.

(2) Former German citizens who, between 30 January 1933 and 8 May 1945, were deprived of their citizenship for political, racial, or religious reasons, and their descendants, shall be regranted German citizenship on application. They shall be considered as not having been deprived of their German citizenship if they have established their domicile (*Wohnsitz*) in Germany after 8 May 1945 and have not expressed a contrary intention.

Art. 117. (1) Law which conflicts with Article 3, paragraph (2), shall remain in force until adapted to this provision of the Basic Law, but not beyond 31 March 1953.

(2) Laws which restrict the right of freedom of movement in view of the present housing shortage shall remain in force until repealed by federal legislation.

Art. 118. The reorganization of the territory comprising the Laender Baden, Wuerttemberg-Baden, and Wuerttemberg-Hohenzollern may be effected notwithstanding the provisions of Article 29, by agreement between the Laender concerned. If no agreement is reached, the reorganization shall be regulated by a federal law which must provde for a referendum.

Art. 119. In matters relating to refugees and expellees, in particular as regards their distribution among the Laender, the Federal Government may, with the consent of the Bundesrat, issue ordinances having the force of law (*Verordnungen mit Gesetzeskraft*), pending settlement of the matter by federal legislation. The Federal Government may in this matter be authorized to issue individual instructions for particular cases. Except where there is danger in delay, the instructions shall be addressed to the highest Land authorities.

Art. 120. (1) The Federation shall bear expenditure for occupation costs and the other internal and external burdens caused as a consequence of the war, as provided for in detail by federal law. So far as these burdens were governed up to 1 October 1965 by federal law, the expenditure shall be borne, in accordance with these federal laws, by the Federation and the Laender proportionally. So far as the Laender, the communes (associations of communes) or other entities carrying out functions of the Laender and the communes have borne the expenditure for burdens caused as a consequence of the war and which were, or are, not governed by federal law, the Federation shall not be obliged to take over any such expenditure even after the above date. The Federation shall bear the subsidies towards the burdens of social insurance, including unemployment insurance and public assistance for the unemployed. The distribution among the Federation and Laender of the burdens caused as a consequence of the war shall not affect the statutory provisions with regard to claims for compensation for consequences of the war.

(2) The revenues shall be transferred to the Federation at the same time as the Federation assumes responsibility for the expenditures.

Art. 120a. (1) Laws concerning the implementation of the Equalization of Burdens legislation may, with the consent of the Bundesrat, stipulate that in the field of equalization benefits, they shall be executed partly by the Federation and partly by the Laender acting as agents of the Federation, and that the relevant powers vested in the Federal Government and the competent highest federal authorities by virtue of Article 85, shall be wholly or partly delegated to the Federal Equalization Office. In the exercise of these powers the Federal Equalization Office shall not require the consent of the Bundesrat; with the exception of urgent cases, its instructions shall be given to the highest Land authorities (Land Equalization Offices).

(2) The provisions of Article 87, paragraph (3), second sentence, shall not be affected hereby.

Art. 121. Within the meaning of this Basic Law, a majority of the members of the Bundestag and of the Federal Convention (*Bundesversammlung*) shall be the majority of the number of their members established by law.

Art. 122. (1) From the time of the first meeting of the Bundestag, laws shall be passed exclusively by the legislative organs recognized in this Basic Law.

(2) Legislative bodies and bodies participating in legislation in an advisory capacity, whose competence ends by virtue of paragraph (1), are dissolved from that date.

Art. 123. (1) Law in force before the first meeting of the Bundestag shall remain in force, insofar as it does not conflict with this Basic Law.

(2) Subject to all rights and objections of the interested parties, the state treaties concluded by the German Reich concerning matters for which,

under this Basic Law, Land legislation is competent, shall remain in force, if they are and continue to be valid in accordance with general principles of law, until new state treaties are concluded by the agencies competent under this Basic Law, or until they are in any other way terminated pursuant to their provisions.

Art. 124. Law affecting matters within the exclusive legislative power of the Federation shall become federal law wherever it is applicable.

Art. 125. Law affecting matters within the concurrent legislative power of the Federation shall become federal law wherever it is applicable:

1. insofar as it applies uniformly within one or more zones of occupation;
2. insofar as it is law by which former Reich law has been amended after 8 May 1945.

Art. 126. The Federal Constitutional Court shall decide desputes regarding the continuance of law as federal law.

Art. 127. Within one year of the promulgation of this Basic Law the Federal Government may, with the consent of the governments of the Laender concerned, extend to the Laender Baden, Greater Berlin, Rhineland-Palatinate, and Wuerttemberg-Hohenzollern any legislation of the Bi-zonal Economic Administration, insofar as it continues to be in force as federal law under Articles 124 or 125.

Art. 128. Insofar as law continuing in force provides for powers to give instructions within the meaning of Article 84, paragraph (5), these powers shall remain in existence until otherwise provided by law.

Art. 129. (1) Insofar as legal provisions which continue in force as federal law contain an authorization to issue ordinances having the force of law (*Rechtsverordnungen*) or general administrative rules or to perform administrative acts, the authorization shall pass to the agencies henceforth competent in the matter. In cases of doubt, the Federal Government shall decide in agreement with the Bundesrat; the decision must be published.

(2) Insofar as legal provisions which continue in force as Land law contain such an authorization, it shall be exercised by the agencies competent under Land law.

(3) Insofar as legal provisions within the meaning of paragraphs (1) and (2) authorize their amendment or supplementation or the issue of legal provisions instead of laws, these authorizations have expired.

(4) The provisions of paragraphs (1) and (2) shall apply *mutatis mutandis* whenever legal provisions refer to regulations no longer valid or to institutions no longer in existence.

Art. 130. (1) Administrative agencies and other institutions which serve the public administration or the administration of justice and are not based on Land law or state treaties between Laender, as well as the Association of Management of South West German Railroads and the Administrative Council for the Postal Services and Telecommunications of the French Zone of Occupation shall be placed under the Federal Government. The Federal Government shall provide with the consent of the Bundesrat for their transfer, dissolution, or liquidation.

(2) The highest disciplinary superior of the personnel of these administrations and institutions shall be the appropriate Federal Minister.

(3) Bodies-corporate and institutions under public law not directly under a Land, and not based on state treaties between Laender, shall be under the supervision of the appropriate highest federal authority.

Art. 131. Federal legislation shall regulate the legal status of persons, including refugees and expellees, who, on 8 May 1945, were employed in the public service, have left the service for reasons other than those arising from civil service regulations or collective agreement rules, and have not until now been employed or are employed in a position nor corresponding to their former one. The same shall apply *mutatis mutandis* to persons, including refugees and expellees, who, on 8 May 1945, were entitled to a pension or other assistance and who no longer receive any assistance or any commensurate assistance for reasons other than those arising from civil service regulations or collective agreement rules. Until the federal law comes into force, no legal claims can be made, unless otherwise provided by Land legislation.

Art. 132. (1) Civil servants and judges who, when this Basic Law comes into force, are appointed for life, may, within six months after the first meeting of the Bundestag, be placed on the retired list or waiting list or be transferred to another office with lower remuneration, if they lack the personal or professional aptitude for their office. This provision shall apply *mutatis mutandis* also to salaried employees (*Angestellte*) whose service cannot be terminated by notice. In the case of salaried employees whose service can be terminated by notice, periods of notice in excess of the periods fixed by collective agreement rules may be cancelled within the same period.

(2) This provision shall not apply to members of the public service who are not affected by the provisions regarding the Liberation from National Socialism and Militarism or who are recognized victims of National Socialism, unless there exists an important reason in respect of their personality.

(3) Those affected may have recourse to the courts in accordance with Article 19, paragraph (4).

(4) Details shall be regulated by an ordinance of the Federal Government, which shall require the consent of the Bundesrat.

Art. 133. The Federation shall succeed to the rights and obligations of the Bi-zonal Economic Administration.

Art. 134. (1) Reich property shall in principle become federal property.

(2) Insofar as the property was originally intended to be used predominantly for administrative tasks which, under the Basic Law, are not administrative tasks of the Federation, it shall be transferred without compensation to the authorities now charged with such tasks, and to the

Laender insofar as it is being used at present, and not merely temporarily, for administrative tasks which under this Basic Law are now within the administrative functions of the Laender. The Federation may also transfer other property to the Laender.

(3) Property which was placed at the disposal of the Reich by the Laender and communes (associations of communes) without compensation shall again become the property of the Laender and communes (associations of communes), insofar as it is not required by the Federation for its own administrative tasks.

(4) Details shall be regulated by a federal law requiring the consent of the Bundesrat.

Art. 135. (1) If after 8 May 1945 and before the coming into force of this Basic Law an area has passed from one Land to another, the Land to which the area now belongs shall be entitled to the property located therein of the Land to which it belonged.

(2) Property of Laender and other bodies-corporate and institutions under public law, which no longer exist, shall pass, insofar as it was originally intended to be used predominantly for administrative tasks or is being used at present, and not merely temporarily, predominantly for administrative tasks, to the Land or the body-corporate or institution under public law which now discharges these tasks.

(3) Real estate of Laender which no longer exist, including appurtenances, shall pass to the Land within which it is located insofar as it is not included among property within the meaning of paragraph (1).

(4) If an overriding interest of the Federation or the particular interest of an area so requires, a settlement deviating from paragraphs (1) to (3) may be effected by federal law.

(5) For the rest, the succession in law and the settlement of the property, insofar as it has not been effected before 1 January 1952 by agreement between the Laender or bodies-corporate or institutions under public law concerned, shall be regulated by a federal law requiring the consent of the Bundesrat.

(6) Interests of the former Land Prussia in enterprises under private law shall pass to the Federation. A federal law, which may also deviate from this provision, shall regulate details.

(7) Insofar as, on the coming into force of this Basic Law, property which would fall to a Land or a body-corporate or institution under public law pursuant to paragraphs (1) to (3) had been disposed of through or by virtue of a Land law or in any other manner by the party thus entitled, the passing of the property shall be deemed to have taken place before such disposition.

Art. 135a. The legislation reserved to the Federation in Article 134, paragraph (4), and in Article 135, paragraph (5), may also stipulate that the following liabilities shall not be discharged, or not to their full extent:

1. liabilities of the Reich or liabilities of the former Land Prussia or liabilities of such other bodies-corporate and institutions under public law as no longer exist,
2. such liabilities of the Federation or other bodies-corporate and institutions under public law as are connected with the transfer of properties pursuant to Articles 89, 90, 134, or 135, and such liabilities of the same as arise from measures taken by the holders of rights defined under item 1,
3. such liabilities of Laender or communes (associations of communes) as have arisen from measures taken by these holders of rights before 1 August 1945 within the sphere of administrative functions incumbent upon, or delegated by, the Reich to comply with regulations of Occupying Powers or to remove a state of emergency due to the war.

Art. 136. (1) The Bundesrat shall assemble for the first time on the day of the first meeting of the Bundestag.

(2) Until the election of the first Federal President his powers shall be exercised by the President of the Bundesrat. He shall not have the right to dissolve the Bundestag.

Art. 137. (1) The right of civil servants, of salaried employees of the public services, of professional soldiers, of temporary volunteer soldiers, and of judges, to stand for election in the Federation, in the Laender, or in the communes may be restricted by legislation.

(2) The electoral law to be adopted by the Parliamentary Council shall apply to the election of the first Bundestag, of the first Federal Convention, and of the first Federal President of the Federal Republic.

(3) The function of the Federal Constitutional Court pursuant to Article 41, paragraph (2), shall, pending its establishment, be exercised by the German High Court for the Combined Economic Area, which shall decide in accordance with its rules of procedure.

Art. 138. Changes in the rules relating to notaries as they now exist in the Laender Baden, Bavaria, Wuerttemberg-Baden, and Wuerttemberg-Hohenzollern, shall require the consent of the governments of these Laender.

Art 139. The legistation enacted for the Liberation of the German People from National Socialism and Militarism shall not be affected by the provisions of this Basic Law.

Art. 140. The provisions of Articles 136, 137, 138, 139, and 141 of the German Constitution of 11 August 1919 are an integral part of this Basic Law.

"*Art. 136.* (*Weimar Constitution*)

"Civil and civic rights and duties shall be neither conditioned nor limited by the exercise of the freedom of religion.

The enjoyment of civil and civic rights and the eligibility for public offices shall be independent of religious creed.

No one shall be obliged to reveal his religious convictions. The authorities shall not have the right to inquire as to a person's membership of a religious society except to the extent that rights or duties depend thereon or that statistical action ordered by law makes it necessary.

No one may be compelled to perform any religious act or ceremony or to participate in religious exercises or to use a religious form of oath.

"*Art. 137.* (*Weimar Constitution*)

"There shall be no state church.

Freedom of association in religious societies shall be guaranteed. The amalgamation of religious societies within the territory of the Reich shall not be subject to any restrictions.

Every religious society shall regulate and administer its affairs independently within the limits of the law valid for all. It shall confer its offices without the participation of the state or the civil commune.

Religious societies shall acquire legal capacity according to the general provisions of civil law.

Religious societies shall remain bodies-corporate under public law insofar as they have been such heretofore. The other religious societies shall be granted like rights upon their application, if their constitution and the number of their members offer an assurance of their permanence. If several such religious societies under public law amalgamate in one organization, such organization shall also be a body-corporate under public law.

Religious societies that are bodies-corporate under public law shall be entitled to levy taxes in accordance with Land law on the basis of the civil taxation lists.

Associations whose purpose is the cultivation in common of a philosophical ideology (*Weltanschauung*) shall have the same status as religious societies.

Such further regulation as may be required for the implementation of these provisions shall be incumbent on Land legislation.

"*Art. 138.* (*Weimar Constitution*)

"State contributions to religious societies, based on law or contract or special legal title, shall be redeemed by means of Land legislation. The principles for this shall be established by the Reich.

The rights of ownership and other rights of religious societies and religious associations in respect of their institutions, foundations and other assets destined for purposes of worship, education, or charity, shall be guaranteed.

"*Art. 139.* (*Weimar Constitution*)

"Sunday and the public holidays recognized by the state shall remain protected by law as days of rest from work and of spiritual edification.

"*Art. 141.* (*Weimar Constitution*)

"To the extent that there exists a need for religious services and spiritual care in the army, in hospitals, prisons, or other public institutions, the religious societies shall be permitted to perform religious acts; in this connexion there shall be no compulsion of any kind."

Art. 141. Article 7, paragraph (3), first sentence, shall have no application in a Land in which different provisions of Land law were in force on 1 January 1949.

Art. 142. Notwithstanding the provision of Article 31, also such provisions of Land Constitutions shall remain in force as guarantee basic rights in conformity with Articles 1 to 18 of this Basic Law.

Art. 142a. The provisions of this Basic Law are not contrary to the conclusion and entry into force of the treaties signed in Bonn and Paris on 26 and 27 May 1952 (Treaty on Relations between the Federal Republic of Germany and the Three Powers and Treaty establishing a European Defence Community) with their related and additional conventions, especially the Protocol of 26 July 1952.

Art. 143. The conditions under which it will be admissible to have recourse to the Armed Forces in case of a state of internal emergency, may be regulated only by a law which fulfils the requirements of Article 79.

Art. 144. (1) This Basic Law shall require ratification by the representative assemblies in two thirds of the German Laender in which it is to apply in the first instance.

(2) Insofar as the application of this Basic Law is subject to restrictions in any Land listed in Article 23 or in any part of such Land, the Land or the part thereof shall have the right to send representatives to the Bundestag in accordance with Article 38 and to the Bundesrat in accordance with Article 50.

Art. 145. (1) The Parliamentary Council shall establish in public session, with the participation of the representatives of Greater Berlin, the fact of ratification of this Basic Law and shall sign and promulgate it.

(2) This Basic Law shall come into force on the expiry of the day of promulgation.

(3) It shall be published in the Federal Law Gazette.

Art. 146. This Basic Law shall cease to be in force on the day on which a Constitution adopted by a free decision of the German people comes into force.

GREECE

SUMMARY

INTERNATIONAL STATUS

Greece is a member of the United Nations (October 25, 1945). It is a member of the European Economic Community and of other international organizations. It was a member of the League of Nations.

Greek independence was proclaimed on March 25, 1821, and there followed a war of independence against the Turks that lasted until 1829. By a protocol of February 3, 1830, the great powers (England, France and Russia) recognized and guaranteed Greek independence in the Peloponnese, the southern mainland (Roumeli), Euboea and the Cyclades. Efforts to incorporate the rest of Greece formed a basic element in Greek policy thereafter. In 1864, the Ionian Islands became part of Greece, in 1881 Thessaly, in 1913 Macedonia, Epirus, Crete and the other Aegean islands, in 1920 eastern Thrace, parts of Asia Minor and in 1947 Rhodes and the Dodecanese.

On January 1, 1882, the first Provisional Constitution was adopted by the First National Assembly meeting near Epidaurus which provided for a republic. The third National (or Constitutional) Assembly at Troezen adopted the Political Constitution of Greece on May 1, 1827, which also provided for a republic. On January 18, 1828, the Constitution was suspended by the President. The London Treaty of May 2–7, 1832, imposed a monarchy on the new state whose frontiers were fixed by the Treaty of Constantinople of July 21, 1832, between Turkey and the three powers. A period of absolute monarchy lasted from 1833 to 1843 when, following an uprising, the First National Assembly of Athens met on November 8, 1843, and voted a Constitution on February 21, 1844, providing for a limited and constitutional monarchy. A revolution in October 1862 expelled the Bavarian King Othon and his dynasty, and the Second National Assembly of Athens voted a new constitution on November 17, 1864. The revisions of 1911 and 1952 did not alter its fundamental provisions. The Treaty of Lausanne in 1923, withdrawing the territories in Asia Minor and Eastern Thrace that had been granted Greece by the Treaty of Sèvres, providing for an exchange of populations between Greece and Turkey, and defining the frontiers, left outstanding as irredentist problems the Dodecanese (returned to Greece after the Second World War), southern Albania (or Northern Epirus) and Cyprus. From 1924 to 1935 Greece was a republic under a constitution of 1927. Greece was invaded by Italy in October 1940 and, after repelling this invasion, was invaded by Germany in April 1941, and occupied by Germany, Italy and Bulgaria. The question of the return of the monarchy after the Second World War was settled by the plebiscite of September 1946. A Communist rising in December 1944 ended with the Varkiza agreements in February 1945. A state of Communist insurrection existed in parts of the country from 1946 to 1949.

FORM OF NATIONAL GOVERNMENT

The Constitution of January 1, 1952[1] is a revision of the Constitution of May 23, 1911, prepared by the Fourth Revisionary Assembly elected in 1946. It states that Greece is a crowned democracy.[2] All powers are derived from the nation.[3] The established religion is that of the Eastern Orthodox Church of Christ.[4] It is forbidden to render into different lin-

[1] Following a military *coup d'état* on April 21, 1967, the Constitution has been virtually suspended, most of the provisions concerning civil rights explicitly so.
[2] Const., Art. 21. [3] Id., Art. 21. [4] Id., Art. 1.

guistic form the text of the Scriptures without the authorization of the Greek Church and of the Oecumenical Patriarchate.[1] A section is devoted to the status and regime of Mount Athos, a self governed part of the Greek state under the administrative jurisdiction of the Greek State and the spiritual jurisdiction of the Patriarchate.[2] Revision of the whole constitution or of certain basic articles is prohibited.[3]

RIGHTS OF THE PEOPLE

The Constitution provides equality before the law, freedom of religion, personal liberty, due process of law, no *ex post facto* punishments, the right to one's lawful judge, the right of petition, assembly, association, inviolability of domicile, freedom of the press, compulsory and free primary education, the right to property, secrecy of correspondence.[4] Greeks must pay taxes and assist in the defence of their country.[5]

LEGISLATIVE DEPARTMENT

Legislative power is exercised by the King and a unicameral Parliament composed of not less than 150 nor more than 300 deputies, elected by universal, direct, secret suffrage for a term of four years subject to dissolution.[6] Deputies represent the whole nation.[7] It meets once a year in regular session.[8] Immunities of deputies are provided.[9] The authoritative interpretation of laws rests with the legislature.[10] There are provisions concerning finance and a Council of Comptrollers.[11]

EXECUTIVE DEPARTMENT

Executive power is vested in an inviolate King and exercised by responsible Ministers appointed by him.[12] The King is the Head of State, commands the Armed Forces, conducts foreign policy, has the power of appointment, promulgates laws, has the right of pardon, grants honors.[13] The Council of Ministers constitutes the government.[14] No member of the royal family may be minister; other incompatibilities are described.[15] The government must enjoy the confidence of Parliament.[16] Ministers have access to Parliament.[17] There are provisions concerning the administration of the state.[18]

[1] Id., Art. 2. [2] Id., Art. 103. [3] Id., Art. 108.
[4] Id., Art. 2–20. But see note 1 on preceeding page. [5] Id., Art. 3.
[6] Id., Art. 22, 66, 68, 69, 37. [7] 67. [8] Id., Art. 54.
[9] Id., Art. 62, 63. [10] Id., Art. 26. [11] Id., Art. 24, 57, 59–61, 98.
[12] Id., Art. 27, 29. [13] Id., Art. 31–41. [14] Id., Art. 76. [15] Id., Art. 77, 71.
[16] Id., Art. 78. [17] Id., Art. 78. [18] Id., Art. 99–102.

JUDICIAL DEPARTMENT

Judicial power is exercised by the courts of law the judges of which are appointed by the King.[1] There is provision for regular administrative courts and for a Council of State.[2] Decisions of the plenum of the Supreme Court and of the Supreme Judicial Council are not subject to appeal to the Council of State.[3]

AREA, POPULATION, ETC.

The area of Greece is 130,918 square kilometres, its population (1964) is 8,510,000. The official language of the State is that in which the Constitution and laws are drawn up.[4] The capital is Athens.

[1] Id., Art. 28, 87. [4] Id., Art. 82–86. [3] Id., Art. 90. [4] Id., Art. 107.

CONSTITUTION of GREECE[1]

January 1, 1952

In the name of the Holy, Consubstantial and Indivisible Trinity.

THE PARLIAMENT OF THE HELLENES, RESOLVES

Religion

Art. 1. The established religion in Greece is that of the Eastern Orthodox Church of Christ; every other known religion is free, and the forms of worship thereof shall be practiced without hindrance under the protection of the laws; proselytism and all other interferences with the established religion being prohibited.

Art. 2. The Orthodox Church of Greece, acknowledging as its head our Lord Jesus Christ, is indissolubly united in doctrine with the Great Church of Constantinople and every other Church of Christ of the same doctrine, observing steadfastly, as they do, the holy apostolic and synodical canons and holy traditions; it is autocephalous, exercising its sovereign rights independently of every other Church, and it is administered by a Holy Synod of bishops. The ministers of all recognized religions shall be subject to the same superintendence on the part of the State as the ministers of the established religion.

The text of the Holy Scriptures shall be maintained unchanged; the rendering thereof into a different linguistic form without the previous sanction of autocephalous the Church of Greece and the Great Church of Christ in Constantinople is absolutely prohibited.

The freedom of religious conscience is inviolable.

The free exercise of religious duties shall not be permitted to offend public order or good morals.

[1] English translation published in the second edition taken from *Revue Hellénique de Droit International*, checked by Editor in light of French translation contained in *Constitution Hellénique* contained in *Publications de l'Institut Hellénique de Droit International et Etranger*. Athens 1963. Supplied by the Ministry of Foreign Affairs in July 1966. The Constitution has been virtually suspended following a military coup d'état on April 21, 1967, see note 1 on page 400. Ed.

Nobody shall, by reason of his religious convictions, be exempt from discharging his obligations to the State or refuse to comply with the laws of the country.

Interpretative Clause: The ecclesiastical situation prevailing in the New Provinces is not contrary to the meaning of this article.

The Public Rights of the Hellenes

Art. 3. Greeks are equal before the law. Greek citizens shall contribute without discrimination towards meeting the public expenditure according to their ability. Only Greek citizens shall be admissible to all public appointments, save in those cases where exceptions are introduced by special laws.

Citizens are those who have acquired or shall acquire the qualifications of citizenship in accordance with the laws of the State

Titles of nobility or distinction are neither conferred upon nor recognized in Greek citizens.

Every Greek able to bear arms is obliged to assist in the defense of the country as provided by the laws.

Art. 4. Personal liberty is inviolable; no one shall be prosecuted, arrested, imprisoned or otherwise confined, except when and as the law provides.

Art. 5. With the exception of persons taken in the act of the committing an offense, no one shall be arrested or imprisoned without a judicial warrant stating the reasons which must be served at the moment of arrest or imprisonment pending trial.

Any person taken in the act or arrested on the basis of a warrant of arrest shall without delay be brought before the competent examining magistrate within twenty four hours of his arrest at the latest, or, if the arrest was made beyond the seat of the examining magistrate, within the time absolutety necessary for his conveyance. Within at the most three days from such appearance, the examining magistrate must either release the person arrested or deliver a warrant for his imprisonment. This time limit shall be extended for up to five days at the request of the person arrested or in the event of *force majeure,* which shall be certified forthwith by a decision of the competent judicial council.

Should both these time limits expire without such action, every jailer or other officer, civil or military, charged with the detention of the person arrested shall release him forthwith. Transgressors of the above provisions shall be punished for illegal confinement and shall be obliged to make good any loss sustained by the injured party and further to give satisfaction to said party by such sum of money as the law provides.

The maximum term of imprisonment pending trial, as well as the conditions under which the State shall indemnify persons unjustly imprisoned pending trial or sentence, shall be determined by law.

Art. 6. In the case of political offenses, the court of misdemeanors may always, on the request of the person detained, allow his release on bail fixed by a judicial order, which shall admit of appeal.

In the case of such offenses, imprisonment pending trial shall under no circumstances be extended beyond three months.

Interpretative Clause

The introduction in the future of general or special laws abolishing or restricting the term of imprisonment pending trial or rendering release on bail mandatory for the judge is by no means precluded. It is further understood that the maximum term of three months set in the second paragraph for imprisonment pending trial shall include the duration of both the entire investigation and the procedure before the judicial councils prior to the final hearing.

Art. 7. No offense shall exist, nor shall any punishment be imposed, unless a law existed prior to commission of the act. A heavier punishment shall never be imposed after commission of the act.

Art. 8. No person shall be withdrawn without his consent from his lawful judge. The establishment of judicial committees and extraordinary courts under any name whatsoever is prohibited.

Art. 9. One person or several persons acting together shall have the right, with due adherence to the laws of the State, to address written petitions to the public authorities, which are obliged to take prompt action and to furnish an answer in writing to the petitioner in accordance with the provisions of the law. Only after the final decision of the authority to whom the petition was made, and with the permission thereof, may action be initiated to determine responsibility of the petitioner for offenses which may be contained in the petition.

Interpretative Clause. By petition is meant recourse to a competent authority and not a request for information which, each authority is, in any case, morally obliged to furnish.

Art. 10. Greeks have the right to assemble peaceably and without arms. The police may be present only at public gatherings. Open air assemblies may be prohibited if danger to public security is imminent therefrom.

Art. 11. Greeks have the right of association, with due adherence to the laws of the State which, however, shall under no circumstances render this right subject to previous permission of the government.

An association shall not be dissolved for violation of the law except by judicial decision.

The right of association in the case of civil servants and employees of semi-governmental agencies and organizations may by law be submitted to certain restrictions.

Strikes of civil servants and employees of semi-governmental agencies and organizations are prohibited.

Art. 12. Each man's house is inviolable. No house searches shall be made except when and as the law directs.

Offenders against these provisions shall be punished for abuse of authority and shall be obliged to indemnify fully the injured party and further to give satisfaction to said party by such sum of money as the law provides.

Art. 13. Every person within the territorial boundaries of the Greek State shall enjoy full protection of his life and liberty irrespective of nationality, creed and language. Exceptions shall be permitted in such cases as are provided for by international law.

Art. 14. Any person may publish his opinion orally, in writing or in print with due adherence to the laws of the State. The press is free. Censorship and every other preventive measure is prohibited. The seizure of newspapers and other printed matter, either before or after publication, is likewise prohibited.

By exception, seizure after publication is permitted:

(a) because of insult to the Christian religion or indecent publications manifestly offending public decency, in the cases provided by law,

(b) because of insult to the person of the King, the successor to the Throne, their wives or their children,

(c) if the contents of the publication according to the terms of the law be of such a nature as to

(1) disclose movements of the Armed Forces of military significance or fortifications of the country,

(2) be manifestly rebellious or directed against the territorial integrity of the nation or constitute an instigation to commit a crime of high treason; but in these cases, the public prosecutor must, within twenty-four hours from the seizure, submit the case to the judicial council which, within a further twenty-four hours, must decide whether the seizure shall be maintained or withdrawn, otherwise the seizure shall be *ipso jure* lifted.

Only the publisher of the item seized shall be allowed to appeal against the judicial order. After at least three convictions of a press offense which admits of seizure, the court shall order the permanent or temporary suspension of issue of the publication and, in grave cases, shall also prohibit the exercise of the profession of journalist by the person convicted. Such suspension or prohibition shall commence from the time that the court decision becomes final.

No person whatsoever shall be permitted to use the title of a suspended newspaper for ten years from the date of the permanent suspension thereof.

Press offenses shall be deemed offenses *in flagrante delicto.*

Only Greek citizens who have not been deprived of their civic rights shall be allowed to publish newspapers.

The manner of rectifying through the press erroneous publications as well as the preconditions and qualifications for exercising the profession of journalist shall be determined by law.

Enforcement by law of special repressive measures directed against literature dangerous to the morals of youth shall be permitted.

The provisions on the protection of the press contained in the present article shall not be applicable to motion pictures, public spectacles, phonograph records, broadcasting and other similar means of conveying speech or of representation. Both the publisher of the newspaper and the author of a reprehensible publication relating to one's private life shall, in addition to being subject to the penalty imposed according to the terms of the penal law, also be civilly and jointly liable to redress fully any loss suffered by the injured party and to indemnify him by a sum of money as provided by law.

Art. 15. No oath shall be imposed except by law determining also the form thereof.

Art. 16. Education shall be under the supreme supervision of the State and shall be conducted by and at the expense of the State or of agencies of local government.

In all elementary and intermediate schools teaching shall be aimed at the ethical and intellectual instruction and the development of the national conscience of youths on the basis of the ideological principles of Greek Christian civilization.

Elementary education shall be compulsory and shall be provided *gratis* by the State. The number of years of attendance shall be determined by law and shall not be less than six.

The higher educational institutions shall be self-administered under the supervision of the State and their professors shall be civil servants.

Private individuals, who have not been deprived of their civic rights, and juridical persons shall, with the previous permission of the authorities, be allowed to establish schools operating in accordance with the Constitution and the laws of the State.

Art. 17. No one shall be deprived of his property except for the public benefit, which shall be duly proved, when and as the law directs and always after full indemnification. The indemnification shall at all times be fixed by the regular courts. In urgent cases indemnification may be provisionally fixed judicially after a hearing or summoning of the beneficiary who may be obliged, at the discretion of the judge, to afford an appropriate guarantee in a manner determined by the law. Prior to the payment of the final or provisional indemnification all the rights of the proprietor shall remain intact and dispossession shall be prohibited.

Special laws determine ownership and disposal of mines, quarries, archeological treasures, and mineral running and subterranean waters.

Ownership and fish-breeding operation and administration of shoals and large lakes shall likewise regulated by law.

Special laws shall regulate requisitioning for the needs of the Armed Forces in the case of war or mobilization or in order to meet immediate social needs liable to endanger public order or health.

Interpretative Clause: The term "property" shall be deemed to include movable property.

Art. 18. Torture and general confiscation are prohibited. Civil death is abolished. The death penalty in the case of political offenses, excepting compound offenses, is abolished.

Art. 19. No previous permission of the administrative authorities shall be required for the trial of State or municipal employees for punishable acts committed in connection with their duties, except in the case of Ministers for whom special provision is made.

Art. 20. The secrecy of letters and of correspondence by any other medium whatsoever shall be completely inviolable.

The Form of Government

Art. 21. The regime of Greece shall be that of a Crowned Democracy.

All powers are derived from the nation and shall be exercised in the manner determined by the Constitution.

Art. 22. The legislative power shall be exercised by the King and Parliament.

Art. 23. The right of proposing laws shall belong to Parliament and the King who shall exercise this right through the Ministers.

Art. 24. No bill, amendment or addition necessitating the expenditure by or a reduction in revenue or property of the State, local government, or other public agencies for the payment of salaries or pensions or, in general, for the benefit of an individual, shall be initiated by Parliament.

Art. 25. A bill rejected by either of the agencies of the legislative power shall not be reintroduced during the same session of Parliament.

Art. 26. The authentic interpretation of the laws shall rest with the legislature.

Art. 27. The executive power shall be vested in the King and exercised by the responsible Ministers appointed by the King.

Art. 28. The judicial power shall be exercised by the courts of law and judicial decisions shall be executed in the name of the King.

The King

Art. 29. The person of the King shall be non-responsible and inviolable; his Ministers shall be responsible.

Art. 30. No act of the King shall have force, nor shall it be executed unless it is countersigned by the competent Minister who shall be rendered responsible by his signature alone. If in the case of a change of the entire

Ministry none of the retiring Ministers consents to sign the decrees dismissing the old and appointing the new Ministry, these decrees shall be signed by the President of the new Ministry after he shall have taken the oath following his appointment by the King.

Art. 31. The King shall appoint and dismiss his Ministers.

Art. 32. The King shall be the supreme Head of the State; he shall command the Armed Forces, declare war, conclude treaties of peace, alliance and commerce, and announce them to Parliament with the necessary clarifications when the interest and the security of the nation permit. However, commercial treaties and such other treaties as embody concessions in regard to which, pursuant to other provisions of the present Constitution, nothing can be determined without a law, or impose a personal burden upon the Greeks, shall be invalid without the consent of Parliament.

Art. 33. No cession or exchange of territory shall be effected without a law.

The secret articles of a treaty shall under no circumstances subvert the published articles.

No foreign army shall be admitted into Greek service, nor shall it remain in or pass through Greek territory without a law.

Art. 34. The King shall confer ranks in accordance with the law upon those serving in the Armed Forces and shall, likewise in accordance with the law, appoint and discharge civil servants save in the case of exceptions provided by law.

Members of the Armed Forces shall be deprived of their rank, honors and pension only when and as the law determines.

Art. 35. The King shall issue the decrees necessary for the execution of the law, but he shall under no circumstances suspend the operation of the law nor exempt anyone from the execution thereof.

During a given parliamentary term and for such time as Parliament is in recess or adjourned the King may issue legislative decrees for the settlement of exceptionally urgent matters with the concurring opinion of a special committee of deputies established at the beginning of each Parliamentary session and functioning until the opening of the new session.

The number of members of the committee shall not be less than one fifth of the total number of Deputies, and the presence of two thirds of its members and a relative majority shall be required for making decisions.

Parliament may from time to time decide to place restrictions on issuance of the legislative decrees referred to above.

Bills submitted by Deputies during the first quarter following the reconvening of Parliament and recommending amendment, repeal or cancellation of these decrees shall, upon the request of at least 15 Deputies, be registered with absolute priority upon the agenda of legislative work.

Art. 36. The King shall sanction and publish the laws passed by Parliament. A law not published within two months from the end of the parliamentary session shall be null and void.

Art. 37. The King shall convoke Parliament in ordinary session once a year, and in extraordinary session whenever he deems advisable; he shall open and close each Parliamentary session in person or by deputy and shall have the right to dissolve Parliament, but the decree of dissolution countersigned by the Ministry shall at the same time comprise the convocation of the electors within forty-five days and of Parliament within three months.

Art. 38. The King shall have the right, once only, to suspend the work of a Parliamentary session, either by postponing the opening or by interrupting the continuance of such work.

The suspension of Parliamentary work shall not exceed thirty days, nor shall it be repeated during a given Parliamentary session without the consent of Parliament.

Art. 39. The King shall have the right to pardon, and to commute and reduce sentences pronounced by the courts of law, except in cases governed by the provisions of the law regarding Ministers. The King shall also have the right to grant an amnesty only in cases of political crimes and under the responsibility of the governmnet.

Art. 40. The King shall have the right to confer the established decorations in accordance with the pertinent provisions of the law.

Art. 41. The King shall have the right to coin money as determined by law.

Art. 42. The civil list shall from time to time be fixed by law.

Art. 43. The King shall attain his majority upon reaching the age of eighteen.

Before ascending the Throne the King shall take the following oath in the presence of the Ministers, the Holy Synod, the deputies who happen to be in the capital, and the other higher authorities:

> "I swear in the name of the Holy, Consubstantial and Indivisible Trinity to protect the established religion of the Greeks, to guard the Constitution and the laws of the Greek nation and to preserve and defend the national independence and integrity of the Greek State."

The King shall convene Parliament within two months at the latest and shall repeat the oath before the Deputies.

Art. 44. The King shall have no powers other than those explicitly assigned to him by the Constitution and by such special laws as are consistent therewith.

Succession and Regency

Art. 45. The Greek Crown and its constitutional rights are hereditary and pass to the legitimate and lawful lineal descendents of King George I by order of primogeniture preference being given to the males.

Interpretative Clause: The true meaning of Article 45 is that the Greek Crown passes by preference to the descendants of the reigning King by order of primogeniture, preference being given to the males.

Art. 46. Should there be no successor to the Throne in accordance with the above stipulations, the King shall appoint one with the consent of Parliament, convoked for the purpose, and by a vote of two thirds of the total number of Deputies taken by open ballot.

Art. 47. Every successor to the Greek Throne shall be required to profess the religion of the Eastern Orthodox Church of Christ.

Art. 48. The Crown of Greece and that of any other state whatsoever shall never unite on one and the same head.

Art. 49. In case of departure of the King from the country, the Regency shall be entrusted by Royal Decree issued at the instance of the Council of Ministers to the heir, if he be of age, or, if there is no heir or he is a minor, to the Queen who shall exercise the full powers of Regent in the name of the King pursuant to the existing laws. Should there be no heir, or if he be a minor, and if the Queen be not living, the King shall be Royal Decree, countersigned by the Council of Ministers, appoint a Representative of the Throne revocable without limitation, who shall exercise the Royal authority in the name of the King. The jurisdiction of the Representative of the Throne shall be determined by the same Royal Decree.

Art. 50. In the event of the death of the King, if the successor be of age and absent, the Council of Ministers shall exercise the Constitutional royal authority until the successor shall have arrived and taken the oath.

If, in the event of the death of the King, the successor be a minor, the Queen, if in a state of widowhood, shall exercise the Royal authority until the successor shall have attained majority.

If the Queen be not alive or remarries, Parliament, even if its term be ended or it be dissolved, shall upon the tenth day following the King's death convene without being summoned and shall elect a Regent who shall be a Greek citizen of the Eastern faith, the Constitutional Royal authority being exercised by the Council of Ministers under its own responsibility until the Regent shall have taken the oath. The foregoing shall also apply in the case of the King's abdication. The details of the Regency shall be determined by special law.

Art. 51. If upon the death of the King his successor be a minor, Parliament, even if its term be ended or it be dissolved, shall convene to elect a guardian who shall, however, be elected only when no guardian is provided for in the will of the deceased King or when the infant successor has not a mother who remains in a state of widowhood, but who, if she so remain, shall be assigned *ipso facto* the guardianship of her son. The guardian of the infant King, whether the be appointed by will or elected by Parliament, shall be a Greek citizen of the Eastern faith.

Art. 52. Should the Throne become vacant, Parliament, even if its term be ended or it be dissolved, shall elect provisionally by open ballot a Greek citizen of the Eastern faith as Regent, and the Council of Ministers shall exercise under its own responsibility the Constitutional Royal authority in the name of the nation until the Regent shall have taken the oath. Within two months at the latest the citizens shall elect representatives equal in number to the Deputies, who shall meet in joint session with Parliament and elect a King by a majority of two thirds of the whole and by open ballot.

Art. 53. Should the King, on account of sickness, deem necessary the establishment of a Regency, he shall by Royal Decree appoint as Regent the successor to the Throne or, if there be no successor or if he be a minor, the Queen. Should the King not be in a position to reign, the Council of Ministers shall forthwith convoke Parliament, even if its term be ended or it be dissolved.

Should Parliament recognize the need for a Regency by a decision taken by a majority of three fourths of the votes cast, the Regency shall be exercised by the successor, if he be of age, or, if there be no successor of age, by the Queen.

If the Queen be deceased, the Council of Ministers shall convoke Parliament which, if there be no successor shall pass a special law on the exercise of the royal authority, or if the successor be a minor, shall by open ballot elect a Regent and, if need be, a guardian of the King.

Parliament

Art. 54. Parliament shall assemble *ipso jure* each year on the 15th day of October in regular session to conduct the work of the year, unless it is summoned earlier by the King for this purpose in accordance with Article 37.

The duration of each regular session shall not be less than three months, which shall not include the period of suspension pursuant to Article 38.

Art. 55. Parliament meets in public in the House of Parliament, but may debate *in camera* upon the request of ten members, provided a decision to this effect is reached in secret session by a majority; it then decides whether to repeat the debate on the same subject in public session.

Art. 56. Parliament cannot debate unless at least one third of the total number of its members are present, nor can it make any decision without an absolute majority of the members present, which majority shall under no circumstances be less than one fourth of the total number of deputies.

In the case of an equally divided vote the motion shall be rejected.

Art. 57. Every bill must have an explanatory report appended thereto and shall be referred to a Parliamentary Committee. After the Committee has submitted its report thereon or the term set for this purpose has expired the bill shall be introduced for discussion following an oral report thereon by the competent Minister or the rapporteur of the committee if no such report was made upon submission of the bill.

Bills designed to amend legislation on pensions or to grant a pension or to recognize services as affording the right to a pension shall be submitted only by the Minister of Finance following a recommendation of the Office of the Comptroller-General. In the case of pensions involving an increase in the budgetary expenditure of semi-governmental agencies the bill shall be submitted by the competent Minister and the Minister of Finance. Such bills on pensions must be specific, the insertion of provisions regarding pensions in laws designed to settle other matters being prohibited.

No bill involving an increase in budgetary expenditure, if submitted by the Ministers, shall be introduced for discussion unless accompanied by a report of the General Accounting Office determining the increase in expenditure or reduction in revenue involved. If submitted by Parliament the bill shall be transmitted before any discussion to the General Accounting Office which shall be obliged to submit its report within fifteen days. If by the end of this time no report has been submitted, the bill may be introduced for discussion without a report.

The same applies to amendments should the competent Ministers ask for a report, in which case the General Accounting Office shall be obliged to submit its report to Parliament within three days. Upon the expiration of this term the discussion may proceed without a report.

Every bill submitted by the Government and involving expenditure or a reduction in budgetary revenue shall be accompanied by a report on the manner of meeting the expenditure or reduction in revenue countersigned by the competent Minister and the Minister of Finance.

Bills submitted by the Government and imposing local or special taxes for the benefit of semi-governmental or private organizations or agencies shall be also countersigned by the Minister of Finance.

A bill designed to amend provisions of a previous law shall not be introduced for discussion unless there is recorded in its explanatory report the entire text of the provision to be amended and in its text the entire new provision as formulated following the amendment.

No addition or amendment to a bill not directly related to the main object of the bill shall be adopted.

No bill shall be adopted unless it has been discussed and voted upon by Parliament twice at two different meetings removed from each other by at least two days, in principle and by article during the first debate and by article and as a whole during the second debate. If during the second debate additions or amendments are adopted, the vote on the whole shall be postponed for twenty-four hours from the distribution of the amended draft.

The vote on a bill as a whole and by article in a single debate shall, by exception, be permitted if requested by the proposer before the bill has been referred to the committee provided for by paragraph 1 of this Article and provided that the committee in question has granted the request of the proposer and that no objection is raised by at least twenty deputies after submission of the bill up to the end of the debate thereon.

The voting of judicial or administrative codes compiled by special committees established under special laws may be effected by a separate law ratifying the codes as a whole.

The codification of existing provisions by a single classification thereof or the re-enactment as a whole of repealed laws, except for taxation laws, may be effected in the same manner.

Art. 58. No one shall without being summoned appear before Parliament to report on any matter either orally or in writing, but petitions may be presented through a Deputy or delivered to the Secretariat. Parliament shall have the right to forward petitions addressed to it to the Ministers, who shall be obliged to furnish the explanation demanded; Parliament may likewise appoint committees of its members for the purpose of conducting inquiries.

Art. 59. No tax shall be imposed or collected without a law. By exception, in the case of the imposition or increase of an import duty, the collection thereof shall be permitted as from the date of presentation to Parliament of the pertinent bill upon the express condition that the law be published at the latest within ten days from the end of the Parliamentary session.

The object of taxation, the rate of the tax and exemptions or exceptions from the tax as well as the granting of pensions may not be made the subject of legislative authorization.

Art. 60. In its annual ordinary session Parliament shall vote the budget for the following year and shall decide on the report on budget returns. All the revenues and expenditures of the State shall be shown in the budget and in the report on budget returns.

The budget shall be brought before Parliament two months before the beginning of the fiscal year, and after having been examined by a special committee of Deputies, it shall be voted once by chapter and article, in sections determined by the Regulations of Parliament, on four different days, the estimates of each Ministry being submitted to a vote by roll call.

Within at the latest one year from the end of the fiscal year the report on the budget returns thereof shall be brought before Parliament. After having been examined by a special committee of Deputies it shall be voted by Parliament in the manner determined by the Regulations of Parliament.

Art. 61. No salary, pension, grant or remuneration shall be either recorded in the budget of the State or granted unless it is provided for by an organizational or other special law.

Art. 62. A Deputy shall not be prosecuted or questioned in any way whatsover on account of an opinion or vote given by him in the exercise of his duties as Deputy.

Art. 63. During a Parliamentary term a deputy shall not be prosecuted, arrested or imprisoned without the leave of Parliament; such leave shall not be required in cases of crimes where the offender is taken in the act. No Deputy shall be subjected to personal detention during a Parliamentary term and four weeks after the termination thereof.

Should a Deputy happen to be under personal detention he shall be released without fail four weeks before the opening of the term.

Art. 64. Before entering upon their duties the Deputies shall take the following oath in the House of Parliament in public session:

"I swear in the name of the Holy, Consubstantial and Indivisible Trinity to observe loyalty to the Country and the Constitutional Monarch, and obedience to the Constitution and the laws of the State and to fulfil my duties conscientiously."

Instead of the invocation "I swear in the name of the Holy, Consubstantial and Indivisible Trinity," Deputies of other religions shall use in their oath the formula of their own religion.

Art. 65. Parliament shall determine by its Regulations how it will perform its duties and all details regarding its personnel.

Art. 66. Parliament shall be composed of Deputies lawfully elected by citizens having the right to vote and by direct, universal and secret ballot.

General elections shall be ordered and held simultaneously throughout the State.

Interpretative Clause: The exercise of the franchise may be rendered mandatory by law.

Art. 67. The Deputies represent the Nation and not only their constituency.

Art. 68. The number of Deputies of each electoral district shall be determined by law according to its population, but the total number of deputies shall in no case be less than 150 or more than 300.

The electoral system and the electoral districts shall be determined by a law voted pursuant to Article 22 hereof.

Art. 69. Deputies shall be elected for four consecutive years starting from the date of the general election; and upon the conclusion of the Parliamentary term, the holding of a general election within forty-five days shall be ordered by Royal Decree; and it shall be mandatory for the new Parliament to be convened in regular session within a further 45 days from the date of the general election.

A Parliamentary seat which becomes vacant during the last year of the Parliamentary term shall not be filled through a by-election, where such an election is required by law, unless the number of vacancies exceeds one quarter of the total number of Deputies.

Art. 70. In order to be elected Deputy one must be a Greek citizen, must have attained 25 years of age and must be a lawfully qualified voter.

A deputy who is deprived of these qualifications shall *ipso jure* forfeit the office of Deputy. Any dispute that may arise in this connection shall by resolved by Parliament.

Interpretative Clause: A law may determine the details for the exercise by women of the right to vote and be elected.

Art. 71. Salaried civil servants, members of the military on active service, mayors, notaries, registrars of mortgages and transfers and employees of semi-governmental agencies or organizations and members of the boards of directors thereof may not be elected Deputies nor nominated as candidates unless they resign before the nomination of candidates.

Their resignation shall be submitted in writing and their return to the office from which they resigned shall be prohibited for one year after elections.

Officers of the Armed and security Forces who resign in order to be elected as Deputies may not be nominated as candidates nor elected as Deputies in a district in which they served for over six months during the last two years before the elections, unless it is the district in which they have exercised their electoral rights; nor can they ever return to the Armed Forces.

Salaried civil servants may not be elected as Deputies nor nominated as candidates in the electoral district in which they were serving during the last three years before their election.

The duties of Deputy shall be incompatible with the functions of a director or other executive representative or salaried legal adviser or employee of a commercial firm or enterprise enjoying special privileges or receiving a regular subsidy by virtue of a special law. Persons coming under any of these categories must, within eight days from the time their election becomes final, declare their choice between the office of Deputy and the above-mentioned functions. Failing such declaration they shall *ipso facto* forfeit the office of Deputy.

It may be established by law that the office of Deputy shall be incompatible with further functions.

Deputies may not rent State-owned agricultural estates or undertake procurement for the State or contracts for the construction of public works or for the collection of public taxes or accept concessions on State-owned estates. Violation of the foregoing provision shall involve forfeiture of the office of Deputy and invalidity of the act.

Such acts shall also be null and void when they are performed by commercial companies or enterprises in which the functions of director or member of the board of directors or legal adviser are exercised by aDeputy or when the Deputy is a general partner or special partner thereof.

The restrictions instituted by paragraphs 3 and 4 shall not be applicable in the first elections to be held after the entry into force of this Constitution.

Interpretative Clauses: (1) The restriction provided under Article 71, paragraph 1, concerning the election as Deputy of members of the boards of directors of semi-governmental agencies and organizations shall become operative from the next general election.

(2) In the case of regular civil servants who do not have life tenure, the restriction provided under Article 71, paragraph 4, concerning election as Deputy or nomination as candidate shall apply only to the electoral district in which their seat is located.

Art. 72. Deputies who assume any of the duties or functions referred to in the preceding article shall *ipso facto* forfeit the office of Deputy.

A Deputy shall have the right to resign from the office of Deputy.

Parliament shall decide upon cases involving forfeiture of the office of Deputy pursuant to the provisions of the preceding and the present article.

Art. 73. The examination and verification of general election results, concerning the validity of which objections may be raised regarding either electoral irregularities during the conduct of the election or lack of qualifications, shall be referred to a special tribunal composed of the President of the Council of State or his substitute and an equal number of members of the Council of State and members of the Supreme Court chosen by lot. The tribunal shall be presided over by the President of the Council of State or should he be unable to attend, by the President of the Supreme Court provided he be a member of the Tribunal. In all other respects, the details regarding the functioning of the tribunal and its entire procedure shall be determined by law.

Art. 74. At the beginning of each Parliamentary session, Parliament shall elect its President, Vice-Presidents and secretaries from among the deputies.

Art. 75. Deputies shall receive from the public treasury compensation to be fixed from time to time by decision of Parliament, and shall be entitled to free travel on railway, street-car, air and automobile public transportation services and on ships flying the Greek flag or owned by Greek shipowners. Deputies shall be exempt from postal, telegraphic and telephone charges.

The regular President of Parliament shall receive a representation allowance equal to the compensation of the Prime Minister.

Should a Deputy be absent from more than five meetings in a month without the permission of Parliament during regular or extraordinary sessions, there shall be withheld for each absence one twentieth of the monthly compensation provided for by the present article.

The Government

Art. 76. The Council of Ministers consisting of the Ministers under the presidency of the Prime Minister constitutes the Government.

One or more Ministers may be appointed Deputy Prime Ministers by a decree issued at the instance of the Prime Minister.

In the absence of a Deputy Prime Minister, the Prime Minister shall, whenever necessary, appoint one of the Ministers as his provisional deputy.

Special legislation may determine the details concerning the office of Under-Secretaries, who shall not necessarily be precluded from being members of the Council of Ministers.

Art. 77. No member of the Royal family may be appointed Minister.

The provisions of paragraphs 5–9 of Article 71 specifying the functions incompatible with the duties of Deputy shall also apply to the duties of Minister and Under-Secretary.

Art. 78. The Government must enjoy the confidence of Parliament.

Upon its formation the Government must, and at any other time may, ask for a vote of confidence from Parliament. If upon the formation of the Government Parliament should be in adjournment, it shall be convened within 15 days in order to express its opinion on the Government.

Parliament may by a decision withdraw its confidence from the Government or from a member of the Government. A motion of lack of confidence may not be submitted before the lapse of two months from the rejection by Parliament of such a motion; it must be signed by at least 20 Deputies and must clearly specify the subjects around which the motion shall center.

A motion of lack of confidence may, by exception, be submitted before the lapse of the above mentioned two month term provided it is signed by half the total number of Deputies.

The debate on the motion of lack of confidence may not be held before two days have elapsed following its submission; nor can it be extended for more than five days.

The vote on a motion of confidence or lack of confidence may be postponed for forty-eight hours upon the request of twenty deputies.

A motion of confidence or no-confidence shall not be adopted unless it has the supporting vote of at least two fifths of the deputies.

The Ministers who are Deputies shall also be entitled to vote on such motions.

Ministers shall have free access to the meetings of Parliament and shall be given a hearing whenever they ask for the floor; they shall vote only if they are members of Parliament.

Parliament and Parliamentary Committees may require the presence of Ministers.

Art. 79. An order of the King, whether in writing or oral, shall under no circumstances release Ministers from responsibility.

Art. 80. Parliament shall have the right to impeach Ministers in accordance with the laws on the responsibility of Ministers before an *ad hoc* tribunal presided over the by President of the Supreme Court and composed of twelve judges chosen by lot by the President of Parliament in public session from among all the memberss of the Supreme Court and of the Courts of Appeal or Presidents thereof, who were appointed prior to the empeachment, in the manner more specifically prescribed by the law.

Interpretative Clause: The details concerning responsibility of Ministers shall be governed by the legislation in force prior to the promulgation of the Constitution of June, 3, 1927, which legislation shall be retained in force and shall be subject to amendment through legislative channels.

Art. 81. The King may grant a pardon to a Minister sentenced pursuant to the above provisions only with the consent of Parliament.

Administrative Justice

Art. 82. All administrative differences (contested administrative jurisdiction) shall be resolved by the regular administrative courts.

Regular administrative courts may be set up from time to time by special laws which shall also determine the cases subject to their jurisdiction.

The provisions of Article 90 shall also apply to the regular administrative judges, the Supreme Judicial Council being composed of members of the Council of State in a manner to be determined by law.

Art. 83. Within the province of the Council of State shall be particularly:

(a) The elaboration of regulative decrees.

(b) The trial of lawfully submitted differences regarding contested administrative jurisdiction.

(c) The annulment, upon petition, of acts of the administrative authorities on account of an exceeding of authority or violation of the law, pursuant to the more specific stipulations of the law.

(d) The petitioning for reversal of final decisions of the regular administrative courts on account of an exceeding of authority or violation of the law.

Further grounds for annulment and reversal may be established by law.

The provisions of Articles 92 and 93 of the Constitution shall be applicable in the cases referred to under (b), (c) and (d).

Art. 84. The number of members of the Council of State shall be determined by law, but may not exceed twenty-five.

The members of the Council of State shall be appointed by decree at the instance of the Council of Ministers and following an expression of the opinion of the Council of State; they shall be appointed for life and their life tenure shall be protected pursuant to the provisions of Article 88 and especially the provisions concerning members of the Supreme Court.

The duties of the members of the Council of State shall be incompatible with the duties of any civil, municipal or ecclesiastical officer whatsoever excepting the duties of professor of a Law Faculty in the University or professor of law or economics in equivalent schools.

The qualifications of the members of the Council of State, the details regarding their retirement and regarding auxiliary personnel as well as all matters relating to the organization and functioning of the Council of State shall be determined by special law.

Art. 85. Conflicts (a) between judicial and administrative authorities, (b) between the Council of State and administrative authorities, and (c) between administrative and common courts shall be tried by a mixed tribunal consisting of an equal number of members of the Supreme Court and of the Council of State presided over by the Minister of Justice or his deputy designated by law.

Art. 86. Administrative differences shall, at present and until such time as regular administrative courts are established, continue to fall within the competence of the regular courts, by which they shall be tried as having priority under the law, except for these cases for which administrative courts are established by special law, which courts shall observe the provisions of Articles 92 and 93 of the Constitution. Until such time as special laws are promulgated the existing legislation on administrative jurisdiction shall be applicable.

Judicial Power

Art. 87. Justice shall badmie nistered by judges appointed by the King according to the law, which shall also determine their qualifications.

The compensation of judicial functionaries must be commensurate with their office.

The details concerning the rank and salary of judicial functionaries shall be determined by special laws.

Art. 88. Judges of the Supreme Court and of Courts of Appeal and of First Instance shall be appointed for life, while Prosecutors, Assistant Prosecutors, Justices of the Peace, judges of Petty Sessional Courts, clerks and assistent clerks of courts and of the offices of Prosecutors, notaries, registrars of mortgages and of transfers shall be permanent provided that the respective services shall exist. Judicial employees enjoying life tenure or permanency may not be discharged without a judicial decision either in consequence of a criminal conviction or because of disciplinary offenses or sickness or inadequacy, duly certified in such manner as the law directs and in accordance with the provisions of Article 92 and 93.

Members of the Supreme Court and Presidents and prosecutors of Courts of Appeal shall mandatorily retire from service upon attaining the age of seventy years, and the remaining salaried judicial functionaries upon attaining the age of sixty-five years.

Registrars of mortgages and notaries shall retire upon attaining the age of seventy-five years.

Art. 89. It shall be possible by law.

(a) to entrust the authorities exercising police duties with the trial of police offenses punishable by fine,

(b) to entrust agrarian security authorities with the trial of misdemeanors relating to farm lands and the personal claims arising therefrom. In both these cases the decisions issued shall be subject to appeal which shall have suspensive force, before the judicial authority;

(c) to settle details concerning juvenile courts, to which provisions of Article 87, first paragraph, and Article 92, 93 and 95 of the Constitution may not be applicable.

(d) to determine that popular judges may also participate in courts which shall try all kinds of labor disputes.

Art. 90. Judicial functionaries and judicial employees, except for personnel below the rank of clerk of the secretariat of courts and offices of prosecutors, notaries and registrars of mortgages and transfers, shall be appointed, transferred, detailed and promoted with the concurring opinion in writing, specifically supported in detail, of a Supreme Judicial Council consisting of members of the Supreme Court, in a manner prescribed by law.

Promotion to the office of President, Vice President and Public Prosecutor of the Supreme Court shall not fall within the competence of the Supreme Judicial Council.

The decisions of the Supreme Judicial Council and of the plenum of the Supreme Court and the administrative acts issued for the execution thereof shall not be subject to appeal before the Council of State.

Art. 91. The King may, on the recommendation of the Council of Ministers in case of a state of war or mobilization due to external dangers or of a serious disturbance of or manifest threat to public order and to the security of the country from internal dangers, suspend by Royal Decree throughout the country or in part thereof the operation of Articles 5, 6, 8, 10, 11, 12, 14, 20, 95 and 97 of the Constitution or certain of these articles and, by putting into effect the law on "state of siege" as this law may apply on each occasion, establish extraordinary tribunals.

This law may not be modified in the course of the work of the Parliament summoned for its application. All measures taken under authority of the present article shall without fail be announced to Parliament for approval or abrogation at its first meeting after their promulgation. If these measures be taken in the absence of Parliament the same Royal Decree shall, under penalty of nullity, summon Parliament to meet within ten days even though its term ended or it be dissolved; in either case Parliament shall decide on maintaining or abrogating the said decree.

The Parliamentary immunity provided for in Article 63 shall enter into effect as from publication of the said Royal Decree.

The effect of the above mentioned Royal Decrees shall not, in the case of war be extended beyond the end thereof; in all other cases their effect shall *ipso facto* terminate after two months from their promulgation unless in the meantime it be extended again with Parliament's permission.

Art. 92. The session of the courts of law shall be public, except when publicity would be detrimental to good morals or public order; but in such cases the courts shall issue a decision to that effect.

Art. 93. All judgments shall be duly supported and shall be pronounced in public sessions.

Art. 94. Trial by jury shall be maintained.

Art. 95. Trial by jury shall be given to criminal and political offenses as well as offenses of the press, whenever such offenses do not concern one's private life, and to any other offenses which may by law be made liable to trial by jury. For the trial of the said offenses of the press, mixed courts may be established by law composed of regular judges and jurors the latter constituting the majority.

Criminal offenses which have thus far been brought within the jurisdiction of the Courts of Appeal by special laws and resolutions shall continue to be tried by such courts provided they are not by law again made liable to trial by jury.

Art. 96. No judge shall be permitted to accept another salaried post except that of University Professor.

Art. 97. The details regarding courts martial of the army, navy and air force, piracy, barratry and prize courts shall be regulated by special laws.

Civilians may not be brought under the jurisdiction of courts martial of the army, navy of air force except for punishable acts affecting the security of the armed forces.

The Council of Comptrollers

Art. 98. The councillors and associates of the Council of Comptrollers shall be appointed for life and shall not be discharged except pursuant to the conditions of Article 88. They shall mandatorily retire from service upon attaining the age of seventy years. The qualifications of councillor and associate shall be prescribed by law.

Appointment or promotion to the posts of councillors of the Council of Comptrollers shall be effected after the Council plenum has given its opinion thereon.

The provisions on the functions incompatable with the office of Councillor of State shall apply also to the members of the Council of Comptrollers holding life tenure.

Decisions of the Council of Comptrollers concerning determination of responsibilities and the granting of pensions shall not be subject to the control of the Council of State.

The Administration of the State

Art. 99. The administrative organization of the State is based on decentralization and local self-government as determined by law.

The election of municipal and communal authorities shall be effected by universal suffrage.

Art. 100. The civil servant shall be loyal and devoted to the Country and the national ideals; he shall execute the will of the State and serve the people.

Ideologies seeking to overthrow the existing political or social regime by violent means shall be absolutely contrary to the status of a civil servant.

Art. 101. The qualifications of administrative civil servants in general shall be prescribed by law.

Regular civil servants shall be permanent so long as the pertinent services and posts shall exist, and, except for cases of dismissal by virtue of a judicial decision, they shall not be transferred without an advisory opinion, or discharged or lowered in rank without a special decision of a council constituted according to law and consisting of at least two thirds of permanent civil servants. Appeal against this decision shall be permitted before the Council of State in a manner more specifically determined by law.

The above provisions shall also extend to the employees of Parliament, who in all other respects shall be governed exclusively by the Regulations of Parliament.

Exemptions from the provisions concerning qualifications and permanence may be introduced by law in the case of persons directly appointed, Ministers Plenipotentiary or Ministers resident, Governors-General, Secretaries General (of Ministries), Prefects, the representative of the State on the Holy Synod, employees of the Prime Minister's Political Bureau and of the private bureaus of Ministers and of the President of Parliament.

The provisions of the present and of the preceding articles shall be applied accordingly also in the case of municipal employees who occupy organic posts pursuant to the by-laws of the municipalities.

The provisions in question may be extended by law to include employees of communes.

Art. 102. No person may be appointed civil servant to a post not provided for by legislation.

No person may be appointed to more than one salaried post in the civil service or in a semi-governmental agency.

No civil servant may participate in more than two councils or committees.

The compensation or any other emoluments whatsoever paid for services rendered in Greece to a salaried civil servant out of the public treasury or treasuries of semi-governmental or private agencies holding a privilege from or contract with the State may under no circumstances exceed in monthly total the regular monthly remunerations of his organic post under penalty of dismissal. The details concerning control of observance of this article shall be determined by law.

Exceptions to paragraphs 2, 3 and 4 may be established by special laws in special cases; but under no circumstances shall it be permitted for a civil servant to be appointed to more than two posts nor for his additional emoluments to exceed twice the amount of his regular compensation from his organic posts.

The incompatibilities established under Article 71, paragraphs 5–9, shall be applicable also in regard to salaried civil servants.

Interpretative Clause: The councils or committees of paragraph 3 of the present article shall be deemed to include the councils, and committees of semi governmental agencies or public utility establishments or banks, but not the service councils of the central service of the Ministry to which the civil servant belongs. The councils or committees of paragraph 3 of the present article do not include the councils whose members receive no additional remuneration for their work nor preparatory legislative committees.

Mount Athos

Art. 103. The Athos peninsula extending beyond Megali Vigla and constituting the district of Mount Athos shall, in accordance with its ancient privileged status, be a self-governed part of the Greek State whose sovereignty thereon shall remain unaffected. Spiritually Mount Athos shall come under the direct jurisdiction of the Oecumenical Patriarchate. All persons residing thereon shall acquire Greek nationality upon admission as novices or monks without any further formality.

Mount Athos shall, in accordance with its regime, be governed by its twenty holy monasteries, among which the entire peninsula is divided, and its territory shall be exempt from expropriation. The administration shall be exercised by representatives of its holy monasteries constituting the Holy Community. No change whatsoever shall be permitted in the administrative system or the number of monasteries of Mount Athos, nor in their hierarchy and their position in regard to their dependencies; and the dwelling there of heterodox or schismatic persons shall be prohibited.

The determination in detail of the Mount Athos regimes and the manner of operation thereof is affected by the Constitutional Charter of Mount Athos, which, with the co-operation of the State representative, is drawn up and voted by the twenty monasteries and ratified by the Oecumenical Patriarchate and the Parliament of the Hellenes.

The correct observance of the Mount Athos regime shall in the spiritual field be under the supreme supervision of the Oecumenical Patriarchate and in the administrative field under the supervision of the State which shall also be exclusively responsible for safeguarding public order and security.

The above mentioned powers of the State shall be exercised through a governor whose rights and duties, as well as the judicial power exercised by the monastic authorities and the holy community, and lastly the customs and taxation privileges of Mount Athos, shall be determined by law.

Transitional Provisions

Art. 104. For the purpose of settling landless farmers and landless small scale breeders of livestock and for a period of three years from the date of entry into force hereof, compulsory expropriation shall be permitted in contravention of Article 17 hereof and in a manner to be determined by law, of the following categories of rural estates:

(a) Tracts of open land of over five hundred stremmas of self-cultivated or two hundred and fifty stremmas of non-self-cultivated land owned entirely or as co-owner by private individuals or private corporations.

(b) Cultivated or arable land as well as grassland or plantations owned by public corporations of any kind whatsoever; in the case of municipalities or communes after their opinion has been heard. The landed property of charitable institutions pursuing educational or philanthropic ends shall be exempt from any compulsory expropriation under the terms hereof.

(c) Grasslands over one thousand stremmas or, if the owner be a livestock breeder, over the area required to meet his present needs or his requirements prior to 1940, in a manner to be prescribed by law.

Expropriation and compulsory renting under the terms hereof of fields, forest land and grassland belonging to the ecclesiastical estate shall be regulated by a law issued once and for all.

Olive groves, vineyards, and gardens as well as urban ecclesiastical property shall be exempt from expropriation and compulsory renting under the term of the present article.

The compensation shall be fixed in terms of the metallic drachma under all circumstances by judicial process at a sum which shall in no case be less than one third of the value of the property expropriated at the time of entry into possession thereof and which shall be paid prior to or after entry into possession, either by instalments or in a manner to be determined by law.

All laws heretofore promulgated on the buying off of long-lease estates, the release from long-term tenancy or quit-rent burdens, and the compulsory renting of lands to landless farmers and livestock breeders, shall be deemed not to be repugnant to the Constitution.

In contravention of Article 17 of the Constitition it shall be permitted by legislation to provide for the adjustment or dissolution of such long term tenancies of fields and quit-rent burdens as may still exist, for the buying off of full ownership by holders of emphyteutic holdings, for the abolition and adjustment of real relations of a peculiar nature, and for the taking of measures against the subdivision or re-establishment of small parcels of landed property being unduly subdivided.

Interpretative Clause: *Plantations shall include also olive groves and olive tree properties* (ἐλαιοκτήματα) *of all kinds.*

Art. 105. All laws and decrees, insofar as they are inconsistent with the present Constitution, are hereby abolished.

General Provisions

Art. 106. The alteration of the contents or conditions of a will or donation, insofar as its provisions in favor of the State or for the public benefit are concerned, is prohibited.

By exception, it shall be permitted by law to make a bequest or donation available for another similar purpose when it becomes absolutely impossible to carry out the will of the donor or testator.

Art. 107. The official language of the State is that in which the Constitution and the laws of Greece are drawn up, and any attempt to corrupt it is prohibited.

Art. 108. Revision of the entire Constitution is prohibited.

The provisions of the present Constitution, which determine the regime as that of a crowned democracy as well as its fundamental provisions, shall under no circumstances be revised.

The non-fundamental provisions of the Constitution may be revised whenever Parliament by two thirds of all its members calls for a revision by a special act which shall specifically designate the provisions to be revised and which shall be voted on two occasions removed from each other by at least one month.

Once the revision has been decided upon by Parliament the following Parliament in its first session shall by an absolute majority of the total number of its members decide on the provisions to be revised.

Every revision of non-fundamental provisions of the Constitution which is adopted shall be issued and published in the *Official Gazette* within ten days from its passage by Parliament and shall be put into effect by a resolution of Parliament.

Art. 109. Co-operatives, both agricultural and urban, are under the protection of the State which shall systematically provide for their development.

Interpretative Clause: The establishment of a compulsory co-operative according to the law is not, in itself, contrary to the Constitution.

Art. 110. Suits of wrongful judgment instituted against members of the Council of State, Supreme Court, Courts of Appeal and of First Instance, prosecutors, assistant prosecutors, judges of administrative courts and life members of the Council of Comptrollers shall be tried by a special tribunal of seven members constituted in such manner as the law directs of members chosen by lot as follows: one member of the Council of State, one member of the Supreme Court, one member of the Council of Comptrollers, three lawyers, who shall be regular substitute members of the Supreme Disciplinary Council and two professors of the Law Faculty of the University of Athens. No permission shall be required to institute a suit of wrongful judgment.

In each case, the member of the particular body upon whose action or omission, on the part of either the entire body or members thereof, the tribunal is called upon to render judgment shall not be included among the members of this tribunal.

Art. 111. Disciplinary authority over the members of the Council of Comptrollers, of the Supreme Court and of the Council of State shall be exercised also by a council, consisting of two members from each of these bodies and two University professors of the Law Faculty, all of whom shall be chosen by lot and presided over by the Minister of Justice.

In each case, those members of the particular body upon whose action, on the part of either the entire body or members thereof, the Council is called upon to render judgment shall not be included among the members of this Council.

Art. 112. A law to be issued once and for all shall provide for the protection of funds imported from abroad for investment in the country.

Art. 113. The present Constitution shall enter into effect upon being signed by the King and the Council of Ministers must publish it in the *Official Gazette* within twenty-four hours therefrom.

Art. 114. Observance of the present Constitution is committed to the patriotism of the Greeks.

HUNGARY

SUMMARY

INTERNATIONAL STATUS

Hungary is a member of the United Nations (December 14, 1955). It was a member of the League of Nations. It is a member of the Council of Mutual Economic Assistence, the Warsaw Treaty and of other international organizations.

The first republic in Hungary was born during the 1848–1849 war of independence when the first representative Hungarian National Assembly dethroned the House of Hapsburg and proclaimed the independence of Hungary on April 14, 1849. After the collapse of the struggle for independence, Hungary again became part of the Austro-Hungarian Monarchy. Within the Monarchy it was, in accordance with the Austro-Hungarian Compromise (*Ausgleich*) of 1867, a state with equal rights, united in a dualist system with Austria by the common dynasty and the affairs recognized as common (foreign affairs, war and finance). Hungary had its own parliament and government. The second Hungarian republic was proclaimed on November 16, 1918, in the course of the 1918 revolution. Its political and legal status was defined by the "Popular Decision" issued by the National Council. A socialist revolution followed on March 21, 1919, and established the Socialist Federated Soviet Republic of Hungary with a constitution adopted by the National Assembly of Councils in July 1919, the first Hungarian constitutional charter which enacted the rights and duties of citizens. After the Soviet Republic had been defeated by force of arms, the kingdom was restored, but no king was elected; the functions of Head of State were exercised by Admiral Horthy as elected Regent.

On March 19, 1944, German troops occupied Hungary and on October 15, 1944, the Regent resigned and the Hungarian Fascists took power with a German army of occupation. On December 21, 1944, the Provisional National Assembly of elected popular representatives was constituted at Debreczen, declared itself the vehicle of Hungarian sovereignty and set up a Provisional Hungarian Government. Soviet troops occupied Hungary in 1945 and on January 17, 1946, the government proclaimed Hungary a republic, the Republic Act becoming effective on February 1st, 1946. The Treaty of Peace between Hungary and the Allied and Associated Powers was signed on February 10, 1947, and restored the frontiers of Hungary as they had existed on January 1st, 1938.

The Hungarian rising which began on October 23, 1956, with a demonstration in Budapest in favor of the same liberties Poland had just achieved, spread to all the country. After an initial success it was suppressed by Soviet troops who returned to the country on November 4. Certain of its claims have since been met.

FORM OF NATIONAL GOVERNMENT

The Constitution of August 20, 1949, declares that Hungary is a People's Republic, a state of workers and working peasants.[1] A section describes the social structure and form of the economy.[2] All power belongs to the working people.[3]

RIGHTS OF THE PEOPLE

The Constitution provides the right to work and remuneration, rest and recreation, protection of health and assistance in the event of disability,

[1] Const., Art. 1, 2. [2] Id., Art. 4–9. [3] Id., Art. 2.

the right to education, equality before the law, equal rights for women and men, forbids discrimination, protects the institution of marriage and the family as well as the interests of young people; safeguards the liberty of conscience of the citizens, freedom of the press, assembly and the right of organization, freedom and inviolability of the person, privacy of correspondence and domicile, the right of asylum.[1] The Constitution admits and protects property acquired as a result of work and ensures the right to succession; private ownership and private enterprise shall not be inconsistent with the interests of the community.[2] Citizens are bound to defend the country.[3]

LEGISLATIVE DEPARTMENT

Legislative power is vested in Parliament which is the highest organ of state authority.[4] Members of Parliament are elected by the population on the basis of universal, equal and direct suffrage by secret ballot for a term of four years subject to dissolution.[5] The Presidential Council of the People's Republic, elected from among the members of Parliament and consisting of a President, two Vice-Presidents, a Secretary and seventeen members, exercises the functions of Parliament when the latter is not in session.[6] It discharges also the functions of Head of State; it may convene Parliament, hold plebiscites, conclude international treaties, award honors.[7] The Presidential Council is responsible to Parliament and its members may be recalled by the latter.[8] The Constitution may be amended only by a two-thirds vote of all the members of Parliament.[9]

EXECUTIVE DEPARTMENT

The highest organ of executive power is the Government, the Council of Ministers whose members are elected and relieved of office by Parliament.[10] The Government is responsible to Parliament, to which it has to render account of its work, and members of Parliament may interpellate the Government.[11] Provision is made for local organs of state power.[12]

JUDICIAL DEPARTMENT

Justice is administered by the Supreme Court and county and district courts.[13] Judges are independent, subject only to the law.[14] Judges of the Supreme Court are elected for a term of six years by Parliament and are accountable to it.[15] Judges are not empowered to modify statutory pro

[1] Id., Art. 45–58. [2] Id., Art. 8. [3] Id., Art. 59–61. [4] Id., Art. 10.
[5] Id., Art. 11, 18, 62, 63. [6] Id., Art. 19, 20. [7] Id., Art. 20.
[8] Id., Art. 21. [9] Id., Art. 15. [10] Id., Art. 22, 23. [11] Id., Art. 27.
[12] Id., Art. 29–35. [13] Id., Art. 36. [14] Id., Art. 41. [15] Id., Art. 39.

visions; the power to annul or modify statutory rules infringing the Constitution or laws rests with the Presidential Council under supervision exercised by Parliament.[1] Provision is made for a Chief Public Prosecutor elected by Parliament for a term of six years to watch over legality.[2]

AREA, POPULATION, ETC.

The area of Hungary is 93,060 square kilometres, its population 10,160,000 (1965). The language is Hungarian; national minorities are free to use their mother tongue before the authorities.[3] The capital is Budapest.

[1] Id., Art. 20. [2] Id., Art. 42, 43. [3] Id., Art. 49.

CONSTITUTION of HUNGARY[1]

August 20, 1949, as amended 1950, 1953, 1954, 1957

The armed forces of the great Soviet Union liberated our country from the yoke of the German fascists, crushed the power of the great landowners and capitalists who were ever hostile to the people, and opened the road of democratic progress to our working people. Having acceded to power in hard struggles fought against the masters and defenders of the old order, the Hungarian working class, in alliance with the working peasantry and with the generous assistance of the Soviet Union, rebuilt our war-ravaged country. Led by our working class hardened in the struggles of several decades, enriched by the experiences of the socialist revolution of 1919 and supported by the Soviet Union, our people began to lay down the foundations of socialism and now our country is advancing towards socialism along the road of people's democracy. The already realized achievements of this struggle and this constructive work, the fundamental changes effected in the economic and social structure of our country, are embodied in the Constitution of the Hungarian People's Republic, which also indicates the direction of our further advance.

SECTION I

THE HUNGARIAN PEOPLE'S REPUBLIC

Art. 1. Hungary is a People's Republic.

Art. 2. (1) The Hungarian People's Republic is a state of workers and working peasants.

(2) In the Hungarian People's Republic all power belongs to the working people. The workers of town and country exercise their power through their elected representatives who are responsible and accountable to the people.

Art. 3. The Hungarian People's Republic defends the power and liberty

[1] ***Constitution of the Hungarian People's Republic, Hungarian Review,*** **Budapest, 1959. Supplied by the Ministry of Foreign Affairs in January 1966. Ed.**

of the Hungarian working people and the independence of the country; it opposes every form of the exploitation of man by man and organizes the forces of society for socialist construction. In the Hungarian People's Republic the close alliance of the workers and working peasantry is made a reality under the leadership of the working class.

SECTION II

THE SOCIAL STRUCTURE

Art. 4. (1) In the Hungarian People's Republic the bulk of the means of production is owned, as public property, by the state, by public bodies or by co-operative organizations. Means of production may also be privately owned.

(2) In the Hungarian People's Republic the force directing the national economy is the state power of the people. The working people gradually dislodge the capitalist elements and consistently build up a socialist system of economy.

Art. 5. The economic life of the Hungarian People's Republic is determined by a state national-economic plan. Basing itself on the publicly owned enterprises, the state banking system and the agricultural machine stations, the state directs and controls the national economy with the object of expanding the forces of production, increasing the national wealth, raising to an ever higher level the material and cultural standards of the working people and strengthening the defences of the country.

Art. 6. The mineral resources, the forests, the waters, the natural sources of power, the mines, the large industrial enterprises, the means of communication, such as railway, road, water and air transport, the banks, the postal, telegraph and telephone services, the wireless, the state-sponsored agricultural enterprises, such as state farms, machine stations, irrigation works and the like, are the property of the state and of public bodies as trustees for the whole people. All foreign and all wholesale trade is carried on by state enterprises, all other trade is under state supervision.

Art. 7. (1) The Hungarian People's Republic recognizes and guarantees the right of the working peasants to the land and regards it as its duty to assist the socialist development of agriculture by establishing state farms and machine stations and giving every support to productive co-operative societies based on voluntary association and joint work.

(2) The state recognizes and supports every genuine co-operative movement of the workers that is directed against exploitation.

Art. 8. (1) The constitution recognizes and protects all property acquired by labor.

(2) Private property and private enterprise must not be such as will run counter to the public interest.

(3) The constitution guarantees the right of inheritance.

Art. 9. (1) In the Hungarian People's Republic labor is the base of the social order.

(2) Every able-bodied citizen has the right, and the duty to work to the best of his ability and is bound in honor to do so.

(3) By their labor, by participation in work competitions, by tightening labor discipline and improving working methods, the workers serve the cause of socialist construction.

(4) The Hungarian People's Republic strives to apply in practice the socialist principle: "From each according to his ability, to each according to his work."

SECTION III

THE HIGHEST ORGANS OF STATE AUTHORITY

Art. 10. (1) The highest organ of state authority in the Hungarian People's Republic is Parliament.

(2) Parliament exercises all the rights deriving from the sovereignty of the people and determines the organization, direction and conditions of government.

(3) In accordance with this its competence, Parliament:

(a) enacts laws,

(b) determines the state budget,

(c) decides the national economic plan,

(d) elects the Presidential Council of the People's Republic,

(e) elects the Council of Ministers,

(f) sets up and abolishes ministries and defines and changes the sphere of activity of the several ministries,

(g) decides upon declaring war and concluding peace,

(h) exercises the prerogative of amnesty.

Art. 11. (1) Parliament is elected for a term of four years.

(2) Members of Parliament may not be arrested or prosecuted without the consent of Parliament, except when taken in the act.

(3) All political, economic or other activity or conduct detrimental to the interests of the workers is incompatible with the quality of a Member of Parliament.

Art. 12. (1) Parliament meets in regular session not less than twice a year.

(2) Parliament must be convened at the written demand of one third of its members or if the Presidential Council of the People's Republic so decides.

(3) Parliament elects a speaker, two deputy speakers and six recorders from among its own members.

(4) The sessions of Parliament are convened by the Presidential Council of the People's Republic.

(5) Parliament lays own its down rules of procedure and agenda.

Art. 13. As a general rule, the sessions of Parliament are held in public. In exceptional cases Parliament may decide to hold a secret session.

Art. 14. (1) The right of legislation is vested in Parliament.

(2) Legislation can be initiated by the Presidential Council of the People's Republic, the the Council of Ministers and by any member of Parliament.

Art. 15. (1) Parliament can take valid decisions only if at least one half of its members are present.

(2) Parliament decides issues by a simple majority.

(3) Changes in the constitution require the votes of two thirds of the members of Parliament.

Art. 16. Acts passed by Parliament are signed by the President and Secretary of the Presidential Council of the People's Republic. New acts are promulgated by the President of the Presidential Council. Promulgation is effected by publication in the official gazette.

Art. 17. (1) Parliament may at need appoint, out of its own members, a committee to investigate any matter.

(2) It is the duty of all public authorities, offices and institutions as well as of all citizens to put at the disposal of such parliamentary committees all the data required by the committee and also to give evidence before the committee if required to do so.

Art. 18. (1) Parliament may pronounce its dissolution before the expiration of its term.

(2) In the event of war or other emergency, Parliament can prolong its mandate for a stated length of time.

(3) In the event of war or other emergency, the Presidential Council of the People's Republic can re-convene a Parliament that has already been dissolved. A Parliament thus convened can itself decide the duration of its mandate.

(4) In the event of dissolution a new Parliament must be elected within not more than three months from the day of dissolution.

(5) The newly elected Parliament must be convened by the Presidential Council of the People's Republic within one month of polling day.

Art. 19. (1) At its first sitting Parliament elects from among its own members the Presidential Council of the People's Republic, consisting of a President, two Vice-Presidents, a secretary and seventeen members.

(2) The Chairman of the Council of Ministers, its Deputy Chairmen and its members are ineligible for election to the Presidential Council of the People's Republic.

Art. 20. (1) The competence of the Presidential Council of the People's Republic extends to:

(a) issuing the writ for a general election;
(b) convening Parliament;
(c) initiating legislation;
(d) holding a plebiscite on matters of national importance;
(e) directing in the highest instance the work of the local organs of state power;
(f) concluding international treaties on behalf of the Hungarian People's Republic;
(g) ratifying international treaties;
(h) appointing diplomatic representatives and receiving the letters of credence of foreign diplomatic representatives;
(i) appointing the higher civil servants and the higher officers of the armed forces, in accordance with the provisions of the law;
(j) awarding the orders and titles instituted by Parliament and authorizing the acceptance of foreign orders and titles;
(k) exercising the prerogative of mercy;
(l) deciding issues specially submitted to its jurisdiction by an Act of Parliament.

(2) The Presidential Council of the People's Republic may annul or modify any by-law, regulation or measure introduced by central or local organs of government, if they infringe the constitution or are detrimental to the interests of the working people.

(3) The Presidential Council of the People's Republic may dissolve any local organ of government the activities of which infringe the constitution or are seriously detrimental to the interests of the working people.

(4) When Parliament is not in session, its functions are exercised by the Presidential Council of the People's Republic; that body cannot, however, change the constitution.

(5) The enactments of the Presidential Council of the People's Republic are law-decrees, which must, however, be submitted to Parliament at its next sitting.

(6) All decisions and measures taken by the Presidential Council of the People's Republic are signed by the President and the Secretary of that body; its decrees must be published in the official gazette.

Art. 21. (1) The term of office of the Presidential Council of the People's Republic expires when Parliament elects a new Presidential Council of the People's Republic.

(2) The Presidential Council of the People's Republic is responsible to Parliament and is under the obligation of rendering an account of its activities to Parliament.

(3) Parliament has the right to recall the Presidential Council of the People's Republic or any member of it.

(4) In order to make valid decisions, at least nine members of the Presidential Council of the People's Republic must be present, in addition to the President and the Secretary.

(5) The Presidential Council of the People's Republic draws up its own rules of procedure, which must be submitted to Parliament.

SECTION IV

THE HIGHEST ORGAN OF STATE ADMINISTRATION

Art. 22. The highest organ of state administration is the Council of Ministers of the Hungarian People's Republic (the Hungarian Revolutionary Workers' and Peasants' Government.)

Art. 23. (1) The Council of Ministers consists of

(a) the Chairman of the Council of Ministers;

(b) the Deputy Chairman or Chairmen of the Council of Ministers;

(c) the Minister or Ministers of State;

(d) the Ministers heading the various ministries, and the President of the National Planning Office.

(2) The Council of Ministers or single members of it are elected to, or relieved of, office by Parliament on the recommendation of the Presidential Council of the People's Republic.

(3) Members of the Council of Ministers who are not members of Parliament may attend the sittings of Parliament and take part in its debates.

Art. 24. The Ministries of the Hungarian People's Republic are listed in a separate statute.

Art. 25. (1) The Council of Ministers:

(a) directs the work of the ministries and of the other organs immediately subordinate to it;

(b) ensures the enforcement of the laws and of the decrees issued by the Presidential Council of the People's Republic;

(c) ensures the fulfilment of the economic plans;

(d) deals with all the matters referred, by provision of law, to its jurisdiction.

(2) In the execution of its duties the Council of Ministers may issue decrees which must not, however, infringe the law or the decrees issued by the Presidential Council of the People's Republic.

(3) Decrees issued by the Council of Ministers are signed by its Chairman. Such decrees must be published in the official gazette.

(4) The Council of Ministers is empowered to annul or modify any statutory provision or measure of any central or local organ of government if such statutory provisions, regulations or measures infringe the Constitution or are detrimental to the interests of the working people.

Art. 26. (1) The Chairman of the Council of Ministers presides over the meetings of the Council, provides for the execution of the orders and decisions of the Council and directs the work of the organs immediately subordinate to it.

(2) The Ministers direct the branches of state administration entrusted to them and the work of the organs immediately subordinate to them, in accordance with the laws and the decrees and decisions of the Council of Ministers.

(3) In the execution of their duties the Chairman of the Council of Ministers and the Ministers are empowered to issue decrees, which may not, however, infringe the laws of the People's Republic or the decrees made by the Presidential Council of the People's Republic or its Council of Ministers. Such decrees must be published in the official gazette.

Art. 27. (1) The Council of Ministers is responsible for its activities to Parliament and must render regular accounts of its work to that body.

(2) The Chairman of the Council of Ministers (or his Deputy) and its members are individually responsible for their actions and conduct. A special law regulates the implementation of this responsibility.

(3) Any member of Parliament may put to the Council of Ministers, its Chairman or members, questions relating to any matter within the competence of the persons named and such questions must be answered by them in the House of Parliament.

Art. 28. (1) The Council of Ministers may take measures on any matter touching state administration either directly or through one of its members.

(2) The Council of Ministers is empowered to take under its own immediate control any branch of the state administration and can set up special organs for this purpose.

SECTION V

THE LOCAL ORGANS OF STATE POWER

Art. 29. (1) For purposes of administration the territory of the Hungarian People's Republic is divided up into counties, districts, towns and boroughs. Larger towns and cities may be subdivided into smaller administrative units.

(2) Changes in the territorial jurisdiction of the various local administrative organs can be made by the organs of state power.

Art. 30. (1) The local organs of state power are the county council, the district council, the town council, the borough council and the town precinct council.

(2) The members of the councils are elected by the voters in the area in question, for a term of four years in accordance with the principles established in connection with the election of members of Parliament.

(3) The members of the local councils can be recalled by their constituents in accordance with the law.

Art. 31. (1) The local councils exercise their administrative functions in their area of jurisdiction in accordance with the constitutionally created laws, decrees and other enactments and within the limits defined by their superior organs.

(2) Local councils:

(a) direct the economic, social and cultural activities in their area;

(b) draw up—within the scope of the state plan of the national economy and the state budget—the local economic plan and budget and supervise their fulfilment;

(c) enforce the laws and the regulations made by superior organs;

(d) direct and supervise the activities of the state administrative and executive organs subordinate to them;

(e) ensure the maintenance of public order and the protection of public property;

(f) protect the rights of the workers;

(g) direct and supervise the activities of economic enterprises of a local character;

(h) give support to the co-operative societies of the workers;

(i) deal with all matters within their competence as defined by a valid enactment.

(3) Local councils can issue regulations within the area of their jurisdiction; but such regulations must not infringe the laws, law-decrees, or decrees issued by the Council of Ministers, the Ministers, or a superior council. The orders issued by local councils must be promulgated according to custom.

(4) Local councils can annul or modify the orders, decisions or measures of the councils subordinate to them, if such orders, decisions or measures infringe the constitution or a constitutionally created enactment.

Art. 32. (1) The local councils exercise their functions in close contact with the population, ensure the active participation of the workers in the work of local government and encourage initiative and vigilance on their part.

(2) Local councils must give an account of their activities to their constituents not less than twice every year.

Art. 33. (1) The executive and administrative organs of the local councils are the Executive Committees, which they elect from among their own members.

(2) The Executive Committee is presided over by a Chairman. Its business is conducted by a Secretary subordinate to the Chairman. The Chairman and his Deputy or Deputies, and the Secretary are elected by the Executive Committee from among its own members.

(3) The Executive Committees are responsible to the local councils that

have elected them, to the higher organs of state power, to the Executive Committees of the superior councils and to the Council of Ministers; in their activities they must comply with the directives of these organs.

(4) Local councils have the right to recall the Executive Committees as a whole or any of their members.

Art. 34. The special administrative functions of the local council are discharged by the special administrative agencies of the Executive Committees; the special administrative agencies are subordinate, on the one hand, to the Executive Committees and, on the other, to the superior special administrative apencies.

Art. 35. Detailed regulations relating to the activities of the local councils and executive committees are the subject of a special Act of Parliament.

SECTION VI

THE JUDICATURE

Art. 36. (1) In the Hungarian People's Republic justice is administered by the Supreme Court of the Hungarian People's Republic, by the county courts and the district courts.

(2) By provision of the law special courts may be set up to deal with specific groups of cases.

Art. 37. The courts are composed of judges and lay members. The law can establish exceptions from this rule.

Art. 38. The Supreme Court of the Hungarian People's Republic exercises the right of supervising in principle the judicial activities and practice of all other courts. For this purpose the Supreme Court can establish directives and take decisions on questions of principle, which are then binding for all courts.

Art. 39. (1) In the Hungarian People's Republic all judicial offices are filled by election and the elected judges may be recalled.

(2) The judges of the Supreme Court are elected for a period of five years, the judges of the county and district courts for a period of three years.

(3) The President and judges of the Supreme Court are elected by Parliament.

(4) The judges are accountable to their electors in respect of their judicial activities.

(5) The election of the judges of the county courts and district courts is regulated by rules laid down in a special enactment.

Art. 40. (1) The hearings before all courts of law are public unless otherwise prescribed by law.

(2) All those accused before the courts are guaranteed the right of defence during the judicial proceedings.

Art. 41. (1) The Courts of the Hungarian People's Republic punish the enemies of the working people, protect and safeguard the state, the social and economic order and the institutions of the people's democracy and the rights of the workers and educate the working people in the observance of the rules governing the life of a socialist commonwealth.

(2) Judges are independent and subject only to the law.

SECTION VII

THE PUBLIC PROSECUTOR

Art. 42. (1) The function of the Chief Public Prosecutor of the Hungarian People's Republic is to watch over the observance of the law.

(2) In the exercise of this function the Chief Public Prosecutor supervises the observance of the law by the ministries, the authorities, offices, institutions and other organs, by the local organs of the state executive and by the citizens.

(3) The Chief Public Prosecutor sees to it that all actions detrimental to, or endangering, the social order, security or independence of the Hungarian People's Republic be consistently prosecuted.

Art. 43. (1) The Chief Public Prosecutor of the Hungarian People's Republic is elected by Parliament for a period of six years. Parliament has the right to recall the Chief Public Prosecutor before the expiration of his term of office.

(2) The Chief Public Prosecutor is responsible and accountable to Parliament in respect of his official activities.

(3) Public prosecutors are appointed by the Chief Public Prosecutor of the Hungarian People's Republic.

(4) The organization of public prosecution is under the control and general direction of the Chief Public Prosecutor of the Hungarian People's Republic.

Art. 44. Public prosecutors proceed independently of the administrative organs and of local state power.

SECTION VIII

THE RIGHTS AND DUTIES OF CITIZENS

Art. 45. (1) The Hungarian People's Republic guarantees for its citizens the right to work and the right to remuneration in accordance with the quantity and quality of the work done.

(2) This right is implemented by the Hungarian People's Republic by means of the planned development of the forces of production and by a manpower policy based on economic planning.

Art. 46. (1) The Hungarian People's Republic ensures the right of rest and recreation for its citizens.

(2) This right is implemented by the Hungarian People's Republic by means of a legally determined working day, holidays with pay and the organization of the rest and recreation of the workers.

Art. 47. (1) The Hungarian People's Republic protects the health of the workers and assists them in the event of sickness or disability.

(2) The Hungarian People's Republic implements this protection and assistance by means of a comprehensive social insurance scheme and the organization of medical services.

Art. 48. (1) The Hungarian People's Republic ensures the right to education for every worker.

(2) The Hungarian People's Republic implements this right by means of an extension to all of the educational facilities, by means of a free and compulsory general schooling scheme, by the provision of secondary and higher schools, by educational facilities for adult workers and by financial aid to those receiving schooling of any kind.

Art. 49. (1) The citizens of the Hungarian People's Republic are equal before the law and enjoy equal rights.

(2) Discrimination of any kind against any citizen on grounds of sex, religion, or nationality is a severely punishable offence.

(3) The Hungarian People's Republic ensures to all nationalities living within its borders the possibility of education in their native tongue and the possibility of developing their national culture.

Art. 50. (1) In the Hungarian People's Republic women enjoy equal rights with men.

(2) The equal rights of women are implemented by the safeguarding of their working conditions on a par with those of men, maternity leave with pay in the event of pregnancy, increased legal protection of mother and child, and a system of maternity and child welfare institutions.

Art. 51. The Hungarian People's Republic protects the institution of marriage and the family.

Art. 52. The Hungarian People's Republic devotes special care to the education and development of the young and accords them special protection.

Art. 53. The Hungarian People's Republic effectively supports all scientific work serving the cause of the working people, as well as the arts which depict the life and struggle of the people, which describe reality, and proclaim the victory of the people. It gives every support to the emergence of intellectual workers loyal to the people.

Art. 54. (1) The Hungarian People's Republic safeguards the liberty of conscience of all citizens and the freedom of religious worship.

(2) In order to ensure the liberty of conscience, the Hungarian People's Republic separates the Church from the State.

Art. 55. (1) In accordance with the interests of the workers the Hungarian People's Republic ensures for its citizens freedom of speech, freedom of the press and freedom of assembly.

(2) In order to implement these freedoms, the state places at the disposal of the workers the material resources required.

Art. 56. (1) In order to develop the social, economic and cultural activities of the workers, the Hungarian People's Republic constitutionally guarantees the right of combination and assembly.

(2) In fulfilling its tasks, the Hungarian People's Republic bases itself on the organizations of the class-conscious workers. In order to defend the people's democracy, promote participation in socialist construction, widen the scope of cultural and educational work, implement the rights of the people and develop international solidarity, the workers establish trade unions, democratic organizations of women and young people as well as other mass organizations, which join their forces in the Democratic People's Front. These organizations put into practice the close co-operation and democratic unity of the industrial, agricultural and intellectual workers. The leading force in such political and social activities is the working class, guided by its vanguard and supported by the democratic unity of the whole people.

Art. 57. The Hungarian People's Republic safeguards the freedom and inviolability of the person, the privacy of the home and the correspondence of its citizens.

Art. 58. (1) The Hungarian People's Republic guarantees these basic freedoms to all workers living within its borders.

(2) Foreign citizens, persecuted for their democratic attitude or their activities in the interests of the liberation of the peoples, enjoy the right of asylum in the Hungarian People's Republic.

Art. 59. It is the fundamental duty of all citizens of the Hungarian People's Republic to defend the property of the people, consolidate social assets, increase the economic strength of the Hungarian People's Republic, raise the living standard and cultural level of the workers and strengthen the people's democratic system.

Art. 60. Military service is the honorable duty of the citizens of the Hungarian People's Republic in accordance with the law on universal military service.

Art. 61. (1) Defence of their country is the sacred duty of all citizens of the Hungarian People's Republic.

(2) Treason, violation of the military oath, desertion to the enemy, espionage and every action detrimental to the military strength of the country—constituting a betrayal of the cause of the country and of the workers—is subject to the severest penalties of the law.

SECTION IX

THE ELECTORAL SYSTEM

Art. 62. (1) Members of Parliament are elected by the citizens of the Hungarian People's Republic on the basis of universal, equal, and direct suffrage by secret ballot.

(2) The elected members are accountable to their constituents.

(3) The constituents have the right to recall their elected member of Parliament.

Art. 63. (1) All citizens of the Hungarian People's Republic who are of age have the right to vote.

(2) Enemies of the working people and those who are unsound of mind are excluded from the suffrage by law.

Art. 64. At elections every citizen entitled to vote has one vote and all votes are equal.

Art. 65. All citizens who have the vote are eligible for election.

Art. 66. Details of the election and recall of members of Parliament are laid down in a special Act of Parliament.

SECTION X

THE COAT OF ARMS, THE FLAG AND THE CAPITAL OF THE HUNGARIAN PEOPLE'S REPUBLIC

Art. 67. The coat of arms of the Hungarian People's Republic is:

An escutcheon with arched sides in the colors red, white and green, in a light-blue field surrounded by a wreath of wheat. The wreath of wheat is wound with a red-white-green ribbon from the left and with a red ribbon from the right. A five-pointed red star in the middle above the escutcheon radiates golden rays onto the field.

Art. 68. The flag of the Hungarian People's Republic is in the colors red, white and green.

Art. 69. The capital of the Hungarian People's Republic is the city of Budapest.

SECTION XI

FINAL PROVISIONS

Art. 70. (1) The Constitution of the Hungarian People's Republic enters into force on the day of its promulgation. Its enforcement is the duty of the Council of Ministers.

(2) The Council of Ministers has the duty of submitting to Parliament the bills required for the implementation of the constitution.

Art. 71. (1) The constitution is the fundamental law of the Hungarian People's Republic.

(2) The constitution as well as all constitutional enactments are obligatory for all organs of state power and all citizens alike.

ICELAND

SUMMARY

INTERNATIONAL STATUS

Iceland is a member of the United Nations (November 19, 1946). It is a member of the Nordic Council and of other international organizations.

The Althing (Parliament) of Iceland was established in 930 and was retained, although with curtailed legislative powers, as a court throughout the period of Iceland's forming part of the Danish Kingdom. The Althing was modernized in 1845, and in 1874, a constitution was granted to Iceland conferring some measure of autonomy. In 1918, the Treaty of Union with Denmark provided that Iceland was an independent state united in personal union with Denmark under the King. Iceland was occupied by British and United States military forces during the second World War. The Treaty of Union with Denmark expired on December 1, 1943, and on June 17, 1944, Iceland was proclaimed a republic.

FORM OF NATIONAL GOVERNMENT

The Constitution of June 17, 1944, as amended August 14, 1959, replaces the Constitution of May 18, 1920 and the Constitutional Acts of March 24, 1934, September 1, 1942 and December 15, 1942. It states that Iceland is a republic with a constitutional government.[1] The Evangelical-Lutheran Church is the State Church.[2]

RIGHTS OF THE PEOPLE

The Constitution guarantees freedom of religion, no detention without judicial ruling, inviolability of the dwelling, the right of private ownership, freedom of employment, public assistance, freedom of the press, association, assembly.[3] Citizens must defend the country.[4] Privileges for nobility, titles and rank are forbidden.[5]

LEGISLATIVE DEPARTMENT

Legislative power is jointly vested in the Parliament (Althing) and the President of the Republic.[6] The Althing is composed of 60 members elected by proportional representation as specified in the Constitution for a term of four years subject to dissolution; these members are then distributed one third into the Upper and two thirds into the Lower House.[7] It meets in one regular session a year.[8] Immunities of Parliament and of members are provided.[9] There are provisions concerning finance.[10]

EXECUTIVE DEPARTMENT

The executive power is exercised by the President and the Ministers who are responsible.[11] The President is elected by direct secret ballot for a term of four years.[12] He has the power of appointment, summons and dissolves the Althing, concludes treaties, has the right of pardon.[13] Ministers may attend meetings of the Althing but may vote only if members.[14]

[1] Const., Art. 1. [2] Id., Art. 62. [3] Id., Art. 63–74. [4] Id., Art. 75.
[5] Id., Art. 78. [6] Id., Art. 2. [7] Id., Art. 24, 31, 32.
[8] Id., Art. 35. [9] Id., Art. 36, 49. [10] Id., Art. 40–43.
[11] Id., Art. 2, 13, 14. [12] Id., Art. 5, 6. [13] Id., Art. 15, 20–24, 29.
[14] Id., Art. 51.

JUDICIAL DEPARTMENT

Judges are guided only by law.[1] The organization of the judiciary is established by law.[2]

AREA, POPULATION, ETC.

The area of Iceland is 102,819 square kilometres, its population (1964) 190,000. The capital is Reykjavik.

[1] Id., Art. 61. [2] Id., Art. 59.

CONSTITUTION of ICELAND[1]

June 17, 1944, as amended August 14, 1959

CHAPTER ONE

Art. 1. Iceland is a republic with a constitutional government.

Art. 2. The legislative power is jointly vested in the Althing (Parliament) and the President of the Republic of Iceland. The executive power is exercised by the President and other governmental authorities in accordance with this Constitution and other laws of the land. The judicial power is exercised by the judiciary

CHAPTER TWO

Art. 3. The President shall be elected by the people.

Art. 4. Any person not less than thirty-five years of age who fulfils the qualifications necessary to vote for the Althing, with the exception of the residence qualification, is eligible for the Presidency.

Art. 5. The President shall be elected by a direct, secret ballot of those who are entitled to vote for the Althing. A presidential candidate shall be formally proposed by not less than fifteen hundred voters and not more than three thousand. The candidate, if there is more than one, who receives the majority of votes, is the legally elected President. If there is only one candidate he is returned unopposed.

Further provisions shall be made by law for the candidature and election of the President, and it may be provided thereby that the number of proposers shall in each quarter of the country be proportionate to the number of voters.

Art. 6. The President's term of office begins on the first day of August and ends on the thirty-first day of July four years later. The election of the President takes place in June or July of the year in which the term ends.

Art. 7. If the President dies or resigns prior to the expiry of his term, a

[1] Published in English by the Information Office of the Ministry of Foreign Affairs, 1948, and supplied by them together with 1959 amendment in January 1966. Ed.

new President shall be elected for a period ending on the thirty-first day of July of the fourth year from the election.

Art. 8. If the office of President becomes vacant or if the President temporarily cannot hold office because of residence abroad, illness, or other reasons, the Prime Minister, the Speaker of the United Althing, and the Chief Justice of the Supreme Court shall exercise the presidential power. The Speaker of the United Althing shall preside at their meetings. In a divergence of opinion the majority shall prevail.

Art. 9. The President must not be a member of the Althing or receive emoluments in the interest of any public or private enterprise.

Allowances from the national treasury to the President or those who execute the presidential authority shall be established by law. It shall be unlawful to reduce presidential allowances during the term of office.

Art. 10. On assuming office the President takes an oath or makes an affirmation to uphold the Constitution. Two identical texts shall be made, one to be preserved by Althing and the second to be enrolled in the National Archives.

Art. 11. The President is not answerable for his official actions. The same applies to those who execute the presidential authority.

The President cannot be prosecuted on a criminal charge except with the consent of the Althing.

The President shall cease to hold office before his term expires if this is approved by a plebiscite held in accordance with a resolution adopted by three fourths of the members of the United Althing. This plebiscite shall be held within two calendar months from the date of adoption of the said resolution, during which period the President shall not hold office.

If the said resolution be defeated in the plebiscite, the Althing shall be immediately dissolved and preparations made for a new election.

Art. 12. The President shall have his residence in Reykjavík or the environs.

Art. 13. The President exercises his authority through his Ministers. The Cabinet has its seat in Reykjavík.

Art. 14. The Cabinet is responsible for all acts of the Government. The responsibility of Ministers is established by law. The Althing may impeach Ministers for the discharge of their official duties. The Court of Impeachment has jurisdiction in such matters.

Art. 15. The President appoints the Cabinet and accepts ministerial resignations. He determines the number of Ministers and assigns their duties.

Art. 16. The President presides over the State Council which is composed of his Ministers.

Laws and important Government measures shall be submitted to the President in Council.

Art. 17. Cabinet meetings shall be held in order to discuss new legislative proposals and important political measures. Furthermore, Cabinet meetings shall be held when one of the Ministers so desires. The Prime Minister shall preside over such Cabinet meetings.

Art. 18. The Minister who has proposed a measure shall, as a rule, submit it to the President.

Art. 19. The Presidential signature countersigned by a Minister validates a legislative measure or an act of Government.

Art. 20. The President shall make the appointments to all such offices as are provided by law.

No person may hold office unless he is an Icelandic citizen. Each official shall take an oath or make an affirmation to uphold the Constitution.

The President may remove from office any official whom he has appointed.

The President may transfer officials from one office to another on the condition that their official income shall not be diminished, and that they shall have an option between such transfer and retirement with a pension or old-age allowance as prescribed by law.

Certain classes of officials in addition to those mentioned in Article 61 may be legally exempted.

Art. 21. The President concludes treaties with other states. Except with the consent of the Althing, he may not make such agreements if they entail renouncement of or servitude on territory or territorial waters or if they imply constitutional changes.

Art. 22. The President shall summon the Althing every year and determine when the session shall close. The Althing must not adjourn till the Budget has been passed. The President may also summon the Althing to extraordinary sessions when necessary.

Art. 23. The President may adjourn meetings of the Althing for a certain period of time, but not for more than two weeks nor more than once a year. But the Althing may authorize the President to deviate from these provisions.

Art. 24. The President may dissolve the Althing. A new election must take place before two calendar months have elapsed from the date of dissolution. The Althing shall reassemble not later than eight calendar months after its dissolution.

Art. 25. The President may have Bills and proposals for resolutions submitted to the Althing.

Art. 26. If the Althing has passed a Bill it shall be submitted to the President for approval not later than two weeks after it has been passed, and upon such approval shall be enforced as law. If the President disapproves a Bill it shall nevertheless become valid but shall as soon as circumstances permit be submitted to a plebiscite by secret ballot and if rejected shall become invalid but otherwise retain its legal force.

Art. 27. All laws shall be published. The form of publication and the enforcement of laws shall be in accordance with the law of the land.

Art. 28. In the event of extreme urgency the President may issue provisional laws in the interval between sessions of the Althing. Such laws must not, however, be contrary to the Constitution and they shall always be submitted to the Althing as soon as it reassembles.

If the Althing does not approve a provisional law it shall become invalid.

A Provisional Budget may not be issued if the Althing has passed the Budget for the fiscal year.

Art. 29. The President may decide that the prosecution for an offence be withdrawn if there are cogent reasons. He grants pardon and amnesty. Except with the consent of the Althing he may not absolve a Minister from prosecution or from the sentence imposed by the Court of Impeachment.

Art. 30. The President grants, either in person or through the Government, exemptions from laws in accordance with the prevailing practice.

CHAPTER THREE

Art. 31. The Althing shall be composed of 60 members elected by the people in a secret ballot. There shall be:

(a) 25 members elected by proportional representation in five constituencies of 5 members each:
West Iceland: Borgarfjord, Akranes, Mýra, Snæfellsness and Hnappadal and Dala districts.
West Fjords: Bardastranda, West and North Isafjord and Strandа districts and Isafjord township.
North-West Iceland: West and East Húnavatn and Skagafjord districts with Saudarkrokur and Siglufjordur townships.
East Iceland: North and South Mula and East Skaftafell districts with Seydisfjord and Neskaupstad townships.
Reykjanes: Gullbringu and Kjosar district with Hafnarfjord, Keflavik and Kopavog townships.

(b) 12 members elected by proportional representation in 2 constituencies of 6 members each:
North-East Iceland: Seydisfjord, North and South Thingeyjar districts with Akureyri, Olafsfjord and Husavik townships.
South Iceland: West Skaftafell, Rangarvalla and Arnes districts with Westman Islands township.

(c) 12 members elected by proportional representation in Reykjavik.

(d) Eleven supplementary members for equalization between parties so that each of them shall be represented as nearly as possible in proportion to the number of votes obtained in the General Election.

Members shall be elected for four years. Each list of candidates shall, as a rule, contain twice the number of members to be elected in the constituency, and deputy members both for constituency and supplementary members shall be as many as those elected from the list.

Art. 32. The Althing is divided into an Upper and a Lower House. One third of the members sit in the Upper House and two thirds in the Lower House. Should the number of members be such as to make impossible a division by thirds the odd members shall sit in the Lower House.

Art. 33. All persons, men and women, who are 21 years of age or older at the time of election, are Icelandic subjects and have been domiciled in the country for 5 years prior to an election, shall have the right to vote. No person shall have the right to vote unless of unblemished character and financially responsible.

A married woman shall be considered financially responsible even though her property be held in the name of her husband.

Further enactments regarding parliamentary elections are laid down in the Election Act.

Art. 34. Every citizen qualified to vote is eligible for the Althing.

Judges who do not hold administrative office are not eligible for the Althing.

CHAPTER FOUR

Art. 35. The Althing shall be summoned for a regular session every year on the fifteenth day of February or, if a holiday, on the following weekday, unless the President has already appointed another date earlier in the year for the opening of the session.

This may be amended by law.

Art. 36. The Althing is inviolate. No person may disturb its peace or violate its freedom.

Art. 37. The Althing shall be convened in Reykjavík, but under special circumstances the President may convene the Althing at some other place in Iceland.

Art. 38. Each House is individually entitled to introduce and pass Bills and proposals for resolutions. Each House individually or unitedly may send addresses to the President.

Art. 39. Each House may appoint committees of its members in order to investigate important matters of public interest. The House may grant authority to such committees to demand reports, oral or written, from Government officials or private persons.

Art. 40. No tax may be imposed, altered or abolished except by law; nor may loans binding upon the State be raised, nor any State property or interest therein be sold or in any other way disposed of except by law.

Art. 41. No disbursements may be made unless authorized in the Budget or the Supplementary Budget.

Art. 42. A Finance Bill for the coming fiscal year containing an estimate of the revenue and expenditure of the State shall be submitted to the Althing immediately on reassembling for a regular session.

Finance Bills and Supplementary Finance Bills shall be introduced in the United Althing and passed in three readings.

Art. 43. The United Althing shall elect by proportional representation three salaried Auditors, who shall annually audit the national revenue and expenditure accounts to ascertain whether the entire revenue has been included and whether any unauthorized disbursements have been made. They may, individually or jointly, request all reports and documents which they may deem necessary. The accounts for each fiscal year shall then be incorporated into one aggregate account and a Bill for the approval thereof be submitted to the Althing together with the comments of the Auditors.

The Auditors are, individually or jointly, entitled to examine the accounts and books of the State Treasurer as well as those of the Ministries for the current or past year. They shall submit their comments, if any, to their successors in writing.

Art. 44. No Bill, with the exception of the Finance and the Supplementary Finance Bill, may be passed without three readings in each House.

Art. 45. The first House which passes a Bill shall submit the Bill in the form in which it was passed to the other House. Should amendments be made here the Bill shall be returned to its source of origin, where, if again amended, the same procedure shall be followed.

Should no agreement be reached both Houses shall meet in a conclave, and the matter be settled in one reading by the United Althing.

When the Althing meets in a joint session more than one half of the members of each House must be present and take part in the voting in order to constitute a quorum, the majority of votes prevailing in all particulars. Bills, other than Finance and Supplementary Finance Bills, shall not be finally passed unless supported by two thirds of the votes cast.

Art. 46. The Althing itself decides whether its members are legally elected and also whether a member is disqualified.

Art. 47. Each new member shall as soon as his election has been approved take an oath or make an affirmation to uphold the Constitution.

Art. 48. Members of the Althing are bound solely by their conviction and not by any orders from their constituents.

Government officials who may be elected to the Althing do not require the permission of the Government to accept election, but they must take measures for the discharge of their functions in a manner deemed satisfacotry by the Government and without expense to the Treasury.

Art. 49. No member may be arrested for debt during a session of the Althing without the permission of the House of which he is a member, nor may he be placed under restraint or an action brought against him unless he is found *in flagrante delicto*.

No member may be made responsible outside the Althing for statements made by him in the Althing, except with the permission of the House concerned.

Art. 50. If a member is disqualified he shall forfeit his seat.

Art. 51. Ministers by virtue of their office have the right to attend meetings of the Althing and are entitled to take part in the debates as often as they may desire, subject to parliamentary procedure; but they have a right to vote only if they are at the same time elected members of the Althing.

Art. 52. Each House and the United Althing elects its own Speaker.

Art. 53. Neither House may pass a resolution unless more than one half of the members of the House are present at the meeting and register their votes.

Art. 54. Each member is at liberty to introduce in the House of which he is a member any matter of general nature and to request a Ministerial report thereon, subject to the permission of that House.

Art. 55. Neither House may admit any matter unless introduced by a member of that House.

Art. 56. If a House does not find any reason to pass a resolution it may refer the subject to a Minister.

Art. 57. The meetings of both Houses and those of the United Althing shall be public. But the Speaker or the quorum stipulated by the rules of the House may demand that all non-members be excluded. The meeting shall then decide whether the matter shall be debated at a public or a closed session.

Art. 58. The rules of procedure of the United Althing and those of both Houses shall be determined by law.

CHAPTER FIVE

Art. 59. The organization of the judiciary cannot be established except by law.

Art. 60. The judges shall settle all disputes as to the extent of the power of administrative officers. But no one seeking a judicial ruling thereunto can evade obeying temporarily an order of the administrative officers by submitting the matter to judicial decision.

Art. 61. Judges shall in the performance of their official functions be guided solely by the law. Judges who do not also hold administrative offices cannot be discharged from office except by a judicial ruling, nor may they be transferred to another office against their will except in the event of re-organization of the judiciary. A judge who has reached the age of 65 may, however, be allowed to resign from office without reduction of salary.

CHAPTER SIX

Art. 62. The Evangelical-Lutheran Church shall be the State Church and as such it shall be supported and protected by the State.

This may be altered by law.

Art. 63. The people are entitled to form societies for the worship of God in conformity with their individual convictions; but nothing may be preached or practiced which is prejudicial to public order and morality.

Art. 64. No person may lose his civil or national rights on account of his religious conviction nor must he therefore refuse to perform any civic duty.

No person is obliged to contribute to any religious worship against his conviction.

If a person is not a member of the State Church of Iceland nor of any other recognized religion he shall pay to the University of Iceland or to a designated scholarship fund of that University dues otherwise payable to the Church.

This may be amended by law.

CHAPTER SEVEN

Art. 65. Any person who is arrested shall be brought before a judge without undue delay, and if not released at once, the judge shall, within 24 hours, give a reasoned ruling as to whether he shall be detained. If the person may be released on bail the ruling shall contain provisions as to its nature and amount.

An appeal to a higher court may immediately be made against a judicial ruling, the procedure of notification and appeal against such rulings being the same as in criminal cases.

No person may be taken into custody for an offence merely punishable by fines or imprisonment.

Art. 66. The home shall be inviolate. Houses may not be searched, nor any letters or other documents be detained and examined, except by judicial warrant or by a special provision of law.

Art. 67. The right of private ownership is inviolate. No one shall be forced to surrender his property unless required by public exigency, in which case a law must be passed and full compensation paid.

Art. 68. No alien may acquire citizenship except by law. The right of aliens to own immovable property shall be subject to law.

Art. 69. No restriction may be imposed upon individual freedom of employment, unless legislated for as being required by the common good.

Art. 70. Whosoever is unable to provide for himself or his dependents shall, subject to duties prescribed by law, be entitled to support from public funds, unless his maintenance rests upon others.

Art. 71. If parents cannot afford to educate their children, or if the children are orphaned or destitute, their education and maintenance must be defrayed from public funds.

Art. 72. Every person has the right to express his thoughts in print, but is responsible for such utterances before the courts. Censorship and other restrictions on the freedom of the press may never be enacted.

Art. 73. Societies may be formed for every lawful purpose without previous authorization. No society may be dissolved by act of Government, but it may be temporarily suspended, in which case an action for dissolution must immediately be brought.

Art. 74. People are entitled to assemble unarmed. The police have the right to be present at all public gatherings. Open-air meetings may be forbidden when it is feared that they may cause riots.

Art. 75. Every person able to carry arms shall be obliged to take part in the defence of the country according to provisions which may be detailed by law.

Art. 76. The right of autonomy of urban and rural communities under the supervision of the Government shall be determined by legislation.

Art. 77. Taxation shall be determined by legislation.

Art. 78. Privileges reserved for nobility, titles and rank must never be enacted.

Art. 79. Proposals, whether amendatory or supplementary to this Constitution, may be introduced at regular as well as extraordinary sessions of the Althing. If the proposal is passed by both Houses, the Althing shall be dissolved immediately and a General Election be held. If both Houses pass the resolution without amendments it shall be ratified by the President of the Republic and come into force as a Constitutional Act.

If the Althing passes an amendment to the status of the Church affairs, according to Article 62, it shall be submitted to a plebiscite by secret ballot for acceptance or rejection.

Art. 80. By this Constitutional Act the Constitution of the Kingdom of Iceland, of the eighteenth day of May nineteen hundred and twenty, the Constitutional Acts of the twenty-fourth of March nineteen hundred and thirty-four, of the first day of September nineteen hundred and forty-two and the fifteenth day of December nineteen hundred and forty-two shall cease to be in effect and become null and void.

Art. 81. This Constitutional Act comes into force when the Althing so resolves, provided that the Act has been passed in a secret ballot by the majority of voters in the country.

TEMPORARY PROVISIONS

Upon the coming into force of this Constitution the United Althing shall elect the President of Iceland for the first time in accordance with the provisions governing the election of the Speaker of the United Althing. The Presidential term of office shall expire on the thirty-first day of July nineteen hundred and forty-five.

Aliens who, prior to the coming into effect of this Constitution have been enfranchised and made eligible for the Althing or have obtained the right to hold public office shall retain the said rights. Danish citizens who under Article 75 of the Constitution of the eighteenth day of May nineteen hundred and twenty would have obtained such rights shall, from the coming into force of this Constitutional Act until six calendar months after negotiations regarding the rights of Danish citizens in Iceland can be commenced, also acquire and retain the said rights.

RESOLUTION

CONCERNING THE COMING INTO FORCE OF THE CONSTITUTION OF THE REPUBLIC OF ICELAND

(Passed by the Althing on the sixteenth day of June nineteen hundred and forty-four)

Whereas the provisions of Article 81 of the Constitution of the Republic of Iceland as to ballot by all voters of the country have been fulfilled,

The Althing with reference to the said Article

Resolves that the Constitution shall come into force upon Saturday the seventeenth day of June nineteen hundred and forty-four with a declaration by the Speaker of the United Althing in session.

In accordance with a declaration by the Speaker of the United Althing, convened at Lögberg on Thingvellir on the seventeenth day of June nineteen hundred and forty-four the Constitution came into force at two o'clock in the afternoon of that same day.

IRELAND

SUMMARY

INTERNATIONAL STATUS

Ireland is a member of the United Nations (December 14, 1955). It is a member of other international organizations. It was a member of the League of Nations.

Ireland became independent by the treaty of December 6, 1921, which created the Irish Free State with Dominion status from the twenty-six counties (the remaining six northern counties with a Protestant majority being governed from London).

The Act of Union with England of 1801, which abolished Ireland's separate parliament, aroused opposition from the beginning, the first result of which was the Catholic Emancipation Act in 1829, permitting Catholics to be elected to Parliament. In 1838, the Fenian brotherhood was formed as a secret society in the United States. Following upon the Great Famine, an attempted rebellion of the "Young Irelanders" in 1848, Fenian activities and pressures, reforms began to be considered: the Church of England was disestablished in 1869, the 1870 Land Act gave tenants security of tenure. The Home Rule League was formed in 1870 and the Land League was founded in 1879. The first two Home Rule bills in 1886 and 1893 were defeated. The third Home Rule bill was introduced in 1912 and passed in 1914 despite the organization of resistance in Ulster. Its application was postponed because of the outbreak of the First World War. The Easter Rebellion of 1916, proclaimed the Irish Republic and was repressed with severity. The Irish members of parliament constituted themselves as an Irish legislature in Dublin in January 1919, and proclaimed the formal constitution of a republic. This led to further British reprisals, guerrilla warfare, the Irish Republican Army. The Home Rule Act of 1920, created two Irish parliaments, one in Belfast and the other in Dublin. Ireland did not recognize the Act and the Parliament did not meet and the Anglo-Irish Treaty of December 1921, created the Free State. Neither partition nor dominion status being acceptable to De Valera and his followers, a civil war ensued upon the creation of the provisional government and the evacuation of British troops, which lasted from July 6, 1922 to May 1923. By the elections of August 1923, the Treaty was accepted by the country. The first constitution came into force on December 6, 1922. The Statute of Westminster of 1926 regulated the form and status of the Commonwealth. In 1936, a Constitutional Amendment Act withdrew all internal authority from the King and the new constitution of 1937, established Ireland as independent and sovereign. On December 2, 1948, with the repeal of the 1936 External Relations Act, Ireland ceased to be a member of the Commonwealth, and on April 18, 1949, it was proclaimed a republic.

FORM OF NATIONAL GOVERNMENT

The Constitution of July 1, 1937, as amended in 1939 and 1941, states that Ireland is a sovereign independent, democratic state and that the national territory consists of the whole island of Ireland, its islands and territorial seas.[1] All powers of government derive, under God, from the people.[2] The Constitution affirms the devotion of Ireland to the ideal of peace and co-operation among nations and its adherence to the principle of the pacific settlement of international disputes by international arbitration and judicial determination.[3] The special position of the Holy

[1] Const., Art. 2, 5. [2] Id., Art. 6. [3] Id., Art. 29.

Catholic Apostolic and Roman Church is recognized and other churches are listed as recognized.[1]

RIGHTS OF THE PEOPLE

The Constitution guarantees due process of law, equality before the law, personal liberty, inviolability of the dwelling, freedom of speech, press, assembly, association, forbids titles of nobility, unlawful detention.[2] It protects the family and marriage and forbids the dissolution of marriage.[3] Freedom of education and free primary education are guaranteed as are the right of private property under social justice, freedom of conscience and religion; discrimination on the grounds of religion is forbidden.[4] A section describes the directive principles of social policy, which are the care of Parliament but not enforceable in court, and include the promotion of welfare through fair distribution of material resources and the safeguarding of the economic interests of the weaker sections of the community.[5]

LEGISLATIVE DEPARTMENT

Legislative power is vested in a bilateral Parliament (the Oireachtas) composed of the House of Representatives (Dail Eireann) and the Senate (Seanad Eireann).[6] It meets in at least one session a year.[7] Immunities of of members are provided.[8] The Dail Eireann is composed of members representing constituencies elected by proportional representation for a term of seven years, subject to dissolution.[9] The Seanad Eireann is composed of 60 members, 11 nominated by the Prime Minister and 49 elected by and as specified in the Constitution for the same term as the Dail Eireann.[10] There are provisions relating to finances.[11] There is provision for submitting bills to referendum.[12]

EXECUTIVE DEPARTMENT

The President is elected by secret direct vote and proportional representation for a term of seven years and is eligible for reelection only once.[13] He has the power of appointment, summons and dissolves Parliament, promulgates the laws, has supreme command of the Armed Forces, the right of pardon.[14] The Prime Minister (Taoiseach) and the ministers form the government which must consist of not less than seven nor more than fifteen members and are appointed by the President; the Government

[1] Id., Art. 44. [2] Id., Art. 38, 40. [3] Id., Art. 41. [4] Id., Art. 42, 43, 44.
[5] Id., Art. 45. [6] Id., Art. 15. [7] Id., Art. 15:7. [8] Id., Art. 15:13.
[9] Id., Art. 16. [10] Id., Art. 18. [11] Id., Art. 17, 20, 21, 22, 33.
[12] Id., Art. 27. [13] Id., Art. 12. [14] Id., Art. 13, 28.

exercises the executive power.[1] It is collectively responsible to the Dail Eireann.[2] Ministers must be members of Parliament.[3] There is provision for a Council of State to aid and counsel the President composed of the Prime Minister and Vice-Prime Minister, the Chief Justice, the President of the High Court, the Chairmen of the two houses of Parliament, the Attorney General, former Presidents, Prime Ministers, Chief Justices and others appointed by the President.[4]

JUDICIAL DEPARTMENT

Justice is administered by judges in the Courts of First Instance and a Court of Final Appeal or Supreme Court.[5] The former include a High Court with original jurisdiction extending to questions as to the validity of any law having regard to the provisions of the Constitution.[6] Judges are appointed by the President for life, are independent in the execution of their judicial functions and may hold no other position.[7] Bills may be referred to the Supreme Court by the President for a decision on whether the bill or any of its provisions are repugnant to the Constitution.[8] There is provision for an Attorney General who is not a member of the Government.[9]

AREA, POPULATION, ETC.

The area of Ireland is 68,894 square kilometres, its population (1964) 2,849,000. The national and first official language is Irish, the second official language is English.[10] The capital is Dublin.

[1] Id., Art. 28:2. [2] Id., Art. 28:4. [3] Id., Art. 28:7. [4] Id., Art. 31.
[5] Id., Art. 34. [6] Id., Art. 34:3. [7] Id., Art. 35. [8] Id., Art. 26.
[9] Id., Art. 30. [10] Id., Art. 8.

CONSTITUTION of IRELAND[1]

July 1, 1937, as amended September, 1939, May 30, 1941

In the Name of the Most Holy Trinity, from Whom is all authority and to Whom, as our final end, all actions both of men and States must be referred,

We, the people of Éire,

Humbly acknowledging all our obligations to our Divine Lord, Jesus Christ, Who sustained our fathers through centuries of trial,

Gratefully remembering their heroic and unremitting struggle to regain the rightful independence of our Nation,

And seeking to promote the common good, with due observance of Prudence, Justice and Charity, so that the dignity and freedom of the individual may be assured, true social order attained, the unity of our country restored, and concord established with other nations,

Do hereby adopt, enact, and give to ourselves this Constitution.

THE NATION

Art. 1. The Irish nation hereby affirms its inalienable, and sovereign right to choose its own form of Government, to determine its relations with other nations, and to develop its life, political, economic and cultural, in accordance with its own genius and traditions.

Art. 2. The national territory consists of the whole island of Ireland, its islands and the territorial seas.

Art. 3. Pending the re-integration of the national territory, and without prejudice to the right of the Parliament and Government established by the Constitution to exercise jurisdiction over the whole of that territory, the laws enacted by that Parliament shall have the like area and extent of application as the laws of Saorstát Éireann and the like extra-territorial effect.

[1] "This text of the Constitution is a copy of the text prepared in accordance with Article 25 and enrolled in the Office of the Registrar of the Supreme Court on the 25th day of March 1942." Published by the Stationery Office, Dublin. Supplied by Departmant of External Affairs in February 1966. Ed.

THE STATE

Art. 4. The name of the State is *Éire*, or in the English language, *Ireland.*

Art. 5. Ireland is a sovereign, independent, democratic state.

Art. 6. (1) All powers of government, legislative, executive and judicial, derive, under God, from the people, whose right it is to designate the rulers of the State and, in final appeal, to decide all questions of national policy, according to the requirements of the common good.

(2) These powers of government are exercisable only by or on the authority of the organs of State established by this Constitution.

Art. 7. The national flag is the tricolour of green, white and orange.

Art. 8. (1) The Irish language as the national language is the first official language.

(2) The English language is recognised as a second official language.

(3) Provision may, however, be made by law for the exclusive use of either of the said languages for any one or more official purposes, either throughout the State or in any part thereof.

Art. 9. (1) 1. On the coming into operation of this Constitution any person who was a citizen of Saorstat Éireann immediately before the coming into operation of this Constitution shall become and be a citizen of Ireland.

2. The future acquisition and loss of Irish nationality and citizenship shall be determined in accordance with law.

3. No person may be excluded from Irish nationality and citizenship by reason of the sex of such person.

(2) Fidelity to the nation and loyalty to the State are fundamental political duties of all citizens.

Art. 10. (1) All natural resources, including the air and all forms of potential energy, within the jurisdiction of the Parliament and Government established by this Constitution and all royalties and franchises within that jurisdiction belong to the State subject to all estates and interests therein for the time being lawfully vested in any person or body.

(2) All land and all mines, minerals and waters which belonged to Saorstát Éireann immediately before the coming into operation of this Constitution belong to the State to the same extent as they then belonged to Saorstát Éireann.

(3) Provision may be made by law for the management of the property which belongs to the State by virtue of this Article and for the control of the alienation, whether temporary or permanent, of that property.

(4) Provision may also be made by law for the management of land, mines, minerals and waters acquired by the State after the coming into operation of this Constitution and for the control of the alienation, whether temporary or permanent, of the land, mines, minerals and waters so acquired.

Art. 11. All revenues of the State from whatever source arising shall, subject to such exception as may be provided by law, form one fund, and shall be appropriated for the purposes and in the manner and subject to the charges and liabilities determined and imposed by law.

THE PRESIDENT

Art. 12. (1) There shall be a President of Ireland (*Uachtarán na hÉireann*), hereinafter called the President, who shall take precedence over all other persons in the State and who shall exercise and perform the powers and functions conferred on the President by this Constitution and by law.

(2) 1. The President shall be elected by direct vote of the people.

2. Every citizen who has the right to vote at an election for members of Dáil Éireann shall have the right to vote at an election for President.

3. The voting shall be by secret ballot and on the system of proportional representation by means of the single transferable vote.

(3) 1. The President shall hold office for seven years from the date upon which he enters upon his office, unless before the expiration of that period he dies, or resigns, or is removed from office, or becomes permanently incapacitated, such incapacity being established to the satisfaction of the Supreme Court consisting of not less than five judges.

2. A person who holds, or who has held, office as President, shall be eligible for re-election to that office once, but only once.

3. An election for the office of President shall be held not later than, and not earlier than the sixtieth day before, the date of the expiration of the term of office of every President, but in the event of the removal from office of the President or of his death, resignation, or permanent incapacity established as aforesaid (whether occurring before or after he enters upon his office), an election for the office of President shall be held within sixty days after such event.

(4) 1. Every citizen who has reached his thirty-fifth year of age is eligible for election to the office of President.

2. Every candidate for election, not a former or retiring President, must be nominated either by

(i) not less than twenty persons, each of whom is at the time a member of one of the Houses of the Oireachtas, or

(ii) by the Councils of not less than four administrative Counties (including County Boroughs) as defined by law.

3. No person and no such Council shall be entitled to subscribe to the nomination of more than one candidate in respect of the same election.

4. Former or retiring Presidents may become candidates on their own nomination.

5. Where only one candidate is nominated for the office of President it shall not be necessary to proceed to a ballot for his election.

(5) Subject to the provisions of this Article, elections for the office of President shall be regulated by law.

(6) 1. The President shall not be a member of either House of the Oireachtas.

2. If a member of either House of the Oireachtas be elected President, he shall be deemed to have vacated his seat in that House.

3. The President shall not hold any other office or position of emolument.

(7) The first President shall enter upon his office as soon as may be after his election, and every subsequent President shall enter upon his office on the day following the expiration of the term of office of his predecessor or as soon as may be thereafter or, in the event of his predecessor's removal from office, death, resignation, or permanent incapacity established as provided by section 3 hereof, as soon as may be after the election.

8. The President shall enter upon his office by taking and subscribing publicly, in the presence of members of both Houses of the Oireachtas, of Judges of the Supreme Court and of the High Court, and other public personages, the following declaration:

"In the presence of Almighty God I do solemnly and sincerely promise and declare that I will maintain the Constitution of Ireland and uphold its laws, that I will fulfil my duties faithfully and conscientiously in accordance with the Constitution and the law, and that I will dedicate my abilities to the service and welfare of the people of Ireland. May God direct and sustain me."

(9) The President shall not leave the State during his term of office save with the consent of the Government.

(10) 1. The President may be impeached for stated misbehaviour.

2. The charge shall be preferred by either of the Houses of the Oireachtas, subject to and in accordance with the provisions of this section.

3. A proposal to either House of the Oireachtas to prefer a charge against the President under this section shall not be entertained unless upon a notice of motion in writing signed by not less than thirty members of that House.

4. No such proposal shall be adopted by either of the Houses of the Oireachtas save upon a resolution of that House supported by not less than two-thirds of the total membership thereof.

5. When a charge has been preferred by either House of the Oireachtas, the other House shall investigate the charge, or cause the charge to be investigated.

6. The President shall have the right to appear and to be represented at the investigation of the charge.

7. If, as a result of the investigation, a resolution be passed supported by not less than two thirds of the total membership of the House of the

Oireachtas by which the charge was investigated, or caused to be investigated, declaring that the charge preferred against the President has been sustained and that the misbehaviour, the subject of the charge, was such as to render him unfit to continue in office, such resolution shall operate to remove the President from his office.

(11) 1. The President shall have an official residence in or near the City of Dublin.

2. The President shall receive such emoluments and allowances as may be determined by law.

3. The emoluments and allowances of the President shall not be diminished during his term of office.

Art. 13. (1) 1. The President shall, on the nomination of Dáil Éireann, appoint the Taoiseach, that is, the head of the Government or Prime Minister.

2. The President shall, on the nomination of the Taoiseach with the previous approval of Dáil Éireann, appoint the other members of the Government.

3. The President shall, on the advice of the Taoiseach, accept the resignation or terminate the appointment of any member of the Government.

(2) 1. Dáil Éireann shall be summoned and dissolved by the President on the advice of the Taoiseach.

2. The President may in his absolute discretion refuse to dissolve Dáil Éireann on the advice of a Taoiseach who has ceased to retain the support of a majority in Dáil Éireann.

3. The President may at any time, after consultation with the Council of State, convene a meeting of either or both of the Houses of the Oireachtas.

(3) 1. Every Bill passed or deemed to have been passed by both Houses of the Oireachtas shall require the signature of the President for its enactment into law.

2. The President shall promulgate every law made by the Oireachtas.

(4) The supreme command of the Defence Forces is hereby vested in the President.

(5) 1. The exercise of the supreme command of the Defence Forces shall be regulated by law.

2. All commissioned officers of the Defence Forces shall hold their commissions from the President.

(6) The right of pardon and the power to commute or remit punishment imposed by any court exercising criminal jurisdiction are hereby vested in the President, but such power of commutation or remission may, except in capital cases, also be conferred by law on other authorities.

(7) 1. The President may, after consultation with the Council of State, communicate with the Houses of the Oireachtas by message or address on any matter of national or public importance.

2. The President may, after consultation with the Council of State, address a message to the Nation at any time on any such matter.

3. Every such message or address must, however, have received the approval of the Government.

(8) 1. The President shall not be answerable to either House of the Oireachtas or to any court for the exercise and performance of the powers and functions of his office or for any act done or purporting to be done by him in the exercise and performance of these powers and functions.

2. The behaviour of the President may, however, be brought under review in either of the Houses of the Oireachtas for the purposes of section 10 of Article 12 of this Constitution, or by any court, tribunal or body appointed or designated by either of the Houses of the Oireachtas for the investigation of a charge under section 10 of the said Article.

(9) The powers and functions conferred on the President by this Constitution shall be exercisable and performable by him only on the advice of the Government, save where it is provided by this Constitution that he shall act in his absolute discretion or after consultation with or in relation to the Council of State, or on the advice or nomination of, or on receipt of any other communication from, any other person or body.

(10) Subject to this Constitution, additional powers and functions may be conferred on the President by law.

(11) No power or function conferred on the President by law shall be exercisable or performable by him save only on the advice of the Government.

Art. 14. (1) In the event of the absence of the President, or his temporary incapacity, or his permanent incapacity established as provided by section 3 of Article 12 hereof, or in the event of his death, resignation, removal from office, or failure to exercise and perform the powers and functions of his office or any of them, or at any time at which the office of President may be vacant, the powers and functions conferred on the President by or under this Constitution shall be exercised and performed by a Commission constituted as provided in section 2 of this Article.

(2) 1. The Commission shall consist of the following persons, namely, the Chief Justice, the Chairman of Dáil Éireann (*An Ceann Comhairle*), and the Chairman of Seanad Éireann.

2. The President of the High Court shall act as a member of the Commission in the place of the Chief Justice on any occasion on which the office of Chief Justice is vacant or on which the Chief Justice is unable to act.

3. The Deputy Chairman of Dáil Éireann shall act as a member of the Commission in the place of the Chairman of Dáil Éireann on any occasion on which the office of Chairman of Dáil Éireann is vacant or on which the said Chairman is unable to act.

4. The Deputy Chairman of Seanad Éireann shall act as a member of

the Commission in the place of the Chairman of Seanad Éireann on any occasion on which the office of Chairman of Seanad Éireann is vacant or on which the said Chairman is unable to act.

(3) The Commission may act by any two of their number and may act notwithstanding a vacancy in their memberschip.

(4) The Council of State may by a majority of its members make such provision as to them may seem meet for the exercise and performance of the powers and functions conferred on the President by or under this Constitution in any contingency which is not provided for by the foregoing provisions of this Article.

(5) 1. The provisions of this Constitution which relate to the exercise and performance by the President of the powers and functions conferred on him by or under this Constitution shall subject to the subsequent provisions of this section apply to the exercise and performance of the said powers and functions under this Article.

2. In the event of the failure of the President to exercise or perform any power or function which the President is by or under this Constitution required to exercise or perform within a specified time, the said power or function shall be exercised or performed under this Article, as soon as may be after the expiration of the time so specified.

THE NATIONAL PARLIAMENT

Constitution and Powers

Art. 15. (1) 1. The National Parliament shall be called and known, and is in this Constitution generally referred to, as the Oireachtas.

2. The Oireachtas shall consist of the President and two Houses, viz.: a House of Representatives to be called Dáil Éireann and a Senate to be called Seanad Éireann.

3. The Houses of the Oireachtas shall sit in or near the City of Dublin or in such other place as they may from time to time determine.

(2) 1. The sole and exclusive power of making laws for the State is hereby vested in the Oireachtas: no other legislative authority has power to make laws for the State.

2. Provision may however be made by law for the creation or recognition of subordinate legislatures and for the powers and functions of these legislatures.

(3) 1. The Oireachtas may provide for the establishment or recognition of functional or vocational councils representing branches of the social and economic life of the people.

2. A law establishing or recognising any such council shall determine its rights, powers and duties, and its relation to the Oireachtas and to the Government.

(4) 1. The Oireachtas shall not enact any law which is in any respect repugnant to this Constitution or any provision thereof.

2. Every law enacted by the Oireachtas which is in any respect repugnant to this Constitution or to any provision thereof, shall, but to the extent only of such repugnancy, be invalid.

(5) The Oireachtas shall not declare acts to be infringements of the law which were not so at the date of their commission.

(6) 1. The right to raise and maintain military or armed forces is vested exclusively in the Oireachtas.

2. No military or armed force, other than a military or armed force raised and maintained by the Oireachtas, shall be raised or maintained for any purpose whatsoever.

(7) The Oireachtas shall hold at least one session every year.

(8) 1. Sittings of each House of the Oireachtas shall be public.

(2) In cases of special emergency, however, either House may hold a private sitting with the assent of two thirds of the members present.

(9) 1. Each House of the Oireachtas shall elect from its members its own Chairman and Deputy Chairman, and shall prescribe their powers and duties.

2. The remuneration of the Chairman and Deputy Chairman of each House shall be determined by law.

(10) Each House shall make its own rules and standing orders, with power to attach penalties for their infringement, and shall have power to ensure freedom of debate, to protect its official documents and the private papers of its members, and to protect itself and its members against any person or persons interfering with, molesting or attempting to corrupt its members in the exercise of their duties.

(11) 1. All questions in each House shall, save as otherwise provided by this Constitution, be determined by a majority of the votes of the members present and voting other than the Chairman or presiding member.

2. The Chairman or presiding member shall have and exercise a casting vote in the case of an equality of votes.

3. The number of members necessary to constitute a meeting of either House for the exercise of its powers shall be determined by its standing orders.

(12) All official reports and publications of the Oireachtas or of either House thereof and utterances made in either House wherever published shall be privileged.

(13) The members of each House of the Oireachtas shall, except in case of treason as defined in this Constitution, felony or breach of the peace, be privileged from arrest in going to and returning from, and while within the precincts of, either House, and shall not, in respect of any utterance

in either House, be amenable to any court or any authority other than the House itself.

(14) No person may be at the same time a member of both Houses of the Oireachtas, and, if any person who is already a member of either House becomes a member of the other House, he shall forthwith be deemed to have vacated his first seat.

(15) The Oireachtas may make provision by law for the payment of allowances to the members of each House thereof in respect of their duties as public representatives and for the grant to them of free travelling and such other facilities (if any) in connection with those duties as the Oireachtas may determine.

Dáil Éireann

Art. 16. (1) 1. Every citizen without distinction of sex who has reached the age of twenty-one years, and who is not placed under disability or incapacity by this Constitution or by law, shall be eligible for membership of Dáil Éireann.

2. Every citizen without distinction of sex who has reached the age of twenty-one years who is not disqualified by law and complies with the provisions of the law relating to the election of members of Dáil Éireann, shall have the right to vote at an election for members of Dáil Éireann.

3. No law shall be enacted placing any citizen under disability or incapacity for membership of Dáil Éireann on the ground of sex or disqualifying any citizen from voting at an election for members of Dáil Éireann on that ground.

4. No voter may exercise more than one vote at an election for Dáil Éireann, and the voting shall be by secret ballot.

(2) 1. Dáil Éireann shall be composed of members who represent constituencies determined by law.

2. The number of members shall from time to time be fixed by law, but the total number of members of Dáil Éireann shall not fixed at less than one member for each thirty thousand of the population, or at more than one member for each twenty thousand of the population.

3. The ratio between the number of members to be elected at any time for each constituency and the population of each constituency, as ascertained at the last preceding census, shall, so far as it is practicable, be the same throughout the country.

4. The Oireachtas shall revise the constituencies at least once in every twelve years, with due regard to changes in distribution of the population, but any alterations in the constituencies shall not take effect during the life of Dáil Éireann sitting when such revision is made.

5. The members shall be elected on the system of proportional representation by means of the single transferable vote.

6. No law shall be enacted whereby the number of members to be returned for any constituency shall be less than three.

(3) 1. Dáil Éireann shall be summoned and dissolved as provided by section 2 of Article 13 of this Constitution.

2. A general election for members of Dáil Éireann shall take place not later than thirty days after a dissolution of Dáil Éireann.

(4) 1. Polling at every general election for Dáil Éireann shall as far as practicable take place on the same day throughout the country.

2. Dáil Éireann shall meet within thirty days from that polling day.

(5) The same Dáil Éireann shall not continue for a longer period than seven years from the date of its first meeting: a shorter period may be fixed by law.

(6) Provision shall be made by law to enable the member of Dáil Éireann who is the Chairman immediately before a dissolution of Dáil Éireann to be deemed without any actual election to be elected a member of Dáil Éireann at the ensuing general election.

(7) Subject to the foregoing provisions of this Article, elections for membership of Dáil Éireann, including the filling of casual vacancies, shall be regulated in accordance with law.

Art. 17. (1) 1. As soon as possible after the presentation to Dáil Éireann under Article 28 of this Constitution of the Estimates of receipts and the Estimates of expenditure of the State for any financial year, Dáil Éireann shall consider such Estimates.

2. Save in so far as may be provided by specific enactment in each case, the legislation required to give effect to the Financial Resolutions of each year shall be enacted within that year.

(2) Dáil Éireann shall not pass any vote or resolution, and no law shall be enacted, for the appropriation of revenue or other public moneys unless the purpose of the appropriation shall have been recommended to Dáil Éireann by a message from the Government signed by the Taoiseach.

Seanad Éireann

Art. 18. (1) Seanad Éireann shall be composed of sixty members, of whom eleven shall be nominated members and forty-nine shall be elected members.

(2) A person to be eligible for membership of Seanad Éireann must be eligible to become a member of Dáil Éireann.

(3) The nominated members of Seanad Éireann shall be nominated, with their prior consent, by the Taoiseach who is appointed next after the re-assembly of Dáil Éireann following the dissolution thereof which occasions the nomination of the said members.

(4) The elected members of Seanad Éireann shall be elected as follows:

i. Three shall be elected by the National University of Ireland.

ii. Three shall be elected by the University of Dublin.

iii. Forty-three shall be elected from panels of candidates constituted as hereinafter provided.

(5) Every election of the elected members of Seanad Éireann shall be held on the system of proportional representation by means of the single transferable vote, and by secret postal ballot.

(6) The members of Seanad Éireann to be elected by the Universities shall be elected on a franchise and in the manner to be provided by law.

(7) 1. Before each general election of the members of Seanad Éireann to be elected from panels of candidates, five panels of candidates shall be formed in the manner provided by law containing respectively the names of persons having knowledge and practical experience of the following interests and services, namely:

(i) National Language and Culture, Literature, Art, Education and such professional interests as may be defined by law for the purpose of this panel;

(ii) Agriculture and allied interests, and Fisheries;

(iii) Labour, whether organised or unorganised;

(iv) Industry and Commerce, including banking, finance, accountancy, engineering and architecture;

(v) Public Administration and social services, including voluntary social activities.

2. Not more than eleven and, subject to the provisions of Article 19 hereof, not less than five members of Seanad Éireann shall be elected from any one panel.

(8) A general election for Seanad Éireann shall take place not later than ninety days after a dissolution of Dáil Éireann, and the first meeting of Seanad Éireann after the general election shall take place on a day to be fixed by the President on the advice of the Taoiseach.

(9) Every member of Seanad Éireann shall, unless he previously dies, resigns, or becomes disqualified, continue to hold office until the day before the polling day of the general election for Seanad Éireann next held after his election or nomination.

(10) 1. Subject to the foregoing provisions of this Article elections of the elected members of Seanad Éireann shall be regulated by law.

2. Casual vacancies in the number of the nominated members of Seanad Éireann shall be filled by nomination by the Taoiseach with the prior consent of persons so nominated.

3. Casual vacancies in the number of the elected members of Seanad Éireann shall be filled in the manner provided by law.

Art. 19. Provision may be made by law for the direct election by any functional or vocational group or association or council of so many members of Seanad Éireann as may be fixed by such law in substitution for an equal number of the members to be elected from the corresponding panels of candidates constituted under Article 18 of this Constitution.

Legislation

Art. 20. (1) Every Bill initiated in and passed by Dáil Éireann shall be sent to Seanad Éireann and may, unless it be a Money Bill, be amended in Seanad Éireann and Dáil Éireann shall consider any such amendment.

(2) 1. A Bill other than a Money Bill may be initiated in Seanad Éireann, and if passed by Seanad Éireann, shall be introduced in Dáil Éireann.

2. A Bill initiated in Seanad Éireann if amended in Dáil Éireann shall be considered as a Bill initiated in Dáil Éireann.

(3) A Bill passed by either House and accepted by the other House shall be deemed to have been passed by both Houses.

Money Bills

Art. 21. (1) 1. Money Bills shall be initiated in Dáil Éireann only.

2. Every Money Bill passed by Dáil Éireann shall be sent to Seanad Éireann for its recommendations.

(2) 1. Every Money Bill sent to Seanad Éireann for its recommendations shall, at the expiration of a period not longer than twenty-one days after it shall have been sent to Seanad Éireann, be returned to Dáil Éireann, which may accept or reject all or any of the recommendations of Seanad Éireann.

2. If such Money Bill is not returned by Seanad Éireann to Dáil Éireann within such twenty-one days or is returned within such twenty-one days with recommendations which Dáil Éireann does not accept, it shall be deemed to have been passed by both Houses at the expiration of the said twenty-one days.

Art. 22. (1) 1. A Money Bill means a Bill which contains only provisions dealing with all or any of the following matters, namely, the imposition, repeal, remission, alteration or regulation of taxation; the imposition for the payment of debt or other financial purposes of charges on public moneys or the variation or repeal of any such charges; supply; the appropriation, receipt, custody, issue or audit of accounts of public money; the raising or guarantee of any loan or the repayment thereof; matters subordinate and incidental to these matters or any of them.

2. In this definition the expressions "taxation", "public money" and "loan" respectively do not include any taxation, money or loan raised by local authorities or bodies for local purposes.

(2) 1. The Chairman of Dáil Éireann shall certify any Bill which, in his opinion, is a Money Bill to be a Money Bill, and his certificate shall,

subject to the subsequent provisions of this section, be final and conclusive.

2. Seanad Éireann, by a resolution, passed at a sitting at which not less than thirty members are present, may request the President to refer the question whether the Bill is or is not a Money Bill to a Committee of Privileges.

3. If the President after consultation with the Council of State decides to accede to the request he shall appoint a Committee of Privileges consisting of an equal number of members of Dáil Éireann and of Seanad Éireann and a Chairman who shall be a Judge of the Supreme Court: these appointments shall be made after consultation with the Council of State. In the case of an equality of votes but not otherwise the Chairman shall be entitled to vote.

4. The President shall refer the question to the Committee of Privileges so appointed and the Committee shall report its decision thereon to the President within twenty-one days after the day on which the Bill was sent to Seanad Éireann.

5. The decision of the Committee shall be final and conclusive.

6. If the President after consultation with the Council of State decides not to accede to the request of Seanad Éireann, or if the Committee of Privileges fails to report within the time hereinbefore specified the certificate of the Chairman of Dáil Éireann shall stand confirmed.

Time for Consideration of Bills

Art. 23. (1) This Article applies to every Bill passed by Dáil Éireann and sent to Seanad Éireann other than a Money Bill or a Bill the time for the consideration of which by Seanad Éireann shall have been abridged under Article 24 of this Constitution.

1. Whenever a Bill to which this Article applies is within the stated period defined in the next following sub-section either rejected by Seanad Éireann or passed by Seanad Éireann with amendments to which Dáil Éireann does not agree or is neither passed (with or without amendment) nor rejected by Seanad Éireann within the stated period, the Bill shall, if Dáil Éireann so resolves within one hundred and eighty days after the expiration of the stated period be deemed to have been passed by both Houses of the Oireachtas on the day on which the resolution is passed.

2. The stated period is the period of ninety days commencing on the day on which the Bill is first sent by Dáil Éireann to Seanad Éireann or any longer period agreed upon in respect of the Bill by both Houses of the Oireachtas.

(2) 1. The preceding section of this Article shall apply to a Bill which

is initiated in and passed by Seanad Éireann, amended by Dáil Éireann, and accordingly deemed to have been initiated in Dáil Éireann.

2. For the purpose of this application the stated period shall in relation to such a Bill commence on the day on which the Bill is first sent to Seanad Éireann after having been amended by Dáil Éireann.

Art. 24. (1) If and whenever on the passage by Dáil Éireann of any Bill, other than a Bill expressed to be a Bill containing a proposal to amend the Constitution, the Taoiseach certifies by messages in writing addressed to the President and to the Chairman of each House of the Oireachtas that, in the opinion of the Government, the Bill is urgent and immediately necessary for the preservation of the public peace and security, or by reason of the existence of a public emergency, whether domestic or international, the time for the consideration of such Bill by Seanad Éireann shall, if Dáil Éireann so resolves and if the President, after consultation with the Council of State, concurs, be abridged to such period as shall be specified in the resolution.

(2) Where a Bill, the time for the consideration of which by Seanad Éireann has been abridged under this Article,

(a) is, in the case of a Bill which is not a Money Bill, rejected by Seanad Éireann or passed by Seanad Éireann with amendments to which Dáil Éireann does not agree or neither passed nor rejected by Seanad Éireann, or

(b) is, in the case of a Money Bill, either returned by Seanad Éireann to Dáil Éireann with recommendations which Dáil Éireann does not accept or is not returned by Seanad Éireann to Dáil Éireann,

within the period specified in the resolution, the Bill shall be deemed to have been passed by both Houses of the Oireachtas at the expiration of that period.

(3) When a Bill the time for the consideration of which by Seanad Éireann has been abridged under this Article becomes law it shall remain in force for a period of ninety days from the date of its enactment and no longer unless, before the expiration of that period, both Houses shall have agreed that such law shall remain in for force a longer period and the longer period so agreed upon shall have been specified in resolutions passed by both Houses.

Signing and Promulgation of Laws

Art. 25. (1) As soon as any Bill, other than a Bill expressed to be a Bill containing a proposal for the amendment of this Constitution, shall have been passed or deemed to have been passed by both Houses of the Oireachtas, the Taoiseach shall present it to the President for his signature and for promulgation by him as a law in accordance with the provisions of this Article.

(2) 1. Save as otherwise provided by this Constitution, every Bill so presented to the President for his signature and for promulgation by him as a law shall be signed by the President not earlier than the fifth and not later than the seventh day after the date on which the Bill shall have been presented to him.

2. At the request of the Government, with the prior concurrence of Seanad Éireann, the President may sign any Bill the subject of such request on a date which is earlier than the fifth day after such date as aforesaid.

(3) Every Bill the time for the consideration of which by Seanad Éireann shall have been abridged under Article 24 of this Constitution shall be signed by the President on the day on which such Bill is presented to him for signature and promulgation as a law.

(4) 1. Every Bill shall become and be law as on and from the day on which it is signed by the President under this Constitution, and shall, unless the contrary intention appears, come into operation on that day.

2. Every Bill signed by the President under this Constitution shall be promulgated by him as a law by the publication by his direction of a notice in the *Iris Oifigiúil*, stating that the Bill has become law.

3. Every Bill shall be signed by the President in the text in which it was passed or deemed to hove been passed by both Houses of the Oireachtas, and if a Bill is so passed or deemed to have been passed in both the official languages, the President shall sign the text of the Bill in each of those languages.

4. Where the President signs the text of a Bill in one only of the official languages, an official translation shall be issued in the other official language.

5. As soon as may be after the signature and promulgation of a Bill as a law, the text of such law which was signed by the President or, where the President has signed the text of such law in each of the official languages, both the signed texts shall be enrolled for record in the office of the Registrar of the Supreme Court, and the text, or both the texts, so enrolled shall be conclusive evidence of the provisions of such law.

6. In case of conflict between the texts of a law enrolled under this section in both the official languages, the text in the national language shall prevail.

(5) 1. It shall be lawful for the Taoiseach, from time to time as occasion appears to him to require, to cause to be prepared under his supervision a text (in both the official languages) of this Constitution as then in force embodying all amendments theretofore made therein.

2. A copy of every text so prepared, when authenticated by the signatures of the Taoiseach and the Chief Justice, shall be signed by the

President and shall be enrolled for record in the office of the Registrar of the Supreme Court.

3. The copy so signed and enrolled which is for the time being the latest text so prepared shall, upon such enrolment, be conclusive evidence of this Constitution as at the date of such enrolment and shall for that purpose supersede all texts of this Constitution of which copies were previously so enrolled.

4. In case of conflict between the texts of any copy of this Constitution enrolled under this section, the text in the national language shall prevail.

Reference of Bills to the Supreme Court

Art. 26. This Article applies to any Bill passed or deemed to have been passed by both Houses of the Oireachtas other than a Money Bill, or a Bill expressed to be a Bill containing a proposal to amend the Constitution, or a Bill the time for the consideration of which by Seanad Éireann shall have been abridged under Article 24 of this Constitution.

(1) 1. The President may, after consultation with the Council of State, refer any Bill to which this Article applies to the Supreme Court for a decision on the question as to whether such Bill or any specified provisions of such Bill is or are repugnant to this Constitution or to any provision thereof.

2. Every such reference shall be made not later than the seventh day after the date on which such Bill shall have been presented by the Taoiseach to the President for his signature.

3. The President shall not sign any Bill the subject of a reference to the Supreme Court under this Article pending the pronouncement of the decision of the Court.

(2) 1. The Supreme Court consisting of not less than five judges shall consider every question referred to it by the President under this Article for a decision, and, having heard arguments by or on behalf of the Attorney General and by counsel assigned by the Court, shall pronounce its decision on such question in open court as soon as may be, and in any case not later than sixty days after the date of such reference.

2. The decision of the majority of the judges of the Supreme Court shall, for the purposes of this Article, be the decision of the Court and shall be pronounced by such one of those judges as the Court shall direct, and no other opinion, whether assenting or dissenting, shall be pronounced nor shall the existence of any such other opinion be disclosed.

(3) 1. In every case in which the Supreme Court decides that any provision of a Bill the subject of a reference to the Supreme Court under this Article is repugnant to this Constitution or to any provision thereof, the President shall decline to sign such Bill.

2. If, in the case of a Bill to which Article 27 of this Constitution applies, a petition has been addressed to the President under that Article, that Article shall be complied with.

3. In every other case the President shall sign the Bill as soon as may be after the date on which the decision of the Supreme Court shall have been pronounced.

Reference of Bills to the People

Art. 27. This Article applies to any Bill, other than a Bill expressed to be a Bill containing a proposal for the amendment of this Constitution, which shall have been deemed, by virtue of Article 23 hereof, to have been passed by both Houses of the Oireachtas.

(1) A majority of the members of Seanad Éireann and not less than one third of the members of Dáil Éireann may by a joint petition addressed to the President by them under this Article request the President to decline to sign and promulgate as a law any Bill to which this Article applies on the ground that the Bill contains a proposal of such national importance that the will of the people thereon ought to be ascertained.

(2) Every such petition shall be in writing and shall be signed by the petitioners whose signatures shall be verified in the manner prescribed by law.

(3) Every such petition shall contain a statement of the particular ground or grounds on which the request is based, and shall be presented to the President not later than four days after the date on which the Bill shall have been deemed to have been passed by both Houses of the Oireachtas.

(4) 1. Upon receipt of a petition addressed to him under this Article, the President shall forthwith consider such petition and shall, after consultation with the Council of State, pronounce his decision thereon not later than ten days after the date on which the Bill to which such petition relates shall have been deemed to have been passed by both Houses of the Oireachtas.

2. If the Bill or any provision thereof is or has been referred to the Supreme Court under Article 26 of this Constitution, it shall not be obligatory on the President to consider the petition unless or until the Supreme Court has pronounced a decision on such reference to the effect that the said Bill or the said provision thereof is not repugnant to this Constitution or to any provision thereof, and, if a decision to that effect is pronounced by the Supreme Court, it shall not be obligatory on the President to pronounce his decision on the petition before the expiration of six days after the day on which the decision of the Supreme Court to the effect aforesaid is pronounced.

(5) 1. In every case in which the President decides that a Bill the subject of a petition under this Article contains a proposal of such national

importance that the will of the people thereon ought to be ascertained, he shall inform the Taoiseach and the Chairman of each House of the Oireachtas accordingly in writing under his hand and Seal, and shall decline to sign and promulgate such Bill as a law unless and until the proposal shall have been approved either

(i) by the people at a Referendum in accordance with the provisions of section 2 of Article 47 of this Constitution within a period of eighteen months from the date of the President's decision, or

(ii) by a resolution of Dáil Éireann passed within the said period after a dissolution and re-assembly of Dáil Éireann.

2. Whenever a proposal contained in a Bill the subject of a petition under this Article shall have been approved either by the people or by a resolution of Dáil Éireann in accordance with the foregoing provisions of this section, such Bill shall as soon as may be after such approval be presented to the President for his signature and promulgation by him as a law and the President shall thereupon sign the Bill and duly promulgate it as a law.

(6) In every case in which the President decides that a Bill the subject of a petition under this Article does not contain a proposal of such national importance that the will of the people thereon ought to be ascertained, he shall inform the Taoiseach and the Chairman of each House of the Oireachtas accordingly in writing under his hand and Seal, and such Bill shall be signed by the President not later than eleven days after the date on which the Bill shall have been deemed to have been passed by both Houses of the Oireachtas and shall be duly promulgated by him as a law.

THE GOVERNMENT

Art. 28. (1) The Government shall consist of not less than seven and not more than fifteen members who shall be appointed by the President in accordance with the provisions of this Constitution.

(2) The executive power of the State shall, subject to the provisions of this Constitution, be exercised by or on the authority of the Government.

(3) 1. War shall not be declared and the State shall not participate in any war save with the assent of Dáil Éireann.

2. In the case of actual invasion, however, the Government may take whatever steps they may consider necessary for the protection of the State, and Dáil Éireann if not sitting shall be summoned to meet at the earliest practicable date.

3. Nothing in this Constitution shall be invoked to invalidate any law enacted by the Oireachtas which is expressed to be for the purpose of securing the public safety and the preservation of the State in time of war or armed rebellion, or to nullify any act done or purporting to be done in time of war or armed rebellion in pursuance of any such law.

In this sub-section "time of war" includes a time when there is taking place an armed conflict in which the State is not a participant but in respect of which each of the Houses of the Oireachtas shall have resolved that, arising out of such armed conflict, a national emergency exists affecting the vital interests of the State and "time of war or armed rebellion" includes such time after the termination of any war, or of any such armed conflict as aforesaid, or of an armed rebellion, as may elapse until each of the Houses of the Oireachtas shall have resolved that the national emergency occasioned by such war, armed conflict, or armed rebellion has ceased to exist.

(4) 1. The Government shall be responsible to Dáil Éireann.

2. The Government shall meet and act as a collective authority, and shall be collectively responsible for the Departments of State administered by the members of the Government.

3. The Government shall prepare Estimates of the Receipts and Estimates of the Expenditure of the State for each financial year, and shall present them to Dáil Éireann for consideration.

(5) 1. The head of the Government, or Prime Minister, shall be called, and is in this Constitution referred to as, the Taoiseach.

2. The Taoiseach shall keep the President generally informed on matters of domestic and international policy.

(6) 1. The Taoiseach shall nominate a member of the Government to be the Tánaiste.

2. The Tánaiste shall act for all purposes in the place of the Taoiseach if the Taoiseach should die, or become permanently incapacitated, until a new Taoiseach shall have been appointed.

3. The Tánaiste shall also act for or in the place of the Taoiseach during the temporary absence of the Taoiseach.

(7) 1. The Taoiseach, the Tánaiste and the member of the Government who is in charge of the Department of Finance must be members of Dáil Éireann.

2. The other members of the Government must be members of Dáil Éireann or Seanad Éireann, but not more than two may be members of Seanad Éireann.

(8) Every member of the Government shall have the right to attend and be heard in each House of the Oireachtas.

(9) 1. The Taoiseach may resign from office at any time by placing his resignation in the hands of the President.

2. Any other member of the Government may resign from office by placing his resignation in the hands of the Taoiseach for submission to the President.

3. The President shall accept the resignation of a member of the Government, other than the Taoiseach, if so advised by the Taoiseach.

4. The Taoiseach may at any time, for reasons which to him seem suffi-

cient, request a member of the Government to resign; should the member concerned fail to comply with the request, his appointment shall be terminated by the President if the Taoiseach so advises.

(10) The Taoiseach shall resign from office upon his ceasing to retain the support of a majority in Dáil Éireann unless on his advice the President dissolves Dáil Éireann and on the reassembly of Dáil Éireann after the dissolution the Taoiseach secures the support of a majority in Dáil Éireann.

(11) 1. If the Taoiseach at any time resigns from office the other members of the Government shall be deemed also to have resigned from office, but the Taoiseach and the other members of the Government shall continue to carry on their duties until their successors shall have been appointed.

2. The members of the Government in office at the date of a dissolution of Dáil Éireann shall continue to hold office until their successors shall have been appointed.

(12) The following matters shall be regulated in accordance with law, namely, the organization of, and distribution of business amongst, Departments of State, the designation of members of the Government to be the Ministers in charge of the said Departments, the discharge of the functions of the office of a member of the Government during his temporary absence or incapacity, and the remuneration of the members of the Government.

INTERNATIONAL RELATIONS

Art. 29. (1) Ireland affirms its devotion to the ideal of peace and friendly co-operation amongst nations founded on international justice and morality.

(2) Ireland affirms its adherence to the principle of the pacific settlement of international disputes by international arbitration or judicial determination.

(3) Ireland accepts the generally recognised principles of international law as its rule of conduct in its relations with other States.

(4) 1. The executive power of the State in or in connection with its exernal relations shall in accordance with Article 28 of this Constitution be exercised by or on the authority of the Government.

2. For the purpose of the exercise of any executive function of the State in or in connection with its exernal relations, the Government may to such extent and subject to such conditions, if any, as may be determined by law, avail of or adopt any organ, instrument, or method of procedure used or adopted for the like purpose by the members of any group or league of nations with which the State is or becomes associated

for the purpose of international co-operation in matters of common concern.

(5) 1. Every international agreement to which the State becomes a party shall be laid before Dáil Éireann.

2. The State shall not be bound by any international agreement involving a charge upon public funds unless the terms of the agreement shall have been approved by Dáil Éireann.

3. This section shall not apply to agreements or conventions of a technical and administrative character.

(6) No international agreement shall be part of the domestic law of the State save as may be determined by the Oireachtas.

THE ATTORNEY GENERAL

Art. 30. (1) There shall be an Attorney General who shall be the adviser of the Government in matters of law and legal opinion, and shall exercise and perform all such powers, functions and duties as are conferred or imposed on him by this Constitution or by law.

(2) The Attorney General shall be appointed by the President on the nomination of the Taoiseach.

(3) All crimes and offences prosecuted in any court constituted under Article 34 of this Constitution other than a court of summary jurisdiction shall be prosecuted in the name of the People and at the suit of the Attorney General or some other person authorised in accordance with law to act for that purpose.

(4) The Attorney General shall not be a member of the Government.

(5) 1. The Attorney General may at any time resign from office by placing his resignation in the hands of the Taoiseach for submission to the President.

2. The Taoiseach may, for reasons which to him seem sufficient, request the resignation of the Attorney General.

3. In the event of failure to comply with the request, the appointment of the Attorney General shall be terminated by the President if the Taoiseach so advises.

4. The Attorney General shall retire from office upon the resignation of the Taoiseach, but may continue to carry on his duties until the successor to the Taoiseach shall have been appointed.

(6) Subject to the foregoing provisions of this Article, the office of Attorney General, including the remuneration to be paid to the holder of the office, shall be regulated by law.

THE COUNCIL OF STATE

Art. 31. (1) There shall be a Council of State to aid and counsel the President on all matters on which the President may consult the said Council in relation to the exercise and performance by him of such of his powers and functions as are by this Constitution expressed to be exercisable and performable after consultation with the Council of State, and to exercise such other functions as are conferred on the said Council by this Constitution.

(2) The Council of State shall consist of the following members:

(i) As *ex-officio* members: the Taoiseach, the Tánaiste, the Chief Justice, the President of the High Court, the Chairman of Dáil Éireann, the Chairman of Seanad Éireann, and the Attorney General.

(ii) Every person able and willing to act as a member of the Council of State who shall have held the office of President or the office of Taoiseach, or the office of Chief Justice, or the office of President of the Executive Council of Saorstát Éireann.

(iii) Such other persons, if any, as may be appointed by the President under this Article to be members of the Council of State.

(3) The President may at any time and from time to time by warrant under his hand and Seal appoint such other persons as, in his absolute discretion, he may think fit, to be members of the Council of State, but not more than seven persons so appointed shall be members of the Council of State at the same time.

(4) Every member of the Council of State shall at the first meeting thereof which he attends as a member take and subscribe a declaration in the following form:

"In the presence of Almighty God I do solemnly and sincerely promise and declare that I will faithfully and conscientiously fulfil my duties as a member of the Council of State."

(5) Every member of the Council of State appointed by the President, unless he previously dies, resigns, becomes permanently incapacitated, or is removed from office, shall hold office until the successor of the President by whom he was appointed shall have entered upon his office.

(6) Any member of the Council of State appointed by the President may resign from office by placing his resignation in the hands of the President.

(7) The President may, for reasons which to him seem sufficient, by an order under his hand and Seal, terminate the appointment of any member of the Council of State appointed by him.

(8) Meetings of the Council of State may be convened by the President at such times and places as he shall determine.

Art. 32. The President shall not exercise or perform any of the powers or functions which are by this Constitution expressed to be exercisable or performable by him after consultation with the Council of State unless, and on every occasion before so doing, he shall have convened a meeting of the Council of State and the members present at such meeting shall have been heard by him.

THE COMPTROLLER AND AUDITOR-GENERAL

Art. 33. (1) There shall be a Comptroller and Auditor-General to control on behalf of the State all disbursements and to audit all accounts of moneys administered by or under the authority of the Oireachtas.

(2) The Comptroller and Auditor-General shall be appointed by the President on the nomination of Dáil Éireann.

(3) The Comptroller and Auditor-General shall not be a member of either House of the Oireachtas and shall not hold any other office or position of emolument.

(4) The Comptroller and Auditor-General shall report to Dáil Éireann at stated periods as determined by law.

(5) 1. The Comptroller and Auditor-General shall not be removed from office except for stated misbehaviour or incapacity, and then only upon resolutions passed by Dáil Éireann and by Seanad Éireann calling for his removal.

2. The Taoiseach shall duly notify the President of any such resolutions as aforesaid passed by Dáil Éireann and by Seanad Éireann and shall send him a copy of each such resolution certified by the Chairman of the House of the Oireachtas by which it shall have been passed.

3. Upon receipt of such notification and of copies of such resolutions, the President shall forthwith, by an order under his hand and Seal, remove the Comptroller and Auditor-General from office.

(6) Subject to the foregoing, the terms and conditions of the office of Comptroller and Auditor-General shall be determined by law.

THE COURTS

Art. 34. (1) Justice shall be administered in courts established by law by judges appointed in the manner provided by this Constitution, and, save in such special and limited cases as may be prescribed by law, shall be administered in public.

(2) The Courts shall comprise Courts of First Instance and a Court of Final Appeal.

(3) 1. The Courts of First Instance shall include a High Court invested with full original jurisdiction in and power to determine all matters and questions whether of law or fact, civil or criminal.

2. Save as otherwise provided by this Article, the jurisdiction of the High Court shall extend to the question of the validity of any law having

regard to the provisions of this Constitution, and no such question shall be raised (whether by pleading, argument or otherwise) in any Court established under this or any other Article of this Constitution other than the High Court or the Supreme Court.

3. No Court whatever shall have jurisdiction to question the validity of a law, or any provision of a law, the Bill for which shall have been rerred to the Supreme Court by the President under Article 26 of this Constitution, or to question the validity of a provision of a law where the corresponding provision in the Bill for such law shall have been referred to the Supreme Court by the President under the said Article 26.

4. The Courts of First Instance shall also include Courts of local and limited jurisdiction with a right of appeal as determined by law.

(4) 1. The Court of Final Appeal shall be called the Supreme Court.

2. The president of the Supreme Court shall be called the Chief Justice.

3. The Supreme Court shall, with such exceptions and subject to such regulations as may be prescribed by law, have appellate jurisdiction from all decisions of the High Court, and shall also have appellate jurisdiction from such decisions of other courts as may be prescribed by law.

4. No law shall be enacted excepting from the appellate jurisdiction of the Supreme Court cases which involve questions as to the validity of any law having regard to the provisions of this Constitution.

5. The decision of the Supreme Court on a question as to the validity of a law having regard to the provisions of this Constitution shall be pronounced by such one of the judges of that Court as that Court shall direct, and no other opinion on such question, whether assenting or dissenting, shall be pronounced, nor shall the existence of any such other opinion be disclosed.

6. The decision of the Supreme Court shall in all cases be final and conclusive.

(5) 1. Every person appointed a judge under this Constitution shall make and subscribe the following declaration:

> "In the presence of Almighty God I do solemnly and sincerely promise and declare that I will duly and faithfully and to the best of my knowledge and power execute the office of Chief Justice (*or as the case may be*) without fear or favour, affection or ill-will towards any man, and that I will uphold the Constitution and the laws. May God direct and sustain me."

2. This declaration shall be made and subscribed by the Chief Justice in the presence of the President, and by each of the other judges of the Supreme Court, the judges of the High Court and the judges of every other Court in the presence of the Chief Justice or the senior available judge of the Supreme Court in open court.

3. The declaration shall be made and subscribed by every judge before entering upon his duties as such judge, and in any case not later than

ten days after the date of his appointment or such later date as may be determined by the President.

4. Any judge who declines or neglects to make such declaration as aforesaid shall be deemed to have vacated his office.

Art. 35. (1) The judges of the Supreme Court, the High Court and all other Courts established in pursuance of Article 34 hereof shall be appointed by the President.

(2) All judges shall be independent in the exercise of their judicial functions and subject only to this Constitution and the law.

(3) No judge shall be eligible to be a member of either House of the Oireachtas or to hold any other office or position of emolument.

(4) 1. A judge of the Supreme Court or the High Court shall not be removed from office except for stated misbehaviour or incapacity, and then only upon resolutions passed by Dáil Éireann and by Seanad Éireann calling for his removal.

2. The Taoiseach shall duly notify the President of any such resolutions passed by Dáil Éireann and by Seanad Éireann, and shall send him a copy of every such resolution certified by the Chairman of the House of the Oireachtas by which it shall have been passed.

3. Upon receipt of such notification and of copies of such resolutions, the President shall forthwith, by an order under his hand and Seal, remove from office the judge to whom they relate.

(5) The remuneration of a judge shall not be reduced during his continuance in office.

Art. 36. Subject to the foregoing provisions of this Constitution relating to the Courts, the following matters shall be regulated in accordance with law, that is to say:

(i) the number of judges of the Supreme Court, and of the High Court, the remuneration, age of retirement and pensions of such judges,

(ii) the number of the judges of all other Courts, and their terms of appointment, and

(iii) the constitution and organization of the said Courts, the distribution of jurisdiction and business among the said Courts and judges, and all matters of procedure.

Art. 37. Nothing in this Constitution shall operate to invalidate the exercise of limited functions and powers of a judicial nature, in matters other than criminal matters, by any person or body of persons duly authorised by law to exercise such functions and powers, notwithstanding that such person or such body of persons is not a judge or a court appointed or established as such under this Constitution.

TRIAL OF OFFENCES

Art. 38. (1) No person shall be tried on any criminal charge save in due course of law.

(2) Minor offences may be tried by courts of summary jurisdiction.

(3) 1. Special courts may be established by law for the trial of offences in cases where it may be determined in accordance with such law that the ordinary courts are inadequate to secure the effective administration of justice, and the preservation of public peace and order.

2. The constitution, powers, jurisdiction and procedure of such special courts shall be prescribed by law.

(4) 1. Military tribunals may be established for the trial of offences against military law alleged to have been committed by persons while subject to military law and also to deal with a state of war or armed rebellion.

2. A member of the Defence Forces not on active service shall not be tried by any court-martial or other military tribunal for an offence cognisable by the civil courts unless such offence is within the jurisdiction of any court martial or other military tribunal under any law for the enforcement of military discipline.

(5) Save in the case of the trial of offences under section 2, section 3 or section 4 of this Article no person shall be tried on any criminal charge without a jury.

(6) The provisions of Articles 34 and 35 of this Constitution shall not apply to any court or tribunal set up under section 3 or section 4 of this Article.

Art. 39. Treason shall consist only in levying war against the State, or assisting any State or person or inciting or conspiring with any person to levy war against the State, or attempting by force of arms or other violent means to overthrow the organs of government established by this Constitution, or taking part or being concerned in or inciting or conspiring with any person to make or to take part or be concerned in any such attempt.

FUNDAMENTAL RIGHTS

Personal Rights

Art. 40. (1) All citizens shall, as human persons, be held equal before the law.

This shall not be held to mean that the State shall not in its enactments have due regard to differences of capacity, physical and moral, and of social function.

(2) 1. Titles of nobility shall not be conferred by the State.

2. No title of nobility or of honour may be accepted by any citizen except with the prior approval of the Government.

(3) 1. The State guarantees in its laws to respect, and, as far as practicable, by its laws to defend and vindicate the personal rights of the citizen.

2. The State shall, in particular, by its laws protect as best it may from unjust attack and, in the case of injustice done, vindicate the life, person, good name, and property rights of every citizen.

(4) 1. No citizen shall be deprived of his personal liberty save in accordance with law.

2. Upon complaint being made by or on behalf of any person to the High Court or any judge thereof alleging that such person is being unlawfully detained, the High Court and any and every judge thereof to whom such complaint is made shall forthwith enquire into the said complaint and may order the person in whose custody such person is detained to produce the body of such person before the High Court on a named day and to certify in writing the grounds of his detention, and the High Court shall, upon the body of such person being produced before that Court and after giving the person in whose custody he is detained an opportunity of justifying the detention, order the release of such person from such detention unless satisfied that he is being detained in accordance with the law.

3. Where the body of a person alleged to be unlawfully detained is produced before the High Court in pursuance of an order in that behalf made under this section and that Court is satisfied that such person is being detained in accordance with a law but that such law is invalid having regard to the provisions of this Constitution, the High Court shall refer the question of the validity of such law to the Supreme Court by way of case stated and may, at the time of such reference or at any time thereafter, allow the said person to be at liberty on such bail and subject to such conditions as the High Court shall fix until the Supreme Court has determined the question so referred to it.

4. The High Court before which the body of a person alleged to be unlawfully detained is to be produced in pursuance of an order in that behalf made under this section shall, if the President of the High Court or, if he is not available, the senior judge of that Court who is available so directs in respect of any particular case, consist of three judges and shall, in every other case, consist of one judge only.

5. Where an order is made under this section by the High Court or a judge thereof for the production of the body of a person who is under sentence of death, the High Court or such judge thereof shall further order that the execution of the said sentence of death shall be deferred until after the body of such person has been produced before the High Court and the lawfulness of his detention has been determined and if,

after such deferment, the detention of such person is determined to be lawful, the High Court shall appoint a day for the execution of the said sentence of death and that sentence shall have effect with the substitution of the day so appointed for the day originally fixed for the execution thereof.

6. Nothing in this section, however, shall be invoked to prohibit, control, or interfere with any act of the Defence Forces during the existence of a state of war or armed rebellion.

(5) The dwelling of every citizen is inviolable and shall not be forcibly entered save in accordance with law.

(6) 1. The State guarantees liberty for the exercise of the following rights, subject to public order and morality:

(i) The right of the citizens to express freely their convictions and opinions.

The education of public opinion being, however, a matter of such grave import to the common good, the State shall endeavour to ensure that organs of public opinion, such as the radio, the press, the cinema, while preserving their rightful liberty of expression, including criticism of Government policy, shall not be used to undermine public order or morality or the authority of the State.

The publication or utterance of blasphemous, seditious, or indecent matter is an offence which shall be punishable in accordance with law.

(ii) The right of the citizens to assemble peaceably and without arms.

Provision may be made by law to prevent or control meetings which are determined in accordance with law to be calculated to cause a breach of the peace or to be a danger or nuisance to the general public and to prevent or control meetings in the vicinity of either House of the Oireachtas.

(iii) The right of the citizens to form associations and unions.

Laws, however, may be enacted for the regulation and control in the public interest of the exercise of the foregoing right.

2. Laws regulating the manner in which the right of forming associations and unions and the right of free assembly may be exercised shall contain no political, religious or class discrimination.

The Family

Art. 41. (1) 1. The State recognises the Family as the natural primary and fundamental unit group of Society, and as a moral institution possessing inalienable and imprescriptible rights, antecedent and superior to all positive law.

2. The State, therefore, guarantees to protect the Family in its consti-

tution and authority, as the necessary basis of social order and as indispensable to the welfare of the Nation and the State.

(2) 1. In particular, the State recognises that by her life within the home, woman gives to the State a support without which the common good cannot be achieved.

2. The State shall, therefore, endeavour to ensure that mothers shall not be obliged by economic necessity to engage in labour to the neglect of their duties in the home.

(3) 1. The State plegdes itself to guard with special care the institution of Marriage, on which the Family is founded, and to protect it against attack.

2. No law shall be enacted providing for the grant of a dissolution of marriage.

3. No person whose marriage has been dissolved under the civil law of any other State but is a subsisting valid marriage under the law for the time being in force within the jurisdiction of the Government and Parliament established by this Constitution shall be capable of contracting a valid marriage within that jurisdiction during the lifetime of the other party to the marriage so dissolved.

Education

Art. 42. (1) The State acknowledges that the primary and natural educator of the child is the Family and guarantees to respect the inalienable right and duty of parents to provide, according to their means, for the religious and moral, intellectual, physical and social education of their children.

(2) Parents shall be free to provide this education in their homes or in private schools or in schools recognised or established by the State.

(3) 1. The State shall not oblige parents in violation of their conscience and lawful preference to send their children to schools established by the State, or to any particular type of school designated by the State.

2. The State shall, however, as guardian of the common good, require in view of actual conditions that the children receive a certain minimum education, moral, intellectual and social.

(4) The State shall provide for free primary education and shall endeavour to supplement and give reasonable aid to private and corporate educational initiative, and, when the public good requires it, provide other educational facilities or institutions with due regard, however, for the rights of parents, especially in the matter of religious and moral formation.

(5) In exceptional cases, where the parents for physical or moral reasons fail in their duty towards their children, the State as guardian of the common good, by appropriate means shall endeavour to supply the place

of the parents, but always with due regard for the natural and imprescriptible rights of the child.

Private Property

Art. 43. (1) 1. The State acknowledges that man, in virtue of his rational being, has the natural right, antecedent to positive law, to the private ownership of external goods.
2. The State accordingly guarantees to pass no law attempting to abolish the right of private ownership or the general right to transfer, bequeath, and inherit property.
(2) 1. The State recognises, however, that the exercise of the rights mentioned in the foregoing provisions of this Article ought, in civil society, to be regulated by the principles of social justice.
2. The State, accordingly, may as occasion requires delimit by law the exercise of the said rights with a view to reconciling their exercise with the exigencies of the common good.

Religion

Art. 44. (1) 1. The State acknowledges that the homage of public worship is due to Almighty God. It shall hold His Name in reverence, and shall respect and honour religion.
2. The State recognises the special position of the Holy Catholic Apostolic and Roman Church as the guardian of the Faith professed by the great majority of the citizens.
3. The State also recognises the Church of Ireland, the Presbyterian Church in Ireland, the Methodist Church in Ireland, the Religious Society of Friends in Ireland, as well as the Jewish Congregations and the other religious denominations existing in Ireland at the date of the coming into operation of this Constitution.
(2) 1. Freedom of conscience and the free profession and practice of religion are, subject to public order and morality, guaranteed to every citizen.
2. The State guarantees not to endow any religion.
3. The State shall not impose any disabilities or make any discrimination on the ground of religious profession, belief or status.
4. Legislation providing State aid for schools shall not discriminate between schools under the management of different religious denominations, nor be such as to affect prejudicially the right of any child to attend a school receiving public money without attending religious instruction at that school.
5. Every religious denomination shall have the right to manage its own

affairs, own, acquire and administer property, movable and immovable, and maintain institutions for religious or charitable purposes.
6. The property of any religious denomination of any educational institution shall not be diverted save for necessary works of public utility and on payment of compensation.

DIRECTIVE PRINCIPLES OF SOCIAL POLICY

Art. 45. The principles of social policy set forth in this Article are intended for the general guidance of the Oireachtas. The application of those principles in the making of laws shall be the case of the Oireachtas exclusively, and shall not be cognisable by any Court under any of the provisions of this Constitution.

(1) The State shall strive to promote the welfare of the whole people by securing and protecting as effectively as it may a social order in which justice and charity shall inform all the institutions of the national life.

(2) The State shall, in particular, direct its policy towards securing

(i) That the citizens (all of whom, men and women equally, have the right to an adequate means of livelihood) may through their occupations find the means of making reasonable provision for their domestic needs.
(ii) That the ownership and control of the material resources of the community may be so distributed amongst private individuals and the various classes as best to subserve the common good.
(iii) That, especially, the operation of free competition shall not be allowed so to develop as to result in the concentration of the ownership or control of essential commodities in a few individuals to the common detriment
(iv) That in what pertains to the control of credit the constant and predominant aim shall be the welfare of the people as a whole.
(v) That there may be established on the land in economic security as many families as in the circumstances shall be practicable.

(3) 1. The State shall favour and, where necessary, supplement private initiative in industry and commerce.
2. The State shall endeavour to secure that private enterprise shall be so conducted as to ensure reasonable efficiency in the production and distribution of goods and as to protect the public against unjust exploitation.

(4) 1. The State pledges itself to safeguard with especial care the economic interests of the weaker sections of the community, and, where necessary, to contribute to the support of the infirm, the widow, the orphan, and the aged.
2. The State shall endeavour to ensure that the strength and health of workers, men and women, and the tender age of children shall not be

abused and that citizens shall not be forced by economic necessity to avocations unsuited to their sex, age or strength.

AMENDMENT OF THE CONSTITUTION

Art. 46. (1) Any provision of this Constitution may be amended, whether by way of variation, addition, or repeal, in the manner provided by this Article.

(2) Every proposal for an amendment of this Constitution shall be initiated in Dáil Éireann as a Bill, and shall upon having been passed or deemed to have been passed by both Houses of the Oireachtas, be submitted by Referendum to the decision of the people in accordance with the law for the time being in force relating to the Referendum.

(3) Every such Bill shall be expressed to be "An Act to amend the Constitution."

(4) A Bill containing a proposal or proposals for the amendment of this Constitution shall not contain any other proposal.

(5) A Bill containing a proposal for the amendment of this Constitution shall be signed by the President forthwith upon his being satisfied that the provisions of this Article have been complied with in respect thereof and that such proposal has been duly approved by the people in accordance with the provisions of section 1 of Article 47 of this Constitution and shall be duly promulgated by the President as a law.

THE REFERENDUM

Art. 47. (1) Every proposal for an amendment of this Constitution which is submitted by Referendum to the decision of the people shall, for the purpose of Article 46 of this Constitution, be held to have been approved by the people, if, upon having been so submitted, a majority of the votes cast at such Referendum shall have been cast in favour of its enactment into law.

(2) 1. Every proposal, other than a proposal to amend the Constitution, which is submitted by Referendum to the decision of the people shall be held to have been vetoed by the people if a majority of the votes cast at such Referendum shall have been cast against its enactment into law and if the votes so cast against its enactment into law shall have amounted to not less than thirty-three and one-third per cent of the voters on the register.

2. Every proposal, other than a proposal to amend the Constitution, which is submitted by Referendum to the decision of the people shall for the purposes of Article 27 hereof be held to have been approved by approved by the people unless vetoed by them in accordance with the provisions of the foregoing sub-section of this section.

(3) Every citizen who has the right to vote at an election for members of Dáil Éireann shall have the right to vote at a Referendum.

(4) Subject as aforesaid, the Referendum shall be regulated by law.

REPEAL OF CONSTITUTION OF SAORSTAT ÉIREANN AND CONTINUANCE OF LAWS

Art. 48. The Constitution of Saorstát Éireann in force immediately prior to the date of the coming into operation of this Constitution and the Constitution of the Irish Free State (Saorstát Éireann) Act, 1922, insofar as that Act or any provision thereof is then in force shall be and are hereby repealed as on and from that date.

Art. 49. (1) All powers, functions, rights and prerogatives whatsoever exercisable in or in respect of Saorstát Éireann immediately before the 11th day of December, 1936, whether in virtue of the Constitution then in force or otherwise, by the authority in which the executive power of Saorstát Éireann was then vested are hereby declared to belong to the people.

(2) It is hereby enacted that, save to the extent to which provision is made by this Constitution or may hereafter be made by law for the exercise of any such power, function, right or prerogative by any of the organs established by this Constitution, the said powers, functions, rights and prerogatives shall not be exercised or be capable of being exercised in or in respect of the State save only by or on the authority of the Government.

(3) The Government shall be the successors of the Government of Saorstát Éireann as regards all property, assets, rights and liabilities.

Art. 50. (1) Subject to this Constitution and to the extent to which they are not inconsistent therewith, the laws in force in Saorstát Éireann immediately prior to the date of the coming into operation of this Constitution shall continue to be of full force and effect until the same or any of them shall have been repealed or amended by enactment of the Oireachtas.

(2) Laws enacted before, but expressed to come into force after, the coming into operation of this Constitution, shall, unless otherwise enacted by the Oireachtas come into force in accordance with the terms thereof.

Dochum Glóire Dé
agus
Onóra na hÉireann.

Note: The Transitory Provisions, Articles 51–63 inclusive, which continue to have the force of law, are, however, omitted from this official text in accordance with the terms of Articles 51 and 52.

ITALY

SUMMARY

INTERNATIONAL STATUS

Italy is a member of the United Nations (December 14, 1955). It is a member of the European Economic Community and of other international organizations. It was a member of the League of Nations until 1935.

The Risorgimento movement began with the *Giovane Italia* movement founded by Giuseppe Mazzini in 1831, after the failure of the 1830 revolutions in Italy under the *Carbonari* movement. A series of insurrections ensued, the Italian popular movement gaining great strength around 1848, when constitutions were granted in Naples, Tuscany, Sardinia, the

Papal States; Milan and Venice expelled the Austrians, and a Republic under a triumvirate headed by Mazzini was proclaimed in Rome in 1849 and joined by Tuscany. French troops defeated the Roman republic, the Austrians regained control and defeated Charles Albert of Piedmont, and general restoration and repression followed. The Charles Albert *Statuto Fondamentale,* the constitution of the Kingdom of Sardinia (Piedmont), was the only constitution retained during the following period, and the idea of a united rather than a federated Italy began to gain ground. Piedmont under Cavour took the head of the national movement. By a secret agreement in 1858, France joined Piedmont in war on Austria in return for Nice and Savoy. Following the Austrian defeat in1859, peaceful revolutions occurred in Tuscany, Parma and Modena. In 1860, different parts of Italy united with the Kingdom of Sardinia (Piedmont), the Bourbons were overthrown in Sicily by the Expedition of the One Thousand under Garibaldi. On March 17, 1861, the first Italian Parliament, meeting in Turin on February 18, conferred the title of King of Italy on Victor Emmanuel of Sardinia (Piedmont). Rome was proclaimed the capital on March 27, 1861, although it was still occupied by a French garrison which did not withdraw until 1870 and not until the Lateran Treaty and Concordat of 1929 was the question of the Pope finally settled, he not having accepted the Law of Guarantees of May 13, 1871. Venetia became part of Italy by the Treaty with Austria of 1866. Trentino and Alto Adige were joined to Italy after the First World War and Trieste in 1948. The Fascist march on Rome occurred on October 28, 1922, and Italy was a fascist corporate state, still a monarchy, until July 25, 1943, when Mussolini was dismissed. Peace was made with the allied powers on September 3, 1943, and war declared on Germany in October. The elections of June 2, 1946 for a Constituent Assembly replaced the monarchy with a republic.

FORM OF NATIONAL GOVERNMENT

The Constitution of December 27, 1947, was drawn up by the Constituent Assembly, meeting from June 25, 1946 to January 31, 1947, following the referendum of June 2, 1946, in which Italy voted for a republican form of Government and the deputies to the Constituent Assembly were elected. It states that Italy is a democratic republic founded on labor; sovereignty belongs to the people.[1] The republic is one and indivisible and local autonomy shall be recognized and promoted.[2] The State and the Catholic Church are each independent and sovereign, their relations regulated by the Lateran Pacts whose constitutional status is recognized.[3] Italy condemns war and agrees to such limitation of sovereignty as may be necessary for a system calculated to ensure peace and justice between nations.[4]

[1] Const., Art. 1. [2] Id., Art. 5. [3] Id., Art. 7. See under Vatican City State.
[4] Id., Art. 11.

RIGHTS OF THE PEOPLE

The Constitution guarantees equality before the law, the right to work, safeguards linguistic minorities, equal freedom of all religious denominations before the law.[1] It guarantees personal liberty and due process of law, inviolability of the domicile, liberty and secrecy of correspondence and communication, freedom of travel and residence, freedom of assembly, association, religion, expression, no deprivation of legal status for political reasons, the right to defence in legal proceedings, no retroactive punishment, no extradition for political offenses.[2] The Republic assists the family, safeguards health, guarantees freedom of instruction and establishes public schools, education is available to all and primary education compulsory and free, labor is safeguarded and social assistance provided, the right to strike recognized, public and private ownership recognized together with State-imposed obligations and limitations on private landed ownership, co-operation and savings are encouraged.[3] Suffrage is universal and the right to petition recognized.[4] All citizens must defend the country, pay taxes and respect the Constitution and laws.[5]

LEGISLATIVE DEPARTMENT

Parliament is bicameral, composed of the Chamber of Deputies and the Senate. The Chamber of Deputies consists of 630 members elected by universal, direct suffrage for a term of five years subject to dissolution.[6] The Senate consists of 315 members elected on a regional basis, also for a five year term subject to dissolution, by direct universal suffrage of voters over 25 years of age, and of former Presidents of the Republic and five members appointed for life by the President.[7] Members represent the whole nation.[8] Parliamentary immunities are provided.[9] Parliament meets in two ordinary sessions a year.[10]

EXECUTIVE DEPARTMENT

The President is elected by Parliament in joint session by a two-thirds majority for a term of seven years.[11] He promulgates the laws, appoints state officials, commands the Armed Forces, grants pardons and honors.[12] The Government of the Republic consists of the President of the Council, appointed by the President of the Republic, and the Ministers, jointly constituting the Council of Ministers which must enjoy the confidence of the two chambers and is responsible to them.[13]

[1] Id., Art. 2–4, 6, 8. [2] Id., Art. 13–28. [3] Id., Art. 29–47. [4] Id., Art. 48–51. [5] Id., Art. 52–54. [6] Id., Art. 55, 56, 60, 88. [7] Id., Art. 57–60, 88. [8] Id., Art. 67. [9] Id., Art. 68. [10] Id., Art. 62. [11] Id., Art. 83–85. [12] Id., Art. 87. [13] Id., Art. 92–96.

A National Council of Economy and Labor is provided as an advisory organ to Parliament and the Government.[1] There is a section relating to local government.[2]

JUDICIAL DEPARTMENT

The judiciary is independent, not subject to any other authority and subject only to the laws.[3] There is a Senior Council of the Judiciary for the appointment, transfer, promotion etc. of judges.[4] There is provision for a Constitutional Court to decide on controversies concerning the constitutional legality of laws, controversies over the constitutional assignment of powers, and to impeach the President and Ministers.[5] There is provision for a Council of State to ensure the legality of public administration and a Court of Accounts.[6]

AREA, POPULATION, ETC.

The area of Italy is 301,224 square kilometres, its population (1964) is 50,955,000. The capital is Rome.

[1] Id., Art. 99. [2] Id., Art. 114–133. [3] Id., Art. 101, 104. [4] Id., Art. 104, 105.
[5] Id., Art. 134. [6] Id., Art. 100.

CONSTITUTION of ITALY[1]

December 27, 1947, as amended March 11, 1953 and February 9, 1963

The Provisional Head of the State, by virtue of the decision of the Constituent Assembly which, on December 22, 1947, approved the Constitution of the Italian Republic and in consideration of the XVIII Final Provisions, proclaims the Constitution of the Republic of Italy as follows:

BASIC PRINCIPLES

Art. 1. Italy is a democratic Republic founded on labor.

Sovereignty belongs to the people who exercise it in the manner and within the limits laid down by the Constitution.

Art. 2. The Republic recognizes and guarantees the inviolable rights of man, both as an individual and as a member of the social groups in which his personality finds expression, and imposes the performance of unalterable duties of a political, economic and social nature.

Art. 3. All citizens are invested with equal social status and are equal before the law, without distinction as to sex, race, language, religion, political opinions and personal or social conditions.

It is the responsibility of the Republic to remove all obstacles of an economic and social nature which, by limiting the freedom and equality of citizens, prevent the full development of the individual and the participation of all workers in the political, economic and social organization of the country.

Art. 4. The Republic recognizes the right of all citizens to work and promotes such conditions as will make this right effective.

Every citizen shall undertake, according to his possibilities and his own choice, an activity or a function contributing to the material and moral progress of society.

[1] *The Constitution of the Republic of Italy.* Presidency of the Council of Ministers, Information and Copyright Service. Supplement to No. 4 of *Italy-Documents and Notes* (July-August) 1965. Supplied by Ministry of Foreign Affairs in August 1966. Ed.

Art. 5. The Republic, which is one and indivisible, recognizes and promotes local autonomy; it applies the fullest measure of administrative decentralization in services dependent on the State and adjusts the principles and methods of its legislation to the requirements of autonomy and decentralization.

Art. 6. The Republic safeguards linguistic minorities by means of special provisions.

Art. 7. The State and the Catholic Church are, each within its own ambit independent and sovereign.

Their relations are regulated by the Lateran Pacts. Such amendments to these Pacts as are accepted by both parties do not require any procedure of Constitutional revision.[1]

Art. 8. All religious denominations are equally free before the law.

Religious denominations other than Catholic are entitled to organize themselves according to their own creed provided that they are not in conflict with Italian juridical organization.

Their relations with the State are regulated by law on the basis of agreeents with their respective representatives.

Art. 9. The Republic promotes the development of scholarship and scientific and technical research.

It safeguards the natural beauties and the historical and aristic wealth of Italy.

Art. 10. Italy's legal system conforms with the generally recognized principles of international law.

The legal status of foreigners is regulated by law in conformity with international rules and treaties.

A foreigner to whom the practical exercise in his own country of democratic freedoms, guaranteed by the Italian Constitution, is precluded, is entitled to the right of asylum within the territory of the Republic, under conditions laid down by law.

The extradition of a foreigner for political offences is not admitted.

Art. 11. Italy condemns war as an instrument of aggression against the liberties of other peoples and as a means for settling international controversies; it agrees, on conditions of equality with other states, to such limitation of sovereignty as may be necessary for a system calculated to ensure peace and justice between Nations: it promotes and encourages international organizations having such ends in view.

Art. 12. The flag of the Republic is the Italian Tricolor: green, white, and red, in three vertical bands of equal dimensions.

[1] By virtue of this Article, Italy recognizes the constitutional status of the Lateran Pacts, consisting of the Treaty, the Concordat and the Financial Agreement. Only modifications agreed upon between the Holy See and the Italian Government may be approved by Parliament with ordinary law. Eventual unilateral changes made by Italy must be approved in a constitutional law. Texts of Latevan Pacts on page 1187 ff.

PART ONE

RIGHTS AND DUTIES OF PRIVATE CITIZENS

Title I. Civil Relations

Art. 13. Personal liberty is inviolable.

No form of personal detention, inspection or search is permitted, nor other restrictions on personal liberty save by order of the judicial authority for which the motive must be stated, and then only in such cases and manner as the law provides.

In exceptional cases of necessity and urgency, strictly defined by law, the police authorities may carry out provisional measures, which must be communicated within 48 hours to the judicial authorities and which, if the latter do not ratify them within the next 48 hours, are thereby revoked and declared null and void.

All acts of physical and moral violence on persons subjected to limitations of freedom are punished.

The law lays down the maximum period of preventive detention.

Art. 14. Personal domicile is inviolable.

Inspection, search and distraint may not be carried out save in cases and in the manner laid down by law in conformity with guarantees prescribed for safeguarding personal freedom.

Special laws regulate verifications and inspections for reasons of public health and safety, or for economic and fiscal purposes.

Art. 15. The liberty and secrecy of correspondence and of every form of communication are inviolable.

Limitations upon them may only be enforced by decision, for which motives must be given, of the judicial authorities with the guarantees laid down by law.

Art. 16. Every citizen has the right to reside and travel freely in any part of the metropolitan territory, save for such limitations as the laws may prescribe in a general way for reasons of health or security. No restrictions may be prescribed for political reasons.

Every citizens is free to leave the territory of the Republic and re-enter it, save for such obligations as are laid down by law.[1]

Art. 17. Citizens are entitled to hold meetings peaceably and unarmed.

No previous notice is required for meetings in places to which the public has access.

For meetings in public thoroughfares previous notice must be communicated to the authorities, who may forbid them only for well established reasons of security or public safety.

[1] Military Service and payment of taxes and duties are compulsory by law.

Art. 18. Citizens are entitled to form associations without authorization for reasons not forbidden to individuals by criminal law.

Secret associations and those which pursue political aims, even indirectly, by means of organizations of a military character, are forbidden.

Art. 19. All are entitled to freely profess their religious convictions in any form, individually or in associations, to propagate them and to celebrate them in public or in private, save in the case of rites contrary to morality.

Art. 20. The religious character and the religious or confessional aims of an association or institution shall not involve special legal limitations or special fiscal burdens for its constitution, legal status or any of its activities.

Art. 21. All are entitled freely to express their thoughts by word of mouth, in writing, and by all other means of communication.

The press may not be subjected to any authority or censorship.

Distraint is allowed only by order of the judicial authorities, for which motives must be given, in the case of offences definitely laid down by the press law, or in the case of violation of the provisions which the said law prescribes for identifying responsible parties.

In such cases, under conditions of absolute urgency and when the immediate intervention of the judicial authorities is not possible, distraint may be applied to the periodical press by officers of the judicial police, who shall communicate the matter to the judicial authorities within 24 hours. If the said judicial authorities do not ratify the measure within the next 24 hours, the distraint is withdrawn and is null and void.

The law may prescribe, by means of provisions of a general nature, that the financial sources of a periodical publication be made known.

Printed publications, performances and all other manifestations contrary to morality are forbidden.

The law lays down proper provisions for preventing and repressing all violations.

Art. 22. No one may be deprived of his legal status, his citizenship, or his name for political reasons.

Art. 23. No personal service or payment may be forced on anyone, save according to law.

Art. 24. All are entitled to institute legal proceedings for the protection of their own rights and legitimate interests.

Defence is an inalienable right at every stage of legal proceedings.

The indigent are entitled, through special provisions, to proper means for action or defence at all levels or jurisdiction.

The law lays down the conditions and methods for obtaining reparation for judicial errors.

Art. 25. No one may avoid proceedings resulting from offences against legislation in force.

No one may be punished save on the basis of a law which has come into force before the offence has been committed.

No one may be subjected to security measures save in such cases as are laid down by law.

Art. 26. The extradition of a citizen is permitted only in cases expressly provided for in international conventions.

Extradition shall never be permitted for political offences.

Art. 27. Criminal responsibility is personal.

The person accused is not considered guilty until final sentence has been passed upon him.

Punishment must not consist of measures contrary to humane precepts and shall aim at reforming the person upon whom sentence is passed.

The death penalty is not admitted save in cases specified by military laws in time of war.

Art. 28. Officials and employees of the State and of public bodies are directly responsible, according to the criminal, civil and administrative laws, for acts committed in violation of rights. In such cases, civil responsibility extends to the State and to public bodies.

Title II. Ethical and Social Relations

Art. 29. The State recognizes the family as a natural association founded on marriage.

Marriage is based on the moral and legal equality of husband and wife, within the limits laid down by the laws for ensuring family unity.

Art. 30. It is the duty and right of parents to support, instruct and educate their children, even those born out of wedlock.

Should the parents prove incapable, the law states the way in which these duties shall be fulfilled.

The law ensures full legal and social protection for children born out of wedlock consistent with the rights of the members of the legitimate family.

The law lays down rules and limitations for ascertaining paternity.

Art. 31. The Republic facilitates, by means of economic and other provisions, the formation of the family and the fulfilment of the tasks connected therewith, with particular consideration for large families.

It safeguards maternity, infancy and youth, promoting and encouraging institutions necessary for such purposes.

Art. 32. The Republic provides health safeguards as a basic right of the individual and in the interests of the community, and grants medical assistance to the indigent free of charge.

No one may be forced to undergo any particular medical treatment, save under the provisions of the law. In no case shall the law violate the limits imposed by proper respect for the human person.

Art. 33. The freedom of art and science and freedom of instruction in them is affirmed.

The Republic lays down general rules for education and establishes public schools of all kinds and grades.

Organizations and private citizens are entitled to found schools and educational institutions which do not involve charges on the State.

The law, in laying down the rights and obligations of private schools which apply for official recognition, must ensure for them full liberty and for their pupils conditions equivalent to those of the public schools.

State examinations are prescribed for admission to the various types and grades of schools, or on the conclusion of educational courses, and for securing diplomas and certificates entitling candidates to exercise a profession or trade.

Institutions of higher learning, universities and academies have the right to draft their own regulations within the limits laid down by State legislation.

Art. 34. Education is available to everyone.

Elementary education, imparted for at least eight years, is compulsory and free.

Capable and deserving pupils, even if without financial resources, are entitled to attain the highest grades of learning.

The Republic gives effect to this privilege by means of scholarships, of contributions to the families of the pupils, and other provisions, to be obtained by competitive examination.

Title III. Economic Relations

Art. 35. The Republic safeguards labor in all its forms and methods of execution.

It provides for the professional or vocational training and advancement of workers.

It promotes and encourages international agreements, and organizations calculated to confirm and regulate the rights of labor.

It admits freedom to emigrate, save for such limitations as are prescribed by law in the general interests, and for the protection of Italian labor abroad.

Art. 36. An employed person is entitled to wages in proportion to the quantity and quality of his work, and in any case sufficient to provide him and his family with a free and dignified existence.

The maximum number of hours of work per day is fixed by law.

An employed person is entitled to a weekly day of rest and to annual holidays with pay: he cannot relinquish this right.

Art. 37. Female labor enjoys equal rights and the same wages for the same work as male labor. Conditions of work must make it possible for them to fulfil their essential family duties and provide for the adequate protection of mothers and children.

The law prescribes the minimum age for paid labor.[1]

The Republic prescribes special measures for safeguarding juvenile labor and guarantees equal pay for equal work.

Art. 38. Every private citizen unable to work and unprovided with the resources necessary for existence is entitled to private and social assistance.

Workers are entitled to adequate insurance for their requirements in case of accident, illness, disability, old age, and involuntary unemployment.

The disabled and persons incapable of employment are entitled to education and vocational training.

The responsibilities laid down in this Article are entrusted to organs and institutions provided or assisted by the State.

The freedom of private assistance is affirmed.

Art. 39. Freedom in the organization of trades unions is affirmed.

No compulsion may be imposed on trades unions except that of registering at local or central offices according to the provisions of the law.

A condition of registration is that the statutes of the unions sanction an internal organization on a democratic basis.

Registered trades unions have a legal status. They may, being represented in proportion to the number of their registered members, negotiate collective labor agreements having compulsory value for all persons belonging to the categories to which the said agreements refer.

Art. 40. The right to strike is exercised within the sphere of the laws concerning the subject.[2]

Art. 41. Private economic enterprise is open to all.

It cannot, however, be applied in such a manner as to be in conflict with social utility or when it is prejudicial to security, freedom and human dignity.

The law prescribes such planning and controls as may be advisable for directing and co-ordinating public and private economic activities towards social objectives.

Art. 42. Ownership is public or private. Economic commodities belong to the State, to public bodies or to private persons.

Private ownership is recognized and guaranteed by laws which prescribe the manner in which it may be acquired and enjoyed and its limitations, with the object of ensuring its social function and of rendering it accessible to all.

[1] Age limits in Italy are subject to the conditions laid down in the Washington (1919) and Geneva (1937) agreements which generally establish that fourteen years is the minimum age for entry to paid employment.

[2] Such a right must be governed by law, which can also limit it. Although the right to strike is recognized, the Constitution does not permit lock-outs.

Private property, in such cases as are prescribed by law and with provisions for compensation, may be expropriated in the general interest.[1]

The law lays down the rules and limitations of legitimate and testamentary inheritance and the rights of the State in relation to same.

Art. 43. For purposes of general utility the law may reserve in the first instance or transfer, by means of expropriation and payment of compensation, to the State, to public bodies or to labor or consumer communities, certain undertakings or categories of undertakings operating essential public services, sources of power or exercising monopolies and invested primarily with a character of general interest.[2]

Art. 44. With the object of securing a rational utilization of the soil and of establishing equitable and rational social relations, the law imposes obligations on, and limitations to, private landed ownership, fixes limits to its extent which vary in the different parts of the country and according to diverse agricultural areas, encourages and imposes land reclamation, the transformation of large estates and the institution of productive units, and assists small and medium sized holdings.

The law prescribes measures in favor of mountainous areas.

Art. 45. The Republic recognizes the social function of co-operation on a basis of reciprocity and devoid of any private speculative aim. The law promotes and encourages such co-operation with suitable provisions and through proper controls ensures its character and objectives.

The law guarantees and provides for the development of artisan trades.

Art. 46. With a view to the economic and social progress of labor and in conformity with the requirements of production, the Republic recognizes the rights of workers to participate in management in the manner and within the limits prescribed by law.

Art. 47. The Republic encourages and safeguards savings in all its aspects and supervises, co-ordinates and controls the issuing of credit.

It encourages the investment of private savings in the purchase of homes or holdings directly farmed by the owners, and direct or indirect investment in large productive enterprise.

Title IV. Political Relations

Art. 48. All private citizens, male or female, who are of age, are entitled to vote.

[1] Article 29 of the Charles Albert Statute established: "All property, without exception, is inviolable" and permitted expropriation only in the public interest. The republican Constitution, on the other hand, recognizes and guarantees private property but authorizes ordinary legislation to be passed concerning methods of acquirement, enjoyments and the limits to be applied, in order to guarantee its social function and to make it accessible to all.

[2] This permits nationalization and take-over of certain enterprise handling essential public services, sources of energy, and monopolies that are of such importance that they are indispensable to national economy.

Votes are personal, equal, free and secret. To vote is a civic duty.

The right to vote may not be limited save on account of civil incapacity or in consequence of an irrevocable penal sentence, or in cases of moral unworthiness established by law.[1]

Art. 49. All citizens have the right to freely form parties in order to contribute by democratic means to national policy.[2]

Art. 50. All citizens may submit petitions to Parliament demanding legislative measures or setting forth general needs.

Art. 51. All citizens of either sex are eligible for public office and for elective positions on conditions of equality, according to the requisites established by law[3].

The law may place Italians who do not belong to the Republic on a par with resident citizens in the matter of admission to public office and elective positions.

Any person called upon to occupy an elective office has the right to claim the time necessary for the fulfilment of such duties without being deprived of his employment.

Art. 52. The defence of the country is a moral duty of every citizen.

Military service is compulsory, within the limits and in the manner laid down by law. The fulfilment of military duty shall not prejudice the employment of the person concerned, nor the exercise of his political rights.

The organization of the Armed Forces is based on the democratic principles of the Republic.

Art. 53. Everyone shall contribute to public expenditure in proportion to his resources.

Fiscal levies shall be on a progressive scale.

Art. 54. All citizens have the duty of fealty to the Republic and shall respect the Constitution and the laws.

Citizens to whom public functions are entrusted shall execute them in a disciplined and honorable manner swearing an oath to fulfil such conditions in those cases prescribed by law.

[1] Apart from the above limitations to the right to vote, the Constitution refers to another two that are contained in the Transitory Provisions, No. XII and XIII.

[2] Article XII of the Transitory Provisions, however, forbids the reorganization of the Fascist Party under any form.

[3] The law may extend this right to persons who are Italian from an ethnical viewpoint but who are not citizens of the Republic.

PART TWO

ORGANIZATION OF THE REPUBLIC

Title I. Parliament

Section I. The Two Chambers

Art. 55. Parliament consists of the Chamber of Deputies and the Senate of the Republic.

Parliament holds joint meetings of members of the Chamber of Deputies and the Senate only in cases laid down by the Constitution.

Art. 56. The Chamber of Deputies is elected by universal and direct suffrage, and is composed of six hundred and thirty Members.

All persons who have reached the age of twenty-five years on the day of the elections are eligible for membership.

Division of seats among the constituencies is obtained by dividing the number of inhabitants registered at the last census by six hundred and thirty and distributing the said seats in proportion to the population of each constituency, on the basis of the quotients and the highest figures below these quotients.

Art. 57. The Senate of the Republic is elected on a regional basis.

Senators number three hundred and fifteen. No region may have less than ten Senators but Molise is attributed two and Valle d'Aosta one. Division of seats among the Regions, on the basis of the terms set out above, is made according to the proportion of the population of the Regions at the last census, with quotients and the highest figures below these quotients.

Art. 58. Senators are elected by direct universal suffrage by voters over twenty-five years of age.

Voters over forty years of age are eligible for election to the Senate.

Art. 59. Any person who has held office as President of the Republic is by right a Senator for Life, unless he refuses to accept the nomination.

The President of the Republic may nominate, as Senators for Life five citizens, who have brought honor to the Nation through their exceptional merits in social, scientific, artistic and literary fields.

Art. 60. The Chamber of Deputies and the Senate are elected for a period of five years.

The term of each Chamber may not be extended save by law and only in the event of war.

Art. 61. Election of the new Chambers must take place within seventy days of the dissolution of the preceding Parliament. The first sitting must be held not later than twenty days after the elections.

The powers of the preceding Chambers shall continue until the newly elected Parliament shall meet.

Art. 62. The Chambers shall meet on the first day of February and October which is not a holiday.

Each Chamber may be convened in extraordinary session on the initiative of its Speaker or of the President of the Republic or of one third of its members.

When one Chamber is called upon to meet in extraordinary session, the other Chamber is also convened *ipso jure.*

Art. 63. Each Chamber elects its Speaker and the members of the Speaker's Office from among its own members.

The Speaker of the Chamber of Deputies and members of the Speaker's Office shall preside whenever Parliament meets in joint session.

Art. 64. Each Chamber drafts its own Standing Orders by an absolute majority of its members.

Sittings are open to the public; nevertheless each of the two Chambers and Parliament in joint session may decide to assemble in private.

The decisions of each Chamber and of Parliament are not valid unless the majority of the members are present, and unless they are voted by a majority of the members present, save where the Constitution provides for a special majority.

Members of the Government, even if they are not members of the Chambers, are entitled to attend meetings and are obliged to be present if called upon. They have a right to be heard whenever they request this right.

Art. 65. The law determines cases of ineligibility or incompatibility with the position of Deputy or Senator.

No person may be a member of both Chambers at the same time.

Art. 66. Each Chamber decides as to the validity of the admission of its own members and as to cases subsequently arising concerning ineligibility and incompatibility.

Art. 67. Each Member of Parliament represents the Nation and carries out his duties without restraint of mandate.

Art. 68. Members of Parliament may not be proceeded against for opinions expressed or votes given in the exercise of their duties.

No member of Parliament may, without the authority of the Chamber to which he belongs, be subjected to criminal proceedings, nor be arrested or otherwise deprived of his personal liberty, nor subjected to search warrants on his person or in his home unless he be caught in the act of committing an offence for which an order of arrest is compulsory.

A similar authority is required to arrest or keep in a state of detention a member of Parliament in the execution of a sentence even if it be irrevocable.

Art. 69. Members of Parliament receive an allowance as laid down by law.

Section II. The Drafting of Laws

Art. 70. Legislative duties are carried out jointly by the two Chambers.

Art. 71. Legislative initiative pertains to the Government, to each member of the two Chambers, and to those organs and bodies on whom it is conferred by Constitutional law.

The people exercise initiative in legislation through the proposal, supported by not less than 50,000 voters, of a Bill drafted in the form of articles.

Art. 72. Every Bill submitted to one of the Chambers is, according to the Standing Orders, examined by a Committee and then by the Chamber itself which approves it, article by article, and subsequently with a final vote. The Standing Orders provide an abbreviated procedure for Bills declared to be urgent.

They also lay down in what cases and in what manner the examination and approval of Bills shall be submitted to committees, including Standing Committees so composed as to reflect the various proportions of the Parliament groups. Furthermore, in such cases, a Bill, until it is finally voted upon, is submitted to the Chamber, if the Government or one tenth of the members of the Chamber or one fifth of the Committee demand that it be debated and voted on by the Chamber itself or submitted to the latter for its final approval with a nominal vote. The Standing Orders decide as to the way in which the work of the Committees shall be divulged.

The normal procedure for the debating and voting of Bills by the Chamber is always applied in the case of Bills of a constitutional and electoral nature and for those delegating legislative power, for authority to ratify international treaties, and for voting on budgets and rectified budgets.

Art. 73. Laws are promulgated by the President of the Republic within a month of their having been voted.

If the two Chambers, each with an absolute majority among its own members, declare a Bill to be urgent, it is promulgated within the time laid down in the Bill itself.

Laws are published immediately after they have been promulgated and come into force on the fifteenth day after their publication, unless the laws themselves provide otherwise.

Art. 74. The President of the Republic, before promulgating a law, may request further discussion by means of a message to both Chambers in which the reasons for such action are set forth.

If the Chambers vote the Bill once more, the law must be promulgated.

Art. 75. A popular Referendum is held to decide on the total or partial repeal of a law or of a measure having force of law if it is demanded by 500,000 voters or by five Regional Councils.

Referenda are not allowed in the case of fiscal or budget laws, amnesties or pardons, or laws authorizing the ratification of international treaties.

All citizens entitled to vote for the election of members of the Chamber of Deputies are entitled to take part in a Referendum.

The proposal submitted to Referendum is approved if the majority of those eligible have participated in the voting, and if it has received a majority of valid votes.

The methods for carrying out a referendum are laid down by law.

Art. 76. The exercise of legislative functions may not be delegated by the Government save by the laying down of principles and criteria and only for a limited period of time and for definite objects.

Art. 77. The Government may not, unless properly delegated by the Chambers, issue decrees having the value of ordinary laws.

When, in exceptional cases of necessity and urgency, the Government issues, on its own responsibility, provisional measures having force of law, it shall on the same day submit them for conversion into law to the Chambers which, even if they have been dissolved, are expressly summoned for that purpose and shall meet within five days.

Decrees lose effect as of the date of issue if they are not converted into law within sixty days of their publication. The Chambers may, however, approve laws to regulate legal questions arising out of decrees not yet converted into law.

Art. 78. The Chambers declare a state of war and confer the necessary powers on the Government.

Art. 79. The right of amnesty and indult are granted by the President of the Republic, on the basis of laws enacted by the Chambers delegating such power.

Amnesty and indult are not applicable in the case of offences committed subsequent to the proposal for delegating such authority.

Art. 80. The Chambers authorize, by law, ratification of international treaties of a political nature, or which provide for arbitration or judicial regulation, or imply modifications to the nation's territory or financial burdens, or to laws.

Art. 81. The Chambers vote the budgets and the audited accounts submitted by the Government each year.

The right to execute the provisional budget may not be granted save by law and for periods of not over four months.

No new taxes or new expenditure can be established by the law approving the budget.

In all other laws implying new or additional expenditure the means for covering it must be set forth.

Art. 82. Each Chamber may order inquiries into matters of public interest.

To this end, it appoints a Committee of its own members so composed as to represent the proportions of the various political groups. The Committee of Enquiry carries out its investigations and examination with the same powers and the same limitations as the judicial authorities.

Title II. The President of the Republic

Art. 83. The President of the Republic is elected by Parliament during a joint session of both Chambers.

Three delegates from every Region, elected by the Regional Council in such a manner as to ensure the representation of minorities, take part in the election.

The Valle d'Aosta is represented by only one delegate.

Presidential elections take place by secret ballot with a majority of two thirds of the Assembly. After the third ballot an absolute majority is sufficient.

Art. 84. Any citizen of fifty years of age enjoying civil and political rights is eligible for election as President of the Republic.

The office of President of the Republic is incompatible with any other office.

The allowances and endowments of the President are established by law.

Art. 85. The Presidential term shall be seven years.

Thirty days before the term lapses the Speaker of the Chamber of Deputies summons Parliament in joint session together with the Regional delegates to elect the new President of the Republic.

If Parliament has been dissolved or is to be dissolved within three months, the election is held within fifteen days of the meeting of the new Chambers. In the interval, the powers of the existing President are prolonged.

Art. 86. Should the President prove to be unable to fulfil his duties, they shall be carried out by the Speaker of the Senate.

In case of permanent incapacity or death or resignation of the President of the Republic, the Speaker of the Chamber of Deputies provides for the election of a new President of the Republic within fifteen days, unless a longer period be foreseen because the Chambers are to be dissolved or because their term has less than three months to expire.

Art. 87. The President of the Republic is the Head of the State and represents the unity of the Nation.

He may send messages to Parliament.

He provides for the election of a new Parliament and authorizes the date of its first meeting.

He authorizes the submission to Parliament of Bills moved by the Government.

He promulgates laws and issues decrees having the value of laws and regulations.

He provides for a referendum in such cases as are laid down in the Constitution.

He appoints, in the cases laid down by the law, the officials of the State.

He accredits and receives diplomatic representatives and ratifies international treaties, provided they be authorized by Parliament whenever such authorization is necessary.

He commands the Armed Forces, presides over the Supreme Defence Council as constituted by law, and declares a state of war when it has been decided by Parliament.

He presides over the *Consiglio Superiore della Magistratura*.[1]

He may grant pardons and commute court sentences.

He confers the honors of the Republic.

Art. 88. The President of the Republic may dissolve one or both Chambers after consultation with their Speakers.

He may not exercise this right during the last six months of his term of office.

Art. 89. No act of the President is legal unless it is countersigned by the Ministers who have submitted it and accept his responsibility.

Measures having the value of law and such others as are laid down by law shall also be countersigned by the President of the Council of Ministers (Prime Minister).

Art. 90. The President of the Republic cannot be held responsible for acts carried out in the exercise of his duties, save in cases of high treason or breaches of the Constitution.

Art. 91. Before taking office the President of the Republic shall swear an oath of loyalty to the Republic and to the Constitution before Parliament in joint session.

Title III. The Government

Section I. The Council of Ministers

Art. 92. The Government of the Republic consists of the President of the Council and of the Ministers jointly constituting the Council of Ministers.

The President of the Republic appoints the President of the Council and the Ministers who are proposed.

Art. 93. Before assuming office the President of the Council and the Ministers shall be sworn in before the President of the Republic.

Art. 94. The Government must enjoy the confidence of the two Chambers.

Each Chamber grants or refuses its confidence by a motion in which it gives its reasons and which is submitted to a nominal vote.

[1] Senior Council of the Judiciary.

Within ten days of its formation, the Government shall present its program to Parliament to obtain its vote of confidence.

The contrary vote of one or of both Chambers on a Government proposal does not necessitate resignation.

A vote of no-confidence must be signed by at least one tenth of the members of the Chamber and can only be debated three days after it has been submitted.

Art. 95. The President of the Council conducts, and is responsible for, the general policy of the Government. He maintains unity in general political and administrative policy, and promotes and co-ordinates the activities of the Ministers.

Ministers are jointly responsible for the decisions of the Cabinet as a whole, and individually for those of their own particular departments.

The law contemplates regulations concerning the Presidency of the Council of Ministers and establishes the number, responsibilities and organization of the various Ministries.

Art. 96. The President of the Council and the Ministers may be impeached by Parliament in joint session for offences committed in the exercise of their duties.

Section II. Public Administration

Art. 97. Public departments are organized according to the provisions of the law, so that proper conduct and impartiality of administration shall be guaranteed.

The competence, duties and responsibilities of public officials are laid down in regulations on public departments.

Appointments in the public administration are secured by competitive entry, unless otherwise laid down by law.

Art. 98. Public officials are exclusively at the service of the Nation

If they are members of Parliament they cannot be promoted save by seniority.

Limitations to the right of registering as members of political parties may be laid down by law for members of the Judiciary, members of the fighting services on active duty, police officials and agents, and diplomatic and consular representatives abroad.

Section III. Auxiliary Bodies

Art. 99. The National Council of Economy and Labor is composed, according to the provisions of the law, of experts and representatives of productive branches, in such a manner that their numerical importance and their qualifications are properly taken into consideration.

It is an advisory organ to Parliament and to the Government for such questions and duties as are attributed to it by law.

It has the right to promote legislation and may contribute to the drafting of economic and social laws according to the principles, and within the limits laid down by law.

Art. 100. The Council of State is an advisory organ on judicial-administrative matters and ensures the legality of public administration.

The Court of Accounts (State Auditor's Department) exercises a form of preventive control on the legitimacy of Government measures and of subsequent control on the management of the budget. It takes part, in the cases and in the manner laid down by law, in the control of the financial management of those bodies to which the State normally contributes. It reports directly to Parliament on the results of the audit so executed.

The law ensures the independence of these two organs and of their members *vis-a-vis* of the Government.

Title IV. The Judiciary

Section I. Jurisdictional Organization

Art. 101. Justice is administered in the name of the people.

The judges are subject only to the laws.

Art. 102. The duties of the judiciary are carried out by permanent judges appointed and governed according to the provisions laid down in regulations on legal structure.

No special judges may be appointed, but specialized sections may be set up and attached to the normal judicial organs for dealing with specific matters, and properly qualified citizens who are not members of the judiciary may participate.

The law lays down the reasons and the manner in which private persons participate directly in the administration of Justice.

Art. 103. The Council of State and other bodies concerned with administrative justice safeguard the legitimate interests of public administration and even those subjective rights that are foreseen by law.

The Court of Accounts (State Auditor's Department) has jurisdiction over matters of public accounts and such other questions as are specified by law.

Military tribunals in war time have jurisdiction as authorized by law. In peace time their jurisdiction is limited to military offences committed by members of the Armed Services.

Art. 104. The Judiciary is an independent structure and is not subject to any other authority.

The President of the Republic is Chairman of the "Consiglio Superiore della Magistratura".

The senior judge and the Public Prosecutor of the Court of Cassation (Supreme Court of Appeal) are *ipso jure* members of it.

Of the other members, two thirds are elected by all regular judges of different categories, and one third by Parliament in joint session, selection being made among professors of law faculties and lawyers of at least fifteen years' standing.

The Council elects an Assistant Chairman from among the members chosen by Parliament.

The elected members hold office for four years and are not immediately re-eligible.

While they are in office they may not be registered on the Rolls of the legal profession, nor be members either of Parliament or of a Regional Council.

Art. 105. According to regulations, the "Consiglio Superiore della Magistratura" is entrusted with the appointment, assignment, transfer, promotion and disciplinary measures concerning the judges.

Art. 106. Entry to the judiciary is by competitive examination.

According to the regulations, honorary magistrates may be appointed, even by election, to perform all the duties attributed to individual judges.

On the proposal of the "Consiglio Superiore della Magistratura", professors of law and lawyers of at least fifteen years standing and registered in the special Rolls entitling them to practise in the senior courts may be appointed. Councillors of the Supreme Court of Cassation for exceptional merits.

Art. 107. Judges cannot be removed from office. They may not be dismissed or suspended from their duties, nor transferred to other courts or duties, save by a decision of the "Consiglio Superiore della Magistratura" taken for reasons and with guarantees for their defence laid down by regulations or with their own consent.

The Minister of Justice is entitled to undertake disciplinary action.

Judges differ from one another only on account of their different functions.

The Public Prosecutor is safeguarded by the guarantees laid down in the regulations.

Art. 108. The rules governing legal structure and every judicial office are established by law.

The law ensures the independence of the judges of special Courts, Public Prosecutors attached to these Courts and other persons taking part in the administration of justice.

Art. 109. The Judicial Police are at the direct disposal of the Judiciary.

Art. 110. Without prejudice to the competence of the "Consiglio Superiore della Magistratura", the organization and operation of services concerned with the administration of law are entrusted to the Minister of Justice.

Section II. Regulations on Justice

Art. 111. Valid reasons must be provided for all legal proceedings.

Appeals to the Supreme Court of Cassation are always allowed against sentences and against measures concerning personal liberty delivered by the ordinary or special courts when violation of law occurs. These provisions may be abolished only in the case of sentences passed by Military Tribunals in time of war.

Appeals to the Supreme Court of Cassation against decisions of the Council of State and of the Court of Accounts (State Auditor's Department) are only allowed for motives concerning jurisdiction.

Art. 112. The public Prosecutor is responsible for instituting penal proceedings.

Art. 113. Claims for protection of rights in matters of legitimate interest before the organs of normal or administrative justice are always allowed against decisions taken by public administration.

Such jurisdictional protection may not be exclusive or limited to special claims or to specific decisions.

The law lays down those jurisdictional organs which may annul decisions of public administration according to the provisions established.

Title V. The Regions, Provinces and "Comuni" [1]

Art. 114. The Republic is divided into Regions, Provinces and *Comuni.*

Art. 115. The Regions are constituted as autonomous territorial units with their own powers and functions according to the principles established by the Constitution.

Art. 116. Particular forms and conditions of autonomy, in accordance with special statutes adopted by constitutional law, are attributed to Sicily, Sardinia, Trentino-Alto Adige, Friuli-Venezia Giulia and the Valle d'Aosta.

Art. 117. Within the limits of the fundamental principles established by the laws of the State, the Region legislates in regard to the following matters, provided that such legislation is not in contrast with the interests of the Nation or of other Regions:

Organization of the offices and the administrative bodies dependent on the Region;

Town boundaries;

[1] This term includes towns, urban and rural districts.

Urban and rural police;
Fairs and markets;
Public charities and health and hospital assistance;
Vocational training of artisans and scholastic assistance;
Museums and libraries of local bodies;
Town planning;
Tourist trade and hotel industry;
Tram and motor coach services of regional interest;
Roads, aqueducts and public works of regional interest;
Lake navigation and ports;
Mineral and spa waters;
Quarries and peat bogs;
Hunting;
Fishing in lake and river waters;
Agriculture and forestry;
Artisanship;
Other matters indicated by constitutional laws;

The laws of Republic may delegate power to the Region to issue norms for their enforcement.

Art. 118. The administrative functions pertaining to the subjects listed in the preceding article reside in the Regions, except those of exclusively local interest which, by the laws of the Republic, may be delegated to the Provinces, "Comuni" or other local authorities.

The State may, by law, delegate the exercise of other functions of an administrative nature to the Region.

The Region normally exercises its administrative functions by delegating them to the Provinces, "Comuni" or other local authorities, or by administering them through their offices.

Art. 119. The Regions have financial autonomy within the forms and limits established by the laws of the Republic which co-ordinate this regional autonomy with the finances of the State. the Provinces and the "Comuni".

The Regions are assigned their own taxes and quotas of Exchequer taxes according to the expenditure necessary to the fulfilment of their normal functions.

The State assigns by law special allocations to single Regions for specific purposes and particularly for the development of southern and insular Italy.

The Region has its own demesne and patrimony according to the requirements of the laws of the Republic.

Art. 120. The Regions may not levy import or export duties or duties on transit between Regions.

The Regions may not adopt provisions which hinder the free movement of persons or goods between Regions.

The Regions may not limit the right of citizens to exercise their professions, employment or labor in any part of national territory.

Art. 121. The official bodies of the Region are: the Regional Council, the Junta and its President.

The Regional Council exercises the legislative and administrative power granted to the Region and all other functions conferred on it by the Constitution and by law. It may propose Bills to Parliament.

The Junta is the executive body of the Regions,

The President of the Junta represents the Region; he promulgates regional laws and regulations and directs the administrative functions delegated to the Region by the State in accordance with the instructions of central government.

Art. 122. The electoral system, and the number and cases of ineligibility and incompatibility of Regional Councillors, are established by the laws of the Republic.

No one may be a member of a Regional Council and a member of either Chamber of Parliament or another Regional Council at the same time.

The Council elects a President from its own members and a President's Office for its functions.

Regional Councillors may not be called upon to answer for opinions expressed or votes cast during the exercise of their duties.[1]

The President and members of the Junta are elected by the Regional Council from among its members.

Art. 123. Every Region has a statute which, in harmony with the Constitution and the laws of the Republic, establishes the norms relative to the internal organization of the Region. The regional statute controls the right of initiative and referendum on laws and provisions of an administrative nature within the Region and the publication of regional laws and regulations.

The Statute is drafted and approved by the Regional Council through an absolute majority of its members and further approved by a law of the Republic.

Art. 124. A Government representative, residing in the capital of the Region, supervises the administrative functions exercised by central government and co-ordinates them with those of the Region.

Art. 125. Control of the legitimacy of administrative decisions in the Region is exercised, in decentralized form, by an organ of central government in the manner and within the limits established by the laws of the Republic. In specific cases, the law may admit re-examination of the merits of the case, but only to the extent of promoting, through a moti-

[1] Under the Constitution, Regional Councillors are not granted parliamentary immunity and they cannot, therefore, enjoy the privilege of avoiding legal proceedings under the term "no authorization to proceed".

vated request, a re-examination of a controversial decision by the Regional Council.

The Regions have their own first degree courts for administrative actions in accordance with the requirements of the laws of the Republic. The courts may have branches in places other than the regional capital.

Art. 126. The Regional Council may be dissolved when it performs acts contrary to the Constitution or commits serious violations of the laws, or fails to respond to the request of the Government to replace its Junta or the President of the Junta when these have committed similar acts or violations.

It may be dissolved when, by reason of resignation or through the impossibility of forming a majority, it is no longer in a position to fulfill its duties.

It may also be dissolved for reasons of national security.

The dissolution of the Regional Council is effected by a decree of the President of the Republic after an opinion has been offered by a Commission composed of Senators and Deputies, formed according to the laws of the Republic on regional affairs.

The Decree of Dissolution is accompanied by the nomination of a Commission composed of three citizens eligible for the Regional Council, which announces the holding of new elections within a period of three months and provides for ordinary administration within the competence of the Junta and for such decisions as cannot be postponed: such decisions are subject to ratification by the new Regional Council.

Art. 127. Every law approved by the Regional Council shall be communicated to the Government representative who, except in the case of opposition on the part of the Government, must approve it within a period of thirty days from its submission.

The law is promulgated within ten days from the date of approval and becomes effective not earlier than fifteen days from its publication. If a law is considered to be urgent by the Regional Council, and the Government of the Republic approves, then its promulgation and date of effect are not subject to the specified periods.

The Government of the Republic, when it considers that a law approved by the Regional Council exceeds the competence of the Region or conflicts with the interests of the Nation or with those of other Regions, returns it to the Regional Council within the period established for approval.

When the Regional Council approves it again by an absolute majority of its members, the Government of the Republic may, within fifteen days of communication of the fact, submit the question of its legitimacy to the Constitutional Court, and that of its merit, in the case of conflicting interests, to the Chamber of Deputies and the Senate. In case of doubt, the Constitutional Court shall decide on the competent body.

Art. 128. The Provinces and the "Comuni" are autonomous bodies within the principles laid down by the general laws of the Republic, which determine their function.

Art. 129. The Provinces and the "Comuni" are also territorial units of State and regional decentralization.

The territory contained within the Province may also be subdivided into districts with exclusively administrative functions, for the sake of further decentralization.

Art. 130. A regional body, constituted in accordance with procedure established by the laws of the Republic, exercises, in a decentralized form, control over the legitimacy of decisions taken by the Provinces, Communes and other local bodies.

In cases specified by law, control of an issue of general merit may be exercised in the form of a reasoned request submitted to the competent assembly for re-examination of decisions taken previously.

Art. 131. The following Regions are instituted:

Piedmont; Valle d'Aosta; Lombardy; Trentino-Alto Adige; Venezia; Friuli-Venezia Giulia; Liguria; Emilia-Romagna; Tuscany; Umbria; Marches; Latium; Abruzzo; Molise; Campania; Apulia; Basilicata; Calabria; Sicily; Sardinia.

Art. 132. By constitutional law, the Regional Council having been heard, arrangements may be made for the merging of existing Regions or the creation of new Regions with a minimum of one million inhabitants, when such a request is made by as many Councils as represent at least one third of the interested populations and when the proposal has been approved by a referendum voted by the majority of the interested populations.

By means of a referendum and by the laws of the Republic, the Regional Council having been heard, consent may be given for Provinces and "Comuni" so desiring to be detached from one Region and attached to another.

Art. 133. Changes of provincial boundaries and the institution of new Provinces within the area of a Region, are established by laws of the Republic, after request from the "Comuni" and the approval of the Region itself.

The Region having heard the interested population, may, by its own enactment, establish new "Comuni" and modify their boundaries and names within its own territory.

Title VI. Constitutional Guarantees

Section I. The Constitutional Court

Art. 134. The Constitutional Court decides:

on controversies concerning the constitutional legitimacy of laws and acts having the force of law, emanating from central and regional government;

on controversies arising over constitutional assignment of powers within the State, between the State and the Regions, and between Regions;

on impeachments of the President of the Republic and Ministers, according to the norms of the Constitution.

Art. 135. The Constitutional Court is composed of fifteen judges, a third of whom are nominated by the President of the Republic, one third by Parliament in joint session, and one third by the members of the ordinary and administrative supreme courts.

The judges of the Constitutional Court are chosen from among the magistrates of the High and Administrative Courts, including those in retirement, professors of law, and lawyers who have been in practice for a minimum period of twenty years.

The Court elects its President from among its members.

Judges are nominated for a period of twelve years and some may be retained in office according to the norms established by law: they are not re-eligible immediately.

The office of judge of the Constitutional Court may not be held concurrently with that of a member of Parliament, a member of a Regional Council, the exercise of the legal profession or with any position or office indicated by law.

Following the same procedure used in the appointment of the judges of the Constitutional Court, Parliament shall draft a list of persons who, in case of necessity, shall be chosen to take part in proceedings following impeachment of the President of the Republic, the Prime Minister and the Ministers.

Art. 136. When the Court declares a norm of law, or an act having the force of law, to be unconstitutional, the norm ceases to have effect from the day following the publication of the decision.

The decision of the Court is published and is communicated to Parliament and the interested Regional Councils in order that provisions may be made in constitutional form where considered necessary.

Art. 137. A constitutional law establishes the conditions, forms and time limits for decisions on constitutional legitimacy and guarantees the independence of the judges of the Court.

All other norms necessary for the constitution and functioning of the Court are established by ordinary legislation.

The decisions of the Constitutional Court may not be contested.

Section II. Amendments to the Constitution. Constitutional Laws

Art. 138. Amendments to the Constitution and other constitutional laws are passed by the Chamber of Deputies and the Senate in two successive sessions at an interval of not less than three months and are approved by an absolute majority of the members of each Chamber after a second reading.

The laws themselves are submitted to popular referendum when, within three months of their publication, a demand shall be made by one fifth of the members of either Chamber or by 500,000 electors or by five Regional Councils. A law submitted to referendum shall not be promulgated unless approved by a majority of valid votes.

A referendum shall not be held if the law has been approved in both Chambers, during a second reading, by a majority of two thirds of the members of each Chamber.

Art. 139. The Republican structure is not subject to constitutional amendment.

TRANSITORY AND FINAL PROVISIONS

I. When the Constitution becomes effective, the Provisional Head of the State shall assume the title of President of the Republic and exercise the attributes of this office.

II. If at the time of the election of the President of the Republic the Regional Councils have not all been constituted, then only the members of the two Chambers shall participate in the said election.

III. By a decree of the President of the Republic, for the first term the Senate will include among its members deputies of the Constituent Assembly who have the necessary qualifications by law for election to the Senate and who:

- have been President of the Council of Ministers, or Speaker or President of legislative bodies;
- have been members of the dissolved Senate;
- have been three times elected, including election to the Constituent Assembly;
- were dismissed during the session of the Chamber of Deputies of November 9, 1926;
- have suffered imprisonment for a period of not less than five years in consequence of sentences passed by the Special Fascist Court for State Defence.

Members of the dissolved Senate who were also members of the National Consultative Assembly are also nominated Senators, by decree of the President of the Republic.

The right to nomination as Senator may be renounced prior to signature of the decree of nomination. Acceptance of candidacy in political elections implies renunciation of the right to be nominated Senator.

IV. In the case of first elections to the Senate, Molise is considered as a Region in itself, the number of its Senators depending on the proportion of its population.

V. The provisions contained in Article 80 of the Constitution, in so far as they concern international treaties which impose charges on the budget or modifications of law, shall be effective from the date of convocation of the two Chambers.

VI. Within five years of the effective date of the Constitution, a revision of the special organs of jurisdiction now existing shall be undertaken, with the exception of the Council of State, the Court of Accounts and Military Tribunals.

Within one year of the said date provision shall be made by law for the reorganization of the Supreme Military Tribunal according to Article 111.

VII. Until such time as new legislation on the Judiciary shall bring it into conformity with the Constitution, the norms at present in force shall continue to be observed.

Until such time as the Constitutional Court shall begin to function, decisions over controversies as under Article 134 shall be rendered according to the forms and limits existing prior to the effective date of the Constitution.

The judges of the Constitutional Court, nominated for the initial composition of that Court, shall not be subject to partial re-election and shall remain in office for a period of twelve years.

VIII. The election of the Regional Councils and the elective organs of provincial administration shall take place within one year of the effective date of the Constitution.

The laws of the Republic regulate, for all branches of public administration, the transfer of central government powers attributed to the Regions. Until provisions have been made for the reorganization and distribution of administrative functions among local government, the Provinces and "Comuni" shall retain the functions they exercise at the present time as well as others which may be delegated to them by the Regions.

The laws of the Republic regulate the transfer of public officials and dependents to the Regions, including those of central government, whenever such transfer shall be deemed necessary because of reorganization.

In setting up their departments, the Regions must, except in cases of necessity, draw personnel from the Civil Service and local public bodies.

IX. Within three years of the effective date of the Constitution, the Republic shall adjust laws according to the requirements of local autonomy and the legislative competence attributed to the Regions.

X. The general norms contained in Title V of Part Two shall be provisionally applied to Friuli-Venezia Giulia referred to in Article 116; the protection of linguistic minorities remains binding as per Article 6.

XI. Other Regions may be formed during the first five year period of the Constitution, by constitutional enactment and in modification of the list contained in Article 131, without recourse to the procedure required under paragraph one of Article 132, but with the obligation to hear the opinions of the interested populations.

XII. Reorganization of the former Fascist Party, under any form whatsoever, is prohibited.

Notwithstanding Article 48, temporary limitations are established by law, for a period of not over five years from the effective date of the Constitution, on the suffrage and eligibility of the responsible heads of the Fascist regime.

XIII. The members and descendants of the House of Savoy are not electors and may not hold any public office or elective position.

Former kings of the House of Savoy, their wives and their male descendants may not enter or remain in Italian territory.

Property within Italian territory belonging to the former kings of the House of Savoy, their wives and their male descendants, revert to the State. Transfers and the establishment of royal rights on such properties, which took place after June 2, 1946, are null and void.

XIV. Titles of nobility are not recognized.

The predicates of those existing before October 28, 1922, serve as part of the proper name.

The Order of Ss. Maurizio e Lazzaro is preserved as a hospital corporation and functions according to the methods established by law.

The law regulates the suppression of the Heraldic Council.

XV. When the Constitution goes into effect, the legislative decree of the Lieutenant of the Realm of June 25, 1944, No. 151 on the provisional organization of the State is held to be converted to law.

XVI. Within one year from the effective date of the Constitution, the preceding constitutional laws, which have not been explicitly or implicitly abrogated, shall be revised and co-ordinated to conform with the Constitution itself.

XVII. The Constituent Assembly shall be convened by its President before January 31, 1948, to decide on the laws for the election of the Senate of the Republic, on the special regional statutes and on the law governing the press.

Prior to the date of the elections, the Constituent Assembly may be convened, whenever there is need to decide on matters within its competence, under Article 2, paragraphs one and two, and Article 3, paragraphs one and two, of the legislative decree of March 16, 1946 No. 98.

The Standing Committees shall continue to function during this period

The Legislative Committees shall submit all Bills transmitted to them, with appropriate observations and proposals of amendments to the Government.

Deputies may question the Government and request written replies.

With reference to Paragraph 2 of this present Article, the Constituent Assembly is convened by its President on the written request of the Government or at least two hundred deputies.

XVIII. This present Constitution shall be promulgated by the Provisional Head of the State within five days of its approval by the Constituent Assembly, and shall come into effect as from January 1st, 1948.

The text of the Constitution shall be deposited in the Town Hall of each "Comune" of the Republic and shall be on view during the whole of 1948 in order that every citizen shall have knowledge of it.

The Constitution, bearing the Seal of State, shall be inserted in the Official Records of the Laws and Decrees of the Republic.

The Constitution shall be faithfully observed as the fundamental law of the Republic by all citizens and organs of the State.

LIECHTENSTEIN

SUMMARY

INTERNATIONAL STATUS

Liechtenstein is not a member of the United Nations. It is a party to the Statute of the International Court of Justice (1950).[1]

Liechtenstein was created a principality in 1719 and was a state of the Holy Roman Empire until 1806. It was a member of the Napoleonic Rhenish Confederation until 1815, of the German Confederation from 1815 to 1866. It was in customs union with Austria from 1852 until 1918 and

[1] And accepts the compulsory jurisdiction of the Court under Article 36 of the Statute.

closely associated with Austria. In 1919, it requested the Swiss Federal Council to assume the diplomatic representation of its interests and maintains, in consequence, a legation only in Berne. Since 1924, it has been in a customs union with Switzerland.

FORM OF NATIONAL GOVERNMENT

The Constitution of October 5, 1921, as amended to 1965, states that the Principality is an inalienable and indivisible whole, a constitutional hereditary monarchy on a democratic and parliamentary basis.[1] The sovereign power is inherent in and issues from the Prince and the people.[2] A chapter relates to the functions of the state, in particular education, maintenance of public health, safeguarding the right to work and assisting agriculture.[3]

RIGHTS OF THE PEOPLE

The Constitution provides freedom of residence, equality before the law, personal liberty, immunity of the domicile, inviolability of correspondence, no extraordinary courts, inviolability of private property, freedom of trade and industry, freedom of religion and conscience, of the press, association and assembly, of petition.[4] All men must defend the country in case of emergency but other than that armed units may not be organized and maintained except for the police service.[5]

LEGISLATIVE DEPARTMENT

The Diet is composed of fifteen representatives, nine elected by the Upper Country (Oberland) and six by the Lower Country (Unterland) by universal, equal, secret and direct suffrage and proportional representation.[6] The term of office is four years, subject to dissolution, and the Diet sits at least every month.[7] Immunities of deputies are provided.[8] The Diet has the right of control over the whole of the State administration.[9] There are provisions concerning finances.[10] The National Council acts in the place of the Diet between sessions and is composed of the President of the Diet and four other members.[11]

EXECUTIVE DEPARTMENT

The hereditary Prince is the Head of State, his person sacred and inviolable, he, through the Government, executes the laws, has the power of

[1] Const., Art. 1, 2.
[2] Id., Art. 2.
[3] Id., Art. 14–27.
[4] Id., Art. 28–43.
[5] Id., Art. 44.
[6] Id., Art. 45, 46.
[7] Id., Art. 47–49.
[8] Id., Art. 56.
[9] Id., Art. 63.
[10] Id., Art. 68, 69, 70.
[11] Id., Art. 71, 72.

appointment and pardon.[1] The whole national administration except educational affairs, is conducted by the Government composed of the Head of the Government and four Government Councillors appointed by the Prince on the proposal and with the concurrence of the Diet.[2] Their term of office is four years.[3] The Head of the Government is also Chairman of the National Board of Education.[4]

JUDICIAL DEPARTMENT

The courts are independent.[5] There is provision for a Lower Court, a High Court and a Supreme Court.[6] The Constitution provides an Administrative Tribunal to which may be appealed all decisions and orders of the Government the judges of which are appointed by the Diet for the same term as the Government.[7] There is a State Tribunal as a court of public law to protect the rights accorded by the Constitution, decide conflicts of jurisdictions and to act as a disciplinary court for members of the Government, the members of which are appointed by the Diet.[8]

AREA, POPULATION, ETC.

The area of Liechtenstein is 160 square kilometres, the population (1963) 18,426. The capital is Vaduz.[9] German is the national and official language.[10]

[1] Id., Art. 3, 7–12. [2] Id., Art. 78, 79. [3] Id., Art. 79. [4] Id., Art. 85, 95.
[5] Id., Art. 99. [6] Id., Art. 101–103. [7] Id., Art. 97. [8] Id., Art. 104, 105.
[9] Id., Art. 1. [10] Id., Art. 6.

CONSTITUTION of LIECHTENSTEIN [1]

October 5, 1921, as amended 1939, 1947, 1958, 1963 and 1965

CHAPTER I

THE PRINCIPALITY

Art. 1. The Principality of Liechtenstein constitutes, by the union of both its regions, Vaduz and Schellenberg, an indivisible and inalienable whole; the region of Vaduz (*Oberland*) consists of the communes of Vaduz, Balzers, Planken, Schaan, Triesen, and Triesenberg; the region of Schellenberg (*Unterland*) consists of the communes of Eschen, Gamprin, Mauren, Ruggell, and Schellenberg.

Vaduz is the capital and the seat of the State authorities.

Art. 2. The Principality is a constitutional, hereditary monarchy upon democratic and parliamentary basis (Articles 79 and 80); the power of the State is inherent in and issues from the Prince and the people, and shall be exercised by both of them in accordance with the provisions of the present Constitution.

Art. 3. The succession to the throne, hereditary in the Princely House of Liechtenstein, the coming-of-age of the Prince Regnant and of the Heir Apparent, as well as any guardianship which may be required, are to be determined by the laws of the Princely House.

Art. 4. Changes in the boundaries of the territory of the State or of individual communes thereof, the creation of new communes, and the joining together of existing ones, may take place only by virtue of a law.

Art. 5. The coat of arms of the State is that of the Princely House of Liechtenstein; the national colours are blue and red.

Art. 6. The German language is the national and official language.

[1] *Constitution of the Principality of Liechtenstein.* Translated at the request of the Government of the Principality by Dr. Pierre Raton (United Nations Legal Office). Published by the Presidential Office of the Princely Government, Vaduz, 1965. Supplied by the Press and Information Department in July 1966. Ed.

CHAPTER II

THE PRINCE

Art. 7. The Prince is the head of the State, and shall exercise his sovereign authority in conformity with the provisions of the present Constitution and of the other laws.

His person is sacred and inviolable.

Art. 8. The Prince shall represent the State in all its relations with foreign countries, without prejudice to the necessary co-operation of the responsible Government.

Treaties which cede national territory, alienate national property, dispose of rights of sovereignty or State prerogatives, assume any new burden for the Principality or its citizens, or contract any obligation to the detriment of the rights of the people of the Principality shall not be valid unless they have been approved by the Diet.

Art. 9. Every law shall require the sanction of the Prince in order to acquire validity.

Art. 10. The Prince shall take, through the Government, and independently of the Diet, the steps required for the execution and administration of the laws, and any action required in pursuance of the powers of administration and supervision, and shall issue the requisite ordinances (Article 92). In urgent cases he shall take the necessary measures for the security and welfare of the State.

Art. 11. The Prince shall appoint the State officials, in conformity with the provisions of the present Constitution. New permanent official posts may be created only with the consent of the Diet.

Art. 12. The Prince shall possess the prerogative of remitting, mitigating or commuting sentences which have been legally pronounced, and of quashing prosecutions that have been initiated.

Only at the instigation of the Diet will the Prince exercise his prerogative of remission or mitigation in favor of a member of the Government sentenced on account of his official acts.

Art. 13. Every successor to the throne will, before receiving the oath of allegiance, declare upon his princely honor and dignity in a written proclamation that he will govern the Principality of Liechtenstein in conformity with the Constitution and the other laws, that he will maintain its integrity, and will observe the rights of sovereignty indivisibly and in like manner.

In the case of a prolonged absence from the country, the Prince Regnant will send a prince of his House to the Principality for a specified period each year, and also as occasion may require, and will empower him to act as his representative and to exercise the sovereign rights appertaining to him.

CHAPTER III

THE FUNCTIONS OF THE STATE

Art. 14. The chief function of the State is to promote the general welfare of the people. For this purpose the State shall provide for the institution and maintenance of the law, and for the protection of the religious, moral and economic interests of the people.

Art. 15. The State shall devote particular attention to education and schooling. These must be so ordered and administered that, as a result of the co-operation of the family, the school and the church, the younger generation may be imbued with religious and moral principles and patriotic feelings, and may be fitted for their future occupations.

Art. 16. The whole field of education and schooling shall be under the supervision of the State, without prejudice to the inviolability of the doctrine of the Church.

Education shall be compulsory for all.

The State shall see to it that adequate compulsory instruction in the elementary subjects is given free of charge in public schools.

Religious instruction shall be given by the church authorities.

All persons having children under their care shall be responsible for seeing that they receive education of the standard prescribed for public elementary schools.

Attendance at continuation schools may be declared compulsory.

The supreme control over education and schooling, which is vested in the State, shall be exercised by the latter through the National Board of Education, the organization and duties of which shall be laid down by law.

Private education shall be allowed in so far as it is in conformity with the legal regulations governing length of schooling, educational aims, and arrangements prevailing in the public schools.

Art. 17. The State shall assist and encourage continuation schools and lower-grade secondary schools (*Realschulen*), as also domestic agricultural and industrial education and training.

It shall provide appropriate scholarships in order to assist children of good intellectual attainments, but without financial means, to attend higher schools.

Art. 18. The State shall promote the maintenance of public health, assist institutions for the care of the sick, and seek by legislation to combat intemperance and to reform alcoholics and work-shy persons.

Art. 19. The State shall safeguard the right to work and shall protect the workers, especially in the case of women and young persons employed in commerce and industry.

Sundays and holidays recognized by the State shall be observed as public days of rest, without prejudice to the legal regulations concerning rest on Sundays and holidays.

Art. 20. In order to increase earning capacity and to advance its economic interests, the State shall promote and assist agriculture, alpine farming, trade and industry. In particular it shall promote insurance against damage to which workers and goods are exposed, and shall take measures to prevent such damage.

It shall pay especial attention to the development of communications in accordance with modern requirements.

It shall assist in the preventive building operations against the effects of mountain torrents (*Rüfeverbauungen*), in afforestation and drainage operations, and shall watch over and encourage every endeavor to open up new sources of wealth.

Art. 21. The State shall possess sovereign rights over waters, in conformity with the laws existing or hereafter to be enacted on this matter. The utilisation and conducting of, and protection from waters shall be legally regulated and promoted, with due regard to the developments of technical science. Rights relating to electricity shall be regulated by law.

Art. 22. The State shall exercise sovereign rights over hunting, fishing and mining; when legislating on these matters it shall protect the interests of agriculture and of communal revenues.

Art. 23. Questions concerning currency and public credit shall be regulated by the State.

Art. 24. The State shall provide, by enacting the necessary legislation, for an equitable system of taxation, which shall exempt incomes below a bare minimum from taxation, and impose heavier burdens on the higher grades of property or income.

The financial situation of the State must be improved to the utmost possible extent, and every effort must be made to open up new sources of revenue to meet the public requirements.

Art. 25. Public poor relief shall be administered by the communes in conformity with specific laws; nevertheless, the State shall supervise their action in this sphere. It may grant appropriate assistance to the communes, especially for the proper care of orphans, the mentally defective, incurables, and aged persons.

Art. 26. The State shall assist and promote insurance against sickness, old age, disability and fire.

Art. 27. The State shall provide for a rapid procedure for legal actions and the execution thereof, under conditions that will safeguard material rights; it shall also provide for a system of dispensing administrative law based on the same principles.

The exercise of the professional representation of parties shall be regulated by law.

CHAPTER IV

THE GENERAL RIGHTS AND OBLIGATIONS OF CITIZENS OF THE PRINCIPALITY

Art. 28. Every citzen of the Principality shall be freely entitled to reside in any locality in the territory of the State and to acquire property of any description, provided that he observes the detailed legal regulations relating to such matters.

The domicile rights of aliens shall be determined by treaties or, in their absence, on a basis of reciprocity.

Persons staying within the territory of the Principality shall be bound to observe its laws, and shall become entitled to the protection afforded by the Constitution and the other laws.

Art. 29. All citizens of the Principality shall be entitled to civic rights in conformity with the provisions of the present Constitution.

Art. 30. The conditions under which citizenship rights may be acquired or forfeited shall be laid down in the laws.

Art. 31. All citizens shall be equal in the eyes of the law. The public offices shall be equally open to them, subject to observance of the legal regulations.

The rights of aliens shall be determined in the first instance by treaties, or, in the absence of such, on a basis of reciprocity.

Art. 32. Personal liberty, the immunity of the home and the inviolability of letters and written matter are guaranteed.

Except in the cases specified in the laws and in the manner thus prescribed, nobody may be arrested or detained in custody, no houses or persons may be searched, and no letters or written matter may be examined or seized.

Persons arrested unlawfully or when obviously innocent, and those who are proved innocent after having been convicted, shall be entitled to full compensation from the State up to an amount to be determined by the courts. The question whether and to what extent the State has a right of recourse against third parties in such cases shall be regulated by law.

Art. 33. Nobody may be deprived of his usual judge; extraordinary courts may not be instituted.

Nobody may be threatened with or subjected to penalties other than those provided by the laws.

Accused persons shall always be entitled to be defended in penal proceedings.

Art. 34. The inviolability of private property is guaranteed; confiscation shall only take place in such cases as are laid down by the law.

Copyright shall be regulated by law.

Art. 35. Where requisite in the public interest, property of any kind may be compulsorily assigned or subjected to an encumbrance, against appropriate compensation, the amount of which in cases of dispute shall be determined by the courts.

The procedure for expropriation shall be regulated by law.

Art. 36. Trade and industry shall be free, within the limits prescribed by the law; the extent to which exclusive commercial and industrial privileges may be admissible for specified periods of time shall be regulated by law.

Art. 37. Religious liberty and freedom of conscience are guaranteed to all persons.

The Roman Catholic Church is the State church and as such enjoys the full protection of the State; other confessions shall be entitled to practise their creeds and to hold religious services so far as is consistent with morality and public order.

Art. 38. The right of ownership and all other proprietary rights of ecclesiastical communities and religious associations in respect of their institutions, endowments and other possessions devoted to worship, education and charity, are guaranteed. The administration of Church property in the parishes shall be regulated by a special law; the assent of the Church authorities shall be sought before the said law is promulgated.

Art. 39. The enjoyment of civil and political rights shall not be dependent on religious belief; nor may the latter constitute a ground for any dereliction of civil obligations.

Art. 40. Every person shall be entitled freely to express his opinions and to communicate his ideas verbally, in writing, in print, or by picture, within the limits of the laws and of morality; no censorship may be exercised except in respect of public performances and exhibitions..

Art. 41. The right of free association and assembly is guaranteed within the limits prescribed by the law.

Art. 42. The right of petitioning the Diet and the National Committee is guaranteed; not only individuals whose rights or interests are affected, but also communes and corporations are entitled to have their wishes and requests brought before the Diet through a member of that body.

Art. 43. The right of complaint is guaranteed. Any citizen shall be entitled to lodge a complaint regarding any action or procedure on the part of some public authority which is contrary to the Constitution, the laws or the official regulations and detrimental to his rights or interests. Such complaint shall be addressed to that authority which is immediately superior to the authority concerned, and may, if necessary, be pursued to the highest authority, except insofar as the right of recourse may be barred by a legal restriction. If a complaint thus submitted is rejected by the superior authority, the latter shall be bound to declare to the complaining party the reasons for its decision.

Art. 44. Every man fit to bear arms shall be liable, up to the completion of his sixtieth year, to serve in the defence of his country in the event of emergency.

Apart from this contingency, no armed units may be organized or maintained, except so far as may be necessary for the provision of the police service and the preservation of internal order. Detailed regulations regarding this matter shall be laid down by law.

CHAPTER V

THE DIET

Art. 45. The Diet is the legal organ representing the whole people of the Principality, and as such has the duty of safeguarding and vindicating the rights and interest of the people in relation to the Government, in conformity with the provisions of the present Constitution, also of promoting as far as is possible the welfare of the Princely House and of the country, while faithfully adhering to the principles laid down in this Constitution.

The rights appertaining to the Diet can only be exercised in the lawfully constituted assembly of that body.

Art. 46. The Diet shall consist of fifteen representatives, who shall be elected by the people by universal, equal, secret and direct suffrage, according to the system of proportional representation. The Upper Country (*Oberland*) and Lower Country (*Unterland*) shall each constitute a constituency. Of the fifteen representatives, nine shall be elected by the Upper Country and six by the Lower Country. In addition to the fifteen representatives, substitutes shall be elected in each constituency by each electoral group. The total number of substitutes in one constituency may not exceed the number of representatives to be elected in that constituency.

The number of substitutes shall be proportional to the strength of the political parties.

Detailed regulations regarding the conduct of the elections shall be laid down in a special law.

Art. 47. Representatives shall be elected for four years, provided that the regular elections shall be held in the February or March of the year when the fourth year of their mandate ends. Representatives shall be re-eligible.

The convention of the electoral groups to which a representative belongs has the right, on the proposal of the parliamentary section of the electoral group concerned, to recall the representative from the Diet, if it has serious grounds for doing so.

Art. 48. The Prince has the right, subject to the exception laid down in the following paragraph, to convene the Diet, to close it, and, on warrantable grounds, which must on each occasion be communicated to the assembled Diet, to prorogue it for three months or to dissolve it. The prorogation, closing or dissolution of the Diet may only be proclaimed before the assembled Diet.

In pursuance of a substantiated written request submitted by not less than six hundred citizens entitled to vote, or of a resolution adopted by the communal assemblies of not less than three communes, the Diet must be convened.

Subject to the same conditions as in the preceding paragraph, nine hundred citizens entitled to vote or four communes which have adopted resolutions to that effect at their communal assemblies, may demand a referendum with regard to the dissolution of the Diet.

Art. 49. The ordinary summons for the convocation of the Diet shall be issued at the beginning of every year in the form of a Princely edict, indicating the place, day and hour of the assembly.

The sittings of the Diet during the course of the year shall be arranged by its President.

When a period of prorogation has expired, a fresh summons convening the Diet shall be issued within one month, in the form of a Princely edict.

Should a representative be prevented from attending one or several consecutive sittings, a substitute from his electoral group shall sit and vote in his place.

Art. 50. Should the Diet be dissolved, new elections must take place within six weeks. The newly elected representatives shall then be summoned to meet within fourteen days.

Art. 51. In the case of an accession to the throne, the Diet shall be convened to an extraordinary sitting within thirty days for the purpose of receiving the declaration of the successor to the throne, as provided in Article 13, and of taking the oath of allegiance.

If the Diet has already been dissolved, the new elections shall be expedited so that it may be convened at the latest on the fortieth day after the change of sovereigns.

Art. 52. At its first regularly convened sitting, the Diet shall proceed, under the chairmanship of its oldest member, to the election of a President and a Vice-President from among its members to direct its affairs for the current year.

The minutes of the sittings shall be drawn up either by two secretaries elected from among its members, or by a Government official, as the Diet may decide.

Art. 53. The representatives shall be bound to attend in person at the seat of the Government in compliance with the summons. If a representative is impeded from attending, he must, on receiving the first summons, promptly notify the Government and subsequently the President, stating the reasons which prevent his attendance. If the impediment is of a permanent character a by-election shall be held, if the representative cannot be replaced by the substitution system.

Art. 54. The Diet shall be opened with due solemnity by the Prince, in person or by attorney. All the new members shall swear the following oath to the Prince or his representative:

"I hereby swear to observe the State Constitution and the existing laws, and to promote in the Diet the welfare of the country, without any ulterior motives, to the best of my ability and conscience. So help me God."

Members subsequently admitted take this oath before the President.

Art. 55. The Diet shall be closed by the Prince, in person or by attorney.

Art. 56. No representative may be arrested while the Diet is in session without the assent of that body, unless he is apprehended *in flagrante delicto.*

In the latter case, the arrest and the grounds therefor must be notified forthwith to the Diet, which shall decide whether the arrest is to be sustained. All papers relating to the case must be placed immediately at the disposal of the Diet if it so requests.

If a representative is arrested at a time when the Diet is not in session, the National Committee must be notified forthwith, and informed at the same time of the grounds for the arrest.

Art. 57. The members of the Diet shall vote solely according to their oath and their convictions. They shall never be made to answer for their votes; for their utterances at sittings of the Diet or its committees they shall be responsible to the Diet alone, and can never be sued before a court of justice in respect thereof.

The exercise of disciplinary powers shall be regulated by rules of procedure to be issued hereafter.

Art. 58. In order that a decision of the Diet may be valid, at least two-thirds of the statutory number of representatives must be present, and it must be adopted by an absolute majority of the members present, except as may otherwise be provided in the present constitution or in the rules of procedure. The same rules shall apply to elections which the Diet has to undertake.

In the case of equality of votes, the President shall give the casting vote: in the case of an election, after the third round of voting, and in all other cases after the first round.

Art. 59. Complaints relating to elections shall be referred to the State Tribunal.

The Diet shall adjudicate on the validity of the election of its members and of the election as such on the basis of the election records and, if applicable, of the decision of the State Tribunal (validation procedure).

Art. 60. The Diet shall adopt its rules of procedure by means of a resolution, having due regard to the provisions of the present Constitution.

Art. 61. Members of the Diet shall receive from the State Treasury a daily allowance and travelling expenses, as prescribed by law, in respect of their attendance at sittings of the Diet and its committees.

Art. 62. The following matters shall fall particularly within the sphere of activity of the Diet:

(a) Participation in the work of legislation, as provided in the Constitution.

(b) Participation in the conclusion of treaties (Article 8).

(c) The establishment of the annual budget and the authorization of taxes and other public dues.

(d) Decisions with regard to credits, pledges and loans chargeable to the State, and regarding the purchase and sale of State property.

(e) The resolution with regard to the report which has to be furnished annually by the Government in respect of the whole State administration.

(f) The making of suggestions and complaints with regard to the State administration as a whole or its various branches.

(g) The impeachment of members of the Government before the State Tribunal for breaches of the Constitution or of other laws.

Art. 63. The Diet shall possess the right of control over the whole of the State administration; it shall exercise this right through a supervisory committee, which it shall elect.

The Diet shall, moreover, be permitted at any time to bring defects or abuses which it has observed in the State administration directly to the notice of the Prince by the submission of memorials or complaints, and to request their redress. The results of the enquiry instituted in respect of such matters and the measures ordered in consequence shall be communicated to the Diet.

The Diet shall be entitled to appoint commissions to ascertain facts.

The representative of the Government must be given a hearing, and shall be bound to answer questions addressed to him by members of the Diet.

Art. 64. The right of initiative with regard to legislation, that is to say, the right of introducing draft laws, shall appertain to:

(a) The Prince, through the procedure of Government bills.

(b) The Diet itself.

(c) Citizens with the right to vote, subject to the following provisions:

If not less than six hundred citizens entitled to vote, whose signatures and qualification to vote are duly certified by the authorities of the commune in which they reside, submit a petition in writing, or if at least three communes do so in the form of resolutions of the communal assembly, in similar terms, requesting the enactment, modification or revocation of a law, such petition must be debated at the next sitting of the Diet.

If a petition from one of the organs referred to under (a) or (c) above concerns the enactment of a law which has not already been provided for in the present Constitution, and the adoption of which would involve public expenditure, whether in a single sum not provided for in the Finance Bill or in payments extending over a longer period, such petition shall only be discussed by the Diet if it is accompanied by proposals for providing the necessary funds.

Should a petition made under the right of initiative affect the Constitution, it must be submitted by not less than nine hundred citizens entitled to vote, or by at least four communes.

Further detailed regulations regarding the popular initiative shall be laid down in a law.

Art. 65. Without the participation of the Diet, no law may be issued, amended, or declared to be in force. For a law to become valid, it must in every case receive the assent of the Diet, be sanctioned by the Prince, countersigned by the responsible Head of the Government or his deputy, and promulgated in the National Legal Gazette (*Landesgesetzblatt*).

In addition, a popular vote (referendum) shall be held under the conditions set forth in the following article.

Art. 66. Every law passed by the Diet which it does not declare to be urgent, as well as every financial resolution which it does not declare urgent, shall, if it involves a new non-recurrent expenditure of 50,000 francs or a new annual expenditure of 20,000 francs, be submitted to a referendum if the Diet so decides, or if not less than six hundred citizens with the right to vote or not less than three communes submit a petition to that effect, according to the procedure prescribed in Article 64, within thirty days of the official publication of the resolution of the Diet.

If the issue affects the Constitution, either as a whole or in part, the demand for a referendum must be made by not less nine hundred citizens with the right to vote, or by not less than four communes.

The Diet is authorized to call for a referendum with regard to the adoption of any of the principles embodied in a proposed law.

The referendum shall be held by communes; the acceptance or rejection of the resolution as to the enactment of the law shall be decided by an absolute majority of the valid votes recorded in the whole country.

Resolutions as to the enactment of laws which are subject to a referendum shall not be submitted to the Prince for sanction until the referendum has been held, or until the statutory period of thirty days within which a petition for a referendum may be submitted has expired without any such action.

If the Diet rejects a bill drawn up in due form and accompanied, if requisite, by proposals for providing the necessary funds, which has been submitted to it through the procedure of the popular initiative (Article 64c), the said bill shall be submitted to a referendum. The acceptance of the bill by the citizens entitled to vote shall then have the same force as a resolution of the Diet, which is in other cases necessary for the adoption of a law.

Further detailed regulations regarding the referendum shall be issued in the form of a law.

Art. 67. Unless it contains any other stipulation, a law shall come into force on the expiry of eight days after the date of its publication in the National Legal Gazette.

Art. 68. Without the approval of the Diet, no direct or indirect taxes or any other public dues or general levies, under any designation whatsoever, may be imposed or collected. The fact that this approval has been given must be expressly mentioned in the tax demand notice.

The system by which all taxes and dues are to be apportioned, their incidence on persons and objects, and the manner in which they are to be collected shall also require the approval of the Diet.

Taxes and dues shall, as a rule, be authorized for the period of one administrative year.

Art. 69. With regard to the State administration, the Government shall submit to the Diet for examination and approval preliminary estimates of all expenditure and revenue for the coming administrative year, accompanied by proposals for the taxation which will be required.

In the first half of each administrative year, the Government shall submit to the Diet an exact statement relating to the preceding administrative year, showing the manner in which revenues approved and collected were applied to the purposes set forth in the preliminary estimates, with the provision, however, that if the latter have been exceeded on justifiable grounds the Diet must give its approval, and that in the absence of justification the Government shall be answerable.

The Government shall be entitled, subject to the same conditions as above, to incur expenditure of an urgent character not provided for in the estimates.

Economies effected in the case of individual items of the estimates may not be applied to cover excess expenditure for other items.

Art. 70. The Diet, acting in agreement with the Prince, shall have the control over the assets of the State Treasury.

CHAPTER VI

THE NATIONAL COMMITTEE

Art. 71. The National Committee (*Landesausschuss*) shall be constituted to act in place of the Diet for any business which requires the participation of the latter or of its committees during the period between the adjournment, closing or dissolution of the Diet and the date of its meeting again, without prejudice, however, to the provisions of Articles 48–51 concerning the time-limits for the reconvocation of the Diet and for the holding of new elections.

Art. 72. The National Committee shall be composed of the President of the Diet, who shall be represented if unable to attend by his deputy, and of four other members, to be elected by the Diet from its midst, equal consideration being given to the Upper Country (*Oberland*) and the Lower Country (*Unterland*).

Opportunity for this election must at all events be afforded to the Diet during the same sitting at which its prorogation, closing or dissolution is announced.

Art. 73. The term of office of the National Committee shall expire when the Diet reconvenes.

Art. 74. The National Committee shall have the following special powers and duties:

(a) To ensure that the Constitution is observed, that steps are taken for the execution of the decisions of the Diet, and, if the Diet should have been dissolved or adjourned, that it is reconvened within the prescribed time.

(b) To audit the accounts of the State Treasury and to transmit same to the Diet, together with its report and proposals.

(c) To append their signatures to acknowledgments in respect of debts and securities made out against the State Treasury, in pursuance of a previous resolution of the Diet.

(d) To carry out special tasks entrusted to it by the Diet in order to prepare the future proceedings of the latter.

(e) In urgent cases, to bring matters to the notice of the Prince, and to make representations, protests or remonstrances in the case of any menace to or violation of constitutional rights.

(f) Should the circumstances require it, to propose the convocation of the Diet.

Art. 75. The National Committee may not incur any permanent obligation on behalf of the Principality, and shall be responsible to the Diet for its conduct of affairs.

Art. 76. The meetings of the National Committee shall take place as required at the seat of the Government, upon convocation by the President.

For its decisions to be valid, at least three members must be present.

Art. 77. During the sessions of the National Committee, its members shall receive the same daily allowance and travelling expenses as the members of the Diet.

CHAPTER VII

THE AUTHORITIES

A. The Government

Art. 78. Subject to the provisions of the present article, the whole of the national administration, with the exception of educational affairs, shall be conducted by the Government as a corporate body responsible to the Prince and the Diet, in conformity with the provisions of the present Constitution and the other laws.

In order to be dealt with independently, specific functions may be transferred by law or by legally binding authorisations to certain official personages, government offices or special commissions, subject to recourse to the corporate Government.

Special commissions for dealing with complaints may be set up by law to act on behalf of the corporate Government.

With a view to taking care of economic, social and cultural obligations, special corporations, institutions and foundations of public law may be established by legislation. They shall remain under the control of the Government.

Art. 79. The corporate Government shall consist of the Head of the Government and four Government Councillors.

The Head of the Government and the Government Councillors shall be appointed by the Prince with the concurrence of the Diet and on the proposal of the latter. Substitutes shall be appointed in like manner for the Head of the Government and for each Government Councillor who may be prevented from attending the meetings of the Government in council.

On the proposal of the Diet, one of the Government Councillors shall be appointed by the Prince as Deputy Head of the Government.

The members of the Government must be natives of Liechtenstein and eligible for the Diet.

When the corporate Government is being appointed, care must be taken that at least two members are chosen from each of the two regions. Their substitutes must be chosen from the same region.

The period of office of the corporate Government shall be four years. Until a new Government is appointed, the previous members shall be responsible for carrying on the Government business.

Art. 80. If a member of the Government should, through his conduct of affairs, lose the confidence of the Diet, the latter may request the Prince to remove the member of the Government in question from his office, without prejudice to its right to bring a charge before the State Tribunal.

Art. 81. For a decision of the corporate Government to be valid, at least four members must be present and a majority of those members present must vote in favor. If the voting is equal, the chairman has the casting vote. Voting is compulsory.

Art. 82. The grounds on which a member of the Government may be debarred from taking part in official business or may be invited to obstain therefrom shall be laid down in the laws.

Art. 83. Government business shall be dealt with partly on a corporate and partly on a departmental basis.

Art. 84. The corporate Government shall issue its rules of procedure in the form of a Government regulation.

Art. 85. The Head of the Government shall also be Chairman of the National Board of Education. He shall preside at meetings of the Government, deal with business directly entrusted to him by the Prince, and countersign the laws, as well as any decrees or ordinances issued by the Prince or a Regent. At public ceremonies he shall be accorded the honors prescribed by the regulations for the representative of the Prince.

Art. 86. The Head of the Government shall submit oral or written reports to the Prince with regard to matters placed under the authority of the Soveriegn.

The texts of the decisions adopted by the Sovereign on his proposal shall be signed by the Prince with his own hand, and shall further be countersigned by the Head of the Government.

Art. 87. The Head of the Government shall take his oath of office before the Prince or the Regent; the other members of the Government and the State officials shall be sworn in by the Head of the Government.

Art. 88. If the Head of the Government should be prevented from attending to his duties, the Deputy Head of the Government shall take over those functions which, according to the Constitution, expressly appertain to the Head of the Government. If the Deputy Head of the Government should also be indisposed, the eldest Government Councillor shall take his place.

Art. 89. The Head of the Government shall sign the decrees and orders issued by the Government in pursuance of its decisions taken in council. He shall further exercise direct supervision over the conduct of business in the Government.

Art. 90. All important matters assigned to the Government, especially the settlement of administrative disputes, shall be dealt with on the grounds of discussion and decision by the Government in council. Certain less important matters may be assigned by law to the appropriate members of the Government in accordance with the distribution of Government business, to be dealt with independently.

Minutes shall be taken at Government meetings by the Government Secretary, or, if he should be prevented from attending, by a substitute to be appointed by the corporate Government.

The Head of the Government is responsible for executing the decisions of the corporate Government. Only if he is of the opinion that a decision is contrary to existing laws or regulations may he delay its execution. He must, however, immediately intimate the matter to the Administrative Tribunal, which, without prejudice to the right of appeal of a party involved, shall determine whether the decision shall be implemented or not.

Art. 91. At the beginning of each period of office, the corporate Government shall distribute its business between the Head of the Government and the Government Councillors in order to prepare the matters to be determined in council and to deal with that business which by law may be treated independently. A system of mutual deputizing shall be arranged for cases of indisposition.

Art. 92. The Government shall be responsible for the execution of all laws and of all such tasks as may be lawfully entrusted to it by the Prince or the Diet. In order to give effect to the laws it shall issue the necessary regulations, which must, however, be confined within the limits of the said laws.

All organs of the national administration must take care to confine their action within the limits of the Constitution and the other laws; even in matters in which the law allows the administrative authorities freedom of judgment, the limits imposed thereon by the law must be scrupulously observed.

Art. 93. The following matters shall fall particularly within the sphere of action of the Government:

(a) Surveillance over all authorities and officials placed under the Government, and the exercise of disciplinary powers in respect of officials.

(b) The allotment of the staff required for the Government and the other authorities.

(c) Supervision of the prisons and of the treatment of persons detained in custody and of convicts.

(d) The administration of buildings belonging to the State.

(e) Supervision of the despatch of business by the Lower Court in order to ensure that it is conducted lawfully and diligently, and the notification to the Court of Appeal of any irregularities observed.

(f) The preparation of the report on its official activities which has to be submitted annually to the Diet.

(g) The preparation of Government bills for submission to the Diet; and the expression of its opinion on proposals submitted to it for that purpose by the Diet.

(h) The decision with regard to urgent expenditure not provided for in the estimates.

Art. 94. The organization of the administration shall be established by law.

B. The National Board of Education

Art. 95. The composition and sphere of action of the National Board of Education (*Landesschulrat*) shall be determined by a law.

Art. 96. (*removed*).

C. The Administrative Tribunal

Art. 97. Except as otherwise provided by law, all decisions or orders of the Government shall be subject to appeal before the Administrative Tribunal. The said Tribunal shall consist of a chairman trained in the law, who shall be appointed by the Prince on the proposal of the Diet, of his deputy, and of four appeal judges and their substitutes elected by the Diet. The chairman and his deputy must be natives of Liechtenstein.

Their term of office shall coincide with that of the Diet, and end at such a time as they are replaced. At its first sitting the Diet shall nominate a chairman and his deputy for the Tribunal and shall elect the appeal judges and their substitutes.

Art. 98. Further detailed instructions for ensuring the judicial independence of the members of the Administrative Tribunal, regarding procedure, abstention, allowances to be paid to the members, and fees to be paid by the parties involved shall be laid down in a separate law.

D. The Administration of Justice

Art. 99. The whole administration of justice shall be carried out in the name of the Prince by responsible judges.

The Courts, within the lawful limits of their powers, and when engaged in judicial proceedings, shall be independent of all interference on the part of the Government. Their decisions and judgements shall be accompanied by a statement of reasons.

Art. 100. The revenue authorities and the officials of the Crown lands shall resort to the ordinary courts to prosecute or to defend claims.

Art. 101. Jurisdiction shall be exercised in the first instance by the Princely Lower Court (*Landgericht*) at Vaduz, in second instance by the Princely High Court at Vaduz, and in third instance by the Princely Supreme Court of Justice.

The organization of the courts, the procedure, and the scale of fees shall be laid down by law.

Art. 102. The procedure in civil disputes shall conform to the principles of oral proceedings, direct hearing and free appraisement of evidence. In penal cases the principle of arraignment shall also be observed.

Civil cases, in first instance, shall be heard by one or by several judges, acting individually.

The High Court and the Supreme Court of Justice are corporate judicial bodies, whose members shall be appointed by the Prince in agreement with the Diet, on the proposal of the latter.

In criminal cases justice shall be administered in first instance in the Lower Court and by that court, or, when required, by the Assize Court, the Criminal Court, or the Juvenile Court.

Art. 103. The judge of the Lower Court (*Landrichter*) shall be in charge of that court, and shall exercise, in first instance, disciplinary authority over the non-judicial officials of the said court.

The High Court shall supervise the administration of justice, and shall exercise disciplinary authority over the judicial officials of the Lower Court; it shall also exercise disciplinary authority in second instance over the non-judicial officials of the Lower Court.

The Supreme Court of Justice shall exercise disciplinary powers over the members of the High Court, and shall also act as a court of appeal in disciplinary questions for the judicial officials of the Lower Court.

E. The State Tribunal

Art. 104. A State Tribunal shall be set up, by a special law, as a court of public law to protect rights accorded by the Constitution, to decide in conflicts of jurisdiction between the law courts and the administrative authorities, and to act as a disciplinary court for members of the Government.

The said court shall have jurisdiction to determine whether laws are in conformity with the Constitution and whether Government regulations are in conformity with the laws; in such cases it may declare their annulment. It shall finally act as an administrative court and as an electoral tribunal.

Art. 105. The State Tribunal shall consist of a President and four other members entitled to vote; the members shall be elected by the Diet in such a manner as to ensure a majority of natives of Liechtenstein; two of its members must be trained in the law. The election of the President, who must be a native of Liechtenstein, shall be subject to confirmation by the Prince.

Art. 106. The members of the State Tribunal shall enjoy the protection of judicial independence.

F. General Provisions

Art. 107. Candidates for employment in the Liechtenstein civil service must possess civic rights in the Principality, without prejudice to any further conditions required by the present Constitution. No exception to this rule may be made without the assent of the Diet.

Art. 108. The organization of the authorities shall be determined by legislation. All authorities must have their seat within the territory of the State; authorities with a corporate organization must include at least a majority of natives of Liechtenstein.

Art. 109. Members of the Government, State officials, and all mayors, their deputies, and the treasurers of the communes shall take the following oath on appointment:

"I swear that I will be loyal to the Prince, that I will obey the laws, and that I will strictly observe the Constitution. So help me God."

The State, the communes, and other corporations, institutions and foundations of public law are liable for damage caused to third persons by individuals acting as their organs who in their official capacity act illegally. In the case of wilful damage or gross negligence, restitution by the responsible persons is reserved.

Individuals acting as organs are answerable to the State, the commune, or other corporation, institution or foundation of public law which they serve, for any damage directly caused to that body through wilful or grossly negligent breach of their official duties.

Further dispositions, in particular those relating to competence, shall be laid down in a separate law.

CHAPTER VIII

COMMUNAL AFFAIRS

Art. 110. Provisions concerning the number, organization and duties of the communes in their own sphere of action and in that assigned to them shall be laid down in the laws.

The laws concerning the communes shall establish the following principles:

(a) Free election of the mayor and of the other officials of the commune by the communal assembly.

(b) Autonomous management of the communal property and administration of the local police, under the supervision of the Government.

(c) Maintenance of a well-ordered poor-relief system, under the supervision of the Government.

(d) The right of the commune to grant citizenship, and the freedom of nationals of the Principality to reside in any commune.

CHAPTER IX

THE MAINTENANCE OF THE CONSTITUTION AND FINAL PROVISIONS

Art. 111. The present Constitution shall be universally binding after its promulgation as a fundamental law of the country.

Any amendments to or interpretations of this fundamental law which may be proposed either by the Government or by the Diet or through the procedure of the initiative (Article 64) shall require the approval of the Diet, either by unanimous vote of the members present, or by a majority of three quarters of the members present at two successive sittings of the Diet.

Art. 112. Should any doubts arise with regard to the interpretation of certain clauses of the Constitution which cannot be removed by agreement between the Government and the Diet, the State Tribunal shall decide in respect thereof.

Art. 113. All laws, regulations and statutory provisions which contradict any express provision of the present Constitution are hereby revoked and declared of no effect; those legal provisions which are inconsistent with the spirit of this fundamental law shall be revised so that they conform with the Constitution.

Art. 114. The Government shall be entrusted with the execution of the present Constitution.

The Government shall prepare the laws provided for in the present Constitution with all possible despatch, and shall proceed with them as laid down in the Constitution.

The Diet as constituted at present shall remain in office until the end of this year.

LUXEMBOURG

SUMMARY

INTERNATIONAL STATUS

Luxembourg is a member of the United Nations (October 24, 1945).[1] It is a member of the European Economic Community, of Benelux, and of other international organizations. It was a member of the League of Nations.

The Duchy of Luxembourg, after four centuries under Burgundian, Spanish, Austrian or French domination, was created by the Congress of

[1] It accepts the compulsory jurisdiction of the International Court under Article 36 of its Statute.

Vienna a Grand Duchy under William I of Holland who was also the Grand Duke of Luxembourg. The 1839 Treaty of London recognizing the independence of Belgium also brought about the independence of Luxembourg which was still, however, ruled by the Dutch King as Grand Duke and was a member of the German Confederation. The 1839 Treaty also ceded the western half of its territory to Belgium which had occupied it in 1830 and then claimed all of Luxembourg. Luxembourg was granted a Constitution in 1841. The Treaty of London of May 11, 1867, after the dissolution of the German Confederation, declared Luxembourg an independent and neutral state, under the protection of the signatories, and required that its fortress be dismantled. In 1890 the first Grand Duke succeeded who was not also King of Holland. Luxembourg was invaded and occupied by Germany in both world wars. The Belgian Economic Union came into force in 1922 and the Benelux Customs Union on January 1, 1948, the Economic Union on February 3, 1958.

FORM OF NATIONAL GOVERNMENT

The Constitution of October 17, 1868, as amended in 1919, 1948 and 1956, replaces that of October 12, 1841. It states that the Grand Duchy is a free, independent and individual state placed under the system of parliamentary democracy.[1] Sovereign power resides in the nation.[2]

RIGHTS OF THE PEOPLE

The Constitution guarantees equality before the law, the natural rights of the individual and family including the right to work, the liberties of trade unions, freedom of commerce and industry and the exercise of the liberal and agricultural professions, individual liberty, due process of law, inviolability of domicile, the right of property, liberty of religion, free primary education, liberty of the press, assembly, association, petition, secrecy of correspondence.[3] The death penalty is abolished in political and civil matters.[4]

LEGISLATIVE DEPARTMENT

Legislative power is exercised by the unicameral Chamber of Deputies the members of which represent the country as a whole.[5] Deputies are elected by universal suffrage and proportional representation for a term of six years subject to dissolution.[6] Immunities of deputies are provided.[7] It meets in one ordinary session a year.[8] A section relates to finances.[9]

[1] Const., Art. 1, 51. [2] Id., Art. 32. [3] Id., Art. 11–28. [4] Id., Art. 18.
[5] Id., Art. 50. [6] Id., Art. 51, 56, 74. [7] Id., Art. 68, 69.
[8] Id., Art. 72. [9] Id., Art. 99–106.

EXECUTIVE DEPARTMENT

The Grand Duke alone exercises the executive power.[1] He promugates the laws, has the power of appointment, the right of pardon, commands the Armed Forces, confers titles and orders.[2] The person of the Grand Duke is inviolable; the members of the government, which must number at least three, are responsible.[3] A section relates to the communes.[4]

JUDICIAL DEPARTMENT

The courts and other jurisdictions may be established only by law; extraordinary commissions and tribunals under whatever name are forbidden.[5] A Supreme Court of Justice is provided for by law.[6] Judges are appointed by the Grand Duke for life.[7]

AREA, POPULATION, ETC.

The area of Luxembourg is 2,586 square kilometres, the population (1965) 331,000. The capital is the City of Luxembourg.[8]

[1] Id., Art. 33. [2] Id., Art. 34–41. [3] Id., Art. 4, 76, 78. [4] Id., Art. 107, 108.
[5] Id., Art. 86. [6] Id., Art. 87. [7] Id., Art. 90, 91. [8] Id., Art. 109.

CONSTITUTION
of
LUXEMBOURG[1]

October 17, 1868, as amended May 15, 1919, April 28, May 6 and 21, 1948, July 27 and October 25, 1956

CHAPTER I

THE TERRITORY AND THE GRAND DUKE

Art. 1. The Grand Duchy of Luxembourg forms a free, independent and indivisible State.

Art. 2. The boundaries and chief towns of judicial or administrative districts, of cantons, and of communes may not be changed except by law.

Art. 3. The crown of the Grand Duchy is hereditary in the family of Nassau, in accordance with the Pact of June 30, 1783, Article 71 of the Treaty of Vienna of June 9, 1815, and Article 1 of the Treaty of London of May 11, 1867.

Art. 4. The person of the Grand Duke is sacred and inviolable.

Art. 5. The Grand Duke of Luxembourg shall reach his majority at the age of eighteen years. When he takes the reins of government, he shall, as soon as possible, in the presence of the Chamber of Deputies or of a deputation appointed by it, take the following oath:

"I swear to observe the Constitution and the laws of the Grand Duchy of Luxembourg, to maintain the national independence and the integrity of its territory, as well as public and individual liberty, and also the rights of all and each of my subjects, and, for the conservation and development of general and particular prosperity to use as a good sovereign should, all the means that the laws place at my disposal. So help me God!"

Art. 6. If, at the death of the Grand Duke, his successor is a minor, the regency shall be exercised in conformity with the Family Pact.

Art. 7. If the Grand Duke is unable to govern, the same regency shall be provided for as in the case of a minority.

[1] French text supplied by the Ministry of Foreign Affairs in November 1965. Translated by the Editor. Ed.

In case of vacancy of the throne, the Chamber shall provide for a temporary regency. A new Chamber, convoked with double the usual number within thirty days, shall provide definitively for the vacancy.

Art. 8. Upon assumption of his functions, the regent shall take the following oath:

"I swear fidelity to the Grand Duke; I swear to observe the Constitution and the laws of the country. So help me God!"

CHAPTER II

LUXEMBOURGERS AND THEIR RIGHTS

Art. 9. The status of Luxembourger shall be acquired, conserved, and lost according to the rules determined by civil law.

The present Constitution and the other laws relating to political rights shall determine what other conditions are necessary for the exercise of such rights.

Art. 10. Naturalization shall be accorded by the legislative power.

A law shall determine the effects of naturalization.

Art. 11. There shall be no distinction of class in the state.

Luxembourgers are equal before the law; they alone shall be eligible for civil and military posts except as may be established by law for particular cases.

The State shall guarantee the natural rights of the individual and the family.

The law shall guarantee the right to work and assure to every citizen the exercise of this right.

The law shall organize social security, health protection and rest of workers and guarantee the liberties of trade unions.

The law shall guarantee freedom of commerce and industry, the exercise of liberal professions and agricultural labor, subject to the restrictions to be established by the legislative power.

Art. 12. Individual liberty is guaranteed.

No one may be prosecuted except in the cases provided for by law and in the form which it prescribes.

Except in cases of *flagrante delicto* no one may be arrested except by virtue of an order issued by a judge, that must be served at the moment of the arrest, or at the latest within twenty-four hours.

Art. 13. No one may be deprived, against his will, of the judge assigned to him by law.

Art. 14. No penalty may be established or applied except by law.

Art. 15. The domicile is inviolable. No domiciliary visit may take place except in the cases provided for by law and in the form which it prescribes.

Art. 16. No one may be deprived of his property except for the public use, in the cases and manner established by law and following a just and prior indemnity.

Art. 17. The penalty of confiscation of possessions may not be established.

Art. 18. The penalty of death in political or civil matters, and of branding are abolished.

Art. 19. Liberty of religion and of public worship and liberty to make known one's religious opinions are guaranteed, subject to the repression of offenses committed on the occasion of the use of these liberties.

Art. 20. No one may be prohibited from participating in any manner whatsoever in the acts and ceremonies of a cult, or from observing its days of rest.

Art. 21. Civil marriage must always precede the nuptial benediction.

Art. 22. The intervention of the State in the appointment and installation of heads of cults, the method of appointment and dismissal of other ministers of cults, the right for one and the other to correspond with their superiors and to publish their acts, as well as the relations of the Church with the State, shall, insofar as intervention by the latter is required, form the object of conventions to be submitted to the Chamber of Deputies.

Art. 23. The State shall provide for every Luxembourger primary education, which shall be compulsory and without charge. Medical and social assistance shall be governed by law.

The State shall create establishments of secondary education and the necessary courses of superior instruction. It shall also establish free professional courses.

A law shall determine the means for meeting the cost of public instruction, as well as the conditions of surveillance by the Government and the communes; it shall regulate, moreover, all that relates to education, and establish a fund for those exceptionally gifted.

Every Luxembourger shall be free to pursue his studies in the Grand Duchy or abroad and to attend the universities of his choice, subject to the provisions of law on conditions of admission to employments or the exercise of certain professions.

Art. 24. Liberty to express one's opinion orally in all matters and liberty of the press are guaranteed, subject to the repression of offenses committed on the occasion of the exercise of these liberties.

Censhorship can never be established.

Surety bonds may not be required of writers, editors, or printers.

The stamp tax on Luxembourg journals and periodicals shall be abolished.

The editor, the printer, or the distributor cannot be prosecuted, if the author is known, if he is a Luxembourger and domiciled in the Grand Duchy.

Art. 25. Luxembourgers have the right to assemble peaceably and without arms in conformance with the laws that regulate the exercise of this right, which may not be made subject to prior authorization.

This provision does not apply to political, religious, or other assemblies in the open air. Such assemblies are entirely subject to the laws and police regulations.

Art. 26. Luxembourgers have the right to form associations. This right cannot be subject to any prior authorization.

The establishment of any religious corporation must be authorized by law.

Art. 27. Everyone has the right to address to the public authorities petitions signed by one or more persons.

Only the constituted authorities have the right to address collective petitions.

Art. 28. The secrecy of correspondence is inviolable.

A law shall determine who are the agents responsible for the violation of the secrecy of letters confided to the mails.

A law shall regulate the guaranty for the secrecy of telegrams.

Art. 29. A law shall determine the use of languages in administrative and judicial matters.

Art. 30. No prior authorization shall be required to bring suit against public officials for acts of their administration, except insofar as is provided with regard to members of the government.

Art. 31. Public officials of whatever branch, members of the government excepted, may be deprived of their functions, honors, and pensions only in the manner determined by law.

CHAPTER III

THE SOVEREIGN POWER

Art. 32. Sovereign power resides in the nation.

The Grand Duke shall exercise it in conformity with the present Constitution and the laws of the country.

He shall have no powers other than those formally vested in him by the Constitution and the special laws passed by virtue of the Constitution, without prejudice to Article 3 of the present Constitution.

Art. 33. The Grand Duke alone shall exercise the executive power.

Art. 34. The Grand Duke shall sanction and promulgate the laws. He shall make known his resolution within three months of the vote in the chamber.

Art. 35. The Grand Duke shall make appointments to civil and military posts, in accordance with the law and subject to the exceptions established by it.

No office salaried by the State may be created except by virtue of a legislative provision.

Art. 36. The Grand Duke shall make the regulations and orders necessary for the execution of the laws without ever being able to suspend the laws themselves, or dispense with their execution.

Art. 37. The Grand Duke shall conclude treaties. No treaty shall enter into force until it has been approved by law and published in the manner prescribed for the publication of laws.

The Treaties provided in Chapter III, Article 49 *bis* shall be approved by a law passed in accordance with the conditions stipulated in Article 114, paragraph 5.

Secret treaties shall be abolished.

The Grand Duke shall make the regulations and orders necessary for execution of treaties in the forms prescribed for executory measures for laws and with the same effects, without prejudice to matters reserved by the Constitution to the law.

No cession, no exchange, no addition of territory may take place except by virtue of a law.

The Grand Duke shall command the Armed Forces. He shall declare war and the cessation of hostilities only after receiving authorization by a vote of the Chamber passed under the conditions stipulated in Article 114, paragraph 5 of the Constitution.

Art. 38. The Grand Duke shall have the right to remit or reduce penalties pronounced by the judges, except as ordered with respect to members of the government.

Art. 39. The Grand Duke shall have the right to coin money in pursuance of law.

Art. 40. The Grand Duke shall have the right to confer titles of nobility without ever attaching any privileges thereto.

Art. 41. The Grand Duke shall confer civil and military orders, observing in this regard that which the law prescribes.

Art. 42. The Grand Duke may be represented by a prince of the blood who shall have the title of Lieutenant of the Grand Duke and shall reside in the Grand Duchy.

This representative shall take the oath to observe the Constitution before exercising his powers.

Art. 43. The civil list shall be fixed at three hundred thousand gold francs a year. It may be changed by law at the beginning of each reign. The budgetary law may grant to the Sovereign House each year the sums necessary to meet representation expenses.

Art. 44. The Grand-Ducal Palace at Luxembourg and the Castle of Berg shall be reserved for the residence of the Grand Duke.

Art. 45. The orders of the Grand Duke must be countersigned by a responsible Counselor of the Crown, with the exception of those that have for their object the honoring of foreigners with decorations not intended to recompense services rendered to the Grand Duchy.

2. Legislation

Art. 46. The assent of the Chamber of Deputies shall be required for every law.

Art. 47. The Grand Duke shall address to the Chamber bills which he wishes to submit for adoption.

The Chamber shall have the right to propose bills to the Grand Duke.

Art. 48. The interpretation of laws by the authorities amy not take place except by law.

3. Justice

Art. 49. Justice shall be rendered in the name of the Grand Duke by the courts and tribunals. Decrees and judgments shall be executed in the name of the Grand Duke.

4. International Powers

Art. 49bis. The exercise of the attributes reserved by the Constitution to the legislative, executive and judicial authorities may be temporarily derogated by treaty to institutions of international law.

CHAPTER IV

THE CHAMBER OF DEPUTIES

Art. 50. The Chamber of Deputies represents the country.

The deputies shall vote without reference to their constituents and may have in view only the general interests of the Grand Duchy.

Art. 51. The Grand Duchy of Luxembourg is placed under the system of parliamentary democracy.

The organization of the chamber shall be regulated by law.

The electoral law shall fixe the number of deputies according to the population. This number may not exceed one deputy for four thousand inhabitants, or be less than one deputy for five thousand five hundred inhabitants.

Elections shall be direct.

The deputies shall be elected on the basis of universal suffrage, pure and simple, by ballot, according to the rules of proportional representation, in conformity with the principle of the smallest electoral quotient, and under the rules to be determined by the law.

The country shall be divided into four electoral districts: the south (Esch and Capellen), the center (Luxembourg city, Luxembourg country, and Mersch) the north (Diekirch, Rédange, Wiltz, Clervaux, and Vianden), and the east (Grevenmacher, Remich, and Echternach).

Voters may be called upon to decide by means of referendum in the cases and conditions to be established by law.

Art. 52. In order to vote, it is necessary:

(1) to be a Luxembourger;

(2) to be in the enjoyment of civil and political rights;

(3) to be at least twenty-one years of age;

(4) to be domiciled in the Grand Duchy.

It is necessary, moreover, to have these four qualities in addition to those which are determined by the law. No tax condition may be exacted.

To be eligible for office, it is necessary to be at least twenty-five years of age and to fulfill the three other conditions enumerated above.

Art. 53. The following may neither vote nor be eligible for office:

(1) those condemned to criminal punishment;

(2) those condemned to imprisonment for theft, swindling, or abuse of confidence;

(3) those in a state of declared bankruptcy, bankrupts, those declared incapable of managing their own affairs, and those for whom legal counsel has been named.

The right to vote may nevertheless be granted as a matter of grace to persons condemned to imprisonment for theft, swindling, or abuse of confidence.

Art. 54. The mandate of deputy shall be incompatible:

(1) with the functions of a member of the Government;

(2) with those of a member of the Council of State;

(3) with those of a magistrate of the judicial order;

(4) with those of a member of the Chamber of Accounts;

(5) with those of a district commissioner;

(6) with those of a receiver or accountant of the State;

(7) with those of a career soldier in active service.

Officials who find themselves in a case of incompatibility shall have the right to choose between the mandate confided to them and their office.

A deputy who has been called to the duties of a member of the Government and who relinquishes those duties shall be reinscribed, as a matter of right, as first substitute on the roll on which he was elected. The same shall apply to a substitute-deputy who, being called to the duties of a member of the government, shall have renounced a deputy's seat devolving upon him during the continuance of those duties.

In the case of conflict between several who are entitled, the reinscription shall be made in the order of the number of votes obtained in the elections.

Art. 55. The incompatibilities recognized in the preceding Article shall be no obstacle to the establishment of others by law in the future.

Art. 56. Deputies shall be elected for six years.

Art. 57. The Chamber shall verify the powers of its members and judge the disputes that occur on the subject.

Upon taking office members shall take the following oath:

"I swear fidelity to the Grand Duke, obedience to the Constitution and to the laws of the State. So help me God!"

This oath shall be taken in public session before the President of the Chamber.

Art. 58. A deputy appointed by the Government to a salaried post that he accepts shall cease immediately to sit, and shall resume his functions only by virtue of a new election.

Art. 59. All the laws shall be submitted to a second vote, unless the Chamber, in accord with the Council of State, sitting in public session, decide otherwise.

There shall be an interval of three months at least between the two votes.

Art. 60. At each session, the Chamber shall name its President and Vice-Presidents and form its secretariat.

Art. 61. The sessions of the Chamber shall be public, subject to the exceptions to be determined by regulations.

Art. 62. Every resolution shall be taken by an absolute majority of the votes. In case of equal division of votes, the proposition under deliberation is rejected.

The Chamber cannot make a resolution unless the majority of its members are present.

Art. 63. Votes shall be given orally or by sitting and standing. On laws as a whole, the vote shall always taken by roll call and orally.

Art. 64. The chamber has the right of inquiry. A law shall regulate the exercise of this right.

Art. 65. A bill may not be adopted by the Chamber except after having been voted article by article.

Art. 66. The Chamber shall have the right to amend and to divide the articles and proposed the amendments.

Art. 67. It shall be forbidden to present petitions to the Chamber in person.

The Chamber shall have the right to refer to members of the Government petitions addressed to it. The members of the government shall give explanations of their contents whenever the Chamber so requests.

The Chamber shall not concern itself with any petition having for its object individual interests, unless it relates to the redress of injuries resulting from illegal acts of the government or the authorities, or unless the decision to intervene is not within the competence of the Chamber.

Art. 68. No deputy may be prosecuted or tried on account of his opinions and votes given in the exercise of his functions.

Art. 69. No deputy may, during the session, be prosecuted or arrested for a punishable matter, without the authorization of the Chamber, except in the case of *flagrante delicto.*

No imprisonment for debt may be carried out against one of its members, during the session, without the same authorization.

The detention or prosecution of a deputy shall be suspended during the session and for its entire duration if the Chamber so requires.

Art. 70. The Chamber shall determine by its regulations the procedure by which it will exercise its powers.

Art. 71. The meetings of the Chamber shall be held where the administration of the Grand Duchy has its residence.

Art. 72. The Chamber shall meet each year in ordinary session at the time fixed by the regulations.

The Grand Duke may convoke the Chamber for extraordinary sessions; he must do so upon the request of one third of the deputies.

Every session shall be opened and closed by the Grand Duke in person, or in his name by a legal representative named for this purpose.

Art. 73. The Grand Duke may adjourn the Chamber. However, the adjournment cannot exceed the period of a month or be repeated in the same session without the consent of the chamber.

Art. 74. The Grand Duke may dissolve the chamber.

New elections shall be held within three months, at the latest, from the dissolution.

Art. 75. The members of the Chamber of Deputies shall receive, in addition to their traveling expenses, an allowance, the amount and conditions of which shall be fixed by the law.

CHAPTER V

THE GOVERNMENT OF THE GRAND DUCHY

Art. 76. The Grand Duke shall regulate the organization of his Government, which shall be composed of at least three members.

There shall be, together with the Government, a Council called to deliberate on bills and amendments that may be proposed, to regulate the questions of administrative disputes, and to give advice on all other questions referred to it by the Grand Duke or by the laws.

The organization of this Council and the manner of exercising its powers shall be regulated by law.

Art. 77. The Grand Duke shall appoint and dismiss the members of the government.

Art. 78. The members of the Government shall be responsible.

Art. 79. Between the members of the Government and the Grand Duke, there shall be no intermediate authority.

Art. 80. The members of the Government or the commissioners who replace them shall have the right of admission to the Chamber and must be heard when they so demand.

The Chamber may require their presence.

Art. 81. In no case may the verbal or written order of the Grand Duke relieve a member of the Government of responsibility.

Art. 82. The Chamber shall have the right to accuse the members of the Government.

A law shall determine the cases of responsibility, the penalties to be inflicted, and the method of procedure, either on the accusation admitted by the Chamber or on prosecution by the injured parties.

Art. 83. The Grand Duke may not pardon the condemned member of the Government except on the request of the Chamber.

CHAPTER VI

JUSTICE

Art. 84. Disputes relating to civil rights shall fall exclusively within the province of the courts.

Art. 85. Disputes relating to political rights shall fall within the province of the courts, subject to the exceptions established by law.

Art. 86. No court and no jurisdiction of litigation may be established except by law. Extraordinary commissions and tribunals may not be created under any name whatever.

Art. 87. The organization of a Superior Court of Justice shall be provided for by law.

Art. 88. The sessions of the courts shall be public unless publicity would be dangerous for order or morals, and in such a case the court shall so declare by a decision.

Art. 89. Every judgment shall contain a statement of the reasons therefor. It shall be pronounced in public session.

Art. 90. The judges of the peace and the judges of the courts shall be appointed directly by the Grand Duke.

The councilors of the Court and the Presidents and Vice-Presidents of the district tribunals shall be appointed by the Grand Duke upon the advice of the Superior Court of Justice.

Art. 91. Judges of the district tribunals and counselors shall be appoint ed for life.

None may be deprived of his place or suspended except by a judgment

The removal of one of these judges may not take place except by a new appointment and with his consent.

However, in case of infirmity or misconduct, a judge may be suspended, revoked, or displaced, in accordance with the conditions determined by the law.

Art. 92. The salaries of members of the judicial order shall be fixed by law.

Art. 93. Subject to the exceptions provided for by the law, no judge may accept salaried functions from the government, unless he exercises them gratuitously, without prejudice however to the cases of incompatibility determined by law.

Art. 94. Special laws shall regulate the organization of military tribunals their attributes, the rights and obligations of the members of these tribunals, and the term of their functions.

There may be tribunals of commerce in the places determined by law. A law shall regulate their organization, attributes, the method of nomination of their members, and the term of the functions of the latter.

Art. 95. The courts and tribunals shall apply general and local resolutions and regulations only in so far as they are in conformity with the laws.

The Superior Court of Justice shall regulate conflicts of prerogatives according to the method determined by law.

CHAPTER VII

THE PUBLIC FORCES

Art. 96. All that which concerns the Armed Forces shall be regulated by law.

Art. 97. The organization and powers of the police force shall be the object of a law.

Art. 98. A civil guard may be formed whose organization shall be regulated by law.

CHAPTER VIII

FINANCES

Art. 99. No tax for the profit of the State may be established except by law.

No loan charged to the State may be contracted except with the consent of the Chamber.

No immovable property of the State can be alienated unless the alienation is authorized by law.

No creation for the benefit of the State of a road, canal, railroad, large bridge, or other considerable building may be decreed except by virtue of a special law.

No charge burdening the budget of the State for more than one fiscal year can be established except by a special law.

No communal charge or tax can be established except with the consent of the communal council.

A law shall determine the exceptions which experience may show to be necessary relative to communal taxes.

Art. 100. Taxes for the benefit of the State shall be voted annually.

The laws which establish them shall be effective for only one year, unless they are renewed.

Art. 101. No privilege in the matter of taxes may be established.

No exemption or abatement may be established except by law.

Art. 102. Apart from the cases formally excepted by law, no payment may be required of citizens or of public establishments except by virtue of a tax for the benefit of the State or the commune.

Art. 103. No pension, no attendance fee, no gratuity charged to the Treasury may be accorded except by virtue of a law.

Art. 104. Each year the Chamber shall draw up the law of accounts and vote the budget.

All the receipts and expenses of the State must be included in the budget and the accounts.

Art. 105. A Chamber of Accounts shall be charged with the examination and liquidation of the accounts of the general administration, and of all those accountable to the public Treasury.

A law shall regulate its organization, the exercise of its powers, and the method of nomination of its members.

The Chamber of Accounts shall see to it that no article of expenditure of the budget be exceeded.

No transfer of one section of the budget to another may be effected except by virtue of a law.

However, the members of the government may effect, within their services, transfers of surpluses from one article to another in the same section, subject to justifying them before the Chamber of Deputies.

The Chamber of Accounts shall settle the accounts of the different administrations of the State and shall be charged with collecting to this effect all the information and all the necessary accountable evidence. The general account of the State shall be submitted to the Chamber of Deputies with the observations of the Chamber of Accounts.

Art. 106. The salaries and pensions of the Ministers of the cults shall be a charge of the State and regulated by law.

CHAPTER IX

THE COMMUNES

Art. 107. In each commune there shall be a communal council elected directly by the inhabitants who qualify to vote; the composition, organization, and powers of this council shall be regulated by law.

The burgomaster shall be appointed and dismissed by the Grand Duke, who may choose him outside the membership of the council.

The communal council shall decide on all that is of purely communal interest, subject to the approval of its acts in the cases and according to the method determined by law.

The communal agents or employees, those of the municipal, forest, and rural police, shall be appointed and dismissed in the manner determined by law.

No communal tax may be established or suppressed without the authority of the Grand Duke.

The accounts and budgets shall be made public.

The Grand Duke may suspend or annul the acts of the communal authorities which exceed their powers, or which are contrary to the law or to the general interest. A law shall regulate the consequences of such suspension or annulment.

The Grand Duke shall have the right to dissolve the council.

Art. 108. The drawing up of acts of civil status and the keeping of the registers shall be exclusively within the powers of the communal authority.

CHAPTER X

GENERAL PROVISIONS

Art. 109. The City of Luxembourg shall be the capital of the Grand Duchy and the seat of the government.

The seat of the government may not be transferred, except temporarily for grave reasons.

Art. 110. No oath may be imposed except by virtue of a law; which shall determine the formula thereof.

All the public civil officials, before taking office, shall take the following oath:

"I swear fidelity to the Grand Duke, obedience to the Constitution and to the laws of the State. So help me God!"

Art. 111. Every foreigner in the territory of the Grand Duchy shall enjoy protection of his person and property, save for the exceptions established by law.

Art. 112. No law, no decree or regulation of general or communal administration, shall be obligatory except after having been published in the manner determined by law.

Art. 113. No provision of the Constitution may be suspended.

Art. 114. The legislative power shall have the right to declare the necessity to proceed to the revision of constitutional provisions as designated by it.

After such a declaration, the Chamber shall be dissolved automatically.

A new Chamber shall be convoked, in conformity with Article 74 of the present Constitution.

This Chamber shall act, in common accord with the Grand Duke, on the points submitted for revision.

In such a case, the Chamber may not deliberate unless three quarters at least of its members are present, and no change shall be adopted without at least two thirds of the votes.

Art. 115. No change of the Constitution may be made during a regency.

CHAPTER XI

TRANSITORY AND SUPPLEMENTARY PROVISIONS

Art. 116. Until it shall be provided by law, the Chamber of Deputies shall have discretionary power to accuse a member of the Government, and the Superior Court, in general assembly, shall judge him, defining the offense and determining the penalty.

However, the penalty may not exceed that of confinement, without prejudice to cases expressly provided for in the penal laws.

The counselors of the Court forming part of the Chamber shall abstain from all participation in the proceedings and the judgment.

Art. 117. Counting from the day when the Constitution shall be executory, all the laws, all the decrees, orders, regulations, and other acts contrary to it shall be abrogated.

Art. 118. The penalty of death, abolished in political matters, shall be replaced by the penalty immediately inferior until a new law shall provide therefor.

Art. 119. While waiting for the conclusion of the conventions provided for in Article 22, the present dispositions relative to cults shall remain in force.

Art. 120. Until the promulgation of the laws and regulations provided for by the Constitution, the laws and regulations now in force shall continue to be applied.

Art. 121. The Constitution of the State of October 12, 1841, is abolished.

All the authorities shall preserve and exercise their powers, until otherwise provided, according to the Constitution.

MALTA

SUMMARY

INTERNATIONAL STATUS

Malta is a member of the United Nations (December 1, 1964). It is a member of the Commonwealth of Nations and of other international organizations.

Malta became independent on September 21, 1964, by the Malta Independence Order 1964.

Malta was a fief of the Order of St. John of Jerusalem from 1530 until seized by Napoleon in 1798. In 1802, Malta asked for British protection (Napoleon having been expelled in 1800) and in 1813 it was annexed by

Great Britain as a crown colony. The 1921 Amery-Milner Constitution provided for a measure of internal self-government. It was suspended in 1930, restored in 1932 and withdrawn in 1933 when crown colony status was again imposed. The 1939 MacDonald constitution providing representative institutions and elected members of the Governor's Executive Council and the Council of Government was suspended during the war. In 1947, a Constitution reinstated responsible government with certain matters such as defence and external affairs reserved to the United Kingdom. In 1955 the London Round Table Conference to consider Malta's constitutional development on the basis of integration with the United Kingdom met with difficulties. In 1958 the Malta government resigned and the island was administered by the governor. The 1959 Malta (Constitution) Order in Council revoked the 1947 Constitution and provided an Executive Council with Maltese non-official members. On August 20, 1962, Malta requested independence within the Commonwealth. The 1963 Constitutional Conference announced Maltese independence for May 31, 1964, at the latest, but the inability of Maltese political parties to agree on the independence constitution made a referendum on the constitution necessary and independence was postponed to September 21.

FORM OF NATIONAL GOVERNMENT

The Constitution of Sentember 2, 1964, as amended October 1965, describes the territory of Malta and contains provisions concerning citizenship.[1] The religion of Malta is the Roman Catholic Apostolic Religion.[2] The source of sovereign power is not stated.

RIGHTS OF THE PEOPLE

The Constitution guarantees protection of the right to life and freedom from arbitrary arrest or detention, from forced labor and inhuman treatment, from deprivation of property without compensation, the right of privacy of the home, due process of law, freedom of conscience, expression, assembly, association, prohibition of deportation, freedom of movement, prohibition of discrimination.[3] A section entitled "Declaration of Principles," which are not enforceable in any court, declares that the State recognizes and will protect the right of all citizens to work, will promote the development of culture and research, safeguard landscape and the patrimony of the nation, attempt to ensure equal rights and wages for women, safeguard the work of minors, provide compulsory and free primary education.[4]

[1] Const., Art. 1, 23–32. [2] Id., Art. 2, 10. [3] Id., Art. 33–48.
[4] Id., Art. 7–22.

LEGISLATIVE DEPARTMENT

Parliament is unicameral consisting of the British sovereign and the House of Representatives. The House of Representatives is composed of fifty members elected by proportional representation for a term of five years subject to dissolution.[1] It meets in at least one session a year.[2] There are chapters relating to finance [3] and the public service.[4]

EXECUTIVE DEPARTMENT

Executive authority is vested in the British sovereign and exercised by a Governor General.[5] The general direction and control of the government of Malta is exercised by a Cabinet which is collectively responsible to Parliament.[6] The Prime Minister and Ministers are chosen by the Governor General from among the members of the House of Representatives.[7] Provision is made for a Leader of the Opposition appointed by the Governor General who must be the person commanding the support of the largest single group of members in opposition to the Government.[8] The Governor General has the prerogative of mercy.[9]

JUDICIAL DEPARTMENT

Provision is made for superior Courts to be provided by law one of which is the Constitutional Court with jurisdiction to hear questions as to the validity of elections and appeals regarding the interpretation of the Constitution and the validity of laws.[10] Judges are appointed by the Governor General on the advice of the Prime Minister and may not be removed from office.[11] Appeals may lie to the Privy Council in the United Kingdom on certain matters.[12]

AREA, POPULATION, ETC.

The area of Malta is 316 square kilometres, its population (1965) 318,000. The national language is Maltese, the official languages Maltese and English.[13] The capital is Valletta.

1 Id., Art. 53, 77.
2 Id., Art. 76.
3 Id., Art. 105–111.
4 Id., Art. 112–118.
5 Id., Art. 79.
6 Id., Art. 80.
7 Id., Art. 81.
8 Id., Art. 91.
9 Id., Art. 94.
10 Id., Art. 96.
11 Id., Art. 97, 98.
12 Id., Art. 103, 104
13 Id., Art. 5.

CONSTITUTION
of
MALTA[1]

September 21, 1964, as amended October 29, 1965

CHAPTER I

THE STATE

Territories

1. Until otherwise provided by law the territories of Malta consist of those territories comprised in Malta immediately before the appointed day, including the territorial waters thereof.

Religion

2. (1) The Religion of Malta is the Roman Catholic Apostolic Religion.

(2) The State guarantees to the Roman Catholic Apostolic Church the right freely to exercise her proper spiritual and ecclesiastical functions and duties and to manage her own affairs.

National Flag

3. The National Flag of Malta consists of two equal vertical stripes, white in the hoist and red in the fly. A representation of the George Cross awarded to Malta by His Majesty King George the Sixth on the 15th April 1942 is carried, edged with red, in the canton of the white stripe.

National Anthem

4. The National Anthem of Malta is "L-Innu Malti" opening with the the words "Lil din l-Art helwa l-Omm li tatna isimha".

Language

5. (1) The National language of Malta is the Maltese language.

(2) The Maltese and the English languages and such other language as

[1] Schedule to *Malta Independence Order 1964*. Published in Supplement to *Malta Government Gazette No. 11, 688*, 18th September 1964. Supplied by Department of Information, Valletta, in December 1965. Ed.

may be prescribed by Parliament (by a law passed by not less than two thirds of all the members of the House of Representatives) shall be the official languages of Malta and the Administration may for all official purposes use any of such languages:

Provided that any person may address the Administration in any of the official languages and the reply of the Administration thereto shall be in such language.

(3) The language of the Courts shall be the Maltese language:

Provided that Parliament may make such provision for the use of the English language in such cases and under such conditions as it may prescribe.

(4) The House of Representatives may, in regulating its own procedure, determine the language or languages that shall be used in parliamentary proceedings and records.

Constitution to be supreme law

6. Subject to the provisions of sections 48(7) and (9) and 67 of this Constitution, if any other law is inconsistent with this Constitution, this Constitution shall prevail and the other law shall, to the extent of the inconsistency, be void.

CHAPTER II

DECLARATION OF PRINCIPLES

Right to work

7. The State recognises the right of all citizens to work and shall promote such conditions as will make this right effective.

Promotion of culture, etc.

8. The State shall promote the development of culture and scientific and technical research.

Safeguarding of landscape and historical and artistic patrimony

9. The State shall safeguard the landscape and the historical and artistic patrimony of the Nation.

Religious teaching in State schools

10. Religious teaching of the Roman Catholic Apostolic faith shall be provided in all State schools.

Compulsory and free primary education

11. Primary education shall be compulsory and in State schools shall be free of charge.

Educational interests

12. (1) Capable and deserving students, even if without financial resources, are entitled to attain the highest grades of education.

(2) The State shall give effect to this principle by means of scholarships, of contributions to the families of students and other provisions on the basis of competitive examinations.

Protection of work

13. (1) The State shall protect work.

(2) It shall provide for the professional or vocational training and advancement of workers.

Hours of work

14. (1) The maximum number of hours of work per day shall be fixed by law.

(2) The worker is entitled to a weekly day of rest and to annual holidays with pay; he cannot renounce this right.

Rights of women workers

15. The State shall aim at ensuring that women workers enjoy equal rights and the same wages for the same work as males.

Minimum age for paid labour

16. The minimum age for paid labour shall be prescribed by law.

Safeguarding labour of minors

17. The State shall provide for safeguarding the labour of minors and assure to them the right to equal pay for equal work.

Social assistance and insurance

18. (1) Every citizen incapable of work and unprovided with the resources necessary for subsistence is entitled to maintenance and social assistance.

(2) Workers are entitled to reasonable insurance on a contributory basis for their requirements in case of accident, illness, disability, old-age and involuntary unemployment.

(3) Disabled persons and persons incapable of work are entitled to education and vocational training.

Encouragement of private economic enterprise

19. The State shall encourage private economic enterprise.

Protection of artisan trades

20. The State shall provide for the protection and development of artisan trades.

Encouragement of co-operatives

21. The State recognises the social function of co-operatives and shall encourage their development.

Application of the principles contained in this Chapter

22. The provisions of this Chapter shall not be enforceable in any court, but the principles therein contained are nevertheless fundamental to the governance of the country and it shall be the aim of the State to apply these principles in making laws.

CHAPTER III

CITIZENSHIP

Persons who become citizens on appointed day

23. (1) Every person who, having been born in Malta, is on the day before the appointed day a citizen of the United Kingdom and Colonies shall become a citizen of Malta on the appointed day:

Provided that a person shall not become a citizen of Malta by virtue of this subsection if neither of his parents was born in Malta.

(2) Every person who, having been born outside Malta, is on the day before the appointed day a citizen of the United Kingdom and Colonies shall, if his father becomes, or would but for his death have become, a citizen of Malta in accordance with the provisions of subsection (1) of this section, become a citizen of Malta on the appointed day.

Persons entitled to be registered as citizens

24. (1) Any person who, but for the proviso to subsection (1) of section 23 of this Constitution, would be a citizen of Malta by virtue of that subsection shall be entitled, upon making application before the expiration of two years from the appointed day in such manner as may be prescribed, to be registered as a citizen of Malta:

Provided that a person who has not attained the age of eighteen years (other than a woman who is or has been married) may not himself make an application under this subsection, but an application may be made on his behalf by the person who according to law has authority over him.

(2) Any woman who on the day before the appointed day is or has been married to a person:

(a) who becomes a citizen of Malta by virtue of section 23 of this Constitution; or

(b) who having died before the appointed day would, but for his death, have become a citizen of Malta by virtue of that section,

shall be entitled, upon making application in such manner as may be prescribed and, if she is a British protected person or a alien, upon taking the oath of allegiance, to be registered as a citizen of Malta.

(3) Any woman who on the day before the appointed day is or has been married to a person who becomes a citizen of Malta by registration under subsection (1) of this section shall be entitled, upon making application within such time and in such manner as may be prescribed and, if she is a British protected person or an alien, upon taking the oath of allegiance, to be registered as a citizen of Malta.

(4) Any woman who on the day before the appointed day has been married to a person who becomes, or would, but for his death, have become entitled to be registered as a citizen of Malta under subsection (1) of this section, but whose marriage has been terminated by death or by such dissolution as is valid under the law of Malta shall be entitled, upon making application before the expiration of two years from the appointed day and in such manner as may be prescribed and, if she is a British protected person or an alien, upon taking the oath of allegiance, to be registered as a citizen of Malta.

(5) The provisions of subsections (2), (3) and (4) of this section shall be without prejudice to the provisions of section 23 of this Constitution.

Persons naturalised or registered as resident before appointed day

25. (1) Any person who on the day before the appointed day was a citizen of the United Kingdom and Colonies:

(a) having become such a citizen under the British Nationality Act 1948 by virtue of his having been naturalised in Malta as a British subject before that Act came into force; or

(b) having become such a citizen by virtue of his having been naturalised or registered in Malta under that Act,

shall be entitled, upon making application before the expiration of two years from the appointed day in such manner as may be prescribed, to be registered as a citizen of Malta:

Provided that a person who has not attained the age of eighteen years (other than a woman who is or has been married) may not himself make an application under this subsection, but an application may be made on his behalf by the person who according to law has authority over him.

(2) Any person who on the day before the appointed day:

(a) was a Commonwealth citizen or a citizen of the Republic of Ireland; and

(b) is descended in the male line from a person born in Malta,

and was on the day before the appointed day ordinarily resident in Malta and had been so resident throughout the period of five years immediately preceding that day shall be entitled, upon making application before the expiration of two years from the appointed day in such manner as may be prescribed, to be registered as a citizen of Malta:

Provided that a person who has not attained the age of eighteen years (other than a woman who is or has been married) may not himself make an application under this subsection, but an application may be made on his behalf by the person who according to law has authority over him.

Acquisition of citizenship by birth or descent by persons born on or after appointed day

26. (1) Every person born in Malta on or after the appointed day shall become a citizen of Malta at the date of his birth:

Provided that a person shall not become a citizen of Malta by virtue of this subsection if at the time of his birth:

(a) neither of his parents was a citizen of Malta and his father possessed such immunity from suit and legal process as is accorded to an envoy of a foreign sovereign power accredited to Malta; or

(b) his father was an enemy alien and the birth occurred in a place then under occupation by the enemy.

(2) A person born outside Malta on or after the appointed day shall become a citizen of Malta at the date of his birth if at that date his father is a citizen of Malta otherwise than by virtue of this subsection or subsection (2) of section 23 of this Constitution.

Marriage to citizen of Malta

27. Any woman who on or after the appointed day marries a person who is or becomes a citizen of Malta shall be entitled, upon making application in such manner as may be prescribed and, if she is a British protected person or an alien, upon taking the oath of allegiance, to be registered as a citizen of Malta.

Dual citizenship

28. (1) Any person who, upon his attainment of the age of eighteen years, is a citizen of Malta and also a citizen of some country other than Malta shall cease to be a citizen of Malta upon his attainment of the age of nineteen years (or, in the case of a person of unsound mind, at such later date as may be prescribed) unless he has renounced his citizenship of that other country and, in the case of a person who is a citizen of Malta by virtue of subsection (2) of section 23 of this Constitution, has made and registered such declaration of his intentions concerning residence or employment as may be prescribed.

(2) A person who:

(a) has attained the age of eighteen years before the appointed day; and

(b) becomes a citizen of Malta on that day by virtue of the provisions of section 23 of this Constitution; and

(c) is immediately after that day also a citizen of some country other than Malta, shall cease to be a citizen of Malta on the expiration of two years from the appointed day (or, in the case of a person of unsound mind, at such later date as may be prescribed) unless he has renounced his citizenship of that other country and, in the case of a person who is a citizen of Malta by virtue of subsection (2) of section 23 of this Constitution, has made and registered such declaration of his intentions concerning residence or employment as may be prescribed.

(3) A citizen of Malta shall cease to be such a citizen if:

(a) having attained the age of eighteen years, he acquires the citizenship of some country other than Malta by a voluntary act (other than marriage); or

(b) having attained the age of eighteen years, he otherwise acquires the citizenship of some country other than Malta and has not, before the expiration of one year after the date on which he acquired the citizenship of that other country, renounced his citizenship of that other country and made and registered such declaration of his intentions concerning residence or employment as may be prescribed.

(4) A person who:

(a) becomes a citizen of Malta by registration under section 24, 25 or 27 of this Constitution; and

(b) is immediately after the day on which he becomes a citizen of Malta also a citizen of some other country,

shall cease to be a citizen of Malta on the expiration of six months after the date on which he acquired citizenship of Malta (or, in the case of a person of unsound mind, at such later date as may be prescribed) unless he has renounced his citizenship of that other country, and made and registered such declaration of his intentions concerning residence or employment as may be prescribed.

(5) For the purposes of this section, where, under the law of a country other than Malta, a person cannot renounce his citizenship of that other country, he may instead make such declaration concerning such citizenship as may be prescribed.

(6) Provision may be made by or under an Act of Parliament extending beyond the period specified in any provision of this section the period in which any person may make a renunciation of citizenship, or make or register a declaration for the purposes of that provision of this section, and if such provision is made that person shall not cease to be a citizen of Malta upon the expiration of the period specified in this section but shall cease to be such a citizen upon the expiration of the extended period if he has not then made the renunciation, or made or registered the declaration, as the case may be.

Commonwealth citizens

29.[1] (1) Every person who under this Constitution or any Act of Parliament is a citizen of Malta or under any enactment for the time being in force in any country to which this section applies is a citizen of that country shall, by virtue of that citizenship, have the status of a Commonwealth citizen.

(2) Every person who is a British subject without citizenship under the British Nationality Act 1948 or who continues to be a British subject under section 2 of that Act shall be virtue of that status have the status of a Commonwealth citizen.

(3) Save as may be otherwise provided by Parliament, the countries to which this section applies are the United Kingdom and Colonies, Canada, Australia, New Zealand, India, Pakistan, Ceylon, Ghana, Malaysia, the Federation of Nigeria, the Republic of Cyprus, Sierra Leone, Southern Rhodesia, the United Republic of Tanzania, Jamaica, Trinidad and Tobago, Uganda, Kenya and Malawi.

Criminal liability of Commonwealth citizens

30. (1) A Commonwealth citizen who is not a citizen of Malta or a citizen of the Republic of Ireland who is not a citizen of Malta shall not be guilty of an offence against any law in force in Malta by reason of anything done or omitted in any part of the Commonwealth other than Malta or in the Republic of Ireland or in any foreign country unless:

(a) the act or omission would be an offence if he were an alien; and

(b) in the case of an act or omission in any part of the Commonwealth or in the Republic of Ireland, it would be an offence if the country in which the act was done or the omission made were a foreign country.

(2) In this section "foreign country" means a country (other than the Republic of Ireland) that is not a part of the Commonwealth.

Powers of Parliament

31. (1) Parliament may make provision:

(a) for the acquisition of citizenship of Malta by persons who do not become citizens of Malta by virtue of the provisions of this Chapter;

(b) for depriving of his citizenship of Malta any person who is a citizen of Malta otherwise than by virtue of:

(i) section 23 or subsection (1) of section 26 of this Constitution; or

(ii) subsection (2) of section 26 of this Constitution in relation to a person born outside Malta whose father at the date of that person's birth is a citizen of Malta by virtue of subsection (1) of section 23 or subsection (1) of section 26 of this Constitution;

(c) for the renunciation by any person of his citizenship of Malta.

(2) Provision may be made by or under an Act of Parliament for ex-

[1] By amendment Act No. XLI of 1965 "Section 29 of the Constitution of Malta shall apply to – (a) the Republic of Zambia; (b) Gambia; (c) Singapore."

tending the period in which any person may make an application for registration as a citizen of Malta, make a renunciation of citizenship, take an oath or make or register a declaration for the purposes of the provisions of this Chapter.

Interpretation

32. (1) In this Chapter:

"alien" means a person who is not a Commonwealth citizen, a British protected person or a citizen of the Republic of Ireland;

"British protected person" means a person who is a British protected person for the purposes of the British Nationality Act 1948;

"prescribed" means prescribed by or under any Act of Parliament.

(2) For the purposes of this Chapter, a person born aboard a registered ship or aircraft, or aboard an unregistered ship or aircraft of the government of any country, shall be deemed to have born in the place in which the ship or aircraft was registered or, as the case may be, in that country.

(3) Any reference in this Chapter to the father of a person shall, in relation to a person born out of wedlock and not legitimated, be construed as a reference to the mother of that person and, in relation to an adopted child whose adoption has been registered under any law in force in Malta, be construed as a reference to the adopter or, in the case of a joint adoption, the male adopter, and references to the parent of such person shall be construed accordingly.

(4) Any reference in this Chapter to the national status of the father of a person at the time of that person's birth shall, in relation to a person born after the death of his father, be construed as a reference to the national status of the father at the time of the father's death; and where that death occurred before the appointed day and the birth occurred on or after the appointed day, the national status that the father would have had if he had died on the appointed day shall be deemed to be his national status at the time of his death.

CHAPTER IV

FUNDAMENTAL RIGHTS AND FREEDOMS OF THE INDIVIDUAL

Fundamental rights and freedoms of the individual

33. Whereas every person in Malta is entitled to the fundamental rights and freedoms of the individual, that is to say, the right, whatever his race, place of origin, political opinions, colour, creed or sex, but subject to respect for the rights and freedoms of others and for the public interest to each and all of the following, namely:

(a) life, liberty, security of the person, the enjoyment of property and the protection of the law;

(b) freedom of conscience, of expression and of peaceful assembly and association; and

(c) respect for his private and family life,

the subsequent provisions of this Chapter shall have effect for the purpose of affording protection to the aforesaid rights and freedoms, subject to such limitations of that protection as are contained in those provisions being limitations designed to ensure that the enjoyment of the said rights and freedoms by any individual does not prejudice the rights and freedoms of others or the public interest.

Protection of right to life

34. (1) No person shall intentionally be deprived of his life save in execution of the sentence of a court in respect of a criminal offence under the law of Malta of which he has been convicted.

(2) Without prejudice to any liability for a contravention of any other law with respect to the use of force in such cases as are hereinafter mentioned, a person shall be not regarded as having been deprived of his life in contravention of this section if he dies as the result of the use of force to such extent as is reasonably justifiable in the circumstances of the case:

(a) for the defence of any person from violence or for the defence of property;

(b) in order to effect a lawful arrest or to prevent the escape of a person lawfully detained;

(c) for the purpose of suppressing a riot, insurrection or mutiny; or

(d) in order to prevent the commission by that person of a criminal offence,

or if he dies as the result of a lawful act of war.

Protection from arbitrary arrest or detention

35. (1) No person shall be deprived of his personal liberty save as may be authorised by law in the following cases, that is to say:

(a) in consequence of his unfitness to plead to a criminal charge;

(b) in execution of the sentence or order of a court, whether in Malta or elsewhere, in respect of a criminal offence of which he has been convicted;

(c) in execution of the order of a court punishing him for contempt of that court or of another court or tribunal or in execution of the order of the House of Representatives punishing him for contempt of itself or of its members or for breach of privilege;

(d) in execution of the order of a court made to secure the fulfilment of any obligation imposed on him by law;

(e) for the purpose of bringing him before a court in execution of the order of a court or before the House of Representatives in execution of the order of that House;

(f) upon reasonable suspicion of his having committed, or being about to commit, a criminal offence;

(g) in the case of a person who has not attained the age of eighteen years, for the purpose of his education or welfare;

(h) for the purpose of preventing the spread of an infectious or contagious disease;

(i) in the case of a person who is, or is reasonably suspected to be, of unsound mind, addicted to drugs or alcohol, or a vagrant, for the purpose of his care or treatment or the protection of the community; or

(j) for the purpose of preventing the unlawful entry of that person into Malta, or for the purpose of effecting the expulsion, extradition or other lawful removal of that person from Malta or the taking of proceedings relating thereto or for the purpose of restraining that person while he is being conveyed through Malta in the course of his extradition or removal as a convicted prisoner from one country to another.

(2) Any person who is arrested or detained shall be informed, at the time of his arrest or detention, in a language that he understands, of the reasons for his arrest or detention:

Provided that if an interpreter is necessary and is not readily available or if it is otherwise impracticable to comply with the provisions of this subsection at the time of the person's arrest or detention, such provisions shall be complied with as soon as practicable.

(3) Any person who is arrested or detained:

(a) for the purpose of bringing him before a court in execution of the order of a court; or

(b) upon reasonable suspicion of his having committed, or being about to commit, a criminal offence,

and who is not released, shall be brought not later than forty-eight hours before a court; and if any person arrested or detained in such a case as is mentioned in paragraph (b) of this subsection is not tried within a reasonable time, then, without prejudice to any further proceedings which may be brought against him, he shall be released either unconditionally or upon reasonably conditions, including in particular such conditions as are reasonable necessary to ensure that he appears at a later date for trial or for proceedings preliminary to trial.

(4) Any person who is unlawfully arrested or detained by any other person shall be entitled to compensation therefor from that person.

(5) Nothing contained in or done under the authority of any law shall be held to be inconsistent with or in contravention of this section to the extent that the law in question authorises the taking during such a period of public emergency as is referred to in paragraph (a) or (c) of subsection (2) of section 48 of this Constitution of measures that are reasonably

justifiable for the purpose of dealing with the situation that exists during that period of public emergency.

(6) If any person who is lawfully detained by virtue only of such a law as is referred to in the last foregoing subsection so requests at any time during the period of that detention not earlier than six months after he last made such a request during that period, his case shall be reviewed by an independent and impartial tribunal established by law and composed of a person or persons each of whom holds or has held judicial office or is qualified to be appointed to such office in Malta.

(7) On any review by a tribunal in pursuance of the last foregoing subsection of the case of any detained person, the tribunal may make recommendations concerning the necessity or expediency of continuing his detention to the authority by whom it was ordered, but, unless it is otherwise provided by law, that authority shall not be obliged to act in accordance with any such recommendations.

Protection from forced labour

36. (1) No person shall be required to perform forced labour.

(2) For the purposes of this section, the expression "forced labour" does not include:

(a) any labour required in consequence of the sentence or order of a court;

(b) labour required of any person while he is lawfully detained by sentence or order of a court that, though not required in consequence of such sentence or order, is reasonably necessary in the interests of hygiene or for the maintenance of the place at which he is detained or, if he is detained for the purpose of his care, treatment, education or welfare, is reasonably required for that purpose;

(c) any labour required of a member of a disciplined force in pursuance of his duties as such or, in the case of a person who has conscientious objections to service as a member of a naval, military or air force, any labour that that person is required by law to perform in place of such service;

(d) any labour required during a period of public emergency or in the event of any other emergency or calamity that threatens the life or well-being of the community.

Protection from inhuman treatment

37. (1) No person shall be subjected to inhuman or degrading punishment or treatment.

(2) Nothing contained in or done under the authority of any law shall be held to be inconsistent with or in contravention of this section to the extent that the law in question authorises the infliction of any description

of punishment which was lawful in Malta immediately before the appointed day.

(3) (a) No law shall provide for the imposition of collective punishments.

(b) Nothing in this subsection shall preclude the imposition of collective punishments upon the members of a disciplined force in accordance with the law regulating the discipline of that force.

Protection from deprivation of property without compensation

38. (1) No property of any description shall be compulsorily taken possession of, and no interest in or right over property of any description shall be compulsorily acquired, except where provision is made by a law applicable to that taking of possession or acquisition:

(a) for the payment of adequate compensation;

(b) securing to any person claiming such compensation a right of access to an independent and impartial court or tribunal established by law for the purpose of determining his interest in or right over the property and the amount of any compensation to which he may be entitled, and for the purpose of obtaining payment of that compensation; and

(c) securing to any party to proceedings in that court or tribunal relating to such a claim a right of appeal from its determination to the Court of Appeal in Malta.

(2) Nothing in this section shall be construed as affecting the making or operation of any law so far as it provides for the taking of possession or acquisition of property:

(a) in satisfaction of any tax, rate or due;

(b) by way of penalty for, or as a consequence of, breach of the law, whether under civil process or after conviction of a criminal offence;

(c) upon the attempted removal of the property out of or into Malta in contravention of any law;

(d) by way of the taking of a sample for the purposes of any law;

(e) where the property consists of an animal upon its being found trespassing or straying;

(f) as an incident of a lease, tenancy, licence, privilege or hypotheque, mortgage, charge, bill of sale, pledge or other contract;

(g) by way of the vesting or administration of property on behalf and for the benefit of the person entitled to the beneficial interest therein, trust property, enemy property or the property of persons adjudged bankrupt or otherwise declared bankrupt or insolvent, persons of unsound mind, deceased persons, or bodies corporate or unincorporate in the course of being wound up or liquidated;

(h) in the execution of judgments or orders of courts;

(i) by reason of its being in a dangerous state or injurious to the health of human beings, animals or plants;

(j) in consequence of any law with respect to the limitation of actions, acquisitive prescription, derelict land, treasure trove, mortmain or the rights of succession competent to the Crown; or

(k) for so long only as may be necessary for the purposes of any examination, investigation, trial or inquiry or, in the case of land, the carrying out thereon:

(i) of work of soil conservation or the conservation of other natural resources of any description or of war damage reconstruction; or

(ii) of agricultural development for improvement which the owner or occupier of the land has been required, and has without reasonable and lawful excuse refused or failed to carry out.

(3) Nothing in this section shall be construed as affecting the making or operation of any law so far as it provides for vesting in the Government of Malta the ownership of any underground minerals, water or antiquities.

(4) Nothing in this section shall be construed as affecting the making or operation of any law for the compulsory taking of possession in the public interest of any property, or the compulsory acquisition in the public interest of any interest in or right over property, where that property, interest or right is held by a body corporate which is established for public purposes by any law and in which no monies have been invested other than monies provided by any legislature in Malta.

Protection for privacy of home or other property

39. (1) Except with his own consent or by way of parental discipline, no person shall be subjected to the search of his person or his property or the entry by others on his premises.

(2) Nothing contained in or done under the authority of any law shall be held to be inconsistent with or in contravention of this section to the extent that the law in question makes provision:

(a) that is reasonably required in the interest of defence, public safety, public order, public morality or decency, public health, town and country planning, the development and utilisation of mineral resources, or the development and utilisation of any property in such a manner as to promote the public benefit;

(b) that is reasonably required for the purpose of promoting the rights or freedoms of other persons;

(c) that authorises a department of the Government of Malta, or a local government authority, or a body corporate established by law for a public purpose, to enter on the premises of any person in order to inspect those premises or anything thereon for the purpose of any tax, rate or due or in order to carry out work connected with any property or installation which is lawfully on those premises and which belongs to that Government, that authority, or that body corporate, as the case may be; or

(d) that authorises, for the purpose of enforcing a judgment or order of a court, the search of any person or property by order of a court or entry upon any premises by such order, or that is necessary for the purpose of preventing or detecting criminal offences,

and except so far as that provision or, as the case may be, the thing done under the authority thereof is shown not to be reasonably justifiable in a democratic society.

Provisions to secure protection of law

40. (1) Whenever any person is charged with a criminal offence he shall, unless the charge is withdrawn, be afforded a fair hearing within a reasonable time by an independent and impartial court established by law.

(2) Any court or other adjudicating authority prescribed by law for the determination of the existence or the extent of civil rights or obligations shall be independent and impartial; and where proceedings for such a determination are instituted by any person before such a court or other adjudicating authority, the case shall be given a fair hearing within a reasonable time.

(3) Except with the agreement of all the parties thereto, all proceedings of every court and proceedings relating to the determination of the existence or the extent of a person's civil rights or obligations before any other adjudicating authority, including the announcement of the decision of the court or other authority, shall be held in public.

(4) Nothing in subsection (3) of this section shall prevent any court or any authority such as is mentioned in that subsection from excluding from the proceedings persons other than the parties thereto and their legal representatives:

(a) in proceedings before a court of voluntary jurisdiction and other proceedings which, in the practice of the Courts in Malta are, or are of the same nature as those which are, disposed of in chambers;

(b) in proceedings under any law relating to income tax; or

(c) to such extent as the court or other authority:

(i) may consider necessary or expedient in circumstances where publicity would prejudice the interests of justice; or

(ii) may be empowered or required by law to do so in the interests of defence, public safety, public order, public morality or decency, the welfare of persons under the age of eighteen years or the protection of the privates lives of persons concerned in the proceedings.

(5) Every person who is charged with a criminal offence shall be presumed to be innocent until he is proved or has pleaded guilty:

Provided that nothing contained in or done under the authority of any law shall be held to be inconsistent with or in contravention of this subsection to the extent that the law in question imposes upon any person charged as aforesaid the burden of proving particular facts.

(6) Every person who is charged with a criminal offence:

(a) shall be informed in writing, in a language which he understands and in detail, of the nature of the offence charged;

(b) shall be given adequate time and facilities for the preparation of his defence;

(c) shall be permitted to defend himself in person or by a legal representative and a person who cannot afford to pay for such legal representation as is reasonably required by the circumstances of his case shall be entitled to have such representation at the public expense;

(d) shall be afforded facilities to examine in person or by his legal representative the witnesses called by the prosecution before any court and to obtain the attendance of witnesses subject to the payment of their reasonable expenses, and carry out the examination of witnesses to testify on his behalf before the court on the same conditions as those applying to witnesses called by the prosecution; and

(e) shall be permitted to have without payment the assistance of an interpreter of he cannot understand the language used at the trial of the charge,

and except with his own consent the trial shall not take place in his absence unless he so conducts himself as to render the continuance of the proceedings in his presence impracticable and the court has ordered him to be removed and the trial to proceed in his absence.

(7) When a person is tried for any criminal offence, the accused person or any person authorised by him in that behalf shall, if he so requires and subject to payment of such reasonable fee as may be prescribed by law, be given within a reasonable time after judgment a copy for the use of the accused person of any record of the proceedings made by or on behalf of the court.

(8) No person shall be held to be guilty of a criminal offence on account of any act or omission that did not, at the time it took place, constitute such an offence, and no penalty shall be imposed for any criminal offence which is severer in degree or description than the maximum penalty which might have been imposed for that offence at the time when it was committed.

(9) No person who shows that he has been tried by any competent court for a criminal offence and either convicted or acquitted shall again be tried for that offence or for any other criminal offence of which he could have been convicted at the trial for that offence save upon the order of a superior court made in the course of appeal or review proceedings relating to the conviction or acquittal; and no person shall be tried for a criminal offence if he shows that he has been pardoned for that offence:

Provided that nothing in any law shall be held to be inconsistent with or in contravention of this subsection by reason only that it authorises any court to try a member of a disciplined force for a criminal offence notwithstanding any trial and conviction or acquittal of that member under the disciplinary law of that force, so however that any court so trying such a member and convicting him shall in sentencing him to any punishment take into account any punishment awarded him under that disciplinary law.

(10) No person who is tried for a criminal offence shall be compelled to give evidence at his trial.

(11) In this section "legal representative" means a person entitled to practise in Malta as an advocate or, except in relation to proceedings before a court where a legal procurator has no right of audience, a legal procurator.

Protection of freedom of conscience

41. (1) All persons in Malta shall have full freedom of conscience and enjoy the free exercise of their respective mode of religious worship.

(2) Nothing contained in or done under the authority of any law shall be held to be inconsistent with or in contravention of subsection (1), to the extent that the law in question makes provision that is reasonably required in the interests of public safety, public order, public morality or decency, public health, or the protection of the rights and freedoms of others, and except so far as that provision or, as the case may be, the thing done under the authority thereof, is shown not to be reasonably justifiable in a democratic society.

Protection of freedom of expression

42. (1) Except with his own consent or by way of parental discipline, no person shall be hindered in the enjoyment of his freedom of expression, including freedom to hold opinions without interference, freedom to receive ideas and information without interference, freedom to communicate ideas and information without interference (whether the communication be to the public generally or to any person or class of persons) and freedom from interference with his correspondence.

(2) Nothing contained in or done under the authority of any law shall be held to be inconsistent with or in contravention of subsection (1) of this section to the extent that the law in question makes provision:

(a) that is reasonably required:

(i) in the interests of defence, public safety, public order, public morality or decency, or public health; or

(ii) for the purpose of protecting the reputations, rights and freedoms of other persons, or the private lives of persons concerned in legal proceedings, preventing the disclosure of information received in confidence, maintaining the authority and independence of the courts, protecting the privileges of Parliament, or regulating telephony, telegraphy, posts, wireless broadcasting, television or other means of communication, public exhibitions or public entertainments; or

(b) that imposes restrictions upon public officers,

and excepts so far as that provision or, as the case may be, the thing done under the authority thereof is shown not to be reasonably justifiable in a democratic society.

(3) Anyone who is resident in Malta may edit or print a newspaper or journal published daily or periodically:

Provided that provision may be made by law:

(a) prohibiting or restricting the editing or printing of any such newspaper or journal by persons under twenty-one years of age; and

(b) requiring any person who is the editor or printer of any such newspaper or journal to inform the prescribed authority to that effect and of his age and to keep the prescribed authority informed of his place of residence.

(4) Where the police seize any edition of a newspaper as being the means whereby a criminal offence has been committed they shall within twenty-four hours of the seizure bring the seizure to the notice of the competent court and if the court is not satisfied that there is a *prima facie* case of such offence, that edition shall be returned to the person from whom it was seized.

(5) No person shall be deprived of his citizenship under any provisions made under section 31 (1) (b) of this Constitution or of his juridical capacity by reason only of his political opinions.

Protection of freedom of assembly and association

43. (1) Except with his own consent or by way of parental discipline no person shall be hindered in the enjoyment of his freedom of peaceful assembly and association, that is to say, his right peacefully to assemble freely and associate with other persons and in particular to form or belong to trade or other unions or associations for the protection of his interests.

(2) Nothing contained in or done under the authority of any law shall be held to be inconsistent with or in contravention of this section to the extent that the law in question makes provision:

(a) that is reasonably required:

(i) in the interests of defence, public safety, public order, public morality or decency, or public health; or

(ii) for the purpose of protecting the rights or freedoms of other persons; or

(b) that imposes restrictions upon public officers,

and except so far as that provision or, as the case may be, the thing done under the authority thereof is shown not to be reasonably justifiable in a democratic society.

Prohibition of deportation

44. (1) Extradition is only permitted in pursuance of arrangements made by treaty and under the authority of a law.

(2) No person shall be extradited for an offence of a political character.

(3) No citizen of Malta shall be removed from Malta except as a result of extradition proceedings or under any such law as is referred to in section 45 (3) (b) of this Constitution.

(4) The provisions made by or under the Fugitive Offenders Act 1881 as for the time being in force in Malta, for the removal of persons from Malta to another country to undergo trial or punishment in that country in respect of an offence committed in that country and any general arrangements for the extradition of persons between Commonwealth countries to which Malta for the time being adheres shall be deemed, for the purposes of subsection (1) of this section, to be arrangements made by treaty, and subsection (2) shall not apply in relation to the removal or extradition of a person under such provisions or arangements.

Protection of freedom of movement

45. (1) No citizen of Malta shall be deprived of his freedom of movement, and for the purpose of this section the said freedom means the right to move freely throughout Malta, the right to reside in any part of Malta, the right to leave and the right to enter Malta.

(2) Any restriction on a citizen's freedom of movement that is involved in his lawful detention shall not be held to be inconsistent with or in contravention of this section.

(3) Nothing contained in or done under the authority of any law shall be held to be inconsistent with or in contravention of this section to the extent that the law in question makes provision:

(a) for the imposition of restrictions that are reasonably required in the interests of defence, public safety, public order, public morality or decency, or public health and except so far as that provision or, as the case may be, the thing done under the authority thereof is shown not to be reasonably justifiable in a democratic society;

(b) for the imposition of restrictions on the freedom of movement of any citizen of Malta who is not a citizen by virtue of section 23 (1) or 26 (1) of this Constitution;

(c) for the imposition of restrictions upon the movement or residence within Malta of public officers; or

(d) for the imposition of restrictions on the right of any person to leave Malta that are reasonably required in order to secure the fulfilment of any obligation imposed on that person by law and except so far as that provision or, as the case may be, the thing done under the authority thereof is shown not to be reasonably justifiable in a democratic society.

(4) For the purposes of this section any person:

(a) who has emigrated from Malta (whether before, on or after the appointed day) and, having been a citizen of Malta by virtue of section 23 (1) or 26 (1) of this Constitution, has ceased to be such a citizen; or

(b) who emigrated from Malta before the appointed day and, but for his having ceased to be a citizen of the United Kingdom and Colonies before that day, would have become a citizen of Malta by virtue of section 23 (1) of this Constitution; or

(c) who is the wife of a person mentioned in paragraph (a) or (b) of this subsection or of a person who is a citizen of Malta by virtue of section 23 (1) or 26 (1) of this Constitution and is living with that person or is the child under twenty-one years of age of such a person;

shall be deemed to be a citizen of Malta by virtue of section 23 (1) or 26 (1) of this Constitution.

(5) If any person whose freedom of movement has been restricted by virtue of such a provision as is referred to in subsection (3) (a) of this section so requests at any time during the period of that restriction not earlier than six months after the order was made or six months after he last made such request, as the case may be, his case shall be reviewed by an independent and impartial tribunal established by law composed of a person or persons each of whom holds or has held judicial office or is qualified to be appointed to such office in Malta:

Provided that a person whose freedom of movement has been restricted by virtue of a restriction which is applicable to persons generally or to general classes of persons shall not make a request under this subsection unless he has first obtained the consent of the Civil Court, First Hall.

(6) On any review by a tribunal in pursuance of this section of the case of a person whose freedom of movement has been restricted the tribunal may make recommendations concerning the necessity or expediency of continuing the restriction to the authority by which it was ordered but, unless it is otherwise provided by law, that authority shall not be obliged to act in accordance with any such recommendations.

Protection from discrimination on the grounds of race, etc.

46. (1) Subject to the provisions of subsections (4), (5) and (7) of this section, no law shall make any provision that is discriminatory either of itself or in its effect.

(2) Subject to the provisions of subsections (6), (7) and (8) of this section, no person shall be treated in a discriminatory manner by any person acting by virtue of any written law or in the performance of the functions of any public office or any public authority.

(3) In this section, the expression "discriminatory" means affording different treatment to different persons attributable wholly or mainly to their respective descriptions by race, place of origin, political opinions, colour or creed whereby persons of one such description are subjected to

disabilities or restrictions to which persons of another such description are not made subject or are accorded privileges or advantages which are not accorded to persons of another such description.

(4) Subsection (1) of this section shall not apply to any law so far as that law makes provision:

(a) for the appropriation of public revenues or other public funds; or

(b) with respect to persons who are not citizens of Malta; or

(c) with respect to adoption, marriage, dissolution of marriage, burial, devolution of property on death or any matters of personal law not hereinbefore specified; or

(d) whereby persons of any such description as is mentioned in subsection (3) of this section may be subjected to any disability or restriction or may be accorded any privilege or advantage which, having regard to its nature and to special circumstances pertaining to those persons or to persons of any other such description and to any other provision of this Constitution, is reasonably justifiable in a democratic society; or

(e) for authorising the taking during a period of public emergency of measures that are reasonably justifiable for the purpose of dealing with the situation that exists during that period of public emergency.

(5) Nothing contained in any law shall be held to be inconsistent with or in contravention of subsection (1) of this section to the extent that it makes provision with respect to qualifications for service as a public officer or as a member of a disciplined force or for the service of a local government authority or a body corporate established for public purposes by any law.

(6) Subsection (2) of this section shall not apply to anything which is expressly or by necessary implication authorised to be done by any such provision of law as is referred to in subsection (4) or (5) of this section.

(7) Nothing contained in or done under the authority of any law shall be held to be inconsistent with or in contravention of this section to the extent that the law in question makes provision whereby persons of any such description as is mentioned in subsection (3) of this section may be subjected to any restriction on the rights and freedoms guaranteed by sections 39, 41, 42, 43 and 45 of this Constitutiton, being such a restriction as is authorised by section 39 (2), 41 (2), 42 (2), 43 (2) or 45 (3).

(8) Nothing in subsection (2) of this section shall affect any discretion relating to the institution, conduct or discontinuance of civil or criminal proceedings in any court that is vested in any person by or under this Constitution or any other law.

(9) Notwithstanding any other provision of this Constitution, no person not professing the Roman Catholic Apostolic Religion shall hold any office entailing the teaching of that religion.

Enforcement of protective provisions

47. (1) Subject to the provisions of subsections (6) and (7) of this section, any person who alleges that any of the provisions of sections 34 to 46 (inclusive) of this Constitution has been, is being or is likely to be contravened in relation to him, or such other person as the Civil Court, First Hall, in Malta may appoint at the instance of any person who so alleges, may, without prejudice to any other action with respect to the same matter that is lawfully available, apply to the Civil Court, First Hall, for redress.

(2) The Civil Court, First Hall, shall have original jurisdiction to hear and determine any application made by any person in pursuance of subsection (1) of this section, and may make such orders, issue such writs and give such directions as it may consider appropriate for the purpose of enforcing, or securing the enforcement of, any of the provisions of the said sections 34 to 46 (inclusive) to the protection of which the person concerned is entitled:

Provided that the Court may, if it considers it desirable so to do, decline to exercise its powers under this subsection in any case where it is satisfied that adequate means of redress for the contravention alleged are or have been available to the person concerned under any other law.

(3) If in any proceedings in any court other than the Civil Court, First Hall, or the Constitutional Court any question arises as to the contravention of any of the provisions of the said sections 34 to 46 (inclusive), that court shall refer the question to the Civil Court, First Hall, unless in its opinion the raising of the question is merely frivolous or vexatious; and that court shall give its decision on any question referred to it under this subsection and, subject to the provisions of subsection (4) of this section, and of section 103 (2) of this Constitution, the court in which the question arose shall dispose of the question in accordance with that decision.

(4) Any party to proceedings brought in the Civil Court, First Hall, in pursuance of this section shall have a right of appeal to the Constitutional Court.

(5) No appeal shall lie from any determination under this section that any application or the raising of any question is merely frivolous or vexatious.

(6) Provision may be made by or under an Act of Parliament for conferring upon the Civil Court, First Hall, such powers in addition to those conferred by this section as are necessary or desirable for the purpose of enabling the Court more effectively to exercise the jurisdiction conferred upon it by this section.

(7) Rules of court making provision with respect to the practice and procedure of the Courts of Malta for the purposes of this section may be made by the person or authority for the time being having power to make

rules of court with respect to the practice and procedure of those Courts, and shall be designed to secure that the procedure shall be by application and that the hearing shall be as expeditious as possible.

Interpretation of Chapter IV

48. (1) In this Chapter, save where the context otherwise requires, the following expressions, shall have the following meanings respectively, that is to say:

"contravention," in relation to any requirement, includes a failure to comply with that requirement, and cognate expressions shall be construed accordingly;

"court" means any court of law in Malta other than a court constituted by or under a disciplinary law and in sections 34 and 36 of this Constitution includes, in relation to an offence against a disciplinary law, a court so constituted;

"disciplinary law" means a law regulating the discipline:

(a) of any disciplined force; or

(b) of persons serving prison sentences;

"disciplined force" means:

(a) a naval, military or air force of the Crown in right of the Government of Malta;

(b) the Malta Police Force;

(c) any other police force established by law in Malta;

(d) the Malta prison service;

"member," in relation to a disciplined force, includes any person who, under the law regulating the discipline of that force, is subject to that discipline.

(2) In this Chapter "period of public emergency" means any period during which:

(a) Malta is engaged in any war; or

(b) there is in force a proclamation by the Governor-General declaring that a state of public emergency exists; or

(c) there is in force a resolution of the House of Representatives supported by the votes of not less than two thirds of all the Members of the House declaring that democratic institutions in Malta are threatened by subversion.

(3) (a) Where any proclamation of emergency has been made, the occasion therefor shall forthwith be communicated to the House of Representatives and, if the House is then separated by such adjournment or prorogation as will not expire within ten days the Governor-General shall by proclamation summon it to meet within five days and it shall accordingly meet and sit upon the day appointed by the proclamation and shall continue to sit and act as if it had stood adjourned or prorogued to that day.

(b) A proclamation of emergency shall, unless it is sooner revoked by the Governor-General, cease to be in force at the expiration of a period of fourteen days beginning on the date on which it was made or such longer period as may be provided under the next following paragraph, but without prejudice to the making of another proclamation of emergency at or before the end of that period.

(c) If at any time while a proclamation of emergency is in force (including any time while it is in force by virtue of this paragraph) a resolution is passed by the House of Representatives approving its continuance in force for a further period, not exceeding three months, beginning on the date on which it would otherwise expire, the proclamation shall, if not sooner revoked, continue in force for that further period.

(4) A resolution such as is referred to in paragraph (c) of subsection (2) of this section shall, unless it is sooner revoked by the Houe of Representatives, cease to be in force at the expiration of twelve months beginning on the date on which it was passed or such shorter period as may be specified therein, but without prejudice to the passing of another resolution by the House of Representatives in the manner prescribed by that paragraph at or before the end of that period.

(5) In relation to any person who is a member of a disciplined force raised under any law in force in Malta, nothing contained in or done under the authority of the disciplinary law of that force shall be held to be inconsistent with or in contravention of any of the provisions of this Chapter other than sections 34, 36 and 37.

(6) In relation to any person who is a member of a disciplined force raised otherwise than as aforesaid and lawfully present in Malta, nothing contained in or done under the authority of the disciplinary law of that force shall be held to be inconsistent with or in contravention of any of the provisions of this Chapter.

(7) Nothing contained in any such law as is specified in the First Schedule to this Constitution and, until the expiration of a period of three years commencing with the appointed day, nothing contained in any other law made before the appointed day shall be held to be inconsistent with the provisions of sections 34 to 46 (inclusive) of this Chapter and, subject as aforesaid, nothing done under the authority of any such law shall be held to be done in contravention of those sections.

(8) Where any provision of law enacted before the appointed day is held to be inconsistent with any of the provisions of sections 34 to 46 (inclusive) of this Chapter, no person shall be entitled to compensation in respect of anything done under the authority of that provision before it was so held to be inconsistent.

(9) Nothing in section 38 of this Constitution shall affect the operation of any law in force immediately before 3rd March 1962 or any law made

on or after that date that amends or replaces any law in force immediately before that date (or such a law as from time to time amended or replaced in the manner described in this subsection) and that does not:

(a) add to the kinds of property that may be taken possession of or the rights over and interests in property that may be acquired;

(b) add to the purposes for which or circumstances in which such property may be taken possession of or acquired;

(c) make the conditions governing entitlement to compensation or the amount thereof less favourable to any person owning or interested in the property; or

(d) deprive any person of any right such as is mentioned in paragraph (b) or paragraph (c) of section 38 (1) of this Constitution.

CHAPTER V

THE GOVERNOR-GENERAL

Establishment of office of Governor-General

49. There shall be a Governor-General of Malta who shall be appointed by Her Majesty and shall hold office during Her Majesty's pleasure and who shall be Her Majesty's representative in Malta.

Discharge of Governor-General's functions during vacancy, etc.

50. Whenever the office of Governor-General is vacant or the holder of the office is absent from Malta or is for any reason unable to perform the functions conferred upon him by this Constitution, those functions shall be performed by such person as Her Majesty may appoint or, if there is no person in Malta so appointed and able to perform those functions, by the Chief Justice.

Oaths to be taken by Governor-General

51. A person appointed to or assuming the functions of the office of Governor-General shall, before entering upon that office, take and subscribe the oath of allegiance and such oath for the due execution of his office as may be prescribed by any law for the time being in force in Malta.

CHAPTER VI

PARLIAMENT

Part 1. Composition of Parliament

Establishment of Parliament

52. There shall be a Parliament of Malta which shall consist of Her Majesty and a House of Representatives.

Composition of the House of Representatives

53. (1) Subject to the provisions of this Chapter, the House of Representatives shall consist of fifty members who shall be elected in the manner provided by or under any law for the time being in force in Malta in equal proportions from the electoral divisions referred to in section 57 of this Constitution and who shall be known as "Members of Parliament."

(2) If any person who is not a member of the House of Representatives is elected to be Speaker of the House he shall, by virtue of holding the office of Speaker, be a member of the House in addition to the said fifty members.

Qualifications for membership of House of Representatives

54. Subject to the provisions of section 55 of this Constitution, a person shall be qualified to be elected as a member of the House of Representatives if, and shall not be qualified to be so elected unless, he has the qualifications for registration as a voter for the election of members of the House of Representatives mentioned in section 58 of this Constitution.

Disqualifications for membership of House of Representatives

55. (1) No person shall be qualified to be elected as a member of the House of Representatives:

(a) if he is a citizen of a country other than Malta having become such a citizen voluntarily or is under a declaration of allegiance to such a country;

(b) save as otherwise provided by Parliament, if he holds or is acting in any public office or is a member of the Armed Forces of the Crown;

(c) if he is a party to, or is a partner with unlimited liability in a partnership or a director or manager of a company which is a party to, any contract with the Government of Malta for or on account of the public service and has not, within one month before the date of election, published in the Gazette a notice setting out the nature of any such contract, and his interest, or the interest of any such partnership or company, therein;

(d) if he is an undischarged bankrupt, having been adjudged or otherwise declared bankrupt under any law in force in Malta;

(e) if he is interdicted or incapacitated for any mental infirmity or for prodigality by a court in Malta, or is otherwise determined in Malta to be of unsound mind;

(f) if he is under sentence of death imposed on him by any court in Malta or is serving a sentence of imprisonment (by whatever name called), exceeding twelve months imposed on him by such a court or substituted by competent authority for some other sentence imposed on him by such a court, or is under such a sentence of imprisonment the execution of which has been suspended;

(g) if he holds or is acting in any office the functions of which involve any responsibility for, or in connection with, the conduct of any election of members of the House of Representatives or the compilation or revision of any electoral register;

(h) if he is disqualified for membership of the House of Representatives by or under any law for the time being in force in Malta by reason of his having been convicted of any offence connected with the election of members of the House of Representatives.

(2) For the purposes of paragraph (f) of subsection (1) of this section:

(a) two or more sentences that are required to be served consecutively shall be regarded as separate sentences if none of them exceeds twelve months, but if any one of them exceeds that term they shall be regarded as one sentence; and

(b) no account shall be taken of a sentence of imprisonment imposed as an alternative to, or in default of, the payment of a fine.

(3) A person shall not be treated as holding, or acting in, a public office for the purpose of paragraph (b) of subsection (1) of this section:

(a) if he is on leave of absence pending relinquishment of a public office;

(b) if he is a teacher at the Royal University of Malta who is not by the terms of his employment prevented from the private practice of his profession or called upon to place his whole time at the disposal of the Government of Malta.

Tenure of office of members

56. (1) The seat of a member of Parliament shall become vacant:

(a) upon the next dissolution of Parliament after his election;

(b) if he resigns his seat by writing under his hand addressed to the Speaker or, if the office of Speaker is vacant or the Speaker is absent from Malta, to the Deputy Speaker;

(c) if he becomes a party to any contract with the Government of Malta for or on account of the public service, or if any partnership in which he is a partner with unlimited liability or a company of which he is a director or manager becomes a party to any such contract, or if he becomes a partner with unlimited liability in a partnership or a director or manager of a company that is a party to any such contract:

Provided that he shall not vacate his seat under the provisions of this paragraph if before becoming a party to the contract or before, or as soon as practicable after, becoming otherwise interested in the contract (whether as a partner with unlimited liability in a partnership or as a director or manager of a company) he discloses to the Speaker the nature of the contract and his interest or the interest of the partnership or company therein and the House of Representatives by resolution exempts him from the provisions of this paragraph;

(d) if he is absent from the sittings of the House of Representatives for such period and in such circumstances as may be prescribed by the Standing Orders of the House;

(e) if he ceases to be a citizen of Malta;

(f) if he ceases to be qualified for registration as a voter for the election of members of the House of Representatives;

(g) subject to the provisions of subsection (2) of this section, if any circumstances arise that if he were not a member of the House of Representatives, would cause him to be disqualified for election thereto.

(2) (a) If circumstances such as are referred to in paragraph (g) of subsection (1) of this section arise because any member of the House of Representatives is under sentence of death or imprisonment, interdicted or incapacitated or adjudged to be of unsound mind, adjudged or otherwise declared bankrupt or convicted of an offence connected with elections and if it is open to the member to appeal against the decision (either with the leave of a court or other authority or without such leave), he shall forthwith cease to perform his functions as a member of the House but, subject to the provisions of this section, he shall not vacate his seat until the expiration of a period of thirty days thereafter:

Provided that the Speaker may, from time to time, extend that period for further periods of thirty days to enable the member to pursue an appeal against the decision, so however that extensions of time exceeding in the aggregate one hundred and fifty days shall not be given without the approval, signified by resolution, of the House.

(b) If, on the determination of any appeal, such circumstances continue to exist and no further appeal is open to the member, or if, by reason of the expiration of any period for entering an appeal or notice thereof or the refusal of leave to appeal or for any other reason, it ceases to be open to the member to appeal, he shall forthwith vacate his seat.

(c) If at any time before the member vacates his seat such circumstances as aforesaid cease to exist, his seat shall not become vacant on the expiration of the period referred to in paragraph (a) of this subsection and he may resume the performance of his functions as a member of the House of Representatives.

(d) For the purposes of this subsection "appeal" means, in the case of an order by a court of voluntary jurisdiction for the interdiction or incapacitation of a member of the House of Representatives, the taking of any action for the review of that order before the Civil Court, First Hall.

Voting at Elections

57. (1) The members of the House of Representatives shall be elected upon the principle of proportional representation by means of the single transferable vote from ten electoral divisions.

(2) No person shall vote at the election of members of the House of Representatives for any electoral division who is not registered under any law for the time being in force in Malta as a voter in that division.

(3) At the election of members of the House of Representatives:

(a) voting shall be by ballot and shall be carried out in such a manner as not to disclose the way in which the vote of any particular voter is given; and

(b) no person shall be permitted to vote on behalf of another:

Provided that provision may be made by law whereby, if a person is unable, by reason of blindness, other physical cause or illiteracy to mark his ballot paper, his ballot paper may be marked on his behalf and on his directions by some other person officially supervising the poll at the place of voting.

(4) Ballot papers shall be drawn up in such a way as to enable illiterates to distinguish between the political parties to which candidates belong.

(5) Candidates and their agents shall be given facilities to watch the transportation of ballot boxes and the sealing and unsealing thereof.

Qualification of voters

58. Subject to the provisions of section 59 of this Constitution, a person shall be qualified to be registered as a voter for the election of members of the House of Representatives if, and shall not be qualified to be so registered unless:

(a) he is a citizen of Malta;

(b) he has attained the age of twenty-one years; and

(c) he is resident in Malta and has during the two years immediately preceding his registration been so resident for a continuous period of one year or for periods amounting in the aggregate to one year.

Disqualification of voters

59. No person shall be qualified to be registered as a voter for the election of members of the House of Representatives if:

(a) he is interdicted or incapacitated for any mental infirmity by a court in Malta or is otherwise determined in Malta to be of unsound mind;

(b) he is under sentence of death imposed on him by any court in Malta or is serving a sentence of imprisonment (by whatever name called) exceeding twelve months imposed on him by such a court or substituted by competent authority for some other sentence imposed on him by such a court, or is under such a sentence of imprisonment the execution of which has been suspended; or

(c) he is disqualified for registration as a voter by or under any law for the time being in force in Malta by reason of his having been convicted of any offence connected with the election of members of the House of Representatives.

Speaker and Deputy Speaker

60. (1) When the House of Representatives first meets after any general election and before it proceeds to the despatch of any other business, it shall elect a person to be the Speaker of the House; and if the office of Speaker falls vacant at any time before the next dissolution of Parliament, the House shall, as soon as practicalbe, elect another person to that office.

(2) The Speaker may be elected either:

(a) from among persons who are members of the House of Representatives, but are not Ministers or Parliamentary Secretaries, or

(b) from among persons who are not members of the House of Representatives and are qualified for election as members thereof.

(3) When the House of Representatives first meets after any general election and before it proceeds to the despatch of any other business except the election of the Speaker, the House shall elect a member of the House, who is not a Minister or a Parliamentary Secretary, to be Deputy Speaker of the House; and if the office of Deputy Speaker falls vacant at any time before the next dissolution of Parliament, the House shall, as soon as convenient, elect another such member to that office.

(4) A person shall vacate the office of Speaker or Deputy Speaker:

(a) in the case of a Speaker elected from among the members of the House of Representatives or in the case of the Deputy Speaker:

(i) if he ceases to be a member of the House:

Provided that the Speaker shall not vacate his office by reason only that he has ceased to be a member of the House on a dissolution of Parliament, until the House first meets after that dissolution;

(ii) if he is appointed to be a Minister or a Parliamentary Secretary;

(b) in the case of a Speaker elected from among persons who are not members of the House of Representatives:

(i) when the House first meets after any dissolution of Parliament;

(ii) if any circumstances arise that would cause him to be disqualified for election as a member of the House of Representatives;

(c) if he announces his resignation of his office to the House of Representatives or if by writing under his hand addressed, in the case of the Speaker to the Clerk of the House and in the case of the Deputy Speaker to the Speaker (or, if the office of Speaker is vacant or the Speaker is absent from Malta, to the Clerk of the House) he resigns that office; or

(d) in the case of the Deputy Speaker, if he is elected to be Speaker.

(5) (a) If, by virtue of subsection (2) of section 56 of this Constitution, the Speaker or Deputy Speaker is required to cease to perform his functions as a member of the House of Representatives he shall also cease to perform his functions as Speaker or Deputy Speaker, as the case may

be, and those functions shall until he vacates his seat in the House or resumes the performance of the functions of his office, be performed:

(i) in the case of the Speaker, by the Deputy Speaker or, if the office of Deputy Speaker is vacant or the Deputy Speaker is required to cease to perform his functions as a member of the House of Representatives by virtue of subsection (2) of section 56 of this Constitution, by such member of the House (not being a Minister or Parliamentary Secretary) as the House may elect for the purpose;

(ii) in the case of the Deputy Speaker, by such member of the House (not being a Minister or Parliamentary Secretary) as the House may elect for the purpose.

(b) If the Speaker or Deputy Speaker resumes the performance of his functions as a member of the House, in accordance with the provisions of subsection (2) of section 56 of this Constitution, he shall also resume the performance of his functions of Speaker or Deputy Speaker, as the case may be.

Establishment of Electoral Commission

61. (1) There shall be an Electoral Commission for Malta.

(2) The Electoral Commission shall consist of a Chairman, who shall be the person for the time being holding the office of Chief Electoral Commissioner and who shall be appointed to that office from the public service, and such number of members not being less than four as may be prescribed by any law for the time being in force in Malta.

(3) The members of the Electoral Commission shall be appointed by the Governor-General, acting in accordance with the advice of the Prime Minister, given after he has consulted the Leader of the Opposition.

(4) A person shall not be qualified to hold office as a member of the Electoral Commission if he is a Minister, a Parliamentary Secretary, a member of, or a candidate for election to, the House of Representatives or a public officer.

(5) Subject to the provisions of this section, a member of the Electoral Commission shall vacate his office:

(a) at the expiration of three years from the date of his appointment or at such earlier time as may be specified in the instrument by which he was appointed; or

(b) if any circumstances arise that, if he were not a member of the Commission, would cause him to be disqualified for appointment as such.

(6) Subject to the provisions of subsection (7) of this section, a member of the Electoral Commission may be removed from office by the Governor-General acting in accordance with the advice of the Prime Minister.

(7) A member of the Electoral Commission shall not be removed from office except for inability to discharge the functions of his office (whether

arising from infirmity of mind or body or any other cause) or for misbehaviour.

(8) If the office of a member of the Electoral Commission is vacant or if a member is for any reason unable to perform the functions of his office, the Governor-General, acting in accordance with the advice of the Prime Minister, given after he has consulted the Leader of the Opposition, may appoint a person who is qualified to be appointed to be a member to be a temporary member of the Commission; and any person so appointed shall, subject to the provisions of subsections (5), (6) and (7) of this section, cease to be such a member when a person has been appointed to fill the vacancy or, as the case may be, when the member who was unable to perform the functions of his office resumes those functions.

(9) In the exercise of its functions under this Constitution the Electoral Commission shall not be subject to the direction or control of any other person or authority.

Electoral Divisions

62. (1) The Electoral Commission shall review the boundaries of the electoral divisions referred to in section 57 (1) of this Constitution at intervals of not less than two nor more than five years and may, in accordance with the provisions of this section, alter such boundaries to such extent as it considers desirable in the light of the review:

Provided that the Commission shall carry out such a review and, in accordance with the provisions of this section, alter the said boundaries whenever Parliament has made provision altering the number of electoral divisions or altering the number of the members of the House of Representatives in such a way that that number is not divisible by the number of electoral divisions; and in addition the Commission may at any time carry out such a review and, in accordance with the provisions of this section, alter the said boundaries to such extent as it considers desirable in consequence of the holding of a census of the population in pursuance of any law.

(2) Any provision by Parliament altering the number of electoral divisions or altering the number of the members of the House of Representatives in such a way that that number is not divisible by the number of electoral divisions shall come into effect when the alteration of the boundaries of the electoral divisions that, in accordance with the provisions of subsection (1) of this section, is consequential thereon comes into effect.

(3) Any alteration of boundaries under this section shall come into effect upon the next dissolution of Parliament after the alteration has been approved by the House Representatives:

Provided that nothing in this subsection shall be construed as as preventing the publication of any electoral register or any other requirement connected with the registration of voters from being carried out in accordance with the alteration, under any law for the time being in force in Malta, before that dissolution.

(4) An alteration of the boundaries of any electoral division under this section shall be made in such manner as secures that, at the time when the Commission carries out its review, the number obtained by dividing the total electorate in the division (as ascertained by reference to the electoral register in force at that time) by the number of members to be returned to the House of Representatives from that division is as nearly equal to the electoral quota as is reasonably practicable:

Provided that any such alteration may be made in such manner that the number of voters in that division is, at the time when the Commission carries out its review, greater or less than the electoral quota multiplied by the number of members to be so returned, but in no case by more than fifteen per centum, in order to take account of means of communication, differences in density of population, parish boundaries and other relevant factors.

(5) For the purposes of any review carried out under this section, "electoral quota" means the number obtained by dividing the total electorate of Malta (as ascertained from the electoral register in force at the time when the Commission carries out that review) by the total number of members to be returned to the House of Representatives at the general election following the next dissolution of Parliament.

(6) The conduct of elections in every electoral division and of any vote taken under the provisions of section 67 (3) of this Constitution shall be subject to the direction and supervision of the Electoral Commission.

Filling of vacancies

63. Whenever the seat of any member of the House of Representatives becomes vacant the vacancy shall be filled in the manner provided by or under any law for the time being in force in Malta.

Determination of questions as to membership

64. Any question whether:

(a) any person has been validly elected as a member of the House of Representatives;

(b) any member of the House has vacated his seat therein or is required, under the provisions of subsection (2) of section 56 of this Constitution, to cease to perform his functions as a member; or

(c) any person has been validly elected as Speaker from among persons who are not members of the House or, having been so elected, has vacated the office of Speaker,

shall be referred to and determined by the Constitutional Court in accordance with the provisions of any law for the time being in force in Malta, and the determination by the Constitutional Court of any such question shall be final.

Clerk to House of Representatives and his staff

65. (1) There shall be a Clerk to the House of Representatives.

(2) The office of the Clerk to the House of Representatives and the offices of the members of his staff shall be public offices.

Part 2. Powers and Procedure of Parliament

Power to make laws

66. (1) Subject to the provisions of this Constitution, Parliament may make laws for the peace, order and good government of Malta.

(2) Without prejudice to the generality of subsection (1) and subject to the provisions of subsections (3), (4) and (5) of this section, Parliament may by law determine the privileges, immunities and powers of the House of Representatives and the members thereof.

(3) No civil or criminal proceedings may be instituted against any member of the House of Representatives for words spoken before, or written in a report to, the House or a committee thereof or by reason of any matter or thing brought by him therein by petition, bill, resolution, motion or otherwise.

(4) For the duration of any session members of the House of Representatives shall enjoy freedom from arrest for any civil debt except a debt the contraction of which constitutes a criminal offence.

(5) No process issued by any court in the exercise of its civil jurisdiction shall be served or executed within the precincts of the House of Representatives while the House is sitting or through the Speaker, the Clerk or any officer of the House.

Alteration of this Constitution

67. (1) Subject to the provisions of this section, Parliament may alter any of the provisions of this Constitution or (in so far as it forms part of the law of Malta) any of the provisions of the Malta Independence Act 1964.

(2) In so far as it alters:

(a) section 5, sections 33 to 48 (inclusive), sections 57, 61, 62, subsection (3) of section 66, sections 92, 96 (other than subsection (2) thereof), 97, 98, 99, 100, 101, 105 to 113 (inclusive), 116, 117, 121 or 122 of this Constitution; or

(b) section 103 of this Constitution at any time within five years from the appointed day; or

(c) section 126 of this Constitution in its application to any of the provisions specified in paragraph (a) or, subject to the limitation therein contained, paragraph (b) of this subsection,

a bill for an Act of Parliament under this section shall not be passed in the House of Representatives unless at the final voting thereon in that House it is supported by the votes of not less than two thirds of all the members of the House.

(3) In so far as it alters:

(a) this section;

(b) sections 2, 3, 4, 49, 52, 58, subsection (2) of section 76, section 77, section 78, subsection (1) of section 79, section 81, and subsection (2) of section 96 of this Constitution;

(c) section 126 of this Constitution in its application to any of the provisions specified in paragraph (a) or (b) of this subsection; or

(d) any of the provisions of the Malta Independence Act 1964,

a bill for an Act of Parliament under this section shall not be presented to the Governor-General for his assent unless not less than three nor more than six months after its passage through the House in the manner specified in subsection (2) of this section it has been submitted to the electors qualified to vote for the election of members of the House of Representatives and the majority of the electors voting have approved the bill.

(4) The provisions of section 57 (3) of this Constitution shall apply to the voting on a bill submitted to the electors under subsection (3) of this section as they apply to voting at the election of members of the House of Representatives, and subject as aforesaid the vote on such a bill shall be taken in such manner as Parliament may prescribe.

(5) In so far as it alters any of the provisions of this Constitution other than those specified in subsections (2) and (3) of this section or, after five years from the appointed day, section 103 of this Constitution, a bill for an Act of Parliament under this section shall not be passed in the House of Representatives unless at the final voting thereon in that House it is supported by the votes of a majority of all the members of the House.

(6) An Act of Parliament altering the number of members of the House of Representatives shall not affect the membership of the House before the dissolution of Parliament next following its enactment.

(7) In this section:

(a) references to any of the provisions of this Constitution or of the Malta Independence Act 1964 include references to any law that amends or replaces that provision; and

(b) references to the alteration of any of the provisions of this Constitution or of the Malta Independence Act 1964 include references to the amendment, modification or re-enactment, with or without amendment or modification, of that provision, the suspension or repeal of that provision and the making of a different provision in lieu of that provision.

Regulation of procedure in House of Representatives

68. (1) Subject to the provisions of this Constitution, the House of Representatives may regulate its own procedure.

(2) The House of Representatives may act notwithstanding any vacancy in its membership (including any vacancy not filled when the House first meets on or after the appointed day or after any dissolution of Parliament) and the presence or participation of any person not entitled to be present at or to participate in the proceedings of the House shall not invalidate those proceedings.

(3) Any provision made in pursuance of subsection (1) of this section for setting up Committees of the House to enquire into matters of general public importance shall be designed to secure that, so far as appears practicable to the House, any such Committee is so composed as fairly to represent the House.

Oath to be taken by members of House of Representatives

69. No member of the House of Representatives shall be permitted to take part in the proceedings of the House (other than proceedings necessary for the purposes of this section) until he has taken and subscribed before the House the oath of allegiance:

Provided that the election of the Speaker and Deputy Speaker may take place before the members of the House have taken and subscribed such oath.

Presiding in House of Representatives

70. (1) There shall preside at any sitting of the House of Representatives:

(a) the Speaker; or

(b) in the absence of the Speaker, the Deputy Speaker; or

(c) in the absence of the Speaker and the Deputy Speaker, such member of the House (not being a Minister or a Parliamentary Secretary) as the House may elect for that purpose.

(2) References in this section to circumstances in which the Speaker or the Deputy Speaker is absent include references to circumstances in which the office of Speaker or Deputy Speaker is vacant.

Quorum in House of Representatives

71. (1) If at any sitting of the House of Representatives any member who is present draws the attention of the person presiding at the sitting to the absence of a quorum and, after such interval as may be prescribed in the Standing Orders of the House, the person presiding at the sitting ascertains that a quorum of the House is still not present, the House shall be adjourned.

(2) For the purposes of this section:

(a) a quorum of the House of Representatives shall consist of fifteen members; and

(b) the person presiding at the sitting of the House shall not be included in reckoning whether there is a quorum present.

Voting

72. (1) Save as otherwise provided in this Constitution, all questions proposed for decision in the House of Representatives shall be determined by a majority of the votes of the members thereof present and voting.

(2) The Speaker shall not vote unless on any question the votes are equally divided, in which case he shall have and exercise a casting vote.

(3) Any other person shall, when presiding in the House of Representatives, retain his original vote as a member and, if upon any question, the votes are equally divided, shall also have and exercise a casting vote.

Mode of exercising legislative powers

73. (1) The power of Parliament to make laws shall be exercised by bills passed by the House of Representatives and assented to by the Governor-General.

(2) When a bill is presented to the Governor-General for assent, he shall without delay signify that he assents.

(3) A bill shall not become law unless it has been duly passed and assented to in accordance with this Constitution.

(4) When a law has been assented to by the Governor-General it shall without delay be published in the Gazette and shall not come into operation until it has been so published, but Parliament may postpone the coming into operation of any such law and may make laws with retrospective effect.

Restriction with regard to certain financial measures

74. Except upon the recommendation of the Governor-General signified by a Minister, the House of Representatives shall not:

(a) proceed upon any bill (including any amendment to a bill) that, in the opinion of the person presiding, makes provision for any of the following purposes, that is to say, for imposing or increasing any tax, for imposing or increasing any charge on the revenues or other funds of Malta or for altering any such charge otherwise than by reducing it, or for compounding or remitting any debt due to Malta;

(b) proceed upon any motion (including any amendment to a motion) the effect of which, in the opinion of the person presiding, would be to make provision for any of the purposes aforesaid; or

(c) receive any petition which, in the opinion of the person presiding, requests that provision be made for any of the purposes aforesaid.

Language of Laws

75. Save as otherwise provided by Parliament, every law shall be enacted in both the Maltese and English languages and, if there is any conflict between the Maltese and the English texts of any law, the Maltese text shall prevail.

Part 3. Summoning, prorogation and dissolution

Sessions of Parliament

76. (1) Each session of Parliament shall be held at such place within Malta and shall commence at such time as the Governor-General may by proclamation appoint.

(2) There shall be a session of Parliament once at least in every year, so that a period of twelve months shall not intervene between the last sitting of Parliament in one session and the first sitting thereof in the next session.

(3) The House of Representatives shall meet not later than two months after the publication of the official result of any general election by the Electoral Commission on a day appointed by the Governor-General.

Prorogation and dissolution of Parliament

77. (1) The Governor-General may at any time by proclamation prorogue or dissolve Parliament.

(2) Subject to the provisions of subsection (3) of this section, Parliament, unless sooner dissolved, shall continue for five years from the date of its first sitting after any dissolution and shall then stand dissolved.

(3) At any time when Malta is at war, Parliament may from time to time extend the period of five years specified in subsection (2) of this section for not more than twelve months at a time:

Provided that the life of Parliament shall not be extended under this subsection for more than five years.

(4) If between a dissolution of Parliament and the next ensuing general election of members of the House of Representatives an emergency arises of such a nature that, in the opinion of the Prime Minister it is necessary to recall Parliament, the Governor-General may be proclamation summon the Parliament that has been dissolved to meet, and that Parliament shall thereupon be deemed (except for the purpose of section 78 and, in relation to the next ensuing general election, sections 62 (3) and 67 (6) of this Constitution) not to have been dissolved but shall be deemed (except as aforesaid) to be dissolved on the date on which the polls are concluded in the next ensuing general election.

(5) In the exercise of his powers under this section the Governor-

General shall act in accordance with the advice of the Prime Minister:

Provided that:

(a) if the House of Representatives passes a resolution, supported by the votes of a majority of all the members thereof, that it has no confidence in the Government, and the Prime Minister does not within three days either resign from his office or advise a dissolution, the Governor-General may dissolve Parliament;

(b) if the office of Prime Minister is vacant and the Governor-General considers that there is no prospect of his being able within a reasonable time to appoint to that office a person who can command the support of a majority of the members of the House of Representatives, the Governor-General may dissolve Parliament; and

(c) if the Prime Minister recommends a dissolution and the Governor-General considers that the Government of Malta can be carried on without a dissolution and that a dissolution would not be in the interests of Malta, the Governor-General may refuse to dissolve Parliament.

General elections

78. A general election of members of the House of Representatives shall be held at such time within three months after every dissolution of Parliament as the Governor-General, acting in accordance with the advice of the Prime Minister, shall by proclamation appoint.

CHAPTER VII

THE EXECUTIVE

Executive authority of Malta

79. (1) The executive authority of Malta is vested in Her Majesty.

(2) Subject to the provisions of this Constitution, the executive authority of Malta may be exercised on behalf of Her Majesty by the Governor-General either directly or through officers subordinate to him.

(3) Nothing in this section shall prevent Parliament from conferring functions on persons or authorities other than the Governor-General.

The Cabinet

80. (1) There shall be a Cabinet for Malta which shall consist of the Prime Minister and such number of other Ministers as may be appointed in accordance with section 81 of this Constitution.

(2) The Cabinet shall have the general direction and control of the Government of Malta and shall be collectively responsible therefor to Parliament.

Appointment of Ministers

81. Wherever there shall be occasion for the appointment of a Prime Minister, the Governor-General shall appoint as Prime Minister the member of the House of Representatives who, in his judgment, is best able to command the support of a majority of the members of that House and shall, acting in accordance with the advice of the Prime Minister, appoint the other Ministers from among the members of the House of Representatives:

Provided that if occasion arises for making an appointment to the office of Prime Minister or any other Minister while Parliament is dissolved, a person who was a member of the House of Representatives immediately before the dissolution may be appointed as Prime Minister or any other Minister as if, in each case, such person were still a member of the House of Representatives, but any person so appointed shall vacate office at the beginning of the next session of Parliament if he is not then a member thereof.

Tenure of office of Ministers

82. (1) If the House of Representatives passes a resolution, supported by the votes of a majority of all the members thereof, that it has no confidence in the Government, the Governor-General may remove the Prime Minister from office:

Provided that the Governor-General shall not do so unless three days have elapsed and he has decided not to dissolve Parliament under section 77 of this Constitution.

(2) The office of Prime Minister shall also become vacant:

(a) when, after any dissolution of Parliament, the Prime Minister is informed by the Governor-General that the Governor-General is about to re-appoint him as Prime Minister or to appoint another person as Prime Minister;

(b) if he ceases to be a member of the House of Representatives otherwise than by a dissolution of Parliament; or

(c) if, under the provisions of subsection (2) of section 56 of this Constitution, he is required to cease to perform his functions as a member of the House of Representatives.

(3) The office of a Minister, other than the office of Prime Minister, shall become vacant:

(a) upon the appointment or re-appointment of any person to the office of Prime Minister;

(b) if his appointment to his office is revoked by the Governor-General, acting in accordance with the advice of the Prime Minister;

(c) if he ceases to be a member of the House of Representatives otherwise than by a dissolution of Parliament; or

(d) if, under the provisions of subsection (2) of section 56 of this Constitution, he is required to cease to perform his functions as a member of the House of Representatives.

Allocation of portfolios to Ministers

83. (1) Subject to the provisions of this Constitution, the Governor-General, acting in accordance with the advice of the Prime Minister, may, by directions in writing, assign to the Prime Minister or any other Minister responsibility for any business of the Government of Malta including the administration of any department of government.

(2) Nothing in this section shall empower the Governor-General to confer on any Minister authority to exercise any power or to discharge any duty that is conferred or imposed by this Constitution or any other law on any person or authority other than that Minister.

Acting Prime Minister

84. (1) Whenever the Prime Minister is unable, by reason of his illness or absence from Malta, to perform the functions of his office, the Governor-General may authorise any other member of the Cabinet to perform those functions (other than the functions conferred by this section) and that member may perform those functions until his authority is revoked by the Governor-General.

(2) The powers of the Governor-General under this section shall be exercised by him in accordance with the advice of the Prime Minister:

Provided that if the Governor-General considers that it is impracticable to obtain the advice of the Prime Minister owing to his absence or illness he may exercise those powers without that advice.

Temporary Ministers

85. (1) Whenever a Minister other than the Prime Minister is unable, by reason of his illness or absence from Malta, to perform the functions of his office, the Governor-General may appoint another member of the House of Representatives to be a temporary Minister:

Provided that if occasion arises for making an appointment while Parliament is dissolved, a person who, immediately before the dissolution, was a member of the House of Representatives may be appointed as a temporary Minister as if he were still a member of that House, but any person so appointed shall vacate office at the beginning of the next session of Parliament if he is not then a member thereof.

(2) Subject to the provisions of section 82 of this Constitution, a temporary Minister shall hold office until he is notified by the Governor-General that the Minister on account of whose inability to perform the functions of his office he was appointed is again able to perform those functions or until that Minister vacates his office.

(3) The powers of the Governor-General under this section shall be exercised by him in accordance with the advice of the Prime Minister.

Exercise of functions of Governor-General

86. (1) In the exercise of his functions the Governor-General shall act in accordance with the advice of the Cabinet or a Minister acting under the general authority of the Cabinet except in cases where he is required by this Constitution or any other law to act in accordance with the advice of any person or authority other than the Cabinet:

Provided that the Governor-General shall act in accordance with his own deliberate judgment in the performance of the following functions:

(a) in the exercise of the powers relating to the dissolution of Parliament conferred upon him by the proviso to subsection (5) of section 77 of this Constitution;

(b) in the exercise of the power to appoint the Prime Minister or remove the Prime Minister from office conferred upon him by section 81 and subsection (1) of section 82 of this Constitution;

(c) in the exercise of the powers conferred upon him by section 84 of this Constitution (which relates to the performance of the functions of the Prime Minister during absence or illness) in the circumstances described in the proviso to subsection (2) of that section;

(d) in the exercise of the power to appoint the Leader of the Opposition and to revoke any such appointment conferred upon him by section 91 of this Constitution; and

(e) in signifying his approval for the purposes of subsection (4) of section 113 of this Constitution of an appointment to an office on his personal staff.

(2) Where by this Constitution the Governor-General is required to act in accordance with the advice of any person or authority, the question whether he has in any case received, or acted in accordance with, such advice shall not be enquired into in any court.

(3) The reference in subsection (1) of this section to the functions of the Governor-General shall be construed as a reference to his powers and duties in the exercise of the executive authority of Malta and to any other powers and duties conferred or imposed on him as Governor-General by or under this Constitution or any other law.

Exercise of Prime Minister's functions

87. (1) Where by this Constitution the Prime Minister is required to exercise any function on the recommendation of any person or authority he shall exercise that function in accordance with such recommendation:

Provided that:

(a) before he acts in accordance therewith he may once refer that recommendation back for reconsideration by the person or authority concerned; and

(b) if that person or authority, having reconsidered the original recommendation under the preceding paragraph, substitutes therefor a different recommendation, the provisions of this subsection shall apply to that different recommendation as they apply to the original recommendation.

(2) Where by this Constitution the Prime Minister is required to perform any function after consultation with any person or authority, he shall not be obliged to perform that function in accordance with the advice of that person or authority.

(3) Where by this Constitution the Prime Minister is required to perform any function in accordance with the recommendation of, or after consultation with, any person or authority, the question whether he has in any case received, or acted in accordance with such recommendation or whether he has consulted with such person or authority shall not be enquired into in any court.

Governor-General to be informed concerning matters of government

88. The Prime Minister shall keep the Governor-General fully informed concerning the general conduct of the government of Malta and shall furnish the Governor-General with such information as he may request with respect to any particular matter relating to the government of Malta.

Parliamentary Secretaries

89. (1) The Governor-General, acting in accordance with the advice of the Prime Minister, may appoint Parliamentary Secretaries from among the members of the House of Representatives to assist Ministers in the performance of their duties:

Provided that if occasion arises for making an appointment while Parliament is dissolved, a person who immediately before the dissolution was a member of the House of Representatives may be appointed as a Parliamentary Secretary as if he were still a member of that House, but any person so appointed shall vacate office at the beginning of the next session of Parliament if he is not then a member thereof.

(2) The provisions of subsection (3) of section 82 of this Constitution shall apply to Parliamentary Secretaries as they apply to Ministers.

Oaths to be taken by Ministers

90. A Minister or a Parliamentary Secretary shall not enter upon the duties of his office unless he has taken and subscribed the oath of allegiance and such oath for the due execution of his office as may be prescribed by any law for the time being in force in Malta.

Leader of the Opposition

91. (1) There shall be a Leader of the Opposition who shall be appointed by the Governor-General.

(2) Whenever there shall be occasion for the appointment of a Leader of the Opposition, the Governor-General shall appoint:

(a) if there is one opposition party whose numerical strength in the House of Representatives is greater than the strength of any other opposition party, the member of the House of Representatives who is the Leader of that party; or

(b) if, by reason of an equality in the numerical strength of the opposition parties in the House or by reason that there is no opposition party, no person is qualified for appointment under paragraph (a) of this subsection, the member of the House who, in the judgment of the Governor-General, commands the support of the largest single group of members of the House in opposition to the Government who are prepared to support one leader.

(3) The office of Leader of the Opposition shall become vacant:

(a) if after any dissolution of Parliament, he is informed by the Governor-General that the Governor-General is about to appoint another person as Leader of the Opposition;

(b) if he ceases to be a member of the House of Representatives otherwise than by a dissolution of Parliament;

(c) if, under the provisions of subsection (2) of section 56 of this Constitution, he is required to cease to perform his functions as a member of the House of Representatives; or

(d) if his appointment is revoked under the provisions of subsection (4) of this section.

(4) If, in the judgment of the Governor-General, a member of the House of Representatives other than the Leader of the Opposition, has become the Leader in the House of the opposition party having the greatest numerical strength in the House or, as the case may be, the Leader of the Opposition has ceased to command the support of the largest single group of members in opposition to the Government, the Governor-General shall revoke the appointment of the Leader of the Opposition.

(5) Subsection (4) of this section shall not have effect while Parliament is dissolved.

Crown Advocate-General

92. (1) There shall be a Crown Advocate-General whose office shall be a public office and who shall be appointed by the Governor-General acting in accordance with the advice of the Prime Minister.

(2) A person shall not be qualified to hold office as Crown Advocate-

General unless he is qualified for appointment as a judge of the Superior Courts.

(3) In the exercise of his powers to institute, undertake and discontinue criminal proceedings and of any other powers conferred on him by any law in terms which authorise him to exercise that power in his individual judgment the Crown Advocate-General shall not be subject to the direction or control of any other person or authority.

(4) Subject to the provisions of subsection (5) of this section, the Crown Advocate-General shall vacate his office when he attains the age of sixty years.

(5) Subsections (2) and (3) of section 98 of this Constitution shall apply to the Crown Advocate-General.

Permanent Secretaries and heads of government departments

93. (1) Where any Minister has been charged with responsibility for any department of government, he shall exercise general direction and control over that department; and, subject to such direction and control, the department may be under the supervision of a Parmanent Secretary:

Provided that two or more departments of government may be placed under the supervision of one Parmanent Secretary.

(2) The Prime Minister shall be responsible for assigning departments of government to Permanent Secretaries.

(3) Power to appoint public officers to hold or act in the office of Permanent Secretary and to remove from office persons holding or acting in such office shall vest in the Governor-General acting in accordance with the advice of the Prime Minister given after the Prime Minister has consulted with the Public Service Commission.

(4) Heads of departments of government other than those whose manner of appointment is specifically provided for in this Constitution shall be appointed from amongst senior public officers by the Prime Minister acting after consultation with the Public Service Commission.

Prerogative of mercy

94. (1) The Governor-General may, in Her Majesty's name and on Her Majesty's behalf:

(a) grant to any person concerned in or convicted of any offence a pardon, either free or subject to lawful conditions;

(b) grant to any person a respite, either indefinite or for a specified period, of the execution of any sentence passed on that person for any offence;

(c) substitute a less severe form of punishment for any punishment imposed on any person for any offence; or

(d) remit the whole or part of any sentence passed on any person for an offence or for any penalty or forfeiture otherwise due to the State on account of any offience.

(2) (a) Where any person has been sentenced to death by any court in Malta, the Governor-General shall cause a written report of the case from the trial judge, or, in the case of a court-martial the person presiding, and such other information derived from the record of the case or elsewhere as the Governor-General may require, to be sent to the Minister responsible for justice.

(b) The said Minister shall send such written report and information (if any) to the Cabinet, and the Cabinet shall advise the Governor-General whether he should grant the offender a pardon or respite in the exercise of the powers conferred on him by this section.

Secretary to the Cabinet

95. (1) There shall be a Secretary to the Cabinet who shall be a public officer designated in that behalf by the Prime Minister.

(2) The Secretary to the Cabinet shall be responsible, in accordance with such instructions as may be given to him by the Prime Minister, for arranging the business for, and keeping the minutes of, the meetings of the Cabinet and for conveying the decisions of the Cabinet to the appropriate person or authority, and shall have such other functions as the Prime Minister may from time to time direct.

CHAPTER VIII

THE JUDICIARY

Part 1. Courts

Superior Courts

96. (1) There shall be in and for Malta such Superior Courts having such powers and jurisdiction as may be provided by any law for the time being in force in Malta.

(2) One of the Superior Courts, composed of the Chief Justice and four other judges of the Superior Courts, shall be known as the Constitutional Court and shall have jurisdiction to hear and determine:

(a) such questions as are referred to in section 64 of this Constitution;

(b) appeals from decisions of the Civil Court, First Hall, under section 47 of this Constitution;

(c) appeals from decisions of any court of original jurisdiction in Malta on questions as to the interpretation of this Constitution other than those which may fall under section 47 of this Constitution; and

(d) appeals from decisions of any court of original jurisdiction in Malta on questions as to the validity of laws other than those which may fall under section 47 of this Constitution:

Provided that if any such question as is referred to in paragraph (c) or (d) of this subsection arises for the first time in proceedings in a court of appellate jurisdiction, that court shall refer the question to the court which gave the original decision, unless in its opinion the raising of the question is merely frivolous or vexatious, and that court shall give its decision on any such question and, subject to any appeal in accordance with the provisions of this subsection and of section 103 (2) of this Constitution, the court in which the question arose shall dispose of the question in accordance with that decision.

(3) The provisions of subsections (6) and (7) of section 47 of this Constitution shall apply to the Constitutional Court and for that purpose references to that section in the said subsections shall be construed as references to this section.

(4) The judges of the Superior Courts shall be a Chief Justice and such number of other judges as may be prescribed by any law for the time being in force in Malta:

Provided that the office of a judge of the Superior Courts shall not, without his consent, be abolished during his continuance in office.

(5) The Chief Justice shall be the President of the Constitutional Court, and there shall be a Vice-President of the Court, who shall be appointed from among the other judges of the Superior Courts in such manner as may be provided by law; and the Vice-President shall among those judges take precedence next to the Chief Justice.

(6) If the Chief Justice is precluded by law from performing the functions of President of the Constitutional Court or is otherwise unable to perform those functions, those functions shall be performed by the Vice-President.

(7) If the office of Vice-President is vacant or if the Vice-President is for any reason unable to perform the functions of his office, those functions shall be performed by such one of the other judges of the Superior Courts as may be designated in that behalf in such manner as may be provided by law.

Appointment of judges

97. (1) The Judges of the Superior Courts shall be appointed by the Governor-General acting in accordance with the advice of the Prime Minister.

(2) A person shall not be qualified to be appointed a judge of the Superior Court unless for a period of, or periods amounting in the aggregate to, not less than twelve years he has either practised as an advocate in Malta or served as a magistrate in Malta, or has partly so practised and partly so served.

Tenure of office of judges

98. (1) Subject to the provisions of this section, a judge of the Superior

Courts shall vacate his office when he attains the age of sixty-five years.

(2) A judge of the Superior Courts shall not be removed from his office except by the Governor-General upon an address by the House of Representatives supported by the votes of not less than two thirds of all the members thereof and praying for such removal on the ground of proved inability to perform the functions of his office (whether arising from infirmity of body or mind or any other cause) or proved misbehaviour.

(3) Parliament may be law regulate the procedure for the presentation of an address and for the investigation and proof of the inability or misbehaviour of a judge of the Superior Courts under the provisions of the last preceding subsection.

Acting Chief Justice and acting judges

99. (1) If the office of Chief Justice is vacant or if the Chief Justice is for any reason unable to perform the functions of his office, then, until a person has been appointed to and has assumed the functions of that office or until the Chief Justice has resumed those functions, as the case may be, those functions shall (except to such extent, if any, as other provision is made by law) be performed by such one of the other judges of the Superior Courts as may be designated in that behalf by the Governor-General, acting in accordance with the advice of the Prime Minister.

(2) If the office of any judge of the Superior Courts (other than the Chief Justice) is vacant or if any such judge is appointed to act as Chief Justice or is for any reason unable to perform the functions of his office, the Governor-General, acting in accordance with the advice of the Prime Minister, may appoint a person qualified for appointment as a judge of the Superior Courts to act as a judge of those Courts:

Provided that a person may be so appointed notwithstanding that he has attained the age of sixty-five years.

(3) Any person appointed under subsection (2) of this section to act as a judge of the Superior Courts shall continue so to act for the period of his appointment or, if no such period is specified, until his appointment is revoked by the Governor-General acting in accordance with the advice of the Prime Minister.

Inferior Courts

100. There shall be in and for Malta such inferior courts having such powers and jurisdiction as may be provided by any law for the time being in force in Malta.

Magistrates

101. (1) Magistrates of the inferior courts shall be appointed by the Governor-General acting in accordance with the advice of the Prime
er.

(2) A person shall not be qualified to be appointed to or to act in the office of magistrate of the inferior courts unless he has practised as an advocate in Malta for a period of, or periods amounting in the aggregate to, not less than seven years.

(3) Subject to the provisions of subsection (4) of this section, a magistrate of the inferior courts shall vacate his office when he attains the age of sixty years.

(4) The provisions of subsections (2) and (3) of section 98 of this Constitution shall apply to magistrates of the inferior courts.

Oaths to be taken by judges and magistrates

102. A judge of the Superior Courts or a magistrate of the inferior courts shall not enter upon the duties of his office unless he has taken and subscribed the oath of allegiance and such oath for the due execution of his office as may be prescribed by any law for the time being in force in Malta.

Part 2. Appeals

Appeals to Her Majesty in Council

103. (1) An appeal shall lie from decisions of the Court of Appeal to Her Majesty in Council as of right in the following cases:

(a) where the matter in dispute on the appeal to Her Majesty in Council is of the value of five hundred pounds or upwards or where the appeal involves directly or indirectly a claim to or question respecting property or a right of the value of five hundred pounds or upwards, final decisions in any civil proceedings; and

(b) such other cases as may be prescribed by Parliament.

(2) Subject to the provisions of section 64 of this Constitution, an appeal shall lie from decisions of the Constitutional Court to Her Majesty in Council as of right.

(3) An appeal shall lie from decisions of the Court of Appeal to Her Majesty in Council with the leave of the Court of Appeal in the following cases:

(a) where in the opinion of the Court of Appeal the question involved in the appeal is one that, by reason of its great general or public importance or otherwise, ought to be submitted to Her Majesty in Council, decisions in any civil proceedings; and

(b) such other cases as may be prescribed by Parliament.

(4) Nothing in this section shall affect any right of Her Majesty to grant special leave to appeal from decisions of the Court of Appeal or the Criminal Court to Her Majesty in Council in any civil, criminal or other matter.

Appeals from Superior Courts in criminal matters

104. (1) As from such date as may be prescribed by law, not being later than three years after the appointed day, there shall be a right of appeal to a Superior Court against any judgement, other than a judgment of acquittal, of any Superior Court given in its original jurisdiction in any criminal matter.

(2) Any such right of appeal shall be exercisable in accordance with such procedure as may be prescribed by law.

CHAPTER IX

FINANCE

Consolidated Fund

105. (1) All revenues and other moneys raised or received by Malta (not being revenues or other moneys payable into some other fund, being a fund established by or under any law for the time being in force in Malta for a specific purpose) shall, unless Parliament otherwise provides, be paid into and form one Consolidated Fund.

(2) No moneys shall be withdrawn from the Consolidated Fund except to meet expenditure that is charged upon the Fund by this Constitution or any other law for the time being in force in Malta or where the issue of those moneys has been authorised by an Appropriation Act or under section 107 of this Constitution.

(3) No moneys shall be withdrawn from any public fund other than the Consolidated Fund unless the issue of those moneys has been authorised by or under any law for the time being in force in Malta.

(4) No moneys shall be withdrawn form the Consolidated Fund or any other public fund except in the manner prescribed by or under any law.

(5) The costs, charges and expenses incidental to the collection and management of the Consolidated Fund shall be a charge on the Fund.

Authorisation of expenditure from Consolidated Fund

106. (1) The Minister responsible for finance shall cause to be prepared and laid before the House of Representatives before, or not later than thirty days after, the commencement of each financial year estimates of the revenues and expenditure of Malta for that year.

(2) The heads of expenditure contained in the estimates (other than expenditure charged upon the Consolidated Fund by this Constitution or any other law for the time being in force in Malta) shall be included in a bill, to be known as an appropriation bill, providing for the issue from the Consolidated Fund of the sums necessary to meet that expenditure and the appropriation of those sums for the purposes specified therein.

(3) If in respect of any financial year it is found:

(a) that the amount appropriated by the Appropriation Act for any purpose is insufficient, or that a need has arisen for expenditure for a purpose for which no amount has been appropriated by that Act; or

(b) that any moneys have been expended for any purpose in excess of the amount (if any) appropriated for the purpose by that Act,

a supplementary estimate showing the sums required or spent shall be laid before the House of Representatives and the heads of any such expenditure shall be included in a supplementary appropriation bill.

Authorisation of expenditure before appropriation

107. Parliament may make provision under which, if the Appropriation Act in respect of any financial year has not come into operation by the beginning of that financial year, the Minister responsible for finance may authorise the withdrawal of moneys from the Consolidated Fund for the purpose of meeting such expenditure as he may consider necessary to carry on the government of Malta until the expiration of four months from the beginning of that financial year or the coming into operation of the Act, whichever is the earlier.

Contingencies Fund

108. (1) Parliament may provide for the establishment of a Contingencies Fund and for authorising the Minister responsible for finance, if he is satisfied that there has arisen an urgent and unforeseen need for expenditure for which no other provision exists, to make advances from that Fund to meet that need.

(2) Where any advance is made in accordance with subsection (1) of this section a supplementary estimate shall be presented and a supplementary appropriation bill shall be introduced as soon as practicable for the purpose of replacing the amount so advanced.

Public debt

109. (1) The public debt of Malta shall be a charge upon the Consolidated Fund and other public funds of Malta.

(2) In this section references to the public debt of Malta include references to the interest on that debt, sinking fund payments and redemption moneys in respect of that debt and the costs, charges and expenses incidental to the management of that debt.

Remuneration of Governor-General and certain other officers

110. (1) There shall be paid to the holders of the offices to which this section applies such salaries as may be prescribed by or under any law.

(2) The salaries and any allowances payable to the holders of the offices to which this section applies shall be a charge on the Consolidated Fund.

(3) The salary payable to the holder of any office to which this section applies and his terms of office, other than allowances, shall not be altered to his disadvantage after his appointment, and, for the purposes of this subsection, in so far as the salary or the terms of service of any person depend upon the option of that person, the salary or terms for which he opts shall be deemed to be more advantageous to him than any others for which he might have opted.

(4) This section applies to the offices referred to in sections 49, 92, 96 (4), 101, 111 and 112 of this Constitution.

Director of Audit

111. (1) There shall be a Director of Audit for Malta, whose office shall be a public office and who shall be appointed by the Governor-General acting in accordance with the advice of the Prime Minister.

(2) Subject to the provisions of subsection (4) of this section, the Director of Audit shall vacate his office when he attains the age of sixty years.

(3) Subsections (2) and (3) of section 98 of this Constitution shall apply to the Director of Audit.

(4) The accounts of all departments and offices of the Government of Malta, including the office of the Public Service Commission, and the office of the Clerk to the House of Representatives, and of all Superior and Inferior Courts in Malta shall be audited and reported on annually by the Director of Audit and for that purpose the Director of Audit or any person authorised by him in that behalf shall have access to all books, records, returns and other documents relating to those accounts.

(5) The Director of Audit shall submit his reports made under subsection (4) of this section to the Minister responsible for finance, who shall cause them to be laid before the House of Representatives within thirty days of the receipt thereof by him, or, if the House of Representatives is not sitting, within thirty days of the commencement of the next sitting of the House of Representatives.

(6) If the Minister fails to lay any reports before the House of Representatives in accordance with subsection (5) of this section, the Director of Audit shall, forthwith on the expiration of the period mentioned in the said subsection, transmit copies of such reports to the Speaker of the House of Representatives (or, if the office of Speaker is vacant or the Speaker is for any reason unable to perform the functions of his office, to the Deputy Speaker) who shall, as soon as practicable, lay them before the House of Representatives.

(7) In the exercise of his functions under the provisions of subsections (4) and (5) of this section the Director of Audit shall not be subject to the direction or control of any other person or authority.

(8) Nothing in this section shall prevent the performance by the Director of Audit of:

(a) such other functions in relation to the accounts of the Government of Malta and the accounts of other public authorities and other bodies administering public funds in Malta as may be prescribed by or under any law for the time being in force in Malta; or

(b) such other functions in relation to the supervision and control of expenditure from public funds in Malta as may be so prescribed.

CHAPTER X

THE PUBLIC SERVICE

Public Service Commission

112. (1) There shall be a Public Service Commission for Malta which shall consist of a chairman, a deputy chairman and from one to three other members.

(2) The members of the Public Service Commission shall be appointed by the Governor-General, acting in accordance with the advice of the Prime Minister given after he has consulted the Leader of the Opposition.

(3) A person shall not be qualified to hold office as a member of the Public Service Commission if he is a Minister, a Parliamentary Secretary, a member of, or a candidate for election to, the House of Representatives, a member of a local government authority or if he is a public officer.

(4) A member of the Public Service Commission shall not, within a period of three years commencing with the day on which he has held office as a member, be eligible for appointment to or to act in any public office.

(5) Subject to the provisions of this section, the office of a member of the Public Service Commission shall become vacant:

(a) at the expiration of five years from the date of his appointment or at such earlier time as may be specified in the instrument by which he was appointed; or

(b) if any circumstances arise that, if he were not a member of the Commission, would cause him to be disqualified for appointment as such.

(6) A member of the Public Service Commission may be removed from office by the Governor-General, acting in accordance with the advice of the Prime Minister, but he may be removed only for inability to discharge the functions of his office (whether arising from infirmity of mind or body or any other cause) or for misbehaviour.

(7) If the office of a member of the Public Service Commission is vacant or if a member is for any reason unable to perform the functions of his office, the Governor-General, acting in accordance with the advice of the Prime Minister, given after he has consulted the Leader of the Opposition, may appoint a person who is qualified to be appointed to be a member, to

be a temporary member of the Commission; and any person so appointed shall, subject to the provisions of subsections (5) and (6) of this section, cease to be such a member when a person has been appointed to fill the vacancy or, as the case may be, when the member who was unable to perform the functions of his office resumes those functions.

Appointment, etc. of public officers

113. (1) Subject to the provisions of this Constitution, power to make appointments to public offices and to remove and to exercise disciplinary control over persons holding or acting in any such offices shall vest in the Prime Minister, acting on the recommendation of the Public Service Commission:

Provided that the Prime Minister may, acting on the recommendation of the Public Service Commission, delegate in writing, subject to such conditions as may be specified in the instrument of delegation, any of the powers referred to in this subsection to such public officer or other authority as may be specified in that instrument.

(2) A delegation of a power under this section:

(a) shall be without prejudice to the exercise of that power by the Prime Minister acting on the recommendation of the Public Service Commission; and

(b) may authorise the public officer or other authority concerned to exercise that power either with or without reference to the Public Service Commission.

(3) (a) An appeal shall lie to the Prime Minister, acting in accordance with the recommendation of the Public Service Commission, from any decision of a public officer or authority to remove any person from a public office in exercise of power delegated under subsection (1) of this section:

Provided that such right of appeal shall be without prejudice to any such other right of appeal as may be provided under section 123 (1) of this Constitution in respect of the exercise of any other power delegated under subsection (1) of this section.

(b) A right of appeal under this section shall be exercised in accordance with such provision relating to procedure as may be prescribed by the Public Service Commission under section 123 (1) of this Constitution:

Provided that any procedure so prescribed shall be the same for all classes of public officers.

(c) Where an appeal is brought under paragraph (b) of this subsection by any public officer he shall, upon the consideration of the appeal by the Public Service Commission, have the right to be heard by the Commission in person and to be assisted by a representative of any trade union to which he belongs.

(4) No person shall be appointed under this section to or to act in any

office on the personal staff of the Governor-General except with the approval of the Governor-General.

(5) The provisions of this section shall not apply in relation to:

(a) the offices referred to in sections 92, 93 (other than subsection (4) thereof), 95, 96 (4), 101, 111, 114 and 115 of this Constitution; or

(b) appointments to act in any public office for two months or less in so far as the recommendation of the Public Service Commission is required for any such appointment; or

(c) appointments to the offices referred to in section 93 (4).

Principal representatives of Malta abroad

114. (1) Power to appoint persons to hold or act in the offices to which this section applies and to remove persons so appointed from any such office shall vest in the Governor-General, acting in accordance with the advice of the Prime Minister:

Provided that in respect of any person selected for appointment from the public service the Prime Minister shall, before giving his advice under the provisions of this section, consult with the Public Service Commission and, on being removed from the office to which he has been appointed under the provisions of this section, the person so appointed shall revert to the rank which he held in the public service immediately before such appointment.

(2) The offices to which this section applies are the offices of any Ambassador, High Commissioner or other principal representative of Malta in any other country.

Appointment on transfer in respect of certain offices

115. (1) Power to make appointments on transfer to and from the offices to which this section applies shall vest in the Prime Minister acting after consultation with the Public Service Commission:

Provided that the person appointed to any such office under the provisions of this section shall, on being transferred from that office, revert to the rank which he held in the public service immediately before his appointment to that office.

(2) The offices to which this section applies are:

(a) offices the holders of which are required to reside outside Malta for the proper discharge of their functions; and

(b) such offices in the Ministry responsible for the external affairs of Malta as may, from time to time, be designated by the Prime Minister.

Protection of pension rights

116. (1) Subject to the provisions of section 117 of this Constitution, the law applicable to any benefits to which this section applies shall, in relation to any person who has been granted, or who is eligible for the grant of such benefits, be that in force on the relevant date or any later law that is not less favourable to that person.

(2) In this section "the relevant date" means:

(a) in relation to any benefits granted before the appointed day, the date on which those benefits were granted;

(b) in relation to any benefits granted or to be granted on or after the appointed day to or in respect of any person who was a public officer before that date, the day before the appointed day; and

(c) in relation to any benefits granted or to be granted to or in respect of any person who becomes a public officer on or after the appointed day, the date on which he becomes a public officer.

(3) Where a person is entitled to exercise an option as to which of two or more laws shall apply in his case, the law for which he opts shall, for the purposes of this section, be deemed to be more favourable to him than the other law or laws.

(4) Any benefit to which this section applies (not being a benefit that is a charge upon some other public fund of Malta) shall be a charge upon the Consolidated Fund.

(5) This section applies to any benefits payable under any law providing for the grant of pensions, gratuities or compensation to persons who are or have been public officers in respect of their service in the public service or to the widows, children, dependants or personal representatives of such persons in respect of such service.

(6) References to the law applicable to any benefits to which this section applies include (without prejudice to their generality) references to any law relating to the time at which and the manner in which any person may retire in order to become eligible for those benefits.

Grant and withholding of pensions, etc.

117. (1) Where any benefits to which this section applies can be withheld, reduced in amount or suspended by any person or authority under any law those benefits shall not be so withheld, reduced in amount or suspended without the concurrence of the Public Service Commission.

(2) The Public Service Commission shall not concur under subsection (1) of this section in action taken on the ground that any person who holds or has held any of the offices referred to in sections 92, 96 (4), 101 and 111 of this Constitution has been guilty of misbehaviour unless he has been removed from office by reason of such misbehaviour.

(3) This section applies to any benefits payable under any law providing for the grant of pensions, gratuities or compensation to persons who are or have been public officers in respect of their service in the public service or to the widows, children, dependants or personal representatives of such persons in respect of such service.

Protection of Public Service Commission from legal proceedings

118. The question whether:

(a) the Public Service Commission has validly performed any function vested in it by or under this Constitution;

(b) any member of the Public Service Commission or any public officer or other authority has validly performed any function delegated to such member, public officer or authority in pursuance of the provisions of subsection (1) of section 113 of this Constitution; or

(c) any member of the Public Service Commission or any public officer or other authority has validly performed any other function in relation to the work of the Commission or in relation to any such function as is referred to in the preceding paragraph, shall not be enquired into in any court.

CHAPTER XI

MISCELLANEOUS

Actions on validity of laws

119. A right of action for a declaration that any law is invalid on any grounds other than inconsistency with the provisions of sections 34 to 46 of this Constitution shall appertain to all persons without distinction and a person bringing such an action shall not be required to show any personal interest in support of his action.

Prohibition of certain associations

120. (1) It shall be unlawful to establish, maintain or belong to any association of persons who are organised and trained or organised and equipped for the purpose of enabling them to be employed for the use or display of physical force in promoting any political object.

(2) The provisions of this section shall be enforced in such manner as may be provided by Parliament.

Broadcasting Authority

121. (1) There shall be a Broadcasting Authority for Malta which shall consist of a chairman and such number of other members not being less than four as may be prescribed by any law for the time being in force in Malta.

(2) The members of the Broadcasting Authority shall be appointed by the Governor-General, acting in accordance with the advice of the Prime Minister given after he has consulted the Leader of the Opposition.

(3) A person shall not be qualified to hold office as a member of the Broadcasting Authority if he is a Minister, a Parliamentary Secretary, a

member of, or candidate for election to, the House of Representatives, a member of a local government authority or if he is a public officer.

(4) A member of the Broadcasting Authority shall not, within a period of three years commencing with the day on which he last held office or acted as a member, be eligible for appointment to or to act in any public office.

(5) Subject to the provisions of this section, the office of a member of the Broadcasting Authority shall become vacant:

(a) at the expiration of five years from the date of his appointment or at such earlier time as may be specified in the instrument by which he was appointed; or

(b) if any circumstances arise that, if he were not a member of the Authority, would cause him to be disqualified for appointment as such.

(6) A member of the Broadcasting Authority may be removed from office by the Governor-General, acting in accordance with the advice of the Prime Minister, but he may be removed only for inability to discharge the functions of his office (whether arising from infirmity of mind or body or any other cause) or for misbehaviour.

(7) If the office of a member of the Broadcasting Authority is vacant or if a member is for any reason unable to perform the functions of his office, the Governor-General, acting in accordance with the advice of the Prime Minister, given after he has consulted the Leader of the Opposition, may appoint a person who is qualified to be appointed to be a member to be a temporary member of the Authority; and any person so appointed shall, subject to the provisions of subsections (5) and (6) of this section, cease to be such a member when a person has been appointed to fill the vacancy or, as the case may be, when the member who was unable to perform the functions of his office resumes those functions.

(8) In the exercise of its functions under section 122 (1) of this Constitution the Broadcasting Authority shall not be subject to the direction or control of any other person or authority.

Function of the Broadcasting Authority

122. (1) It shall be the function of the Broadcasting Authority to ensure that, so far as possible, in such sound and television broadcasting services as may be provided in Malta, due impartiality is preserved in respect of matters of political or industrial controversy or relating to current public policy and that broadcasting facilities and time are fairly apportioned between persons belonging to different political parties.

(2) The function of the Broadcasting Authority referred to in subsection (1) of this section shall be without prejudice to such other functions and duties as may be conferred upon it by any law for the time being in force in Malta.

Powers and procedure of Commissions

123. (1) Any Commission established by this Constitution may, with the consent of the Prime Minister or such other Minister as may be authorised in that behalf by the Prime Minister by regulation or otherwise regulate its own procedure and confer powers and impose duties on any public officer or authority of the Government of Malta for the purpose of the discharge of its functions.

(2) Any Commission established by this Constitution may act notwithstanding any vacancy in its membership or the absence of any member and any proceedings thereof shall be valid notwithstanding that some person who was not entitled so to do took part therein.

(3) Any question proposed for decision at any meeting of any Commission established by this Constitution shall be determined by a majority of the votes of all the members thereof, and if on any such question the votes are equally divided the member presiding shall have and exercise a casting vote.

(4) For the purposes of subsection (3) of this section, the references to a member of the Electoral Commission shall be construed as including a reference to the Chairman of that Commission.

(5) The provisions of this section shall apply to the Broadcasting Authority established by this Constitution.

Resignations

124. (1) Any person who is appointed, elected or otherwise selected to any office established by this Constitution (including the office of Prime Minister or other Minister or Parliamentary Secretary) may resign from that office by writing under his hand addressed to the person or authority by whom he was appointed, elected or selected.

(2) The resignation of any person from any such office as aforesaid shall take effect when the writing signifying the resignation is received by the person or authority to whom it is addressed or by any person authorised by that person or authority to receive it.

Reappointments, etc.

125. (1) Where any person has vacated any office established by this Constitution (including the office of Prime Minister or other Minister or Parliamentary Secretary), he may, if qualified, again be appointed, elected or otherwise selected to hold that office in accordance with the provisions of this Constitution.

(2) Where by this Constitution a power is conferred upon any person or authority to make any appointment to any public office, a person may be appointed to that office notwithstanding that some other person may be holding that office, when that other person is on leave of absence pending

relinquishment of the office; and where two or more persons are holding the same office by reason of an appointment made in pursuance of this subsection, then for the purposes of any function conferred upon the holder of that office the person last appointed shall be deemed to be the sole holder of the office.

Interpretation

126. (1) In this Constitution, unless the context otherwise requires:

"Act of Parliament" means any law made by Parliament;

"the appointed day" means 21st September 1964;

"the Cabinet" means the Cabinet established by section 80 of this Constitution;

"the Commonwealth" means Malta, any country to which section 29 of this Constitution applies and any dependency of any such country;

"the Consolidated Fund" means the Consolidated Fund established by section 105 of this Constitution;

"Constitutional Court" means the Constitutional Court established by section of this Constitution;

"financial year" means the period of twelve months ending on the thirty-first day of March in any year or on such other date as may be prescribed by Parliament;

"Gazette" means the Malta Government Gazette or any other official journal substituted therefor published by order of the Government of Malta;

"House" means the House of Representatives established by section 52 of this Constitution;

"law" includes any instrument having the force of law and any unwritten rule of law and "lawful" and "lawfully" shall be construed accordingly;

"Malta" means the Island of Malta, the Island of Gozo and the other islands of the Maltese Archipelago, including the territorial waters thereof;

"oath of allegiance" means the oath of allegiance set out in the Second Schedule to this Constitution or such other oath as may be prescribed by Parliament;

"Parliament" means the Parliament of Malta;

"public office" means an office of emolument in the public service;

"public officer" means the holder of any public office or a person appointed to act in any such office;

"the public service" means, subject to the provisions of subsections (2) and (3) of this section, the service of the Crown in a civil capacity in respect of the Government of Malta;

"session" means the sittings of the House of Representatives beginning when it first meets after the commencement of this Constitution or after the prorogation or dissolution of Parliament at any time and terminating when Parliament is prorogued or is dissolved without having been prorogued;

"sitting" means a period during which the House of Representatives is sitting continuously without adjournment and includes any period during which the House is in committee;

"the Speaker" and "the Deputy Speaker" mean respectively the Speaker and the Deputy Speaker elected under section 60 of this Constitution.

(2) In this Constitution, unless the context otherwise requires, "the public service" includes service in the office of judge of the Superior Courts, service in the office of magistrate of the inferior courts and service in the office of a member of the Malta Police Force.

(3) In this Constitution "the public service" does not include service in the office of:

(i) Prime Minister or other Minister, a Parliamentary Secretary, Speaker, Deputy Speaker, a member of the House of Representatives, a member of a Commission established by this Constitution;

(ii) save where the holder of the office is selected from the public service, an Ambassador, High Commissioner or other principal representative of Malta in any other country; or

(iii) save in so far may be prescribed by Parliament, a member of any council, board, panel, committee or other similar body established by or under any law.

(4) For the purposes of this Constitution a person shall not be regarded as holding a public office by reason only of the fact that he is in receipt of a pension or other like allowance in respect of public service.

(5) In this Constitution, unless the context otherwise requires:

(a) a reference to an appointment to any office shall be construed as including a reference to an appointment on promotion or transfer to that office and to the appointment of a person to perform the functions of that office during any period during which it is vacant or during which the holder thereof is unable (whether by reason of absence or infirmity of body or mind or any other cause) to perform those functions; and

(b) a reference to the holder of an office by the term designating his office or by reference to the provision of this Constitution establishing that office shall be construed as including a reference to any person for the time being lawfully performing the functions of that office.

(6) Where power is vested by this Constitution in any person or authority to appoint any person to act in or perform the functions of any office if the holder thereof is himself unable to perform those functions, no such appointment shall be called in question on the ground that the holder of the office was not unable to perform those functions.

(7) References in this Constitution to the power to remove a public

officer from his office shall be construed as including references to any power conferred by any law to require or permit that officer to retire from the public service;

Provided that:

(a) nothing in this subsection shall be construed as conferring on any person or authority power to require any person holding any of the offices referred to in sections 92, 96 (4), 101 or 111 of this Constitution to retire from the public service; and

(b) the provisions of this subsection shall not apply to any power conferred by any law to permit a person to retire from the public service where that person has requested permission to retire from the public service on proved medical grounds.

(8) Any provision in this Constitution that vests in any person or authority power to remove any public officer from his office shall be without prejudice to the power of any person or authority to abolish any office or to any law providing for the compulsory retirement of public officers generally or any class of public officers on attaining an age specified therein.

(9) Where any power is conferred by this Constitution to make any proclamation, order, rules or regulations or to give any directions or to make any designation, the power shall be construed as including a power, exercisable in like manner, to amend or revoke any such proclamation, order, rules, regulations, directions or designation.

(10) No provision of this Constitution that any person or authority shall not be subject to the direction or control of any other person or authority in exercising any functions under this Constitution shall be construed as precluding a court from exercising jurisdiction in relation to any question whether that person or authority has performed those functions in accordance with this Constitution or any other law.

(11) Where a person is required by this Constitution to make an oath he shall be permitted, if he so desires, to comply with that requirement by making an affirmation.

(12) Any reference in this Constitution to a law made before the commencement of this Constitution shall, unless the context otherwise requires be construed as a reference to that law as in force immediately before the appointed day.

(13) Any reference in this Constitution to a law that amends or replaces any other law shall be construed as including a reference to a law that modifies, re-enacts, with or without amendment or modification, or makes different provisions in lieu of that other law.

(14) The Interpretation Act 1889 as in force on the appointed day shall apply, with the necessary adaptations, for the purpose of interpreting this

Constitution and otherwise in relation thereto as it applies for the purpose of interpreting, and in relation to Acts of Parliament of the United Kingdom.

SCHEDULES TO THE CONSTITUTION

Not reproduced

MONACO

SUMMARY

INTERNATIONAL STATUS

Monaco is not a member of the United Nations. It is a member of other international organizations.

Monaco, a principality under the House of Grimaldi since the tenth century except for a period during the French Revolution when the line was deposed, was a protectorate of France until 1815 when it became a protectorate of the Kingdom of Sardinia (Piedmont) until 1860. Its independence was recognized in 1861 and it was placed again under French protection. It was granted a Constitution by the Prince in 1911. On

January 29, 1959, the Prince suspended the constitutional guarantees and dissolved the two assemblies of the Principality. In 1961, a National Assembly with appointed members was created. In March 1962, the two Councils were reestablished with elected members and the new Constitution promulgated in December 1962 provides that it cannot be suspended by the sovereign.

FORM OF NATIONAL GOVERNMENT

The Constitution of December 17, 1962, replacing the Constitution of January 5, 1911, as amended to 1946, states that Monaco is a sovereign and independent state within the general principles of international law and of particular conventions with France.[1] It is a hereditary and constitutional monarchy.[2] The principle of the separation of the administrative, legislative and judicial powers is provided.[3] The Roman Catholic religion is the religion of the State.[4]

RIGHTS OF THE PEOPLE

The Constitution provides equality before the law, individual freedom and due process of law, no retroactive punishment, the inviolability of the domicile, secrecy of correspondence, freedom of religion, inviolability of property, freedom to work, social assistance, free primary and secondary education, trade union rights, the right of assembly, association and petition.[5] The death penalty is abolished.[6]

LEGISLATIVE DEPARTMENT

Legislative power is exercised by the Prince and the National Council composed of 18 members elected by universal, direct suffrage and proportional representation for a term of five years subject to dissolution.[7] Immunities of deputies are provided.[8] The National Council meets in two ordinary sessions a year.[9] There are provisions concerning finance.[10]

EXECUTIVE DEPARTMENT

Executive power is exercised by the Prince whose person is inviolable.[11] He represents the Principality in foreign affairs, signes treaties, grants pardons after consultation with the Council of the Crown, grants honors and titles.[12] Government is exercised, under his authority, by a Minister of State and a Council of Government who are responsible to the Prince.[13]

[1] Const., Art. 1. [2] Id., Art. 2. [3] Id., Art. 6. [4] Id., Art. 9.
[5] Id., Art. 17–31. [6] Id., Art. 20. [7] Id., Art. 4, 53, 74.
[8] Id., Art. 56. [9] Id., Art. 58. [10] Id., Art. 70–73, 33–42.
[11].dI , Art. 3. [12] Id., Art. 12–16. [13] Id., Art. 43, 50.

Counselors of the Government may not be members of the National Council but may take part in its debates.[1] A Council of State is provided with consultative status.[2] A Council of the Crown is provided composed of seven members appointed by the Prince for a term of three years which meets at least twice a year and must be consulted regarding international treaties, dissolution of the National Council, requests for naturalization, re-integration, pardons and amnesty.[3] Provision is made for communal administration, the territory of the Principality forming a single commune.[4]

JUDICIAL DEPARTMENT

Judicial power is exercised by courts whose organization is fixed by law.[5] There is a Supreme Court which rules on the rules of procedure of the National Council, on appeals concerning the rights and freedoms provided in the Constitution, as a court of appeal in administrative matters and on all conflicts of jurisdiction.[6]

AREA, POPULATION, ETC.

The area of Monaco is 368 acres, the population (1961) 20,441. French is the official language.[7]

[1] Id., Art. 54, 65. [2] Id., Art. 52. [3] Id., Art. 75–77. [4] Id., Art. 78–87.
[5] Id., Art. 5, 88. [6] Id., Art. 89, 90. [7] Id., Art. 8.

CONSTITUTION
of
MONACO[1]

December 17, 1962

Rainier III, by the Grace of God Sovereign Prince of Monaco.

Considering that the institutions of the Principality should be perfected, both to satisfy the needs of good administration of the country and to satisfy the new requirements arising out of the social evolution of its population;

We have resolved to grant a new Constitution to the State which by our sovereign will shall henceforth be considered as the fundamental law of the State and may be modified only according to the terms we have decreed;

We have ordained and We ordain:

TITLE I

THE PRINCIPALITY, THE PUBLIC AUTHORITIES

Art. 1. The Principality of Monaco is a sovereign and independent State within the framework of the general principals of international law and of particular conventions with France.

The territory of the Principality is inalienable.

Art. 2. The principle of government is that of a hereditary and constitutional monarchy.

The Principality is a State under law devoted to the respect of the fundamental liberties and rights.

Art. 3. The executive power is exercised under the high authority of the Prince.

The person of the Prince is inviolable.

Art. 4. The legislative power is exercised by the Prince and the National Council.

[1] *Constitution de la Principauté de Monaco* (*17 decembre 1962*), Reproduced in *Notes et Etudes Documentaires, No. 3.028*, 14 October 1963, from *Journal de Monaco* of 17 December 1962. Confirmed as in effect by letter from the Secretary General of the *Conseil National*, Monaco, of July 1966. Translated by the Editor. Ed.

Art. 5. The judicial power is exercised by the courts and tribunals.

Art. 6. The separation of the administrative, legislative and judicial functions shall be ensured.

Art. 7. The princely flag shall be formed of the arms of the Grimaldi House on a white background.

The national flag shall be formed of two equal horizontal stripes, the upper stripe red and the lower one white.

The use of these flags shall be regulated by the provisions of the Sovereign Ordinance of April 4, 1881.

Art. 8. French is the official language of the State.

Art. 9. The Apostolic Roman Catholic religion is the religion of the State.

TITLE II

THE PRINCE, THE TRANSMISSION OF THE CROWN

Art. 10. After death or abdication, succession to the throne shall take place within the direct legitimate line of the reigning Prince by primogeniture, priority being given to males within the same degree of relationship.

If there is no legitimate heir, an adopted child or an adopted child's legitimate descendants may succeed.

Art. 11. The age of majority for the exercise of the sovereign powers shall be fixed at twenty-one years.

The organization and conditions for the exercise of a Regency during the minority of the Prince or where he is unable to exercise his functions shall be fixed by the statutes of the Sovereign Family.

Art. 12. The Prince shall exercise his sovereign authority in accordance with the provisions of the Constitution and the laws.

Art. 13. The Prince shall represent the Principality in its relations with foreign powers.

Art. 14. After consultation with the Council of the Crown, the Prince shall sign and ratify treaties and bring them before the National Council. Treaties which affect constitutional organization, however, shall be ratified only by a law.

Art. 15. After consultation with the Council of the Crown, the Prince shall exercise the right of pardon and of amnesty, of naturalization and of resumption of nationality.

Art. 16. The Prince shall grant orders, titles and other honors.

TITLE III

FUNDAMENTAL RIGHTS AND LIBERTIES

Art. 17. Monegasque citizens are equal before the law. There shall be no privileges among them.

Art. 18. All individuals born in Monaco or abroad of a Monegasque father shall be Monegasque.

A law shall regulate other ways to acquire Monegasque nationality.

A law shall establish the conditions under which nationality which has been acquired by naturalization may be withdrawn.

In all other cases, the law may envisage loss of Monegasque nationality only as a result of the volontary acquisition of another nationality or of illegal service in a foreign army.

Art. 19. Individual liberty and security are guaranteed. Noone may be prosecuted except in the cases, before the judges, and in the manner prescribed by law.

Except in cases of *flagrante delicto,* noone may be arrested except by a judge's order giving the reasons therefor which must be shown at the time of the arrest or, at the latest, within twenty four hours. An interrogation must precede any detention.

Art. 20. No penalty may be established or applied except by law.

The criminal laws must ensure respect for human personality and dignity. Noone may be subjected to cruel, inhuman or degrading treatment.

The penalty of death is abolished.

The criminal laws may not have retroactive effect.

Art. 21. The domicile is inviolable. No domiciliary visit may take place except in the cases and under the conditions prescribed by law.

Art. 22. Everyone has the right to respect for his private and family life and the secrecy of his correspondence.

Art. 23. Freedom of religion, of its public exercise, and the freedom to express opinions on all matters are guaranteed, except that offences committed in the exercise of these liberties may be suppressed.

Noone may be forced to take part in the acts and ceremonies of any religion nor to observe its days of rest.

Art. 24. Property is inviolable. Noone may be deprived of his property except for legally attested public use and against a fair indemnity, decided and paid in accordance with the law.

Art. 25. Freedom of work is guaranteed. Its exercise shall be regulated by law.

Priority of access to public and private employment is guaranteed to Monegasque citizens under the conditions prescribed by law or by international conventions.

Art. 26. Monegasque citizens have the right to State assistance in case of poverty, unemployment, sickness, disablement, old age and maternity, under the conditions and in the manner prescribed by law.

Art. 27. Monegasque citizens have the right to free primary and secondary education.

Art. 28. Everyone may defend the rights and interests of his profession or activity by trade union action.

The right to strike is recognized within the framework of the laws relating thereto.

Art. 29. Monegasque citizens have the right to assemble peacefully without arms in accordance with the laws which may regulate the exercise of this right without, however, making it subject to prior authorization. This freedom does not extend to meetings in the open air which remain subject to police laws.

Art. 30. Monegasque citizens have the right of free association subject to respect for the rules of the Constitution.

Art. 31. Everyone may address petitions to the public authorities.

Art. 32. Foreigners shall enjoy in the Principality all the public and private rights which are not formally reserved to nationals.

TITLE IV

THE PUBLIC DOMAIN AND PUBLIC FINANCES

Art. 33. The public domain is inalienable and indefeasible.

The transfer of an asset belonging to the public domain may be effected only by a law which places the transferred asset within the private domain of the State or of the Commune as the case may be.

The composition of and rules regarding the public domain shall be determined by law.

Art. 34. The assets of the Crown shall be applied to the exercise of sovereignty.

They are inalienable and indefeasible.

Their composition and the rules regarding them shall be determined by the statutes of the Sovereign Family.

Art. 35. Landed rights and properties belonging to the private domain of the State are inalienable only insofar as the law so provides.

Art. 36. Empty properties without an owner shall belong to the private domain of the State.

Art. 37. The national budget shall include all the receipts and expenditures of the Principality.

Art. 38. The national budget shall express the economic and financial policy of the Principality.

Art. 39. The budget shall be the subject of a bill which shall be passed and promulgated as a law.

Art. 40. The expenses of the Sovereign House and of the Princely Palace shall be established by the budget law and shall constitute a prior claim on the general receipts of the budget.

Art. 41. Any excess of receipts over expenditures which is found after the execution of the budget and closure of the accounts shall be placed in a constitutional reserve fund. Any excess of expenditures over receipts shall be covered by drawing on this fund in accordance with a law.

Art. 42. Control over the management of the finances shall be ensured by a High Commission of Accounts.

TITLE V

THE GOVERNMENT

Art. 43. The government shall be exercised, under the high authority of the Prince, by a Minister of State assisted by a Council of Government.

Art. 44. The Minister of State shall represent the Prince. He shall direct the executive services. He shall have control over the civil police. He shall preside, with a casting vote, over the Council of Government.

Art. 45. Sovereign ordinances shall be considered in the Council of Government. They shall contain mention of the deliberations relating thereto and be presented to the Prince under the signature of the Minister of State. They shall be signed by the Prince, which signature shall be executory.

Art. 46. The following Sovereign ordinances do not require consideration by the Council of Government nor presentation by the Minister of State:

those relating to matters that fall within the control of judicial services;

those appointing members of the Sovereign House, of the diplomatic and consular services, of the Minister of State, of Counsellors of the Government and similar officials, of magistrates of the judicial order;

those granting *exequatur* to consuls;

those dissolving the National Council;

those conferring honorary distinctions.

Art. 47. Ministerial decrees shall be considered in the Council of Government and signed by the Minister of State; they shall contain mention of the deliberations relating thereto. They shall be transmitted to the Prince within twenty-four hours of their signature and become executory ten days after their transmission by the Minister of State if there has been no express opposition by the Prince within this period.

The Prince may, however, inform the Minister of State that he will waive his right of opposition for certain decrees or categories of decrees, which shall then have executory force from the time of their signature by the Minister of State.

Art. 48. Except where legislation to the contrary exists, the division of subjects between Sovereign ordinances and ministerial decrees shall be made by a Sovereign ordinance.

Art. 49. Deliberations of the Council of Government shall be contained in minutes recorded in a special register signed, after a vote, by the members present. The minutes shall mention the vote of each member. They shall be transmitted within five days from the meeting to the Prince who may object under the conditions provided in Article 47.

Art. 50. The Minister of State and the Counsellors of the Government shall be responsible toward the Prince for the administration of the Principality.

Art. 51. The fundamental obligations, rights and guarantees of officials and their civil and criminal responsibilities shall be fixed by law.

TITLE VI

THE COUNCIL OF STATE

Art. 52. The Council of State shall give its advice on all bills and ordinances submitted to it by the Prince.

It may be consulted on other matters.

Its organization and functioning shall be fixed by a Sovereign Ordinance.

TITLE VII

THE NATIONAL COUNCIL

Art. 53. The National Council shall be composed of eighteen members elected for five years by universal direct suffrage and proportional representation.

All citizens of both sexes of at least twenty one years of age who have possessed Monegasque nationality for at least five years shall have the right to vote with the exception of those persons deprived of the right to vote for any of the reasons provided by law.

Art. 54. All Monegasque citizens of both sexes of at least twenty five years of age who are eligible to vote shall be eligible for office unless they have been deprived of their eligibility for any of the reasons provided by law.

The following offices shall be incompatible with the office of National Counsellor: member of the Sovereign House, Counsellor of Government, diplomatic or consular agent, magistrate of the judicial order.

The following offices are also incompatible:
the Commissioner-General of the Department of Public Works and Social Affairs;
the Comptroller-General of Expenditures;
the Commissioner-General of Health;
the Director of the Budget and the Treasury;
the Administrator of the Domains;
the Chief Engineer for public works;
the Government Commissioner attached to monopoly companies;
the Treasurer-General of finances;
the Secretary-General of the judicial services;
the Private Secretary to the Minister of State;
the chief secretary of the Mayor's office;
officials of the legislative services of the State;
officials forming the secretariat of ministerial departments;
members of the High Commission of Accounts;
agents of the police and security forces.

Art. 55. Control over the regularity of elections shall be confided to the courts under the conditions provided by law.

Art. 56. Members of the National Council shall incur no civil or criminal responsibility for their opinions or votes in the exercise of their functions.

Except with the authorization of the Council, they may not be prosecuted or arrested during a session for crimes or misdemeanors except in cases of *flagrante delicto*.

Art. 57. The newly elected National Council shall meet on the eleventh day after the elections to elect its secretariat. The oldest National Counsellor shall preside at this meeting.

The powers of the preceding National Council shall, subject to Article 74, expire the day the new one meets.

Art. 58. The National Council shall meet automatically each year in two ordinary sessions, on the first working day of the months of May and November.

The duration of sessions may not exceed two months. Closure shall be pronounced by the President.

Art. 59. The National Council shall meet in extraordinary session, either on the convocation of the Prince or, at the request of at least two thirds of its members, on the convocation of its President.

Art. 60. The secretariat of the National Council shall be composed of a President and Vice-President elected each year by the Assembly from among its members.

The functions of mayor shall be incompatible with those of President of the National Council.

Art. 61. Subject to constitutional and, where appropriate, legislative provisions, the organization and functioning of the National Council shall be determined by the rules of procedure drawn up by the Council.

Before being put into force, these rules of procedure must be submitted to the High Court which shall pronounce on their conformity to constitutional and, where appropriate, legislative provisions.

Art. 62. The National Council shall draw up its agenda, which shall be communicated to the Minister of State at least three days in advance. At least one meeting out of two must, at the request of the Government, be devoted to bills tabled by the Prince.

The agenda of extraordinary sessions convoked by the Prince, however, shall be contained in the notice of convocation.

Art. 63. Meetings of the National Council shall be public.

The Council may, however, decide by a two-thirds majority of the members present, to sit *in camera.*

The report of public sessions shall be printed in the *Journal de Monaco.*

Art. 64. The Prince shall communicate with the National Council by messages which shall be read by the Minister of State.

Art. 65. The Minister of State and the Counsellors of the Government shall have their entrance and their places reserved at meetings of the National Council.

They must be heard if they so request.

Art. 66. A law implies an agreement reached between the will of the Prince and that of the National Council.

The Prince shall have the right to initiate laws.

The National Council shall have the right to deliberate and pass laws.

The Prince shall have the right to approve laws and by their promulgation give them obligatory force.

Art. 67. The Prince shall sign bills which shall be presented to him by the Council of Government under the signature of the Minister of State.

The National Council shall have the right to propose laws which shall follow, where appropriate, the procedure provided in the preceding paragraph.

Art. 68. The Prince shall issue the necessary ordinances for the execution of laws and for the application of treaties and international agreements.

Art. 69. Laws and Sovereign ordinances shall become applicable on the day following their publication in the *Journal de Monaco.*

Art. 70. The National Council shall pass the budget.

No direct contribution may be established except at the wish and with the consent of the National Council.

No indirect contribution may be established except by a law with the exception of those resulting from an international treaty.

Art. 71. The budget bill shall be presented to the National Council before 31 October.

The budget law shall be voted during the course of the November session of the National Council.

Art. 72. The budget shall be voted upon chapter by chapter. Transfers from one chapter to another shall be forbidden except in the cases authorized by law.

The budget shall include under expenses, in particular, the sums placed at the disposition of the Communal Council for the coming financial year in accordance with Article 87.

Art. 73. If the credits requested by the Government in accordance with Article 71 have not been passed before December 31, the credits corresponding to the services passed may be opened by Sovereign ordinance with the agreement of the Council of State.

The above shall apply also to receipts and expenditures resulting from international treaties.

Art. 74. The Prince may, after consulting the Council of the Crown, pronounce the dissolution of the National Council. New elections must then take place within three months.

TITLE VIII

THE COUNCIL OF THE CROWN

Art. 75. The Council of the Crown shall consist of seven members of Monegasque nationality appointed for a term of three years by the Prince.

The President and three other members shall be freely appointed by the Prince.

Three members shall be appointed upon the nomination of the National Council and from outside its midst.

The functions of Minister of State and of Counsellor of Government shall be incompatible with those of President or member of the Council of the Crown.

Art. 76. The Council of the Crown shall meet at least twice a year on the convocation of the Prince. The Prince may convene it whenever he considers it necessary either on his own initiative or at the suggestion of the President of the Council of the Crown.

Art. 77. The Council of the Crown may be consulted by the Prince on matters touching the higher interests of the State, and it may present its suggestions to the Prince.

The Council of the Crown must be consulted about the following matters: international treaties, dissolution of the National Council, requests for naturalization or resumption of nationality, pardons and amnesty.

TITLE IX

THE COMMUNE

Art. 78. The territory of the Principality shall form one single commune.

Art. 79. The commune shall be administered by a municipality consisting of a Mayor and associates appointed by the Communal Council from among its members.

All citizens of both sexes of at least twenty-one years of age who hav possessed Monegasque nationality for at least five years shall have the right to vote, with the exception of those persons deprived of the right to vote for any of the reasons provided by law.

Art. 80. The Communal Council shall consist of fifteen members elected for four years by universal direct suffrage and by proportional representation.

There shall be no incompatibility between the office of Communal Counsellor and that of National Counsellor.

Art. 81. The Communal Council shall meet every three months in ordinary session. The duration of each session may not exceed fifteen days.

Art. 82. Extraordinary sessions may be held at the request and with the authorization of the Minister of State for specific purposes.

Art. 83. The Communal Council may be dissolved by ministerial decree containing the reasons therefor, after notifying the Council of State.

Art. 84. In case of dissolution or of the resignation of all the members of the Communal Council, a special delegation shall, by ministerial decree, be entrusted with its functions until the election of a new Council. Such election shall take place within three months.

Art. 85. The Mayor shall preside over the Communal Council or, in his absence, his assistant or the counsellor replacing him in order of the roll.

Art. 86. The deliberations of the Communal Council on the affairs of the commune shall be public. Its decisions shall be executory fifteen days following their transmission to the Minister of State unless there has been objection in the form of a ministerial decree stating the reasons therefor.

Art. 87. The communal budget shall be met by the revenue from communal properties and the ordinary resources of the commune. If there is an excess of expenditures, the National Council shall, each year when the budget is tabled by the Communal Council, consider what credits can be placed at the disposal of the commune.

TITLE X

JUSTICE

Art. 88. The judicial power belongs to the Prince who, by this Constitution, delegates the full exercise thereof to the courts and tribunals.

The courts shall render justice in the name of the Prince.

The independence of judges is guaranteed.

The organization, jurisdiction and functioning of the courts and the statute of the judges shall be fixed by law.

Art. 89. The Supreme Court shall be composed of five regular members and two substitutes.

Members of the Supreme Court shall be appointed by the Prince in the following manner:

one regular member and one substitute nominated by the National Council from without its midst;

one regular member and one substitute nominated by the Council of State from without its midst;

one regular member nominated by the Council of the Crown from without its midst;

one regular member nominated by the Court of Appeal from without its midst;

one regular member nominated by the civil court of first instance from without its midst.

Each of the bodies listed above shall make two nominations for each place.

If the Prince does not agree to the nominations he may request new ones.

The President of the Supreme Court shall be appointed by the Prince.

Art. 90.A. In constitutional matters the Supreme Court shall pronounce final judgment on:

(1) the conformity of the rules of procedure of the National Council with constitutional and, where appropriate, legislative provisions in accordance with Article 61;

(2) the annulment, upon petition, of the validity of verdicts in questions of threats to the rights and freedoms guaranteed by Title II of the Constitution which do not fall under paragraph B of this article, and on the granting of indemnities arising therefrom.

B. In administrative matters the Supreme Court shall pronounce final judgment on:

(1) the annulment, upon petition, of acts of the administrative authorities of sovereign ordinances issued for the execution of laws on account of an exceeding of authority and on the granting of indemnities arising therefrom;

(2) the petitioning for reversal of final decisions of the regular administrative courts;

(3) the petitioning for interpretation and appeals on questions of validity concerning decisions of the various administrative authorities and of supreme ordinances taken for the execution of laws.

C. The Supreme Court shall rule on conflicts of jurisdiction.

Art. 91. The Supreme Court shall meet either in plenary assembly of all five members or in administrative section of three members.

It shall meet in plenary assembly for the following matters:

(1) constitutional questions;

(2) to decide on conflicts of jurisdiction;

(3) administrative questions transferred to it by the President of the Supreme Court or decided upon by the administrative section.

It shall meet in administrative section for all other cases.

Art. 92. A Sovereign ordinance shall establish the organization and functioning of the Supreme Court, including in particular the qualifications required for membership, activities incompatible with membership, the statute for members, rotation of members of the administrative section, procedure to be followed before the Court, the effects of appeals and decisions, the procedure and effects of conflicts of jurisdiction and the transitional measures required.

TITLE XI

AMENDMENT OF THE CONSTITUTION

Art. 93. The Constitution may not be suspended.

Art. 94. Total or partial amendment of the Constitution must be the result of a common agreement of the Prince and the National Council.

Art. 95. Where the National Council initiates amendment the decision must be taken by a majority of two thirds of the normal membership of the assembly.

TITLE XII

FINAL PROVISIONS

Art. 96. All former constitutional provisions shall be abrogated.

The present Constitution shall enter into effect immediately.

Renewal of the National Council and of the Communal Council shall take place within three months.

Art. 97. Laws and regulations at present in effect shall remain applicable insofar as they are not contrary to this Constitution. Should the latter be the case they must be brought into harmony with the Constitution as soon as possible.

Given in Our Palace in Monaco the seventeenth of December one thousand nine hundred and sixty two.

GPSR Compliance

The European Union's (EU) General Product Safety Regulation (GPSR) is a set of rules that requires consumer products to be safe and our obligations to ensure this.

If you have any concerns about our products, you can contact us on ProductSafety@springernature.com

In case Publisher is established outside the EU, the EU authorized representative is:

Springer Nature Customer Service Center GmbH
Europaplatz 3
69115 Heidelberg, Germany

Batch number: 10830941

Printed by Printforce, the Netherlands